BUS 870

ACPL ITEM
DISCARDED

3 1833 01627 9694

ALLEN COUNTY PUBLIC LIBRARY

658.3 R137w
RAMBO, WILLIAM W.
WORK AND ORGANIZATIONAL
BEHAVIOR

S0-BWR-760

2116

DO NOT REMOVE
CARDS FROM POCKET

ALLEN COUNTY PUBLIC LIBRARY

FORT WAYNE, INDIANA 46802

You may return this book to any agency, branch,
or bookmobile of the Allen County Public Library.

DEMCO

WORK
AND
ORGANIZATIONAL
BEHAVIOR

WILLIAM W. RAMBO
OKLAHOMA STATE UNIVERSITY

WORK
AND
ORGANIZATIONAL
BEHAVIOR

HOLT, RINEHART AND WINSTON
New York   Chicago   San Francisco   Philadelphia   Montreal   Toronto
London   Sydney   Tokyo   Mexico City   Rio de Janeiro   Madrid

Allen County Public Library
Ft. Wayne, Indiana

TO AVIS

Library of Congress Cataloging in Publication Data

Rambo, William W.
Work and Organizational Behavior

Bibliography: p.
Includes index.
1. Organizational behavior.   2. Personnel management.
I. Title
HD58.7.R35   658.3   81-20025

ISBN 0-03-056133-7   AACR2

Copyright © 1982 by CBS College Publishing
Address correspondence to:
383 Madison Avenue
New York, N.Y. 10017
All rights reserved
Printed in the United States of America
Published simultaneously in Canada
2 3 4 5   144   9 8 7 6 5 4 3 2 1

Cover and Book Design by
GLORIA GENTILE

CBS COLLEGE PUBLISHING
Holt, Rinehart and Winston
The Dryden Press
Saunders College Publishing

Preface

If one were to take a long view of the developments that have taken place in the behavioral sciences, some of the most significant signs of progress would be found in the expansion of the number of issues that have been given experimental attention. To be sure, progress of a linear type has been made, but over the years the field has broadened its scope dramatically to include aspects of behavior that were previously ignored by those who carry out research. Nowhere is this trend more evident than in the subject matter that is the main concern of this book. The study of work behavior is a discipline that has experienced a substantial growth in the number of issues that have been brought under its jurisdiction. What was once an area of study dominated by a concern for personnel administration and work efficiency has now become an area that deals with almost every facet of psychological adjustment.

As the field developed it began to organize its subject matter into two major divisions. The first, industrial psychology, focuses on the techniques of personnel administration; the second, organizational behavior, places emphasis on the complex of social variables that make up the environment of work. For some these two lines of interest exist as separate disciplines; for others they represent integrated subdivisions of a single field. From this latter point of view, industrial psychology serves as the methodological foundation for a scientific approach to work behavior. Its techniques of measurement (for example, the questionnaire, interview and rating scale) generate much of the data studied by those who are interested in organizational behavior. On the other hand, the application of these techniques to practical personnel problems requires that one be aware of organizational dynamics that surround their use.

This text has been written on the assumption that a first course in work behavior should present the student with a broad view of the field. This means that topics drawn from both industrial psychology and organizational behavior can be selected to form appropriate combinations for the beginning student who is seeking a representative overview of the area. The coverage of the text is extensive enough, however, to provide instructors with some freedom in constructing a course that reflects their particular orientation. By selecting chapters and topics within chapters the relative emphasis placed on industrial psychology and organizational behavior themes can be fitted into an instructor's course objectives.

In preparing each chapter an attempt was made to retain the conceptual "flavor" of each topic area. For instance, for a topic involving considerable technical detail an attempt was made to present the material in a fashion that is accessible to the advanced undergraduate and beginning graduate student for whom the book was prepared, but in doing so no effort was made to avoid an idea because it requires the student to deal with technical concepts. Hence, the book contains several chapters that involve the details of behavioral methodology; however, these chapters presuppose no previous work in statistical methods or test construction.

The literature on work behavior is one that is scattered across many areas of the social sciences. Psychology, sociology, management science, labor economics, and industrial engineering all contribute to the research that is done in the field. As a result, while the main emphasis of the text is psychological, the material presented has been drawn from a wide range of social science sources. The study of work behavior is an enterprise shared by a number of disciplines, and to ignore any of them would seriously distort one's view of the field. Specialization, if it is desired, can be sought in subsequent courses. An important function of the first course is to enhance students' curiosity about an area of study, and convince them that the field holds potential for interesting and challenging problem solving. I believe that these objectives are best met by taking a broad look at one's subject matter.

The list of those who have contributed to the final version of this book is a long one, and my intellectual debt to them is high. But, debts of this type enrich rather than impoverish, and it is with gratitude that I acknowledge the generous contributions others have made to my work. Norman Gekoski and C.H. Lawshe introduced me to the field and guided me through the early phases of my training. They were warm and supportive teachers whose influence can be found on every page of this book. My colleagues Roy Gladstone, Bob Helm, Mark MacNeil and William C. Scott read parts of the manuscript and were generous in their efforts to contribute to the text. William Jaynes was most helpful in supplying me with materials on discriminatory selection practices, and James L. Phillips, my department chairman, supported my need for autonomy, and thereby created the working climate that made this work possible.

The editorial staff of Holt, Rinehart and Winston has been a source of substantial support, and I am particularly indebted to Arlene Katz, Betty Poor, and Sheree Rhinehardt who managed to mix competence with warmth and make bearable a process that I shall never comprehend.

I can never fully express my gratitude to the professional staff of the Oklahoma State University Library for the many services and courtesies extended to me. I would particularly like to thank Edward Hollman, Jill Holmes, Elizabeth Struble, John Phillips, and Vicki Phillips who made innumerable contributions to the research that went into this text. On many occasions I used the resources of the library at the University of Oklahoma in Norman. Karl Rambo was my "man in Norman" who was always ready to assist in my search for materials. For this, I thank him.

The Houghton Mifflin Company has been most generous in permitting me to reprint excerpts from I.L. Janis's book, *Victims of Groupthink*. Similarly, The Society for Applied Anthropology and Dr. Joy Roy have been very cooperative in allowing excerpts from Donald Roy's article, *Banana Time*, to be reprinted in my chapter on the work group. To them, and to all whose work has been cited, I acknowledge my indebtedness.

My loyal assistant in preparing the manuscript was Evelyn Ferchau. With admirable composure she endured my fretting and through it all managed to produce a steady stream of accurate work. For all this I am deeply grateful.

Finally, to my wife, Avis, good friend and gentle critic, I dedicate this book. I cannot remember how many times I followed her about reading the latest version of some opaque paragraph; and I cannot forget the many ways she balanced my fragile ego with her encouragement that I not lose sight of the student for whom all this is intended.

Contents

1

Introduction

Work is a central part of our lives. Apart from its obvious economic significance, the general environment of work contains much that is socially and psychologically important to the individual. Work plays an influential role in the development of the adult personality and makes a significant contribution to the quality of the life we lead. The term ''work'' is used to refer to both an activity and a place: as an activity it involves us in tasks that draw on our talents and energies, and in doing so exposes us to experiences that shape the impressions we have about our identity and about our general level of competence; as a place it involves us in a social environment that can be both rewarding and threatening. Often it places us in an organization large in size and complex in its social structure. It is also the setting for a major portion of our waking hours.

It is not difficult to find information regarding the size of our personal investment in work. For instance, in spite of what currently seems to be an increasing national concern with leisure, paid employment has been involving a growing portion of the population. In 1978 almost 69 percent of the adult population (age 16 and above) was employed sometime during the year (Young, 1980), and during the same period approximately 50 percent of

the nation's children under 18 had mothers who were employed (Waldman et al., 1979). Along similar lines, Hedges and Taylor (1980) estimate that the average full-time employee works 2060 hours every year; and in keeping with this, in 1979 the average yearly vacation per full-time worker was only 2.0 weeks.[1] Figures such as these testify to the extent to which the adult social role is dominated by work. Furthermore, work has become an even more prominent part of daily life, since with increasing frequency the American family must contribute eighty—not forty—hours of work each week in order to achieve its social and economic objectives.

TRENDS IN WORK

Like most aspects of the society, work has been subjected to a number of influences that have brought about significant changes in its character. In many respects, what is meant by work today is radically different from the meaning associated with the concept several decades ago. Working conditions, income provisions, job duties, and the number and kind of people participating in paid employment have undergone continuous and dramatic change. Corresponding to this has been a set

[1]In both France and West Germany the law requires that every worker receive at least one month of vacation every year. In addition to a much shorter average vacation time, American workers are absent from work much less than their European counterparts. Lost work hours in America tend to vary from 3.0 to 3.5 percent of the usual working hours, whereas comparable figures from West Germany are 11.0 percent, 10.0 percent in Holland, and 15.0 percent in Italy (Taylor, 1979).

of changes in people's orientation toward work, and in the objectives they seek in entering the labor force. As a case in point, many employees are becoming more concerned about the quality of their work lives, and a growing number believe that a career should provide them with opportunities to satisfy personal needs that extend beyond those directly relating to the wages that are earned.

Changes both in the kind of work carried out and in the characteristics of persons entering the labor force have also been accompanied by changes in the pattern of work careers. For example, there is evidence that people are more mobile; that is, they move from job to job more than in the past. Rosenfeld (1979) reports that about 11.6 percent of all employed persons changed occupations during the one-year period from January 1977 to January 1978. Sekscenski (1979) found that in 1978 median job tenure for all workers was only 3.6 years; only 25 percent of those employed during this time had been on the same job for more than ten years.

It is difficult to trace the origins of many changes that have taken place in the nature and conditions of work. In part they can be found in the development of new technologies that have been changing the duties of jobs. In part they represent an expression of our changing view of life and what is reasonable to expect from it. Whatever their origins, however, these changes in the character of work have led to new directions in the research literature that deals with work behavior and the organizational influences that surround the work we do. Paralleling the changes occurring in work, the research literature has shifted its focus toward a new set of topics. For example, what previously had been an area of research that was heavily influenced by an interest in improving the efficiency of performance has now become more concerned with the psychological and social consequences of work. What was initially a primary concern with work methods and the physical conditions surrounding the job has become an area of research that recognizes the importance of motivational influences and the social-organizational context within which they function.

Research on Work Behavior

During the recent past there has been a significant increase in the amount of research activity carried out on problems relating to work behavior. This growth can be found in both the number of studies being reported in the research literature and in the substantial increase in the range of topics being investigated. Topics are now being researched that until recently had received relatively little attention. Social problems and a heightened social awareness have provided a stimulus for much of this new research, and many of the issues being considered are those that approach work not only from management's perspective but also from the point of view of individual workers and the society in which they live. For example, the growth in size and complexity of governmental and industrial organizations has made people more aware of the significance of these larger social units. This awareness has made it clear that the social variables that affect a worker's job experience are not all to be found within the relatively close circle formed by the immediate work group. Rather, there exists an entire realm of organizational variables that are associated with the structure and function of the large social units that make up a business firm. These variables operate to influence the effectiveness with which a business organization achieves its objectives. They are also important factors influencing the conditions under which individuals perform their job duties. Recognition of the significance of these variables has led to the development of an area of research referred to as *organizational behavior,* which is an area of study that deals with the behavior of people who are working within these complex social structures. It also deals with the behavior and interaction of groups that range in size and complexity from the small task group to the entire business organization.

While the field of work behavior has broadened its scope to include these more complicated topics, it still has retained an active interest in many of the more traditional lines of research. For example, questions concerning supervision and leadership still receive a considerable amount of attention. Also, issues surrounding the nature of job satisfaction continue to be actively studied. As a consequence, one finds the study of work behavior involving an amalgamation of the more traditional topics with the newer topics that emphasize the significance of organizational variables. In essence, the field is moving more closely to what may be called a social psychology of work, and as it is presently constituted, it is an area of research that pays close attention to the interaction that takes place between the social and psychological variables found in the work environment. The field is also becoming more interdisciplinary, and the chapters that follow will present a cross section of these newer and traditional topics and discuss them in the context of the research reported from the fields of psychology, sociology, management, and labor economics. But before considering the general plan of the text, it may be worthwhile to give brief consideration to several different points of view concerning the nature of work and its general significance for the worker and the society. The purpose of this discussion is to emphasize the fact that in studying work behavior one is never far removed from social philosophy and humanistic values. Hence, research in this area, either directly or indirectly, has implications for social policy; and as a consequence, it often relates to the basic beliefs held by the individual reader.

Beliefs about the Nature of Work

There is something less than complete agreement in the social science literature concerning the fundamental nature of work and its social and psychological significance. One might think that a scientific literature would be immune from these more philosophical and value-oriented considerations, but they do in fact play an important role in such things as the selection of questions to be researched and in determining the appropriateness of the various experimental techniques available to the social scientist. In the case of the literature on work behavior one can find that often there is associated with a particular theoretical point of view an implicit set of beliefs concerning the nature and purposes of work. For example, there are those who support models of management that permit broad worker participation in the decision-making activities that take place on the job. There are those who contend that the most effective source of worker motivation is to be found in the self-actualizing potentials of working, and there are scientists who see narrow work specialization as a condition that leads to employee alienation. All of these positions, while they receive some support from research, are closely related to sets of more fundamental beliefs concerning the aims of work and the basic psychological characteristics of the worker. As a result, it is important that one keep these different orientations in mind when considering the research that has been carried out in this area, and this is particularly true of the type of research that leads to programs of action and policy recommendations.

Buchholz (1977) contends that there are sets of basic beliefs concerning the nature of work and its relationship to those who engage in it. These points of view serve to provide a basic orientation to the study of work behavior, and one may find these ideas being expressed, either directly or indirectly, in much of the research that can be found in the social sciences literature. He identifies five such belief structures, and among them the *Work Ethic* is the one most closely associated with traditional and conservative management philosophies. Furthermore, in spite of the fact that this point of view is often interpreted as being nonprogressive in its perception of work and the worker, it still expresses a set of values and beliefs that are widely held.

The Work Ethic contends that the character and the value of individuals are expressed in the work they do. Hard work and dedication to a job are an expression of a set of highly valued human attributes that collectively are referred to as virtue. But the relation of work to human virtue is cyclical, in that working tends to bring the individual into contact with experiences that in and of themselves are capable of building character. Hence, work is an expression of virtue as well as being an experience that leads to the development of high levels of human character.

Although work is its own reward, dedication to hard work leads to the accumulation of material rewards and social position. Therefore, unless the individual is functioning within a defective social system, material wealth and well-being reflect virtue and commitment to work. Work is also seen as an obligation that all possess, and those who shun work are idlers whose membership in the community is tenuous at best.

Organizational Belief Systems. The Work Ethic poses a set of beliefs that form a sharp contrast with those found in what Buchholz calls the *Organizational Belief System*. From the perspective of this latter point of view, the significance of work is found in its contribution to the organization within which the individual functions. Commitment to the organization transcends one's commitment to work, and loyalty to the group and its management leadership combines with adherence to the behavioral norms of the organization to create the conditions that lead to success and upward mobility. As will be demonstrated in later sections of the text, there is experimental support for this point of view, although it would be a mistake to assume that these organizational considerations universally exert more influence than productivity in determining the distribution of rewards in a work organization. Nevertheless, the study of executive mobility, organizational communication, and the variables that relate to financial incentives often moves quite close to ideas that are consistent with this organizational belief system.

Humanistic Belief Systems. From the standpoint of the *Humanistic Belief System* work is an activity that enables an individual to achieve a sense of fulfillment and actualization. It is within the work setting that workers are able to exercise their talents and skills, and in so doing obtain the satisfaction of realizing their potentialities. Congenial work involves activity that permits personal growth and the freedom to pursue the satisfaction of the higher human needs. Work is sterile if it denies workers the opportunity to draw on their full range of strengths.

Humanistic belief systems view the design of work as a principal consideration determining worker happiness and productivity. Absences, turnover, low rates of productivity, and poor quality are often symptoms of work that has been poorly designed. Unlike the Work Ethic, this orientation focuses on external factors such as the duties of the job, work rules, and machine pacing as sources of job dissatisfaction. As a consequence, many problems faced by workers can, from this point of view, be solved by the judicious redesign of the work and the job environment.

Marxist-Related Beliefs. Apart from their obvious political and economic implications, there are many Marxist concepts that are sociological in their scope. In many instances these ideas overlap those found in systems that Buchholz labels humanitarian. In the literature on work behavior, for instance, the concept of alienation is drawn on widely in discussions of the negative consequences of certain technological innovations. In general, this set of beliefs views work not merely as a means for earning a living but as an activity through which individuals express their basic nature. Furthermore, because workers do not own the means of production nor control the means by which work is accomplished, they tend to feel alienated from the work they do. Alienation is a negative motivational force that has broad-reaching social and psychological consequences. Its continued presence leads to deteriorating mental health and a reduced level of commitment to the demands of the work situation. Finally, Marxist concerns with ownership of the means of production translate into ideas that advocate increased worker participation in the affairs of the organization, but this is a position that may be found in a variety of general approaches to work that are not Marxist in their character.

The Leisure Ethic. Of the different orientations to work, the one expressed by the leisure ethic is the most pessimistic. From this perspective, work serves little function except to provide the basic economic resources required to support one's life. The concept of work is heavily seasoned with the concept of toil, and there is little prospect for redesigning work so that it satisfies higher human needs. Self-expression and creativity are exercised during leisure time and not through work; hence, the good life is one that frees the individual from work and expands the amount of free time that is available to pursue more rewarding activities. Therefore freedom, the availability of leisure, is one of the prime objectives of social planning.

Beliefs of the types outlined in the above sections are much too general to be thought of as research hypotheses, but they are important considerations, since they often serve to give direction to the development of research questions. They can also serve as a link between the results obtained from a group of studies and the recommendations made for action programs. It is not usual for the results of a study to be so opaque that they lend themselves to a multitude of divergent interpretations; but when one is considering the results of a series of studies, one's beliefs concerning the nature of work can play a role in bringing such a complex literature into an organized system. Therefore, in dealing with this literature it would be helpful to consider one's own point of view, since it functions to influence the reader's reaction to the research that is reported.

THE ORGANIZATION OF THE TEXT

The text is organized into five main topic areas and under each there is a group of chapters dealing with different facets of the main theme.

Fitting the Worker to the Job

The first topic area concerns issues involved in achieving a satisfactory fit between the worker and the job. Workers choose jobs and organizations choose workers, and within this personnel allocation system one may find many of the important variables that determine the level of success with which workers adjust to their jobs. One chapter in this section considers the problems and procedures that are associated with the recruitment, selection, and placement of job applicants. Here within an organizational framework we will discuss the techniques that are available to augment the decisions

management must make in staffing the work organization. A second chapter in this section concerns the organization's efforts to train workers to meet the demands of work. Here the concern is with formal programs to modify the behavior of the worker so that it fits in more comfortably with the requirements of the job situation. Finally, a third chapter discusses one of the most controversial and difficult phases of worker-management relationships, the evaluation of work performance. Performance evaluation concerns the distribution of the rewards and punishments that are available at work. It contributes to management's efforts to pinpoint organizational problems. It deals with information that is fed back to employees concerning the adequacy of their work. It involves a whole range of interpersonal relationships that operate within the political dynamics of the firm, keeping the grapevine active and the anxiety level high. In short, these procedures reflect work values and social norms that operate within a given work setting.

Work and the Individual

The second major division of the text concerns the pluses and minuses of work. Here the discussion will be focused on the positive and negative motives and emotions that are associated with a job. For example, the first chapter will deal with the psychological importance of work, that is, the extent to which the work environment contains events that contribute to the quality of an individual's life. This section also contains a chapter concerning the stress and anxiety generated under certain job conditions. This chapter also considers the broader question of emotional mental health as it is influenced by variables found at work. Following this there is a chapter concerning the psychological signficance of financial incentives, which is included to serve as a framework within which to discuss the question of work motivation. Rather than considering worker motivation in abstraction, the text will discuss the topic within the context of the wages paid on a job. The basic principles of human motivation do not change for different types of incentives, and wages are an interesting and important aspect of work. Finally, the section is concluded with a chapter on job satisfaction and the variables that have been found to influence a worker's affective reaction to the job. This topic refers to one of the primary objectives of the study of work behavior. While not disregarding production effectiveness, to understand the variables that contribute to worker satisfaction is to comprehend one of the most important factors determining the general quality of the life an individual will lead.

The Social Conditions of Work.   Work organizations are fascinating places. For the individual worker they serve as a model that is used to gain an understanding of the more remote and complex institutions operating in the society. Increasingly, workers are becoming organization persons whose skills and energies are exercised within the complicated and often frustrating confines of these large social units. In addition, success at work requires that the worker be successful in adapting to the social requirements of the work organization; and as individuals move up the chain of command, the care and maintenance of this organization assume a more significant role in their daily activities.

Basically, the work organization is a social system that contains an intricate network of rules, standards, and interpersonal relationships. The first chapter of this section outlines a number of behavioral models that have been applied by social scientists to bring a sense of order to the behavior of these complex social systems. Following this, there is a chapter on organizational communications, which reviews work that has been done in both laboratory and field settings. It is through a study of the communication system that one may gain an important perspective on the dynamics of organizational activity, and in this chapter an effort will be made to consider certain aspects of how organizations function and how they exert an influence on the individual worker.

A third chapter in this section concerns the role of the immediate work group. There is an abundant research literature which demonstrates the importance of the work group in establishing and maintaining an extensive set of behavioral standards that govern the conduct of the workday, and it will

be with this aspect of group functioning that the chapter will be concerned.

Finally, there is a chapter on the labor union. Union membership and union-management relations are facts of life in a large number of work settings, and the influence of union activity extends across the entire field of work. In addition, the psychology of union membership is an interesting aspect of organizational life, since it involves workers in two competing groups that vie for their loyalties.

Work Leadership.   The section on the social conditions of work concentrates its attention on the psychology of individual workers as they are influenced by the immediate work group and the larger social units that make up the work environment. Of all the organizational influences, however, none is more significant than the authority system. The boss, the organizational superior, is a potent and psychologically central part of work, and it is with work leadership that the next section is concerned. A chapter on supervision summarizes the attempts made by social scientists to describe different styles of work supervision and uncover some of the psychological and organizational variables that are associated with each. From a psychological perspective the work leader plays a role that is associated with significant levels of power. It is through their control of job incentives that leaders exert such a substantial influence on the behavior of those who work under them. But supervisors are dependent on the support of their subordinates, so an interactive dependency is maintained between workers and leaders. Supervisors influence the behavior of the group members who, in turn, influence the behavior of the supervisor, and it is in this interaction that one can find many of the ingredients that enter into the general level of effectiveness that is characteristic of a group.

A chapter on the business executive is included in order to extend our consideration of work leadership up the organizational hierarchy and deal with it at levels where power is concentrated and where policy-making influences extend throughout the entire firm. Although the research literature does not dwell on different styles of executive leadership, there is a wealth of information concerning the nature of the executive's job, and the characteristics of those who move into these positions and the routes they follow to the top of the firm. This chapter, therefore, is as much a discussion of the workings of a large organization as it is a study of executive leadership.

Changing Conditions of Work. The final section of the text involves two current issues that relate to important changes taking place in the field of work. The first concerns the rapidly accelerating technological innovations that are changing the nature of the work we do and altering the psychological consequences of working. Many view these changes as a negative force that has been robbing jobs of their challenge and autonomy. There are others who view these technical innovations in work as a source of hope that workers will be freed from the routine and confinement of empty jobs. Of course, there is no simple resolution to these two points of view, but it is interesting to learn how far social scientists have progressed in their efforts to understand the many and complicated consequences of these changes.

To some extent as the result of new technology, but also reflecting a host of other social and economic influences, the impressive increase in the number of women entering the job market is a major development. The final section of the text contains a chapter on this increased rate of women's participation in work. This is an area of research activity that is as active as any other being considered today, and in general this literature has been able to provide some new insights into the social and psychological dynamics of women's adjustment to work. This chapter will present a discussion of this topic within the framework of the socialization processes that play such a significant role in determining women's approach to work and their experiences with paid employment. The family consequences of dual work careers will also be considered.

An Interdisciplinary Approach

The chapters that follow will consider topics in the light of the research literature that is available from several areas of the social-behavioral sciences. The study of work behavior is not located within the exclusive jurisdiction of any one discipline, and students in this area who confine their attention to a single field will receive a distorted view of the status of the subject matter. For example, while the psychological laboratory has contributed much to our understanding of the operation of wage incentives, the field of survey research and the methods of the labor economist all give a broader view of the motivational significance of the wages received for work. Along similar lines, organizational research that relies heavily on questionnaire data has provided some important insights into the dynamics of communications as they take place within a real work environment. The laboratory, however, has provided us with a setting where communication structures have been carefully studied, and the results of these studies have vastly improved our understanding of the significance of structural properties of a communication network.

One could continue to point out examples of the multimethod and multidiscipline approaches that have been taken in studying work behavior, but the main point is that an exclusive allegiance to one discipline or to one methodology will lead to a narrow view of a very complex subject matter. In the chapters that comprise the remainder of this text information has been sought across several fields of study, and for each topic an attempt has been made to present a representative cross section of the many studies that are available. The principal commitment has been to try to present the main ideas that are currently active in the field of work behavior, and not to present an exhaustive review of all the research that has been done on this subject. It is hoped that this approach will serve as a beginning point for the reader's continued interest in this fascinating area of social science inquiry.

1
FITTING THE WORKER TO THE JOB

2
Employee Selection and Employment

One of the more widely accepted ideas in the field of work behavior is that a close fit between the psychological makeup of an individual and the requirements of a job leads to a successful adjustment to work. In attempting to improve the fit between employees and jobs, work organizations often rely on training, job redesign, and work incentive programs that strive to modify either the worker or the job. Effective as these programs may be, many managers would argue that effective recruitment, selection, and placement can make a much more substantial contribution to a company's efforts to staff its ranks with competent personnel.

This point of view assumes that some of the more important variables influencing work performance may be found in the personal attributes brought to the job by an employee. It is assumed that job potential is related to certain skills that have developed over the years; and at the time of employment, these skills exist as well-established parts of the individual's psychological makeup. These attributes are extremely difficult to modify, but they can be identified at the time an individual makes application for employment. Information concerning these attributes, collected when the job application is made, gives an organization a certain amount of insight into how the individual will adjust to the work and meet its requirements. Hence, one of the objectives of the employee-selection process is to obtain an accurate measurement of

these behavioral indicators. Once these data are available, prediction schemes can be developed that give both employer and job applicant early access to information concerning the applicant's prospects for job success.

The problems considered in this chapter are ones that all work organizations face. As a result of either expansion or attrition, organizations are constantly engaged in a quest for competent employees. Within limits, jobs can be modified to better accommodate the available employees, but effective selection and placement programs can make an additional and significant contribution to an organization's staffing efforts. Each firm must make a choice concerning the type of personnel program it maintains. For example, selection can be dealt with in a rather informal manner that relies on advertisements in the local newspaper and the impressions formed by a supervisor when applicants are interviewed. Selection procedures can also involve a series of systematic procedures that include job analysis, psychological testing, and standardized interviews. In this latter approach, the hiring process is a multistage procedure that involves a sequence of decisions regarding the suitability of the job applicant. At each stage of this sequence, additional information is sought from the applicant, and at each step a different personnel procedure is used.

Personnel practices vary widely from one organization to another and from job to job within the same organization, and as a result it will be impossible to identify the "typical" procedures followed in hiring employees. Nevertheless, the present chapter will discuss a cross section of the more frequently used procedures in an effort to demonstrate the range of available technical options. Many of these approaches are rather quantitative in nature, relying on measurement and statistical tools that are often quite advanced. The underlying ideas are, however, not difficult, and it is possible to present a general overview of these techniques without being drawn into material that is beyond the reach of the nontechnical reader.

WORKERS SELECT JOBS

Before beginning our discussion of the formal personnel procedures that are used to select employees, we should recognize that there are unplanned factors at work that bring jobs and people together. As a result of these informal influences, chance is not the only factor that brings individuals into an organization in search of a particular type of job. For a variety of reasons, individuals who come into a company's employment office tend to bring with them sets of skills, interests, and work values that approximate the requirements of the positions that are open. Additionally, those who accept job offers do not represent a random sample of all who receive offers. We should give job applicants considerable credit for insight into what they want in a job and what they can bring to it in the way of talents and commitments. Granted, this is a factor that varies from one person to the next, but as a group, the people who seek and accept particular jobs tend to be better suited for those jobs than would a group of applicants randomly selected from the population.

Theories of Job Recruitment

There are a number of different theoretical orientations that have been developed to deal with the early phases of the employment process. In general, these theories contend that in making application for employment and in selecting a job, individuals tend to engage in some kind of accounting process in which job characteristics are evaluated in the light of the individual's personal objectives in seeking work. Theories differ, however, in identifying the principal factors that enter into these evaluations; Behling, Labovitz, and Gainer (1968) have identified three views of this process.

Objective Factor Theories.   Some contend that a job applicant's orientation toward a position is the outcome of an assessment of a group of *objectively measurable* job factors such as wages, promotion opportunities, geographical location, and fringe benefits. The applicant's selection of a job is seen to be the result of a weighted summation of the advantages and disadvantages associated with this set of objective job factors. Applicants may or may not have accurate information about each of these factors; but in the absence of accurate facts they often rely on hearsay and vague impressions to construct a view of the personal consequences of a given job choice.

Subjective Factor Theories.   The subjective-factor point of view emphasizes the applicant's perception of an organization's potential for satisfying the higher-order and less objectively measurable needs. The theory identifies the attraction of an applicant to an organization with a process of "psychological advantage seeking" in which one perception of one's own psychological makeup is matched with the image of the firm as an environment that contains certain potentials for personal fulfillment. A decision to seek work with a firm is not the result of an accounting of the objective advantages of the job, but is based on considerations that are personal and emotional in their nature.

Critical Contact Theory.   From the critical-contact perspective, attraction to an organization is based on a set of real and often brief encounters with the firm during the time of application for work. The typical job seeker is seen as being unable to differentiate among work organizations on the basis of objective incentives and working conditions. In the competition for attractive recruits, work organizations tend to create a rather uniform picture of the advantages associated with employment. As a result, applicants often find themselves basing their job-selection decisions on impressions formed when they are in direct contact with representatives of the firm.

Research. Although there is not an abundance of information bearing on these theoretical positions, there is a small group of studies that tend to support their perception of the reward potential of a job. For example, several studies have shown that employees prefer work organizations and occupations that are perceived as providing access to the goals they are seeking in their job search (Pieters, Hundert, & Beer, 1968; Vroom, 1976[a]; Sheard, 1970; Wanous, 1972). In a related study, Tom (1971) has shown that a preference for different work organizations is related to the similarity of one's own personality and one's perception of the personality image of an organization. This finding bears directly on the theory by Super (Super et al., 1963; Super & Crites, 1962) which maintains that vocational choice involves an effort on the part of the individual to actualize his or her personality in the job that is selected. Super contends that people tend to associate different personality characteristics with individuals who are found in different occupational classifications. Efforts to obtain jobs in a particular vocation are, therefore, seen as an expression of applicants' efforts to secure a work environment that is compatible with their self-concept.

Perhaps one of the most influential variables directing people into various occupational categories is the social prestige associated with different jobs. For example, applicants from white-collar, middle-class backgrounds often refuse to consider employment in blue-collar occupations in spite of the fact that many of these positions pay higher salaries than do the white-collar jobs available (Glenn, Ross, & Tully, 1974). This is especially true if the individual is a male. Hence, entire segments of the job market are considered inappropriate because the social background and career interests of the job seeker preclude even considering jobs that are associated with a blue collar and a lunch pail.

There are other factors that contribute to the selectivity workers display in applying for jobs. For example, educational and training experiences, the courses taken, and the individual's success in these courses result in an orientation toward work that leads a worker toward certain occupational classifications. The end result of all this is that before a company makes any effort to select individuals for the jobs that are vacant, a considerable amount of selectivity has already taken place. But selectivity of this sort still does not ensure that all who apply for a job will be successful in it; a considerable range of talent visits the employment office looking for work. Hence, this process of self-selection is open to many sources of error, and as a result, an employer cannot rely on it to bring him into contact with only those who are suitable job applicants. The employer must actively recruit job applicants who are then selected on the basis of a number of screening techniques that are used as part of the hiring process.

Accepting a Job Offer. There is, of course, another aspect of a worker's selection of a job, and that occurs when an offer of employment is received. Now a whole set of working conditions and economic considerations enter into the worker's choice. These factors also interact with the impressions that were formed during the brief time the applicant was in contact with the personnel office (Schmitt & Coyle, 1976). Relatively little is known about how these factors combine to produce a final decision, and the little evidence that is available leaves many aspects of this question unanswered.

Several studies have attempted to manipulate the amount and accuracy of information given about a job during the application period, and one of these (Reilly, Tenopyr, & Sperling, 1979) was successful in demonstrating that such preview information does have an effect on the rate at which applicants accept job offers. This was a study done with applicants for telephone operator jobs, and it was found that those applicants who were given a realistic preview of the nature of this position declined job offers at a higher rate than did those who received a completely favorable preview or no preview at all. There are other studies that have attempted similar preview efforts without finding any significant effects on the rate of job acceptance (Farr, O'Leary, & Bartlett, 1973; Wanous, 1973). Reilly et al. (1979) suggests that the impact of job preview information is probably greatest for jobs involving more complicated duties and responsibilities; and in all probability, job market conditions play a role in determining the effectiveness of preview information. In any event, there is some support for the critical contact theory, but at the present time there is still much to be learned about the significance of early contacts with a work organization on decisions to accept or reject a job offer.

One possibility should be recognized, however, and that is that all decisions to accept a job are not identical. Often when accepting a job a worker will be playing out a strategy that will determine the kind of tenure commitment he will make to a job (Hom, Katerberg, & Hulin, 1979). Some may enter into a job with little intention of remaining for more than a short time. Others may accept a job on a trial basis in order to determine whether it meets their requirements for promotion, pay, and the like. Still others may take a job with little thought to a tenure strategy. Hence, when a worker accepts a job it is often unclear whether this selection involves an expectation that the position will be a lasting one or whether it is viewed in a number of ways that imply a temporary affiliation. It is difficult to anticipate these strategies at the time of hiring, but a company can accumulate data concerning the characteristics of long- and short-term employees and perhaps discover some of the characteristics of those employees who accept work but whose short tenure makes them a costly investment to the organization (Lee & Booth, 1974).

PREDICTING WORK BEHAVIOR— GENERAL PRINCIPLES

In selecting job applicants organizations are faced with the problem of predicting future job performance. Viewed from this perspective, the entire selection process can be seen as one whose basic objective is to secure information that will throw light on an applicant's prospects for successful adjustment to the job. There are many alternative procedures that can be used to supply information about the applicant; but underlying all is a set of ideas that are fundamental to the prediction process, and one of the more basic of these considerations concerns the nature of individual differences.

Individual Differences

Whether one considers physical attributes like height or weight, psychological characteristics like intelligence and personality or whether one is observing performance on a specific task, one is confronted with considerable person to person variation. It is this fact that serves as the primary objective of all behavioral research and measurement. The basic purpose of research, for example, is to explain why these differences occur and to identify the factors that give rise to them. Along similar lines, psychological measurement involves a description of these differences, many times using scales that express observations in quantitative terms.

In the social sciences, explanation of behavioral events often draws on the relationships that exist between two or more measures of individual differences, one set of behavioral differences being explained in terms of a second set of differences. For instance, differences in job performance might be attributed to differences in the extent to which workers possess certain psychological attributes thought to be underlying requirements of the job. Hence, explanation of one set of differences (performance) involves a reference to another set of differences—the psychological attributes.

Differences in Job Performance.   One need not have had much experience with work to recognize that differences in work performance can be substantial. These differences exist between workers and within a single worker from one time period to the next (Rothe, 1978). Furthermore, it is not unusual to find that within a given work group the range of performance differences extends from high levels of efficiency down to levels of work that represent economic losses to the company. For example, in many work situations the most productive member of a group may be found out-performing the least productive by a two-to-one ratio.

The production data presented in Table 2.1 provide an example of individual differences in work performance. These data are actual production figures taken from a group of sewing machine operators whose output is expressed in terms of the average hourly earnings calculated on a piece-rate basis. There is a guaranteed minimum for this job, $3.10 per hour, and if the worker's output does not yield this amount, the company pays the differential and considers this payment a loss. Referring to the table, notice the range of production earnings during each of the eleven weeks. In most instances, the output of the most productive worker is twice that of the least productive operator. Furthermore, notice the frequency with which certain employees meet the production standard of $3.10 while other operators do not. Operators 1, 5, and 6 regularly stand at the top of the weekly earnings while operators 4 and 7 are rather consistently producing at a rate that is not earning the wages that they are being paid. Hence,

for some operators the company consistently earns a profit; for others the company consistently sustains a loss, and it is this kind of situation that leads companies to invest in selection programs that attempt to identify the characteristics of successful and unsuccessful performers at the time they are considered for employment. What is a cost connected with hiring new employees can be a profitable investment if the selection program succeeds in identifying competent employees.

Variance and Common Variance. The term "variance" is a statistical concept referring to the magnitude of individual differences in a set of observations. Variance statistics increase in size as the differences between observations become larger. As a general rule, the variance in a set of behavioral measures is a reflection of the influence of a number of factors that combine to produce the behaviors observed. For example, the variation in the levels of production that we observed in the group of sewing machine operators is probably the result of variation in a number of variables that combine to determine the output observed. Different workers possess different amounts of the basic skills that contribute to production levels, and then there is a whole set of motivational influences that operate to determine the extent to which these

TABLE 2.1 Average Hourly Earnings During an Eleven Week Period for a Group of Sewing Machine Operators[1]
(Dollars)

Operator	Week 1	2	3	4	5	6	7	8	9	10	11
Simpson	5.02	5.05	5.00	5.25	5.09	5.06	5.02	4.98	5.07	5.09	4.61
Thomas	3.03	2.72	3.24	3.28	3.20	3.17	3.27	3.33	3.00	3.26	3.01
Gladstone	3.39	3.21	3.40	3.40	3.40	3.24	3.38	3.42	3.46	3.71	3.60
McKennan	2.97	2.68	3.09	2.67	2.09	2.39	2.88	3.39	3.11	2.99	3.09
Ditman	5.35	5.39	5.09	5.10	5.04	4.59	5.03	5.28	4.98	5.52	5.42
Chadwick	5.34	5.49	5.52	4.87	5.33	5.30	5.48	5.51	5.30	5.50	4.85
Scott	1.75	1.95	2.27	2.19	2.07	1.77	1.66	2.04	1.82	1.94	2.04

[1]Each employee is paid on a piece-rate basis, but there is a guaranteed minimum of $3.10 per hour. If during any week an employee's output does not average $3.10 per hour, the company pays the differential and considers this payment a loss. For example, Scott's output during week 1 averaged $1.75/hour. She worked a forty-hour week; therefore, her output earned $70.00, but she was paid ($3.10 × 40 hrs.) = $124.00

FIGURE 2.1   Variance Components of a Selection Test and a Measure of Job Performance

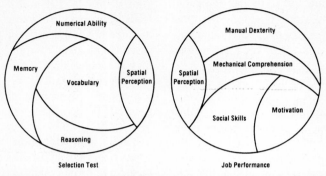

(A) The areas marked off in each circle represent the relative contribution made by a set of basic skills to the variation among test scores and measures of job performance. Notice that both measures reflect the influence of spatial perception skills.

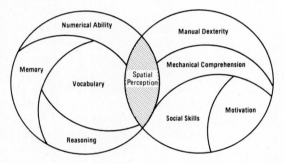

(B) The spatial perception factor accounts for the relationship between test score and job performance measure. This factor accounts for the common variance shared by these two measures.

skills are effectively utilized. In addition, there is a set of past experience and training variables that vary from one worker to the next, and these also contribute to the variance in output. Variance in work performance is, therefore, an expression of the fact that workers vary in the extent to which they possess the basic psychological skills and energies that underlie their work behavior.

The term ''common variance'' means that the individual differences found in one measure reflect influences that in some way are related to individual differences in another variable. For example, if we look at scores on a mental ability test given to a group of college students, we will probably see considerable variation in these scores. If we also look at the grade-point averages of these same

students, we will also see a range of differences. Why do some students have higher grades than others? To some extent it is because some students have higher levels of mental ability than others. The skills and aptitudes that produce individual differences in mental ability scores also contribute to the individual differences we see in grades. Variation observed in one measure, mental ability, seems to be associated with some of the same influences that are underlying variations in a second measure, grade-point. Hence, we say that the two measures share common variance.

Much of what is meant by selection procedures consists of methods for developing and evaluating sources of information that contain common variance with the scales that are used to measure the effectiveness with which an individual performs a job. Job performance scales may be output records, the number of absences or accidents, merit ratings obtained from supervisors, or any of a number of indications bearing on some aspect of the worker's behavior on the job. Whenever it can be demonstrated that the data collected at the time of hiring shares common variance with these performance measures, then an opportunity exists for predicting these aspects of job performance from the information that is gathered before an applicant is hired.

An Index of Common Variance. The index most frequently used to express the extent to which variables share common variance is the *Pearson coefficient of correlation.*[1] Symbolized by r, this coefficient is an index number that varies in both magnitude and sign. The range of values for r begins with -1.00, extends through 0.00, and ends with $+1.00$. The magnitude of the coefficient expresses the *strength* of the relationship between two variables while the sign refers to the *direction* of the relationship. A coefficient of 1.00, regardless of its sign, tells us that the two variables contain only common variance, and that there is a perfect relationship between them that permits completely accurate prediction. A zero coefficient tells us that the two variables share no common variance. In this case, information regarding a person's position on variable 1 gives no information concerning that person's status on variable 2.

Coefficients falling between zero and one indicate that while two variables share some common variance, they each contain variance that is not shared by the other. A convenient way to interpret different values of r is to compute r^2. This value tells us the proportion of variance that is shared by variables 1 and 2. Hence, a coefficient $r = .50$, indicates that one quarter of the variation ($r^2 = .25$) observed in variable 1 is shared with variable 2. If this coefficient were found to describe the relationship between a measure of job performance and salary, for example, we might conclude that of the total magnitude of the differences between workers' salaries, 25 percent of this variation is related in some way to the differences we see in their job performance. Conversely, 75 percent of the variation in salaries is *not* related to the differences we see in the measures of job performance that are being used.

The sign of the correlation coefficient indicates the direction of the relationship between two variables. A positive coefficient indicates that high scores on variable 1 tend to be found accompanying high scores on variable 2. A negative sign indicates that high scores on one variable are associated with low scores on the second variable. For example, a positive r might be obtained if we observe the relationship between the scores on a manual dexterity test and the number of units produced each hour on an assembly task of some sort. If, however, we were to take the same test scores and correlate them with the number of rejected units produced each hour, the obtained coefficient would be negative. Here high scores that indicated high levels of manual dexterity would be associated with *low* scores on a performance scale, when performance is measured in terms of the number of production rejects turned out.

There is one final and very important consideration that must be taken into account when considering the Pearson r: the coefficient accurately describes only linear relationships. In other words,

---

[1]The computational formula for r is:

$$r_{xy} = \frac{N\Sigma XY - (\Sigma X)(\Sigma Y)}{\sqrt{[N\Sigma X^2 - (\Sigma X)^2][N\Sigma Y^2 - (\Sigma Y)^2]}}$$

Where Σ = summation
ΣXY = sum of the $X \cdot Y$ cross products
ΣX = sum of the X values
N = number of XY pairs or number of subjects

ΣX^2 = sum of the squared X values
ΣY = sum of the Y values
ΣY^2 = sum of squared Y values

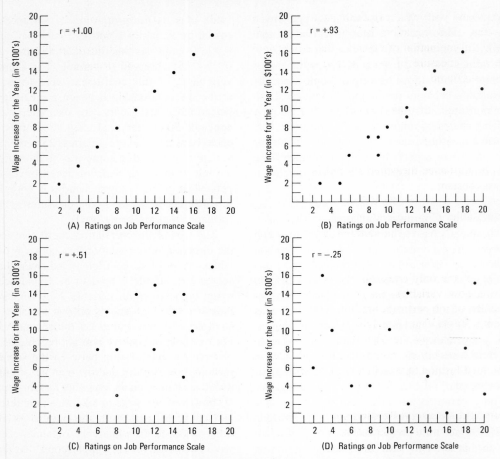

FIGURE 2.2   Groups of workers were evaluated by their supervisor, and subsequently wage increases were given. Each of these four scattergrams depicts a different relationship between performance ratings and wages. Graph (A) represents a perfect (r = 1.00) correlation between the two. Graphs (B) and (C) show weaker positive relationships between the wages awarded and performance, and graph (D) shows a weak negative relationship between the two. Here there is a slight tendency for those who received higher performance scores to have been given smaller wage increases.

this coefficient should be used only when the relationship between two variables can best be described by a straight line (See Figure 2.3). In those instances in which a relationship is nonlinear, the Pearson r provides an underestimation of the relationship between the two variables.

Weighting Predictors

It should be recognized that in a selection situation, as in all other prediction efforts, the dif-

ferent types of predictor information collected do not all share the same common variance with job performance measures. We might find, for example, that the information gathered in the employment interview contributes less to our prediction efforts than do scores obtained from psychological tests. One obvious solution to this problem is to combine the various sources of predictor information in a weighted fashion, the weights being calculated to reflect the magnitude of common variance found between *predictor* and *predicted* measures. The equation below represents this weighted combination of variables that combine to predict the measure of work performance that is being considered.

$$P_i = A + w_1V_1 + w_2V_2 + \ldots + w_kV_k$$

where:

P_i = performance measured for individual i
A = a constant
$w_1, w_2, w_3 \ldots w_k$ = the weight assigned to each variable
$V_1, V_2, V_3 \ldots V_k$ = the value of each predictor variable

This is not the only equation that can be used to describe how variables are combined to yield a prediction of job performance, but it does serve to present a basic idea underlying efforts to predict work performance—the idea being that information from a variety of sources can be combined in a weighted fashion to predict a worker's future job performance.

Errors and Actuarial Predictions.   Since every phase of behavioral measurement is subject to error, the predictions that are made from these measurements also contain inaccuracies. As a consequence, predictions are not made as exact forecasts of future behavior, but are expressed in terms of probabilities that an applicant will perform at a given level of efficiency. The situation faced by selection systems is similar to that faced by an insurance company when it writes a policy. Here the company is aware of certain variables that influence the probability that there will be a claim against the policy; and as a result, premiums are set to take these probabilities into account. For example, a company may find that automobile drivers between the ages of 16 and 25 have a higher probability of having an accident than do drivers between 26 and 35. This does not mean that the company predicts that any one driver will have an accident, but that, as a group, these

FIGURE 2.3   A Nonlinear Relationship between Performance Ratings and Wage Increases.

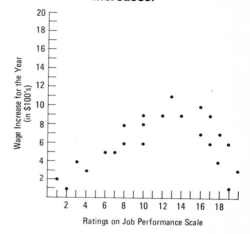

younger drivers are a higher risk. They must, therefore, all pay higher premiums, even though some may never have an accident.

A given score on a selection instrument is comparable to the age of the driver in the above illustration. All who make this score will not display the same job performance, but probabilities that they will perform at an acceptable level can be computed. As a result, selection procedures permit us to make actuarial-type predictions in which estimates are made of the probabilities that a job applicant will or will not adjust successfully to a job. Since these probabilities never reach zero or unity, there is associated with every prediction the risk of error that the predicted outcome will not actually be observed. But, just as insurance companies have found that losses can be reduced by attending to variables like age, geographic location, and state of health, so too can a corporation reduce its costs of personnel procurement by attending to the probabilities that are associated with the information that is generated by selection instruments.

Moderator Variables.   The relationship between the scores on a selection device and a measure of job performance is sometimes found to change as a function of changing values of a third variable. For example, a given selection instrument may display a strong relationship with some aspect of job performance when the group observed consists of male employees. The same instrument may show little relationship with the same measure of performance when the group of applicants observed are women. In this instance we say that the sex of the applicant is a variable that moderates the relationship between selection scores and job performance. Hence, we are dealing with what is called a *moderator variable.*

Blum and Naylor (1968) define a moderator variable as any variable whose value influences the magnitude of the relationship between two other variables. In some instances the presence of a moderator variable is viewed as a nuisance, since it is seen as obscuring the relationship between two variables. In these cases the moderator can be controlled by statistical techniques. Generally, the presence of a moderator gives us added information concerning the nature of the relationship being investigated. For example, the presence of a moderator may *signal* that biases of one sort or another are operating in some facet of the selection system. Suppose sex was found to be moderating the relationship between scores on a selection test and a set of performance evaluation measures: the test was found to predict job performance (measured by the performance evaluation scale) for males but not when it was used with women. This situation may be an indication of the fact that the evaluation of work performance is not being applied to men and women in a uniform fashion (Flaugher, 1978; Haefner, 1977). Biasing influences may be operating to contaminate the performance evaluation of women, and as a result, the selection instrument may not show a significant relationship with this biased performance measure. When the same instrument is applied to a group of male applicants, however, it may show a substantial relationship with the now uncontaminated evaluations of job performance. Hence, the *differential predictability* moderated by the sex variable is interpreted to indicate the presence of biasing influences in the evaluation of women's job performance.

EMPLOYEE SELECTION, EQUITY, AND SOCIAL POLICY

During the recent past there has been a growing concern that selection procedures can at times function to deny certain groups of people access to jobs for which they are qualified (Dunnette & Borman, 1979). Selection biases of this sort may be unintended consequences of a particular employment procedure, or they may represent intended outcomes of a set of hiring practices that have been constructed to discriminate against certain job applicants (Plotkin, 1972). In either case, discrimination in employment that is based on race, religion, sex, age, or national origin is illegal (Byham & Spitzer, 1971), and employers are discouraged from pursuing any hiring practice that does not provide equal access to job vacancies to all who are sufficiently qualified for the work.

The primary legal basis for this proscription is Title VII of the Civil Rights Act of 1964, which forbids discrimination in a wide range of social activities including employment. The so-called Tower amendment to this act [Section 703 (h), U.S.C. 2000e (2) (h)], however, expressly permits the use of professionally developed ability tests in selecting employees, and much of the concern and discussion surrounding the employment implications of Title VII relate to the interpretation and implementation of the language of this amendment. The amendment reads:

> . . . Nor shall it be an unlawful employment practice for an employer to give and to act upon the results of any professionally developed ability test, provided such test, its administration or action upon the results is not designed or used to discriminate because of race, color, religion, sex or national origin.

The government agency given the responsibility for enforcing the provisions of Title VII is the Equal Employment Opportunities Commission (EEOC), and this agency has issued a number of directives dealing with the employment procedures that legally may be used under the provisions of the law. In 1966, and then again in 1970 and 1978, the EEOC developed a set of guidelines on employee-selection procedures, and in 1971 in *Griggs v. Duke Power Co.* the Supreme Court laid down a series of rulings that together with the EEOC guidelines have played a significant role in defining acceptable personnel-selection practices. For example, in the Griggs case the Court struck down the use of employment procedures that are adopted without any meaningful evidence of their relationship with job performance. It also declared illegal selection procedures that have an *adverse impact* on members of minorities seeking employment.

Adverse Impact

The definition of this concept, adverse impact, has proved to be a difficult problem for those responsible for administering selection programs, and in the discussions surrounding the issue there have emerged several points of view regarding what is meant by fairness in selection (Darlington, 1971; Thorndike, 1971; Cole, 1973; Gross & Su, 1975; Hunter & Schmidt, 1976; Flaugher, 1978). Many of these positions are highly technical, relying on statistical concepts to derive their definition of fairness, but the basic intent of all these different approaches is to develop a standard that may be used to identify the presence of bias in selection procedures. Several of the more psychometrically oriented standards look for the presence of moderator variables (for example, race, sex, and so on) functioning to change some aspect of the relationship between test scores and measures of job performance. The standard applied by the EEOC focuses on the proportion of minority and nonminority applicants hired. We will consider this approach first.

When does a selection procedure have adverse impact on the employment opportunities of minorities? In attempting to gauge these negative effects, the EEOC applies what is called the "four-fifths rule" to the selection decisions that are made by a work organization. This rule states:

A selection rate for any race, sex or ethnic group which is less than four-fifths (⅘) (or eighty percent) of the rate for the group with the highest rate will generally be regarded by the Federal enforcement agencies as evidence of adverse impact, while a greater than four-fifths rate will generally not be regarded . . . as evidence of adverse impact. (Federal Register, 1978)

The computations required by this rule are quite simple. Consider an organization selecting employees from groups of black and white job applicants. The four-fifths rule requires that the proportion of black workers selected from among the total group of black applicants be not less than 80 percent of the proportion of white workers selected from the group of white applicants. For example, suppose 25 white workers and 15 black workers apply for a job. The company selects 10 of the white applicants (that is, 40 percent of the 25 white applicants) and 5 black workers (that is, 33 percent of the 15 black applicants). Since the ratio formed by these two percentages is greater than 80 percent—that is, $\frac{33\%}{40\%} \simeq .82$, these selection decisions are not seen by the EEOC as having an adverse impact on the black minority.

Guion's Definition. Guion (1966) applies another standard to identify an unfair selection technique. He states:

Unfair discrimination exists when persons with equal probabilities of success on the job have unequal probabilities of being hired for the job (p. 26).

Cole (1973) refers to this definition as the *equal risk model,* since all job applicants who have the same prospects for job success should have the same prospects for being hired. In adopting a hiring standard from the perspective of this definition, a company would be taking the same risk in hiring people from each applicant group being considered. An employer is never certain that a given applicant will prove to be satisfactory when placed on the job; the risk of making an error is associated with every hiring decision. Guion's standard, however, requries that an employer not be willing to take a higher risk in hiring people from one group than from another. Female applicants, for example, should not have to demonstrate higher qualifications than males in order to be considered good prospects for employment.

Cleary's Regression Model.   Called a regression model in reference to the mathematical function describing the relationship between test scores and measures of job performance, this definition of selection bias states:

> A test is biased for members of a subgroup of the population if, in the prediction of a criterion for which the test is designed, consistent nonzero errors of prediction are made for members of the subgroup (Cleary, 1968, p. 115).

This model contends that selection bias exists in those instances in which consistent over- or underpredictions of job performance are made for one but not another applicant group. Hence, the errors of prediction would tend to operate in one direction for the one group, and consistently under- or overestimate the job potential of its members.

The Incidence of Selection Bias

There is no definitive information concerning the frequency with which individuals are denied employment because of the biases that operate in a selection system. One can find evidence in the research literature, however, suggesting that every phase of the selection process can unfairly restrict employment opportunities to certain groups of applicants. Beginning with the insertion of a "help wanted" advertisement (Bem & Bem, 1973) and extending through the evaluation of an applicant's work resumé (Newman, 1978; Newman & Krzystofiak, 1979), the employment interview (Cohen & Bunker, 1975), the application blank (Pace & Schoenfeldt, 1977) and employment tests (Ruda & Albright, 1968; Farr, O'Leary & Bartlett, 1971, Hamner et al., 1974), one can find numerous instances of selection bias functioning to screen out

minority group applicants. There is little information, however, that can be used to form a picture of how frequently selection instruments function in a biased fashion.

In one rather extensive study of selection test bias Farr, O'Leary, and Bartlett (1971) analyzed the manner in which selection systems functioned as they were used by a group of government agencies. In general, these authors found evidence of some type of bias in approximately one-third of the comparisons that were made among different ethnic groups. Further analyses, however, revealed that the most frequently occurring patterns of bias did not result in any decrease in the frequency with which minority group members were hired. In fact, one of the two most frequent patterns of bias denied employment opportunities to applicants who were members of the majority group.

Differential Prediction.   We will consider the concept of validity in more detail at a later point in the chapter, but for the time being consider the term as referrring to the accuracy with which a selection device predicts job performance. Differential prediction is a general term that is used to refer to situations in which a selection device is capable of predicting future job performance with a different level of accuracy for one ethnic group than for another (Boehm, 1972; 1977). Evidence of differential prediction indicates that separate prediction equations should be developed for the various ethnic groups. Traditionally, all data from selection instruments and job performance measures were combined to estimate a single prediction equation that describes the relationship between the two. If, however, the selection instrument is capable of predicting job performance for only some but not all of the applicant groups, there exists a potential source of bias in the selection procedure.

Boehm (1977) reviewed thirty-one different selection studies in which 583 pairs of validity indexes were available, and in 75 percent of these comparisons there was no evidence of differential prediction. Furthermore, there was considerable evidence that when it did occur, differential prediction tended to be found in studies whose research methodologies deviated from commonly endorsed test evaluation practices. Boehm concludes that a continuing focus on differential prediction does not appear to be a worthwhile approach to the general area of selection and equal employment opportunities (Boehm, 1977, p. 1953; Linn, 1978).

JOB ANALYSIS AND CRITERION DEVELOPMENT

There are two fundamental requirements that apply to all employment selection systems: First, the system must be built upon reliable knowledge of the positions that are to be filled; and second, the system must include provisions for measuring the effectiveness of job performance. The first requirement involves a wide range of data collection procedures that are referred to collectively as *job analysis*. The second requirement is known as *criterion development,* which refers to procedures that are used to determine the accuracy of the hiring decisions.

These procedures should not be seen as peripheral or auxiliary parts of employment selection; rather they are central aspects of a system of interrelated data-collection procedures. If one aspect of this system is weak, the effectiveness of the entire program will be diminished. As a result, both job analysis and criterion development are factors that must be taken into consideration in the early phases of selection program development. Every step in the selection sequence is guided by a job analysis and is directed toward a criterion measure.

Job Analysis

Work organizations need accurate information about the jobs involved in their operations. As a general rule, effective management is built on knowledge of what people should be doing in their work roles, and virtually every phase of the management process has its own requirements for job information. Personnel administration is no exception, and the programs that are carried out in this area are all guided by the data that are obtained through job analysis. Job analysis refers to any systematic effort carried out to collect information about jobs. This is a broad term that does not identify a narrow range of techniques (McCormick, 1976); rather, it includes approaches to information gathering that are as diverse as interviewing, time and motion study, and the use of psychological tests. The one basic requirement of job analysis is that the steps taken to collect information be systematic. This means that the procedures to be followed should be planned and the rules of measurement and observation established before any study is initiated.

In those instances in which job analysis information is to be used in conjunction with a hiring program, the data sought is of a type that will shed light on the employee characteristics that contribute to job performance. In these situations the job analyst observes the job, reviews its technical and skill requirements, and interviews supervisors and employees who are knowledgeable about the work. From these data a *job description* is prepared. The job description contains a list of *job requirements,* that is, attributes thought to be necessary to do the job. Steps are then planned to obtain a satisfactory measure of these attributes, and these measures will constitute the predictor instruments that will be used to predict future job performance. This step of moving from a job description to a trial set of predictor instruments is largely a matter of judgment, since there are few objective techniques that aid in this process (McCormick, DeNisi, & Shaw, 1979). A well-developed job description, however, based on accurate information, is a substantial help in choosing instruments and procedures that will be useful in selecting new employees.

Uses of Job Analysis

Information collected in a job analysis may be put to many purposes. The data collected from any study of jobs may reflect the request for informa-

FIGURE 2.4   Sources of Workers

U.S. DEPARTMENT OF LABOR
BUREAU OF EMPLOYMENT SECURITY
UNITED STATES EMPLOYMENT SERVICE

JOB ANALYSIS SCHEDULE

1. Job title ___TOOL DESIGNER___   2. Number ___9901613___

3. Number employed M ___4___ F ___0___   4. Establishment No. ___99-95-40___

6. Alternate titles ___junior tool designer___   5. Date ___March 10, 1964___

___senior tool designer___   Number of sheets ___4___

_____   8. Industry ___Construction Machinery Mfg.___

_____   9. Branch ___Concrete Mixers, Conveyor Equip.___

7. Dictionary title   ___TOOL DESIGNER 0-48.41___
and code   10. Department ___Tool Design___

11. Work Performed:

Designs special tools, dies, jigs, and fixtures for use on all types of production
machines to machine parts from raw material through finished stages.

   1. Studies tooling problem to determine the basic part and machine specifications
governing the design of the tool: (3-25%) (See Comments.)

      a. Reads Tool Order, examines blueprint of finished part, and
analyzes Sequence of Operations Sheet to determine machining
operations required of new tool.

      b. Studies part and part blank and computes the dimensions of part
or parts before and after machine operation for which tool design is required.
(See Comments). Sketches part in relationship to tool as guide to tool design.

      c. Examines machine for which tool is to be made and confers with shop foreman
to gather information to make decisions relative to designing the tool needed to
perform the necessary machining operations. Draws sketches of machine and
part incorporating basic decisions made, including dimensions, clearances, and
tolerances.

   2. Designs the tool: (3-30%)

      a. Develops the form and shape of the tool by studying tool design drawing
of other similar tools, by comparing own ideas of the tool's design with
accumulated part and machine specifictaions, and by drawing rough and
semidetailed sketches.

      b. Calculates final detail dimensions, clearances, and tolerances
of tool, using *Design Reference Book,* machinists' handbook,
mechanical engineers' handbook, trigonometry, slide ruler, and
standard formulas.

      c. Draws general assembly drawings of complete tool showing top,
front, and side views, tool, machine, and part in actual use, and
all dimensions, tolerances, and clearances.

(CONTINUE ON SUPPLEMENTARY SHEETS)

Analyst ___N. Devers___   Reviewer ___Miss T. Day___

Abbreviated job analysis schedule used by U.S. Department of Labor.

FIGURE 2.4   Sources of Workers

12. Experience: None _____ Acceptable ___ TOOL DESIGN DRAFTSMAN

13. Training data: Minimum training time— a. Inexperienced workers.
    b. Experienced workers.   6 months

TRAINING	SPECIFIC JOB SKILLS ACQUIRED THROUGH TRAINING
In-plant (on job) training TOOL DESIGNER APPRENTICE	Fundamental principles of tool designing. Experience designing tools. Calculating dimensions and reading blueprints and specifications. Knowledge of algebra and other mathematics that are helpful in computations.
Vocational training Technical school or vocational school. Course must include algebra, geometry, trigonometry, mechanical drawing, machine shop practice, and shop mathematics.	
Technical training	
SRW Eng. General education	
Activities and hobbies Metal Working, Wood Working	Fundamentals of designing and knowledge of calculations

14. Apprenticeship: Formal ___X___ Informal _____ Length required __5 yrs. DESIGN DRAFTSMAN__

15. Relation to other jobs:
    a. Promotions from and to, transfers, etc; From DETAILER or DESIGN DRAFTSMAN; promotion
       to LEADMAN (GROUP LEADER)

    b. Supervision received: General ___X___ Close _____ By CHIEF TOOL DESIGNER
                                                                        (Title)

    c. Supervision given: None _____ Number supervised __3__ Titles DESIGN DRAFTSMAN

The following items must be covered on supplementary sheets

PERFORMANCE REQUIREMENTS

16. Responsibility (consider material or product, safety of others, equipment or process, cooperation with others, instruction of others, public contacts, and the like).
17. Job knowledge (consider pre-employment and on-the-job knowledge of equipment, materials, working procedures, techniques, and processes).
18. Mental application (consider initiative, adaptability, independent judgment, and mental alertness).
19. Dexterity and accuracy (consider speed and degree of precision, dexterity, accuracy, coordination, expertness, care, and deftness of manipulation, operation, or processing of materials, tools, instruments, or gages used).

COMMENTS

20. Equipment, materials, and supplies.
21. Definition of terms.
22. General comments.

Abbreviated job analysis schedule used by U.S. Department of Labor.

tion that has been received from a number of departments in the organization. The following represents a list of the more important uses for job analysis data:

1. Recruitment and Hiring

Knowledge of the duties and requirements of a job is an essential first step in developing a selection system. The nature of the jobs determines the kinds of data that will be collected. As a general rule, a job analysis gives an organization valuable leads concerning the kind of behavior needed for job success.

2. Placement

Hiring and placement decisions are often made simultaneously. There are times, however, when placement is a separate step that is taken after the decision to hire has been made, and the problem now becomes one of matching applicant characteristics with the requirements of the positions that are vacant. A careful job analysis provides information concerning these requirements.

3. Criterion Development

It is apparent that an organization must have good information concerning the requirements of a job before it can develop adequate measures of the success with which these requirements are being met.

4. Training

Job analysis can be geared to collect information that will go into the construction of an industrial training program. Job analysis is used to provide information regarding the skills and knowledge that are involved in satisfactory job performance.

5. Job Evaluation

Decisions must be made concerning the wages that are to be paid for a job. An organization must establish its own wage structure, just as it must set prices for its goods and services, and job evaluation procedures are techniques that attempt to estimate the worth of each job. They involve judgmental procedures that evaluate the information generated by a job analysis. These evaluations are then translated into dollars and cents.

6. Employee Relations

It is important that employees have a clear idea of their jobs and their obligations. Do electricians change light bulbs or is this the janitor's job? Who moves materials from one location to the next; is it a teamster's job or is it the responsibility of each work crew? These are the kinds of questions that are answered in labor negotiations that are based on job analysis information.

7. Performance Evaluation

Before one can determine whether an employee is doing a good job, there must be an accurate description of the standards and objectives of work activities. Merit-rating programs involve an evaluation of the extent to which an employee meets the requirements of a job as it is defined by job analysis procedures. Merit ratings often serve as a source of criterion data.

Methods of Job Analysis

Just as there are many uses for job analysis information, there are also many data collection methods that can be adapted to a job analysis study. The objective is to obtain accurate information concerning a job, and conceivably any of the observational tools used by behavioral scientists may be employed to collect this information. McCormick (1976) lists eleven general approaches to collecting information about jobs:

1. Observation
2. Individual interview with current job holders
3. Group interview with work teams
4. Technical conference with experienced personnel
5. Questionnaire—structured
6. Questionnaire—open-ended
7. Diary records of work activity
8. Critical incidents—records of exceptionally good or poor job performance
9. Equipment design information
10. Recordings of job activities—films, time and motion study, etc.
11. Company records

FIGURE 2.5   Checklist Used To Describe Physical Demands of Work.

DEPARTMENT OF LABOR
BUREAU OF EMPLOYMENT SECURITY
UNITED STATES EMPLOYMENT SERVICE

PHYSICAL DEMANDS FORM

Job Title ___TOOL DESIGNER___   Occupational Code ___0-48.41___

PHYSICAL ACTIVITIES		WORKING CONDITIONS	
1 _X_ Walking	16 _O_ Throwing	51 _X_ Inside	66 _O_ Mechanical hazards
2 _O_ Jumping	17 _O_ Pushing	52 _O_ Outside	67 _O_ Moving objects
3 _O_ Running	18 _O_ Pulling	53 _O_ Hot	68 _O_ Cramped quarters
4 _O_ Balancing	19 _X_ Handling	54 _O_ Cold	69 _O_ High places
5 _O_ Climbing	20 _X_ Fingering	55 _O_ Sudden temperature	70 _O_ Exposure to burns
6 _O_ Crawling	21 _O_ Feeling	changes	71 _O_ Electrical hazards
7 _X_ Standing	22 _X_ Talking	56 _O_ Humid	72 _O_ Explosives
8 _O_ Turning	23 _X_ Hearing	57 _O_ Dry	73 _O_ Radiant energy
9 _O_ Stooping	24 _X_ Seeing	58 _O_ Wet	74 _O_ Toxic conditions
10 _O_ Crouching	25 _O_ Color vision	59 _O_ Dusty	75 _X_ Working with others
11 _O_ Kneeling	26 _O_ Depth perception	60 _O_ Dirty	76 _X_ Working around others
12 _X_ Sitting	27 _O_ Working speed	61 _O_ Odors	77 _O_ Working alone
13 _O_ Reaching	28 ___	62 _O_ Noisy	78 ___
14 _O_ Lifting	29 ___	63 _X_ Adequate lighting	79 ___
15 _O_ Carrying	30 ___	64 _X_ Adequate ventilation	80 ___
		65 _O_ Vibration	

DETAILS OF PHYSICAL ACTIVITIES:

   Sits (90%). Reaches for blueprints, specifications, and designing
equipment. Reads blueprints and makes calculations. Stands and walks
10% to and from other personnel to assign work or to confer with them.

DETAILS OF WORKING CONDITIONS:

   Inside (100%). Works in constant contact with others in adequately
lighted and ventilated room.

DETAILS OF HAZARDS:

   None.

Within each of these eleven items is an assortment of individual methods, but perhaps the most commonly used approach involves the direct observation of the work task, aided by an observational schedule which the analyst uses to identify the components of work activity (See Figures 2.4 and 2.5). Considerable progress has recently been made in developing questionnaires that provide a detailed breakdown of job activities, and these instruments serve a useful role in analyzing jobs down into their constituent parts. Of these instruments, the most promising appears to be the *Position Analysis Questionnaire* (PAQ) developed by E.J. McCormick and his students (McCormick, Jeanneret, & Meacham, 1972; McCormick, 1976).

The Position Analysis Questionnaire. The PAQ describes jobs in terms of a set of 187 elements that are thought to represent the "building blocks" of job performance. These elements cover a range of human activities that combine in different patterns to form the duties of various jobs. The individual elements have been classified into six clusters or divisions that are presented below, accompanied by one of the elements found in each.

Division	*Element*
1. Information input	1. Use of written materials
2. Mental Processes	2. Reasoning in problem solving
3. Work output	3. Handling objects/materials
4. Relationships with others	4. Instructing
5. Job context	5. Low temperatures
6. Other job considerations	6. Specified (controlled) work pace

The PAQ requires that jobs be observed and rated on each of the 187 scales associated with the behavioral elements, and statistical procedures have been developed to collect the individual ratings into a smaller set of job activity components. As a rule, jobs are described in terms of the scores obtained on each of the six divisions identified above. Hence, a profile of scores can be presented for different jobs as a representation of the behavioral content. Jobs can be compared, grouped according to common activity elements; and what is more important for the present chapter, knowledge of the content of a job, especially when it is in precise quantitative form, can lead to the selection of more effective hiring instruments. Consider, for example, psychological tests. Knowledge of the performance requirements of a test, coupled with a job's PAQ profile, will give a personnel department useful information concerning the predictive potential of the test.

One major problem with the procedures involved with the PAQ is the complex nature and time-consuming requirements for a description of job content. For instance, Ash and Edgell (1975) found the readability level of the PAQ to reach the college graduate level of difficulty. But complex activities require complicated measurements, and the PAQ represents a major resource for an organization that seeks a detailed and quantitatively based system of job analysis. The PAQ will be considered again in this chapter when the concept of content validity is discussed.

The Criterion

Smith (1976) defines a criterion as "a measure for judging the effectiveness of persons, organizations, treatments, or predictors of behavior, results and organizational effectiveness" (Dunnette, 1976, p. 745).

When industrial psychologists talk about a criterion they are referring to a measurement of performance that is being used to define the level of success with which an employee carries out the duties of a job. The information collected by a selection system attempts to predict this criterion measure; and as a consequence, criterion scores are often referred to as the *predicted variables* in a selection system. The principal role played by a criterion in a selection program is as a source of feedback concerning the predictive accuracy of the different components of the hiring program. Those selection instruments that show a significant relationship with these measures of job success are retained and used to help in the framing of hiring decisions.

Types of Criterion Data.　Numerous sources have been drawn on to supply criterion data, and each work situation will suggest a different set of criterion measures. The following list, however, probably encompasses the major sources of this type of information (Brogden & Taylor, 1950):

1. Production records (including sales)	5. Work sample tests
2. Merit ratings—subjective performance appraisals	6. Public relations effectiveness
3. Tenure and absences	7. Reactions of subordinates and peers
4. Progress in training programs	8. Dollar criteria

The last item on the list, a dollar criterion, refers to a measure of job performance that has been translated into dollars-and-cents equivalents. This approach places the measurement of all criterion elements on a common, dollar-value, scale.

In looking at this list one may question whether the data obtained from these different sources are not just measures of one underlying performance factor. For example, if employees consistently produce at high levels, isn't it safe to conclude that they will also place high on most of these other measures? The answer to this appears to be no. The research literature has tended to show that many measures of work performance are not closely interrelated with one another (Buel, 1960; Turner, 1960; Taylor et al., 1965; James, 1973); it is probably safe to assume that the different sources and types of criterion measures do provide different views of job performance. Hence, criterion measures can consist of weighted elements that are brought together to provide a more complete coverage of the complex psychological events that enter into job performance. This can be a demanding procedure since criterion measures must meet a relatively large number of standards that concern both technical and organizational considerations. As a result, the choice of a set of criterion measurements is not an easy task, nor is it one that is directed solely by the principles of good measurement.

The choice of a criterion usually represents a compromise of some sort between the values of the organization, the availability of data, and the measurement strength of the available data. Blum and Naylor (1968, p. 182) list the requirements for an adequate criterion.

Although these fourteen properties are interrelated and overlapping, the list does succeed in impressing one with the complex nature of criterion development. In the final analysis, however, there are not right or wrong criterion measures, except those like sex, race, and so on that are proscribed by law as sources of performance evaluation. There are measurement weaknesses that may lead an organization to reject a given criterion measure, but first and foremost the criterion reflects the value orientation of a work organization. That which defines a successful employee is largely a matter for management determination, although there would doubtless be considerable agreement among managers regarding their definition of success for any given job. Disagreement over these definitions probably increases, however, as one moves up the organizational hierarchy to consider the performance effectiveness of higher-level management personnel.

A major problem in criterion development involves the attempts to translate management's concepts of success into an effective and accurate measurement scale. The available performance records maintained by a company may at times serve as a convenient and tempting alternative to the costly efforts required to construct criterion measures that are more closely tuned to management's value system. For example, research and development personnel may easily be evaluated by calculating the number of research reports each scientist has prepared, but a measure of research creativity may fall closer to management's definition of performance effectiveness. The problem is that such measures may not be readily available; hence the criterion chosen is one that may not be able to satisfy completely management's desire to translate value judgments into accurate measurement (Guion, 1961).

1. Reliable	8. Predictable
2. Realistic	9. Inexpensive
3. Representative	10. Understandable
4. Related to other criteria	11. Measurable
5. Acceptable to job analyst	12. Relevant
6. Acceptable to management	13. Uncontaminated and free of bias
7. Consistent from one situation to the next	14. Discriminating

The Dynamic Nature of Criteria. Psychologists actually know little about long-term performance consistency in work situations (Rothe, 1978), but the available evidence indicates that it is not impossible to find some rather significant fluctuations in criterion scores from one time period to the next. For example, Ghiselli and Haire (1960) found considerable inconsistency in the performance of 56 taxicab drivers whose production records were observed over an 18-week period. Along similar lines, Scott and Hamner (1975) found that different patterns of change in performance seemed to exert different influences on the performance ratings that were made on a group of people working in a laboratory setting. Hence fluctuations over time and the pattern of change in performance are factors that can enter a criterion measure, perhaps as an unwanted source of variance. As a consequence, it is clear that criterion measures must involve a sample of time as well as behavioral elements, and any such measure must be interpreted with reference to both these dimensions.

Criterion Relevance. Thorndike (1949), Guion (1961), and others used the term "ultimate criterion" to refer to a measure of performance that is a complete and final index of job success. The ultimate criterion is that measure of job performance containing every conceivable factor related to success on a given job, and it is a measure that extends into time to include all possible sources of information concerning how well an individual performs. Such a criterion measure is purely hypothetical in nature, but the concept does serve as a reference against which one may evaluate the available criterion scores that are being used in a selection study.

Criterion relevance is defined with reference to the ultimate criterion, and it is identified as the extent to which the available criterion corresponds to the ultimate criterion. Criterion relevance is a concept that concerns both the accuracy and completeness of the measures used to define successful job performance. There are a number of ways in which information regarding criterion relevance may be collected (James, 1973), but the hypo-thetical nature of the ultimate criterion makes it almost inevitable that the evidence assembled will be incomplete. In the final analysis human judgment and data bearing on the content characteristics of the job and the criterion measure appear to be the most practical sources of information concerning this important question of criterion relevance.

Criterion Deficiency. Criterion deficiency refers to a source of bias that occurs whenever the actual criterion does not contain all the behavioral elements that are identified with the ultimate criterion. Most often, the elements missing are those that are most difficult to measure, and this includes the broad range of personality, social, and motivational variables that contribute to job success. Furthermore, since the ultimate criterion is, in a practical sense, unattainable, all criterion measures that one finds in use in a real work setting are deficient.

Criterion Contamination. This type of bias refers to the presence of unwanted behavioral elements in the criterion measure. In this instance, the actual criterion scale is tapping behaviors that do not form part of the ultimate criterion, and people are differentiated, in part, on the basis of behaviors that are considered to be irrelevant to the successful performance of the job. Several types of criterion contamination have been identified. For example, *opportunity bias* refers to differences in job performance that can be attributed to unequal opportunity to perform successfully. Variation in sales performance, for instance, may reflect differences in the territories that may make it difficult to achieve high levels of sales in some but not others.

Another type of contamination is sometimes called *knowledge of predictor bias*. Here a supervisor has knowledge of the selection information that led to the hiring of an employee, and this knowledge influences the supervisor's ratings of job performance that are used for the criterion. Bias of this sort can operate in a positive or negative direction. It also can function along with opportunity bias to complicate criterion measurement. For instance, knowledge of the information that led to hiring a highly recommended employee might lead a supervisor to assign the new employee to a position where job success is more readily attainable. Subsequent criterion ratings will, therefore, reflect these compounding biases.

One could go on assigning names to different sources of contamination that may enter criterion measurements, but the principal point to be made is that care should be taken to detect the presence of unwanted sources of systematic variance in criterion scores, because their presence will tend to distort the information that is generated to evaluate the effectiveness of the selection system.

SELECTION INSTRUMENTS

It is now time to consider the selection procedures that are used during the time the applicant is in contact with the work organization. Psychological tests, interviews, application blanks, and assessment center programs are, perhaps, the more prominent members of a long list of procedures that may be used to gather information regarding the suitability of job applicants. In this section we will consider these techniques along with some ideas that are important to the evaluation of their effectiveness.

The Application Blank

The application blank is a widely used instrument which, when properly constructed, can make a significant contribution to a company's selection program. Essentially, the application blank is a form that solicits personal background information from each job applicant (see Figure 2.6). Some of

this information, such as age, address, number of dependents, and social security number is used in the admininistration of medical, retirement, and vacation programs. Some of the entries can also be used as a starting point for an employment interview. Here information concerning such things as past employment experience and reasons for terminating previous jobs can be followed up by an interviewer who is attempting to construct an accurate picture of an applicant's employment record. Used in this fashion, the application blank gives direction to further efforts to secure information about an applicant, but there are more rigorous functions that may be served.

Data taken from application blanks frequently has been found to be related to future job performance. For example, the author recently had contact with a company involved in the production of textile products. At several of its plants the company had been experiencing employee turnover that was approaching 100 percent each year. An examination of the information collected on application blanks revealed that certain personal characteristics were associated with a very high probability of early termination. Age was one such variable. Turnover was very high among employees who were under twenty-one when they were hired. For instance, at one plant, 80 percent of these younger workers quit before they had been employed six months. Another application blank item, length of tenure on previous jobs, was also found to be a significant indicator of future employment tenure (Table 2.2). In both plants, as an applicant's tenure on the previous job increased there was a corresponding increase in the percent who remained on their present jobs for at least six months.

TABLE 2.2　Past Employment Stability and Present Job Tenure[1]

Time on Previous Job:	0–6 months	7–12 months	Over 12 months
Plant I	35.3	54.6	67.6
Plant II	35.9	45.4	76.8

[1]Cell entry: percent who remained on their present jobs for at least six months.

FIGURE 2.6

EMPLOYMENT APPLICATION **ABC INC.** XYZ Division	Job Salary	Do Not Write in This Space Supervisor Availability

Name				Today's Date
Last	First	Middle		Home
Present Address				Phone

How Long Lived At This Address	Distance to Our Plant	How Will You Get to Work	Nearest Phone not at your home
Previous Address		How Long Lived There	Soc. Sec. Number

PERSONAL

Type Work for Which You Are Applying	Do You Want Full Time Work	☐ Yes ☐ No	Earnings Expected	
Other Work in Which You Are Interested	Will You Work Daily Overtime If Needed	☐ Yes ☐ No	Will You Work Some Weekends If Asked	☐ Yes ☐ No
Birth Date	(The Age Discrimination in Employment Act of 1967 prohibits discrimination on the basis of age.)		☐ Right Handed ☐ Left Handed	

Citizen of U.S.?	If No, Do You Have Work Permit?

List Any Physical
or Health Problems

Amount of Time Lost from Work or School in Past Year	Reason

How Were You Referred?	Have You Worked for ABC before?	☐ Yes ☐ No	When

In Emer- gency Who Should We Notify?	Name ———————————— Phone ——————— Address ———————————————	Please Check ☐ Spouse ☐ Minor Child If This Is ☐ Parent ☐

EDUCATION (Specific academic level or achievement not needed for consideration for employment.)

School	Name	Location	Major	Dates From	Dates To	Years Completed	Diploma, Degree Certificate	Grade Average
Grade								
High								
College								
Graduate								
Vocational Apprentice								
Other								

GENERAL

List leadership positions held in past.
(Exclude racial, religious, or nationality groups)

Have you ever been convicted of a crime? (Other than a traffic violation)	Reason	When

(Criminal record does not automatically disqualify applicant for consideration for employment.)

PLEASE TURN OVER

FIGURE 2.6

WORK EXPERIENCE-Including Military Service

Company Name & Address (Begin With Most Recent)	Dates and Wages		Nature of Your Work	Reason for Leaving
1.	From	To		
	Wages			
	Beginning	End	Supervisor	
2.	From	To		
	Wages			
	Beginning	End	Supervisor	
3.	From	To		
	Wages			
	Beginning	End	Supervisor	
4.	From	To		
	Wages			
	Beginning	End	Supervisor	
5.	From	To		
	Wages			
	Beginning	End	Supervisor	

By Number List Those Companies We Should Not Contact and State Reason.	For reference purposes, if you worked at any above places under a different name, list name and place of employment.

Do You Hold Seniority With Any Other Company? ☐ Yes ☐ No   How Much?

IF APPLYING FOR OFFICE JOB, PLEASE ANSWER	Typing Speed	Shorthand Speed	Office Machines You Operate

REFERENCES (other than relatives)

Name	Address	Phone	Occupation

I affirm that all answers to the foregoing questions are correct to the best of my ability and knowledge. I hereby authorize ABC Inc. to verify and investigate this information and understand that failure to complete this application, concealment of information, intentional omissions or misrepresentation will be grounds for refusal of employment or immediate dismissal.

Signature_____

TABLE 2.3 Comparison of Item Responses by Long- and Short-Tenure Office Employees

Items on Application Blank	Percentage of	
	Short-Tenure Group	Long-Tenure Group
Local address	39	62
Within city	50	36
Outlying suburbs		
Age	35	8
Under 20	38	32
21–25	8	2
26–30	7	10
31–35	11	48
35 and over		
Previous salary	31	30
Under $2000	41	38
$2000–3000	13	12
$3000–4000	4	4
Over $4000		
Age of children	12	4
Preschool	53	33
Public school	35	63
High school or older		

Source: Adapted from E.A. Fleishman and J. Berniger. One way to reduce office turnover. *Personnel,* American Management Association, 1960, *37,* 63–69. Copyright 1960 by the American Psychological Association. Adapted by permission of the author and publisher.

Relatively simple procedures are needed to identify items that are related to future job performance. Evidence of significantly different levels of job performance observed among those who make different responses to a given item suggests that the item is tapping information that will prove useful in selecting applicants. Consider, for example, the data presented in Table 2.3 that was obtained from the application blank responses of a group of 120 women clerical workers who had been classified according to the length of time they remained in their jobs. Notice the tendency of women with young children to be found more frequently in the short-tenure group that had quit their jobs within two years. Information of this sort signals an employment office to recognize the risks in hiring applicants who fall into this category. One caution should be exercised, however, when using the application blank for selection purposes. There is continuing need for the relationship between job performance and application blank items to be reevaluated, since changes in the labor market and in the conditions and duties of work may alter the usefulness of the information collected. As a consequence, the use of an application blank, as is the case with all types of selection instruments, requires a commitment to a continuing program of development and evaluation. Selection programs require more than just the initial development phase.

Application Blanks and Fair Employment Practices. Application forms that are used to select people for jobs are subject to the same legal requirements as are tests or any other component of the selection system (Pace & Schoenfeldt, 1977). This means that a company using such an instrument should be able to show that the items on the blank are job-related and do not have an adverse impact on protected minority groups. When adverse impact is in evidence, then the organization must be able to demonstrate that the instrument maintains a significant relationship with a clearly defensible criterion of job performance. Hence, as part of the development of application forms a company must invest considerable care in avoiding items that do discriminate against groups of applicants who represent protected minorities.

Effectiveness of the Application Blank.
There is a considerable body of research evidence indicating that the application blank has been used successfully in hiring employees (Asher, 1972). In a wide variety of work situations application blanks have proved to yield data that are related to some aspect of future job performance. For example, a number of studies have found that employee turnover can be predicted from the responses made to an application blank (Lee & Booth, 1974; Cascio, 1976), and Nevo (1976) has been able to show significant relationships between these kinds of data and promotion success in a military setting.

Some express concern regarding the possibilities that job applicants will consciously distort the information they supply on the application blank, and there are a few studies, for example, Goldstein (1971), that have found this to be a problem. But the weight of the research evidence (Cascio, 1975) suggests that high levels of accuracy are usually found in the information recorded on the application blank. Hence, with proper care in its construction and with attention to EEOC considerations, the application blank is a useful tool for making employment decisions.

Psychological Tests

Perhaps the most widely recognized but not necessarily the most widely used technique for personnel selection is the psychological test. Testing has many advantages to offer a company that wishes to improve the quality of its selection program. Primarily, the psychological test can give an organization information about basic skills, aptitudes, and personality dimensions that are not easily observable in the interview. In addition, a test can provide this information at relatively little

cost and within a short period of time. As a consequence, psychological tests are important and potentially useful additions to the selection program of an organization that has available the technical competence needed to install and use these instruments effectively.

There are several general properties of psychological tests that should be considered before dealing with their specific application to an industrial setting. These are characteristics that are independent of the content of the test, and in a broad sense they refer to the characteristics of tests as they function as observational tools. For instance, psychological tests are *standardized*. By this is meant that there are certain aspects of administration and scoring that remain the same each time the test is given: on each administration of a given test the same items are presented, they are in the same order, the instructions do not change, and the time limits do not vary. Standardization is an important property of tests, since it permits us to view different individuals against the common background created by the testing situation. The fact that certain important aspects of the situation have been standardized permits us to interpret differences in test performance in terms of individual differences in psychological makeup rather than in terms of the results of a changing situation.

A psychological test is an observational tool. The test creates a behavior situation within which an individual's responses can be observed. These observations are then translated into a system of numbers that forms the scale of measurement associated with the test. This scoring system is not dependent on the subjective values of the individual scoring the test, and so we say that the test is *objective*. Objectivity, therefore refers to an observational system in which the values, desires, and biases of the observer do not play a significant role in determining the scores that are obtained. Most tests used in employment situations tend to be objective.

A test is also a *sample of behavior*. Psychological tests consist of items that account for a relatively small cross section of the behavioral domain that is of interest to the psychologist. On the basis of performance on this small set of items, inferences are drawn that estimate an individual's performance capabilities on all possible items that could be constructed from the domain under consideration. Hence, an individual's performance on the sample of items is generalized to the larger domain, and an inference is made that performance on the sample is representative of the level of performance across the entire measurement domain.

Selecting a Test.   After the job analysis has been completed and the criterion measures have been developed, an organization must choose the psychological tests that will be used. This is a choice that in large measure is based on knowledge of the technical literature, a knowledge of the job conditions, and the criterion measures under consideration. Guion (1961) uses the term "hunch" to describe this judgment; but whatever it is called, this choice has not been reduced to formulas or a set of strict rules that make the decision a matter of routine calculation. There are no well-established procedures for selecting tests; but on the basis of a careful job analysis, realistic hypotheses can be constructed concerning the likelihood that a particular test will prove to be successful in selecting competent employees. Once a test has been selected, there follows a series of procedures whose principal purpose is to evaluate the effectiveness with which the test functions in selecting new employees. Hence, a poor choice of tests leads an organization into an elaborate data collection procedure, the outcome of which will indicate that the chosen test is, in fact, ineffective.

One must look to many different sources of information in choosing a test, and in the final analysis, the choice must rely on competent professional judgment. The following list contains some of the more important considerations that enter into this judgment:

Information about the job, the criteria, and the applicant pool come from the preliminary work that has been done by the technical staff. Information concerning tests that are commercially available may be obtained from the technical literature. For example, the standard index of available tests is the *Eighth Mental Measurements Yearbook* (Buros, 1978). This is a reference source that lists and reviews 1184 psychological tests that are available for a variety of measurement purposes. *Psychological Abstracts* is another source of information regarding the research that is reported each year in all areas of psychological inquiry. Among the topics considered are those that involve the application of psychological tests to the employment setting. It is here that one may find the most current information concerning the effectiveness of certain tests as they have been observed in selection problems.

Assessing a Test's Usefulness.   There is no guarantee that a test will make a contribution to a company's selection program. Careful study of the job and knowledge of the research that has been done on individual tests will improve the chances that a test that is chosen for a tryout will show a healthy relationship with job performance. The ultimate check on a test, however, involves empirical studies that estimate the relationship between test scores and criterion scores. Although there are many factors that can contribute to the accuracy of a test, there are two basic concepts that are applied to the evaluation of the effectiveness of a psychological test. These concepts are *validity* and *reliability*.

Validity.   In general, the concept of validity refers to the nature of the behaviors tapped by a test. Cronbach (1971) defines validity in terms of the extent to which accurate inferences can be drawn

1. The requirements of the job
2. The nature of the performance criteria
3. The characteristics of the applicant pool
4. The technical properties of the tests
5. The past effectiveness of the test
6. EEOC guidelines

from the scores of the test. This definition contends that high test validity implies that the behavioral statements that are made on the basis of test scores tend to be accurate. Hence, a test is valid to the extent to which it measures the behaviors that are the intended subject matter of the test. For example, if a test is constructed to measure certain dimensions of mental ability, then a demonstration of validity requires evidence that the test does, in fact, measure these abilities. Validity has often been defined as the extent to which the test measures what it purports to measure. There are several approaches to the evaluation of test validity, however, and each gives us a somewhat different view of this concept. Therefore, we will consider each of these separately as a different perspective on the more general idea.

Predictive Validity. Of all the approaches to validity determination, predictive validity is probably the most crucial to those who intend to apply a test to an employment selection problem (Guion, 1976). Predictive validity refers to the extent to which a test is capable of predicting future performance on the job. To demonstrate this one must be able to test a number of job applicants and place them on the job without reference to their performance on the test. In other words, during the period in which a test is being introduced and adapted to an employment situation, applicants must be hired without regard to their performance on the test. This will permit the company to view the workings of the test over a broader range of job performance than would be the case if only the high scoring applicants were selected. After the applicants are hired, trained, and permitted to adjust to the job, a measurement of job performance is collected. Statistical procedures will then enable the company to detemine whether the test scores that had been collected several months earlier are related to the level of performance demonstrated by the employees.

Time is a key factor in demonstrating the predictive validity of a measuring instrument. There must be a time interval of some length separating the collection of test data and the determination of the quality of work performance. While there are no firm rules governing the length of this interval, a good guideline to follow is that the time period should enable individuals to achieve a stable level of job performance commensurate with their potential.

It is inappropriate to talk about the predictive validity of a test as if it were a single parameter reflecting a stable property of the measuring instrument. Predictive validity is a concept that embraces an entire prediction situation, involving a test, a subject pool, and a criterion. Significant changes in any of these factors will often produce a changing picture of the predictive capabilities of the test. Hence, what is meant by predictive validity is a concept that summarizes the predictive effectiveness of a test as it is applied to a variety of situations and subject populations. As a result, rather than a single index of predictive validity, we can think of a large number of such indexes each reflecting a different predictive situation.

Validity Generalization. Validity generalization concerns the extent to which one may extend evidence of validity across different employment situations. Is it realistic to conclude, for example, that a test that has demonstrated acceptable levels of validity in one situation will show comparable levels of validity in another situation? At first impression, one is tempted to conclude that when the jobs and employees involved in the two situations are similar, it is safe to infer validity in the second situation from the evidence of validity obtained from the first. Yet it is commonly thought that such an assumption is extremely risky, and that each new application of a measurement instrument requires a complete validation study. Those who advocate this point of view cite evidence of a lack of stability in the validity coefficient across what seemed to be similar work settings.

Schmidt and Hunter (1980) have argued that under the appropriate experimental conditions, the predictive capabilities of a test tend to be more stable than many psychologists are willing to acknowledge. They point out that the typical validation study employs too few workers, and as a consequence the statistical estimates derived are of low power and fail to show the true predictive strength of the test (Schmidt, Hunter & Urry, 1976). These authors contend that predictive validity studies require sample sizes "often ranging above 200 or 300" workers before a stable estimate of predictive validity can be obtained. As a consequence, good quality predictive validity studies are often technically unfeasible, and organizations should rely on alternative validation approaches. There are, however, numerous routes to achieving statistical power, and restricting validity studies to prohibitively large samples ignores these alternatives that may be achieved through a carefully designed and well-controlled experimental procedure. The evidence that some use to discourage validity generalization may, according to Schmidt and Hunter, be obtained from those studies that involve small samples but strong experimental designs. This is a hopeful and important argument, and it warrants much more attention from psychologists in their future research.

Concurrent Validity.   In one important respect concurrent validity is similar to predictive validity; that is, concurrent validity concerns the relationship between test performance and job performance. Unlike predictive validity, however, concurrent validation procedures collect job performance data at the same time test scores are obtained. This procedure has been called the *present employee method* (McCormick & Ilgen, 1980) because the test scores and performance data are obtained from workers who are already on the job and experienced in its requirements. As a consequence, the subjects on whom test validity is determined have been selected not only by the company's previous selection procedures but also by selective attrition that has probably led unsatisfactory employees to leave the job in higher numbers than workers whose performance is more satisfactory. A principal difference, therefore, between predictive and concurrent validity procedures is that the workers involved in the latter tend to form a group that is more homogeneous in job

performance. In most cases, concurrent validation procedures involve subjects who are likely to cluster toward the satisfactory end of the job performance scale. A test administrator under these circumstances may find it difficult to differentiate among these employees, and hence the test may appear to be less valuable than it would be if it were used in screening job applicants who form a group possessing a wider range of talent. As predictive validity studies extend the time between applicant testing and performance evaluation, the results of the two procedures should become more comparable.

The distinction between predictive and concurrent validity studies also involves the motivational climate surrounding test administration. In concurrent validation studies tests are given to present employees who have already secured jobs for which the hiring program is being constructed. In predictive studies the individuals involved are applicants who are attempting to secure jobs. Whether these two situations result in motivational differences, and if they do, whether these differences in test-taking motives influence test scores, are matters that have not been established empirically. Probably, the impact of these motivational factors depends on the nature and content of the test, and on the instructions that are used to present the tests to the study participants.

Content Validity.   Content validity refers to evidence indicating that a test is tapping the behaviors that it sets out to measure. A number of approaches may be adopted to demonstrate this type of validity. Frequently a test constructor will present evidence for content validity by pointing to the methods whereby the items on the test were selected or constructed. For example, a test of mechanical comprehension, where items are drawn from technical manuals dealing with mechanical operations, may claim that the method of item selection substantiates the content validity of the test.

Another approach may involve a demonstration that a test correlates with other tests whose content is well established. There are no real limits on the methods that may be drawn on to obtain content validity information. Logic and reason applied to a set of data can lead one to the conclusion that the content of a test is as it is specified. Of course, this logic must be made available to test users, who can accept or reject the rationale as they see fit.

Construct Validity. Construct validity refers to any procedure used to give support to the theoretical constructs on which a test is built. Evidence is gathered to strengthen a rational argument that a test taps the measurement components that it says it contains. For example, one approach to estimating construct validity is to examine the interrelationships between the test under evaluation and other tests. When the pattern of these interrelationships forms a logical structure that is consistent with the theoretical *constructs* that underlie the test, then a claim of construct validity can be made.

Campbell (1976) suggests a number of alternative approaches one may adopt in attempting to assess construct validity—for example, the use of *process analysis,* which involves interviews with those who have taken the test. The interview attempts to ascertain why people respond the way they did when they took the test. When these reports indicate that people do, in fact, draw on the behaviors that are consistent with the purported content of the test, there is then evidence of construct validity. Another possible approach uses the test scores to deduce how people will respond when placed in a given experimental situation. Confirmation of these deductions is interpreted as evidence of construct validity. This last approach illustrates what Bass and Barrett (1981) refer to as the network of ideas that surround psychological tests, ideas that form a logical system from which behavioral predictions can be deduced. Experimental confirmation of these predictions reflects back on the test and permits a conclusion that the test is a valid measure of its content domain.

Reliability. The reliability of a measurement instrument refers to the extent to which it is free from certain types of measurement errors. There

are two major kinds of errors that influence a measurement instrument. The first type can be called *bias,* which consists of all kinds of unwanted influences that affect a test score in a systematic fashion. A bias may involve, for example, culture-bound influences that might give an advantage to some and a disadvantage to others who take a test. A bias may operate in an employment interview in the form of prejudicial attitudes held by the interviewer that result in a consistent lowering of the interview ratings for certain types of applicants.

A second variety of measurement error is unsystematic in its nature and affects a test score in a random and unpredictable fashion. Random error is a major concern of those who are interested in the measurement of behavior. A random error occurs when an unintended influence affects the outcome of a test in a completely coincidental fashion. For example, a momentary distraction may cause a subject to miss an item. A person may misread a question and miss it, or may not have the slightest notion of the correct answer and guess correctly. These and a myriad of other chance occurrences may combine to produce a random increase or decrease in a subject's test score.

We can define reliability in terms of freedom from random influences of this sort, and unreliability in terms of *randomly generated* influence that produces a discrepancy between the score we observe and the score that would have been obtained if we had an error-free instrument.

Recall the use of the concept of variance in our discussion of individual differences. Variance refers to the amount of variation one observes in a set of measurements, and it is possible to break variance estimates down into different components, each component representing a different source of influence affecting the measurement. Now if we take the variance of a set of test scores, σ_t^2, we can think of this being composed of two independent components. The first, σ_∞^2, refers to differences between the scores that are a function of variation in the extent to which people possess the skills or traits measured by the test. This is called the *true variance*. A second component contains all the random variables that produce the measurement errors associated with the test. This component, σ_e^2, is called the *error variance*. Given these terms, Thorndike (1949) defines the reliability of a test, r_{tt}, in terms of the following equation:

$$r_{tt} = \frac{\sigma_\infty^2}{\sigma_t^2}$$

or

$$r_{tt} = 1 - \frac{\sigma_e^2}{\sigma_t^2}$$

In other words, the value of the reliability index associated with a test corresponds to the proportion of variance in test scores that is due to true differences between individuals in the quality being evaluated by the test (Thorndike, 1949, p. 72). There are several routes one may follow to obtain an index of test reliability. Each taps a somewhat different set of random influences, but as a rule they all reflect the level of measurement accuracy that is associated with a test.

Test-Retest Reliability. One indication of measurement reliability is found in the consistency with which a test gives the same results when it is used to obtain repeated measurements from the same subject, which is one of the more basic requirements of a good test. Consider the lack of confidence one would have in a measurement of length if each time an object was measured a different number were obtained. Or consider the implications if one were to give an intelligence test to a person on a Monday and then again on a Tuesday and obtain an I.Q. of 147 on the first day and 98 on the second.

Test-retest reliability is determined by readministering a given test, to the same subjects, after a passage of time. A close relationship between the two sets of scores is an indication of high reliability. Here the concept is defined in terms of the stability of the scores that are obtained from the test. High test-retest reliability indicates that one can have a certain amount of confidence that the

scores generated by a test are not unique to the specific instance in which the test was given. Furthermore, since many psychological traits are considered to be relatively stable over time, evidence of high test-retest reliability contributes to a *general argument* that the test scores do in fact reflect this behavioral property.

Alternate-Forms Reliability. In constructing a test it is often useful to develop enough items to produce two or more forms of the same instrument. Although each form has the same general type of item, the individual items vary from form to form. A strong relationship between these alternate forms is desirable because it indicates they are measuring the same things. As a consequence, a subject may be retested with a completely new set of items that are comparable to those used on the first testing. Retesting, therefore, can be made *relatively* free of the effects of practice on the first set of items.

A high correlation between alternate forms of a test is also interpreted to indicate test reliability. In this case there is evidence that a person's score is not dependent on the particular set of items included in the form of the test that was given. When alternate forms are given in sessions that are separated by time, evidence is presented that bears on the stability of the scores over different samples of items as well as over time.

Internal Consistency. Evidence of test reliability can also be obtained by demonstrating that the score from one part of a test is related to the score obtained from a second part. In certain respects this type of reliability is similar to that just referred to as alternate-forms reliability. Here, however, two tests are constructed by subdividing the one form of a test into two or more subtests, and a separate score is obtained from each. Evidence that subjects obtain similar scores on both subtests suggests that the content of the two halves is homogeneous. Sometimes this is called split-half reliability to refer to the fact that the subtests are constructed from the first and second halves of the test. If the two subtests are constructed by using every other item, then the estimate is called odd-even reliability.

There is one other variant of this method, which involves correlating each item with every other item in the test. High interrelationships among the items suggests that they are all tapping a rather homogeneous domain of measurement—that is, they all tend to be measuring the same behavior. There are several ways these item interrelationships can be calculated, but the main thing to remember is that when items show signs of being highly related to one another, there is evidence that the instrument is relatively free from random error. Hence, the instrument shows evidence of high reliability.

Relationship between Reliability and Validity. The validity of a test is limited by its reliability. Tests of low reliability contain a substantial amount of random error that cannot relate significantly to any measure of job performance. To use a test that is "perfectly unreliable" would be equivalent to predicting job performance by drawing a subject's "test" score from a table of random numbers. Of course, no usable predictions could come from such a source. As test reliability increases, the amount of random error in the test score decreases and the potential for accurate prediction increases. Note that we said the *potential* for accurate prediction, since high reliability tells us only that the test is measuring something with reasonable accuracy. Of course this something may not be related to the measure of job performance that is being used; hence, the predictive validity of the test may be low, while the reliability is high. Reliability is a necessary condition for validity, but it does not ensure high validity. On the other hand, a test cannot show evidence of high validity if it has low reliability.

Criterion Reliability and Test Validity. The reliability of the criterion is a factor that exerts a significant influence on the *apparent* validity of a selection instrument such as a psychological test. If the criterion is itself highly unreliable then it will be impossible for a test to provide accurate

predictions of job performance. A given test may measure exactly what it intends to measure, and these behaviors may in fact be those that are essential for job success. If the procedures used to measure job performance are unreliable, however, then the test will *appear* to have low validity.

Because of variation in the characteristics of the criterion measures used, a psychological test may appear to show varying degrees of validity from one situation to the next (Ghiselli & Haire, 1960). One of the factors that gives rise to this apparent variation in test validity can be found in the reliability of the criterion measures that are used in different situations. Hence, an unsuccessful testing program might well be as much the result of an inadequate measure of job performance as it is a function of a psychological test that does not measure accurately.

Selection programs are installed in order to improve a company's capabilities of identifying applicants who will eventually be able to perform a job successfully. As a result, one of the requirements of a systematic selection program is that the company must develop a definition of job success. This seems like an obvious and relatively simple problem, but as we have seen there are aspects of it that are not as simple as they first appear. For example, virtually every facet of job performance can be incorporated into a definition of success. Productivity, relations with superiors, absentee rate, tenure, and promotability are but a few of the more obvious dimensions of performance that may enter a company's definition of job success. Some choices have to be made, since not every conceivable dimension can be included. To be useful, those dimensions of performance that are selected must be measurable in a reliable and valid way. Furthermore, some decision must be made concerning the weights to be assigned to each facet of job performance, since they are probably not all considered to be of equal importance in establishing the worth of an employee.

As a rule, what can be a complicated and time-consuming problem usually receives little attention. The most likely solution is to select a single index of job success—for example, number of units produced—and have the selection program concentrate on trying to predict this aspect of work performance. In a great many instances the criterion used probably relates to some of the other aspects of job performance that were not considered; therefore, a test that predicts one might also predict the other. One cannot count on this (James, 1973), however, and as a result considerable care should be invested in defining and measuring those performance dimensions that are used for the criterion. To invest time and energy in the development of selection techniques without giving adequate attention to the development of criterion measures is running the risk that the techniques will give the appearance of being inadequate, while in reality the problem is one of an inadequate job criterion.

Other Factors Affecting the Usefulness of Selection Techniques.   One of the factors that influence the extent to which a selection technique can make a contribution to a personnel program is the number of present employees considered to be successful in their work. It's obvious that if everyone now on the job were considered to be successful, then a new selection instrument could not possibly increase the accuracy of a program that is already maximally accurate. A test would have the greatest opportunity of making a significant contribution to a program if in the past this program had very low accuracy in finding competent employees. Hence, as the number of successful employees selected by an old method decreases, there is increased opportunity for a new method to improve the accuracy of prediction.

Consider the following diagrams found in Figure 2.7. The first diagram, (A), shows a coordinate system, the baseline of which forms a scale made up of test scores from a selection test. The vertical axis is a scale that measures job performance. Each employee has a score on each scale, and the ellipse contains all the score combinations obtained from a group of employees. In the next diagram, (B), we have the same ellipse, but now the baseline has been divided by a vertical arrow that represents the minimum test score the applicant needs in order to be hired. Applicants falling to the right of this arrow are hired, those falling to the left are rejected. The horizontal arrow drawn on the scale of job performance divides successful and unsuccessful performance. Those who fall above this horizontal line show successful performance, those falling below do not perform their jobs successfully.

FIGURE 2.7   Relationship between Test Scores and Job Performance.

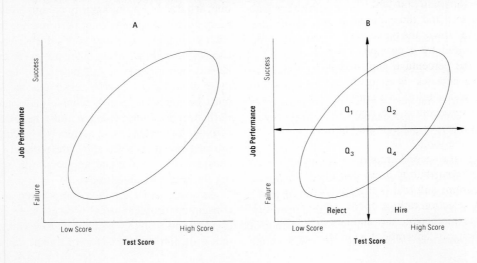

The two arrows divide the points in the ellipse into the four quadrants that are defined below the figure. If we were to hire everyone without regard to performance on the test (this is the situation that existed before the test was introduced into the selection program) then the percentage of successful applicants would be:

$$\frac{Q_1 + Q_2}{Q_1 + Q_2 + Q_3 + Q_4} \times 100$$

= percent successful without test.

If we were to hire only those who score above the test cutoff, our percent accuracy would be:

$$\frac{Q_2}{Q_2 + Q_4} \times 100 = \text{percent successful with test.}$$

The difference between these two values is an indication of the contribution the test will make to the accuracy of our selection decisions.

How much improvement in the accuracy of selection can be expected when a new test is introduced into a selection program? One important factor involved in answering this question is the percentage of present employees considered to be successful. To what extent are present selection techniques succeeding in hiring employees who prove to be satisfactory? It can be shown that with other factors held constant (that is, the validity of the new test and the minimal score required for hiring), the lower the percentage of successful employees hired by a previous method, the higher will be the percentage gain in selection accuracy when the new test is used. A test will make its greatest contribution to a company whose present selection procedures are not successfully identifying employees who make satisfactory adjustments to the job.

There is a second important factor that influences the contribution a test can make to a selection program, and that is the size of the *selection ratio*. A selection ratio is expressed as the number of people hired over the number of people who apply for a job. This ratio is an index of selectivity.

$$sr = \frac{\text{number of applicants hired}}{\text{total number applicants}}$$

The closer this index approaches unity, the greater the proportion of applicants hired. A selection ratio equaling one describes a situation in which every applicant is hired, and as a consequence no differential selectivity is possible. The selection ratio is often a reflection of the condition of the local labor market (the number of people seeking work) and the effectiveness of the company's recruitment program.

When all factors except the selection ratio are held constant, decreasing the selection ratio leads to an improvement in the percentage of successful employees hired. Refer to Figure 2.8 which represents the same data presented in the previous figures. As the selection ratio is decreased, a company will be in a position to hire applicants who score higher on the selection test. This is represented by the three vertical arrows on the figure. Beginning with the lowest arrow (the highest selection ratio) we compute the value: $\frac{Q_2}{Q_2 + Q_4}$. This is the proportion of hired applicants who are successful on the job. We next compute this value for

FIGURE 2.8   The Relationship between Selection Ratio and the Utility of a Selection Test.

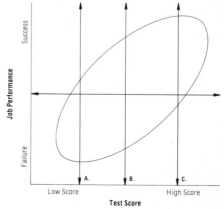

A, B, C Minimum Acceptable Score

situations defined by the remaining two arrows, and find that it increases as the minimum score needed to be hired increases. Hence, with a low selection ratio, a company will derive more accuracy from its selection tests than it will when the ratio is high. In other words, if a company can fill its vacancies by hiring only those applicants who score at the very highest points on the test scale, then the probability of hiring a person who is unsuccessful on the job decreases.

The Taylor-Russell Tables. By taking three pieces of information—the validity of a test, the percentage of present employees judged to be satisfactory, and the selection ratio—one can estimate the percentage of newly hired workers who will be satisfactory employees. The calculations required for this estimate have been summarized in a series of tables called the Taylor-Russell tables

(Taylor & Russell, 1939). Each table in this series refers to a different proportion of present employees considered to be satisfactory. For example, Table 2.4 refers to a situation in which 60 percent of the present employees are considered to be carrying out their work satisfactorily. The rows of the table identify different validity coefficients. These coefficients are Pearson correlation coefficients, and let's assume that they refer to the magnitude of the relationship between test scores and the criterion. The columns of the table refer to different selection ratios.

Let's consider a situation in which an organization must hire 80 percent of all individuals who apply for a given job. Let's also assume that these applicants are hired on the basis of a test that has a validity coefficient of .45. Entering the table at the row labeled .45 and moving over to the column labeled .80, we locate a cell containing the entry

TABLE 2.4   Proportion of Employees Considered Satisfactory = .60 Selection Ratio

r	.05	.10	.20	.30	.40	.50	.60	.70	.80	.90	.95
.00	.60	.60	.60	.60	.60	.60	.60	.60	.60	.60	.60
.05	.64	.63	.63	.62	.62	.62	.61	.61	.61	.60	.60
.10	.68	.67	.65	.64	.64	.63	.63	.62	.61	.61	.60
.15	.71	.70	.68	.67	.66	.65	.64	.63	.62	.61	.61
.20	.75	.73	.71	.69	.67	.66	.65	.64	.63	.62	.61
.25	.78	.76	.73	.71	.69	.68	.66	.65	.63	.62	.61
.30	.82	.79	.76	.73	.71	.69	.68	.66	.64	.62	.61
.35	.85	.82	.78	.75	.73	.71	.69	.67	.65	.63	.62
.40	.88	.85	.81	.78	.75	.73	.70	.68	.66	.63	.62
.45	.90	.87	.83	.80	.77	.74	.72	.69	.66	.64	.62
.50	.93	.90	.86	.82	.79	.76	.73	.70	.67	.64	.62
.55	.95	.92	.88	.84	.81	.78	.75	.71	.68	.64	.62
.60	.96	.94	.90	.87	.83	.80	.76	.73	.69	.65	.63
.65	.98	.96	.92	.89	.85	.82	.78	.74	.70	.65	.63
.70	.99	.97	.94	.91	.87	.84	.80	.75	.71	.66	.63
.75	.99	.99	.96	.93	.90	.86	.81	.77	.71	.66	.63
.80	1.00	.99	.98	.95	.92	.88	.83	.78	.72	.66	.63
.85	1.00	1.00	.99	.97	.95	.91	.86	.80	.73	.66	.63
.90	1.00	1.00	1.00	.99	.97	.94	.88	.82	.74	.67	.63
.95	1.00	1.00	1.00	1.00	.99	.97	.92	.84	.75	.67	.63
1.00	1.00	1.00	1.00	1.00	1.00	1.00	1.00	.86	.75	.67	.63

Source: Taylor, H. C., and Russell, J. T. The relationship of validity coefficients to the practical effectiveness of tests in selection. *Journal of Applied Psychology*, 1939, *23*,565–578

.66. This indicates that 66 percent of the applicants who are hired on the basis of their test scores will prove to be satisfactory employees. Since there are already 60 percent of the present employees who are satisfactory, the use of the test will improve the percentage of satisfactory employees by 6 percent.

If the organization could improve its recruitment efforts and bring enough applicants into the employment office so that the selection ratio was .50, then the use of the test would yield 74 percent satisfactory new hires, and a 14 percent improvement in the percentage of satisfactory employees.

There are assumptions and limitations associated with the use of the Taylor-Russell tables. To use them accurately the following conditions should be taken into consideration:

1. The relationship between the test and the criterion must be linear.
2. A single criterion score separating satisfactory and unsatisfactory performance must be established.
3. The tables do not take into consideration hiring errors that occur among the rejected applicants. Table entries refer only to the group of applicants who were hired and for whom criterion data are available.

The Usefulness of Psychological Tests.   There are many reasons why a work organization should consider adopting tests for selection of job applicants. Tests provide information about specific skills and aptitudes that is difficult to obtain from other sources, and as a result, they provide an additional source of information of the type that is basic to the assessment of an applicant's job potential. A testing program also provides information that is objectively determined, so that it is relatively free from the personal biases that sometimes enter into other personnel procedures such as the interview and letters of reference.

The costs involved in introducing a test into the selection process are usually rather modest. It is often quite costly, however, to recruit and train a new employee, and as a consequence preventable turnover is a financial burden that many organizations would like to reduce. If the use of test information can lead to a significant reduction in the number of unsuitable employees hired, then a substantial economy can be realized. The effective use of selection tests can also contribute to a reduction in the human costs that are associated with job dissatisfaction, failure, and turnover. It is in the employee's interest, as well as in the interest of the employer, to obtain work that is within his or her capabilities. To the extent that personnel tests do improve the prospects for a congenial fit between worker and job, a company's investment in a testing program is a major investment in good human relations.

More attention is currently being paid to the economic implications of selection tests, and in many instances the findings have been quite encouraging (Schmidt, Hunter, McKenzie, & Muldrow, 1979; Dunnette & Borman, 1979). Using sets of equations whose characteristics are beyond the reach of this text, these studies have attempted to estimate the productivity increases that are associated with the selection of employees on the basis of test scores. These estimates are then translated into dollars and cents with the result that surprising economies appear to be within the reach of those organizations that use selection tests of moderate validity.

Schmidt et al. (1979) estimated the national economies that are associated with using a selection test to hire computer programmers. The results of their computations are summarized in Table 2.5. This table indicates that the use of a selection test known as the Programmer Aptitude Test (PAT) could produce savings in the U.S. economy ranging from $93 million to $1605 million, depending on the selection ratio and the validity of the previous procedures. Schmidt et al. estimated that the validity of the PAT was rather high (.76); hence, with tests of lower validity, the

TABLE 2.5　Estimated Productivity Increase From 1 Year's Use of Programmer Aptitude Test to Select Computer Programmers in U.S. Economy (in Millions of Dollars)

Selection ratio	True validity of previous procedure				
	.00	.20	.30	.40	.50
.05	1,605	1,184	973	761	550
.10	1,367	1,008	828	648	468
.20	1,091	804	661	517	373
.30	903	666	547	428	309
.40	753	555	455	356	257
.50	622	459	376	295	213
.60	501	370	304	238	172
.70	387	285	234	183	132
.80	273	201	165	129	93

Source: Schmidt, F. L., et al. Impact of valid selection procedures on work force productivity. *Journal of Applied Psychology*, 1979, *64*, 609–626. Copyright 1979 by the American Psychological Association. Published by permission of the author and publisher.

estimates in Table 2.4 have to be reduced. The point is, however, that such an analysis into dollar savings is possible, and early results suggest that psychological testing is quite capable of achieving improvements in productivity and attractive savings for organizations that use them for selection purposes.

The question now remains, do tests actually work as selection devices? It would be a mistake to believe that all testing programs have been successful, but there is an accumulation of information in the research literature (Ghiselli, 1966; Guion, 1965, 1976) that clearly indicates that a testing program is a realistic consideration for management. It has sometimes been disappointing to see the rather modest relationships existing between single tests and complex criteria of job performance, but with the use of a battery of tests, criterion coverage improves and the predictive capabilities of test information increase. Using a test battery does not imply that an extensive number of individual tests are needed to reach acceptable levels of predictive accuracy. Relatively few tests that require only a modest amount of time to take

often lead to quite usable levels of selection accuracy.

Finally, one should always bear in mind that the psychological test is only one component of a series of information sources that combine to produce a selection decision. To view the predictive accuracy of tests as if they were the only type of information available overlooks the fact that a test may supplement and extend the information that is found in the application blank, letters of recommendation, and the interview.

The Employment Interview

Of all the procedures available for hiring and placing employees, none is used more widely or with greater reluctance than the interview. Although it exists in many different forms, the interview is basically a conversation that has a well-defined set of objectives. When used in a selection situation, the interview serves as an additional source of information that bears on the suitability of a job applicant. Ideally, the interview will function very much like a psychological test, in that from it will come a score that can be used to enhance the predictive capabilities of those responsible for hiring. In reality, the interview often provides general impressions of the personality and social skills of the applicant. Functioning in this fashion, the interview gives management some security against hiring an applicant who will not fit in with the social climate of the organization.

The interview serves purposes other than obtaining information about the applicant. It also provides a means whereby information about the job and working conditions is given to the applicant. This is an important function, since an applicant's decision to accept a job, if one is offered, should be based on an accurate understanding of the nature of the work and the conditions under which it will be done. Therefore, we may think of a well-planned interview as a social situation in which information is exchanged between applicant and employer. As this information moves in either direction, it should contribute to both kinds of prediction that are being made at the time of hiring.

Management predicts a candidate's job potential; the applicant seeks information that permits him to anticipate some of the personal consequences of accepting a job with the organization.

In addition to its role as a selection instrument, the interview also serves a public relations function. The employment interview is the first, and on many occasions the only direct contact an individual has with a company; hence, many of the impressions concerning an organization are based on an individual's experience with an employment interviewer. The reputation of the company as an employer is an important factor influencing the availability of labor in the local community and a company's employment office can be a place where much of this reputation is formed. Hence, one of the functions of an employment interview is to help create positive attitudes toward the company as an organization that has congenial working conditions.

Types of Interviews. The format of the employment interview varies widely from one organization to the next; and unlike tests, where there is a wide range of instruments that may be purchased, it is probably safe to say that most companies construct their own interviewing schedules. There are two interrelated dimensions of an interview that can be used to classify the different formats used. The first deals with the extent to which the interviewer maintains discretionary control over the interview session. There are some interviewing procedures in which such things as the questions asked and the length and general focus of the conversation are decided upon by the interviewer during the course of the interview. There are other approaches to interviewing in which the interviewer has little or no control over these matters. This type of interview is completely planned, putting the interviewer in a situation where his principal job is to read a set of prearranged questions and then record the interviewee's responses. There are also interview formats that represent a compromise between these two extremes.

A second consideration regarding the format of the interview concerns the manner in which information is scored. This varies from the global summary statement, which expresses the interviewer's overall evaluation, to an analytical, item-by-item score that is recorded for each facet of information collected. The final evaluation of the interview data generated by both approaches is a score of some sort, but in the summary evaluation this overall score is obtained directly, as expressed by the interviewer. In the more analytical approach, the final score is calculated by combining the individual scores obtained from the separate parts of the interview.

The Unstructured Interview. The content of the unstructured interview is largely determined by the interactions that take place between the participants. With this approach, each interview provides a new opportunity for the interviewer to direct the content and flow of the conversation. It is in this relative freedom, however, that one finds both the strengths and weaknesses of this type of interview. The unstructured approach is often cited for its lack of reliability and its susceptibility to a variety of biases. Furthermore, since the content of the interview is not standardized, there may be little that is comparable in the data obtained from different applicants. As a consequence, it is difficult to devise a satisfactory scheme to incorporate interview evaluations into test scores and other sources of information about the applicant. Potentially, each interview views each new applicant from a different perspective, making it difficult to compare applicants.

Although rarely recommended, the unstructured interview is frequently used; and in some instances its use may be justified by the characteristics of the jobs being filled. There is a substantial social component associated with many of the jobs that are found in managerial and professional areas. In such jobs interpersonal relationships play a significant role in determining an individual's general effectiveness, and these social skills are given an opportunity to appear in the freewheeling exchanges that take place in these interviews. In this respect, one may think of the unstructured interview as a situational test, since it exposes the applicant to a social situation that is not unlike those found on the job. Being able to present oneself in a favorable manner, the ability to express one's ideas, to project confidence, and to persuade another person are all important ingredients in many white-collar jobs. These are all variables that can be observed in the unstructured interviews, and as a result many managers, scientists, and technicians are given unstructured interviews so that employers have an opportunity to observe behaviors that may indicate how the applicant will "fit in" with the social climate of the organization.

None of this, however, reduces the many problems that are connected with the unstructured interview. All the reliability problems, together with the potential for personal biases, must be taken into account by anyone who chooses to use this type of interviewing format.

The Area Interview. An area interview is one that presents the interviewer with a number of topics about which information is being sought. Interviewers begin by asking general questions that are designed to encourage the applicants to talk freely about their background and experience, but if in the course of such a conversation the applicant does not voluntarily provide information regarding the desired areas, the interviewer is instructed to ask questions about these matters at the close of the session. In one approach, there are a series of questions that the interviewer must answer about the applicant's status in each of the areas under consideration (see Figure 2.9). For example, one question may concern the interviewer's appraisal of the applicant's training. At the conclusion of the interview, the interviewer must answer each of these questions, and from these responses determine an overall score that describes the applicant's suitability for the job.

There is much that recommends the area interview. It retains some of the freedom and spontaneity of the unstructured interview, but it also ensures that each interview provides a common core of information on which an evaluation may be computed. It also provides a framework within which the interviewer can work, thereby ensuring

that the planned purposes of the conversation are kept in mind throughout the course of the interview. Although the structure imposed on the interview does not completely guarantee adequate reliability, there is some assurance that the content of the interview remains somewhat stable from one applicant to the next. This is a major improvement over the lack of content reliability that is seen as being one of the primary weaknesses of the unstructured interview.

The Standardized Interview. The standardized interview stands at the opposite pole from the unstructured interview. Like a psychological test, the standardized interview presents the interviewer with a series of questions that must be asked each job applicant. Question wording and the order in which questions are presented are predetermined. After each question the responses are recorded and scored according to a prearranged scoring key.

In many respects the standardized interview is a questionnaire that is read to each applicant. Its use ensures that the information obtained from different applicants taps the same areas of background and experience. Furthermore, the standardized interview offers the personnel department opportunity to analyze each item with respect to its relation to the criterion and thereby guarantee that the items entering into the conversation have some bearing on future job behaviors. The cost for this is a loss of spontaneity that is often thought to be a source of useful insights into the social competence of the interviewee. Furthermore, being committed to a set number of carefully worded questions, the interviewer is not free to follow up on interesting leads that may come up during the course of the interview. As a consequence, many suggest that the completely standardized interview is actually a questionnaire that could more efficiently be administered as part of the application blank.

Sources of Interview Error. In spite of its wide use in employment settings, the interview is often viewed with considerable apprehension. Direct attempts to evaluate the reliability and validity of the

FIGURE 2.9   Patterned Interview Guide

Name of applicant _____   Address _____

Position _____   Telephone _____

Department _____

Area	Comments

I Work History
  a. Titles of previous jobs
  b. Duties
  c. Reasons for leaving
  d. Military experience
  e. Satisfaction with work	

II Educational History
  a. Formal schooling
  b. Specialized awards
  c. Special awards
  d. Extra-curricular activities and leadership	

III Avocational activities
  a. Reading (materials and amount of time)
  b. Hobbies
  c. Community and church activities	

IV Career interests and goals
  a. Objectives (5 years)
  b. Objectives (long term)
  c. Expectancies concerning company
  d. Plans for future development	

V Health
  a. Childhood health
  b. Present health (serious
    illness, impairments)	

EVALUATION: Ratings;

        5 = Well above average
        4 = Above average
        3 = Average
        2 = Below average
        1 = Well below average

	Weight	Rating	Score	Comments

1. Appropriateness of
   applicant's work history
   for job being considered
	2	x _____	= _____	

2. Adequacy of training	2	x _____	= _____	
3. Work significance of avocational activities	1	x _____	= _____	
4. Career interests and goals, motivational significance	2	x _____	= _____	
5. Health history	1	x _____	= _____	
		TOTAL SCORE	_____	

Recommendations:

interview have yielded disappointingly low coefficients, and there is an extensive research literature showing the technique to be vulnerable to a
variety of contaminating influences. Mayfield
(1964) reviewed the research literature and concluded that even in those instances in which the
interview had high reliability, the data obtained
often showed low validity. Schmidt (1976), in a
later review, was unable to find that the employment interview has displayed levels of reliability
and validity comparable to those associated with
psychological tests.

To be sure, there have been instances in which
interviews have shown accpetable measurement
strength, and there may be certain well-structured
interviewing procedures that show high levels of
reliability. The point is, however, that as a general
rule the interview has been unable to demonstrate
levels of reliability and validity that engender a
high degree of confidence in its outcomes. As a
consequence, much of the research that has been
done in this area has focused on the sources of
contamination that affect the decisions made on
the basis of interviewing data.

Positive and Negative Information.   Hiring decisions are often based on information about an
applicant that is both positive and negative. It is
not unusual for a job applicant's background to
contain negative information found within an otherwise positive record, and in many of these instances the applicant would be able to make a satisfactory adjustment to the job if hired and given
a chance to succeed. Yet the presence of negative
information can be very damaging to an applicant's job prospects. For example, there is considerable research evidence suggesting that interviewers often assign much heavier weights to negative
information than they do to positive items of information (Springbett, 1958; Bolster & Springbett,
1961). Early work by Springbett (1958) indicated
that a single unit of unfavorable information in an
otherwise positive interview would significantly
increase the number of decisions to reject a job
applicant. Hollman (1972) offers a slightly different interpretation, contending that interviewers
tend to assign accurate negative weights, but do

not place sufficient weight on positive information.
Whatever the case, there appears to be considerable evidence that interviewers assign different
weights to the two types of information, and there
is a good likelihood that a single item of negative
information in an applicant's credentials will lead
to a decision to reject the individual for employment.

Why negative information carries this inordinately heavy influence has been discussed by a
number of authors (Kanouse & Hanson, 1972;
Constantin, 1976), and there seem to be several
interesting points of view regarding the issue. For
example, some contend that people generally believe they live in a world where most outcomes
are positive, and within this context negative
events create strong contrasts and carry greater influence. From this perspective, an employment interviewer operates in the belief that most human
events and most dimensions of a given person are
positive. It is the presence of negative attributes
that plays a major role in differentiating one person
from the next. If this is the case, then one would
expect that a negative fact would carry greater
weight than a positive one, since it brings with it
more information that serves to differentiate one
applicant from another.

A second possibility, pointed out by Constantin
(1976) is that interviewers tend to be held to higher
levels of accountability in instances in which they
recommend hiring an applicant who subsequently
proves to be unsuccessful. Rejecting potentially
successful applicants or hiring successful applicants does not receive the attention from management that the hiring of an unsuccessful applicant
does, and under these circumstances interviewers
are more sensitive to the presence of negative information that signals a high risk of hiring an unsatisfactory employee.

At the present time the dynamics of the information processing that goes on in an employment
interview are not well understood, but on the basis
of the research that has been done it seems reasonably clear that interviewers tend to maintain an
orientation that leads them to weight positive and
negative items of information differentially. It is
not clear, however, whether this differential

weighting is always a factor that contributes to the low validity coefficients often associated with the interview. One could reason that the heavy weight carried by negative information is comparable to the weight often carried by negative facets of job performance. In many instances a manager's view of the unsatisfactory employee may involve only a single or limited number of negatives. If this is true, then the interviewer who decides to reject an applicant on a single negative consideration might very well be expressing a weighting system that operates in the performance evaluations that take place after applicants are placed on a job. Of course, this is all quite speculative, and more research will be required before we are in a position to determine whether an interviewer's reactions to positive and negative information undermines or enhances the validity of the employment interview.

Order Effects. The order in which information is presented in an interview has also been shown to have an influence on the evaluations of the applicant (Peters & Terborg, 1975). Springbett (1958) concluded that information presented early in the interview carried more weight in the decisions to hire or reject an applicant. When this decision is made, subsequent information is not attended to (Farr, 1973) or is responded to selectively (Anderson, 1960). Some contend that during the early phases of the interview the interviewer sets up different causal models that are used to link the applicant with past events. For example, Tucker and Rowe (1979) suggest that interviewers who develop an unfavorable expectation early in the session tend to give an applicant less credit for past accomplishments and attribute more responsibility for past failures. Their data indicate that to a lesser extent the opposite is true for interviewers who establish a positive orientation early in the session. This type of bias has been called the *halo effect,* to refer to an error of generalization in which a limited set of impressions are found to color the entire interview. Here responses during one phase of an interview are interpreted in a manner that is consistent with the interviewer's evaluations of earlier phases. The interview then be-

comes a method whereby the interviewer attempts to confirm evaluations previously made, rather than proceeding to collect information that is not biased by prior observations.

Order effects have not been confined to primacy, since there is also evidence suggesting that under certain circumstances information that is presented late in an interview session plays a significant role in the hiring decision (Stewart, 1965; Hendrick & Costantini, 1970). This *recency effect* has been found most frequently in interviews in which the interviewer is required to make a sequence of judgments based on the accumulating information that is presented as the session unfolds. It is suggested by some (Farr, 1973) that this series of judgments encourages the interviewer to pay closer attention to all phases of the interview and as a result, those events taking place later in the interview are retained to exert an influence on the judgments. The important point, however, is that both primacy and recency effects do represent potential sources of error to which the employment interview is subject. The higher reliability of the standardized interview may, in part, reflect the fact that these order effects have not been eliminated, but have become a standardized, hence systematic, part of the procedure.

Stereotypes and Contrasts. The decision to hire an applicant may arise from a comparison that an interviewer makes between personal impressions of an applicant and an idealized model of a successful employee. This stereotype of the successful worker serves the interviewer as a point of reference, and the closer the applicant approaches this stereotype, the greater the likelihood that the interviewer will make a positive recommendation. The stereotype may be unique to a given interviewer (Mayfield & Carlson, 1966) and it probably varies from one job to the next. Hakel, Hollman, and Dunnette (1970) asked groups of employment interviewers, certified public accountants and students to express their views concerning the interests held by those who are employed as accountants. The results showed two different perceptions of the accountant, and to the extent that hiring decisions would depend on how closely an applicant fits a stereotype, then these two different perceptions would result in the selection of two different sets of applicants.

The job of the employment interviewer often requires an individual to interview a group of job applicants who appear in a given order. One would expect that the impressions and judgments established by the interviewer when considering one applicant might carry over to influence the perceptions and judgments made on the next applicant. This *contrast effect* has been demonstrated in several studies (Carlson 1970; Heneman et al., 1975), but it has not always appeared as a major source of influence in interview results (Hakel, Ohnesorge, & Dunnette, 1970). To the extent that these order effects do operate to influence hiring decisions, we see yet another contaminating influence entering into the results of this widely used employment technique.

Comment.   Other unwanted factors have been found to influence the hiring decision made on the basis of the interview, and all serve to point out the complex nature of the employment interview. We can end this discussion by referring to a point made at the beginning. The interview is a conversation between people, and as such it involves the whole range of social and psychological variables that are usually associated with this type of interchange. As a measurement technique it is an extremely complicated process, but it is one that for a variety of reasons, some more emotional than rational, organizations are reluctant to abandon.

As a consequence, the procedure calls for a program of continuing research and development.

The Assessment Center

The assessment center approach refers to a coordinated series of standardized activities that are used to obtain information about job potential (Finkle, 1976). In one of its common forms, an assessment center involves one or several group sessions in which applicants are brought together and put through a sequence of activities that have been constructed to generate information about their work skills. Although the procedure has been applied to the selection of salespersons (Bray & Campbell, 1968), police officers (Dunnette & Motowidlo, 1975) and stockbrokers (Hellervik, Hunt & Silzer, 1976), its principal application has been for the selection of management personnel.

The exercises involved in a typical assessment-center program include individual activities like the ''in-basket'' procedure, which confronts a participant with a stack of correspondence of the type managers find on their desk. Each piece of correspondence requires a reaction decision, and an assessment is made of the individual's handling of these real-life decisions. Group exercises may involve problem-solving sessions or a ''leaderless group discussion.'' Kraut (1976) estimates that the typical assessment-center program requires about two full days of activities such as these.

Perhaps the best way of describing what an assessment center is, and what it is not, is to quote Kraut (1976) who lists the following:

An Assessment Center Is
1. A group of assessment procedures one of which is a simulation of a work situation.
2. A procedure using multiple assessors.
3. An approach that pools information from different assessors and different exercises.
4. A procedure in which the final evaluation is made at a separate time from the observation of behavior.
5. An approach using extensively pretested techniques.
6. An approach that evaluates behaviors relevant to job performance.

An Assessment Center Is Not
1. A panel interview or series of interviews as the only technique used.
2. A specific technique used as the sole basis for evaluation.
3. A battery of psychological tests.
4. An assessment made by a single assessor.
5. Individual assessments are not pooled.

Evidence for the validity, reliability, and utility of assessment centers tends to be quite encouraging (Huck, 1973; Finkle, 1976; Cascio & Silbey, 1979), and it would appear that the approach puts to use a variety of individual selection techniques in an effective fashion. One of its limitations is its expense, which might limit its application to certain non-rank-and-file positions; however, the assessment center has had considerable success in selecting managerial and staff positions, and at present time its popularity as a selection and promotion system appears to be growing. We will consider this technique further in Chapter 14.

METHODS OF COMBINING SELECTION DATA

Once an applicant has passed through the various steps of the selection procedure, the company is faced with the problem of combining these separate pieces of information into a composite evaluation that will serve as the basis for the final employment decision. There are several methods available to bring these data together to form a total score, and these will be considered in the sections that follow. As a general rule, these procedures require statistical competence that extends beyond the scope of this book, and as a consequence, we will consider only their most elementary outline. They all lead, however, to a decision that is relatively simple—that is, whether to hire or reject an applicant. In doing this, a critical score is established, which represents the *minimum value* that one may obtain from the combined selection procedures and still be considered suitable for the job. This critical score reflects value judgments on the part of management, and it is a direct extension of the definition of what does and what does not constitute successful performance on the job. In large measure this critical score is established on the basis of available knowledge concerning the selection scores of present employees who are considered to be successful in their jobs.

In considering the whole process of decision making in an employment setting, one must not forget the practical considerations. These practical matters will sometimes lead a company to revise the decision-making strategies that were first established during the planning stages of a selection program. What may appear as a textbook-type procedure in these early tryout stages may later be modified and adapted to fit changing circumstances. Methodological purity is often a luxury that a real-life personnel program may not be able to afford. Changing conditions of work and varying factors in the labor market often combine to create circumstances that did not exist when a personnel program was planned. Hence, the discussions of methodology that follow should be recognized as general cases that will require further technical input before they can be adapted to the requirements of a given situation.

Statistical Methods Perhaps the most elegant method of combining predictor information is one involving a statistical analysis that determines the weighted combination of variables and maximizes the accuracy with which job performance is predicted. The details of this method are beyond the

FIGURE 2.10 Interrelationships between Two Tests and a Measure of Job Performance.

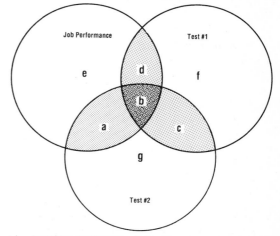

a, d	Common variance, the unique contributions of Test #1 and #2 to predicting job performance
b	Common variance, duplicate contributions of Test #1 and #2 to predicting job performance
c	Common variance, shared only by Test #1 and #2
e, f, g	Non-common variance, specific to each measuring instrument

scope of this book, but in general they involve computing a linear equation that assigns a weight to each source of predictor information. The weighted sum of these separate variables yields a value that is the predicted criterion scores. This equation represents an additive combination of data in the sense that the score from a predictor is multiplied by its weight and the product of these two values is *added* to the products of other predictor-weight combinations. The equation represented on page 19 represents such an equation, and it will be reproduced here in somewhat different form in order to more clearly show its role in combining selection data:

$$\text{Predicted job Performance} = \begin{array}{l} \text{Constant} + (\text{Weight 1} \times \text{Test Score}) \\ + (\text{Weight 2} \times \text{Interview Score}) \\ + (\text{Weight 3} \times \text{Application Blank Score}) \\ + \ldots \end{array}$$

The weights in this equation are obtained from the calculations that are required by the statistical methods.[1]

Notice that each predictor *adds* its contribution to the overall prediction, but what is not apparent is that the statistical technique permits each new variable to add to the equation only the information that has not been accounted for by variables already in the equation. Figure 2.10, for example, illustrates this. Suppose there is considerable overlap in the information obtained from two selection tests, but both relate to job performance. If the Test 1 score is put into the equation, its added contribution will involve only that part of the job performance measure represented in area d; the area labeled b has already been accounted for by Test 2. All this means that the weight assigned to a given source of employment information doesn't necessarily represent its entire relationship with the criterion, but only the part that is unique. Hence, a company might extend its selection procedures to include an additional technique, but if this new technique taps an area of job performance already predicted, it will make little or no contribution to the selection of employees.

This approach to combining selection information is a quantitative one, and as a consequence each separate source of data input must be expressed in quantitative form. This presents no particular problem for the scores obtained from psychological tests; they are in quantitative form to begin with. Application-blank and reference-letter data, however, must be translated into numbers, and this is an operation that is important to the usefulness of these instruments. Valuable selection information can be wasted if care isn't exercised in expressing interview, application-blank, and reference-letter data in numerical form.

Multiple Cutoff Method. The multiple cutoff method establishes a minimum score for each separate procedure used in the selection process, and to be considered for employment an individual must score above those minimum values on each technique used. Regardless of how high an applicant may score on every other scale, if he fails to reach the critical value on one of the procedures, he is considered unacceptable for hiring.

The most frequent complaint voiced about this approach is that it does not recognize the possibility that an individual may compensate for deficiencies in one area by showing considerable strength in another. This approach also does not solve the problem of what is to be done when there is a surplus of applicants who satisfy these minimum standards. The method does not tell us how to combine scores that have passed all the cutoff values. Perhaps a statistical equation like the one considered above could be fitted to data that satisfy the multiple cutoff standard, but we now must face

---

[1]The general method involved here is called a multiple regression procedure, and it may be found in any standard text in statistics (for example Hays, 1973).

the fact that after we eliminate those who miss at least one of the critical values, there will remain only a relatively homogeneous group of applicants. Finally, it is difficult to establish the lower limit scores in a way that will not eliminate applicants who would have succeeded, had they been placed on the job.

A conservative approach to setting these critical limits may lead to a reasonable application of this procedure. This involves setting the cutoff scores quite low, so that relatively few are eliminated. For many jobs there are real and compelling requirements that must be met by the employees before the job can be successfully carried out. Technical jobs often demand a certain level of formal training; certain kinds of experience may be essential for higher level management positions; skilled trades require certain minimum levels of apprenticeship training. By setting critical scores at conservatively low levels, the multiple cutoff method is a reasonable strategy for combining employment information obtained from several sources. Those surviving these multiple criteria, will be screened by other techniques.

Profile Analysis. Another approach to using predictor information that comes from several sources is to prepare a graphic profile of an individual's scores on each of the various selection instruments. Similar information is available from all present employees who are considered to be successful in their jobs, and an average score is computed from each separate predictor. A plotting of these average values represents a profile that is used as the standard against which the profile of each applicant is compared. Applicants whose profiles consistently lie above the points on the standard profile or who accumulate the smallest negative deviations are considered more suitable for hiring.

Sequential Multiple Cutoff. Selection procedures are administered to the applicant successively. A screening interview often follows the submission of a completed application blank, and this may be followed by the administration of psychological tests. It is possible to devise a scheme in which a decision whether or not to reject an applicant is made after each step in the hiring sequence. If the applicant is not rejected, he is permitted to go on to the next phase of the selection procedure.

This type of strategy can be extended into the period of training that immediately follows hiring. In other words, if the applicant successfully passes each step in the hiring process, he might then be assigned to a training program. His status at the end of this program will determine whether he is permitted to go on to placement in a department. After remaining in the department for several months, the new employee is evaluated by his supervisor. If this evaluation is satisfactory he is now considered a successful employee who has passed through all the evaluational procedures involved in selection, training, and the trial period of work. At each step in this procedure a decision to discharge or retain the employee is made. The contract with the labor union will probably specify the duration of this assessment period.

SUMMARY COMMENTS

Much that enters into successful work involves employee characteristics that are developed over many years. Personality and social behaviors, basic skills, and aptitudes make substantial contributions to an individual's potential for job success. These are attributes that are brought to the job by new employees; and although they can be modified to some extent by training, they often operate as a well-established base on which much job performance is built. Job design, incentive programs, and employee training programs all serve an important role in influencing the general level of employee performance, but an effective selection program brings into the organization employees whose basic makeup substantially increases the likelihood that these other personnel programs will be successful.

The main idea underlying employee selection concerns collecting information at the time of hiring that has been shown to have a relationship with job performance. This information can be collected and assembled in a relatively short time, and it provides insight into behaviors that can become available only after an employee is hired, trained, and placed on the job. Hence, personnel selection represents a forecasting activity; it gathers information that improves the accuracy of the predictions implicit in all hiring situations.

One may ask whether experience with these selection programs has indicated that they contribute to prediction accuracy. It is difficult to answer this question, since research bearing on this issue is so widely scattered. There is also considerable variation from one work setting to the next in the strength of the relationship between selection device and work performance. One of the more ambitious efforts to assess the validity of occupational tests has been reported by Ghiselli (1966) who examined 45 years of published research literature for validity information. Ghiselli concludes that when considering all tests and all jobs, the chances are quite good (3 to 1) that the validity coefficient will be high enough to have some practical value for an employer. Some caution should be used, however, since different types of tests have shown variation in the strength of their association with various facets of work behavior. For example, tests of motor ability have not been quite as successful in predicting job proficiency as have tests of intelligence or tests of spatial and mechanical abilities. One should be aware of this sort of information before adopting a test for use in a work setting.

There is one final note: a test may show accuracy in predicting an employee's success in a training program, and be of little use in predicting performance on the job. The opposite relationship may also be found. Ghiselli found that in some areas of work (for example, trades and crafts, industrial occupations) there was very little relationship between a test's ability to predict training performance and its ability to predict job performance. Furthermore, scanning across all tests, Ghiselli found that occupational tests seem to have a slightly better record in predicting success in training. Why this is so is open to speculation, but one good possibility is that it is a function of the nature of the criteria used in the two areas. Often a measure of success in training is less complex and easier to obtain than is a measure used to express an evaluation of a worker's job performance. We need more information concerning the adequacy of selection techniques; but more important than this, we must acknowledge that in all instances the development of a selection system requires an experimental approach in which data are collected and evaluated for each specific situation.

3
Training for Work

Many managers contend that there is a limited supply of competent workers in the labor market and that the ultimate success of a work organization rests on its ability to attract these people to its ranks. In seeking qualified employees, companies often calculate work potential in terms of the amount and type of formal education possessed by a job applicant, and many business organizations have active programs that recruit and hire those who possess the certificates and diplomas that testify to high levels of formal training. Yet it is not uncommon to hear new workers reporting that their schooling did not adequately prepare them for the work they do. In large measure this complaint reflects the fact that school and college curricula do not include the variety of specific skills and knowledge that one may find required in the many different fields of work. It also points up the fact that work organizations have to make some provisions to train employees before they are able to perform the duties of their jobs. Although effective recruitment, selection, and placement programs can contribute to a company's efforts to secure successful employees, training programs must also be available to develop the individual skills and knowledge required for most jobs.

On first impression, a company training program may appear to be an extravagance for all but the largest corporations, but whether formally recognized or not, the training function is a real and important part of every personnel program. Some of this training may be narrow in scope, some of it broad; some well organized, some almost casual; but regardless of their structure, training programs represent a major concern for those involved in the management of work organizations.

This chapter will consider industrial training in the light of its psychological and organizational implications. When viewed from a psychological perspective, training is seen as an application of the principles of human learning and motivation to an industrial setting. Effective training implies efficient learning, and knowledge of some basic learning principles that have evolved from laboratory research is considered an essential part of the training specialist's preparation. But the learning that goes on in many training sessions often concerns more than the objective skills and knowledge required by a job. Training activities may also be viewed as part of an organization's attempt to maintain an orderly and secure social environment within its boundaries. In many instances training programs serve to transmit information concerning the values, attitudes, and expectations held by a management group. From this point of view, training is a control mechanism that operates within a corporation; and its objectives are often a reflection of the internal politics that constitute the social dynamics of the organization. This chapter will take up these considerations.

We will also consider the methods and techniques of industrial training. Over the years a surprisingly broad array of training procedures have been adapted to an industrial setting, and an attempt will be made to select a representative cross section of these approaches and discuss their principal characteristics. The chapter will also discuss some of the important antecedent and consequent activities that are essential to effective training. That is to say, we will describe the procedures that are used to estimate training needs and the steps required to assess the extent to which a training program reaches its objectives. First, however, it would be prudent to take up some of the basic behavioral principles that are useful in dealing with the development and implementation of instructional activities. This refers to concepts concerning learning and performance that have been generated by psychological research.

PRINCIPLES OF LEARNING AND PERFORMANCE

The scientific literature on human learning is an extensive one (cf. McKeachie, 1974; Wittrock & Lumsdaine, 1977); but in spite of this, the psychologist has still been unable to set down rigorous scientific principles that account for the intricate details of how people learn. There is, however, good agreement among psychologists concerning some of the *general* conditions that seem to improve the *efficiency* of learning, even though there is less than good agreement concerning how some of these mechanisms work. But learning is only one aspect of a successful training program. A worker must utilize the skills and knowledge learned in training, and there are conditions that should be met before it is realistic to expect training experiences to translate into job performance. In large measure these are conditions that exist away from the training site, and their importance points to the fact that the concerns of a training program extend beyond the immediate site where instruction takes place. Many programs have failed, not because the trainees did not learn, but because they did not translate their new learning into job performance. Hence, in thinking about industrial training one must consider instruction, learning, and a variety of supporting conditions that are found out on the work floor.

The Nature of Learning— Gagne's Model

There are few behavioral events that are more complicated than learning, and the development of a successful training program requires that attention be given to each facet of this intricate process. One of the better learning models is one developed by Gagne (1974) to depict the sequence of events that constitute a single act of learning (see Figure 3.1). This model maintains that every act of learning involves a series of phases that occur over time. Associated with each phase is a psychological process that is operative during that period.

FIGURE 3.1 The Phases and Psychological Processes Associated with a Single Act of Learning

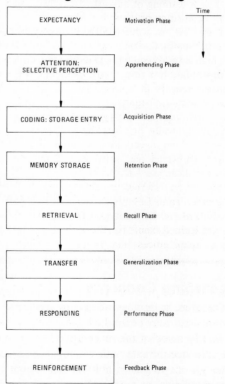

Source: Gagne, R. M. *Essentials of learning for instruction.* Hinsdale, Ill.: Dryden Press, 1974, p. 28. Copyright 1974, published by permission.

Hence, Gagne's model depicts learning as a complex sequence of events that occur within the individual. Each of these events is in itself a complicated process, and the successful acquisition of new behaviors can be facilitated or disrupted by conditions influencing any phase of this sequence. The following eight phases are involved in each single act of learning:

1. *The motivation phase:* At the onset of learning the individual must establish an expectation that a reward of some sort will be available as a consequence of learning activities. Trainers can establish this expectation by communicating to the learner the outcomes that might be expected as the result of learning. These outcomes may involve wages, recognition, or merely the ability to carry out a job with greater competence and ease.

2. *The apprehension phase:* In order to learn, the learner must attend to the relevant part of the learning situation. The learner must selectively perceive those aspects of the total situation that are involved in the efficient learning of the task.

3. *The acquisition phase:* It is during this phase that the events that are perceived are mentally transformed in such a way that they can be stored. This transformation is called coding, and it can involve translating the learning task into words, visual images, or even movements. In this phase, the first steps in the act of memory are begun.

4. *Retention phase:* Memory, as the term is used informally, typically involves the long-term storage of events. Some events may be stored for periods of time that extend over many years, while other events tend to disappear with the passage of time. Memory may also be disturbed through interference generated by other learned events.

5. *Recall phase:* One criterion for learning is that the event learned should be accessible to recall. Through a complex process that is not well understood, a mental search is carried out through the materials stored in long-term memory. The retrieval of an event from memory may be facilitated by external cues that aid recall. Past experiences have led to the formation of associations linking learned events together. Subsequently, the advent of one event leads to the recall of other associated events.

6. *Generalization phase:* Material that has been learned in one situation can be extended and applied to other situations. This process, known as *transfer,* accounts for the fact that each new situation does not ordinarily require that a person begin anew and learn every detail. Previously learned materials can often be transferred to the new situation.

7. *Performance phase:* It is through performance that learning is inferred, although there are many instances in the classroom or at work in which the performance that is observed is not consistent with the objectives of training.

8. *Feedback phase:* The feedback phase involves the transmission of information concerning the consequences of learning. When the learner becomes aware that the desired learning objectives have been met, then the learned act is said to be reinforced. Reinforcement is a concept that refers to the change in probability that the learned act will occur again, and it is a process that is generated by the consequences of learning. According to Gagne, reinforcement occurs when the expectations established during the motivational phases are confirmed. The concept is closely related to the concept of reward.

Learning Concepts

There are a number of general principles and concepts that may be applied to learning situations to identify some of the more important conditions that influence the rate with which learning occurs. Although one might be able to find exceptions to these principles, as a general rule they do serve as useful representations of the variables that play a significant role in the acquisition of new behaviors.

Individual Differences. There are wide individual differences in the ability to learn any skill, and an individual with one skill may show considerable difficulty in learning another. This appears to be an obvious fact, but it is one that should receive considerable attention whenever training programs are developed to involve the members of a group of employees who usually vary widely in their ability to learn.

Attention. Instructional procedures must direct the learner's attention to the pertinent elements of the learning task. For example, there is research support for the use of a set of pertinent questions that precede the material that is to be learned (Frase, 1973, 1975). These *prequestions* focus the learner's attention on certain aspects of the task and often improve the learning and retention of the material involved in the questions asked (Bull & Dizney, 1973; Snowman & Cunningham, 1975).

The rate of learning has also been found to change when the instructional materials identify the objectives of the learning task (Duell, 1974). Stated objectives are thought to direct the learner's attention to the critical aspects of the task, but there is some question whether the use of these objectives retards learning of material that is not directly included in the objectives (May & Lumsdaine, 1958; Frase & Kreitzberg, 1975). But whatever the case, and much probably depends on the type of material to be learned, the learner should be able to discriminate the important aspects of a problem in order to progress efficiently toward the goals of the learning task.

Motivation. Learning occurs most efficiently when trainees are motivated to learn (Otto & Glaser, 1970). The desire to learn is a factor that is essential in achieving reasonable speed in acquiring new knowledge or skill, and this motivation to learn tends to originate from two sources. First, if learning is perceived as leading to the attainment of some desired external goal, the rate of progress tends to be more rapid. For example, if employees see such things as job security, wages, or promotion being related to learning the material presented in training, there is an increased likelihood that they will learn efficiently. Motivation of this sort is said to be *extrinsic,* since it lies outside the task in the form of incentives that reinforce learning.

There may also be instances in which the task itself generates positive motives to learn. Here the trainee finds that there is satisfaction in performing the task, and his continued efforts to learn are motivated by the interest he has in the task itself.

DeCharms (1968) contends that a person who perceives that the causes of personal behavior are found within the self is intrinsically motivated. The intrinsically motivated learner, therefore, is one who sees the acquisition of new skills to be the result of personal efforts and talents. Furthermore, perceptions of this sort are more probable in tasks that have high interest values and that do not rely on external rewards to motivate performance.

Intrinsic motivation is often seen as being more desirable than motivation associated with extrinsic incentives (Deci, 1975; Notz, 1975). It is not always possible, however, to rely on intrinsic sources, especially early in training when trainees tend to be functioning at low levels of competence. As skill and competence improve, the prospects improve for intrinsic sources of motivation to begin exerting more influence on the rate of learning. In all probability, most practical training situations rely on both intrinsic and extrinsic sources of trainee motiviation.

Reinforcement and Knowledge of Results. Reinforcement is a concept that has figured prominently in discussions of learning. A reinforcer is an event that follows a response and strengthens the probability that the response will again appear under similar conditions. Often a reinforcer is thought of in terms that are quite similar to the general concept of reward. Hence, learning that leads to behaviors that produce reward is often found to progress more rapidly than does learning that is not linked to a reward system (Otto & Glaser, 1970; Wittrock & Lumsdaine, 1977).

Reinforcement refers to one of the consequences of learning, and in practical learning situations these consequences most often take the form of some sort of feedback of knowledge of the results of a learner's efforts to learn. This information concerns the degree of success or failure associated with a person's learning efforts, and learning is often found to progress most efficiently when knowledge of results is fed back to the learner.

Provisions should be made in all training sessions to provide the trainee with knowledge of results. Information of this sort serves several functions. First, if after each attempt at learning the trainee receives this type of feedback, the characteristics of correct and incorrect behaviors can more easily be identified (Surber & Anderson, 1975). Second, since learning is encouraged by management, knowledge of the results of successful performance is often a rewarding experience for the trainee. Knowledge of results therefore serves as a reward for progress in learning as well as a cue for correct performance during the training exercise.

Transfer of Learning. Learning of one skill often facilitates the learning of another, and thus individuals tend to build on the knowledge and skills they have previously acquired. As a consequence, some training programs can proceed more efficiently than others as a result of the fact that those being trained possess previously acquired competencies in related areas. There are times when trainees reach a point in their general level of proficiency when they are capable of learning certain kinds of new material with relatively little help from the trainer. It is a mistake to assume that formal instruction must be given in each and every facet of a skill area. Along similar lines, if a learner practices in a variety of different settings, this will tend to broaden the range of situations to which the learning will apply.

There are instances in which transfer effects are negative in the sense that previously learned behaviors interfere with the acquisition of new responses. There are times when previous behaviors must be "unlearned" before new learning can proceed efficiently. In these situations one refers to *negative transfer effects*. Maximum negative transfer can be produced when a new and dissimilar response must be attached to the original training situation (Avery & Cross, 1978).

Progress of Learning. Learning often progresses rather rapidly at first, but then as practice continues, the rate of acquisition tends to become slower. This fact has great motivational significance for those who plan training programs. The general optimism, experienced in the early phases of learning when progress is most rapid, often gives way to disappointment when each new learning trial fails to produce noticeable improvements in performance. It is during these difficult phases that the trainer must give added support and encouragement to the trainee.

It should also be recognized that there is no such thing as a standard curve describing the rate of learning in all situations. Different tasks will generate different curves, and within a given task one usually finds wide individual differences in the shape of the curve that shows performance changes as a given trainee moves from one learning trial to the next. Experienced trainers are often familiar with these differences, and they adopt procedures that are appropriate for the individual case.

Length of Practice Sessions. It is often more efficient to space learning out over many short sessions rather than concentrate practice in a few long sessions. When there is too great an increase in the amount one tries to learn in a single session, there comes a point where learning efficiency begins to suffer. Much depends on the nature of the task and the ability of the learner, but massing practice trials within a single session can overburden the learner and make the progress of learning more difficult.

Comment. In considering general principles such as these, one should bear in mind that their application to practical training situations does not guarantee efficient learning. For example, Gagne (1962) in a widely cited paper reports a number of instances where the application of some generally accepted learning principles did not lead to rapid learning. Gagne contends that a thorough analysis of the task to be learned is often more important than strict allegiance to basic principles of learning. The analysis of a complex learning task into its elemental parts is essential for effective instruction, but once this is done it is unwise to ignore the fundamental principles that direct the course of learning. What all this means is that there exists no simple formula permitting the direct extension of a set of highly general principles to all learning problems. These principles must be interpreted in the light of a task analysis that has been carried out in order to identify the basic nature of the training task. Nevertheless, when training programs are developed, there are questions of practice, reinforcement, transfer, and motivation that must be considered; and it would probably be profitable if they were considered from the perspective of general principles of the type outlined above.

Performance

To be successful, a training program must be able to demonstrate that trainees not only have learned the content of the course, but that they have carried this learning over into their job performance. Learning refers to the acquired capability to make certain kinds of responses, while performance refers to the actual occurrence of these responses. In many training programs the nature of the course material is such that there is little question that the trainees will successfully learn. A major problem concerns the extent to which

trainees will translate their new learning into on-the-job performance (Fleishman, Harris & Burtt, 1955; Allen & Silverzweig, 1976). The solution to this problem is found largely in the conditions that exist on the job and not in the structure or conduct of the training sessions themselves (Lawson, 1974).

Hinrichs (1976) discusses what he calls maintenance systems that support and sustain the learning and performance that is the objective of training. One set of these maintenance variables is found within the individual. Here Hinrichs refers to the ability, personality, and motivational variables that play an important role in supporting the learning that takes place in training. A second general type of maintenance factor is external to the individual learner. These variables reside in the organization and within the systems that form the social context of work. These external influences function to sustain the behaviors that are acquired during training, and they play a key role in determining whether the performance objectives of training are met.

We can state several general principles that can be applied to better ensure the transfer of learning into job performance.

1. Performance reflecting the content of a training program is more likely to occur if this behavior is incorporated into the systems of reward maintained by the organization. There should be an increase in the likelihood that workers will receive a positive incentive of some sort whenever they perform in a fashion consistent with training. For example, if supervisors are trained in certain human relations skills, then management should provide a positive incentive (in the form of merit ratings, pay, promotions, and so forth) to those who succeed in displaying these skills in their relationships with subordinates.

2. The connection between rewards and the desired performance must be perceived by the trainees. In a later chapter (Chapter 7) we will discuss more completely the concept of *perceived instrumentality*. For the present, it is sufficient to say that trainees must perceive that the behaviors learned in training lead to desired goals. To the extent that this perception exists, there is an increased likelihood that training will carry over into job performance.

PURPOSES AND OBJECTIVES OF TRAINING

A training program is an agent of change that is maintained in order to improve the likelihood

that certain organizational objectives will be met. The most fundamental purpose of training is behavioral change, and the primary objective is to demonstrate that employees behave differently after they have participated in a training exercise.

Some argue (Planty, McCord, & Efferson, 1948) that every training program, regardless of its emphasis, is directed toward changes in three behavioral components: skills, information, and attitudes. Hence, from this point of view the general purposes of industrial training are to develop skills, impart information, and modify attitudes. A program set up to train employees in the operation of a piece of office equipment, for example, might have as its principal objective the development of a new set of manual skills. At the same time, however, a considerable amount of new in- formation will be transmitted along with the new sets of attitudes about the specific task and about the organization.

Within the framework of these general objectives one may list a number of more specific goals for industrial training. Ultimately, each contributes to the basic economic and social goals of the organization, but in many instances they are also directed at improving the general level of work adjustment of the individual. The following is a representative set of objectives that are usually associated with industrial training:

1. Helping worker adapt to new position
2. Improve worker productivity
3. Maintain up-to-date job skills
4. Reduce waste and repair costs
5. Improve product quality
6. Improve operational efficiency
7. Better utilization of equipment and supplies
8. Broaden range of skills possessed by worker
9. Increase worker versatility
10. Reduce number of grievances and improve morale
11. Reduce absences and turnover
12. Improve communications
13. Reduce dependence on supervision
14. Lower levels of work tension and job stress
15. Lower rate of accidents
16. Meet the special needs and provide support for the disadvantaged worker.

This list is by no means complete, but it does represent a major portion of the objectives that motivate training activities. From this list one may see the many functions served by a training department, although there are other personnel procedures—for example, selection, placement—that contribute to achieving each of these aims. As a consequence, a training program is best thought of as a single facet in an integrated personnel *system* whose general purpose is to improve the efficiency of work performance and increase the quality of work life (Goldstein, 1980).

ASSESSING TRAINING NEEDS

Determining the need for training often requires data collection of the sort that enters into job analysis procedures (McCormick, 1976). Training needs are not always self-evident, and it is unwise and potentially expensive for an organization to launch a program without first collecting information that will shed light on both the need for training and the content and structure of the program. Organizational problems can often be solved by the effective use of training, but it is easy to be misled into thinking that training is a solution, when more effective selection procedures or a change in the incentive system may really be called for (Thayer & McGehee, 1977).

Apart from determining the need for training, a needs analysis will provide guidance in the construction of the program. The determination of the content of the program and the selection of instructional techniques should stem from a systematic effort to collect data on training needs. Common sense, always a valuable tool in personnel work, should be tempered with available information concerning the status of training needs in the organization.

Training Needs Indicators

Training needs are most often indicated by a discrepancy of some sort (Mager & Pipe, 1970; Moore & Dutton, 1978). Information reflecting existing conditions is compared with statements regarding the conditions that are desired, and discrepancies suggest the possible need for training. A review of production records might indicate a problem that should be dealt with by further training. Merit ratings, reports from time-study engineers, interviews with supervisors, accident data, morale surveys, and an analysis of the company's performance records might all signal the need for further training. The initial indication of the need often comes from an analysis of materials collected for purposes other than training. Any record that reflects on the performance of the organization or its personnel is a potential source of training needs information. It often happens that these data are called to the attention of the personnel department by a supervisor who is responsible for the performance of one or more departments. Periodic interviews with employee and supervisory personnel by the training department is also a useful source of information concerning training needs.

McGehee & Thayer (1961) define training needs determination in terms of three types of analyses:

1. Organizational analysis—determining where in the organization training activities should be focused
2. Operations analysis—identifying the content of training by determining the performance requirements of a work task
3. Man analysis—identifying skills, knowledge, or attitudes possessed by those holding jobs.

A comparison of information obtained in operations and man analyses provides data representing performance deficiencies.

Organizational Analysis.   It is rare that an analysis of organizational records can provide a diagnosis of a problem. It can locate places in the firm where problems exist, but it is often inadequate in pinpointing the causes of these difficulties. An organization may be generating an inordinate amount of scrappage, and the company records can identify one department as the origin of the problem. Poor work quality, however, may result from a variety of causes, many of which have little to do with the behavior of the employees in a department. Inadequate equipment, faulty engineering layout, and poor materials may lie at the bottom of the problem, and there is little available in the organizational records to spotlight these causes. Hence, an inspection of the many performance records kept by a company may show where problems exist, but not why they exist.

An organizational analysis can, however, be directed at obtaining information concerning the goals and objectives of the organization. Furthermore, it can provide data regarding the distribution of manpower over the various departments of the company. Both deficiencies and oversupply of manpower can produce symptoms that suggest the need for training. The locus of this type of problem, however, may not be in the departments where the poor performance occurs. The low morale, poor productivity, and high turnover that may be characteristic of a department that is over- or understaffed can probably be best corrected by action taken at places in the organization where staffing decisions are made. Here, training that concerns itself with manpower needs may be most effectively directed outside the departments where the performance problems are occurring.

An organizational analysis may draw on many different sources of data that provide information regarding the location of situations that might profit from training. Moore and Dutton (1978) identify a number of these data sources, among them:

1. *Organizational goals and objectives*—A review of these statements is a starting point in identifying discrepancies that indicate the need for training.
2. *Manpower inventory*—Identifies where training is, or will be, needed to fill gaps caused by expansion, retirement, turnover, and so on.
3. *Skills inventory*—Enumeration of employees in various skill categories.
4. *Organizational climate indicators*—Includes such indexes as turnover, grievances, suggestions, accidents, productivity, attitude surveys, and customer complaints.
5. *Analysis of efficiency indexes*—Considers such things as labor costs, cost of materials, equipment down time, repairs, and late deliveries.
6. *Exit interviews*—Work problems reported by those terminating employment.
7. *Inventory of technological changes*—Listing of new equipment and changes in procedures that may require training.
8. *Management requests*—A survey of management judgment concerning departments and work groups in need of training.

Organizational analysis might also include the collection of information bearing on what Bahn (1973) calls *countertraining*. This refers to the existence of organizational impediments that discourage participation in training or the utilization of skills imparted during a training program. Access to information concerning these organizational constraints is not always easy, but follow-up interviews of the trainees and their supervisors may provide clues regarding the presence of countertraining influences. This topic will be discussed again in conjunction with our consideration of the organizational dynamics of training activities.

Operations Analysis. The techniques used in an operations analysis tend to be quite similar to those employed in a job analysis. The operations analysis has as its principal concern the behavioral requirements that a job places on the worker. Skills, knowledge, and attitudes combine into patterns of performance that identify how the job should be carried out.

The military services have made important contributions to the development of procedures useful in operations analysis. For example, Christal (1974) developed a *job inventory* procedure that is useful for these purposes. This job inventory consists of two sections:

1. A section involving questions concerning a worker's education, time on the job, tools used, job location, equipment worked on, training schools attended, pay grade, and so on.
2. A section containing a list of all the significant tasks that may be performed by a worker in a given occupational area.

Christal contends that if this task list is properly constructed, then all workers in the occupation will be able to define their jobs in terms of the subset of tasks that are included in the list. Hence, with this approach, a questionnaire format is employed (see Figure 3.2). This questionnaire is given to those who are currently holding the job being analyzed, and these workers describe the operations performed by checking the appropriate task item on the inventory.

Ammerman and Essex (1977) propose another method that employs descriptions of work operations supplied by workers and supervisors who are close to the job. The content of training is determined by asking these persons for their judgment on what Ammerman calls *inclusion* and *em-*

FIGURE 3.2 Survey of Supervisory Training Needs

Name _____

Bureau _____

Please indicate your level of supervisory responsibility by checking one
of the following:

F = first-line supervisor (the employees you supervise do not supervise others)
S = second-line supervisor (you supervise employees who also have supervisory responsibilities)
M= management level

I. Please indicate by checking the appropriate column the degree of need
you think exists for training first-line supervisors only.

	Great Need	Some Need	Little Need
1. Communications			
2. Interviewing			
3. Counseling			
4. Disciplining			
5. Hiring Procedures			
6. Termination Procedures			
7. Developing Employees			
8. Motivating			
9. Human Relations			
10. Handling Complaints/Grievances			
11. Planning/Organizing			
12. Performance Appraisal			
13. Decision Making			
14. Leadership			
15. Functioning in the Organization			
16. Delegation			
17. Management Methods (e.g. M.B.O.)			
18. Budgeting			
19. Time Management			
20. Conducting Meetings			
21. Reporting Systems (written information)			
22. Safety (e.g. OSHA, First Aid)			
23. Affirmative Action/E.E.O.			

II. Please indicate any other supervisory skills for which you feel there may
be a need. List them below and check the appropriate box indicating the
degree of need.

	Great Need	Some Need	Little Need
1.			
2.			
3.			
4.			
5.			

**Source: Culbertson, K., & Thompson, M. An analysis of supervisory training needs. *Training and Development Journal*, 1980, *34*, 58–62.
Reproduced by special permission from the American Society for Training and Development, copyright, 1980.**

phasis. Inclusion concerns whether a task should receive some consideration in training, and emphasis concerns the level of ability that should be sought through training. Ammerman, like Christal, uses a task inventory questionnaire that lists the operations to be performed. In addition, for each task that is associated with a job, data are obtained concerning the frequency with which it occurs, its rated importance, and where and when it should be learned.

It should be clear from the above examples, that what is meant by operations analysis is a series of job-analysis-like procedures that are specially designed to collect information bearing on behaviors associated with a job, and that are potentially amenable to training (cf. Goldstein, 1974).

Man Analysis. If operations analyses draw on job-analysis procedures, man analysis seeks information of the type that resembles merit-rating data. A man analysis concerns both a *description* and an *evaluation* of the attributes and work performance of individuals. Information is sought concerning the level of skill and knowledge found among those who are on the job, or among those who are being considered for a training program. Numerous sources of information may be drawn on. Moore and Dutton (1978) list the following sources of man analysis information:

1. Performance data
2. Interviews
3. Questionnaires
4. Psychological tests of skills, knowledge, and achievement
5. Attitude surveys
6. Rating scales and critical incident
7. Business games and simulation procedures
8. Assessment centers

One could list other sources, but the point is that the information generated by a man analysis provides insight into training needs when it is related to the information obtained from an operations analysis that describes how the work should be performed and specifies the knowledge and skills that should be possessed by those who occupy a given position. Hence, as is the case with most personnel techniques, we find that training-needs assessment procedures form a system that yields interrelated information concerning an important aspect of work behavior. The organizational analysis provides information concerning the environmental setting of work, the operations analysis provides a picture of the tasks that are associated with a job, and man analysis generates information concerning the characteristics of the workers who are available to perform the job.

Determining the Content of Training. Once a set of training needs has been identified, there remains the problem of translating them into the specific details of a training program. In large measure, this problem is one that relies either on the judgment of professionals or on the perceptions of those who will participate in training (Wilson, 1980). In many instances, judgments of this sort are reasonably accurate, since the instructional implications of a given set of training needs are often quite clear; but this is not always the case.

The basic problem here is one of selecting an instructional strategy that will be effective in achieving the behavioral objectives that are obtained from the training-needs analysis. The solution to this problem begins with an analysis of a complex learning task into a set of simpler learning units that will form the segments of the training sessions. These simplified task units make the job of selecting instructional procedures easier, but the choice of techniques still depends on good judgment, and better yet, a research literature that will provide clues as to which training procedures will be most effective in developing the desired behaviors. There is at present a growing body of knowledge concerning the science of instruction (cf. Gagne, 1974; Gagne & Briggs, 1974; Fleishman, 1975; Scandura, 1977) that will eventually put the training director on much firmer ground in choosing instructional techniques. As matters now stand, however, the translation of training needs into teaching strategies is still a process that relies on the experience and judgment of those who develop instructional programs.

APPROACHES TO INDUSTRIAL TRAINING

When a company organizes a training program, decisions must be made regarding a number of factors in addition to the nature of the materials and topics to be presented. For example, one important decision involves the location of the training activities within the organization. Much training is done on the job, using the same facilities that are ordinarily used for production purposes. There are also program alternatives that place training in a number of different off-the-job settings. Some of this training takes place in the plant, but away from the areas where day-to-day production work is going on. In other instances, instruction is given at locations outside the plant, some being conducted by public or private contractors.

Program-to-program differences can also be found with respect to the personnel who assume responsibility for instruction. In some instances, a program may rely on the rank-and-file employees in each department to undertake the job of instruction, and in other instances it is the supervisor who assumes this role. In still other cases, a professional training staff is brought into the department to do the training. Finally, training teams involving all three types of personnel can be constructed in order to draw on the strengths of each.

On-the-Job Training

There are authors (McGehee & Thayer, 1961) who contend that some component of on-the-job training must be included in every training program, and it is probably true that this approach accounts for a large portion of all industrial training. The decision to train employees at the job site is a natural one, since all the equipment and facilities needed for the job are available and the training environment is identical to the conditions surrounding the job the trainee will eventually perform. In many of these programs a period of time is established during which the employee's training status is recognized and the normal standards of production and piece rates are suspended. As the trainee acquires proficiency on the job, he is brought into the normal set of rates and regulations that apply to others.

On-the-job training by no means limits instructional responsibilities to those who are directly involved with the work, but probably predisposes the organization toward this choice of instructors. Usually on-the-job training is carried out by members of the work group to which the trainee has been assigned. Staff personnel from the training department can be made available to assist in the instruction and to evaluate the trainee's progress in the program.

Advantages.   The primary advantage of an on-the-job training program is that training experiences are closely related to the actual duties, requirements, and conditions of the job. This approach to training is often used to introduce new employees to their job assignments. Here social orientation—for example, introduction and assimilation into a work group—takes place together with the learning of new job skills (Lefkowitz, 1970). Furthermore, as training progresses and trainees acquire competence, they gradually become productive members of their work groups. This has advantages for both learner, who gains an increasing sense of work team membership, and management, which shares the benefits of the worker's productivity.

Being close to the ongoing work of the department, on-the-job training exposes the trainee to the many job-related skills that are often essential for effective membership in a work team. This type of material not only includes the informal rules and standards that govern the behavior of the work group but also involves work shortcuts, knacks for doing things, and a number of minor insights that have been accumulated over the years and that often make the job easier to handle.

Disadvantages. Perhaps one of the most serious drawbacks found in on-the-job programs is the quality of the instruction that is available from the members of a work group (Goldstein, 1974). A given work group may be fortunate in having a member who can do a competent job of training, but this is somewhat a matter of chance, since employees are rarely chosen because of their skills in training. Of course, a company should make preparations for an on-the-job training program by training those who will be assigned a teaching role, and supervisors or staff members from the training department should monitor all teaching activities. Members of the training staff could also do the training, provided they had the manual and technical skills to do so.

There is another major disadvantage to on-the-job training, and that is found in the tendency of departments to look at training as a secondary responsibility (Strauss, 1967). It is often quite easy for a supervisor to perceive that production goals are more important than the training of new employees. As a consequence, training is assigned as an incidental part of a present employee's job, and the trainee receives inadequate instruction from a trainer who is busy with production matters. The solution to this problem requires that upper levels of management give encouragement and support to the training function, and develop rules and procedures that do not penalize people for committing themselves to doing a good job in training.

Job Rotation Plans. A program that has been used in training entry-level management personnel involves a systematic transfer of trainees from one department to another. Programs of this type are often intended for both training and placement purposes. Not only are the trainees exposed to the range of operations that occur in the organization, but individual departments are permitted to bid for the services of individual trainees after the pro-

gram has been completed. From a training perspective, job rotation programs give the trainee an overview of the work process. They also expose the trainee to the social dynamics of the organization, and it is knowledge of these processes that is vital to the effective performance of the middle- and upper-level manager.

Off-the-Job Training

There are a number of alternatives that locate training activities away from the job site. Programs of this type can be conducted in separate facilities located within the plant, or they can be set up at locations away from the home base. Much off-the-job training is carried out with tenured employees, and much of it is of relatively short duration. Management and supervisory personnel frequently participate in short courses and conferences, many of which take place away from the plant. Apprentice programs also employ off-the-job training, combining classroom training with the experience trainees obtain from working closely with a journeyman. In instances where the primary objectives of a program involve the development of human relations skills or the transmission of information, off-the-job training sites are frequently used.

Vestibule Training. A vestibule facility is one in which the materials and equipment found at the job site are made available in a special training room. Away from the pressures of the work floor, training can proceed without the interruptions caused by production schedules and other organizational commitments. Usually a special training staff is assigned to these vestibule courses; and as might be expected, facilities of this sort are most often established for jobs where there is a continuing demand for newly trained employees. For example, cutting and sewing operations in garment work often employ large numbers of workers who are doing similar kinds of work. It is also not unusual to find high turnover among these employees, and this requires a continual source of newly trained employees. A vestibule facility is ideal for jobs of this sort. Lefkowitz (1970) reports that a program that combined a vestibule facility with on-the-job training was quite effective in training sewing machine operators.

Short Courses and Conferences.   Much of the training done at upper levels of management involves relatively brief courses that consist of several long sessions that occupy the better part of one or two days. Courses of this type provide managers with an opportunity to interact with management personnel from other organizations, since this type of training is often carried out by a consultant or contractor who services many business firms.

Although programs of this sort can serve a worthwhile function, they can be quite expensive, since they often involve considerable travel and maintenance expenses in addition to tuition costs. Alternatives that are much less expensive can usually be found, with many of the same results. Conference telephone calls, written summaries of the pertinent information, and taped presentations circulated in the mails are all effective substitutes. In an era of modern telecommunications it is often unnecessary to move trainees bodily to distant cities in order to receive information that can be transmitted through more efficient channels. The social aspects of these training junkets, however, may sometimes assume a more important role than training objectives, and management should exercise restraint in using this approach when other more efficient formats can be made available. In any event, management should require reasonable evidence that programs of this type are making a contribution to the general objectives of the organization.

Formal Classroom Training.   The pace of technological change is such that business organizations must use the facilities of vocational schools and universities in order to maintain up-to-date contact with the technical facets of their work. Engineers and accountants are often among those who are encouraged to continue their formal training by enrolling in further courses of instruction in order to expand their area of specialization.

Apprentice Programs.   Apprentice programs usually involve combinations of many different kinds of training. For a major portion of the program, the trainee assumes the role of helper to a journeyman, but there is also a component of formal off-the-job classroom instruction. Many apprentice programs involve the collaboration of union and management, with the union being primarily responsible for the general organization and content of the training. Evaluation of trainees is often left in the hands of the labor union.

Strauss (1967), considering some of the problems associated with apprentice programs, contends that journeymen and supervisors are often unwilling to provide the apprentice with careful instruction and guidance. In these instances little care is taken to ensure that the trainees are exposed to a broad range of work situations, and often the trainee is held responsible for meeting production levels that interfere with effective learning. Finally, Strauss found that in certain fields like electronics, where rapid technical changes take place, training in new skills and complicated concepts is difficult to carry out while the apprentice is on the job. The classroom is often a more appropriate setting for such instruction.

INSTRUCTIONAL TECHNIQUES

Once a site has been chosen for training, a decision needs to be made regarding the instructional approach to be used. To some extent this choice is limited by the content of the program and the nature of the subject matter to be presented; but even when these considerations have been established, there is still a wide assortment of instructional techniques that may be adopted. It would be comforting to believe that the knowledge exists to enable a program developer to choose the exact instructional techniques best suited for the training objectives that have been adopted. There is some information available concerning the more popular techniques, but this information is incomplete. At any rate, there is evidence (Carroll, Paine, & Ivancevich, 1972) indicating that so-called expert judgment is often not based on the limited amount of research that has been done. As a result, the selection of the most appropriate training techniques still seems to be a matter of opinion.

This section will describe a number of the more popular instructional techniques and consider the research evaluating their effectiveness. Since there are many variants of a single technique, only a broad descriptive outline will be presented, containing the basic characteristics of each method. In considering these descriptions, the reader must realize that there is broad latitude in adapting a technique to a specific work situation. Furthermore, it is often the case that a combination of procedures proves more effective than a single technique. As a consequence, the reader must bear in mind the possibility that a particular technique may show considerable utility when used in conjunction with other methods, even though when used alone it makes little contribution.

Behavior Modeling

One of the most effective sources of instruction can be found in the behavior of an instructor who provides an example of the skills and performance sought in training. Skill training, for example, often consists of a direct one-on-one coaching process in which the instructor provides a model of correct performance and gives frequent guidance and feedback to the trainee. Frequently, these modeling activities are spontaneous and unplanned, as might be the case in an apprentice program where the trainee is told to watch the journeyman and "pick up" whatever he or she can. Behavior modeling can, however, be brought into a systematic instructional program, and in these instances it represents a useful tool in training for certain types of skills.

Basically a behavior-modeling approach involves three important components:

1. A demonstration of master performance
2. Guided trainee practice
3. Feedback concerning the effectiveness of trainee performance (Tosti, 1980)

The content and complexity of the training material may vary considerably, but the above three activities constitute the central core of a behavior-modeling approach. Behavioral modeling refers to a process of *observational learning* in which the behavior of the model serves as a stimulus and a guide for the performance of others (Marlatt & Perry, 1975). The technique places heavy reliance on imitation as a process whereby individuals learn new behaviors; and unlike many other approaches to instruction, behavior modeling is grounded in a well-established theory of social learning (Bandura, 1971).

In large measure, the behavior modeling approach has been employed to train supervisory personnel. Used primarily to improve interpersonal skills, the technique was first employed in industry by Sorcher (1971; Goldstein & Sorcher, 1974) in a program sponsored by the General Electric Company, which attempted to reduce turnover among socially disadvantaged employees by improving relations with their supervisors. This program involved four components:

1. Modeling—trainee sees films of model persons performing correctly in a problem situation.
2. Role playing—trainee practices the behavior demonstrated in the films.
3. Feedback—trainee's performance given constructive feedback by trainer or members of training class.
4. Transfer of training—while on the job the trainee is encouraged to utilize modeled behavior.

This program led to a marked improvement in trainee performance. For instance, after a six-month training program involving both employees and supervisors, there was a significant improvement in the turnover rates for those who had been trained. Of the trainees who worked for supervisors who had also been trained, 72 percent remained on the job, whereas only 28 percent of those who had not been trained were still employed.

Burnaska (1976) reports on the outcome of another modeling program for middle managers, in which modest success was achieved in improving their listening skills and in upgrading their ability to establish responsibility for problems that were dealt with by subordinates. American Telephone and Telegraph has also installed a behavior-modeling program following Sorcher's approach (Moses & Ritchie, 1976). Evaluation studies for this program indicated that supervisors trained by this method improved their ability to solve certain kinds of personnel problems. Finally, Smith (1976) reports on a study done at IBM in which behavior modeling resulted in a variety of positive changes, including improved morale and better customer relations.

It appears that one can find a considerable amount of evidence pointing to the effectiveness of the modeling approach to training, but the technique is not without its detractors. Locke (1977), for example, argues that modeling is a procedure for translating abstract principles into applications within a specific situation. If these general principles are not made clear to the trainees, as is often the case, then they will find it difficult to apply what is learned to situations that differ from those represented in the training exercise. As a result, behavior modeling will not encourage a broad transfer of training to a variety of job situations. If this contention of Locke's is correct, then this is a serious drawback of the behavior-modeling technique. At the present time, however, Locke's argument has not received the research attention that it deserves.

Lecture Method

There seems to be a general mistrust of the lecture method in much of the training literature. Perhaps because of the reliance placed on this approach by schools and colleges, it is often referred to as the "conventional method" of instruction. Common sense suggests that it is an efficient approach to teaching, since it can be adapted to large groups, and it is a reasonable approach whenever the content of training involves abstract concepts and general principles. Lecturing is a difficult skill, however, and the availability of a competent lecturer is frequently a problem. Furthermore, the method makes it difficult to accommodate the range of individual differences one might encounter in a group of trainees. Nevertheless, with care in organizing a group, and with ample opportunity for interaction between instructor and trainee, this problem can be dealt with.

Carroll et al. (1972) carried out an interesting survey that involved 117 training directors who were employed by the *Fortune 500* companies with the largest number of employees. The survey asked these directors to express their evaluations of nine training methods, with regard to the extent to which they achieved each of six training objectives. Table 3.1 shows the ranking of each method considered in the light of each objective. As can be seen, the lecture method did not receive high rankings. Notice the differences in ranking received by the lecture approach and a conference technique that involved discussion among trainees. Yet Carroll et al. point out that the research that has been reported comparing these two methods has not demonstrated differences in the effectiveness with which they transmit knowledge. Furthermore, the research literature indicates that the lecture method has been found to be successful in achieving trainees' acceptance of the materials presented. As a consequence, there may be a tendency on the part of training directors to dismiss a method that can make a positive contribution to the objectives of a training program.

TABLE 3.1   Training Director's Ranking of the Effectiveness of Nine Training Methods for Six Training Objectives

Method	Knowledge Acquisition	Changing Attitudes	Problem Solving Skills	Inter-personal Skills	Participant Acceptance	Knowledge Retention
Case Study	2	4	1	4	2	2
Conference-Discussion	3	3	4	3	1	5
Lecture with Questions	9	8	9	8	8	8
Business Games	6	5	2	5	3	6
Films	4	6	7	6	5	7
Programmed Instruction	1	7	6	7	7	1
Role Playing	7	2	3	2	4	4
Sensitivity Training	8	1	5	1	6	3
Television Lecture	5	9	8	9	9	9

Abstracted from Carroll, S., et al. The relative effectiveness of training methods—expert opinion and research. *Personnel Psychology,* 1972, *25,* 495–509.

Group Discussion

When properly led, it has been found that group discussion can be quite successful in encouraging participants to adopt courses of action that are consistent with the objectives of the training techniques. Care must be taken in selecting and training those who assume the role of discussion leader, and Maier (1963) maintains that supervisory personnel can learn the interpersonal skills needed to assume this role. These skills involve behaviors that create a climate of acceptance and techniques that encourage trainee participation within a group that is not dominated by its discussion leader. Group-discussion methods have persuasion as their major objective. They have found extensive use in situations where problem solving is an important part of the training exercise.

Films

Films combine lecture and demonstration, and can be used as part of a modeling program. Films can be expensive, but they often provide a carefully prepared, standardized demonstration that permits trainees to view materials and skills at a number of different speeds and from close up. Unless tailor-made for a specific situation, films obviously suffer from not being able to reflect many of the situational conditions found in a particular plant. But film-making skills tend to be readily available, so there is little to prevent organizations from constructing films for their own training purposes.

Programmed Instruction (PI)

Programmed instruction presents the learning task in a detailed step-by-step sequence that represents a careful development of the material to be learned. After each step learners are asked to respond to a question that tests their understanding of the material just presented. Correct answers advance the learner to the next unit; incorrect answers inform the trainee that the material needs to be reconsidered (see Figure 3.3). The technique places considerable emphasis on constant feedback that keeps trainees informed about their learning progress as they move through the many steps that lead to the completion of the task. Programs are of two different types: a linear type, which moves the learner through the steps in a fixed order, and a branching type, which moves the learner to a place in the program that is determined by the nature of the response to each question. For example, a particular type of error response may move the learner back only a single step in the program.

FIGURE 3.3   Four Frames of a Programmed Text

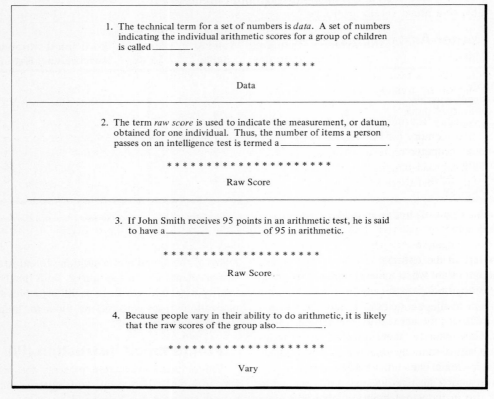

1. The technical term for a set of numbers is *data*. A set of numbers indicating the individual arithmetic scores for a group of children is called _____.

* * * * * * * * * * * * * * *

Data

2. The term *raw score* is used to indicate the measurement, or datum, obtained for one individual. Thus, the number of items a person passes on an intelligence test is termed a _____ _____.

* * * * * * * * * * * * * * * * * *

Raw Score

3. If John Smith receives 95 points in an arithmetic test, he is said to have a _____ _____ of 95 in arithmetic.

* * * * * * * * * * * * * * * *

Raw Score

4. Because people vary in their ability to do arithmetic, it is likely that the raw scores of the group also _____.

* * * * * * * * * * * * * * * *

Vary

Source: F. F. Elzey *A Programmed Introduction to Statistics.* Belmont, Cal.: Wadsworth, 1966.

Another error response may move the trainee back to the beginning of an entire section or to a subroutine designed to correct the misunderstandings.

In large measure, programmed instruction is a self-teaching device. Once trainees are familiar with the details of the routine, the responsibility for instruction rests completely with the learning program. PI may be presented mechanically by a device that presents the trainee with one frame of the lesson at a time, or it may be presented on a printed page that has been divided into a number of frames (see Figure 3.3). In this latter format the learner moves a card down the page uncovering one unit at a time. In all cases, the rate with which the trainee progresses through the program is self-determined.

Nash, Muczyk and Vettori (1971) reviewed a large number of studies evaluating programmed instruction compared with more conventional procedures. Their results indicated that PI "almost always" reduced training time to an extent that was significant from a practical perspective. The method did not, however, demonstrate consistent superiority over conventional approaches when trainee learning and retention were considered. When these latter findings are considered in conjunction with Nash et al.'s contention that the development of program material can be quite expensive, there seems to be little room for unreserved optimism concerning the technique. In specific situations in which very complex tasks are to be learned, however, the detailed task analysis carried out for PI, coupled with the feedback provisions involved, can result in a learning task that is accessible to a broad variety of trainees.

Computer-Assisted Instruction (CAI)

The computer has been called upon to provide technical support for training in a number of practical situations (cf. Patrick & Stammers, 1977). With its capacity for information storage, rapid response, and memory for the performance of the trainee, the computer represents an instructional device that has broad-ranging possibilities. Seltzer (1971) contends that there are three principal advantages attached to the use of the computer. First, the computer permits highly individualized pacing and sequencing of material. Second, it removes many of the negative interpersonal influences that may operate in the training sessions. This is particularly important when trainees represent a social group whose background contrasts with the instructor's. Finally, the computer takes over much of the drill and practice required by learning, and frees the instructor for more interesting and creative parts of the training sequence.

There is some question whether computer-assisted instruction justifies the expenses connected with its use in industrial training, but there have been instances in which CAI has proved to be quite economical. For instance, a training program at British Airways was carried out for ticket agents who were scattered over a wide area. Training materials presented on visual display units located at each travel agency resulted in efficient learning at a substantial savings over a conventional program that would have involved considerable staff travel (Simmons, 1975).

CAI has also been found to be successful when used to train employees in electronic troubleshooting, and when employed as part of an aircraft simulator (Caro, 1969). In both of these areas of training one may find an enormous number of complex alternatives, and the storage capabilities of the computer make it an ideal training device in these situations. Finally, CAI has been used rather widely in a variety of management and business games that simulate problems faced in an industrial setting. Here, once again, the computer can accommodate real-life problem solving. Hence, in spite of its cost limitations, there are training situations in which the computer can make a cost-efficient contribution.

Sensitivity Training (T-group)

Sensitivity (T-group) training is an instructional approach that focuses on the human relations abilities of people. The technique draws on a large variety of behavioral exercises that have been constructed so as to provide participants with an opportunity to learn about themselves and about how their behavior impacts on others (Cooper & Mangham, 1971). T-group procedures are carried out in a small-group setting in which a group undertakes a task or exercise of some sort. The exercise may be one requiring self-disclosure, physical contact, conflict resolution, or any of a number of activities that require close interaction among the members. They often are of a no-holds-barred variety, in which participants consider each other's strengths, weaknesses, and behavioral strategies. During and after these exercises the members are encouraged to attend to the workings of their own behavior and the behavior of other members of the group. While doing this it is expected that there will develop an improved understanding of person-to-person skills and an ability to achieve a more honest and spontaneous approach to interpersonal relationships.

Efforts that have been made to evaluate sensitivity training within an industrial setting have not yielded strong support. For example, Dunnette and Campbell (1968) reviewed the research literature and concluded: ''(Sensitivity training) has not been shown to bring about any marked change in one's standing on objective measures of attitudes, values, outlook, interpersonal sensitivity'' (p. 23). These same authors, however, acknowledge that research has indicated that those who receive this type of training are more likely to be seen as modifying their job behavior. Why this is so, in view

TABLE 3.2   Behavioral Changes Reported after Sensitivity Training—A Summary of Research Results

Type of measure	Changes immediately after training			Changes at follow-up		
	Intended effects found	Total N	Percent successful	Intended effects found	Total N	Percent successful
Global self-concept[a]	17	28	61	2	6	33
Self as the locus of casuality	10	17	59	1	3	33
Prejudice and open-mindedness	10	20	50	2	5	40
Orientation toward participative behaviors	14	22	64	2	9	22
Other aspects of personality	9	19	47	2	5	40
Perception of others	5	13	38	1	2	50
Others' perception of trainees	18	22	81	2	4	50
Organizational behavior	10	13	77	10	11	90
Number of studies[b]	78	100	78	21	31	68

[a]Of 28 studies that examined changes in global self-concept, 17 found positive effects.
[b]Number of studies comprises the sum of the preceding columns because some studies included more than one type of measure.
Source: Smith, P. B. Controlled studies of the outcome of sensitivity training. *Psychological Bulletin*, 1975, *82*, 597–622. Copyright 1975 by the American Psychological Association. Reprinted by permission of the publisher and author.

of the apparent lack of change in self-awareness, interpersonal sensitivity, and so on mentioned above, is not clear. Perhaps the problem stems from the complex demands T-group objectives place on the measurement techniques and experimental designs that are available to evaluate the effects of training. The measurement inadequacies associated with efforts to quantify constructs such as self-awareness combine with the always difficult problems associated with designing a study to evaluate training outcomes.

In spite of these design and measurement difficulties, work has continued beyond the Dunnette and Campbell review (Smith, 1975), and the accumulation of this later evidence indicates that sensitivity training does appear to produce positive effects on a variety of behavioral measurements

(see Table 3.2). Smith, however, contends that important questions concerning the persistence of these effects and whether they occur in all kinds of groups have not been resolved, and this represents some of major work remaining to be done before the T-group approach can be evaluated in any satisfactory fashion.

Simulation Techniques

Simulation refers to the creation of a training environment that contains many of the essential components that are found in the real-life operating conditions. Gagne (1961) states that all simulation procedures have three things in common:

1. An attempt to represent a real situation in which operations are carried out
2. A provision for certain controls over the simulated task
3. A design that deliberately omits certain components of the real situation

From this perspective many, if not all, industrial training procedures are simulational in nature, and any attempt to limit membership in this category must appear to be arbitrary. Perhaps the clearest example of simulation in a work setting is found in the use of machine simulators that represent a ''mock-up'' of the equipment that is operated on the job. Training in the maritime, aircraft, and trucking industries often use model representations of the expensive equipment that is under an operator's control. In other work settings simulation procedures are used in an off-job program in which a mock-up of expensive equipment is made available to trainees. Although they may be quite elaborate, these simulators are often less expensive than the actual operating equipment, and yet they provide the trainee with many of the important aspects of the actual operation. They also do so within a relatively low-risk, secure environment.

Miller (1974) uses the term *fidelity* to describe the extent to which a simulator contains the various elements found in the real situation. He argues that as fidelity increases, there is a tendency for both learning value and the cost of the simulator to increase. There is, however, a point of diminishing returns where further increases in fidelity add substantially to costs, without a proportionate increase in learning value. Hence, building a high-fidelity simulator may not result in the most training value for the cost. A principal concern is with the transfer value of a simulator. To what extent does the learning that takes place on the simulator carry over into the work situation? Miller contends that military research has indicated that higher fidelity rarely if ever results in poorer transfer. There is, however, evidence from this research indicating that relatively low-cost machine simulators often are able to make an effective contribution to a training program.

Case Study.   The case study is a simulation procedure requiring trainees to consider in depth the full range of events that enter organizational or human relations problems. Trainees are given a detailed written description of a problem situation and asked to develop a course of action. These solutions may be developed in a group setting, or individual trainees may be asked to formulate their own plans before entering into a group discussion concerning the issue. This method permits trainees to consider and cope with problems that are representative of those that actually occur in a work environment. It also permits them to compare their solutions with those developed by other trainees. This provides both the organization and the trainee with a source of feedback and insight into the nature and effectiveness of the individual's strategy and mode of problem solving.

The case study method lays heavy emphasis on situational diagnosis. There is a substantial element of ''troubleshooting'' in management problem solving where complex situations occur, and a manager's first task is to analyze the event in order to identify the problem's central issues. These main elements then contribute to a search for the resources that may be used in a solution. All these facets are incorporated in the case-study method, and if well conducted, these sessions can provide a valuable source of training for managerial personnel.

The extent to which case-study experiences generalize to other work related situations is a question that may be raised concerning this approach to training. Transfer from training to job is a problem. Trainees may participate in an exercise involving a case and find that they receive little of value that can be applied to a real-life situation. Although there are probably underlying principles that extend through a large portion of all management situations, they still require translation into the requirements of each individual episode. In this respect, the case-study method may be viewed as a training procedure in which general principles of problem solving can be developed. The method is not complete in itself; it requires additional on-the-job experience. Since there are no training techniques that can be expected to prepare managers for each specific problem situation, the best that might be done is to develop skills in general problem-solving strategies. The case-study method is constructed for this purpose.

Role Playing.   Role playing, a type of simulation technique, is a training procedure in which trainees are placed in a fictitious problem situation that involves interaction among people who occupy different organizational positions or who possess conflicting points of view. Roles are assigned to the trainees, who proceed to enact the drama as if it were a real-life happening. Although role-playing exercises usually involve a situation in which attitudes and emotions lie at the heart of the problem, they can be adapted to the kinds of organizational problems that are often put into case-study approaches (Lawshe, Bolda, & Brune, 1958; 1959).

Participation in a role-playing exercise is highly ego-involving and puts a trainee in a position of responsibility for the public presentation of a point of view. Often this point of view is not one endorsed by the role player. Hence, from this new perspective, the trainee is in position to view the problem from another person's angle. As a consequence, advocates of this approach argue that participants gain a broader understanding of the problem. This understanding includes attitudinal and emotional elements, which are often important but which usually do not enter into case-study and business-games situations.

In-Basket Technique.   An interesting variation of the role-playing procedure is called an in-basket project. The term, in-basket, refers to the receptacle found on many desks that holds in-coming written documents. In this type of exercise, a trainee assumes the role of a person occupying a specified position in the organization. The trainee receives pertinent information about this position and the organization, and is then given in-basket materials. This material involves letters, forms, memos, and a variety of documents, all of which require some form of decision and response. Hence, the trainee is confronted with a range of problems requiring a reaction, the response usually being in written form. The types and variety of problems presented in this exercise represent the daily responsibilities of many management personnel.

A variety of different instructional formats may be adopted in conjunction with an in-basket exercise, one being a group discussion that follows the completion of each set of decisions. As with other simulation techniques, in-basket procedures have also been used in the assessment of management personnel (Byham, 1970). Here the quality of an individual's response is taken as an indication of management proficiency.

Business Games.   Simulation procedures called business games have become quite popular in training programs concerned with management decision making and organizational control. With this approach, simulations in the form of a model of a business organization are brought into the training room, and management trainees are given responsibility for the conduct of the affairs of the company. Resource allocation, for example, may be a primary objective in one type of game. Here trainees are presented with certain kinds of market and investment situations, and they attempt to assign company resources so that certain organizational objectives (for example, profits, inventory levels, and so on) are met.

In spite of the popularity of the business game, there appears to be very little evidence concerning its value as a training device. Hinrichs (1976) mentions several problems associated with these procedures:

1. They limit the behavior of the trainee to those reactions that are programmed into the situation.
2. Trainees can become too much involved in "playing the game" and ignore the general principles that should be learned.
3. Some question the degree of fidelity of the gaming situation when it is compared with the trainee's real-life circumstances.
4. The expense associated with this approach may be high.

These concerns, coupled with the universal concern over transfer of training into the job setting, leave one with many reservations. This approach does, however, provide a way to come to grips with training in an area that is beset with many difficulties. Management decision making can probably profit from training of some sort, but at the present time the social scientist is in need of much more information before a clear sense of direction can be established for this field.

THE EVALUATION OF TRAINING OUTCOMES

From a strictly practical standpoint, the need to evaluate training is a direct function of the costs associated with a program and the organizational significance of the behaviors involved. Too often an organization will invest substantial amounts in an elaborate program, and little or nothing in an effort to evalute the extent to which training objectives have been achieved. In some instances it is assumed that the content and structure of the program is adequate validation, and in certain respects there is merit in this kind of thinking. Recall the concept of content validity that was applied to the evaluation of psychological tests (see Chapter 2). From the same point of view, a training program whose content is consistent with its objectives has a claim to being effective.

One might argue, however, that there are other assessment criteria that are more important than the content and structure of the program, and these are found in the behavior of the employees who have been trained. The primary objective of training is to modify the behavior of those who have been trained; hence the evaluation of training must include the performance of those who are involved in the program, and ultimately their performance when they return from the training sessions and resume their positions on the job.

Methods of Evaluation

In planning to evaluate a training program there are two general, necessary considerations. The first concerns the design of the evaluation study, and the second, the sources of data that will be used. Study design refers to the general plan to be followed in collecting data. Matters to be decided include who will be observed in the study, and at what time prior to, during, and after the training sessions observations will be taken. For example, since training evaluation concerns whether changes have taken place in the trainee's behavior, some point of reference must be used to measure these changes. One such reference might involve a group of trainees who have not been trained. If properly carried out, a comparison between those trained and those who were not provides information about the success of training. Another possibility is to permit trainees to serve as their own points of comparison. Here, measures taken on the trainees before they enter the program and then again after they complete it show the effects of training. This latter approach probably has more practical value than the first, since it is often difficult to find an adequate comparison group of non-trained employees; however, both of these designs carry with them other problems, since they are vulnerable to sources of contamination that may distort the results of an evaluation study.

With regard to the time at which the data are collected, there are several study designs one may use. In some instances a single measure taken at the close of the training session will be sufficient. In some other instances a before-and-after-training design is more appropriate; and under still other circumstances, measures should be taken before training, then again at the close of the session, and again after the trainees have been back on their jobs for a period of time. Much depends on the knowledge that is available concerning the trainees' status before the program begins. Obviously, if the program is designed to impart completely new information or if it is intended to teach job skills to new operators, a before-and-after design is not called for. Whenever there is, however, a question regarding the transfer of course materials to job performance, observations should be taken both at the immediate close of the training sessions—to gauge the effectiveness of learning—and then after the trainees are back on the job, to gauge the effectiveness of transfer.

The above discussion may leave one with the impression that the design of an evaluation study is an easy task, but by no means is this true. It is quite difficult to construct an experiment that provides a clear view of the behavioral outcomes that can be attributed solely to the training an individual has received. One group of problems stems from the fact that much training research is not carried out under laboratory conditions, where all extraneous sources of variation are either held constant or are dealt with through randomization that permits their influence to enter the experiment in an unbiased fashion. For example, it is often impossible to ensure that no other changes are taking place in the work environment during the time training is being carried out or when its effects are being measured. There is danger, under these circumstances, that what appears to be a training outcome is really the result of these other changes that are occurring.

Design Alternatives

It would be impossible to consider all the design alternatives that might be applied to training evaluation studies, but an introduction to this topic can be presented from the perspective of the more common designs that are used in training research. As a point of departure, the first three experimental designs will be those recognized by Cook and Campbell (1976) as leading to results that are uninterpretable. These designs, while frequently used in evaluation studies, often yield data that are ambiguous in the sense that training effects can not be separated from other influences that may have been occurring during the time period covered by the study.

To describe these designs a notation system will be adopted in which T will be used to refer to a training activity, O will represent a measure of behavior, and the subscripts 1, 2, . . ., n refer to an observation. Thus:

$$O_1 T O_2 O_3$$

refers to a study in which a behavior measure (O_1) is made before training (T) begins, and this is fol-lowed by two posttraining measurements (O_2 and O_3).

Three Common Designs.　　The first two designs suffer from a common deficiency, the absence of a control group that can be used as a basis for comparison with the training group. In training-evaluation studies, a control group is one that does not receive training, but is otherwise treated in the same fashion as the group that does. Hence, the control group is exposed to all the influences, save the training, that may produce changes in the performance of the training group. Significant differences between the control and training groups, therefore, suggest that training effects are present over and above the effects of these other variables that might be affecting the behavior being observed.

Cook and Campbell (1976) refer to the first of these designs as a "one group, posttest only" design, described by the following sequence:

$$T O_1$$

Here a group is given training and then a performance measure is administered sometime after training activities have been completed. In many instances this study design is completely inadequate for evaluating the effectiveness of a training program. In the first place, it does not provide a measure of the performance status of the trainees before the training activities were begun. As a consequence, one is not sure that the observations taken at O_1 are the result of training or merely a representation of the pretraining status of the group. Also, the absence of a control group prevents one from concluding either that the behavior observed at O_1 is a function of training or that it is the result of other work-related influences that took place in the organization during the training period.

The pretest-posttest design using a single group corrects one of the above problems, but still suffers from the lack of control group. This study design is described as follows:

$$O_1 T O_2$$

The addition of a control group to this design yields an arrangement that is probably one of the more frequently used experimental designs. This is a pretest-posttest design with a control group that does not receive training. This arrangement appears as follows:

Training Group	$O_1 T O_2$
Control Group	$O_3 \; O_4$

Differences between the posttest scores obtained from experimental and control groups (O_2 versus O_4) may be interpreted as reflecting the influence of the training period, assuming that the two groups were equivalent when they were subjected to the pretest measure. Another, and perhaps more satisfactory alternative involves computing change scores ($O_2 - O_1$) and ($O_4 - O_3$). Then these change scores are compared and differences interpreted in terms of the influence of the training sessions.

Although this two-group design is satisfactory for many purposes, a number of researchers have expressed reservations concerning its inability to detect one course of unwanted variation (Solomon, 1949; Campbell & Stanley, 1963). In some cases the effect of training may be influenced by the fact that a pretest was administered before the training activities were begun. For example, in training programs directed toward attitude changes, the presentation of the pretest instrument may sensitize trainees to certain aspects of the training and result in a change in their perceptions of the meaning and significance of the material presented. The two-group design is also unable to detect the influence of events, not part of the training program, that might take place between the pretest and the posttest.

Responding to these problems, Solomon (1949) suggested the use of a four-group design that extends the two-group approach in the following manner:

Experimental Group	$O_1 \; T \; O_2$
Control Group I	$O_3 \quad O_4$
Control Group II	$T \; O_5$
Control Group III	O_6

This design offers many possible comparisons that bear on the effects of training, pretesting, and extraneous influences, and Campbell and Stanley (1963) suggest an arrangement of the data that gives a convenient set of comparisons relating to training effects and pretest effects:

	No T	T
Pretested	O_4	O_2
Unpretested	O_6	O_5

From the means of the two columns, $(O_4 + O_6)/2$ and $(O_2 + O_5)/2$, one estimates the effect of no training and training, respectively. The effects of the pretest are obtained by comparing the mean of the first row $(O_4 + O_2)/2$ with the mean of the second row $(O_6 + O_5)/2$. More detailed analyses are available with this design, but one can see from the above that the use of several control groups gives the program director access to information bearing on some of the major variables that are of interest to the training evaluator.

The number of design alternatives is large (cf. Cook & Campbell, 1979), and the selection of an appropriate experimental layout depends in large measure on the need to control or estimate the influence of variables other than training effects. Burgoyne and Cooper (1975) contend that the evaluation designs advocated by many American social scientists are those that have the high precision required by pure research. Designs of this type yield data having scientific status, and therefore lead to conclusions that have a general significance that extends beyond the situation from which the data were obtained. One must bear in mind, however, that the practical realities of many evaluation studies preclude the use of a design that satisfies all the requirements of experimental precision. Burgoyne and Cooper maintain that the European approach to evaluation tends to strike a compromise that balances costs and experimental resources with the need for high-quality information. The use of three- or four-group designs involving several control groups might be an impossibility in all but a few work settings. In this case, the number of available trainees may place a serious limitation on the number of groups that can be formed. Furthermore, the requirement that the members from experimental and control groups do not interact with each other during the period of the study is a condition that may be difficult to achieve in many work organizations. Consequently, a company may find itself sponsoring a study that provides only partial information regarding the efficacy of a given training program.

There are other sources of information that may be drawn on to establish the validity of a training program, and even though they are not experimental in their origin, they cannot be ignored. In addition, there is sometimes the possibility of conducting a follow-up study if the results of an initial study support the continuation of the program. The evaluation of training activities does not have to be completed in a single research effort. A realistic approach to training evaluation often finds one piecing together information, some of which may not be of the highest quality, in order to arrive at a decision concerning the merit of the program.

Evaluation Criteria.   Time is a factor that must be considered when selecting the criterion measures that will be used in training evaluation. Performance data reflecting the effects of training become available at different points in time, and each time segment provides a different perspective on the program. For example, behavioral data may be available at the end of each unit or lesson. Measures may be taken of performance at the close of the training program, and additional information obtained after the workers have been back on the job several weeks or months after training. Criterion measures that are obtained from behaviors that occur during or immediately after training are referred to as *internal criteria*. These measures reflect the influence that training variables have on the behavior that is observed in the training envi-

ronment. Measures that are taken after the conclusion of the program and when the trainees have returned to their jobs are called *external criteria*.

External criterion measures reflect the transfer value of a particular training activity. They concern the extent to which behaviors acquired during training are translated into on-the-job performance. In many respects, external criterion measures are an expression of the primary purposes of industrial training activities; that is, to modify behaviors that are involved in the performance of a job. One must, however, exercise some caution in using these data, since the extent to which a training program is followed by real on-the-job changes is sometimes a function of conditions that are not a part of the training activities. Transfer from training to job depends first on whether the worker has acquired the appropriate behaviors, but it also depends on the climate of support and incentives in the plant or office that encourage the utilization of these behaviors. Hence, the absence of positive results when an external criterion is used may cast a shadow on the training received, or it may signal the existence of suppressor conditions that operate on the job to inhibit the display of behaviors learned in training. Positive results with an internal criterion, when coupled with negative findings for the external criterion, increase one's suspicion that the problem lies outside the boundaries of the training program.

TRAINING AND THE ORGANIZATION

There have been relatively few social scientists who have expressed interest in the organizational significance of industrial training. The mechanics of training seems to have dominated the concerns of those working in the area, but a training department is immersed in the full flood of organizational politics and social relationships. From this perspective, training begins to appear as a mechanism of control that operates within an organization to shape and mold the social climate and to perpetuate the social traditions of the firm. One of the functions of training is to indoctrinate an individual into a work culture that is found within the place of employment. Training objectives reflect the values of the organization and its management, and the content of many training programs expresses management's view of work and its expectations concerning how it should be carried out.

It is through a training program that those who possess organizational power can communicate what they want done by those below them. In transmitting these messages through training channels, it is possible to give the full force of organizational legitimacy to the goals, activities, and behavioral styles that are a part of the training objectives. While in the planned environment of a training session it is easy for the trainee to feel enveloped in organizational pressures that discourage dissent and foster overt displays of commitment and eventual compliance. The training department delivers the message; it presents the organizational line that expresses the company's expectations concerning a wide range of work behaviors. Training, therefore, can be viewed as an active component in the company's machinery for work socialization. Inherent in much training material, especially that concerning attitudes, supervisory affairs, and interpersonal relations, is a set of company directives as to how an individual should behave. Resistance to these directives is often difficult, and can expose the offender to the organizational sanctions that are reserved for those who are "not team players."

Training frequently costs substantial amounts of money, and as a consequence, members of the training staff often have a high personal investment in the outcome of these activities. Not only is there concern that the instructional activities succeed in achieving their behavioral objectives; there is also a high level of concern that the training objectives themselves fit in with the values of the management group that directs the organization. As a result, the training personnel are themselves variables that exert a significant influence on the design and the evaluation of these activities. Sjoberg (1975) points out that one should not forget that the social scientist who participates in these activities is a member of the sponsoring organization.

Operating within this social context, these professionals may unwittingly carry the values and preferences of the organization into the training activities under their supervision. Sjoberg cites a number of well-known experiments (Orne, 1962; Rosenthal, 1966) whose results point out the effect that an individual's values and beliefs exert on the outcome of supposedly objective experiments. By analogy, the same processes might be at work in instances when training departments are involved in the construction and evaluation of training programs. To the extent that this is true, there is an inherent organizational bias that may enter training and influence its structure.

Counter Training

All this does not say that resistance to training objectives never happens, and there are several reports in the literature that describe instances in which a variety of pressures operate in the organization to counter the training efforts that had been made (Baumgartel & Jeanpierre, 1972; Bahn, 1973; Charner, 1980). Bahn (1973) uses the term *counter training* to refer to an organizational "counterforce" that encourages behaviors that are contradictory to those that are acquired through formal training. These negative influences may be an expression of a general resistance to change that has often been noted in work settings. The fear of unknown events combines with a commitment to well-established habit patterns to produce a reluctance on the part of individuals and groups to explore new ground and sample new experiences. Bahn also contends that this resistance to change stems from what he calls the *N.I.H. syndrome*. N.I.H. means "not invented here," and it is applied to the tendency of people to resist ideas that have not originated within their own organization. Counter training also derives from a built-in inertia found in social systems that is the result of well-established behavioral expectations, social roles, and traditions that place the group member within a social unit whose behaviors are regular and predictable.

Perhaps the most familiar counter training theme is the message that goes through the grapevine prophesying that "it won't work" or "it's too complex. It's sure to be outmoded before we can get it installed and shake the bugs out of it." Another familiar counter training theme is, "they'll never accept it," with little effort to define the "they." These are all messages that signal the presence of social mechanisms that are operating to discourage the implementation of training objectives.

Bahn (1973) recommends the following alternatives that may be employed to minimize the effects of counter training:

1. Train all levels of an organization that will be affected by the new behaviors.
2. Make training materials directly applicable to the work setting that will be affected by training outcomes.
3. Some attempt should be made to blend the training and work environments.
4. Training groups should be made up of individuals coming from similar work backgrounds.
5. Trainers should be familiar with each specific work situation and its social structure.
6. The benefits of change should be clearly explained.
7. Trainees should be warned of the symptoms of counter training and told that they are often a natural consequence of attempts to introduce change into a work environment.

Finally, one way of interpreting the presence of counter training influences is to see them as a reflection of management's misperception of the social dynamics of the organization. To the extent that training departments and management groups are in touch with the social realities of the firm, the prospects of these negative factors are reduced. All of this, of course, resides within the realm of judgment, but an organization that maintains open channels of communication creates social situations that encourage accurate judgment.

TRAINING AND THE HARD-CORE UNEMPLOYED

Thus far our discussion has not considered problems associated with training activities that are carried out for workers who bring special problems into the work environment. In all these instances training must be designed to accommodate the special needs of those who participate, and nowhere is this more important than when the trainees are individuals who have experienced persistent difficulties in establishing themselves in the job market. The hard-core unemployed (HCU) present training departments with particularly vexing problems, coming to work as they do with a long his-

tory of work failure and unemployment. Under these circumstances, industrial training must broaden its objectives to include a wide assortment of support activities that are needed before the HCU can integrate the values and routines of work into their lives.

Several major programs, jointly sponsored by business and government, have been set up to facilitate the HCU's entry into the job market. For example, the National Alliance of Businessmen's JOBS program involved the expenditure of over $100 million in an effort to provide jobs, training, counseling, and support services to the HCU. These efforts, although not without some success, met many problems that often prevented them from achieving their major objectives. Both Shlensky (1972) and Triandis, Feldman, and Weldon, (1974) conclude that training activities for the HCU have largely been ineffective. These failures have not been the consequence of the HCU's inability to learn, but rather, they stem from the absence of a whole variety of support behaviors that seem to prevent these individuals from adapting to the requirements of work. Shlensky contends that it is behaviors such as these that were ignored by many training programs that tended to concentrate their efforts on skills that were more directly involved with doing the work. It was because of this that these programs failed.

Work-Support Behaviors

Successful employment requires more than the skills and knowledge considered necessary to carry out the duties of a job. Work requires that an individual assume responsibility for such things as getting to work on time, regular attendance, and learning the social norms of the workplace. These are habits that are often taken for granted, being thought of as behaviors that are possessed by most adults. Yet it is with respect to the development of these work-supporting behaviors that the HCU experiences the greatest set of difficulties. Shlensky (1972) interviewed supervisors and training personnel in six JOBS programs and found that nearly everyone mentioned attendance as the most serious problem of the HCU. Conformity to the norms of the organization was the next most serious problem. Dress habits, using appropriate language, sensitivity to interpersonal relationships, and practicing acceptable social behaviors created difficulties that often prevented HCU from making an acceptable adjustment to a work role.

As can be seen from these reports, the primary problem faced by the HCU largely involved adopting behaviors that are required for membership in a white middle-class culture. Wellman (1968) summarizes this in describing a program designed to assist the HCU in securing work:

> The real problem was what the program demanded of the young men. It asked that they change their manner of speech and dress, that they ignore their lack of skills and society's lack of jobs, and that they act as if their arrest records were of no consequence in obtaining a job. It asked, most important, that they pretend *they* and not society bore the responsibility for their being unemployed. (The program) didn't demand much of the men: only that they become white. (p. 13)

Evaluations of the performance of the trainees may also focus on behaviors that relate more to the social aspects of work than to its content. Beatty (1973) studied a program designed to de-velop black supervisors, and found that employers tended to evaluate these trainees on factors that were not related to the content of the program or on task-related behaviors, but rather on the basis of social behaviors that contributed to the employer's impression of the trainee. Under these circumstances the HCU, bringing with them a set of social habits completely foreign to those of a middle-class management, find themselves in a work setting where the prospects of repeated failure and eventual discouragement are very high.

Ecosystem Distrust. Ecosystem distrust (Triandis, et al., 1975) refers to a cluster of negative attitudes which express an individual's general orientation toward the people, things and institutions that make up his or her environment. Attitudes such as these are thought to result from an environment in which punishments are far more frequent than rewards, and many believe that this condition represents an accurate description of the psychological climate of ghetto life. Triandis, Feldman, and Weldon (1975) present evidence indicating that some ghetto blacks experience a general distrust of their environment, and that this expresses itself as a basic suspicion of people, a rejection of established authority, whether black or white, and feelings of unimportance. It is clear that attitudes such as these provide a poor foundation upon which to build a firm commitment to work. They tend to lead an individual to impose a negative interpretation on the behavior of others; and operating within this framework, it is extremely difficult for the HCU to make a comfortable adjustment to work.

These attitudes are difficult to deal with under the best of circumstances, but within a work setting where supervisory and training personnel are unprepared to cope with them, they create obstacles that are often impossible to overcome. There are no final solutions to problems such as these, but those solutions that suggest themselves from the research literature indicate that the training of the chronically unemployed person requires that adjustments be made in the internal climate of an organization before the more conventional training methods can work effectively to bring the individual into the labor market.

Solutions

What course of action might be followed in attempting to train the HCU for work? Friedlander and Greenberg (1971) report findings that indicate that the sole correlates of the HCU's effectiveness at work are found in variables that reflect the amount of support given to the new worker by an organization. This study dealt with a large number of HCUs who were put through a two-week training program in which participants were assigned to counselors who worked with them individually and in groups. When placed on a job many of these trainees soon quit, but in those organizations whose climate was judged to be more supportive of the new worker, the retention rate was 82 percent.

One of the more surprising outcomes of this study was the fact that employees who were rated by their supervisors as being the most reliable, that is, were not frequently late or absent, were the ones who had the *shortest* retention rates. Friedlander and Greenberg contend that this finding reflects the fact that the HCU tends to cope with a nonsupportive work climate in one of two ways. First, they may have a high incidence of lateness and absences; they may simply show resistance to the time routines of work while still remaining on the work rolls. On the other hand, workers who are reliable while on the job may cope with an unsupportive work situation by quitting and leaving the field. Hence, an unsupportive work climate can lead to two patterns of negative adjustment, worker unreliability and turnover.

It is widely recognized that a solution to the low retention rate frequently found among HCU trainees requires that revisions be made in the attitudes and expectations of those who are in established positions in an organization. These psychological changes should be such as to place established workers in positions where they can relate effectively to workers coming from completely different social backgrounds. The principal emphasis in many HCU training efforts is to adapt the trainee to a new and often foreign work culture. Additional effort should be made to adapt an organization and its personnel to the culture of the new employee. Along these lines, Triandis et al. (1975) recommend that supervisory personnel be trained to look at events from the perspective of the HCU's background, and Bass et al. (1976) describe a program that showed evidence of improving awareness and understanding of racial issues among a group of over two thousand supervisory personnel.

But there are more specific variables that have been identified as factors that contribute to an improved retention rate among the HCU. For example, Goodman and Salipante (1976) have identified a number of organizational reward systems that, when properly administered, seem to improve retention rate. Good pay is an important factor, and when combined with reasonable prospects for promotion, was found to be associated with longer tenure among the HCU. Cohn and Lewis (1975) found that paying a high starting salary did not reduce turnover, but Goodman and Salipante (1976) found that fairly early increases in pay seemed to provide the support needed to encourage the HCU to remain on the job. Finally, in those organizations where the number of minority workers was high, the greater the percentage of minority supervisors, the better the retention rate. This is an employment pattern that suggests good promotional opportunities for the entering HCU. On the other hand, in organizations hiring few minority workers, the higher the percentage of minority supervisors, the *lower* the retention rate. Goodman and Salipante contend that this latter pattern of work assignments suggests to the HCU that those minority workers chosen for supervision represent highly selected individuals, and this perception, when combined with their initial feelings of insecurity, discourages their continued employment. In a firm hiring many minority workers, the presence of a high percentage of minority supervisors is seen by the HCU to be representing an opportunity for upward mobility.

A final study in this area is one reported by Salipante and Goodman (1976). Using the same sample employed by the study just considered, these authors found that retention rates among HCU workers did not vary as a function of whether or not training programs were offered by the organization, but rather, they varied as a function of the content of the training. Programs that emphasized job-skills training appeared to improve retention rates. The degree of job-skills emphasis could, however, exceed an optimal boundary, and it was found that a very high concentration of skills training (80 percent or more) was associated with lower retention rates. In addition, some types of attitudinal training also related to higher turnover among HCU workers. More specifically, the use of role playing seemed to relate to low retention. Perhaps this outcome was a function of the personal threat that may be experienced when the HCU trainee is required to participate in a potentially revealing and embarrassing public performance of the type required by role-playing exercises. Nothing is certain in this area except that the problems faced by these disadvantaged workers require organizations to try to understand better the psychological orientation of the new workers. Individual counseling has shown itself to be a valuable adjunct to training programs designed for the HCU (Salipante & Goodman, 1976), and with special effort and increased experimentation with program alternatives, industry may find itself in an improving position to make a significant contribution to this very difficult social and psychological problem.

SUMMARY COMMENTS

Few workers enter a work organization fully prepared to assume a productive role. In all but a few instances some type of training is an essential part of fitting the worker to the job. Hence, in spite of the significant increase in the educational level of the workforce, there continues to be a need for job-specific training that is relatively narrow in scope and practical in its objectives. Much of the instruction that takes place in a work setting builds on the formal schooling the worker brings to the job. It focuses on the duties of a specific job and

has as its principal objective the development of skills, knowledge, and attitudes that lead to competent work performance.

Effective industrial training requires attention to the organization and presentation of course materials. These are the mechanics of teaching, and they strive for clarity, orderliness, and completeness. But over and above the mechanics of presenting ideas and skills, there is a variety of psychological variables that are important in determining the efficiency with which material is learned. It is quite possible to develop a training exercise in which the material is relatively simple to grasp, is well presented, and yet the trainees fail to learn. Here we are talking about problems that might stem from the motivational climate within which learning takes place. Learning tends to be most efficient when its consequences are relevant to the needs and desires of the learner. Hence, a good learning situation uses feedback mechanisms of some sort, which provide learners with indications that personal objectives are being met as they improve their grasp of the training subject matter.

Training programs often require support from other units of the organization if they are to be successful in modifying on-the-job behaviors. Trainees can learn the content of a training program but fail to transfer this learning into day-to-day performance. In instances such as this the problem often lies in the lack of support given by superiors to those who do show evidence of training in their job performance. Hence, although a training program may be directed toward a single level of the organization, other levels must take an informed interest in seeing that the program receives the support needed on the job.

Little has been said about the characteristics of the learner apart from the discussion of general learning and motivation variables. How does an organization choose individuals for a training program? There are techniques that are being developed to select people for training, and in large measure the procedures followed are similar to those used to select employees for a job. All types of selection instruments can be used to predict employee responses to a training program, but there has been one interesting approach that recently has been receiving some attention. This approach, called *trainability testing,* involves actually training a prospective employee to perform a sample of tasks that are part of a job. Following this brief training period, the applicant is asked to perform these tasks, and his ability to do so is measured (Siegal & Bergman, 1975; Robertson & Downs, 1979). This performance is used to predict the trainee's effectiveness in future training activities. Thus far, encouraging results have been reported in connection with this technique; and although further research is needed, trainability testing appears to be a useful addition to the techniques available for choosing trainees.

4
Evaluating Work Performance

Most organizations develop performance evaluation procedures that are used to measure the effectiveness with which work is being carried out. As a general rule, programs of this type require supervisors to conduct a periodic appraisal of the work of their subordinates; and in most cases, the results of this review are fed back to the employee, who is given opportunity to consult with the individual making the assessment. Once completed, performance evaluations become a part of the employee's personnel record and may be used for a variety of purposes. For example, in some instances this information contributes to the many decisions management must make about the individual worker. In other instances the organization draws on these records to obtain criterion data that are used to assess the effectiveness of various personnel programs. Performance evaluations also provide information that can be used to assess certain kinds of training needs.

From the perspective of the individual worker, performance evaluations are an important part of the motivational climate of work, since they play a significant role in determining who receives the rewards an organization provides its members. Job security, pay increases, work assignments, and promotions are all calculated on the basis of management's appraisal of the worker's contribution to the organization. Of these, promotion is probably the most significant. There is some evidence,

for example, that promotion is often viewed as an organization's most important reward since it is correlated with so many other incentives. Kanter (1977), in her study of the social dynamics of corporate life, quotes one salary administrator's comments about the incentive system in his firm: "Money is not a motivator anyway. It's just a way for the company to cut its losses by ensuring that people do their jobs at all. The reward we really control is the ability to promote." (p. 129)

In this organization salary was limited by one's corporate position, as were the opportunities for personal independence, growth, a sense of challenge, and a chance to learn. All these, plus a host of other desirable perquisites, were linked to a promotion system that functioned as an end point of a set of evaluations, both formal and informal, of each employee's performance. Promotions were meted out to those whose work was visible to others, and whose performance was highly valued by those who were in established positions of power. From this it is apparent that the performance evaluation program is of considerable importance to an organization, its management, and its employees. It is both an information system and an incentive system, and from either perspective it is essential that the program function in a manner that is both accurate and reliable.

In an effort to obtain acceptable measurements of job performance, social scientists have developed a large number of rating techniques that have been adapted to work situations. Although these procedures may assume a number of different forms, they all draw on the subjective judgments of a rater who is in a position to observe and evaluate the job performance of the ratee. Throughout the years the literature on performance evaluation has given major emphasis to these rating procedures; however, largely because of their reliance on subjective processes, they have been found to be susceptible to a variety of biasing influences. As a consequence, considerable effort has been expended in developing rating scales that are less vulnerable to these unwanted influences. This problem of bias is one of the most difficult issues in the area of psychological measurement, and in this chapter we will attempt to summarize some of the more interesting rating scale formats that have been developed to insulate performance appraisals from these influences.

Not all performance evaluations are based on subjective ratings. There are job situations in which the work leaves behind palpable evidence of merit, and in these cases performance evaluations can be obtained from those aspects of production that can be counted, graded, or weighed. In other instances, evidence of merit can be obtained from personnel records that contain information on tenure, absences, latenesses, and accidents. With these data a measure of merit can be obtained in a relatively objective fashion; and although there are important pitfalls, the process of evaluation appears to be simple and direct. But even on jobs that do produce material things, there may be important dimensions of performance that are not reflected in the objects produced or in the records maintained in the personnel office. Promotability, knowledge of company practices, and interpersonal skills may be facets of worker performance that are not visible in these data. Hence, in using objective sources of appraisal data, one often finds oneself dealing with data that give an incomplete picture of the individual's contribution to the organization. This does not mean, however, that objective information sources are of no value, and this chapter will discuss these types of merit

evaluation data, along with some of the problems associated with their use.

To begin the chapter we will consider the organizational setting within which a performance evaluation system functions. This is important, since to understand some of the problems inherent in this type of measurement, one must understand how these rating systems fit into the social-political affairs of the organization. For instance, the performance evaluation system is one of the principal tools an organization uses to arrive at decisions regarding the distribution of rewards. Related to this, it is also a system that, under EEOC guidelines, provides information that serves to justify the personnel decisions that are made. As a consequence, one finds performance appraisal programs functioning in areas of organizational activity where there is a considerable emotional investment and where competition is high. Hence, in studying performance evaluation one must not lose sight of the social-organizational climate that surrounds these procedures. Such influences can play a significant role in the outcome of these measurements; therefore, to think of this area strictly in terms of the available rating techniques overlooks a crucial aspect of the process.

PERFORMANCE APPRAISAL AND ITS ORGANIZATIONAL CONTEXT

Over the years there has been a disappointing lack of research interest in the organizational variables that influence the evaluation of work performance. Yet it is generally recognized that these evaluations are an important part of the political system that operates within the firm. For example, Gandz and Murray (1980) asked a large group of management personnel to describe an actual work situation, involving either themselves or others, that was a good example of workplace politics in action. These narratives were analyzed for their content, and it was found that two themes, one involving the assessment of work performance and the other concerning promotion, accounted for the largest proportion of the political happenings taking place in these organizations.

Little is known about the politics of work organizations. Gandz and Murray (1980) reviewed this literature and found only a handful of articles; yet it is a topic that one frequently hears mentioned when people talk about work. Scholars writing about the topic tend to think of organizational politics in terms of competition for scarce resources or in terms of behaviors that are consciously self-serving. In all cases it is an issue that is firmly enmeshed in the interpersonal relationships of the organization, especially those relationships involved in the distribution of rewards and punishments. From this perspective, therefore, it would be expected that performance evaluations would be perceived as being involved in the politics of the organization, and this is what a large number of Gandz and Murray's subjects reported.

Performance Evaluation and Power

That performance evaluations were seen as being so closely tied in with the political dynamics of the organization is probably a reflection of the fact that they are an integral part of the power system that functions within the firm. The performance evaluation program is one of the principal mechanisms used by an organization to control the behavior of its members (Halaby, 1978; O'Reilly & Weitz, 1980). The control of employee ratings gives supervisors a tool with which they can influence the behavior of subordinates. Hence, the more discretion supervisors have in the assignment of merit evaluations, the more power they possess. Evaluations that rely on subjective opinions tend to give the rater more discretionary control over the outcome of the evaluations, whereas merit appraisal that is drawn from objective records gives less control to the rater.

In instances where management power is weak or unstable, there is evidence that the performance evaluations used tend to draw more heavily on the subjective opinions of the supervisor (Halaby, 1978). In organizations where power is more sta-ble and firmly held, performance evaluations tend to rely more on objective sources of data. We know little about this relationship that Halaby's study reports; it is probably mediated by a number of task and organizational factors. It is clear, however, that when a subordinate's status on an evaluation is determined by the opinions of others, he or she tends to be more fully exposed to the social forces that operate in the organization. Under these circumstances, one may think of the subordinate's work role as being more highly politicized, and we may conjecture that this type of evaluation system tends to sensitize the employee to the social norms in the immediate work environment.

Evaluations and Uncertainties about Work

In certain respects, when there is uncertainty concerning work assignments and work roles, there is an increase in the likelihood that work relationships will become disorganized and power relationships will be weakened. Under these circumstances, Halaby's study would lead us to expect that the evaluation system would be more likely to involve subjective ratings than objective sources of information. In keeping with these expectations, Keeley (1977) found that in organizational units in which there was considerable uncertainty regarding the content and duties of jobs, performance evaluations were more heavily weighted with subjective opinions. Objective standards—that is, evaluations involving the direct empirical measurement of work performance—tended to operate more influentially in those units in which supervisors were more certain about the duties and objectives of jobs.

In a related study Nieva (1976) reports that when uncertainty does exist, the assignment of more highly favorable ratings and more attractive rewards is related to the degree of similarity that exists between the supervisor and the subordinate. Nieva measures similarity in terms of background, attitudes, and personality, and finds that when supervisor and subordinate are more alike in terms of these variables, the subordinates receive more favorable treatment in the evaluation system. Furthermore, this relationship is stronger among jobs for which there are higher levels of uncertainty about their content. From a study such as this we see that performance evaluations are open to the influence of factors that reside in the interpersonal relationships between rater and ratee. It is also clear that there are organizational variables that relate to the extent to which these interpersonal considerations influence the evaluations.

Bidirectional Influences

There is need for much more research before a clear picture can be formed of the organizational variables affecting the outcome of merit evaluations. Many lines of research suggest themselves; for example, one may conjecture that raters often construct a strategy that involves the consequences of the ratings they make. These outcomes involve the impact of the ratings on those being evaluated, but they also involve the consequences for raters. Under these circumstances raters may follow a strategy of rating that is calculated to minimize their costs, while at the same time attempting to provide accurate evaluations of subordinates. For instance, a supervisor may generate a certain distribution of ratings in order to create a favorable impression of supervisory ability. Another rater may be convinced that there are a large number of unsatisfactory workers in the group, but may be reluctant to make a large number of negative ratings for fear that this will be interpreted as a reflection of incompetent supervision. Still another supervisor may give high ratings to a subordinate who is a popular and influential member of the work group. Fear of group reprisals may lead to all sorts of rating distortions.

It would be impossible to anticipate all of the strategies that might be adopted by an individual who is responsible for performance ratings, but the point is clear that the implications of the ratings are bidirectional. The consequences of ratings impact on both rater and ratee, and this points up a unique property of this type of measurement: there are few measurement procedures that operate to affect the status of both the observer and the person measured. One of the consequences of this set of bidirectional influences is to lead to the construction of defensive strategies on the part of the rater, and we sometimes can get a glimpse of these behaviors by examining the distribution of ratings that are made. An inordinate number of high ratings (leniency) or a concentration of ratings in the center of a scale (central tendency) may be symptomatic of strategies that are calculated in terms of their organizational consequences to the rater. We will consider these types of biases from another perspective later in this chapter.

PERFORMANCE EVALUATION TECHNIQUES[1]

A distinction has already been made between performance evaluation procedures that rely on objective sources of data and those that draw on the subjective judgments of the observer. The first approach will be called *objective performance appraisal,* since the values and motives of the evaluator do not influence the measurement operations. The second approach is usually applied to those aspects of work that do not result in tangible units of production. Supervisory and management jobs, maintenance work, and technical jobs are among many such activities, for which objective standards of merit are difficult to establish. Hence the evaluation of performance in these jobs requires the exercise of judgment by someone who is in a position to observe the performance of the person being evaluated. Since this approach to performance evaluation often involves the use of subjective rating scales, we will refer to it as *merit rating.*

Objective Performance Appraisal

Although there are many advantages associated with the use of objective procedures, there are also

---

[1]The terms ''evaluation'' and ''appraisal'' will be used interchangeably in this chapter.

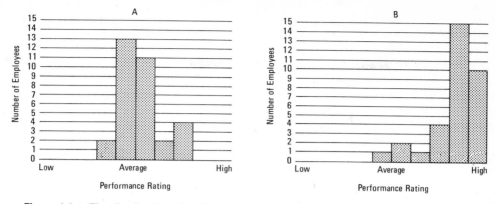

Figure 4.1 The distribution of performance ratings in diagram (A) shows the ratings tending to cluster in the center of the evaluation scale. This suggests the possibility of a central tendency bias operating in the rating system. Diagram (B) shows ratings clustering at the upper end of the scale, and this suggests the possibility of a leniency bias operating in the system.

shortcomings that should not be disregarded. As a rule, this type of evaluation relies on the records that are kept as a regular part of management's responsibilities. Production or sales records are a convenient and meaningful index of work performance. In addition, such records as scrappage rate, training courses completed, absences, and tardiness may all contribute to a measure of the individual's worth to the organization. There are occasions when objective data are obtained from direct observation of the work task. Work-sample tests are a case in point. Here workers are observed actually doing their jobs, and an appraisal is made of the success with which the tasks are performed (Asher & Sciarrino, 1974).

Along similar lines, the evaluation of management personnel can involve work-sample tests that attempt to simulate actual job situations. In-basket procedures, business games (Chapters 3 & 14), and the assessment-center approach (Chapter 14) all provide a means whereby the performance of managers may be evaluated in a relatively objective fashion. The important requirement of objective appraisal is that one move from actual performance to a set of measurements without employing personal values or decisions. Usually

this merely requires that the evaluator collect records that are kept as a direct representation of the worker's performance. If the quality of these records is good, then objective standards of this type are valuable sources of information about job merit. They require little training on the part of those who will make the evaluations, and they are relatively free of the personal biases that plague subjective merit-rating procedures.

Problems with Objective Procedures. Although objective procedures seem accurate and direct, there are a number of serious problems associated with their use. One of the more important of these difficulties involves the fact that merit evaluations of this sort usually give an incomplete picture of the total worth of an employee. This is particularly true in those jobs that have a complex set of duties. Managers, for example, may be evaluated by considering the production and sales records accumulated by those working under them. Valid as such indicators may be, there are many who would argue that there are other dimensions of managerial performance that are not to be found in production figures. Hence, although production records may be accurately assembled and conveniently available, they are *deficient* in their coverage of the many dimensions of job performance that enter an organization's definition of managerial success.

One must also avoid making the assumption that objective performance records are without measurement defects. Researchers who have studied them report that they are frequently inaccurate and poorly maintained (cf. Ilgen, 1977). Variations in accuracy and completeness will probably be found from plant to plant and between departments within the same organization. Finally, production data are often obtained from the employees themselves, and this may result in some distortion.

Recently there has been a discussion in the literature concerning the adequacy of attendance and absence records as a source of reliable information on job performance (Latham & Pursell, 1975; Ilgen, 1977). In this discussion it is pointed out that absence data, information that appears to be objective and unambiguous in its content, is sometimes confounded with turnover data. Workers sometimes quit their jobs without informing their employers, and when this happens the first days or weeks after their departure are recorded as absences. Furthermore, absences often reflect a number of different behaviors, only some of which can logically be tied in with performance effectiveness. For example, work-related injuries that cause absences combine with absences that result from poor work attitudes and low job commitments. Hence, what may appear to be a direct and clear indication of work merit is in reality a conglomeration of different behaviors, only some of which may be acceptable to the organization's definition of job performance.

There are other problems associated with objective performance evaluations. Apparent differences in performance, as found in the records, may be associated with factors that are not under the control of the worker. The differences in sales observed in a group of salespersons may reflect differences in ability and commitment, or it may indicate that the sales territories vary in their potential for sales. One salesperson may be working in a well-established territory, another may be trying to sell in a comparatively new area. Hence,

differences in sales *opportunities* are found to influence the differences seen in performance records.

In considering objective performance records, one must not lose sight of the problems associated with them. Problems of deficiency, contamination, and opportunity may underlie what otherwise seems to be an accurate indicator of an employee's value to the organization. It is also true that specific objective measures can be selected to serve certain political aims that relate to the organization, but this, along with the problems mentioned above, is not unique to objective measures. In fact, subjective systems are usually thought to be more vulnerable to these unwanted influences.

MERIT-RATING SCALES

Merit-rating scales are instruments that give guidance to a rater who is asked to express a judgment regarding the merit of another employee. A merit-rating scale is not like a psychological test in which responses are interpreted in terms of the individual who responded to the instrument. It is, instead, a descriptive device that refers to an individual other than the one who is responding to it. Hence, a merit-rating scale is a tool that is used to assist in the subjective evaluation of another individual's performance. The essential part of all such procedures is the subjective judgment of the rater, and although the rating task can be made easier by the scales that are used, in the final analysis the accuracy of the evaluation depends on the soundness of the evaluator's judgment.

Perhaps an interview with the evaluator or a prepared written statement serves as a form of merit evaluation. In essence, this unstructured approach is equivalent to asking a supervisor to prepare a reference letter for each employee. Although such an approach may generate useful information, there can be problems in trying to account for the differences in verbal facility among supervisors. What may appear as differences in employee merit may, in fact, be a difference in the ability of various supervisors to express themselves in writing. In addition, the problem of assigning numbers to these statements is difficult to solve.

In comparison to the free-responding, unstructured approach, the merit-rating scale provides for a better organization and definition of the rating task. It specifies the facets of behavior to be considered; and provided the rater follows instructions, a merit-rating scale requires the raters to give consideration to each of the performance dimensions. Usually the responses required by rating scales are quite simple; and compared with the evaluations that rely on narratives, the rating scale does not place heavy verbal responsibilities on the rater. Rating scales are easier to use and less time-consuming than unstructured evaluations. The scale lends itself to a quantitative scoring system, but scores presented in this form may provide limited guidance to the supervisor who, faced with an appraisal conference with the ratee, is expected to analyze performance deficiencies and make recommendations for corrective actions. We will comment further on this matter later in the chapter.

There are numerous types of rating scales; for each type there are many variations in content and format that may be applied to a specific work setting. In the sections that follow, only the more widely used techniques will be considered, along with a few of the current revisions that have been developed in order to improve the measurement characteristics of merit evaluation.

Graphic Rating Scales

As a general rule, a graphic merit-rating scale presents the rater with a figure that depicts varying degrees of quality in work performance. These scales are often presented in the form of a straight line that has been segmented into categories representing different degrees of merit (see Figure 4.2). Linked with each scale is a statement or a word that identifies the dimension of performance that is to be evaluated. This statement may refer to an overall, summary appraisal of work, or one may find a series of scales each referring to a specific part of an employee's job performance.

Located near these identifying statements there is a graphic rating scale that is actually a response scale, since it provides a means by which a rater can respond to the performance dimension. For the moment we will not concern ourselves with the different types of identifying statements, but rather confine our attention to the form of the response scale. For example, a typical scale consists of a straight line, beneath which appears a series of words and/or numbers (called scale anchors), which identify portions of the line. When making a rating, the rater considers each dimension of performance and places a mark over the segment of the scale that best represents the quality of the ratee's performance. Although there are several methods available for translating scale anchors into score values, simply assigning consecutive numbers to the scale categories has proved a satisfactory scoring system for most purposes.

Number of Response Categories. A decision must be made concerning the number of categories to be included in each scale. Experience has usually indicated that five or seven response alternatives are optimal (Guilford, 1954). If too few categories are used, the scale will not permit raters to fully utilize their ability to differentiate employees according to their merit. If too many categories are used, the scale exceeds the ability of the rater to perceive differences among employees, and this tends to increase the unreliability of the ratings. Much depends on the ability of the raters and the traits to be evaluated. For some clearly defined, concrete behaviors, raters may be able to make a large number of reliable discriminations. For highly complex and abstract traits—for example, leadership, adaptability—a rater may be able to utilize accurately only a small number of categories.

Empirical evidence concerning the appropriate number of categories indicates that the use of too few or too many categories can result in lower scale reliabilities (Bendig, 1953, 1954; Lissitz & Green, 1975; Jenkins & Taber, 1977). Although the results of these studies have not been completely consistent, a reasonable range might be between three- and seven-response categories (Finn, 1972).

FIGURE 4.2   Examples of Rating-Scale Formats

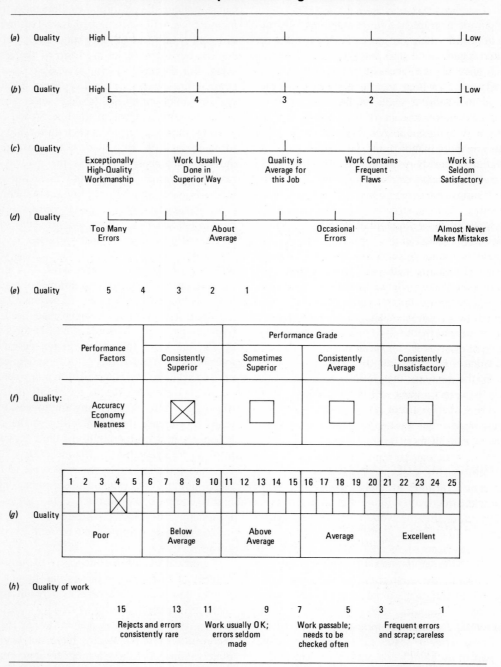

Source: Guion, R. M. *Personnel testing.* New York: McGraw-Hill, 1965. Copyright 1965, published by permission of McGraw-Hill Book Company.

Scale Anchors. Figure 4.2 shows different types of anchors that may be used to identify the segments of a graphic rating scale. Perhaps the most frequently used are sets of consecutive numbers and adjectives that express the degree or frequency with which the rated performance occurs. Both types of anchors require the rater to determine their meaning in terms of the behavior rated; both types have been used successfully. Some readers may express concern that the abstractness of these anchors makes them less useful than others that are more sharply defined, but with proper rater training, anchors of this type tend to be adequate for most rating purposes.

Graded Behavioral Statements. One potential source of confusion associated with a graphic rating scale is found in the interpretation of scale anchors. The distinction between such terms as *seldom, sometimes,* and *never,* for example, is often left to the evaluator, and variations in the interpretation of terms such as these contribute a source of error to the ratings. In an effort to reduce this type of error, some researchers have suggested using anchors that consist of a series of graded behavioral statements. These statements supposedly define each segment of the scale in terms that refer to concrete, easily identifiable behaviors, and therefore reduce the ambiguities associated with adjectives and abstract numbers. An example of this type of scale can be found in Figure 4.2. Another form can be seen in Figure 4.3, which is taken from a military efficiency report for company grade officers.

The idea underlying scale anchors of this type is an attractive one. To ask a rater to choose among a set of specific statements about behavior tends to simplify his job of translating observations of the ratee's performance into an appropriate scale category. A major problem, however, is in building a set of anchors of this type. Here one has to develop a group of statements that vary according to degree and not according to the type of behavior involved. For example, although the item in Figure 4.3 is a good one in many respects, it still displays some aspects of this problem. Notice the fact that the first category on the left refers only to the nature of the situation, that is, its routine character. The next category brings in a new, qualitatively different dimension—stress. Hence, as one moves across categories, not only is behavior varying in terms of degree; it is also changing in its qualitative content.

One final problem associated with the construction of scales of this type is found in trying to develop a set of categories that are equally spaced. This is not a problem unique to the behaviorally anchored scales, but it is a difficult one to solve with anchors that are this complex. It is especially difficult to solve when the different categories do not refer to the same behaviors, as in the case of Figure 4.3.

Anchors can be scaled in a number of ways, and psychologists have developed a wide variety of scaling procedures that may be selected for these purposes (cf. Edwards, 1957; Torgerson, 1958). Later in the chapter we will consider an extension of these traditional graphic rating scales

FIGURE 4.3.   A Set of Graded Behavioral Anchors Representing Different Degrees of Adaptability

ADAPTABILITY					
NOT ○ OBSERVED	Unable to perform adequately in other than routine situations	Performance declines under stress or in other than routine situations	Performs well under stress or in unusual situations	Performance excellent even under pressure or in difficult situations	Outstanding performance under extreme stress meets the challenge of difficult situations

FIGURE 4.4   A Person-to-Person Graphic Rating Scale

Eric Keith	Carol Otey	Karl Vernon	David Edwards	Lynn Jones

Instructions to Raters: Considering overall job performance, compare the ratee with each of the names appearing above. Place a check mark on the scale expressing your judgment of the ratee's job performance relative to those employees named above. Your check mark may be placed at any point on the line depending on where the ratee stands relative to the other employees.

that has received considerable attention in the literature. This type of instrument, called a behaviorally anchored rating scale (BARS) might have been included in the present discussion, but since it often uses techniques that we have not yet discussed—for example, critical incidents—we will defer its consideration.

Person Anchors.   One interesting variation involves the use of employees' names as standards for the different segments of the scale (see Figure 4.4). These anchors can be developed in a number of ways (Guilford, 1954), but a reasonable approach begins by asking supervisors to select the most outstanding and the least competent members of a group. Names for which there is good agreement among the supervisors are selected as anchors. After the two end anchors are chosen, the supervisors are asked to select employees who fall midway between the two extremes. Once again a name is chosen for which there is general agreement regarding its midpoint location. Finally, names are selected that are judged to lie midway between the center anchor and the two end anchors.

Once the anchors have been selected, the scale presents an evaluator with a rating task that involves comparing each ratee with each of the scale anchors. As each anchor is considered, the evaluator must decide which member of the pair, ratee or anchor person, is higher in merit. When the point on the scale is reached where the anchor is judged to have higher merit than the ratee, the ratee is then placed in the preceding category and

given the numerical value assigned to it (see Figure 4.4).

Paired-Comparison Ratings

The paired-comparison rating procedure asks the evaluator to consider pairs of employees and indicate which member of each pair displays better performance. The procedure presents the rater with all possible pairs of employees, and the rater goes through the pairs selecting the member of each that is seen to rate higher in the trait being evaluated. On any single trait, a fair approximation of an individual's final standing can be obtained by counting the number of times he is chosen over others. There are more elaborate methods for computing an employee's final standing in the group (Torgerson, 1958; Baird & Noma, 1978), but this simple method will give a reasonably good approximation of what might be obtained from these more advanced analyses.

Consider a situation in which a foreman is asked to rate five employees in terms of the overall quality of their job peformance. The rating assignment is presented to the foreman in the following way:

INSTRUCTIONS: Before you is a deck of cards, and on each card you will find the names of two of your employees. Consider each pair, and draw a line under the member of each who you believe is doing the best overall job for your department.

Let's assume the following employees are involved in the evaluation:

Smith
Monroe
Hennessey
Ginsburg
Luis

The pairs would consist of:

Smith vs. Monroe
Smith vs. Hennessey
Smith vs. Ginsburg
Smith vs. Luis
Monroe vs. Hennessey

Monroe vs. Ginsburg
Monroe vs. Luis
Hennessey vs. Ginsburg
Hennessey vs. Luis
Ginsburg vs. Luis

In preparing this set of comparisons, the names are randomly assigned to the first or second position on the card to avoid the possibility of a bias occurring because a particular name was always first in each pair.

As you can see, the paired-comparison method presents a rater with a relatively easy task. At any one time the rater is faced with a choice that involves only two workers. This is quite a bit easier than trying to decide, for example, who is the best worker in a group. There a rater is faced with a situation in which he must consider all the workers simultaneously. To say that someone is first also says something about everyone else in the group—that is, they are not first. Hence, the paired-comparison rating task confines a rater's attention to two employees at a time, and in that sense the task is a simple one. Some of these pairs may, however, present the rater with a difficult choice. In our example, both Luis and Smith may be viewed by the supervisor as being exceptionally good workers, yet the procedure demands that a choice be made between them when they are paired together.

One problem with the paired-comparison method is that it becomes cumbersome when the number of employees to be rated is large. If N is

TABLE 4.1   Number of Pairs in a Paired-Comparison Rating

Number of Ratees	Number of Comparisons
5	10
6	15
10	45
15	105
20	190

the number of employees, then a complete pairing of all ratees generates $N(N - 1)/2$ pairs. Table 4.1 gives evidence of how rapidly the rating task increases as the size of the group expands. There are procedures, however, that may be used to reduce the number of pairs (McCormick & Bachus, 1952), and they have proved rather successful in reducing the size of the rating task without seriously disturbing the value of the ratings (Rambo, 1959a, 1959b).

There is much that commends the use of paired comparisons. It is a procedure that provides a wide range of data analysis alternatives (Torgerson, 1958), and it can yield much information about both the rater and the ratee. It can be used with global evaluations of work proficiency, or a series of paired comparisons can be undertaken, each dealing with a different facet of performance. The method does require a little more technical information when one attempts to analyze the ratings, but this is an easy obstacle to overcome. Hence, paired-comparison procedures offer a useful alternative to those who are responsible for the performance evaluations carried out in a work organization.

Ranking Procedures

Employees can be evaluated by asking supervisors to rank them in some order of merit. If several supervisors are available to rate a group of workers, median ranks are computed for each ratee. For example, consider a situation in which an eight-person work group is evaluated for overall job performance by three supervisors. Three separate sets of ranks are produced as below:

Employee	Rater A	Rater B	Rater C	Median Rank
Chadwick	3	1	4	3.0
Simpson	6	5	7	6.0
Wooler	8	6	6	6.5
Scott	4	3	1	3.0
McKenna	2	4	3	3.0
Stein	1	2	2	2.0
Czappo	5	7	5	5.5
Tinsley	7	8	8	8.0

Since ranks express only order, they provide no information concerning the magnitude of the performance differences that exist between employees. Median ranks are computed, and tied ranks can be adjusted in a conference of those involved in the ratings. In any event, the use of order of merit data is probably not a serious deficiency, since for many merit-rating uses, information concerning order will satisfy the needs of the organization. A supervisor may have to select the top three or four members of a work group, but in many instances is not asked to provide a precise estimate of *how much* better one worker is than another.

The rating-task requirements of the ranking methods appear to be simple, but can become clumsy and difficult as the number of ratees increases. Remember, to determine the rank of any one employee, that person's position must be compared with all others. As the number of ratees increases, the comparisons become more difficult. Also ranks become more difficult to establish as one moves from the extremes to the center of the ranks (Guilford, 1954). In a group of 100 ratees, it is often easier to select the top three and bottom three employees than it is to assign people to rank 50, 51, and 52.

The rank-order method is probably a useful approach when one considers many of the day to day personnel decisions that must be based on merit considerations. There are instances when merit-rating data are used in the evaluation of selection and placement instruments, and ranks may place some limitations on the kinds of statistical analyses that can be performed. A set of ranks also does not provide much guidance for an appraisal interview, but for many purposes, ranking employees on merit satisfies an organization's need for performance appraisal information.

Checklists

Although they come in several forms, checklists usually consist of a number of statements, each of which concerns a different aspect of job performance. It is usually recommended that these statements refer to actual behaviors that have been observed in the job setting. One approach to developing checklist statements asks supervisors to write essay descriptions of the behaviors that have been observed in high- and low-merit employees, and checklist statements are drawn from these essays.

Unlike the behavioral statements used to anchor graphic rating scales, checklist items are not graded according to the degree of merit they express. Statements are usually given equal weights, and a ratee's standing is determined by counting the number of statements checked. In this respect the checklist approach is similar to the scoring used with psychological tests, where a person's score is the number of items passed. It is possible to develop more elaborate weighting systems in which checklist items are given weights other than +1 and 0 (Edwards, 1957; Torgersen, 1958; Baird & Noma, 1978); but before investing in the added labor required by this, one should have good reason to suspect that these weights will improve measurement accuracy and be fairly stable over time and work groups.

The following items are taken from a checklist used to evaluate the performance of supervisory personnel (Rambo, 1958):

INSTRUCTIONS TO RATERS: Consider your immediate supervisor in the light of each of the following statements. Place a check beside each statement that you believe to be descriptive of your supervisor's behavior.

1. Is thoughtful of others
2. Frequently checks subordinates' work
3. Is fair in dealing with subordinates
4. Takes time to listen to gripes
5. Keeps people informed

Other types of checklist items can be developed; for example, some checklists consist of sets of adjectives that are descriptive of performance (see below).

INSTRUCTIONS TO RATERS: Consider your immediate supervisor in the light of each of the following terms. Place a check beside each term that you believe to be descriptive of your supervisor's behavior.

Adaptable	Efficient
Flexible	Helpful
Aggressive	Suspicious
Versatile	Impatient
Undependable	Stern
Capable	Intolerant
Demanding	Sensitive
Thoughtful	Realistic
Considerate	Slipshod
Organized	Reliable

There is little information concerning the relative merits of different checklist formats, but an important consideration concerns the reliability of the scales that consist of these different types of items. We need research on this question before we can make realistic choices between different checklist formats.

Forced-Choice Scales

The forced-choice merit-rating scale represents an approach to subjective judgment that attempts to obscure the scale's scoring key from the rater. Obscuring the scoring key means that the scales are constructed in such a fashion that the rater cannot tell by looking at the instrument which of the items increase the ratee's merit score and which of the items do not. On most other types of merit-rating scales, a rater can easily determine whether his response will increase or decrease the ratee's merit status. Hence, if an item reads: "Worker is

insolent and insubordinate," it would probably be a good bet that an affirmative response would be harmful to the ratee's standing in the merit evaluation. Because of the transparency of many merit-rating scales—that is, a rater knows whether an item carries positive or negative weight—one must worry about the possibility of conscious biases entering into the evaluations. In other words, in the usual merit-rating case, if a rater sets out to do a good turn for the ratee, it is not very difficult to see which of the scale items will achieve this purpose.

Construction. A major complaint about the forced-choice approach concerns the involved set of construction procedures that are required. These procedures are based on an idea that the appearance of an item—for example, whether it is a favorable or an unfavorable statement—should not necessarily relate to its ability to differentiate high and low performers. A statement may represent a very favorable comment to make about an employee, but it may apply equally to good and poor workers. Another equally favorable statement may be applied much more frequently to superior performing employees. If these two statements are paired, a rater who must choose between them in an attempt to rate an employee is unable to determine which of the two implies high merit. If the nondiscriminating statement is chosen, the ratee's score remains unchanged. If the discriminating item is used to describe the ratee, he receives an increase in his merit score.

Guilford (1954) outlines the steps required to build a forced-choice scale:

1. Supervisors are asked to identify the very best and the poorest workers in their group. They are then asked to write essay descriptions concerning the behaviors of these individuals.
2. These descriptions are used as the basis for constructing a set of behavioral statements or adjectives.
3. These statements are given to another group of supervisors who are asked to describe employees who have been classified into high and low merit groups. Supervisors do this by checking

items thought to be descriptive of a given employee's behavior.

4. For each statement a discrimination index and a favorability index is determined. A discrimination index is an indication of an item's ability to differentiate high and low merit employees. A favorability index is obtained from a set of ratings which evaluate the extent to which an item expresses a socially favorable or unfavorable comment about a person.

5. Items are then paired. Those having similar favorability indexes are brought together, one of these items having a high discrimination index, the other not. Statements having unfavorable content are also paired. Once again, one of these items carries a high discrimination index, the other does not.

6. One favorable pair and one unfavorable pair are brought together to form a tetrad. This tetrad contains two discriminating items which carry a non-zero weight (probably 1) and two non-discriminating items which carry a scoring weight of 0. For example:

	Scoring Weight
Is friendly and cooperative	0
Is supportive and encouraging	+1
Plays favorites	−1
Frequently complains	0

7. Raters are instructed to consider each tetrad and select the one item that best describes the ratee and the one that is least descriptive.

8. Scores are determined for each tetrad, and its ability to discriminate high and low merit employees is determined.

9. Discriminating items are retained and assembled into a final form. Scoring weights are determined, and a scoring key constructed.

To the extent that these construction procedures are successful, the forced-choice scale presents raters with a set of choices that are difficult to bias in a desired direction. Not being able to anticipate the scoring consequences of any response, raters find themselves in a position in which they more likely report their unbiased observations of ratees' performance. Hence, in these circumstances the scale becomes a descriptive instrument that is free

from one of the major sources of contamination that plagues most other merit-rating procedures.

Evaluation.   The question remains, to what extent are forced-choice scales immune from the influence of raters who consciously set out to fake their responses to the scale? Is it possible to see through these pairs and select the statement that carries the nonzero score? A number of studies have been reported in which raters have been given a forced-choice scale with instructions to fake the results (Waters, 1965). The drift of these studies suggests that the forced-choice procedure is not completely insulated from the influence of bias, but there does seem to be reason to suspect that the procedure succeeds in reducing the magnitude of this influence. There is also some evidence that neutral items may be more effective in reducing bias than are items that express positive or negative assessments (Isard, 1956; Obradovic, 1970).

Leniency bias, the tendency for the rater to assign ratings toward the high end of the scale, seems to be less evident in the forced-choice format (Taylor, Schneider, & Clay, 1954; Sharon & Bartlett, 1969), but efforts to compare forced-choice and graphic rating-scale reliabilities and validities have not demonstrated a clear-cut superiority for the procedurally more demanding forced-choice approach (Lepkowski, 1963; Cozan, 1959). Hence, whether in any given situation the success achieved in reducing rater bias compensates for the added effort required to construct a forced-choice scale is a matter that depends on the seriousness of rater bias. In many situations, and with adequate training, conscious rater biases may be of little concern. In these situations, the procedural requirements of the forced-choice instrument would probably discourage its use.

Critical-Incident Ratings

The critical-incident technique is a procedure that can be used to develop the checklist items used in performance evaluation. The primary objective of this approach is to identify, in clear behavioral terms, the critical requirements of a job (Flanagan, 1949; 1954). These critical requirements are obtained from direct observation of work activities, and to be considered critical, the behavior must be seen as being responsible for outstandingly effective or clearly unsatisfactory performance on the job.

Beginning with a well defined and thoroughly understood definition of the aims and objections of a task, the procedure asks supervisors to prepare statements that describe in terms of actual behaviors the activities they believe to be critical to success or failure in achieving these objectives. Therefore, supervisors generate a large group of statements that tell in direct terms what a worker did or did not do in successfully meeting or failing to meet the requirements of the job. These statements are reviewed by a group of judges who rate behaviors in terms of their critical significance to job performance. Statements for which there is good agreement among the judges are retained and entered into a rating form that consists of a list of these critical activities.

It is often recommended that critical-incident ratings be carried out continuously. That is to say, a supervisor is given a checklist for each subordinate and is instructed to make a record of critical incidents at the time they occur. For example, suppose on a given day a supervisor becomes aware of an event that reflects one of the behaviors that are listed as positive critical incidents. The supervisor will record on the checklist the fact that these behaviors occurred and write down some of the details surrounding the event. This type of merit evaluation, therefore, requires that the rater serve merely in the role of observer and recorder. The rater is not put in a position in which evaluation of the degree of merit associated with different behaviors is required. Rather, the rater has a list of critical incidents, and the task is merely to indicate when these incidents occur. Hence, the rater does not carry a heavy evaluation responsibility. Furthermore, since ratings are not carried out at fixed time intervals, the continuous nature of critical incidents takes much of the burden off memory as a factor that influences an employee's status on a merit evaluation.

The procedure is not, however, without problems. One of the most serious drawbacks associated with this approach is found in the fact that critical incidents tend to occur infrequently. As a result, the typical distribution of critical-incident ratings involves a large number of employees with no incidents and a small group with one or two. In these circumstances, the technique does not do a satisfactory job in discriminating among workers in terms of their performance effectiveness—unless, of course, the purpose of the evaluation is to identify the top or bottom few employees in the group.

There is also a sizable judgment factor involved in the technique, and little is known about its significance and how it operates. Both in the preparation of the scale, and especially in the application of the technique, supervisors must exercise considerable judgment in translating day-to-day observations into critical-incident items. Considering the complexity and specific qualities of a given behavioral act, the supervisor must judge when a given behavior fits a critical incident that is listed on the scale and when it does not. Little is known about the presence of bias in these decisions, but intuition would lead one to suspect that they are not completely free of these influences.

Mixed-Standard Rating Scales

The mixed-standard rating scale (Blanz & Ghiselli, 1972) requires the rater to evaluate employees in each of a number of traits. For each trait, a set of three statements describing high, average, and poor performance is developed (see Table 4.2), and then all statements are arranged in random order on the scale. By randomly assigning traits and levels of performance to positions on the scale, this technique attempts to reduce the effects of some types of rater bias that are thought to occur more frequently when items are grouped together in a systematic fashion (Landy & Farr, 1980). One finds in this approach, therefore, an example of the psychologist's effort to combat rater bias by manipulating the format of a rating instrument.

Once the rating form has been prepared, raters are asked to respond to the items by indicating whether the ratee is better than each statement, fits

TABLE 4.2   Scoring Systems for Set of Three Statements

Statements			Points
I	II	III	
+	+	+	7
0	+	+	6
–	+	+	5
–	0	+	4
–	–	+	3
–	–	0	2
–	–	–	1

+ = ratee is better than the statement
0 = ratee fits the statement
– = ratee is worse than the statement
Source: Blanz, F., & Ghiselli, E. E. The mixed standard scale: A new rating system. *Personnel Psychology*, 1972, *25*, 185–199. Published by permission, copyright 1972.

TABLE 4.3   A Set of Behavior Descriptions Measuring Diligence

Scale Location	Performance Level	Statement
9	High	A real workhorse. He works much harder than his job really requires.
45	Average	He is sufficiently industrious and earnest in his work. You cannot accuse him of being lazy; nevertheless, you wouldn't say he is exceptionally diligent.
27	Poor	He has a touch of laziness. He does just what he is required to do, but no more.

the description in the statement, or is worse than the description. As a consequence, each item can receive one of three responses, and each set of three statements measuring a single trait can generate a number of different response patterns. Table 4.2 illustrates the logically consistent response patterns that can be given to any set of three items. In this table, statements labeled I, II, and III refer to high, average, and poor performance, respectively.

Apart from providing a range of different scoring outcomes, this response system permits the assessment of the logical consistency of a rater's answers. For example, suppose a rater were to describe a ratee as being better than the average description but worse than the poorest description of a trait. This would represent an inconsistent response that would call attention to the possibility that the ratings were of questionable utility.

Blanz and Ghiselli (1972) describe a mixed-standard scale that was used by 23 high management officers to rate 100 middle management personnel employed by an aluminum company. The scale contained 18 traits, and for each a high, average, and poor performance description was prepared. As an example of the items developed to measure one trait, diligence, consider the three behavioral descriptions in Table 4.3.

To illustrate the random arrangement of traits and performance levels that appear on the mixed-standard scale, Table 4.4 shows the trait/performance level combinations that make up the first five items on the Blanz and Ghiselli scale:

TABLE 4.4   Arrangement of Items in a Mixed-Standard Scale

Item Position	Trait Measured	Performance Level
1	Self-confidence	Average
2	Enthusiasm for Work	Poor
3	Delegation of Authority	High
4	Efficiency	Average
5	Carefulness	Poor

As the rater moves from one item to the next, he moves across a random assortment of the traits being measured, and this nonsystematic arrangement of traits and levels of performance continues through the entire 54 items of the scale.

Evaluation. At present there is little evidence concerning the measurement effectiveness of the mixed-standard scale. Blanz and Ghiselli examined a distribution of ratings generated by their scale and found what appeared to be a reduced tendency on the part of raters to bias their evaluations toward the lenient end of the scale. They also present evidence suggesting that there is reasonably good agreement among raters who are evaluating the same worker. In another study, Saal and Landy (1977) applied a mixed-standard scale to the performance evaluation of police officers, comparing these ratings with others obtained from a behaviorally anchored scale. The evidence from this study indicated that the mixed-standard scale did appear to generate ratings that were less influenced by several types of rater bias, but there was a general tendency for interrater reliability coefficients to be much too low to be useful. If evidence

of low levels of reliability continues to appear in subsequent studies, this would represent a fatal defect in the procedure. At present, however, we must await this future research and reserve judgment.

BARS/BES

Merit-rating procedures can be developed by bringing together combinations of steps required by the techniques that have been described in the preceding sections. One such procedure is the *behaviorally anchored rating scale* (BARS),[2] the development of which is usually attributed to Smith and Kendall (1963). This technique, which has received considerable attention in the literature (Dunnette & Borman, 1979; Landy & Farr, 1980), borrows procedures used in critical-incident rating and combines them with construction procedures that are usually associated with attitude-scale development.

Latham, Fay, and Saari (1979) describe the following steps that enter into construction of a BARS:

1. Critical incidents are collected from judges who know the objectives of a job and who have had opportunity to observe the work.
2. A group of workers who presently hold these jobs are asked to classify these incidents into different categories (job knowledge, interaction with supervision, etc.). Each category will serve as a separate dimension of the standard that will be used to evaluate an employee.
3. Another group of present job holders are given both the set of incidents and the categories that were developed in the previous steps, and they are asked to assign incidents to the categories judged to be appropriate for the content of each incident. Incidents are retained when there is high agreement among the judges concerning the job category to which they refer.
4. Another group of persons familiar with the job are given the set of categories under which are listed the incidents judged to identify each. These judges are asked to rate each incident on the degree to which it represents good, average or poor performance. Once again, incidents are retained if there is good agreement among the judges concerning the degree of merit expressed.
5. The surviving incidents are assigned a scale value that is the average of the individual values assigned by the judges. These incidents serve as anchors for a rating scale, each job category having its own scale.

Smith and Kendall (1963) describe the format of their scale as involving a set of continuous graphic rating scales that are presented vertically on the page. Positions on the scale are identified

---

[2]The term *behavioral expectation scale* (BES) is sometimes applied to this and similar procedures.

by the behavioral descriptions that are printed beside the scale. In making ratings of job proficiency, raters are asked to decide whether the behaviors they have observed in the ratee would lead them to *expect* any of the behaviors that appear along the scale. The rating task, therefore, asks the rater to make inferences about the likelihood of the behaviors described by the various scale anchors when these inferences are based on the specific on-the-job behaviors that have been observed by the rater. Hence, unlike the ratings required by many other techniques, the BARS is not necessarily concerned with behaviors that have actually occurred, but with behavioral inferences that are derived from actual behaviors. Parenthetically, Landy et al. (1976) found ''strong objections'' to the use of a scale that required such inferences when they were dealing with a group of police officers. One cogent argument raised by these officers was that an appeal of a rating based on behavior that *might happen* was likely to be upheld. An important provision of the procedure is that raters are asked to support the check mark they place on the scale with notes concerning the actual observed behaviors that led to the ratings. This latter provision is not found on all BARS instruments, but it is a useful supplement, since it clarifies the inferential decisions a rater makes in expressing a rating.

Evaluation. From the foregoing it is evident that a BARS is an involved and possibly expensive instrument to construct. Furthermore, its use of a number of independent judgment groups may represent a condition that cannot be met in many work organizations. Hence, one may question whether the approach has been able to demonstrate advantages over other rating scales whose construction procedures are less complicated.

We can begin our answer to this question by noting that BARS have been used successfully in a number of rating situations (Smith & Kendall, 1963; Landy & Guion, 1970; Landy et al., 1976). When compared with other scales, however, the evidence does not give the BARS clear superiority. There is, in fact, a mixed pattern of results that

sometimes gives BARS the advantage in reducing certain kinds of rater bias (cf. Campbell et al., 1973; Burnaska & Hollmann, 1974) and sometimes gives other rating scales the edge in reducing these unwanted influences (Borman & Vallon, 1974; Bernardin, Alvares, & Cranny, 1976). In a number of instances the differences observed between scales were very small (Borman & Dunnette, 1975) and in other instances the differences disappeared when more rigorous procedures were used to develop the items for the BARS (Bernardin, 1977). Landy and Farr (1980), after reviewing the research evidence, concluded that the added effort required by these procedures has not been rewarded with significantly improved ratings. It may be premature to dismiss the BARS technique as a potential contributor to an organization's performance appraisal program; but until additional information regarding its cost-benefit value is available, the decision to construct such a scale should be made only after a careful consideration of the less complex alternatives.

PEER ASSESSMENT

Performance evaluation is usually an activity that falls within the jurisdiction of those who occupy supervisory and management positions. There are many reasons for this. Evaluation and its consequences generate a potent source of power that reinforces the leadership role. Also, those who occupy leadership positions are often well acquainted with the norms and objectives of an organization; and in all probability, there is a belief shared by those in power that their judgment is more accurate than that of those who are in follower roles. As a consequence, the rater is usually an individual who is in an organizational position that is superior to the one held by the ratee.

Peers can, however, provide an alternative source of information concerning performance effectiveness. One could easily argue that such ratings would be more accurate than those submitted by superiors, since peers occupy a vantage point from which to observe the performance of other members of the work group. On the other hand, many have expressed misgivings about this type of evaluation, contending that such ratings can be confounded with the friendship ties that are found within the group.

These and other similar arguments have been considered in a number of programs that have been developed to utilize peer-assessment procedures. Peer ratings have been given considerable attention by the military services, while relatively little interest has been shown in this approach by work organizations. Why this is so is open to conjecture, but over the years the armed services have shown great interest in all types of performance appraisal systems, and they have sponsored a considerable amount of research that has made a substantial contribution to this area.

Methods of Peer Assessment

Kane and Lawler (1978) have identified three principal methods of peer assessment.

---

1. *Peer Nominations*—Group members are asked to identify a specified number of people who are judged to be at the top of the performance scale. In some cases, a similar number of the poorest performers are nominated. Individuals who are placed in these end groups are usually ranked in order of their standing on the rating dimension.
2. *Peer Ratings*—Using any of the rating scales that have been discussed, each group member rates every other member of the group. Average ratings are usually used to represent an individual's final standing on the rating dimension.
3. *Peer Rankings*—Similar to peer ratings, except that a ranking scale is used. Here each member is ranked by all other members, and median ranks are computed.

Of these three approaches, rankings have received less attention in the literature, while nomination and rating techniques have been studied extensively. As one might expect, the efforts made to evaluate the different approaches have produced a complicated and not totally consistent set of results. The general trend of these studies, however, has provided enough encouraging evidence concerning the effectiveness of peer assessment to indicate that continued attention should be given to its application to a work setting (Lewin & Zwany, 1976).

Nomination Techniques. Peer nomination techniques have generally displayed rather high reliability. Kane and Lawler (1978) report median internal consistency and test-retest reliabilities to be .89 and .78, respectively, in one set of studies they reviewed. These coefficients are quite high, although one might expect high reliability from a technique that focuses on the extreme positions of a distribution, since these positions are often most easily identified.

Efforts to assess the validity of peer nomina-tions have also been quite encouraging, especially when the nominations involve leadership performance as a predictor of future leader effectiveness. There have been, however, reports of negative reactions and resistance from those who have been asked to make peer nominations (Webb, 1955; Downey, Medland, & Yates, 1976). Furthermore, there is evidence that nominations are influenced by friendship considerations and halo errors. Finally, nomination techniques contribute little to efforts to provide constructive feedback to those being evaluated, although there appears to be no reason why the techniques can not be supplemented with sets of written statements concerning the specific observations that led to an employee's positive or negative nomination.

Peer Ratings. There is little information regarding the reactions of individuals participating in peer rating programs, but there are some who argue that this technique is more useful than nominations for employee counseling. Although these are important considerations, they are secondary to concerns about the basic measurement properties of the ratings. In this regard, peer ratings compare rather poorly with nomination procedures. The Kane and Lawler (1978) review of the studies in this area estimates that the median internal consistency reliability of peer ratings has been a disappointing .45. In this instance, internal consistency refers to the extent to which raters agree in assigning ratings to their associates. Apparently, higher interrater agreement can be achieved when peers are asked to nominate the top and bottom portion of the merit scale than when they are asked to locate the position of each member of the group on the rating dimension.

Although there have been numerous occasions when peer ratings have yielded evidence of useful levels of validity, when compared with nominations such ratings have proved somewhat less valid. Little information is available concerning the influence of rater bias, but Brehm and Festinger (1975) reported a tendency for raters to move both low and high performers toward the middle of the scale. Finally, it has been reported that peer ratings tend to be vulnerable to racial biases, although this problem may be overcome if training is given prior to the ratings (Cox & Krumboltz, 1958; Schmidt & Johnson, 1973).

In summary, it is difficult to draw any conclusions from comparisons of peer ratings and nominations. In the first place, peer ratings undertake a more difficult task when they ask each rater to assign an evaluation to all members of the group. Second, there is a wide assortment of individual rating procedures that can be put in the hands of peer raters. The procedural alternatives that are applicable to peer nominations are decidedly limited. As a consequence, comparisons between the two approaches yield results that vary as a function of the relative merits of the specific scaling techniques used.

Finally, peer ratings have been compared with supervisory ratings, and in most instances the two approaches have led to different outcomes (Borman, 1974). For example, several studies (Rothaus, Morton, & Hanson, 1965; Zedeck et al., 1974) have found more lenient ratings being generated by peers. It seems reasonable to expect differences between these two sources of evaluation information, since supervisors and peers tend to view performance from different perspectives.

Peer Rankings.   Little can be said with confidence about the effectiveness of peer rankings, since so little research has been done on this approach. What has been reported concerning reliability has been quite encouraging, but the limited amount of information regarding validity and freedom from bias prevents any conclusions.

Summary Comments

Peer assessment represents an interesting alternative to supervisory ratings; but rather than viewing it as an alternative, it may be more realistic to consider peer assessment as a supplement to supervisory evaluations. Following this line of argument, one might also look to ratings from subordinates as still another source of appraisal information (cf. Klimoski & London, 1974). How one might combine information coming from these different sources is, at the moment, a difficult question to answer, but the logic of the argument leads one to conclude that such evaluations would give a more complete view of the performance effectiveness of an employee. There is much work that needs to be done before evaluations from those different sources can be combined into an overall appraisal of the individual.

ERRORS IN SUBJECTIVE EVALUATIONS

Whenever rating scales are compared, a frequent concern involves the extent to which they are susceptible to the different types of bias that plague subjective measurements. Questions of reliability and validity, although given some attention, are often secondary to the interest shown in a procedure's ability to generate ratings that are free from rater bias. Sadly, little is known about the psychological mechanisms that underlie these biasing factors; and as a consequence, efforts to eliminate these influences through revisions in the format of the scale or through training programs have not met with high levels of success. The problem lies in the fact that these errors stem from a number of different sources, not the least of which being the complicated nature of the rating task. To translate day-to-day behavior, considering all of its many varieties and subtleties, into the format of a rating scale is a complex assignment. This difficulty is compounded by the fact that the merit rating system carries with it costs and benefits for both ratee and rater, and as a result it involves a system of measurement that is deeply embedded in a complicated social psychology of interpersonal relationships.

Consider the fact that negative merit ratings may inflict harm on the job status and career prospects of the ratee. In making these ratings the rater is placed in a social situation that may carry with it substantial costs for the ratee. As a consequence, one finds a negative or threatening work situation that can be mitigated or avoided altogether by submitting a set of ratings that are biased toward the high end of the scale. There is evidence that people try to avoid transmitting negative messages to others (Blumberg, 1972; Tesser & Rosen, 1975), and one way of doing this is to make the ratings more positive.

Ratings that will not affect the status of the ratee should be less lenient than those that will have a bearing on the individual's employment. For instance, ratings that are carried out strictly for research purposes carry with them fewer personal consequences than ratings made for administrative purposes. Borresen (1967) found that evaluations tend to be more lenient when made for administrative purposes than when made for research. One probable reason for this finding is that raters tend to anticipate the personal costs that they incur when they make ratings that will inflict harm on a work associate. Fisher (1979) reports that a group of raters anticipated that feedback of negative evaluations would result in unpleasant reactions from their subordinates. Related to this, she found that raters were more lenient when they were

responsible for a face-to-face meeting with the ratee during an appraisal interview.

Reluctance to make negative evaluations may have its origin in a fear of reprisal from those receiving low ratings. The college instructor may fear giving stringent grades because of the prospects of student retaliation in course evaluations. Jones (1966) found that a system of reciprocity seemed to be operating in a situation in which people were asked to rate each other. In this case, a person who received positive evaluations from another rater reciprocated and assigned positive ratings to that person. The same general rule applied to negative ratings, with negative evaluations tending to trigger negative evaluations in return. It is not difficult to imagine a work setting in which a supervisor refrains from negative ratings lest a worker or the entire group retaliate in a variety of ways.

Social distance and power differentials also play a part in influencing the distribution of ratings that are obtained. When a person who possesses substantial power unfavorably evaluates a person having little power, the costs to the rater may be relatively slight. When, on the other hand, a peer makes a negative rating, there may be substantial personal costs associated with this action. As a case in point, there are a number of studies that have found that organizational superiors tend to be less lenient with their ratings of subordinates than are the peers of the ratee (Rothaus et al., 1965; Zedeck et al., 1974; Schneier & Beatty, 1978). The social distance separating supervisor from subordinate may render doing harm less unpleasant, and the power differential may insulate the rater from retaliatory actions from the ratee. From a general point of view, merit rating is an activity that forms a part of the relationships that exist between people. Variation in any of the large number of factors that characterize these relationships or influence their nature can lead to changes in the orientation of the rater who is evaluating the performance of another. As more uncertainty surrounds the rating task and as the prospects for objective verification recede, there is probably an increased probability that the ratings will become more vulnerable to these social and organizational influences (Nieva, 1976).

Types of Errors

Efforts to reduce these sources of rating bias by revising the format of the rating scale may seem to be futile, and there is much in the research literature that suggests this may be true. There are, however, other sources of bias that influence the scale that cannot be described as conscious strategies to achieve a certain social-organizational objective. For example, unusual rating distributions may be generated by neutral statements, since they tend to be more ambiguous than more extreme statements (Edwards, 1957). In addition, the tendency for some raters to favor certain positions on the rating scale and the carry-over effects from one item to the next on a rating scale may exert a biasing influence on the results of the ratings. Perhaps it is this type of bias that is most effectively removed by alterations in the format of the rating scale. But whatever the case, the research literature has a long way to go before the problem of rating bias is solved, and until that point is reached it would be well for the social scientist to invest more research attention in a study of the basic social and psychological mechanisms that combine to produce the different types of bias one finds operating in merit-rating scales.

Errors of Leniency.[3] Errors of leniency are usually detected by examining the distribution of ratings and finding a large number of evaluations falling at the favorable end of the scale. Of course, the distribution of ratings will reflect the distribution of work performance that is characteristic of a work group, and since selective attrition may, over time, homogenize a group at the high end of the performance continuum, the appearance of a high number of favorable ratings may testify to the operation of a good personnel program. Within a research setting, however, it is possible to create experimental situations where the distribution of task performance is known (Borman, 1979), and under these conditions the presence of leniency biases is easy to detect. In practical work situations one may have supplementary information concerning job performance, and when this does not agree with the distribution of ratings, then one may suspect the presence of biasing factors.

Some suggest that the use of a *forced distribution* procedure might be an appropriate solution for leniency errors, and this is a reasonable suggestion, provided there are some rational grounds for the distribution chosen. A forced distribution technique is really not a scaling procedure in the usual sense of the word, but rather a constraint placed on the distribution of ratings that requires raters to limit the number of ratings they make to the various segments of the scale. Figure 4.5 illustrates a forced distribution approach that at one time was used by the U.S. Air Force in its ratings of officers. Above each of the rating categories there appears a cluster of figures that identifies the prescribed proportion of ratings that should appear in each part of the scale. Notice that ratings assigned to upper and lower categories must be accompanied by a written explanation of the rationale that led to the assignment. This is another technique that may function to discourage leniency errors from operating in the ratings.

Errors of leniency may also reflect a rater's inability to interpret in behavioral terms the attributes being evaluated. For example, raters asked to evaluate subordinates in terms of abstract traits such as leadership, judgment, and adaptability may find it difficult to draw sharp distinctions among ratees. Under these circumstances, raters may develop a judgmental strategy that leads them to concentrate their judgments in a given area of the scale. This difficulty may be dealt with by sharpening the definition of the scale anchors and tying them more closely to observable behaviors. Training raters in observational and rating techniques may also be effective (Spool, 1978).

---

[3]Severity errors are the complement of leniency errors. This type of bias shows itself in an inordinate number of low ratings.

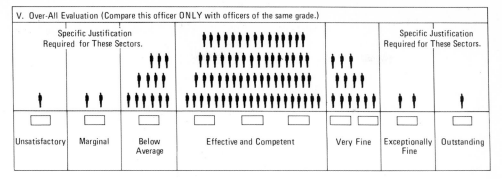

FIGURE 4.5   A forced-distribution scale used to rate Air Force officers. The recommended distribution of ratings is depicted by the small human figures in the sectors above the rating categories. Notice that specific, that is, written justification is required whenever a ratee is assigned to the lower three sectors and the top two sectors.

Source: Air Force form 475, *Training Report* **(discontinued).**

Central Tendency Bias.   This type of bias results in a distribution of ratings that concentrates in the middle regions of the rating scale. Distributions of this sort may reflect a number of different problems in the evaluation system, one of which being a reluctance on the part of the rater to commit himself to extreme ratings that might require some additional justification. The middle categories of rating scales can also serve as a ''dumping ground'' for uncertain judgments. Ambiguous behavioral anchors, ill-defined performance dimensions, and employees whose performance is inconsistent—that is, sometimes effective, sometimes inept—all may lead to ratings that concentrate in the middle of the scale.

Halo Errors.   We have already mentioned the halo effect in connection with the discussion of interviewing procedures. Briefly, a halo effect is a bias that occurs when judgments made with respect to one aspect of an individual's performance influence the judgments made with respect to other dimensions of performance. In many instances this type of error probably progresses from the general to the specific. A supervisor may form a general impression of the quality of an employee's per-

formance and then proceed to assign a rating to specific job dimensions in a manner that is consistent with the overall evaluation. There is also little to prevent halo error from originating in aspects of an employee's relationship with the rater that should not enter the rating task. Personal biases, of one sort or another—for example, attitudes toward women, blacks, or a particular style of behavior—may serve as the foundation on which a whole set of specific ratings are built.

Halo errors can also stem from a situation in which the rater is unable to clearly define or successfully differentiate among the traits that are to be considered. Here, once again, care in the selection of traits and anchors, coupled with a training session that attempts to clearly identify the behavioral implications of each trait, may be of some help in overcoming halo errors. The signal to consider the possibility of halo errors operating in a merit-rating program comes from an examination of the interrelationships among the individual scales. High correlations among these scales indicate that the scales tend to be tapping similar aspects of performance, and that there is a redundancy in the measurement. Perhaps, under these circumstances, some of the individual scales can be eliminated without affecting the final standing of the ratees. Whatever the course of action taken, it is essential that one be aware of the pattern of interrelationship among scale items, since this pattern may reflect the presence of an unwanted halo error that is influencing the evaluations that are being made.

Problems of Definition.   A serious problem in psychological research results from the many alternatives that may be used to measure certain behavioral concepts. By approaching a concept from different sets of measurement operations, psychologists often end up measuring different facets of behavior while thinking about them as if they were identical. A case in point is found in the rating literature where Saal, Downey, and Lahey (1980) found considerable lack of uniformity in the conceptual and operational definitions used by researchers to identify a given type of rating error. For example, these authors found that four different conceptual and three different operational definitions of leniency/severity bias have been used in studies evaluating the measurement quality of rating scales. As a result, when different rating-scale formats were compared with respect to their susceptibility to leniency/severity errors, the relative superiority of a given format varied as a function of the methods by which the errors were measured. All this gives the research literature the appearance of considerable inconsistency and results in the kind of confusion that might be expected when people apply a single concept to different facets of behavior. It is apparent from this, that a meaningful analysis of the psychology of subjective judgment will depend on the progress that is made in reaching some clear conceptual and operational definitions of the terms that are involved.

Scale Format and Bias

One of the objectives of scale construction procedures is to reduce the influence of rater bias. The critical-incident technique attempts to create a situation in which the rater serves as an objective observer rather than an evaluator. The forced-choice procedure strives for a similar outcome by attempting to obscure the scoring key that underlies the ratings. The behaviorally anchored scale seeks to reduce bias by clarifying the definition of the behaviors to be evaluated. Hence, the elimination of subjective bias is an objective shared by many rating procedures; and in the light of this, one may question whether the format of the scale does, in fact, have a bearing on the accuracy of ratings. For example, is it realistic to rely on the format of the instrument to improve the accuracy of ratings and reduce the halo and leniency biases that plague merit evaluation programs?

In turning to the research that has been done on this topic (cf. Landy & Farr, 1980; Cascio & Valenzi, 1977; Bernardin, 1977; Dunnette & Borman, 1979), one finds no clear indication that any one rating format is consistently superior to others. In fact, what one does find is that the relative merits of one or another of these scales seem to vary from one rating situation to the next. For example, Borman (1979) carried out a study that compared ratings obtained from five different scale formats. Three of the formats used a series of graded behavioral statements; a fourth involved a set of personal traits that were found to be important for effective performance. A fifth format used a simple numerical scale that required the rater to rate performance in terms of a set of scales that identified several dimensions of the task. Numerical ratings were made for each dimension.

The results of the study revealed that no single format was consistently superior to the other four. The relative effectiveness of any given technique seemed to vary with the job being evaluated. In addition, within a given job, some performance dimensions were evaluated better with one format than with another. One result was of particular significance: there seemed to be little relationship between the sophistication of the scaling procedure and its general effectiveness. The BARS-type scales, for example, performed no better than a simple numerical rating scale. Hence, the substantial investment in construction effort required by behaviorally anchored scales did not lead to ratings that were consistently more accurate than those obtained from a graphic rating scale employing a set of abstract numerical anchors. One of the more consistent results of the Borman study was that certain dimensions of job performance were more accurately rated than other facets of work performance. It seems, therefore, that the characteristics of the behavior to be evaluated may be more important than the format of the instrument used to make the evaluations.

Perhaps the best way to summarize the status of our knowledge regarding scale format and bias is to quote Landy and Farr (1980, p. 89), who, after reviewing the research in the area, maintain that after ''more than 30 years of serious research, it seems that little progress has been made in developing an efficient and psychometrically sound alternative to the traditional graphic rating scale.'' To be sure, our understanding of the measurement requirements of effective rating has been advancing, but one of the rewards of this progress has been a broadening awareness of the complexity of the problem. This is an important step, and the research going on today is doing a better job of incorporating the complexities of the merit evaluation task into its experimental designs. In the light of this, there is reason to expect continued progress in the area.

Bias and the Rater

In order to understand the complexities and frailties of merit evaluation one must consider the role of raters and the conditions under which they function. We have already discussed some of the social-political factors that influence the outcome of merit ratings. Recall from that discussion that the rater may perceive the evaluation task as an activity that contains many threats and few benefits for the individual who attempts to carry out the ratings with accuracy and objectivity. In all probability, many of the more difficult problems encountered in merit ratings stem from perceptions such as this. To avoid these problems it is essential for the rater to believe that ratings are being made for purposes that are constructive and personally beneficial. To see a threat to one's own job in these evaluations virtually ensures that the ratings

will be distorted and inaccurate. No easy prescription can be written for the kind of psychological climate required, but it seems clear that effective merit ratings must be built on a tradition of good employee relations. In organizations that have not maintained these cordial relationships, it may be impossible to construct and implement a good evaluation program.

In addition to these general considerations, there are other variables associated with the rater that have been found to influence the rating process. For example, raters vary among themselves with regard to the standards they use to evaluate performance. In some instances, raters may use their own job performance as a basis upon which the performance of others is evaluated. In line with this it is sometimes found that raters who are themselves comparatively competent tend to apply higher standards than do raters whose performance is lower in effectiveness. A study by Bass (1968) bears on this point. In this study Bass asked graduate business students to make a set of wage recommendations for a group of engineers whose performance in a fictitious company was described. When asked to rate these employees, raters who were lower in intelligence and achievement tended to assign higher salary increases than did raters who appeared to be more able. Kirchner and Reisberg (1965) and Mandell (1956) also report that supervisors who have a relatively poor job performance tend to be poorer raters of others. Hence, we must recognize that among the many anchors that may be used to make merit evaluations, the personal attributes of the rater can serve as a point of reference on which to base the ratings.

Multiple Ratings. In view of the importance of merit evaluations to an employee's career, it is often valuable to obtain ratings from more than a single rater. In some respects, evaluations that are a product of several judges are more acceptable, since multiple ratings provide some protection against the biased or inaccurate supervisor who misevaluates an employee. One is more likely to feel confident in the face of a clear consensus among several independent raters, although interrater agreement in and of itself does not guarantee accuracy.

In theory, two or more raters who are well acquainted with both the ratee and the performance criteria should arrive at essentially the same evaluations. That this does not always happen is the result of several factors that are often difficult to control. For example, even though raters have equal opportunity to observe and are focused on the same aspects of behavior, they may still differ widely in the standards of performance they hold. What is excellent performance to the foreman may only be average performance to the general foreman. There are a number of studies (Zedeck et al., 1974; Schneier, Beatty, & Beatty, 1976; Schneier & Beatty, 1978) that demonstrate different rating standards operating at different levels of an organization. For example, Schneier and Beatty (1978) had employees and supervisors rate the extent to which a group of 138 critical incidents expressed meritorious performance. They also used the same incidents to evaluate a group of rank-and-file employees. When rating the incidents themselves, the supervisors assigned higher scale values than did their subordinates. This suggests that the superiors perceived these behaviors as expressing higher levels of performance than did their subordinates. When actually using these incidents to evaluate subordinate behavior, however, the superiors tended to assign lower ratings than did rank-and-file employees who were rating their peers. Hence, both in the perception of the rating standards used and in the evaluation of performance, there were significant differences between raters who occupied different positions in the organization.

Results such as these illustrate the difficulties one encounters in trying to obtain comparable ratings from several evaluators. Individuals who occupy different positions in the organizational structure not only observe the work of an employee from different vantage points, but in filling their various organizational roles they may be led to approach the rating task with a different judgmental orientation and a different set of rating standards.

Ability to Rate.   There is one final consideration regarding the influence of a rater on the outcome of merit evaluations: that raters vary widely in their ability to observe and evaluate behavior. For example, Schneier (1977) has reported a study that first measured the ability of raters to perceive complex behavior. Next, he gave these raters two scales, one requiring complex observations, the other requiring relatively simple perceptions. Schneier found that those raters who were more able to deal with complexities could rate more effectively when using the complex scale. Those who were less able tended to produce a higher number of leniency and halo errors when using this complex scale.

The results of this study lead us to think about the level of compatibility existing between the rater and the judgment task. It also suggests that within a single organization one can find supervisors who vary widely in their ability to observe and evaluate behaviors that are beyond certain levels of complexity. Perhaps with training these differences would disappear, but we have already seen that training is no absolute guarantee that ratings will be carried out effectively.

Reliability of Ratings

Large components of unsystematic error in a set of merit ratings indicates that a problem of scale unreliability exists. Low levels of reliability indicate that the scores obtained from a scale are being influenced by sets of random factors that are obscuring the behaviors the scale is attempting to measure. Low reliability shows itself in ratings for which there is little agreement among different raters, or in ratings of a single rater who is inconsistent from one rating period to the next. Evidence of adequate levels of reliability is essential if a scale is to yield meaningful information.

Although a large amount of evidence has been accumulated regarding the reliability of merit-rating procedures, it would be difficult to make an overall appraisal of the measurement status of these scales. Reliability is not an intrinsic property of a given scale, but is an expression of the accuracy of measurement that is obtained from an entire work setting. This setting involves a specific group of ratees and a group of raters who are reporting on a specified set of behavioral dimensions. A given scale may, therefore, display good reliability in one situation and unacceptable reliability in another. For example, a well-constructed rating scale used to evaluate a clearly defined behavioral dimension may show low agreement among raters. The reason for this apparently low scale reliability might be traced to the fact that these raters differ in the perspective from which they view these behaviors. A foreman and a general foreman may show low agreement in their ratings, not because of any inherent unreliability in the rating instrument or in the behaviors being evaluated, but because they view these behaviors from different organizational vantage points (Schneier & Beatty, 1978). Hence, reliability estimates, when applied to merit rating procedures, express a summary of the measurement accuracy one might expect from an entire situation of which the rating scale is only a part.

In view of these complexities, it would seem reasonable to ask, what are the highest levels of reliability one might expect using one of the standard merit-rating procedures? Borman (1978) attempted to answer this question in a study that estimated the upper limits of reliability one might obtain from job performance ratings made under ideal circumstances. Using BARS in a laboratory setting, trained raters eveluted work performance that had been carefully recorded on videotape. Under these ideal conditions Borman found evidence of reliability that approached the high levels often achieved by standardized psychological tests. For example, evidence of interrater reliability appeared to be quite high on a majority of the behavioral dimensions evaluated.

There were problems, however. In spite of the good overall agreement among raters, there were instances in which large rater disagreements occurred, even under conditions that were conducive to good evaluation. For instance, while rating performance on a seven-point scale, there were oc-

casions in which two raters disagreed on a rating by as much as five scale points. Nevertheless, even though the ratings in Borman's study did not reflect perfect reliability, the levels observed placed these scales well within a range that can be considered acceptable.

PERFORMANCE APPRAISAL FEEDBACK

Up to this point our discussion has been primarily concerned with the measurement aspects of performance evaluation. In earlier sections we did consider some of the organizational influences affecting appraisal systems, but thus far little attention has been given to the psychological consequences of these programs. Usually, when one thinks about how people react to performance appraisals, interest begins to focus on the feedback mechanisms that are used to transmit information about the outcome of an evaluation. Feedback activities generally involve some type of interview between superior and subordinate and, as a rule, performance evaluation programs set up procedures for this kind of meeting. For example, a nationwide survey of work organizations conducted by the Bureau of National Affairs (1974) found that 91 percent of these firms had provisions for discussing performance appraisals with their employees, and the most typical arrangement was an appraisal interview.

The appraisal interview may be thoroughly planned or its content may be left to the discretion of the supervisor. One program, described by Latham and Wexley (1981), used an appraisal interview that encouraged employees to adopt performance goals that would lead them to attain excellence in their work. Excellence was defined by a group of critical incidents that were prepared and incorporated into a behaviorally based rating scale. Both supervisor and subordinate completed the scale, and the results were discussed in terms of setting performance goals that would achieve higher scores in the next rating period.

Latham and Wexley report that when specific

goals were set there was a significant improvement in job performance. During the six-month interval following the interview, individuals who achieved or exceeded their goals received rewards that involved money, praise, or public recognition. Rewards were found to increase the level of performance (money was the most effective); however, the largest performance gains were not attributed to rewards but to the goal-setting activities that took place in the feedback sessions. Feedback without goal setting was no more effective in improving performance than was no feedback at all. Hence, we find in this report evidence of the potential motivational consequences of a performance evaluation program. When evaluations are used in conjunction with appropriate reward and goal setting techniques, it is possible that improved performance levels may be observed in a work group.

Appraisals and Communications

Throughout the chapter. performance evaluation has been referred to as an information system. From this perspective, merit rating scales are seen as instruments that are used to gather information, and it is in the feedback process that this information is transmitted to others in the organization. Hence, a performance evaluation program can be thought of as being one of the channels of communication that operates within the firm; and when viewed from this perspective, the system may be analyzed into three basic components of a communications act—source, message, and recipient. Ilgen, Fisher, and Taylor (1979) have done this, and in doing so have given us a convenient structure within which to study the psychological processes operating in feedback mechanisms.

Source.   An employee may receive feedback from a number of different sources, and there is evidence suggesting that these sources are not equivalent in their influence on behavior. This evidence comes from a study by Greller and Herold (1975), which asked workers in a number of organizations to indicate the extent to which they relied on five different sources of feedback. The sources considered were:

1. The organization (that is, performance appraisal)
2. The supervisor
3. Coworkers
4. The task
5. One's self

The self emerged as the source that was seen as being the most influential in providing information concerning the effectiveness of the individual's work. Furthermore, the general pattern of results suggests that workers tend to rely on feedback sources that are close to them rather than on those that operate within the formal structures of the organization.

Does this mean that the feedback workers receive from a company's performance evaluation program is always less important than their own assessment of job performance? Probably not, since much depends not only on the proximity of the feedback source but also on its credibility, power, and trustworthiness. Proximity of the source may, therefore, be a factor that is influential in determining the consequences of feedback, but these other variables produce another set of influences that must be taken into consideration. Hence, a powerless source that is close to the recipient may exert less influence than a distant organizational source that possesses considerable power.

Message.   Ilgen, Fisher, and Taylor (1979) identify three properties of the feedback message that play a role in determining its consequences—time, sign, and frequency. Time refers to the interval between performance and feedback, and as a general rule, the longer the delay between performance and feedback, the less effective is the feedback. When viewed from the perspective of an appraisal program, a set of evaluations often serve to summarize behavior that has taken place over a considerable period of time. Conceivably, some of the behaviors that enter into a given rating may have occurred several months earlier. This may create problems, rendering the impact of the feedback less potent; however, we do not know much about how time influences the probability of a behavior entering into the rating scheme of the evaluator. Intuition would lead one to guess that behaviors occurring near the end of the evaluation period will exert more influence on the *evaluator*—that is, will carry greater weight—than will events that occurred several months earlier in the rating period. This is a question that should receive some research attention.

Whether feedback is positive or negative is an important factor in determining its impact on the employee. For example, Ilgen, Fisher, and Taylor (1979) cite information indicating that positive feedback is more accurately perceived and more readily accepted than is negative feedback. The relationship is complex, however, and no simple generalizations concerning the consequences of praise and reproof appear to be warranted. The general drift of the findings seems to give support to the superior benefits of positive feedback (cf. Latham & Wexley, 1981), yet O'Reilly and Weitz (1980) report that the more frequent use of informal warnings, formal warnings, and dismissals seem to be associated with higher levels of performance among groups of workers whose job conduct has been marginal. On the other hand, Greenberg (1977) found that an individual's general orientation toward work was a factor that played a role in determining the behavioral consequences of positive and negative feedback. Individuals with a high commitment to the Protestant Work Ethic improved task performance after *both* positive and negative feedback. Persons with low commitment to the work ethic also improved their performance after positive feedback, but displayed a significant decline in performance after receiving negative feedback.

Finally, studies carried out at General Electric (Kay, Meyer, & French, 1965) found that criticisms by the supervisor during the appraisal interview were less likely to result in improved work performance. Furthermore, as the number of criticisms increased, there was also a significant increase in the number of defensive reactions shown by the employee. Hence, in summary, it appears that praise during an appraisal interview is more constructive than reproof; but reproof, especially if it is accompanied by a constructive effort to help the employee improve performance, is a tactic that can, under some circumstances, be used with some hope of success.

The frequency with which performance evaluations are made is a factor that influences their behavioral impact. How many times during the year should an employee be subjected to a work appraisal? Much, of course, depends on the consistency of work performance, and this is a subject about which social scientists know little (Rothe, 1978; Rambo, Chomiak, & Price, 1981). Ilgen, Fisher, and Taylor (1979) say that more frequent feedback leads to improved performance, and Landy, Barnes, and Murphy (1978) find that employees perceive more frequent feedback as being fairer. Yet if too frequent, feedback may be perceived by the employees as a threat to their autonomy. The supervisor who is always making evaluative comments may be perceived as providing little freedom for the work group. Finally, workers may become dependent on the directions that are given by the feedback, and hence, too frequent feedback may stifle employee initiative and independence. The evidence suggests that there is some optimal range for the number of feedback sessions each year, but at the present it would be hazardous to prescribe the exact numbers defining this range. Remember, however, that formal merit evaluations are but one of a number of different sources from which workers obtain feedback; quarterly or semiannual evaluations do not represent the only information an employee obtains about job performance. Basically, they represent management's formal view of this performance.

The Recipient.   The recipient is the most complicated of the components in the feedback cycle.

FIGURE 4.6   Model of the Effects of Feedback on Recipients.

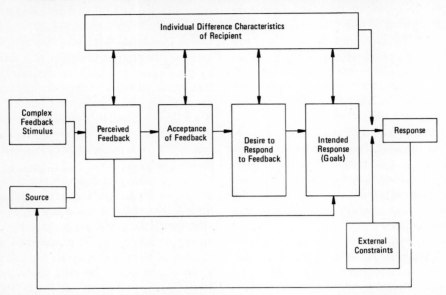

Psychological processes linking feedback stimuli with the worker's response. Notice the contribution of individual difference variables to the feedback system.

Source: Ilgen, D. R., Fisher, C. O., & Taylor, M. S. Consequences of individual feedback on behavior in organizations. Copyright 1979 American Psychological Association. Reprinted by permission.

Although the source and the message are important determinants of the outcome of a feedback system, the perception of these two elements by the recipient is the main link in the chain (see Figure 4.6). The employee's personality is an important aspect of the psychology of feedback, and there is some evidence that workers differ in the extent to which they are dependent upon sources of feedback that are internal or external to themselves. The personality variable, *locus of control* (Rotter, 1966), is one likely prospect for this relationship. There is a considerable amount of evidence indicating that people differ according to how they perceive the agents of change that influence the events taking place in their lives. There are some, called *internals,* who tend to perceive life events as being the result of their own behavior. Others, called *externals,* tend to attribute these events to luck, to the intervention of more powerful individuals, or to forces they cannot understand. Considering the five sources of feedback studied by Greller and Herold (1975), the worker with a high internal ori-

entation will probably be more responsive to feedback that comes from the task or from self-evaluations; the external will depend more on feedback coming fom supervisory or organizational sources. Self-esteem, confidence, and anxiety are additional variables that probably relate to the perception of feedback information, and Ilgen, Fisher, and Taylor (1979) conclude their search of this research by maintaining that the perception of feedback is selective, being fitted within the personal frame of reference of each individual employee. To understand feedback mechanisms, therefore, the supervisor must be able to develop a sensitivity to the individual personality characteristics of those whose work will be evaluated.

Summary Comments.   Perhaps the best way to conclude this discussion of work appraisal feedback is to list the characteristics of a good feedback system. This is a list developed by Burke, Weitzel, and Weir (1978), who maintain that a good feedback program involves:

1. High levels of subordinate participation in the appraisal and development process
2. A helpful and constructive attitude on the part of the supervisor
3. Mutual setting of specific goals to be achieved by the subordinate
4. Solving problems that may be hampering the subordinate's current performance
5. Restraint on the number of criticisms given by the supervisor
6. Opportunity for the subordinate to talk and express his or her views

When a performance evaluation system is supported by an effective training program, these characteristics appear to be well within a work organization's reach; and this brings us to another consideration, the effectiveness of the training activities that are used to teach raters how to carry out their evaluations.

TRAINING RATERS

It is generally assumed that a merit rating program will include a training component that is used to prepare raters for their assignment. In addition to the obvious need to prepare raters in the specific procedures that will be used, it is not unusual for these programs to attempt to reduce the influence of the common types of rating bias that plague subjective evaluations. In addition, special efforts are sometimes make to improve the accuracy of the ratings by instructing the raters in the techniques of behavioral observation (Bernardin & Pence, 1980; Spool, 1978).

Effectiveness of Training

There have been numerous studies carried out in order to determine whether training is really effective in improving the general quality of ratings, and the results thus far seem to indicate that it is possible to improve some aspects of the ratings, while other dimensions have not readily given way to training efforts. For example, rater training has frequently been able to reduce rating biases such as leniency and halo errors (Bernardin, 1977, 1978; Bernardin & Walter, 1977; Bernardin & Pence, 1980; Borman, 1975, 1979). In one of these studies, Borman (1979) used a series of films that depicted different degrees of merit in the per-

formance of two tasks—recruitment interviewing and managers solving problems involving a troublesome employee. The construction of these films relied on carefully prepared scripts for the performers, who were subjected to a set of ratings by experts who judged the merit of each performance according to a well-developed set of criteria. Associated with each performance, therefore, was a "true" score that had been obtained from these expert ratings. As a consequence, it was possible to calculate how far other individual raters missed these true scores in situations where only some of the raters had received training. This permitted a determination of the accuracy of the ratings under different training conditions.

Two groups of raters, one receiving three hours of training on observational errors and rating biases, the other receiving no training, rated different levels of performance depicted for the two jobs. Ratings used several different rating formats, and estimates of bias were calculated. The results showed that the training sessions seemed to reduce halo errors, but this was true only for the recruiter job and not for the managers' job. *Furthermore, accuracy of the ratings did not improve with training.* It would appear, therefore, that a training program may not be equally effective for all jobs, and that it may be necessary to adapt training to the particular set of jobs to be evaluated during any given period.

There are further complications. First, a number of studies have found that the effects of this type of training tend to dissipate quite rapidly over time (Bernardin, 1978; Ivancevich, 1979), and may not transfer readily out of the training sessions to improve ratings that are made in an on-the-job situation (Warmke & Billings, 1979). Also, in instances in which it is possible to obtain an estimate of the accuracy of ratings, that is, the extent to which ratings are related to the true quality of work performance, there is little evidence that training is effective in improving this aspect of the evaluations (Borman, 1979). Spool (1978) reports a review of training studies that have attempted to improve the accuracy of ratings. He finds that the training designs that have been employed usually involve some mix of lecture, demonstration, practice, and feedback. Spool maintains that these studies indicate that the accuracy of ratings can be improved by training. There have, however, been too many instances of failure in this area to warrant general optimism about the effectiveness of training in improving the accuracy of ratings. In fact there have been several reports in which training actually had a negative effect on the ratings (Crow, 1957; Bunney & Hamburg, 1963; Borman, 1975; Bernardin & Pence, 1980). Much may depend on the content of training.

Content of Training

Bernardin and Pence (1980) maintain that the typical program to improve the quality of performance evaluations involves training that attempts to change the rater's response distribution, thereby avoiding errors of leniency and halo. In these instances, trainees are presented with graphical representations of the rating distributions that are characteristic of the various types of errors (see Figure 4.7). Training is directed toward avoiding these types of distributions, since they signal the presence of biasing influences.

A second general approach to rater training focuses on developing observational skills that improve the accuracy of ratings. Bernardin and Pence name this type of training *rater accuracy training* (RAT), as contrasted with *rater error training* (RET), which involves familiarizing raters with the distributions of ratings that are associated with different types of bias. They describe a RAT program that consisted of the following components:

1. A lecture describing the multidimensional characteristics of most work. The need to keep these dimensions separate when observing work was emphasized.
2. The importance of fair, unbiased ratings was stressed.

3. Trainees then developed and defined dimensions that applied to the job they were going to evaluate. They discussed critical examples of high, medium, and low behaviors for each dimension.

Bernardin and Pence (1980) compared RET and RAT training in a study where students evaluated performance of classroom instructors. A third group received no training prior to making their ratings. The results indicated that the RET training did succeed in reducing both leniency and halo errors when these ratings were compared with those obtained from the RAT and control groups. When ratings were evaluated for accuracy, the RET group was found to be significantly less accurate than the RAT group and the control group that had received no training. Hence, RET training appeared to result in ratings that were less accurate then were those that were obtained from a group that received no training at all; however, there was

also no significant difference between this control group and the RAT group that had been trained specifically to improve its accuracy.

This is a disappointing result, and one that bears further consideration by researchers. The Bernardin and Pence study clearly indicates that the content of a training program can significantly influence the errors of rating, but these authors were apparently unable to design a program that improved accuracy any better than that observed with no training at all. They did, however, find that training in reducing rating errors tended to result in *lower* levels of rating accuracy while also reducing the frequency of rating bias.

The general impression one gets from this train-

FIGURE 4.7 Material Used To Train Raters To Identify the Consequences of Leniency and Halo Errors

Halo Error	Dimension ratings on one ratee						
Rater	A	B	C	D	E	F	G
1	9	9	8	9	8	9	8
2	9	6	4	5	6	4	8
Who is commiting halo error, Rater 1 or 2?						(Answer: Rater 1)	

Leniency Error	Ratees						
Rater	A	B	C	D	E	F	G
1	9	3	6	5	4	8	2
2	9	8	9	7	8	7	9
Who is commiting leniency error, Rater 1 or 2?						(Answer: Rater 2)	

Source: Bernardin, H. J., & Pence, E. C. Effects of training: Creating new response sets and decreasing accuracy. *Journal of Applied Psychology*, 1980, *65,* 60–66. Copyright 1980 by the American Psychological Association. Reprinted by permission.

ing literature is that a performance evaluation program, to be carried out in a manner that serves the interests of both employer and employee, requires a considerable investment in time and effort. It is always tempting to work up a rating form of some sort and pass it out to supervisors under the assumption that their job experience qualifies them to provide accurate personnel evaluations. Unfortunately, this is not always true, and as a consequence every performance evaluation system should involve a variety of personnel procedures to ensure that the system functions in a way that was intended. One of these procedures is a well constructed training program. At the present time, however, there is need for additional research that will give us guidance in structuring the content of these programs. Spool (1978) suggests, and Bernardin and Pence's study demonstrates, that in order to be successful in improving the validity of ratings, training must involve more than just a lecture on the types and causes of rating error.

LEGAL CONSIDERATIONS

One of the potential consequences of performance evaluation is a set of personnel decisions that operate to deny employees equal opportunity as defined by federal law. Performance evaluations are particularly vulnerable to claims that they are being manipulated to prevent qualified people from receiving fair treatment, and federal laws and regulations have been written to deal with this problem.

The legal considerations surrounding performance evaluations are basically the same as those that apply to selection and placement procedures (see Chapter 2). Fundamental to the proper application of these appraisal procedures is the availability of evidence concerning their validity and reliability. The standards of *adverse impact,* as defined in the 1978 EEOC Guidelines, also serve as a principal test of the legality of these procedures. Furthermore, legislation recently passed into law specifically refers to the use of performance appraisal systems. This law, the Civil Service Reform Act of 1978, contains regulations that govern employee evaluation in many federal agencies. The act directs these agencies to develop appraisal systems, and it prescribes that these procedures should possess the following characteristics:

1. Appraisal systems should be developed with employee participation in the construction of performance standards.
2. Evaluations must be conducted *at least* on an annual bias.
3. All appraisals should be recorded in writing.
4. Standards used should be based on elements that are critical to the performance of the job.
5. The procedures followed in developing performance standards should be recorded in writing, and employees should be informed of the nature of these standards before evaluations are made.
6. Evaluations must be based on critical job elements.
7. Decisions regarding personnel actions, such as promotion, demotion, and reassignment, must be based on the results of the appraisal.
8. Employees should have opportunity to ask for a review of their ratings done by an employer in a higher level position before the ratings become final.
9. Training must be provided to those who supply the evaluations, and the program must be subject to periodic review to determine its impact and general effectiveness.

These appear to be stringent requirements, but most of them are not far removed from standard practices that would normally be pursued by professionally run evaluation systems. In essence, they require only that the system function as its purpose dictates. Under these circumstances, both employee and work organization benefit. Still, one must recognize that the involvement of governmental influences in merit-assessment programs might serve as a further sociopolitical consideration that might enter into the rating strategies adopted by those who are responsible for personnel appraisal.

SUMMARY COMMENTS

Great strides have been made in the development of sophisticated measurement procedures useful in merit evaluation. Forced choice, BARS, and paired comparisons are a few of the more advanced techniques available to an organization wishing to measure performance quality. In spite of developments in scale format, however, there has been little progress in extending our understanding of the complicated social and motivational factors that influence the outcome of merit ratings. In their simplest form, merit ratings involve a measurement procedure that operates within the relationship between two people. In their most complex form, merit ratings take place within the social-political dynamics of the entire work organization. Hence, to consider only the construction of a rating instrument and the technical details of its format is to overlook many of the more important variables that influence the quality of merit ratings.

In spite of the many problems that have been discussed in this chapter, one should not ingnore the fact that merit rating scales have frequently proved to yield accurate and reliable information concerning work performance. Furthermore, an organization usually has no alternative to making an investment in a carefully constructed performance evaluation system. Performance evaluations take place regardless of whether they are systematized or not; therefore, it is essential that adequate attention be given to developing a good program. Such a program not only has built-in checks and balances that protect both employees and employer from unfair and inaccurate assessment, but it also serves as a source of constructive feedback that gives guidance to employees who desire to serve an organization more effectively. Hence, a merit rating system contributes to a program of employee counseling that is directed toward strengthening employees' performance and improving their general adjustment to work.

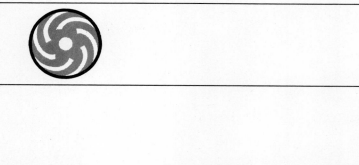

2
WORK
AND
THE
INDIVIDUAL

5
The Psychological Importance of Work

The expectation that one will eventually join the labor force and take a job develops out of our early social learning. Work is the bedrock of a culture, and the general understanding that a person will one day assume a work role permeates every facet of the social world in which the individual is reared. The appearance of behaviors that anticipate formal work may be found quite early in childhood. For example, one can point to the play activities of young children (Cass, 1971) as evidence of the early antecedents that lead to an adult work role. Children's games often take on an occupational theme reflecting an early interest in the requirements of work.

Although the period of childhood play may be followed by one in which the person engages in part-time work such as a newspaper route, garden work, and the like, the time arrives when the individual enters the labor market in search of full-time employment. For many this step is associated with certain events, such as leaving school or marriage, that are involved in assuming an adult role in the community. But whatever the events surrounding one's entry into a career, it soon becomes evident that the job requires a substantial investment of the individual's psychological resources. The job becomes a major part of the individual's life.

But how important is work to the individual? To what extent do people see a job as a central focus of life? One may find that for many there are family, community, and recreational alternatives that may serve as the primary object of personal interest. For others work may be the most important aspect of their lives. It is apparent that individuals vary widely in the personal investment they make in work, and it is this fact that serves as the subject matter of the present chapter. The primary question to be raised is, is it possible to describe the extent to which workers are committed to their jobs; and if we can, what are the factors that underlie this involvement with work?

JOB INVOLVEMENT

The topic of job involvement is of fundamental importance to the study of work behavior. The level of job involvement is a factor that relates to a worker's motivational orientation toward a specific job and the work role. It concerns both the amount a worker invests in the job and the general importance of the psychological consequences of working. Job involvement, therefore, refers to both inputs and outcomes. Related to this, an individual's commitment to a job is a factor that must be considered if one is to understand how various aspects of work impact on the individual worker. For example, individual differences in the level of job involvement probably underlie the differences one observes in workers' responses to incentive systems. The prospect of promotion may exert a substantial motivational pull on an employee who has a high commitment to work, whereas similar prospects may be insignificant to the employee with low commitment. In this sense job involvement may be thought of as a generalized motivational orientation that plays a role in influencing an employee's response to a job.

Job involvement itself is also an outcome of work. Rabinowitz and Hall (1977) cite evidence suggesting that the experience of success in a task will increase involvement. A worker who finds important sources of satisfaction and success in a job is likely to become more involved in it. In a similar vein, negative job experiences may also lead to heightened job involvement. For instance, a worker attempting to cope with such things as work pressures may display an increased involvement in work. These topics will be considered in more detail later, but for the moment it is clear that a study of the job involvement literature will provide some insight into one of the interesting consequences of both positive and negative work experience.

Throughout the chapter several terms will be used to refer to the psychological importance of work. Two of these terms, involvement and commitment, will be used interchangeably in dealing with the *degree* to which a person perceives work to be an important aspect of life. A closely related question concerns whether work is *the most important* setting in which the individual carries out his daily activities. From this perspective, the psychological importance of work is approached by *ordering* different behavioral settings, for example, home, work, community. The setting ranked most important is referred to as the central life interest; and when this idea is applied to jobs, the term *work centrality* is often used.

Commitment to work, or job involvement, concerns the extent to which an individual invests psychological resources in a job. Psychological resources include time, talents, and energies. They also relate to the extent to which an individual's feeling of well-being and self-esteem are connected to the outcomes of work. The question here is, does the worker care about the outcomes of his

work? In addition, one of the more important indicators of job commitment is the extent to which an individual sees work as a place where one may achieve the personal goals of one's life plans.

Research by social scientists has given us a considerable amount of information that bears on these issues. Some of this literature involves a direct approach in which workers are asked for their judgments regarding the relative importance of work to their lives. One aspect of this research considers whether work is *the* central life interest of the individual.

Work—the Central Life Interest

Generally speaking, it is easy to be led into thinking that work serves as the central point of focus in an individual's life. At first glance, work roles seem to command so much of our energies that one might automatically conclude that an individual's job serves as the most important psychological commitment. The research available on this subject, however, has not been able to marshal a great deal of support for this point of view. In fact, the balance of the literature seems to point in a different direction.

For example, in one of the more widely cited studies, Dubin (1956) administered a questionnaire to a group of blue-collar industrial workers who were employed in three midwestern manufacturing plants. This instrument consisted of a series of items, each of which specified an activity. The respondents were asked to indicate whether they preferred to engage in each activity within a work setting, within a nonwork setting, or whether they were indifferent to the place where the activity took place. The results indicated that for almost 75 percent of the subjects, work was *not* the central life interest. To be sure, there were areas of their lives that they preferred to carry out in a work setting, but there were also many activities that they would rather have occur away from work. For instance, more than 90 percent preferred to have their social contacts in settings away from the job, whereas a large majority preferred to have their relations with formal organizations and with

TABLE 5.1   Central Life Interests of Industrial Workers, Middle Managers, and Specialists

Central Life Interest	Industrial Workers (Dubin, 1956) Percent	Middle Managers Percent	Technical Specialists Percent
	(N=491)	(N=404)	(N=96)
Work	24	43	41
Nonwork	76	57	59
Informal Relations			
Work	9	14	18
Nonwork	91	86	82
General Experience			
Work	15	45	34
Nonwork	85	55	66
Formal Organization			
Work	61	88	87
Nonwork	39	12	13
Technological Experience			
Work	63	79	85
Nonwork	37	21	15

Source: Dubin, R. S., and Goldman, D. R. Central life interests of American middle managers and specialists. *Journal of Vocational Behavior,* 1972, *2,* 133–141. Copyright, 1972, Academic Press. Published by permission of the author and publisher.

technical activities within the context of the job. As an example of the latter, these workers reported that they would prefer to receive awards or some type of recognition from their jobs than from some nonwork organization.

Work Centrality and Job Level.   In a second study, Dubin and Goldman (1972) administered a revised form of the *Central Life Interest* instrument to a group of middle managers and a group of technical specialists. Here it was also found (see Table 5.1) that a majority of these white-collar employees reported that their central life interests focused principally on nonwork activities. There was, however, a significant shift in the percent of those responding in this fashion. Whereas only 24 percent of the blue-collar workers saw their central life interests in their jobs, 43 percent of the middle-management employees and 41 percent of the technical specialists did so. Hence, even though a majority of the workers participating in these two studies did not define their fundamental life interests in terms of work, a significant increment in

those who did was found as one moved from a blue-collar to white-collar, management-specialist positions.

Along the same line, Goldman (1973) in a study of middle managers and specialists reports that 58 percent of his sample indicated that work did not serve as a central life interest. A second variable, however, the extent to which the employee expressed interest in upward mobility—that is, promotion and high status—significantly influenced these commitments. Goldman found that for the majority of those managers who placed high value on promotion, the job did in fact represent the fundamental commitment of their lives. For those who were upwardly mobile, work was seen as a medium through which one moves to achieve personal objectives. The job and job performance are perceived as being instrumental in attaining those opportunities for social success that are so highly valued, and under these circumstances work tends to move more toward the center of an individual's psychological world.

TABLE 5.2   Professional Nurses' Responses to Central Life Interest Instrument N = 150

Total CLI	Percent
Work	79
Nonwork	21
Informal Relations	
Work	45
Nonwork	55
General Relations	
Work	67
Nonwork	33
Formal Organization Relations	
Work	91
Nonwork	9
Technological Relations	
Work	87
Nonwork	13

Source: Orzack, L. H. Work as a central life interest of professionals. *Social Problems,* 1959, 7, 125–132.

Professional Work.   In a professional setting one would probably expect to find a higher frequency of those for whom the job is a central life interest. The years of formal preparation, the intellectual content of this type of work, and the increased personal autonomy are factors that may contribute to a work situation that is both rewarding and likely to receive a major investment in psychological resources. In a replication of Dubin's original work, Orzack (1959), surveying registered nurses, found that these suppositions were in fact true. Administering the *Central Life Interest* scale to a group of 150 professional nurses, Orzack found that almost 80 percent of those responding gave evidence that work was the central commitment of their interests. Orzack's results, found in Table 5.2, indicate that with the exception of informal social relations, these professionals reported that work was the principal social setting in which they preferred to carry out many of their daily activities.

These results suggest that it is within the content of the job that one may find the important influences that lead to high work centrality. Intuition would predict that jobs having more demanding skill requirements and greater variety would tend to occupy a more central position in an individual's life than would jobs whose skill requirements are low and whose duties are routine. In support of this supposition, Mannheim (1975) reports that workers on jobs having high scientific and technical content tend to indicate that work is a central life interest, whereas those in service-type jobs show significantly lower degrees of job involvement. Yet job content is only one factor underlying an individual's job involvement, and a worker's psychological makeup and background probably combine with the job situation to produce a given level of work involvement (Rabinowitz & Hall, 1977).

Comment.   When asked directly, workers often report that there are areas of their lives outside of work that they consider to be more central to their interests. Dubin (1956) contends that for many workers, attachment to work primarily involves those activities that are *required* by the job. Job involvement tends to revolve around the obligational aspects of work; and as work settings become more bureaucratized and impersonal, the principal basis for attachment is found in the technical components of work and in the organizational aspects of the work setting. Congenial social relationships are sought primarily in nonwork settings, or not sought at all.

The Pattern of Human Concerns

Another interesting source of information regarding the psychological significance of work may be found in a study of personal aspirations and human concerns that was carried out by Cantril (1966). International in its scope, the study surveyed opinions in eleven countries around the world using a survey instrument that included these two basic, open-ended questions:

a. "When you think about what really matters in your life, what are your wishes and hopes for the future?"

b. ". . . what are your fears and worries about the future?"

Space does not permit a summary of the broad results of this study; however, Table 5.3 reproduces Cantril's findings from the sample of 1549 cases obtained from the United States. Here we see that issues relating to work and working conditions fall well down on the list of aspirations and fears reported by these respondents. Concerns about health matters seem to head the list, and family and economic matters also seem to occupy high rankings. As might be expected, there was variation within the sample studied. With regard to fears concerning employment, Cantril found that it was not individuals in the lower-status occupations who were most concerned about employment, but rather those with a college education and higher status jobs who seemed to be most concerned with this aspect of their lives. This parallels the reports that work is a more central interest to those in higher-level jobs. Furthermore, only a very small percentage of older respondents, that is, those over fifty, reported concern over employment.

This study is particularly interesting in that it bears on the question of the psychological importance of work from a slightly different perspective. Instead of providing respondents with just two or three alternatives, such as work or nonwork, Cantril utilized an interviewing procedure in which the respondents had considerable freedom to construct their own responses. Here, people were asked what their hopes and fears were, and in response

they indicated that it was not in work but in the other areas of their lives that their aspirations and apprehensions lay. The major positives and negatives of their lives seemed to revolve around events that do not concern jobs and the work situation.

Choosing the Work Role

It is one thing to argue that a job is not the central life concern for many individuals, but it is quite another to maintain that work and the work role are of little psychological consequence. Granted, it is extremely difficult to obtain reliable direct evidence regarding the psychological importance of work, but there is a substantial amount of indirect data from which inferences can be drawn. For example, there are several studies available in which people have been given a choice between a job and nonwork with equivalent economic security. The weight of the evidence here seems to indicate that the majority of those confronted with this choice select work over nonwork.

In a survey employing a national sample of employed men, Morse and Weiss (1955) asked subjects whether they still would want to work if they were independently wealthy. Of a sample of 393 men responding to this question, 80 percent responded that they would continue to work in spite of this new-found wealth. It was only among the unskilled and older workers that the study found noticeable departures from this response; and even with these groups, a majority still opted for work.

TABLE 5.3 Personal Aspirations and Human Concerns

General Categories on the Personal Hopes of Americans	Percent	General Categories on the Personal Fears of Americans	Percent
Economic	65	Health	56
Health	48	Economic	46
Family	47	Family	25
Personal Values	20	International Situation, World	24
Status Quo	11	No Fears	12
Job or Work Situation	10	Job or Work Situation	5
International Situation, World	10	Political	5
Social Values	5	Personal Values and Character	3
Political	2	Social Values	3

Source: Cantril, H. *The pattern of human concerns.* Copyright © 1965 by Rutgers, The State University. Reprinted by permission of Rutgers University Press.

When asked why they chose this option, over two-thirds of the respondents gave reasons that indicated that desirable goals were to be found within the work situation; hence, work to them represented a goal-approach setting. Work was seen as a place where one could pursue a wide range of personal objectives. For the remaining one-third, the choice of work represented an avoidance of negative consequences. The majority of those responding indicated that work meant something more to them than earning a living. A job was seen as providing a more interesting life, a sense of contribution to the community, and a connection that certified their membership in society.

Similar results are reported by Tausky (1969), in a study that found that 82 percent of a national sample of blue-collar workers would continue to work even if economic considerations did not require it. Along the same lines, Kaplan and Tausky (1972) cite an unpublished study in which a sample of 151 middle-management personnel responded to a similar question. In this instance, 89 percent chose work over nonwork. Finally, in a study using 275 chronically unemployed persons, Kaplan and Tausky (1972) report that 84 percent of this group said that they would hold a job even if they had independent wealth.

This latter finding is of considerable interest, since it deals with people, living in poverty, for whom the employment market had proved to be a source of considerable failure and frustration. Under these circumstances some might expect that economic privation would displace the typical commitment to work in favor of what might be a more readily available source of income support, welfare. This was not the case in this instance, although when asked what is the most important thing about a job, 61.9 percent responded that a job represented a source of income to them. Nevertheless, the social status implications of job holding were still in evidence, as is seen in the response to a question that asked the respondent to choose between a job that was low paying but respectable and an average paying job that was held in low regard by one's friends. The majority of the sample, 57 percent, chose the low paying job.

Many might look at chronic unemployment in terms of motivational problems that stem from defects in the character and values of the individual. The individual with a long history of unemployment is frequently perceived as one who possesses a different orientation to work than does one who has a history of steady employment. This is not the case, according to the results of a study reported by Goodwin (1972), who stated his findings as follows:

> Poor people—males and females, blacks and whites, youths and adults—identify their self-esteem with work as strongly as do the non-poor. They express as much willingness to take job training if unable to earn a living and to work even if they were to have an adequate income. . . . This study reveals no differences between poor and non-poor when it comes to life goals and wanting to work. (p. 112)

It is also not the case according to a study that compared the work values of chronically unemployed persons with those expressed by successfully employed rank-and-file workers. Here Searls, Brauch, and Miskimins (1974) report no significant differences between the employed and the unemployed groups.

Much of the literature seems to suggest that in many respects the work orientations of the poor and the chronically unemployed are similar to those of persons in more affluent positions. Of particular interest is the *New Jersey Guaranteed Work Incentive Experiment* (Watts & Rees, 1977; Cogan, 1978) that was carried out to evaluate the consequences of a negative income tax program. In this experiment, families living in poverty were guaranteed an annual income, paid to those who chose not to work. For those who did work, the welfare portion of their income was reduced as their wages increased. Comparisons were made with a control group that did not receive these supplemental payments.

The result of the experiment indicated that the supplemental payments did serve as a *disincentive* to work. On the average, people receiving these payments worked fewer hours than did those in the control group. The guaranteed annual wage did not, however, result in any massive outflow of workers from the labor force. Job turnover for those who had jobs was significantly reduced; and although there was about a 2 percent increase in unemployment levels of male heads of households, younger participants seemed to be more successful in finding higher-status jobs.

This experiment, and several more like it, touched off an explosion of controversy (Anderson, 1978); but ignoring the public policy implications, the results of these studies all show that the commitment to the work role is still substantial even when the income benefits of work are available to those who choose to remain outside the labor force. The results are also of considerable interest in that they report on individuals facing a set of real-life alternatives. The previous studies we have considered presented individuals with a choice between work and nonwork, but these choices were purely hypothetical. Obviously, it is one thing to opt for work when the consequences of the choice have little bearing on the individual's life circumstances. It is another thing to choose work when a real and reasonably secure nonwork alternative is available. In choosing work under these circumstances, the individual is making a clear statement concerning the psychological importance of the work role as a commitment that carries with it implications other than income maintenance.

One should recognize that these results, agreeing as they do with the questionnaire data, also confirm another proposition: that verbal behavior, what others tell us, by and large represents a reasonably good approximation to their view of reality. This does not mean that one should accept the results of questionnaire research without caution, but one should not dismiss all such research as being meaningless and irrelevant.

Retirement Choices. There is one final aspect of the choice between work and nonwork that should be mentioned in passing. This is the choice an increasing number of workers face in considering early retirement, and the consequent decision to take on a second career after retiring. Of course these decisions may reflect as much the adequacy of a particular retirement program as they do a commitment to work itself. Nevertheless, large numbers of workers do continue to work after they are eligible to retire. For example, the *Monthly Labor Review* (1966) reports that 77 percent of all United Automobile Workers who were eligible for an early retirement program chose to continue working, and Messer (1964) reports that 8 percent of all those employed in Civil Service jobs were working beyond their retirement tenures. Of those retired, furthermore, he finds that approximately 58 percent had begun a second career. Along similar lines, Biderman (1964) reports that 80 percent of a sample of military retirees held some type of job, and 3 percent were in school in preparation for a second career.

Granted, this line of evidence is difficult to interpret, since income considerations figure so prominently in decisions to continue to work beyond the retirement age. As an example, Messer found that the majority of those who retire from the Civil Service continue to work because retirement income is seen as being inadequate for their needs. But apart from this, it is probably reasonable to assume that many who do not take early retirement or seek a new job after retiring from another do so because they are reluctant to abandon the work role. Not knowing how to spend their free time, not wanting to feel useless, and the fear that idleness will hasten death are factors that keep people in the work role. From this perspective we may view the data on retirement choices as a source of evidence that reflects some of the psychological significance of work and the work role.

Comment. The fact that work is an important aspect of many lives is hardly a revelation. What is more interesting is the evidence concerning the breadth of work commitment. It is not just specific things like wages or the social stimulation one receives from work associates, but it is also the work role itself that appears to serve important social-psychological functions. These functions are varied and complex, and many are not well understood. It does seem clear, however, that any serious effort to develop an understanding of worker motivation must consider the level of commitment made to the work role. This general orientation can be viewed as a background against which the more specific motivational pushes and pulls operate to produce a particular pattern of work behavior.

JOB INVOLVEMENT—EXPERIMENTAL STUDIES

Thus far the discussion has concentrated on survey-type studies that have attempted to assess the psychological importance of work. Now attention will shift to studies of a more experimental nature. These studies differ from surveys in that they use more integrated measurement scales. Scales of this type are comprised of series of items, each tapping an aspect of job involvement and each contributing to a total score that represents an individual's general orientation to work. Experimental studies also attempt to manipulate variables associated with the individual or the job in order to observe the contribution of these variables to the level of job involvement.

Recall that job involvement was previously defined as the extent to which an individual invests psychological resources in a job. Investing psychological resources means the extent to which an individual commits energies, talents, and his sense of self-esteem to the job. One important dimension of job involvement relates to the extent to which the individual is concerned about the consequences of his job performance. Indifference to performance outcomes implies low levels of job involvement; but when the worker sees job performance as being instrumental to the attainment of status and self-esteem, this constitutes a high level of involvement.

A related definition of job involvement deals with the extent to which an individual identifies with his work (Guion, 1958). By this we mean the degree to which individuals employ the work role, and their performance in it, to answer the question, "Who am I?" We would conclude that an individual who refers to his job and his work performance to support his feelings of self-importance and competence is highly involved with the work.

Some say that job involvement results from early social experiences in which the individual learns about the importance of work and its implications for the individual and the community (Lodahl, 1964). Hence from this point of view, job involvement relates to the value system maintained by the individual, and as such it is a characteristic that is relatively stable, not changing as the person faces one situation or another (Hall & Mansfield, 1971). Studies of industrial executives (Warner & Abegglen, 1955a; Powell, 1963; DeSola-Pool, 1964) indicate that this is characteristic of those who have been successful in moving up the organizational hierarchy. For many successful executives there is a history of high involvement with work that extends from the early teens up through the mature phase of their work careers.

A second point of view maintains that the level of job involvement is largely determined by the content of the job and the characteristics of the work organization. From this perspective, job involvement is a psychological reaction that is dependent upon the characteristics of the work situation. Hence, there is something about the job— its duties, its social setting, its opportunities for personal accomplishment—that generates the level of involvement experienced by the worker. Current concerns regarding the alienated worker are frequently traced to jobs that discourage personal involvement. Technological change has often been accused of removing from work the freedom and autonomy that encourage a high degree of personal commitment. Hence, it may well be that the problems of low job involvement are essentially engineering problems that revolve around the design of the job, and that programs of job enlargement and enrichment are the prescriptions for what is seen as worker alienation.

A third point of view sees both psychological and situational factors combining to produce a given level of job involvement. Lawler and Hall (1970) have argued for this interaction approach.

FIGURE 5.1 A Model of Job Involvement-Alienation.

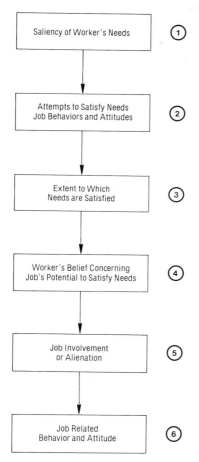

This model identifies job involvement-alienation as part of a motivational process that results from job behaviors and attitudes (Box 2) leading to need satisfaction (Box 3) and the worker's perception of a job's potential for satisfying needs (Box 4). The Kanungo model is more complete than the one presented above since it includes family and community involvement as alternative areas within which the individual may seek out the gratification of salient needs.

Source: Adapted from Kanungo, R. N. The concepts of alienation and involvement revisited. *Psychological Bulletin,* 1979, *86,* 119-138.

These authors acknowledge the significant role past learning plays in the individual's orientation toward work; these influences, however, come into contact with the conditions found on a specific job, and the level of worker commitment is seen to be the result of these two sets of variables interacting with one another. Studies reported by Herman and Hulin (1972), Herman, Dunham, and Hulin (1975), Newman (1975) and Saal (1978) all present evidence indicating that job involvement is related to both the characteristics of the job and the psychological characteristics of the worker. As is the case with most complex behavioral variables, it is probably most realistic to view job involvement from the perspective of this interaction model.

The Kanungo Model

Perhaps the most elaborate formulation of the job-involvement concept has been presented by Kanungo (1979). In this model, job involvement is one end of a bipolar scale that has job alienation as its negative pole. Both are states of the same phenomenon. Involvement is seen as a set of beliefs held by an individual concerning his or her identification with a job. Identification depends on two things: the relative importance of the various need states experienced by the person, and the belief that a job has the potential for satisfying needs, especially those needs that are psychologically most important to the individual. Figure 5.1 is a simplified version of the model presented by Kanungo. As represented here, the model applies only to the work role, although it can be extended to include other aspects of life.

Begin considering this model by recognizing that at any one point in time an individual's behavior is under the influence of a variety of psychological needs. These needs may be ordered according to their potency, and this varies from time to time and from one environment to another. A person functioning within one environment—work, for example—may be influenced more significantly by some needs than others. If the person moves to another environment—for example, family—other needs emerge as more important influences. The need for certain kinds of affection may be a more important motivational force while a person is functioning within the family than it is when that person is on the job. Psychologists talk about the *saliency of needs* to express the fact that both time and environmental circumstances affect the relative importance of need states as they influence our behavior.

In Kanungo's model the saliency of needs that function at work is the consequence of two sets of influences: past socialization (previous learning) and the individual's present beliefs concerning a job's potential for satisfying needs. In response to these salient needs (Box 1), the individual initiates job activities and attitudes (Box 2) which attempt to achieve satisfaction. To the extent that these needs are met (Box 3), the worker develops beliefs concerning the job's potential for satisfying these needs in the future (Box 4). From these beliefs there develops a sense of identification with the job that is either involving or alienating (Box 5). Finally, work involvement or alienation has sig-

nificant effects on subsequent job behavior and job attitudes (Box 6).

From the perspective of this model it is clear that Kanungo places emphasis on the motivational implications of job involvement. In doing so, he defines the concept in terms of the extent to which an individual believes that a job has the potential for satisfying important needs; thus, job involvement is a cognitive construct. The psychological state implied by high job involvement—or its opposite, alienation—is a system of beliefs that deal with motivational concerns. When these beliefs are optimistic, job involvement is said to be high; when they are pessimistic, a worker's orientation toward a job is described in terms of alienation.

Measurement of Job Involvement

One of the more useful measures of job involvement comes from a study (Lodahl, 1964) in which groups of automobile and electronics workers were interviewed with regard to the way they looked at

---

TABLE 5.4   The Lodahl-Kejner Job Involvement Scale

I'll stay overtime to finish a job even if I'm not paid for it.	I live, eat, and breathe my job.
You can measure a person pretty well by how good a job he does.	I would probably keep working even if I didn't need the money.
The major satisfaction in my life comes from my job.	Quite often I feel like staying home from work instead of coming in.
For me, mornings at work really fly by.	To me, my work is only a small part of who I am.
I usually show up for work a little early to get things ready.	I am very much involved personally in my work.
The most important things that happen to me involve my work.	I avoid taking on extra duties and responsibilities in my work.
Sometimes I lie awake at night thinking ahead to the next day's work.	I used to be more ambitious about my work than I am now.
I'm really a perfectionist about my work.	Most things in life are more important than work.
I feel depressed when I fail at something connected with my job.	I used to care more about my work, but now other things are more important to me.
I have other activities more important than my work.	Sometimes I'd like to kick myself for the mistakes I make in my work.

Source: Lodahl, T. M., & Kejner, M. The definition and measurement of job involvement. *Journal of Applied Psychology*, 1965, *49*, 24–33. Copyright 1965 by the American Psychological Association. Published by permission.

their work. In analyzing these interviews, it was observed that a significant job involvement theme ran through the conversation of both groups. Submitting these interviews to extensive statistical analyses, it was discovered that this job involvement dimension appeared to be independent of both the workers' satisfaction with the work and their level of work motivation. In other words, the study yielded evidence that indicated that a worker could be highly involved with his job, yet not particularly satisfied or highly motivated. This observation suggested that it would be worthwhile to construct a scale that could measure this facet of worker behavior; so, in what is probably the most widely cited study in this area, Lodahl and Kejner (1965) built such a scale, employing a series of scale construction and factor analytic techniques (See Table 5.4). The scale gives the respondent four response categories with which he can express varying degrees of agreement with each statement. Lodahl and Kejner have reported that the scale is reasonably reliable, and there is some evidence that the instrument does successfully differentiate occupational groups. Additional evidence of the scale's validity has been reported from a study of government research workers (Goodman, Furcon, & Rose, 1969).

Job Involvement and Job Satisfaction

One of the more interesting aspects of the early studies in this area is the evidence suggesting that job involvement is independent of job satisfaction. Intuition would lead one to expect that a worker who is satisfied with his job will also show a high level of commitment to it. Yet Lodahl's study indicated that this is not necessarily the case. Lodahl and Kejner (1965) did find a low but statistically significant correlation between the two variables, when they observed a group of engineers; the two variables functioned independently, however, with groups of professional nurses and students. Lawler and Hall (1970), in a study of scientists, found that job involvement was uncorrelated with satisfaction with work and with work motivation.

There are, however, studies that show a positive relationship between job satisfaction and job involvement, but in most of these instances the relationship holds for only certain facets of job satisfaction. Schwyhart and Smith (1972) found job involvement correlating with satisfaction with one's company, and Hall, Schneider, and Nygren (1970) found that the positive relationship was confined to satisfaction of needs for self-fulfillment and autonomy.

Perhaps the pattern of these research findings points to the fact that the relationship between job involvement and job satisfaction is a complicated one. For instance, since job satisfaction is a complex factor involving a number of separate dimensions, job involvement may be associated with only certain aspects of job satisfaction and not with others. Weissenberg and Gruenfeld (1968) have found this to be the case with a group of Civil Service supervisors. These authors contend that job involvement is found to be associated with those sources of job satisfaction that reside in the job itself, rather than in those facets of work that seem peripheral to the job duties. For instance, job involvement was found to be associated with the recognition offered by the job, and with achievement and responsibility, but it was not associated with such things as satisfaction with pay, security, and company policy.

Wood (1974), in a study of skilled and semi-skilled papermakers, tends to agree with this interpretation. He contends that high job involvement points to an individual's concentration on the specific duties that are inherent in the work. This contention is based on the observation that the high job-involved employees in his study did not display satisfaction with an extrinsic set of rewards manipulated by a company performance appraisal system. Those who are deeply involved with their work, Wood maintains, derive their principal sources of gratification from actually doing the work, and thus they are less responsive to the external rewards that surround work. Wood does report, however, that this relationship was most pronounced for the employees in skilled jobs; hence, it might be more realistic to talk about varieties of job involvement, which vary as a function of both the nature of the job and certain psychological characteristics of those employed.

At this point it would probably be wise to reserve judgment on the question of the nature of the involvement-satisfaction relationship. The weight of the evidence would suggest that job involvement relates to certain facets of job satisfaction. In all probability, sources of satisfaction found in the work itself will prove to correlate most closely with job involvement. This relationship will vary, however, from one situation to the next, and it will be the objective of future research to determine the variables that mediate these changing relationships.

Involvement and Job Performance. In a recent study Saal (1978) attempted to describe the relationship between job involvement and a large set of personal, situational, work outcome, and performance variables. Significant relationships with job involvement were found in each class of variables except one, performance. Of seven performance measures, not one was found to relate to the level of job involvement expressed by a group of rank-and-file employees of a manufacturing firm. Cummings and Manring (1977) report finding a *negative* relationship between a measure of job involvement and performance. In a study carried out with a group of blue-collar employees holding a variety of forging jobs, supervisors were asked to rate each employee on the effort expended and on job performance. Correlations with job involvement measures indicated a weak but significant tendency for high rated workers to express low levels of job involvement. Rabinowitz and Hall (1977) in their review of the work done in this area failed to find any clear relationship between job involvement and performance.

At first glance it is disturbing to learn that workers whose involvement with a job is high are not necessarily among the successful and productive employees. If one considers, however, the complexity of most work situations, it becomes clear that a worker's commitment to the work role may attach itself to any one or combination of dimen-

sions that make up the total work environment. For example, taking part in the social-political affairs of work may not result in high levels of productivity, but may result in high psychological involvement with the work setting. It's possible, therefore, to explain the absence of a relationship between involvement and performance; it is imperative, however, that research explore this situation further.

Absences. There is one aspect of job behavior that has been shown to relate to job involvement. As a rule research indicates that high levels of job involvement accompany lower rates of absences and turnover. In fact there are several studies (Farris, 1971; Patchen, 1961) in which this relationship was moderately high. Doubtless there are situations in which high job involvement may be a condition necessary for movement into high-prestige organizations that can provide more attractive working conditions. In these situations it is the highly involved individual who moves most from job to job.

Social and Psychological Factors

Does an employer hire workers with different levels of job involvement or does the employee's commitment to work develop out of his experience with the job? One would probably think that whether individuals are highly involved with the work is, at least in part, a reflection of their psychological makeup. From this point of view, job involvement is an expression of something workers bring into the workplace, and has its roots in their personality and social background. In considering this question it might be useful to separate psychological characteristics from social background factors, since job involvement may not show the same degree of relationship with these two types of variables.

Social Factors. Job involvement has a social basis, and it is in both the immediate social environment of work and the social background of the worker that one may search for variables that underlie a worker's commitment to a job. However,

TABLE 5.5 Association between Work-Role Involvement and Selected Variables for Two Supervisory Levels

Variable	Bottom-level supervisors	Middle-level supervisors
Age	−.00	.08
Age at first job	−.11	.13
No. dependents	−.01	−.17
Occupational level of father	−.11	.16
Occupational level of father-in-law	−.01	.22
Education—self	.01	.13
Education—wife	−.10	.15
Education—mother	.00	.04
Income	.03	.09
Company tenure	−.07	.00
Position tenure	−.08	−.05
Plant size	.01	.20
Organizational commitment	.12	−.15
Perceived mobility chances	.14	.08
Mobility aspiration	.22**	.41**

**Pearson correlation coefficient significant at *p* less than .01.

Source: Maurer, J. G. *work role involvement of industrial supervisors.* East Lansing, Mich.: Michigan State University, 1969, p. 57. Copyright 1969, Michigan State University.

in the few instances in which this search has extended into the worker's social background, the relationships obtained have not been particularly strong. Maurer (1969), for example, has correlated job involvement with a number of background variables in a study that dealt with supervisory personnel. In this study Maurer was unable to find any relationship between job involvement and such things as the occupation of the worker's father, the educational attainment of the mother, or the age at which the worker took his first job. In fact, the general pattern of Maurer's results suggests that job involvement does not relate to many of the variables that can be used to describe an individual's social background (see Table 5.5).

Currently, it seems that the social variables most closely relating to job involvement are to be found in the social environment one finds surrounding a worker's present job. Lodahl (1964) found that commitment to a job appears to be linked to the extent to which an employee is involved with a work team, and also to the number of individuals found working nearby. Lodahl and Kejner (1965) cite evidence indicating that job involvement is highest when a person works closely with others and has a large number of contacts with other people during the day. Finally, we will learn shortly that job involvement relates to the number of friends one has at work (Parker, 1964) and to the worker's interest in getting ahead.

Hence, it would seem that job involvement is influenced most significantly by those social factors that are more immediate to the present work situation. Variables, like those studied by Maurer, which refer to aspects of the social background that have been of long standing, do not predict the current level of job involvement. To a large degree, job involvement means involvement in the rich set of interpersonal dealings that take place on every job. This seems to be particularly true for those social relationships that are perceived by the worker as having career, and more specifically, promotion implications.

Psychological Factors. There is very little information available linking job involvement with those basic intellectual and personality factors typically studied by the psychologist. As a result, we are presently in no position to say that such factors as intelligence, extroversion, or neuroticism make a contribution to the level of involvement workers have in their jobs. Much of the information that is available regarding psychological factors concerns either individuals' attitudes toward work or their aspirations for upward mobility.

Lodahl maintains that workers who are involved in their jobs tend to possess behavioral attributes that make them more responsive to the requirements of the job and to the demands of the work organization. In large measure these attributes originate in social conditions that are found quite early in the worker's life, since it is during this period that the basic attitudes and values concerning work are laid down. Lodahl and Kejner see involvement with work as an expression of the *Protestant Work Ethic,* which is a cluster of beliefs concerning the value and moral significance of work.

Basically, the Protestant Work Ethic holds that there is dignity and moral virtue in work, and those who gain worldly position and comfort are those who earn these rewards through their industry and skill. A life of moderation and diligent work will lead to prosperity on earth and entrance into heaven in the afterlife. Essentially, we are talking about a belief that there is a broad range of instrumentalities surrounding work. Those who subscribe to these beliefs maintain that *in the long run* commitment to work leads to desirable payoffs, both on the job and in the individual's general state of happiness. On beliefs such as these rests the individual's general orientation toward work.

A number of studies have presented us with evidence indicating that the extent to which an individual subscribes to the Protestant Work Ethic relates positively to the level of job involvement (Rabinowitz & Hall, 1977). These studies demonstrate that whether individuals are interested in their jobs and concerned about the quality of their work is, in part, a function of a set of values and attitudes that concern the meaning and importance of work. Those who endorse the belief that hard work is a characteristic of a virtuous person tend to show high levels of psychological involvement with the work they do.

Other Psychological Factors.   One of the more consistent characteristics found to be associated with the level of job involvement is the mobility aspirations of the worker (Kahn et al., 1964; Maurer, 1969; Goldman, 1973). As might be expected, those workers who aspire to move up through the ranks of their company tend to be more highly involved in their work than are those who do not place high value on promotion. Their involvement with work indicates a high drive for social status, and they see the job as the social channel that offers the best opportunity for upward mobility. Since these people are interested in promotion, and since promotion is significantly influenced by interpersonal relations, then we would also expect to find highly involved workers being more active in the social activities surrounding work.

This expectation has been verified in a study by Parker (1964), which involved a large group of men and women who were employed in a number of business and service positions. These employees were asked to indicate the number of close friends they had on the job, and their responses were correlated with the attitudes the employees held toward their work. Parker found that the workers who had the greatest number of friends on the job also indicated that they were positively identified with their work and considered their jobs to be a central life interest.

Along somewhat different lines, Maurer (1969) has shown that individuals who are highly involved in their work tend to consider as very important those aspects of a job that relate to higher personal needs such as desire for esteem, autonomy, and self-actualization. It is of interest to note that even though job involvement correlated with an individual's perception of the importance of these needs, it did not correlate with the extent to which these needs were being met by the job. Here again is evidence that job satisfaction and job involvement are not strongly related. Job involvement has, however, been shown to be related to the extent to which the individual is satisfied with the company in which he works (Schwyhart & Smith, 1972). Hence, although the degree to which individuals are involved with their work may not always be closely associated with their satisfaction with work, it does appear that job involvement is related to the social components of work, including the individual's pride in and satisfaction with the work organization.

Another factor found to be associated with job involvement concerns the worker's expertise-achievement orientation (Katz & Kahn, 1978.) An orientation such as this refers to the person who sees in his work challenging tasks that draw on valued personal skills. Katz and Kahn find that workers who approach their jobs with this orientation tend to become more highly involved in their work. Further, the effect of this orientation seems to vary as a function of the level of anxiety possessed by the individual. It was for high anxious subjects that the contribution of expertise-achievement orientation was found to be most significant in influencing job involvement.

Anxiety and Job Involvement

Findings like those above point to the possibility that anxiety levels may prove to be another important factor that leads to high job involvement. The research literature might leave one with the impression that job involvement means a positive attraction to some aspects of the work. In many instances, this is quite true. One must not, however, overlook the possibility that job involvement may also function as a coping mechanism that is responding to the threats and anxiety that exist in many work settings. The individual for whom work is a dominant concern, the person who brings his work home from the office or shop, who talks work and finds it difficult to psychologically disengage himself from the job, may not necessarily be a person who is happily distracted from other aspects of his life by the job. Rather, we may be viewing the behavior of an individual who is wrestling with a problem—a threat or the fear of failure—which motivates him to assume a work role of high expertise and involvement. The social factors that we have just studied can be considered in terms of job tensions. The informal activities surrounding work, the drink before going home, lunching with the people at the office, the immersion in the social-political intrigues of the firm, may possibly be manifestations that derive not from genuine friendships but from a situation that is threatening and anxiety-producing.

When we look at the experimental literature, we can find abundant, although indirect, support for the contention that high anxiety tends to focus an individual's attention on certain aspects of his experience to the exclusion of others. Research both on animals (Bruner, Matter, & Papanek, 1955) and on humans (Silverman, 1954; Easter-

brook, 1959; Fenz, 1964) indicates that one of the possible consequences of anxiety is to lead individuals to focus on the central elements of their perceptual world and to be less responsive to peripheral events. Easterbrook (1959), for example, concludes that emotional arousal consistently acts to restrict the range of cues used by an individual who is responding to a complex event. Other researchers agree (Fenz, 1964; Postman & Bruner, 1948) that anxiety has a significant effect on the individual focusing on the threatening aspects of the situation, and those things that are not relevant to the threat are not attended to.

Thus far we have found that job involvement seems to be associated with certain social dimensions of work. Interest in social mobility, status orientation, and friendship affiliations have all been shown to relate to the individual's involvement in work. The research literature also shows us that social behaviors such as these relate to another important psychological process, that is, anxiety. Schachter (1959) in a widely cited study reports that subjects who were exposed to an anxiety-producing situation during one phase of an experiment tended, when given the chance, to affiliate with others more than did subjects not exposed to these stressful conditions. Similar results have been obtained by Sarnoff and Zimbardo (1961), although these authors draw a distinction between fear—a real perceived threat—and anxiety, a response to repressed motives, contending that it is fear that produces the tendency to seek affiliation.

There is one final study that bears on this discussion of job involvement and psychological tensions. Matthews and Saal (1978) measured the extent to which a group of subjects displayed what is known as Type A behavioral patterns. Type A behavior is thought to be a consequence of the tensions that come from a continual struggle to attain a large number of goals in a limited period of time. It is a manifestation of time pressures that gives the individual a chronic sense of urgency that is accompanied by displays of competitiveness, achievement striving, and free-flowing hostility. This type of behavior has been closely associated with a heightened risk of coronary problems. In their study, Matthews and Saal found there was a positive relationship between the extent to which students displayed Type A behaviors and the extent to which they were involved in their work. Although this study does not trace the origin of these Type A behaviors to conditions associated with the work task, the fact that high tensions and involvement are related suggests that the factors contributing to high job involvement may not all stem from positive experiences.

On the basis of indirect support such as that just presented, we hypothesize that job anxiety, an experience widely reported by workers (Katz & Kahn, 1964) may give rise to patterns of adjustment that include a tendency toward affiliation and a tendency to bring the threatening situation into the central regions of the individual's psychological world. This pattern is seen lying at the heart of what we have been referring to as job involvement, and although it would be hazardous to see in the level of job involvement a sure sign of anxiety, one should keep the prospects of this relationship in mind in considering these aspects of worker behavior.

Age and Involvement

Although a few studies have obtained nonsignificant correlations (Gurin, Veroff, & Feld, 1960; Mannheim, 1975), the trend of the evidence suggests that there is a positive relationship between the level of job involvement and age (Schwyhart & Smith, 1972; Jones, James, & Bruni, 1975; Hall & Mansfield, 1975; Saal, 1978). In a variety of job settings, older workers have been found to express higher levels of involvement in their work than have their younger associates. The nature of age as a research variable makes it difficult to settle on a single interpretation of this relationship. Perhaps alternative job opportunities are more readily available to younger workers, making it more likely that they consider their present jobs as just one of a number that might be held. In the absence of this perception of mobility, the older workers may be more prone to invest their energies and resources in the present job. It may also be that as

workers grow older and acquire tenure on a job, the conditions of work, relations with supervisors, pay, job duties, and so on may improve, making it more likely that the worker will identify with the work and invest more heavily in its activities. With increasing age, family commitments change, health status may deteriorate, and a number of other personal and social changes may take place. The list of factors that might serve as linkages between age and job involvement is a long one indeed, but the consequence of this is that it is impossible at the present time to arrive at a single explanation for the frequently noted positive relationship that exists between the two variables.

Rabinowitz and Hall (1977) recommend that future studies follow people through their work careers, noting the changes that take place in their commitment to work. Studies of this type could collect auxiliary information concerning other changes that might be taking place, and such information would serve to clarify the age-involvement relationship. At present the evidence encourages one to operate on a purely descriptive level; and at this stage in our understanding, the interpretations of relationships should be viewed as hypotheses for future research.

Job Design Factors

In spite of the substantial evidence linking the level of job involvement to psychological variables, it still seems reasonable to look for additional factors in the characteristics of the job itself. Many of the studies that have correlated involvement with psychological variables have reported that the relationships observed tended to be relatively weak. This suggests that other sets of variables may also be significant in explaining the level of worker involvement with a job. Furthermore, it would be difficult to imagine that a worker would maintain the same level of involvement, regardless of the characteristics of the job.

There appears to be a growing number of persons who are convinced that it is in the design of the job that one finds the principal correlates of job satisfaction and worker alienation. Impressed by the rapid changes that have been taking place in the technology of work, many believe that these changes have led to a general deterioration in the social and psychological climate of work. Technology with all of its demand for narrowing specialization has, in the minds of many, tended to dehumanize work and make jobs increasingly more meaningless and psychologically sterile. We will consider the general literature bearing on this question at a later point in this book (see Chapter 15). For the present we will consider only one aspect of this job design problem, the relationship between job characteristics and the extent to which people become involved in their jobs.

Participation in Decision Making. Jobs vary in the extent to which they permit the employee to make decisions concerning the directions and conduct of the work. The degree to which a worker is given opportunity to participate in work decisions has been found to be postively related to the level of job involvement (White & Ruh, 1973). Participation in group problem solving serves an ego-involving function, since under these conditions group activities reflect decisions to which the individual has made a contribution. Hence, the worker has a psychological investment in the consequences of the decision, and is therefore more likely to be supportive of the activities that follow the decisions that have been made.

Wickert (1951) found that job involvement is strengthened in those cases where the job provides opportunity to make decisions, thereby giving the worker the feeling that he is making an important contribution to the success of the organization. Jobs that permit the individual to set his own pace (a decision-making function) and that provide opportunity for recognition and achievement also encourage the worker to become involved with the job. In the absence of these job features, Wickert reports that employees tend to leave the job.

Lawler and Hall (1970) substantiate Wickert's findings when they report that job involvement is more likely to be found in jobs on which workers can influence what is going on in their departments. Finally, in a study that involved a large number of employees in a manufacturing organi-

zation, Siegel and Ruh (1973) found a substantial positive correlation existing between participation in decision making and the level of employee involvement in the job.

This is probably the most clearly established relationship in the entire area of job involvement. To design a job in such a fashion that it permits employees to take an active role in deciding how some of the important aspects of their work will be carried out and evaluated is a step that will improve employees' commitment to the job and better ensure that they will be concerned about the quality of their performance. The psychology of ego-involvement is a powerful consideration in determining workers' orientation to the job and their general level of interest in seeing that it is carried out effectively.

Job Level and Content. As one moves up the ranks of an organization one may expect to find jobs that are more interesting and congenial. With higher-level jobs an increased opportunity to plan and control one's work is often combined with duties that are more varied and challenging. As a consequence, one would expect jobs of this type to be more involving than jobs at the lower levels of the organization, where freedom is more restricted and duties more routine. The available evidence tends to confirm that job *content* is an important factor underlying a worker's involvement with the job. Studies that have correlated job involvement with job *level*, however, have not been able to obtain consistent results. Rabinowitz and Hall (1977) cite several studies that were unable to find any relationship between the level of a job and the degree of involvement shown by the employees. Therefore, on the basis of the current evidence, the assumption that people in higher level jobs display more commitment to their work than do those in low-level positions is unwarranted.

The main question concerning job content is not whether it maintains a significant relationship with job involvement, but what dimensions of a job have shown a significant correlation with this variable. One important dimension related to involvement is the extent to which jobs permit workers to use the skills and talents the workers value most highly in themselves. Lawler and Hall (1970) found that positions that permit individuals to draw on abilities that they see as being highly developed in themselves and jobs that allow creative activities are the ones that are more involving to the worker. Vroom (1962) agrees with this point of view, contending that individuals will become ego-involved in their work to the extent that their performance is seen as expressing aptitudes and abilities that are central to their self-concepts. It is the exercise of highly valued skills that leads to an increased commitment to a job, and to have a job that utilizes these talents is to have a job that provides opportunity for self-actualization. Hence, we might conclude that job involvement is a direct function of the extent to which workers can see in their work a manifestation of the talents and abilities that enhance their feelings of self-esteem and competence. Pride in one's work is approval of oneself, and self-actualization refers to a task that generates outcomes that reflect a positive image of the self.

Interaction between Worker and Job

Job or personality factors alone are probably insufficient to explain the extent to which workers are committed to their jobs. Job involvement depends upon combinations of job design factors and personality variables. The wide range of individual differences in job involvement that one can usually find on any given job testifies to the significance of the interaction between these two sets of factors. For example, Guion and Landy (1972) found that work that was meaningful to the employee seems to encourage higher levels of involvement; this was not true, however, for all workers. These authors found that workers whose behavioral style was characterized by low levels of general activity tended to become most involved with work when the job possessed characteristics that made for a meaningful set of activities. On the other hand, a worker whose behavior expressed a high activity level, "seems to reserve some portion of his efforts for work and to express that portion *regard-less of the meaning the work might have,*" (Guion & Landy, 1972, p. 337; italics added). Hence, whether or not a work task is meaningful is not important to job involvement when the worker has an energy level that leads to high levels of general activity. That worker tends to become involved in work regardless of its meaningfulness. The job involvement of workers whose activity level is usually low, however, requires a task that is meaningful.

Along somewhat similar lines, Kahn et al. (1964) suggest that there are several varieties of job involvement, both flexible and rigid, that stem from the worker's personality makeup. The flexible individual's involvement with a job revolves around the dimensions of work that concern variability of experience, opportunity for introducing significant change, and development of interpersonal relationships. Jobs that permit greater opportunity for these activities prove highly involving for the flexible personality. Kahn and his associates report a series of interviews with management personnel, one of which is presented below to illustrate the job perspective of a flexible manager who was asked what makes for a good job:

> Well a job—well, such as I have now—that brings me into contact with people, gives me a certain degree of authority and responsibility, and is far from routine, always something new developing, something new every day, and working with essentially pretty congenial decent people. I like working together with people as a team, as a coordinated group.
>
> I think the fact that I'm dealing in, well, an extremely interesting business—a fascinating business—growing all the time, dealing with situations all over the world, in some pretty strange places—makes it interesting and a joy.
>
> I couldn't stand a general routine job. For example, I could never take a job dealing with figures all the time, such as an accountant. I don't think I could take that at all. (Kahn et al., 1964, p. 287)

People with rigid personalities, on the other hand, tend to involve themselves in aspects of work that are highly structured, consistent, orderly, and stable. They become most involved in job dimensions that assign them to well-defined tasks. Kahn et al. quote one such manager who was questioned about how often he initiated changes in his own activities:

> No sir, I do not. Any major changes are handed down to me by instruction. Certain type jobs may carry on in the same method and in the same procedures, but that doesn't mean that they will carry on indefinitely because the model changes and the operations change. We *have* to change for those because that is what's required and is necessary. Personally, in my opinion, any man who is that stubborn to stick to one golden rule and thinks he's the only one that's right, he's *wrong*. We can all learn something new every day. I know I do. But that doesn't mean we have to have a lot of changes all the time. I know that changes have to happen, but we shouldn't have any more than necessary. (Kahn et al., 1964, p. 292)

Admittedly, there is not a surfeit of information concerning those combinations of job design and psychological attributes that tend to produce high levels of job involvement. These patterns are likely to be varied and possibly complex. Nevertheless, at the present time the reader should bear in mind the likelihood that the extent to which workers are psychologically involved with their work is a function of both job design factors and sets of psychological attributes, each interacting with the other.

Summary Comment. Looking back now on the research dealing with job involvement, we see running through all studies evidence of a wide distribution of individual differences in the extent to which people are psychologically involved with their jobs. Furthermore, it seems reasonably clear that an individual's involvement with the job is significantly influenced by the social events the worker confronts on a daily basis. This is particularly evident in those instances in which an employee maintains high interest in promotion and places high value on status position. One must rec-

ognize, however, that interest in promotion in and of itself may not be sufficient to encourage high levels of job commitment on the part of the worker since reasonable opportunities for promotion probably must also be perceived.

In addition, we must not overlook the possibility that the duties of the job may serve as a factor that results in high job involvement. The literature is not particularly clear with regard to the characteristics of work that tend to be associated with more intensely committed workers. There appears to be evidence that work that permits a certain amount of personal autonomy and participation in decision making tends to be more highly involving. Also, jobs that contain some opportunity for creativity and self-actualization are more likely to encourage higher levels of worker involvement than do jobs that do not provide these opportunities. Much more work is needed in this area, and as the research thus far reported suggests, job factors most likely interact with personal factors to determine the level of job involvement evident in the performance of a worker.

Finally, one must not overlook the potential influence of psychologically negative factors in influencing the extent to which workers are involved with their jobs. The tensions and anxieties of work may well require a considerable investment of psychological resources that appear in the form of high job involvement.

Time Budgeting

There is one often neglected source of evidence that bears on the question of the psychological importance of work. Several large-scale surveys have attempted to determine how people allocate time to various areas of activity that fill their days. The investment of time in an activity has broad social and psychological significance. In fact, of all the indexes of psychological importance, a good argument could be advanced that time budgeting is the most direct expression of an individual's psychological involvement with the various events that make up that person's life. Time can be thought of as one of the more important psychological resources, and the allocation of this resource is an indication of the values, obligations, and costs surrounding a given activity (Meier, 1959). To find different patterns of time utilization among groups of individuals is to discover important social and psychological differences among them.

Naturally, much of the time budgeted for a particular activity does not reflect a willing commitment but rather an obligation that is imposed on the individual by an external source. State law, for instance, prescribes the length of the school day, and company policy dictates the duration of the work spell. Furthermore, the distribution of activity segments over the day is shaped by external determinants. Work begins at eight o'clock in the morning, movies begin at seven o'clock in the evening, and lunch is eaten at noon. Hence, the budgeting of time and the sequencing of events over time are often in response to external demands that obligate the allocation of time rather than putting time completely at the person's disposal.

Work for the most part must be considered an obligation in the sense that the time committed to its purposes is fixed by social institutions. But regardless of its obligatory nature, the investment of large segments of time in work activities does reflect a substantial expenditure of this most valuble psychological resource; hence, it represents a substantial cost imposed on people who work.

At present, to contend that time allocation gives us direct access to job involvement behaviors, as they are defined in the current research literature, would be unwarranted. There is one study (Gechman & Wiener, 1975) reporting that more highly involved school teachers devoted more personal time to their work. Until more evidence of this type is presented, however, time allocation should be viewed as an alternative source of data bearing on the broad question of the psychological importance of work. It may very well turn out that the use of time, especially discretionary time, is closely correlated with the measures of job involvement that are taken from current questionnaire-type instruments. Intuition would lead one to suspect that high job involvement is related to a tendency to engage in work and work-related activities. This is a matter that can be resolved by

further research. At its most fundamental level, however, time allocation is a measure of duration of exposure to an activity and an environmental setting. This in itself has psychological significance. The fact that workers invest nine or ten hours of every working day in getting ready to work, traveling to the job, working, and returning home, is something that cannot be overlooked when one considers the importance of work in the lives of many individuals.

Time Utilization and Work.   There have been a number of attempts to survey samples of adults in the United States in an effort to estimate the amount of time they invest in a variety of activities (see Szalai, 1966a). The results of these studies point very clearly to the conclusion that work accounts for a substantial portion of the individual's waking hours, and that employed persons report relatively small amounts of time available to them for discretionary use.

Robinson and Converse (1966), for example, conducted a time-budget survey that involved 1244 adults in a national urban sample. The methods used included a series of questionnaires and a diary in which the respondent recorded information concerning time utilization. Survey results indicated that sleep and work received the major allocation of time. Employed men averaged 7.6 hours each weekday for both work and sleep, and 4.2 hours were allocated to leisure time activities. Employed women averaged the same amount of time for sleeping, 7.6 hours, but worked fewer hours, 5.7, and reported fewer leisure-time hours, 3.6.

A more recent study by Hammer and Chapin (1972) reports on a survey of the time budgets of 1667 adults in the Washington, D.C. area. In this instance an interview method was used, with respondents recalling the budgeting of time during two recent days. Table 5.6 reproduces the results of one phase of this project. Notice the similarity of estimates obtained in this and the Robinson and Converse survey. People reported spending on the average 7.77 hours working and 7.46 hours sleeping. Discretionary time accounted for only 4.72 hours during the 24-hour day.

TABLE 5.6   Mean Durations and Participation Rates for Activities in the 38-Code Activity Classification System, Weekdays (*n* = 1667)

Activity Category		Proportion Engaging in Activity	Mean Hours Allocated Per Activity Participant		Mean Hours Allocated Activity and Travel, Per Person in Sample
Code Number	Brief Title		To Activity	To Travel	
Obligatory					
01	Miscellaneous	.40	0.54	0.04	0.23
02	Main Job	.58	7.77	0.97	5.06
03	Other Income	.03	3.39	0.45	0.13
04	Personal Care	.84	0.89	0.00	0.75
05	Eating	.96	1.63	0.11	1.67
06	Shopping	.36	1.02	0.57	0.57
07	Health	.06	2.03	0.34	0.14
08	Maintenance	.11	1.65	0.01	0.19
09	Housework	.66	3.46	0.00	2.28
10	Chores, Pet Care	.06	0.76	0.05	0.05
11	Business	.24	0.80	0.14	0.22
12	Education	.04	4.84	0.57	0.20
					(11.49)
Discretionary					
13	Child-centered	.10	1.12	0.08	0.11
14	Family Social	.06	1.80	0.14	0.12
15	Oversee Child	.04	0.99	0.03	0.04
16	Family Outing	.01	2.26	0.11	0.03
17	Other Family	.17	1.28	0.02	0.22
18	Visit at Home	.22	1.46	0.00	0.32
19	Visit Neighbors	.04	1.43	0.03	0.06
20	Visit Others	.14	1.64	0.25	0.26
21	Other Social	.04	1.95	0.50	0.11
22	Nap and Loaf	.21	1.78	0.00	0.38
23	Read Misc.	.46	1.23	0.00	0.56
24	Read Book	.06	1.49	0.00	0.08
25	Cultural	.06	1.61	0.19	0.11
26	Movies	.02	2.28	0.64	0.05
27	Television	.67	2.46	0.01	1.65
28	Radio	.06	1.00	0.01	0.06
29	Hobbies	.03	1.90	0.02	0.06
30	Walk	.03	0.98	0.00	0.03
31	Drive Around	.01	0.90	0.00	0.01
32	Part. Sports	.06	1.50	0.21	0.10
33	Spect. Sports	.01	1.90	0.51	0.02
34	Out-of-Town	.02	7.16	0.00	0.17
35	Other Rec.	.02	1.18	0.03	0.03
36	Religious	.04	1.66	0.26	0.08
37	Organizations	.01	1.97	0.46	0.03
38	Civic	.01	2.02	0.43	0.03
					(4.72)
	Travel	.83	1.40	—	1.16
	Sleep	.99	7.50	0.00	7.46

Source: Hammer, P. G., & Chapin, F. S. *Human time allocation: A case study of Washington, D.C.* Center for Urban and Regional Studies, University of North Carolina, 1972.

It is interesting to examine the results of a time survey conducted in the Soviet Union in 1959 (Szalai, 1966b). For men, the results of this survey are in substantial agreement with studies previously cited. Time allocations for women, however, contrast sharply with those reported from U.S. samples. For example, men averaged 7.17 hours working, 7.48 hours sleeping, and 3.39 hours discretionary time. Women, on the other hand, averaged 7.20 hours at work, 6.97 hours sleeping, and only 2.42 hours were budgeted in discretionary activities. The road to socialism appears to be a bit more arduous for some than for others.

In general, time-budget surveys tend to confirm the general conclusion that work accounts for a substantial investment of the time available during a day. In terms of time, we may conclude that work accounts for approximately one-half of the waking hours available to an individual, and that when work is combined with other obligational time categories, individuals retain relatively little time that may be utilized according to their own discretion. DeGrazia (1962) in a widely quoted study estimates that the amount of free time available during a workday lies somewhere between 1.0 and 2.5 hours. Furthermore, he estimates that work time takes up an average of 10 hours and 40 minutes a day when one includes the work spell, travel time, and the after-hours work that one does about the house and in moonlighting.

Work Time, Job Level, and Occupation. A mail survey of 3176 executives carried out by Heckscher and DeGrazia (1959) confirms this high investment of time in work. On the average, these executives reported that 55 hours of their week were devoted to work-related matters, with 43 hours being directly allotted to the office. It is interesting, however, that 73 percent of this group indicated rather clearly that they desired more leisure time than was available to them. A study of 43 managers employed in an engineering department (Burke, 1973) revealed that there was a general desire in this group for more leisure time and for less time for work.

There is really no clear picture available concerning differences in time allocation to work, as one moves from one occupation to the next. The evidence coming closest to this question concerns the variation in time investments in work as a function of the social prestige level of the occupation. For example, Wilensky (1961) maintains that gains in leisure time that have taken place over the recent past have been enjoyed primarily by workers in private, nonagricultural, industrial jobs. Professionals, executives, and the self-employed have benefited little in obtaining increased release time from work. Wilensky estimates, for example, that a professional worker's lifetime total of 96,000 work hours exceeds that of the blue-collar worker who invests 94,000 hours in work, even though the latter tends to remain on the job longer (47 years) than does the individual in a profession (40 years). Robinson and Converse (1966) in their previously cited nationwide survey of time usage, report a slight trend in the opposite direction, with lower ranked blue- and white-collar workers investing slightly more time in work than their higher-status blue- and white-collar counterparts. There are numerous studies of executives, however, that support Wilensky's findings that people who are in high positions at work tend to invest time far in excess of the 40 hours that define the typical workweek of the blue-collar worker.

SUMMARY COMMENTS

Questions concerning the psychological importance of work are at once obvious and elusive. To begin with, one must accept the obvious fact that there is a wide range of individual differences regarding the extent to which individuals are psychologically engaged in their work. The research literature leaves little room for argument on this point. Furthermore, we might tentatively conclude, along with Dubin, that work is not *the* central life interest for the majority of those in the labor force. Other areas of life such as family, neighborhood friends, recreation, and the community often receive a more substantial investment of personal aspirations and concerns. It also appears reasonable to contend that the work role is a highly valued one, and that typical adults tend to choose the work role over nonwork whether they be affluent or poor, white- or blue-collar.

Work can be thought of from many perspectives, but the social implications of holding a job are a consideration that must figure prominently in any inquiry into the importance of work. This role is sought and highly valued for many reasons. Income provisions of work are perhaps the first to suggest themselves as the principal motive underlying the individual's assumption of the work role, and for many, especially the poor, this is the case. To earn a living, to gain access to the basic necessities of life through work is of obvious importance; we will consider wage incentives in some detail in a later chapter. Work must also be seen, however, as providing an individual with a place in society—a location in the social structure, a sense of contribution, and a feeling of membership. It is well recognized that there is an extensive range of status and prestige differences existing between jobs, but the mere fact that an individual holds a job, almost any job, serves as the foundation upon which increments in social status are based. To work is to be certified as a contributing member of the community; not to work sets an individual apart from the directive forces that operate in the community. Work, therefore, is a fundamental role that gives the individual entry into adult society; hence it is no wonder that we see in the research literature a broad-range commitment to job holding.

A job also gives an individual something to do. Work provides a variety of the social, intellectual, and physical activities that are required to maintain a satisfactory level of psychological health. We tend to think about these aspects of work in terms

of an outlet for an individual's skills, talents, and energies. This is quite probably true. It is through the exercise of valued skills and physical resources that one gains an important source of insight into who one is and what one can do. But over and above these considerations there lies one aspect of the job that should receive mention: there are compulsory aspects of work that require the individual to meet the demands of events that are under external control. The job involves events that day in and day out compel the worker to react rather than to initiate behavior. Job demands carry the worker through the day, establishing a tempo of activity largely determined by factors external to the individual. The daily routine, job exigencies, and the social milieu of work all place workers in settings in which they are not required to draw continuously on their own internal initiative in order to maintain the level of resource expenditure and environmental stimulation required for psychological health. Without jobs individuals are more likely to find themselves in situations in which they carry greater responsibility for stoking their own fires; whereas jobs reduce this burden by imposing on workers sets of external demands to which they are compelled to respond. A job, therefore, serves to combat one of the more persistent problems plaguing adult life—boredom.

Of course, the level of external direction may reach such a point on a particular job that it stifles the individual and creates problems that are best solved by quitting. Hence, in the above discussion we are referring to some optimal range. As an alternative to nonwork, however, the work role is in its fundamental sense valued by many, partly because it is in this role that individuals find those external stimuli that help them overcome a persistent psychological inertia.

6

The Costs of Work: Tensions and Industrial Mental Health

Although survey data indicate that a large number of individuals are generally satisfied with the work they do (see Chapters 8 and 15), there are probably few jobs completely free of tension and worry. At one time or another most people experience psychological stress associated with their work. Usually these instances are short-lived, and the tensions generated tend to be confined to each single happening. Once past, the events are largely forgotten, leaving behind little that influences one's perception of the job or one's mental health. There are other times, however, when job conditions result in negative experiences that persist and lead to more serious psychological problems. Such conditions do not inevitably produce emotional tensions in every worker. Within broad limits, tensions result from the interaction of a job condition and the personality of the individual worker; and as a consequence, we usually find that individuals differ widely in their reactions to any particular type of work pressure. Nevertheless, there do seem to be certain kinds of working conditions that increase the likelihood that the given worker will experience tension, and it is these conditions that will be the subject of the present chapter.

EFFECTS OF STRESS

Consider the following cases which illustrate work situations that resulted in different types of psychological distress. In the first, Walker (1957) describes the pressures reported by a worker regarding his experiences in adjusting to the work changes that were brought about by moving to a new highly automated mill:

> There's just that pressure, pressure, pressure, on the fellows all the time. You have the pressure of the machines and the pressure of the bosses, I just hate to go to work there every day. In the old mills when we knew we were going to have a good run coming up, why I just couldn't wait to get in that mill and get things going. On Number 4 I just feel like I'm going in there to a concentration camp every day. (p. 50)

In another case, Brodsky (1976) describes more serious consequences of job pressures in the situation faced by Bill, a department head:

> After ten years in his position . . . where he was highly respected and extremely successful, he requested an evaluative survey of his entire program. He expected the results to be positive and had requested the study because he believed the program so successful that the survey would serve as a basis for increased budget requests. It never occurred to him that the results would be anything but good. The survey was a disaster. The evaluation team focused only on the negative aspects of his work. The study attacked him as unqualified, stressing his lack of formal education instead of his great experience. The survey so

undid him that it brought on severe headaches, memory loss, numbness in the arms and legs, and respiratory problems. His diabetes became uncontrollable and within six months he was declared disabled and left work. (p. 74)

Finally, Jackall (1978) describes an instance in which job tensions carried over to influence the interpersonal relations of a posting clerk in a large bank:

> There's too much pressure. It makes me sick. I go home and cry. I was crying in bed Friday night. You really use your head in this. The work makes me depressed; it gives me headaches. I get nasty and then I get annoyed with little things my husband does, then I apologize because it's not his fault, then I feel bad and feel guilty. (p. 28)

These cases illustrate job situations that have resulted in a variety of psychological problems. Ranging from extremely negative attitudes toward work to psychological depression and physical disablement, these work experiences have contributed to a deterioration in the mental health of the workers.

The frequency with which such happenings occur is very difficult to determine; however, many who study work behavior believe that job conditions are important contributors to an individual's psychological health. Evidence supporting this belief comes from two major sources. First, case studies such as those presented above indicate that workers do perceive a connection between their on-the-job experiences and their emotional adjustment. Second, there is accumulating evidence that certain types of physical illness are associated with the characteristics of work and the nature of the job environment. These physical complaints are those, like coronary heart disease and high blood pressure, that often are the result of persistent and excessive tensions.

A surprising amount of time lost from work has been attributed to emotional problems. For example, Aldridge (1970) cites data indicating that during a single year 22.8 million workdays were lost in Great Britain as the result of emotional dis-

orders of one sort or another. This lost time exceeded that resulting from industrial accidents. Along similar lines, in a single year (1957–1958) coronary heart disease accounted for 12 percent of all time lost from work by the working population of the United States (Felton & Cole, 1963). Greenwood (1978) estimates that the annual cost of executive stress in the United States is between $10 and $20 billion. He points out that this figure is higher than the gross revenues of any one of all but three of the largest corporations found in the *Fortune 500* list. Finally, Von Wiegan (1976) contends that a conservative estimate is that 6 percent of the labor force is suffering from alcoholism, a disease largely attributable to the operation of psychological stresses.

Estimates of this sort are often indirect and approximate. For example, figures relating to coronary heart disease reflect genetic, physiological, and psychological influences. To infer that the incidence of this disease is a reflection of the level of psychological pressures in a given environment is to focus on one set of causes while ignoring others. The whole problem of tracing the factors underlying stress symptoms is a very complicated one. In all probability, emotional problems are always the result of multiple causes; furthermore, it is often impossible to separate out these individual causes, since many of them lie far back in the early experiences of the worker. As a consequence, we might conclude, not by citing facts but by making an assumption, that the quality of emotional life is significantly but not exclusively influenced by the conditions under which an individual works.

In the present chapter we will consider the emotional costs of work. In certain respects this chapter is a continuation of our study of the psychological importance of work that was taken up in the last chapter. Here, however, we will be concentrating on the negatives of job experiences and asking questions about job characteristics that seem to be linked to psychological tensions. For instance, one important question to be raised is whether individuals in high-status jobs show a frequency of emotional problems different from that shown by persons employed in lower-level positions. Is higher-status work frequently accompanied by greater pressures and increased psychological tensions? Is there a difference between individuals who occupy high- and low-level positions in the effectiveness with which they adjust to life stresses? Is there something about the content of job duties that increases the risk of psychological problems? Do workers on a dull, repetitive job experience more tension or are they relatively free from pressures, since the job is well learned and offers no threat of failure?

These and other questions will be considered in the light of the research literature dealing with industrial mental health. There has been some interesting work reported in this area, and although the research problems involved are very complicated, there has been some encouraging progress made in our understanding of the effects of work on the general quality of an individual's emotional life.

Measurement and Definition

The measurement of psychological stress and mental health is a very difficult undertaking. One approach relies on the self-report of the individual. Workers are either interviewed with regard to their work experiences or are given a questionnaire that asks them to report the presence or absence of tension-related symptoms like headaches, insomnia, and feelings of fear and anger. Interview records are given to psychiatrists or clinical psychologists who make an evaluation of the mental health of the person interviewed. Evidence of mental health and stress can also be inferred from information concerning stress-related physical complaints. An index of this type, which has figured prominently in stress research, is evidence of coronary heart disease and one of its predisposing conditions, the level of serum cholesterol in the blood.

None of these measures is completely satisfactory; each looks at a different facet of mental health and each faces the problem of measuring a highly complicated behavioral system that is composed of a number of separate components. Perhaps the best way to see the multidimensional nature of mental health is to consider some of the definitions that have been used to deal with the concept. We will consider only two of these definitions, selected because they have come out of studies that have dealt with the problems of mental health in a work setting. The first is a definition that has been presented by Kornhauser (1965) in his classic study of mental health among automobile workers. Kornhauser contends that behaviors that indicate good mental health involve the following characteristics:

1. Freedom from anxiety and its related symptoms such as excessive nervousness, insomnia, and overconcern with one's health
2. High self-esteem and self-confidence; freedom from extreme discouragement, a positive feeling of accomplishment, and confidence in the future
3. Freedom from excessive and persistent hostility
4. An active and positive outlook regarding other people; tendency to seek social contacts rather than withdraw from social situations
5. Trust and confidence in others, a positive outlook regarding interpersonal relations

French and Kahn (1962) provide us with another set of behavioral dimensions, which they use in their definition of mental health. These authors contend that in measuring mental health, one should take the following behaviors into consideration:

1. Attitudes and perceptions toward the self
2. Growth, development, and self-actualization
3. Integration
4. Perception of reality
5. Interpersonal competence
6. Autonomy
7. Affective states
8. Physiologic states
9. Disease entities
10. Criteria of job performance
11. Adjustment and adjustability

Each of the dimensions listed above presents formidable measurement problems, and the prospects of combining these many facets into a reliable global measure of mental health is challenging indeed. Yet we do find in these definitions a clear statement of the kind of behaviors that enter the concept. Mental health involves a combination of

658.3
R137W

CALL NUMBER

Staff use:

STOR

LOCATION

Title:

Author:

instances of distress and no assumption will be made that these individual symptoms stem from a more basic underlying condition that is called mental disease.

THEORIES OF WORK ADJUSTMENT AND MENTAL HEALTH

Behavioral scientists frequently construct theoretical models to deal with the complex events they study. A model can be thought of as an abstraction of real happenings. It is a system of logic, a set of ideas that is thought to parallel a set of real behaviors. The relationships between the parts of this logical system represent the relationships found in the real world of ongoing behavior. When this is true, the model permits us to explain the behaviors that are observed. In its most elegant form, the scientific model is expressed in precise mathematical terms, the equations of which permit us to predict behaviors that will occur in the future. In its most usual form, however, a model is a general approximation to real events. It frequently serves as a point of reference that gives the observer a way of looking at the welter of events that enter behavioral situations. We will deal with ...hion, considering a model ...ermits us to consider com- ...ng a set of reference con- ...nize our observations. We ...ding that it is probably not ...of truth, but a system that ...roximations to real events ...e moment.

...rk Adjustment

...videly accepted idea con- ...ork adjustment is one that ... thinking of industrial psy- ...rly beginnings of the field ...iteles, 1932). The gist of ...adjustment may be thought ...nt to which the job fits the ...r fits the job. Perhaps the best recent statement of this point of view can be found in a theory of work adjustment presented by Lofquist and Dawis (1969). Briefly put, this theory maintains that the worker brings to a job certain abilities and certain psychological needs. The job, in turn, confronts the worker with certain demands on his abilities and a set of potentials for satisfying the individual's needs. Worker adjustment to the job can then be thought of in terms of the extent to which the worker fulfills the requirements of the work situation and the extent to which the work situation satisfactorily meets the psychological needs of the worker.

When placed on a job, a worker actively seeks out a harmonious relationship with the work environment, trying to meet the demands of the job and achieve the rewards and satisfactions the job makes available. As a worker remains on the job, this relationship between job and worker begins to stabilize and there emerges a pattern or style of behavior that characterizes what Lofquist and Dawis call the work personality. This is defined as a cluster of needs and abilities that play a part in the worker's effort to cope with the job. If these needs and abilities form a harmonious relationship with the job, then the worker remains on the job; a satisfactory adjustment has been made.

Lofquist and Dawis do not think of worker adjustment in terms of some permanent matching of the worker with a job that remains fixed over time. Instead, they deal with worker adjustment as a continuing and changing process. Work adjustment is continuous and dynamic, with the job imposing varying demands on the worker, and the worker facing the job with changing abilities and changing psychological needs. As one might suspect, the relative stability of the correspondence between worker and work varies from one individual to the next and from one situation to the next.

The theory speaks of satisfactoriness and satisfaction. Satisfactoriness refers to the extent to which individual workers fulfill the requirements of the work environment, and is measured through the observations and judgment of others who have opportunity to appraise their job performance. Satisfaction refers to the extent to which the work environment fulfills the psychological needs of the workers, and is measured in terms of the workers' own appraisal of their work experience. In the words of Lofquist and Dawis, the basic process of work adjustment may be thought of in terms of the day-to-day *correspondence* between job satisfactoriness and job satisfaction.

One finds in this model a very general approach to the process of work adjustment. The fit between a worker and the job is a consideration that is basic to much thinking that goes on about industrial mental health, and the Lofquist-Dawis model has served as a useful tool in dealing with this area of work behavior.

Subjective Aspects of Worker Adjustment

A worker's adjustment to the job environment has just been described as a process that has two aspects—the worker's subjective satisfaction and the extent to which job requirements are fulfilled. A model will next be considered that deals specifically with one of these components, the worker's feeling of satisfaction. This model, developed by Bradburn (1969), attempts to describe the structure of psychological well-being. It deals with the manner in which positive and negative experiences come together to influence a person's general feelings of happiness. Although Bradburn's model was not specifically developed with reference to an industrial situation, he and his associates (Noll, 1968) have extended it to the work setting; therefore it will be considered in this context.

Bradburn maintains that there are two sources of subjective input that determine a person's position on a scale of psychological well-being. One of these includes those experiences that lead to positive affect (positive emotions) and the other includes those experiences that lead to negative affect. Furthermore, and this is important, it is thought that these two dimensions of subjective experience are independent of one another. In other words, the extent to which individuals experience positive emotions in some area of their lives does not usually enable us to predict the extent to which they also experience negative feelings; the two are independent. The extent to which individuals avow happiness—that is, the degree to which they experience a general feeling of psychological well-being—is a function of the algebraic sum of these positive and negative emotional states. In Bradburn's (1968) words,

> A person's position on the dimension of psychological well-being is seen as a resultant of the individual's position on two independent dimensions—one positive affect and the other negative affect. The model specifies that an indivdual will be high in psychological well-being in the degree to which he has an excess of positive over negative affect and will be lower in well-being in the degree to which negative affect predominates over positive. (p. 9)

One interesting implication of this idea is that we cannot, with anything that approaches certainty, infer individuals' general feelings of well-being on the basis of the frequency with which they are faced with events that produce negative emotions. Since they may also experience a compensating, or even a larger number of instances of positive affect, individuals may report large numbers of negative experiences and still feel that they are generally happy and well adjusted in the situation.

An example might help translate these ideas into an industrial setting. Suppose we find a worker who is repeatedly exposed to the pressures and abuses of a thoughtless supervisor. As we listen to him talk about these work experiences we might be led to assume that we are dealing with an unhappy worker. When inquiring a bit further, however, we learn that this person experiences numerous social contacts with fellow workers that are both congenial and rewarding. We find that the negative experiences have no direct bearing on these positive experiences, since the positive character of the contacts with work associates is not diminished by the negative character of experiences with the supervisor. If the positive experiences overbalance the negative ones, then the net result of these two sets of events might well be a worker who in general, overall terms maintains a feeling of positive well-being with regard to the job.

Another interesting aspect of Bradburn's model is the contention that positive experiences are related to different things than negative experiences. In other words, there are areas of an individual's life that tend to contribute to the experience of positive affect; there is a different set of life situations that tend to relate to the experience of negative affect. Extending these ideas to the work environment, one might predict that there are facets of the job that tend to be associated with feelings that are positive; there are other areas of the job that tend to correlate with negative feelings. Variation of the conditions found in the former set of job facets results in variation in one's feelings, ranging from neutral to positive; they tend not to produce negative emotions; variation here results in changes in feelings ranging from neutral to

negative, with positive affect rarely expected to be associated with these events.

We can summarize the main ideas in Bradburn's theory by noting that according to this approach, psychological adjustment reflects the sum of an individual's positive and negative experiences. Feelings of well-being are the result of this combination of plus and minus experiences. Furthermore, there are certain aspects of the individual's life that are more likely to be involved in positive feelings; there are other aspects that are more involved with negative experiences. These are interesting ideas that we will take up in more detail when we consider job satisfaction (see Chapter 8). For the moment, however, we have a very general model that provides a framework for thinking about the nature of psychological adjustment.

A Theory of Occupational Status and Mental Health

Those who write about worker behavior have shown an increasing interest in the idea that the jobs individuals hold play significant roles in shaping and supporting their self-concepts. It is thought that individuals obtain considerable information on self-identification through the experiences they have at work, and a good job environment is one in which the positive and more highly valued dimensions of the self are actualized in the work. In other words, if workers can see in their jobs a reflection of the talents and skills they value most highly, then the work is thought to be psychologically healthy. One facet of this general process concerns the perceived status of occupations. It is thought that an individual's feelings of self-worth, an important factor in mental health, is significantly influenced by the prestige level of the job he holds.

A group of researchers from the Institute for Social Research at the University of Michigan have developed an interesting model that ties occupational prestige to mental health (French and Kahn, 1962; Kasl and French, 1962; Zander and Quinn, 1967). Based on research findings, the theory begins by pointing out that there is reasonably good evidence indicating that jobs distribute themselves along a scale of social prestige (Taylor, 1968; Slocum & Musgrave, 1967) and that people frequently agree about the things that determine the prestige of jobs. Such matters as income, educational requirements, the job's contribution to social welfare, and so forth, appear to be the factors that people use in assessing the social status of occupations. Furthermore, research points out that individuals generally agree on the location of occupations along a scale of social status (Simpson & Simpson, 1960), and that these prestige ratings have shown amazing stability over time (Hodge, Siegel, and Rossi, 1964) and across cultures (Inkeles & Rossi, 1956).

On the basis of this background research, it is hypothesized that the personal characteristics of job holders are inferred, in part, from the characteristics of the jobs they hold. Furthermore, just as the characteristics of the jobs themselves are valued differently by people, so too are the personal characteristics that are attributed to those who hold the jobs. Individuals who hold high-status jobs are seen as possessing more highly valued personal characteristics. Executives, for instance, may be seen as having high intelligence, strong leadership skills, and sound judgment. As a consequence, public esteem—that is, a person's status as perceived by others—is imputed to an individual as a result of the public evaluation of the job and the personal characteristics attributed to those who hold the job. The higher the status of the occupation, the higher the status of the individual.

The theory goes on to assume that individuals become aware of the level of public esteem they hold by seeing this expressed in the behavior of others who interact with them. One's public esteem contributes significantly to the development of the person's own feelings of worth and esteem, and the higher the level of self-esteem, the more likely it is that the individual will experience good mental health. As a consequence, the theory predicts that we should find more evidence of positive mental health as we move up to higher levels of job status. We will look at the research support for this prediction later in this chapter, but first we

should look at one final theory, which considers problems of work tensions and mental health within the setting of a large, complex work organization.

A Theory of Organizational and Individual Response to Stress

Organizations, like individuals, are sometimes exposed to threats and tensions that require some sort of adaptation. Shrinking revenues, a shake-up in management, mergers, and the like produce the kind of tensions that may reverberate throughout an entire organization, resulting in profound changes in the psychological climate of work. Organizational stress carries over to place pressures on the individual, and if conditions are severe enough, these organizational stresses can lead to tensions experienced by the individual workers.

Hall and Mansfield (1971) have presented a theoretical outline that draws a parallel between the processes of stress that involve organizations and the tensions that are transferred from the organization to the individual. This model contends that the sequence of events associated with organizational stress have characteristics that are also found associated with personal stress.

The theory defines stress an an external force operating on a system, and strain is the internal changes that result from these external influences. Organizational stress—that is, threats that originate outside the organization—transform into organizational strain—that is, changes in the internal workings of the company. The organization will attempt to mobilize its resources to come to grips with these internal strains, but in doing so both the internal strains and the coping mechanisms adopted by the organization to deal with them alter the working environment and may result in conditions that expose the individual worker to stresses that are internalized as personal strain. The individual then initiates coping behaviors in order to adapt to these external pressures, and depending on circumstances—for example, the level of stress and its persistence—the individual may adopt behaviors that themselves serve as a new source of

FIGURE 6.1   The Cycle of Organizational Stress and Individual Strain

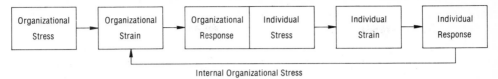

Source: Hall, D. T., & Mansfield, R. Organizational and individual response to external stress. *Administrative Science Quarterly*, 1971, *16*, 533–547. Published by permission of Administrative Science Quarterly.

organizational stress. The cycle then repeats itself. Figure 6.1 summarizes this model as presented by Hall and Mansfield (1971).

It is hypothesized that during the early phases of the stress cycle, an organization will concentrate on achieving its own goals, often to the exclusion of its concern for the needs of its individual members. As a result, the individual worker experiences reduced identification with the organization, and in attempting to adapt to the threat he faces, the worker is less likely to be concerned about the needs of the organization. Conditions that produce internal stress for the organization now exist.

An Example.   Hall and Mansfield present a study that reflects a stress cycle that occurred in a group of research and development organizations. Although the situation described is more complex and detailed than can be presented here, a brief sketch of the study will serve to illustrate the central ideas of the model.

The principal source of organizational stress operating in this situation resulted from a substantial decrease in the financial resources available to a group of scientist-technicians who were employed in this research and development setting. Market conditions and a reduction in government support for research put these organizations under considerable external stress. As Hall and Mansfield indicate, stress transforms into strain, and in this instance this meant a heightened awareness within the organization that expenses had to be reduced and that additional revenues were needed. The organization began to cope with these tensions by encouraging its scientists to work on problems not of their own choosing, but on those that had

more immediate prospects for funding and practical payoff. In addition, the organizations began to adapt to these strains by reducing budgets and generally initiating economy measures.

The organizational stress cycle transferred to the individual scientists; personal stress took the form of reduced job security, reduced pay and promotion opportunities, and less opportunity for self-fulfillment. This translated into internal strains, as individuals reported decreased satisfaction with a variety of job dimensions. Finally, as the researchers began to cope with these problems, there was a noticeable decrease in organizational identification and, in some groups, a decrease in motivation to work. These, of course, are conditions that impose another form of stress on the organization, and the cycle begins again.

The Hall and Mansfield theory is an interesting one because it represents a tension exchange relationship that exists between an individual and a work organization. There is a transfer of tensions from organization to individual and from individual to organization. As these cycles of stress begin to build and accumulate, we see that the concept of mental health can be applied to both the individual and the organization. The internal climate of an organization and the cycle of tensions set up between the organization and its members may show many of the same signs of pathology most usually associated with the individual alone.

WORKING UNDER PRESSURE

What do workers tell us when they are asked to describe, either through interviews or by means of questionnaires, the conditions of work perceived to be responsible for the tensions they experience? As a general rule, we find that job pressures are not limited to a small set of pathogenic working conditions. Almost every facet of work, its social context and the personalities of the workers, have at one time or another been associated with work stress. To be sure, there are aspects of the job environment that carry comparatively greater potential for stress, but the experience of psychological distress is most frequently the result of combinations of several factors, some residing in the worker, some in the work environment.

Beyond the background and personality of the employee, stress-producing job pressures can be found in the duties and demands of work, in its physical surroundings, among the persons who constitute the work group, and in the characteristics of the organization in which the job is carried out. In regard to this latter aspect, several authors (Buck, 1972; Jackall, 1978) have pointed out that work pressures, especially those found in white-collar jobs, can be an expression of a management philosophy that views high levels of pressure as a condition that is desirable for increased levels of production. As a result, pressure is induced by managerial styles that consciously attempt to create a climate of tension. In Buck's terms, job pressures can become part of an organizational strategy.

The Duties and Demands of Work

There have been numerous reports from workers indicating that the stress they experience is the result of difficulties growing out of their understanding (or lack thereof) of what is expected of them on the job. The understanding of one's work assignment and its objectives is referred to as the perceived work role, and it is with regard to this aspect of work that much tension seems to be generated. Ambiguity surrounding work roles is a problem that is particularly acute in management positions, where job duties are often ill defined and the objectives of work projects are obscure. Managers often report considerable pressure stemming from their confusion regarding areas of re-

sponsibility and authority. Responsibility refers to areas of work activity in which the manager is held accountable for outcomes. Authority refers to areas of jurisdiction, that is, activities in which the manager can legitimately make decisions and manipulate resources (power) to achieve work goals. Managers frequently report instances in which they are held accountable for certain outcomes, although uncertain whether they have the authority to adequately influence the events that lead to these outcomes. As an example, managers are responsible for the effectiveness of their subordinates' performance, but often there is considerable uncertainty whether the company will "back up" the personnel decisions the manager would like to make.

Overloading the work role creates another situation in which the prospects for tension are high. The pressures stemming from role overload have been observed in a variety of employment situations (Whyte, 1948; Walker & Guest, 1952; Buck, 1972; Jackall, 1978). The salesperson faces an overload of customer requests during rush hours, the assembly-line worker complains about the speed of the line, the executive claims there is too little time in the day to meet the demands of the job, and the schoolteacher protests classrooms with excessively large enrollments.

French and Caplan (1973) have differentiated two types of role overload, quantitative and qualitative. Quantitative overload refers to situations of the type just described, where the worker has too much to do in the time available. Qualitative overload refers to a situation in which the requirements of the job exceed the worker's knowledge and talents. One can think of many instances of this latter problem, but one important cause of the difficulty is the rapid changes in technology, which make skills and knowledge become obsolete. Increasingly one hears of workers who at one time possessed the necessary skills and knowledge to meet the demands of a job, but who, because of the introduction of new technology, were rather rapidly put in a position where these technical skills became overloaded.

Finally, workers report that tensions often arise

from sets of conflicting demands. Conflicts between personal ethics and business practices, competing loyalties to peers and superiors, and conflicts between the requirements of quality work and career aspirations create tensions with which the worker must cope. One of the more threatening sources of tension is found in the decisions that managers must make regarding personnel. For example, Baumhart (1968) found that managers frequently experience significant personal conflict in conjunction with firing and layoffs. Baumhart (p. 29) quotes one executive as saying, ''Employees with long, good records, and whose work becomes inefficient. How long can I carry them on the payroll? What is the measure of my loyalty to a man who helped build my business?'' Guilt, loyalty, and insecurity combine to make decisions concerning people a persistent pressure in the lives of those who lead work groups.

The Physical Environment of Work

There is an accumulation of evidence indicating that there are limits beyond which there is an increasing risk that the physical environment of work will produce tension and stress (Poulton, 1978). The intensity of light, noise, temperature, smells, and other atmospheric pollutants can all reach levels where workers find working conditions unpleasant and stress-producing. The stress associated with the physical environment is often inferred from performance levels or on the basis of employee subjective ratings of the relative unpleasantness of a specific condition. The more global mental-health effects of a poor work environment have been demonstrated, but the amount of information in this area is not very substantial. Nevertheless, poor mental health has been associated with such things as exposure to danger and health hazards, tiring and physically demanding work, and long hours (Kasl, 1978).

Work Specialization

One of the basic requirements of satisfying work is that it must be meaningful. By this we mean that the worker should be able to construct

a rationale for the work that explains the purposes and objectives of the job in a way the individual can accept. In jobs that have been highly specialized, where the duties are narrow and routine, workers often have difficulty justifying the work they are doing. This is especially true as their years on the job increase, and the persistent sameness of work leads them to question the reasons for continuing on a job that has become empty and monotonous. Such circumstances often lead to the worker experiencing tension and anxiety.

Highly routinized work is most often associated with blue-collar production jobs. Sewing-machine occupations, small-scale assembly, canning and food processing, assembly-line production, all clearly reflect the engineering efforts that have been made to improve the efficiency of performance through job specialization. White-collar work has not been immune from these influences, however; Jackall (1978) reports on an extensive series of interviews carried out on a sample of bank clerks whose jobs had been highly standardized and segmented in the same fashion as many blue-collar production jobs. One clerk told Jackall, ''What do I like about this job? Are you kidding? This is a very boring job. I feel like I am already a robot, a machine'' (p. 34). The nature of this type of highly routinized work creates pressures with which each individual worker must cope. In some instances workers reported that they took steps to artificially complicate their work in order to combat the boredom of standardized work.

> How do I cope with this job? Well I've developed my own system for things, even for things nobody was really interested in having systematized. I do this because I was so damned bored. I just keep adding variables until it is terribly complicated. . . . It doesn't make the job more interesting, but it does make it less boring. (Jackall, 1978, p. 36)

The interviews revealed that the workers were basically ambivalent about their jobs. The jobs were relatively secure and the pay was important to them, but they also saw their work as being tedious and unchanging. How did these workers legitimize this work? How did they make sense out of what they were doing? A wide variety of mechanisms were adopted to cope with these problems, with each worker developing a personal set of defensive rationalizations to excuse or justify many of the pressures and stresses of the job. For example, one defensive theme involved the understanding that the job was a temporary one and that the worker could find more suitable employment whenever desired. Others adopted the belief that they intended to take action that would place the job more tightly under their control. Some threatened to join unions or go on strike. Others developed a justification for their dull jobs by acknowledging that there is routine and uniformity in all jobs, and as a result, there was no reason to believe that their present problems would change on any other job.

The list of defensive strategies that may be adopted to cope with the tensions of standardized work is limited only by the ingenuity of the worker. The important thing to remember, however, is not how any one worker comes to grips with this problem, but that a fundamental condition of work that produces psychological distress can be found in the absence of acceptable justification legitimizing the work being done. It is important that workers be able to account for their jobs in a way that gives the position meaning and importance. If the individual is unable to do this, then job experiences become disorderly and, eventually, stressful.

Interpersonal Pressures—Harassment

It is in the relations between people that we often find significant work-related tensions. People threaten one another; they dispense the rewards and punishments of work, they provide guidance and support on which much of an individual's general security is based. Hence, interpersonal relations play a pivotal role in an individual's efforts to maintain a satisfactory adjustment to work.

Reports of job tension often contain anxiety about social relations. Brodsky (1976) interviewed a large number of workers who had filed claims for workmen's compensation as the result of being unable to work because of difficulties with other people. Numerous instances of harrassment were involved in these cases in which one person or a group put another in an uncomfortable position. These pressures led the individual to leave the job, and often the target of this harassment experienced severe and debilitating psychological problems.

Often harassment is a reflection of the competition that exists among the members of a group. In many instances these pressures lead to relatively mild forms of aggression, such as teasing and exposing the worker to minor embarrassment. There are other times when the level of competition is high and the psychological consequences more distressing. Superiors, peers, and subordinates have all been found to be involved in harassing other workers. Name calling, shunning, and hostile practical jokes from peers; undesirable assignments, constant checking of work, and public reprimands from superiors; rudeness and insubordination by subordinates—all are found in the cases studied by Brodsky.

Usually the harassment of one worker by another represents an effort by one individual to gain a competitive advantage over another. Sometimes the harassment is organized and purposeful, as might be the case when a work group turns on one of its members who may have violated some group norm. Sometimes supervisors harass workers whom they do not like in order to force their resignation. At other times however, harassment is an unplanned consequence of a work situation that generates competition that results in persistent pressures and anxieties. Whatever the causes or consequences, Brodsky's report demonstrates the significance of negative interpersonal relationships in influencing the climate of tensions that exist in a work environment. A good adjustment to work involves satisfactory relations with one's work associates.

Personality Factors

Although our emphasis has been on factors that are external to the worker, the wide individual differences observed in reaction to a given job situation testify to the importance of personality factors in the experience of work tensions. The fact that two workers facing the same set of job pressures may report completely different levels of tension leads us to look at the background and personality of these individuals to find an explanation for these differences.

Buck (1972) finds that it is the cautious, fearful individual who is predisposed to experience job tensions. Among workers and managers alike, Buck found that those who experienced high levels of job pressure were individuals who displayed well-developed tendencies toward self-protection. Whether this guarded personality type results in a plodding and defensive approach to work that lowers effectiveness and increases work pressures, or whether it merely lowers a person's threshold for the pressures that are imposed on everyone on a job, is a matter that Buck's results do not resolve. Nevertheless, this study clearly demonstrates that a person with high need to avoid failure, humiliation, and blame, while at the same time possessing a well-formed degree of egocentricity, is an individual who is likely to report job pressures. Hence, personality factors, which are often well established at the time an individual enters a job, combine with job design variables to create a condition that produces psychological tensions experienced at work.

RESEARCH IN INDUSTRIAL MENTAL HEALTH

Currently there is a large number of people who are convinced that while pursuing the narrow objectives of production efficiency, work organizations have designed many jobs in a way that neglects some of the more important psychological needs of the worker. Immediately the assembly line comes to mind as a symbol of both modern technology and the psychological sterility of work. High levels of production efficiency are obtained from jobs that are routine, repetitive, unchanging, and machine-paced. Jobs of this sort create a negative picture for observers, especially those whose background and work experience are foreign to blue-collar production. But beyond the moving line and the lunch pail there is also a white-collar world that can appear to be equally empty and

unrewarding. Here work is not only segmented and routine, but is entangled in a stupifying bureaucracy. Commenting on such conditions, Sheppard and Herrick (1972) state:

> In today's highly regimented, increasingly automated, and deeply impersonal industrial society, the human being who has found fulfilling work is indeed among the blessed. . . . But more and more workers—and every day this is more apparent—are becoming more disenchanted with the boring, repetitive tasks set by a merciless assembly line or by bureauracy. They feel they have been herded into economic and social cul-de-sacs.

Although one might be hard pressed to find convincing evidence for such a negative view of contemporary work, this statement does illustrate both a rising apprehension over the adjustment problems many workers face and a widely shared conviction that a principal source of stress is to be found in the design of a job rather than in the individual personality the worker brings to the job.

Although aware of the importance of environmental factors, the behavioral scientist traditionally has associated emotional difficulties with personality characteristics, the foundations of which had been set down quite early in life. Few would challenge the validity of this point of view. What we are now considering in dealing with industrial mental health, however, is a shift in emphasis, the current emphasis being that work tensions and stress do not arise exclusively from a defective personality, but from deficiencies that are inherent in the structure of a job. It should be pointed out there really is no serious effort in the field to downgrade the importance of workers' early experiences or the many signficant events in their lives that occur away from the workplace. Nor would any serious student of industrial behavior suggest that what Lofquist and Dawis call job-worker correspondence is not an important factor in the worker's emotional adjustment. What we are referring to at the moment is a change in focus, a shift in interest toward variables that are associated with the design of the job.

Job Design Variables

Perhaps a good place to begin our consideration of job content factors is with the widely cited study reported by Kornhauser (1965). This was a rather intensive study of the mental-health status of a group of blue-collar workers who were employed in thirteen automobile manufacturing plants in the Detroit area. Workers were interviewed with regard to a variety of work, background, and attitude considerations, and each interview was scored on a scale that reflected the status of their mental health. Data analysis revealed that there was a clear relationship between the skill level of workers' jobs and their score on the mental-health scale. Generally, it was observed that the workers whose jobs required skill and had a greater variety of operations were the ones who scored higher on the mental-health scale. Furthermore, when these workers were classified according to their age, the same general trends were found for both young and middle-aged workers, although there was a tendency for high mental-health scores to occur less frequently among younger workers who held repetitive semiskilled jobs.

Job Status.   Other studies give us results indicating that the level of job skill may make an important contribution to the general mental health of the worker. Kasl and French (1962), in conjunction with their theory of occupational status and mental health, report two studies that were carried out on large groups of blue-collar and supervisory personnel. They measured mental health in a rather interesting fashion by determining the number of times a worker visited the company dispensary during a specified period of time. These authors cite evidence (Sainsbury, 1960) indicating that individuals with emotional problems tend to seek medical aid more frequently than do those having better psychological adjustment. Hence, if dispensary visits varied among jobs with different skill levels, this would suggest that there was a relationship between mental health and the skill content of work.

Two studies were carried out, one involving 5389 production and supervisory personnel employed by a communications company, the other involving 625 supervisory and nonsupervisory employees of an aircraft factory. The results of both studies revealed, as was predicted, that workers on jobs with higher skill requirements tended to visit the dispensary less frequently than did workers who were in low-skill jobs. It is interesting to note that this finding held up when supervisory positions were studied separately. Furthermore, these relationships remained basically unchanged when the frequency of dispensary visits was adjusted by disregarding visits involving injury or accidents; hence, even after making adjustment for differences in job hazards, skill level and dispensary visits still showed a strong negative relationship.

These results lend support to Kornhauser's study, although Kasl and French view them from a somewhat different perspective, since they placed more emphasis on the fact that the variations in skill level of jobs tend to be accompanied by variations in the social status of the job. Furthermore, in keeping with their theoretical position, they linked the social status of a job with the individual's self-esteem, arguing that it was this high self-regard that led to better mental health.

Kornhauser acknowledged that there is a close relationship between skill level and job status. He attempted to isolate and study job status, and he found that perceived job status was, in fact, related to the mental health of these automobile workers. For example, for workers in routine low-skill jobs, twice as many who saw their positions as lacking importance were found in the low mental-health category as those who saw their jobs as important.

Hence, at this skill level, there appears to be a rather clear relationship between the status of the job, *as it is perceived by the job holder,* and the level of mental health. A similar analysis was inconclusive at the higher-skill levels, primarily because so few workers at these levels perceived their jobs as being unimportant. This, of course, in itself testifies to the association between skill level and job status.

Job Differences.   More work needs to be done before we will be able to make separate statements about these two variables; at present it would probably be reasonable to conclude that both make a significant contribution to the mental health of the worker. When individuals are forced to grapple with a dull, low-status job, discontentment with work can eventually transform into tension and poor mental health. It would be unwise, however, to expect every time one observes two jobs, one more complex than the other, that the mental-health status of the employees will reflect the relative level of skill and of the two positions. Even though dull, routine work duties may produce a predisposition to feelings of tension, other job conditions may compensate for the monotony of the task and make the job situation reasonably satisfactory (Kennedy & O'Neill, 1958; Turner & Lawrence, 1965; Chinoy, 1955).

As an example, a study by Turner and Miclette (1962) involved employees who were assembling very small electronic components. The job was routine and repetitive, but it did require the worker to acquire a knack in manipulating the components. In spite of the routine nature of the work, these employees were found to maintain relatively healthy attitudes toward work, largely stemming from such things as their pride in the product and their *perception* of the job as requiring high skill. Hence, in the view of these workers, their jobs provided them with assignments in which they could take pride and exercise a competent level of skill.

There are also reports of wide individual differences in responses to job design factors. Some workers are able to adjust their approach to a dull job so as to make their work more satisfying. They may enrich their work by improvising more interesting job activiites (Jackall, 1978), lowering their expectations, or focusing on some aspect of the position (for example, income, work associates) that compensates for dull work. Furthermore, some workers find security in jobs they know can be mastered and that are unlikely to change. A ''good steady job'' can confront the worker with little that is difficult and provide a reliable paycheck. But in spite of these possibilities, the evidence currently available indicates that this kind of worker does not represent a large segment of the labor force. Rather, it seems reasonable to conclude that variety and challenging levels of skill

are factors that increase the probability of a more contented worker who is not burdened by costly tensions and poor mental health.

Social Class and Mental Health

There are some (for example, Zaleznik, Ondrack, & Silver, 1970) who contend that in placing emphasis on job design as a factor in mental illness, the influence of social class has not been adequately taken into consideration. Of course, a major difficulty confronting much of the research done on industrial mental health lies in the interrelationships among the variables that are manipulated. To vary components of the job, such as skill content, without also varying a host of other correlated factors is oftentimes a difficult, or impossible, task to accomplish. For instance, higher levels of occupational skill tend to be associated with other factors, such as income level and education, that enter into the measurement of socioeconomic class. Hence, in looking at jobs having varying levels of skill, indirectly one will also be looking across different levels of socioeconomic status. Furthermore, the different levels of socioeconomic status vary in terms of a large number of other factors that have a bearing on the psychological adjustment of the individual.

A number of studies have considered the relationship between mental health and the broader concept of social class. These studies relate to our interest in jobs and worker behavior, since in most cases occupational status plays a central role in defining the social class of the groups observed. Furthermore, the studies contain some interesting insights that may be applied to the interpretation of the results of studies that are done within an industrial setting.

As a group, these studies confirm the relationship reported from the industrial studies—that is, higher social status is associated with higher levels of mental health. For example, Hollingshead and Redlich (1958) conducted a survey of individuals in the community of New Haven, Connecticut. These authors report a definite relationship between social class and the likelihood of being a psychiatric patient. As one moves up the social classes, one finds a decreasing proportion of patients under psychiatric care. Hence, it is beginning to appear that we are dealing with a very general phenomenon. Individuals who hold highly valued positions, at work or in the community, tend to show evidence of higher mental health. People who are in low-status positions tend to show evidence of lower mental health.

Perhaps the most interesting confirmation of this point of view is found in a cross-cultural study reported by Inkeles (1960). In this instance, data collected by a variety of authors were drawn from a number of national surveys. Responses dealing with such things as job satisfaction, avowed happiness, life satisfaction, and the like were considered in relation to the status structure of the various countries from which data were obtained. On the basis of his analysis, Inkeles concluded that in all modern societies there seems to be a fairly consistent relationship between people's social position and many of their more important psychological characteristics. There were, to be sure, country-to-country differences in the percentage of people found at different levels of satisfaction and happiness, but in all countries similar shifts occurred in these variables as the study moved across different income, educational, and occupational levels. The direction of these shifts was similar across countries, with high-status individuals appearing to be better adjusted psychologically. It seems to be a general rule that an individual's social status is related to a number of psychological characteristics, some of which, like avowed happiness and life satisfaction, are a direct expression of mental health. Hence, what we observe in work settings regarding mental health, and the skill and status of jobs, is probably a reflection of a broader relationship that extends throughout a culture.

Langner and Michael's study.   One may wonder why these relationships exist. Why should we find evidence of better mental health as we move up into more highly skilled and statusful jobs? The first explanation to come to mind is that higher-status positions, whether in industry or in the community, carry with them lower exposure to stress. For those in lower-ranked positions, life includes more stress, perhaps stemming from the fact that

the circumstances surrounding these positions provide fewer opportunities to satisfy one's needs. Levitan (1971) presents evidence to suggest that high public esteem is related to better opportunities to satisfy needs. Levitan also presents evidence indicating that good mental health is related to opportunities one has to fulfill one's needs.

Langner and Michael (1963) report on a study that bears directly on this idea. The study was part of the Midtown Community Mental Health Project (Rennie & Srole, 1956), which involved an extensive set of mental health interviews conducted with persons living in New York City. Langner and Michael obtained from their data the usual relationship between social status and measures of mental health. As they moved up from low to high socioeconomic levels they found a substantial improvement in the mental health of their subjects. Furthermore, mental health seemed to be related to the *number* of stresses to which an individual was exposed, but not to the specific kinds of stresses that were present in the environment. In other words, it didn't seem to matter what *kind* of pressures an individual experienced; it was the *number* of different sources of stress that related to the quality of his mental health.

These results appear to support the hypothesis that explains the mental health differences found among different status positions in terms of the number of stresses to which people in these positions are exposed. Yet, when Langner and Michael examined frequency of exposure to stress, they found that the differences among the social classes were relatively small. People in the higher social classes were being exposed to just as many stresses as those in lower classes. This led them to suggest that it is not exposure to stress that differentiates high- and low-status individuals, but the availability of means for coming to grips with the stresses they face. For example, when the investigators looked at the data on how these individuals attempted to cope with stress, they found that high-status individuals tended to draw on what the psychiatrists believed to be more effective methods. People in low-status levels tended to use psychological coping mechanisms (for example, fantasy, escape) that were less effective in dealing with the problems they faced. Hence, Langner and Michael suggest that the poorer quality of mental health often observed among people in low-status positions might well be a function of *how* they adjust to stress and not the *number* of stresses they must face. This is an interesting idea, since it associates mental health with the competency level of people's coping behaviors and not with an environment that bombards them with numerous stresses. It doesn't rule out, however, the possibility that high-status positions carry with them a more effective set of alternatives with which the individual can contend with stress.

Work Implications

These findings suggest an interesting analogy for the work setting. Recall that Buck (1972) found that rank-and-file workers and managers did not differ in the job pressures they felt. Based on this, we hypothesize that the *number* of job pressures does not change signficantly as one moves up in jobs that are ordered according to skill content, education, income, or any other factor related to social status. Therefore, the fact that low-skill or low-status jobs are often found associated with poorer mental health may indicate that workers holding these jobs have available to them fewer and less effective means of adjusting to the work stresses they experience.

As an example, the person on a routine, machine-paced job is in a situation in which spatial movements are limited, opportunities for improvisation and variation in the work task are restricted, and the daily schedule is fixed and routinized. Face-to-face social contacts occur within work groups that are relatively weak with respect to power and influence, and modest skills deny workers attractive job alternatives, should they choose to leave their present positions. Furthermore, the available alternatives to these workers may not be as effective in meeting their problems as are those available to individuals in higher-status jobs.

The low-status worker does not have ready access to one of the mechanisms that plays an important role in people's attempts to cope with threats to their welfare. This worker cannot as

readily create organizations, change organizations, or learn how to deal more effectively with the alternative channels of an organization. Those with jobs at higher skill and status levels may well have a wider range of these organizational alternatives to draw on in order to cope with the psychological problems they face at work. The whole picture shows higher-status workers having a broader set of defensive measures that provide relief for the job pressures they experience.

There is one more interesting possibility that may explain the poorer mental-health scores among low-skill and low-status workers. Upward mobility in an organization may be selective, based in part on how effectively an individual copes with stress. Langner and Michael (1963, p. 156) conclude, ''The elites in our society are those who are emotionally elite in a broad sense.'' We can speculate that similar selection factors function in a work organization. There are many psychological attributes that influence the probability that a person will be moved up the ranks, and one of these factors involves the general style and effectiveness of coping strategies. Emotional competence, as well as other aptitudes, figures into the selection of people for more challenging and statusful positions in a work organization. We are thus led to the question, is the state of a worker's mental health signficantly influenced by the content of the job, or is the job held a consequence of the state of the worker's mental health? We have already seen that job content factors have an influence on a worker's mental health. There is also evidence (Miner & Anderson, 1958; Segal, 1961; Galinsky, 1962; Super et al., 1963; Holland, 1966) indicating that personality and emotional variables play a role in the selection and placement of people in jobs. Hence, our answer is that job content can influence mental health, but at the same time, the state of an individual's mental health is also a factor determining the level of job held.

Status Incongruity

Within the set of duties defining an individual's job we can usually find a large number of functions and responsibilities that may be described in terms of social status. There may be a considerable range of differences between these elements of status, and in certain instances one status position may be incongruent with another. For example, incongruities may exist between the educational requirements of a job and the wages it pays. Disparity may exist between skill requirements and power to influence work-related decisions. One source of psychological stress is thought to be found in the pattern of status incongruities associated with an individual's job. This follows from the fact that status influences people's views of how they should behave and how others should behave toward them. Individuals with jobs whose duties and work roles carry *both* high and low status are faced with competing and incompatible expectations concerning their own and others' behaviors (Kasl & Cobb, 1967). Such circumstances are thought to be associated with an increased likelihood of psychological stress.

A case in point may be found in a study by Exline and Ziller (1959). These authors set up a laboratory situation in which congruence-incongruence was established between individuals' ability status and their power to influence group decisions. The results indicated that groups whose members experienced status incongruity found themselves functioning in less congenial social climates than were groups whose members were not exposed to these incongruities. In addition, in the incongruity situations there appeared to be more competition among members as they attempted to control group decision making. Under these circumstances, it may be reasonable to expect heightened psychologial stress.

In a work setting, Erickson, Pugh, and Gunderson (1972) attempted to study the relationship between status incongruity and psychological stress among a group of 2080 Navy enlisted men. Status incongruity was determined by considering the degree to which individual's advancement in their jobs was commensurate with the number of years worked, age, and marital status. Life stress was measured by a questionnaire procedure. These authors report that there was a significant correlation obtained between status incongruity and reported psychological stress. Furthermore, life stress seemed to maintain a linear relationship with the absolute degree of status incongruity; as status incongruity increased, there was a proportionate increase in the level of life stress.

Jackson (1960), considering the level of incongruity among ranked occupational, educational, and racial-ethnic backgrounds, found that only certain patterns of status incongruity—for example, males with high occupational status and low educational attainment—were associated with symptoms of psychological strain.

Finally, there appears to be some relationship between indicators of psychological stress and the congruity that exists between present status and aspirations (Kleiner and Parker, 1963). Mahone (1960) has shown that students with unrealistically high occupational aspirations show greater evidence of high levels of anxiety. Coupled with this was the finding that these students appear to have more problems in giving realistic estimates of their abilities.

We see, therefore, that the relationship between the status elements that define an individual's occupational and social role may be a factor that contributes to the psychological tensions experienced. Although the Kornhauser study (1965) failed to find evidence supporting this status-incongruity hypothesis, there appears to be enough evidence in the research literature to suggest that at least under some circumstances incongruent status positions predispose the individual to experience psychological tensions.

Role Conflict

Just as a worker's job is identifiable in terms of a number of status positions, it may also be described with regard to the number of different roles required of those who hold the position (Kahn, 1974). By role is meant a set of activities that are to be performed by those who hold a particular job. A role expectation refers to what others believe an occupant of a job should or should not do.

In a study that involved a national cross section of the labor force, Kahn et al. (1964) found that one relatively common source of work tension is traceable to the conflicting role expectations one finds surrounding a job. Rank-and-file employees, for example, are expected by their supervisors to maintain high production standards, but at the same time they may be expected to adhere to a lower production standard held by their work-group peers. Middle managers are often caught in the middle of conflicting expectations that pit their commitment to doing good creative work against their commitment to serve the career aspirations of their superiors. Almost half of those interviewed in the Kahn et al. study indicated that their jobs exposed them to conflicting role expectations of one sort or another, and in the large majority of instances (88 percent), these conflicts involved the worker with someone who held a higher position in the organization.

A second significant source of role difficulty was found in role overload, a conflict among legitimate tasks or problems involved with the ordering of priorities. Almost 50 percent of those interviewed indicated that their jobs involved these kinds of problems. Role ambiguity, uncertainty concerning work roles, was a third source of psychological tension in work. Almost 40 percent of those in the sample felt that they were frequently given inadequate information with which to perform their jobs in a satisfactory fashion. Among the emotional costs of role conflict and role ambiguity were low levels of job satisfaction, decreased self-confidence, a high sense of futility, and a high incidence of job-related tensions.

Stress and Social Relations

The friendships one establishes at work can serve as a useful mechanism for coping with stress (Newman & Beehr, 1979). For example, the pressures experienced by new employees are often reduced by seeking out friends who hold similar positions in the organization (Mansfield, 1972). The loss of a job is also associated with higher levels of stress (Cobb & Kasl, 1972), but there is evidence (Gore, 1973) indicating that people who lose their jobs stand up better under the stress when they have social support from friends and associ-

ates. Hence, the mechanisms of psychological adjustment can be found in the support one receives from the members of one's social group.

The group can also be a source of considerable tension (Brodsky, 1976). There is evidence that individuals can find themselves in work settings in which the social environment becomes a significant personal problem. One of the more interesting studies done on this topic has been reported by Mettlin and Woelfel (1974). This study revealed a positive relationship between number of associates and amount of stress experienced. When asked to identify people who served as a source of influence in their lives, individuals who listed a greater number of these acquaintances tended to report experiencing higher levels of psychological tensions. Furthermore, reported levels of stress became even higher when this group of acquaintances did not share a uniform set of expectations regarding the person's behavior.

Perhaps Mettlin and Woelfel were observing a form of social overload in which, as the circle of acquaintances grows larger, individuals' capacity to meet their social obligations is reached and passed. It becomes more costly to manage the social world, and consequently, higher levels of tension result. This condition can be aggravated as the composition of the social group becomes increasingly more heterogeneous, particularly as this relates to the group's expectations of the individual. Mettlin and Woelfel suggest that membership in a large work organization that exposes the individual to a large number and wide variety of other people may be stress inducing by virtue of the complexity of the social setting.

REACTIONS TO STRESS

Thus far we have considered the impact of work tensions on the broader aspects of mental health. Now we will turn our attention to studies that have attempted to see how stress affects the performance of an individual who is involved with a job. The basic question is, what does stress do to us as we try to carry out the duties of a job? There have been quite a large number of studies done in this general area, but unfortunately for our purposes, few have dealt with an industrial setting. As a result, we will look briefly at the general literature and then go on to spend a bit more time with those studies that have been carried out with work groups. Specifically, we will consider four questions. The first deals with the effects of stress on the tendency of people to move psychologically closer together. The second concerns the effect of stress on performance levels, and the third will consider individual differences in response to stress.

There is one additional reaction to stress that will be considered. Research has shown that exposure to stress appears to be one of the factors contributing to the risk of coronary heart disease. Associated with this is a pattern of behavior, called Type A behaviors, that is thought to contribute to this disease process. There is a large and growing list of research studies bearing on this topic, and a brief consideration of these findings will be presented.

Stress and Group Cohesiveness

There have been a number of interesting nonindustrial field studies that describe people's reactions to a variety of stressful situations. (Bettelheim, 1943; Janis, 1951, 1958; Schmideberg, 1942; Wolfenstein, 1957; Radloff & Helmreich, 1968). With reasonably good consistency these studies have found that individuals confronted by substantial levels of stress appear to have an increased tendency to affiliate with others and to derive considerable psychological benefit from their association with the members of a group. Furthermore, when exposure to stressful events extends over a long period of time, there appears to be a tendency for individuals to become more dependent on those who hold leadership positions.

Bettelheim (1943), for example, reports that as their confinement continued, prisoners in Nazi internment camps became increasingly responsive to their guards. Modeling the behavior of their captors—for example, wearing clothing and insignia similar to those of the Gestapo officers—a number of the inmates displayed many of the authoritarian behaviors that were characteristic of their oppressors.

Radloff and Helmreich (1968) report a parallel set of results from a psychological investigation of the men who participated in the SEALAB II experiments. The SEALAB project established an underwater environment for a group of men who lived 200 feet beneath the surface of the sea for periods of approximately two weeks. Living conditions were cramped and the men were continuously exposed to uncomfortable and stressful circumstances. Under these conditions, Radloff and Helmreich report that the stresses of the underwater lab increased the dependency the individual members displayed toward their leaders. As reports of stress increased, there was a tendency for the men to show reduced independence and an increased reliance on their leaders.

Studies of the type just described show us that heightened stress and tension can produce an effect on the interpersonal relationships in a group. Leadership styles can more clearly be seen reflected in the behavior of the members, and interpersonal dependency becomes a more influential social force operating in the group. There are instances reported in the literature (Schmideberg, 1942; Janis, 1958) where, when functioning under stress, individuals have been denied affiliation with other members of the group. In these instances individuals report that they experienced considerable anxiety and increased apprehension. Contact with the leader may provide an important source of security, and as the levels of tension increase, there is an increased need for interaction with figures of authority and power.

Laboratory Studies.   Related findings have been reported from laboratory studies in which subjects were exposed to stressful conditions and then were given a choice to affiliate with others or remain alone. Perhaps the most widely cited study in this area is one by Schachter (1959), who brought subjects into an experimental setting and informed them that they would soon be asked to participate in a task that would expose them to painful electric shocks. They were also told that periodically samples of blood would be removed from their arms. After exposure to these threatening instructions, subjects were then given the choice of waiting in a room with other subjects or waiting alone for the experiment to begin. The results of the study revealed that these subjects, confronting stressful events, tended to choose affiliation with others more frequently than did subjects who had been introduced to the experiment by being informed that the electric shock they would receive would "resemble more a tickle or a tingle than anything unpleasant."

Hence, Schachter suggests that when exposed to tension-producing events the individual experiences an increase in the need for affiliation. In other studies that were carried out in the series, he finds that this tendency seems to be independent of the opportunity to communicate with others; just being in close proximity to people appears to be the important ingredient of this response to stress. Furthermore, the data indicate that when given a choice, anxious subjects tend to prefer affiliation with others who share a similar lot (Mansfield, 1972). Schachter suggests that one of the principal motives involved in these affiliational tendencies is found in the need to seek information concerning the appropriateness of one's own behavior, and this one finds through observation of the behavior of others.

Comment. It seems quite reasonable to argue that environmental tensions should encourage people to seek out one another as a means of coping with problems. The field and laboratory studies we have considered thus far have supported this hypotheses. On reflection, however, it is possible to think of situations where these tendencies toward affiliation could be reversed. Consider a situation in which the source of tension is from within a group. Much job pressure, for example, is generated by competition between group members. In these instances, tensions would logically be expected to decrease the cohesion of the group, although affiliation needs might be displaced to other persons or groups in the immediate vicinity.

Consider another situation in which, when responding to outside pressures, individuals are encouraged and rewarded for competing with one another. As a case in point, pressures on salesmen during a sales promotion often throw them into competition with each other. This is an instance in which high levels of pressure can undermine the solidarity of a group of workers. Much seems to depend on whether increased or decreased group solidarity leads to a reduction in work tensions. There are studies reported in the industrial literature that illustrate these possibilities.

Industrial Studies. Seashore (1954) reports a study carried out with 228 section-shift groups working for a company engaged in the manufacture of heavy machinery. In this setting he found that the highest levels of group cohesiveness were not associated with high levels of tension, but were observed when tensions and anxieties were low. When work pressures were high, workers reported less commitment to their groups. There were a few exceptions, and these were obtained from 9 work groups whose average rate of production was considerably below both the company standard and the standard that the group members themselves considered reasonable. Although reporting that they were experiencing high pressures to increase their productivity, these nine groups were highly cohesive. Remember, however, these were 9 groups out of a total of 228 that participated in the study. Hence, even though Seashore found a few instances in which high pressures were associated with high group cohesion, the main drift of his evidence indicated that when workers were under high levels of pressure, their solidarity with their work group tended to be low.

Klein's Study. There is a series of studies by Klein (1971) that give us insight into the conditions under which high tensions will lead to a reduction in group cohesiveness. The first of this series is an interesting study because it was carried out in a plant that had recently initiated a program designed to increase substantially the rate of production obtained from its employees. Industrial engineering studies revealed that the plants forming this company had been producing on the average at 60 percent of the rate considered standard on the basis of time-and-motion studies. Management, seeking to raise production rates, installed a program that raised production standards and placed workers under increased pressures to improve the work rates. At the time the data were collected, a number of employees in these plants had not yet come under the new higher work standards, and as a result there was considerable variation among workers in the extent to which they had been exposed to the new production pressures.

Klein, on the basis of his literature search, hypothesized that the higher the work pressures, the more cohesive would be the behavior of the workers. Unexpectedly, however, Klein's data reveal just the opposite relationship. Conforming to the result reported by Seashore, Klein found a tendency for those groups exposed to the more severe work pressures to be *less* cohesive than were those workers who had not been exposed to the new program of increased production.

These unanticipated results led Klein to look back into his data for clues that might explain the relationships he obtained. In doing so, he discovered that in this particular work situation, high pressures to produce were associated with a reward system that tended to encourage competitive behavior among the members of the work group. Increased rates of production translated into competition and intragroup conflict, and under these circumstances, the climate for forming a cohesive work group was not particularly good.

These additional findings led Klein to undertake a second study, which attempted to replicate the first in all major details. Recall that in the first study the work pressures represented relatively recent changes in the climate of work. The second study was carried out in a company that had a tradition of high production pressures, and the production process was maintained at a high rate that had been increasing gradually over the years. Nevertheless, these work pressures were not uniform for all workers, thus providing Klein with an opportunity for studying how different levels of pressure were associated with variation in measures of group cohesiveness.

The data were collected from 93 production departments and involved 1356 employees. By and large the procedures followed were similar to those followed in the first experiment, and Klein's results were quite consistent with those of his first study. Figure 6.3 has been taken from Klein (1971) to show that he found once again a clear tendency for high cohesive behavior to be observed under conditions of low work pressures. In addition, Figure 6.2 demonstrates a significant relationship between work pressures and evidence of competitive behavior among the members of the work group. Klein found that there were aspects of a reward system operating in the company that seemed to link together work pressures and competitiveness. For instance, in those departments in which work pressures were high, Klein found workers reporting that their supervisors actually encouraged competition among workers. Also, workers in high pressure situations tended to report that helping other workers had little bearing on receiving wage increases.

What we have seen in these studies reported by Klein are groups under pressure from their work who are operating within a system of rewards that tends to reinforce competition and discourage cohesiveness and cooperation. In broad outline, then, we may think of these pressures as a crisis that requires workers to adopt means for coping with these influences. Whether they adopt a pattern of increased cohesiveness, or whether they adopt a pattern of increased competition and decreased cohesion, depends in large measure on the reward system that operates to encourage one or the other pattern of accommodation. Just the fact that tensions and pressures are present in a given situation may not in itself permit us to anticipate the resulting course of group behaviors. We must also look to the structure of the reward system surrounding affiliational behaviors on the one hand, and the structure of the reward system surrounding competitive behaviors on the other, before we can predict the social consequences of work pressures.

Along similar lines, whenever the individual

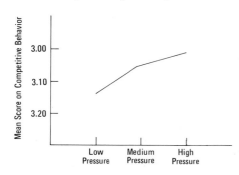

FIGURE 6.2 Relationship between Work Pressure and Competitive Behavior
(F = 2.51, P < .10)

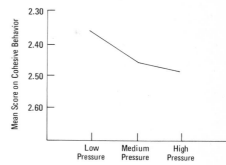

FIGURE 6.3 Relationship between Work Pressure and Cohesive Behavior
(F = 3.30, P < .05)

Source: Klein, S. M. *Workers under stress.* Lexington: University of Kentucky Press, 1971, p. 111.
© 1971 by the University Press of Kentucky.

faces a threatening situation in which pressure-reducing responses are unavailable for whatever reason, then we may expect a pattern of adjustment that is affiliational in its nature. Rabbie (1963), for example, carried out an experiment in which pressures were quite high but were operating in a situation in which subjects had difficulty determining what would be an appropriate response. Under these conditions, Rabbie found that people facing ambiguous pressures chose to affiliate with others with a higher frequency.

The field studies that were considered earlier involved situations in which the severity of threat and its scope were much greater than in the industrial studies. In addition, individuals involved in these situations tended to report a feeling of considerable helplessness regarding the nature and consequences of the tensions they were experiencing. In the laboratory studies the source of tension was generated by the anticipation of a highly painful and clearly defined event; however, the subjects were placed in a situation in which the range of behavioral options they had available was severely restricted. Under both of these conditions, research revealed that the general pattern of adjustment included increased tendencies toward affiliation.

Work Pressures and Performance

The effects of work pressures on job performance have received surprisingly little attention (Beehr & Newman, 1978). This is probably attributable to the difficulties encountered when one attempts to vary work pressures in any controlled fashion within the ongoing activities of an industrial setting. There is, however, an extensive amount of experimental work available from laboratory studies (Drabek & Hass, 1969; McGrath, 1976) that indicate that the relationship between stress and performance is an extremely complicated one. Martin (1961) suggests that two considerations, the nature of the task and the level of stress, are important in influencing this relationship. According to Martin, research results indicate that as the task involves better established and more numerous responses that compete with one another, the presence of stress in a situation results in a greater impairment of performance.

We might find an example of this hypothesis in a work situation in which workers are facing a change in the methods of production. In these instances we would expect that well-developed work habits and performance skills that were once appropriate for the older method may actually compete with those habits and skills required by the new method. It is under considerations such as these that one may expect to see the effects of stress resulting in a reduction in performance efficiency.

We are fortunate in having a study, done in industry, that deals with this question. Reported by Schachter et al. (1961), this study described the impact of work stress on the performance of workers engaged in assembly line work. The study was carried out in three separate replications, each involving matched pairs of assembly-line work groups performing identical operations. One group in each pair was designated "Disfavored"; the other group was designated "Favored." During a three-week period the disfavored groups were exposed to a prearranged pattern of persistent and continuous incidents that were intended to be both annoying and stressful. These pressures built up to a maximum at the end of the three-week period. For three weeks the favored group basked in a climate in which they were frequently praised and flattered for their good work. During this period management personnel took considerable pains to be friendly and helpful, and to recognize these employees for any suggestions they made.

At the end of this three-week interval, all experimental manipulations ceased, and the work groups were subjected to identical changes in their work procedures. Employees had been notified of these changes a few days before they were introduced, and from the workers' perspective, the changes were associated with the production of a new product or the rebalancing of the line in order to produce a different number of units per day.

Surprisingly, during the period in which the annoying work pressures were operating, no significant changes in the quality or quantity of work performance were noted. All groups, whether favored or disfavored, performed at comparable levels. Schachter and his associates viewed this prechange period as one in which work performance was highly stereotyped, with workers drawing on well practiced and well established sets of job behaviors. The advent of the stressful work pressures during this period, although there was evidence that they were annoying to the workers, failed to translate into a decline in job performance.

It was during the time when changes in working procedures were taking place that the favored and disfavored groups began to separate in terms of work performance. The groups that previously had been subjected to work pressures consistently produced work of lower quality than did the groups that had been working in a climate relatively free of stress and pressure. Furthermore, in those instances in which quantity of work was not machine paced, the favored groups displayed higher production rates than did the disfavored groups, although for both quality and quantity, differences between groups began to disappear as the workers adjusted to the new working situation. This study indicates that when asked to undergo change that requires the acquisition of new skills and procedures, workers who have been subjected to stressful harassment from management are unable to adapt as readily as those who have not been stressed. It is also apparent from this study that during times of stress, workers may not always display a reduction in their performance. When work skills and habits are well developed, employees may be able to undergo considerable tension before it becomes visible in production levels. We might speculate that stress reduces the flexibility of behavior and impedes a person's ability to cope with changing events. It is during times of change that the effects of stress may more clearly be seen in workers' performance, although it must be kept in mind that the change itself may be an added source of stress that compounds pressures already in the workplace.

Levels of Stress. With regard to the performance effects of different levels of stress the research literature indicates that moderate amounts of tension seem to facilitate performance, while low levels and extremely high levels of stress seem to impair performance. Lazarus (1966), in his review of the research in this area, cautions that this relationship may be modified by many mediating variables, and there are numerous studies that indicate that both personality factors (Sales, 1970;

Lyons, 1971; Beehr, Walsh, & Taber, 1976) and situational factors play a role in determining the impact of different levels of job pressures on an individual's performance. As a case in point, Sales (1970) reported that the effects of overload-induced stress is a function of the personality of the worker. Persons with a high need for achievement reported that they made an effort to try harder under conditions of role overload, but as the pressures of the overload increased, these high-achievement subjects performed at a lower rate. Hence, increasing levels of overload stress had a different effect on workers as a function of the level of their achievement motives. Results such as this show us that a simple statement describing what happens to performance as the level of stress increases does not usually fit what really happens in a work situation. To assume that a given level of stress always exerts a positive, or a negative, motivational influence on behavior is not justified by what is known about the number of variables that enter into the relationship between stress and performance. Of course, at very high levels, stress rather uniformly reduces performance effectiveness, especially if the task requires memory, precision, or complex control.

Other Field Studies

Before leaving this topic, there is one unusual set of studies that we might consider. Sponsored by the U.S. Army, these studies (Berkun et al., 1962) were carried out in order to study the effects of high levels of stress on the performance of military personnel. These authors contend that laboratory studies many times do not succeed in inducing high tension states, since subjects employ cognitive defenses that lead them to deny that the experimenter would deliberately expose them to danger. Such attitudes thwart the experimenter's attempts to generate the high levels of stress that are characteristic of real-life crises. In order to avoid this problem, these authors constructed a series of highly stressful situations that were part of real-life training exercises. Performance measures used were such that they appeared to be reasonable parts of a response to the threatening situation.

In one experiment, for example, subjects were passengers in an airplane that ostensibly had suffered mechanical failure that forced it to go through maneuvers preparatory to crash landing. The men assigned to these experimental groups were being flown on a training mission, when at a prearranged time the aircraft lurched and one of the two engines ceased to function. Prearranged communications to the passengers and the control tower informed the subjects that the airplane was preparing to crash land, and the pilot ordered the flight steward to prepare for a crash landing in the sea since the landing gear was malfunctioning. These preparations consisted of having all on board fill out the Emergency Data Form, a purposely complicated form that asked for a description of, and instructions for the disposition of, the individual's personal property in the event of death. A second instrument, the Official Data on Emergency Instructions, was an achievement test dealing with the retention of airborne emergency instructions that the subjects had read as a standard operating procedure before the flight. This latter test was given under the pretext that it would provide evidence to insurance companies that proper emergency precautions had been followed during the period preceding the anticipated crash. The papers were to be placed in a waterproof container and thrown from the plane prior to the crash landing.

Urine tests, made after the plane had safely landed, revealed the presence of secretions that indicated that the subjects had indeed been exposed to a real threatening event. Performance measures used considered the accuracy with which the subjects filled out the two test instruments that had been completed during the emergency. Comparisons made with control groups that had not been subjected to these severe stresses revealed a clear and statistically significant deterioration in the accuracy of performance of the experimental groups.

Other experiments performed in this series exposed subjects to a situation in which artillery shells appeared to be falling short, endangering the subjects who were located in a spotting bunker. In other instances subjects were implicated in an accidental explosion. Postexplosion intercommunications led the subjects to believe that the accident had resulted in personal injuries, and circumstances were such that the subjects' conduct could have been a factor underlying the accident. Once again subjects were given a series of complicated forms to fill out, and once again those subjects who had been exposed to the high levels of stress showed a marked deterioration in their performance.

One may raise questions concerning the ethicality of research of this sort. Although subjects were given a complete explanation of the nature and purposes of the research, the potential psychological costs of this type of research are too high to recommend that further research along these lines be carried out, regardless of the value of the results. Be that as it may, the studies were reported, and the results do confirm the generalization that under very high levels of psychological stress one may reasonably expect to observe a reduction in the accuracy of performance.

Stress, Type A Behavior and Coronary Heart Disease

In adjusting to a job individuals tend to adopt certain behavioral patterns, which, if successful in meeting their needs, become incorporated into the personality as a more or less stable response style. Under certain job conditions there is a tendency for these behaviors to emerge in a form that is symptomatic of the tensions and pressures that exist in the work environment. These stress-induced behavioral patterns probably serve a function that is psychologically adaptive, but there is growing evidence that they are also associated with an increased risk of coronary heart disease (Cooper & Marshall, 1976). Hence, according to this point of view, there are behavioral patterns that seem to occur in stressful work environments, and carry with them an increased risk of heart disorders.

These are interesting ideas, and ones that have received considerable attention in the recent literature. Numerous correlational studies have been

carried out, and the general drift of the findings has been quite encouraging. Little progress has been made, however, in gathering support for the proposed causal sequence that leads to coronary heart disorders; that is, that jobs create conditions that lead to the development of certain patterns of behavior, which in turn lead to coronary heart disease. What is cause and what is effect may not be clearly apparent from the studies that have been reported, but the fact that relationships exist among jobs, behaviors, and heart disease is a step toward a better understanding of the operation and consequences of stress.

Job Variables. In keeping with this correlational approach, studies have shown that coronary heart disease is related to a variety of working conditions, personality characteristics, and to a set of nonwork conditions such as family problems and life crises. Figure 6.4, from Cooper and Marshall (1976), summarizes some of the more important variables that have been found to be related to coronary heart disease. Machine pacing, for example, is a condition that has been linked with these disorders (Kritsikis, Heineman, & Eitner, 1965). Role conflict has also been found to increase the incidence of coronary heart disease (Shirom et al., 1973), as have working conditions that require an individual to assume high responsibility for other peole (Wardwell, Hyman, & Bahnson, 1964). At the present time the amount of available research is insufficient to enable us to specify a single cluster of working conditions that serve to increase the risk of heart disorders, but there is reason to believe that any aspect of work exposing an individual to prolonged stress is a potential risk factor.

Type A Behavior. In addition to job conditions, there is an interesting behavior configuration that has been associated with high levels of coronary heart disease. Referred to as Type A behaviors, these patterns are characterized by a chronic sense of urgency that seems to originate in individuals' perceptions that they face pressures to complete work within time periods that are insufficient for the task. Time pressures, a sense of being con-

FIGURE 6.4 A Model of Stress at Work

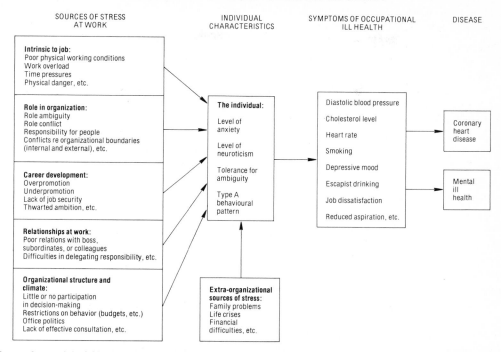

Source: Cooper, C. L., & Marshall, J. Occupational sources of stress: A review of the literature relating to coronary heart disease and mental health. *Journal of Occupational Psychology*, 1976, *49*, 11–28. Copyright 1976 by the British Psychological Society.

stantly hurried, is a central component of Type A behaviors, but the pattern also includes chronic competitiveness, a high need for achievement, and a tendency to be in conflict with others (Howard, Cunningham, & Rechnitzer, 1977).

There are a number of studies (for example, Friedman & Rosenman, 1974; Rosenman, 1974) reporting that people whose behavior reflects the Type A pattern tend to have a higher incidence of coronary heart disease. For example, in one study involving 3500 men, Rosenman and Friedman (1971) found that Type A persons ran twice the risk of coronary heart disease and double the rate of fatality due to heart disorders. Evidence of this sort provides support for the contention that behavioral patterns can serve as factors that increase the risk of coronary heart disease.

Relationship between Job Conditions and Type A Behaviors. Thus far evidence has been reported showing the relationships among coronary

heart disease and job conditions and behavioral patterns. There still remains a question whether job conditions lead to the Type A behaviors that supposedly cause higher rates of heart disease. The evidence here is not particularly abundant, but a case that suggests that this relationship is a plausible one can be pieced together. For example, one study (Howard et al., 1977) reports that jobs that require higher supervisory responsibility for people and that impose excessive workloads and conflicting demands are the ones that tend to encourage the development of Type A behaviors. Positions that bring the worker into competition with others were also found to be associated with higher levels of Type A behavior. This study also found that high-growth companies tend to create situations that give rise to Type A behaviors, and jobs that require considerable travel and long hours may also be associated with the development of Type A patterns.

There are other variables associated with Type

A behaviors that may be thought of as reflecting job conditions, even though they express themselves in the form of an individual's reaction to work. For example, Matthews and Saal (1978) report that high job involvement is related to Type A behaviors. Jenkins (1971) suggests that this high involvement of Type A individuals leads them to ignore other aspects of life. Finally, there are some indications that job dissatisfaction is associated with Type A behaviors (Howard et al., 1977).

Comment. Job conditions, Type A behaviors, and coronary heart disease display a pattern of interrelationships that indicates that they function as part of some type of disease process. There is some suggestion that this process can be represented by a causal sequence that begins with stress inducing conditions that lead to the development of Type A behaviors, which lead to an increased risk of coronary heart disease (See Figure 6.4). At the present time our understanding of cause-and-effect relationships is very limited, and in all probability what will finally emerge from the research carried out in this area is a complicated model containing many components and feedback loops that interconnect each factor with every other one. Whatever the outcome of these efforts, however, it has become clear that the consequences of job induced stress include not only typical psychological symptoms such as anxiety and depression, but also a full range of physical disorders. Many of these disorders are burdensome, others may be debilitating, but there are others, such as coronary heart disease, that can be fatal.

SUMMARY COMMENTS

Perhaps one of the most difficult tasks facing the behavioral scientist is to describe the causes of psychological disorders. In large measure this difficulty stems from the fact that psychological distress oftentimes is the result of a long history of experiences that combine to produce the disorder. Hence, it is in the past that the roots of emotional difficulties are found, and what we see in the present as causes might best be considered to be precipitating factors. Yet psychologists are rarely certain about the relative contribution of the past and the present to the behavior being observed. As a consequence, when studying the behavior pathology associated with a particular set of conditions, one must be prepared to find a considerable amount of individual difference in reactions to these conditions.

Often when trying to deal with the apparent inconsistencies in people's response to pressures, personality variables are found to moderate the relationships among the job-related variables studied. Personal attributes that have developed over a lifetime of experiences play an important role in determining an individual's susceptibility to work pressures. We do find, however, that the design of the job can increase the prospects that an individual worker will experience tensions and apprehensions, and can demonstrate job-to-job differences in the incidence of emotional problems among workers.

The concept of role has proved useful in describing the circumstances that seem to precipitate psychological distress of one sort or another. Each job is viewed as a more or less complicated set of role assignments that define not only workers' responsibilities to the duties of the job but also a set of expectations regarding how they should behave with respect to the social relations that exist at the workplace. Large numbers of workers have reported that these expectations are frequently in conflict with one another or are unclear or burdensome. When this is the case, tension is a probable consequence.

Job pressures commonly arise whenever workers are rushed for time. Sales clerks, restaurant workers, assembly-line employees often report the pressures of time that accumulate on a job on which there is more work to perform than time will permit. At the other end of the scale, however, one can find reports of psychological distress on jobs that provide too much time for the work that is available. In addition, routine work, especially if it is of a repetitive nature, may also be found stressful, and jobs that involve responsibility for the performance and welfare of other people frequently lead to personal tensions.

If one were to attempt to list the many job characteristics that have been associated with work tensions, the list would be a long one indeed. If, on the other hand, one were to consider the therapeutic procedures that are available to deal with the consequences of stress, the list of those that have received any careful scrutiny would be surprisingly short (Newman & Beehr, 1979). It is a fact that many different programs for stress management have been suggested, but unfortunately we have very little research-based information concerning their therapeutic value. Personal strategies, ranging from retraining and withdrawal from stress to the development of new life philosophies and meditation, have all been advocated as effective means for coping with the psychological problems generated by work pressures. A broader understanding of organizational dynamics and human adjustment is also a reasonable approach to the prevention of stress.

Organizational programs that view the techniques of selection and placement from a perspective that includes job-person fit represent a potentially fruitful step that might lead to the reduction of work stress (Gavin, 1977). Finally, the whole range of supervisory training programs that are designed to improve the human relations capabilities of management personnel can serve as a reasonable strategy for combatting stress at work. But whatever the program, efforts in this direction must in large measure be based on opinion rather than experimental support. As a consequence, the construction and implementation of such programs must rest largely on intuition and common sense, since at the present time this area of occupational therapy is more an art than a science. Workers and work organizations both have a substantial investment in any efforts made to extend the reach of science into this area of work behavior. The prevention and care of occupational tensions would represent a major step in our efforts to improve the overall quality, and probably the length, of an individual's life.

7

THE REWARDS OF WORK: FINANCIAL INCENTIVES

Of all the rewards in a work situation, pay is often thought of as the most important. On the face of it, it seems obvious to assume that people work primarily to *earn a living,* and that economic motives play a dominant part in much of the behavior observed at work. But once saying this, and there may be reason to challenge the statement, there still remain many questions regarding the motivational climate of work and the part financial rewards play in shaping it. For example, one could ask whether pay is closely tied in with the quality of an individual's work and the effort expended in carrying out a job. Can we encourage people to work harder and more effectively by increasing their wages? What constitutes a fair wage, and to what extent are workers satisfied with the wages they receive? Along the same lines, one may wonder about what constitutes an attractive increase in wages, and what factors seem to relate to the satisfaction one has with pay.

The present chapter will attempt to answer these and other questions concerning the motivational significance of the paycheck. Fortunately, there is at present a fairly large and active research literature dealing with pay incentives, and recently there has been a promising increase in the theoretical developments that have taken place in this area. An effort will be made to present the highlights of this work, and in doing so it will become evident that the study of pay incentive applies to the whole range of motivational systems that operate in a work setting. What we know about wage incentives, therefore, is useful in understanding the workings of other sets of rewards that are available to people who work.

In starting out to study wage incentives, it might be prudent to comment briefly on the general psychological functions served by wages. Basically, the pay an individual receives can be thought of as both a secondary reinforcer and an incentive. A secondary reinforcer is a reward whose psychological value has been significantly influenced by the individual's past experience; it is a stimulus whose reward value has been learned. As a rule, a secondary reinforcer is a one-time neutral stimulus that has been repeatedly presented in close connection with events that gratify the primary needs of the individual. Money, early in life, is essentially a neutral stimulus, serving no significant function in the need systems of the individual. As time progresses, however, it is often present in one form or another at times when basic needs are being met. Through repeated association with things that gratify basic needs, money begins to acquire psychologically rewarding properties of its own, and eventually it begins to function as a reinforcer of behaviors in much the same fashion as the so-called primary reinforcers such as food, sex, and water.

Money can also be thought of as an incentive. Here we are talking about its role as a goal object toward which behavior is directed. The anticipation of financial reward often serves as a stimulus to performance, and typically work is seen as being instrumental in attaining this financial goal. Pay, in turn, is instrumental in achieving other personal objectives, such as food, shelter, status, and so the motivational role of money is traceable to its association with a wide range of events that serve psychological needs. This association is, however, learned; therefore, the motivational impact of pay is a product of an individual's past experience. Since there are broad differences in past experience, so too are there broad individual differences in the psychological importance of pay.

THE PSYCHOLOGICAL IMPORTANCE OF PAY

How important is pay? When one considers the large list of potential incentives that are available to job holders, what rank does pay hold among motivational factors? For instance, does the typical worker value interesting and challenging work more than the wages received? Would the worker swap high wages for better job security? Perhaps the most direct route to answering these questions would be to ask workers to report their own feelings about the relative importance of the incentives they find in their work; and this, in fact, has been done in a large number of industrial studies.

One of the most widely cited studies of this type is a survey carried out at Sears Roebuck (Worthy, 1950) in which 12,000 employees were asked their opinions concerning the psychological importance of a group of work incentives. Responses to this survey indicated that pay ranked eighth in a list of fourteen factors. In another study, Jurgensen (1947) had job applicants rank a list of ten incentives and found that pay tended to be ranked near the middle of the list. Throughout a thirty-year period, Jurgensen (1978) continued to collect rankings of this type from individuals applying for work at the Minnesota Gas Company in Minneapolis. During this time 57,000 applicants provided information about their preferences for the ten incentives, and generally these rankings

remained relatively stable. Although wages seemed to increase slightly in their standing, over the three-decade interval they rather consistently held to a middle position in the list of ten job factors. During the last period for which results were reported, 1971–1975, pay held a rank of five in the list of ten. Over the years it became rather fashionable to point to results such as these to demonstrate that financial incentives do not necessarily play the most important role in determining the level of motivation found operating in a work setting. For every study that found pay ranking low, however, there were several that found pay appearing near the top of the list (Centers & Bugental, 1966; Lawler, 1966a).

Lawler (1971) presents the most complete summary of this kind of research. Gathering together forty-nine studies from which an estimate of the status of pay can be obtained, Lawler finds that in approximately two-thirds of the reports, pay was ranked one of the three most important job incentives. The average number of incentives ranked by each study was twelve, and only two of the forty-nine reported pay ranking below six. In approximately one of every four, pay was found in the first rank; therefore, when asked directly, workers often acknowledge the high importance of pay as a job-related incentive.

The Changing Importance of Pay

Lawler's survey reveals that over the years pay seems to have varied in its status in relation to other work incentives. In the studies reported between 1945 and 1949, for example, pay maintained an average rank of 4.1, while between 1950 and 1955 the average rank rose to 2.6. During the 1960s pay underwent a significant shift in rank, compared to other incentives. In the first half of the decade pay held an average rank of 3.4, while during the latter half the average moved up to 2.1.

These figures must be interpreted with caution, since the studies differ both in the composition of the samples and the number of incentives ranked. Yet the comparisons do serve to suggest that the psychological importance of wages probably

TABLE 7.1   Reported Importance of Pay and Percent of Work Stoppages Involving Wages as a Major Issue

Year	Importance of Pay as Incentive, Average Rank[1]	Percent Work Stoppage with Pay Major Issue[2]
1945–1949	4.1	46
1950–1954	2.6	50
1960–1964	3.4	48
1965–1969	2.1	54

[1]Source: Lawler, E. E. *Pay and organizational effectiveness.* New York: McGraw-Hill, 1971.
[2]Source: *Statistical Abstract of the United States, Bicentennial Issue.* Washington, D.C.: Bureau of the Census, Department of Commerce, 1976.

undergoes change from one time period to the next. What factors underlie these changes is open to speculation. The state of the economy is doubtless a factor, but there are probably social and psychological variables that are involved as well.

Interestingly, one can find parallel changes taking place in the percentage of strikes that involve wages as a major issue. For instance, as the perceived importance of wages increased between the first and second half of the 1960s, there was in the United States a corresponding increase in the percentage of work stoppages that involved wages as a major issue. Table 7.1 gives these figures for the four periods for which there were sufficient industrial studies to compute average rank for the reported importance of pay. Here we see further evidence suggesting that the psychological importance of pay is not static, but changes from time to time. Table 7.1 also suggests that workers' reports of pay importance rise and fall with the data representing strike issues. For the periods included in the table, as the behavioral studies reported pay assuming a higher ranking—that is, as pay was reported to be more important to the workers—there was an increase in the percentage of strikes that involved pay as a central issue. As pay dropped in relative importance, so too was there a drop in the percent of strikes involving wages.

For a number of methodological reasons, some have criticized studies that have attempted to rank the importance of work incentives (Lawler, 1971; Opsahl & Dunnette, 1966), but the relationship seen in Table 7.1 suggests that workers' responses

to these surveys do in fact show a relationship with real, overt work behavior. What workers say about their job benefits and what enters the national climate of labor grievances appear to be related. Hence, there may be more substance to workers' reports concerning their perception of wage incentives than some are ready to acknowledge.

Reasons for Fluctuations.   Apart from economic reasons, one can only speculate as to why the perceived importance of pay incentives seems to fluctuate from one period to the next. One interesting hypothesis is that the importance of pay is influenced by the general level of social and psychological tensions that exist during a given time period. As the general climate of social tension changes, so too does the relative importance of wage incentives.

According to this line of reasoning, the motivational value of money is associated with its role as an anxiety reducer (Brown, 1961). It is believed that in early life the absence of money is often associated with expressions of anxiety and distress on the part of a child's parents. Such events expose the child to a learning experience in which money's absence is associated with negative emotional states. At the other end of the relationship, it is during times when money is present and being spent that the child is given security and affection. As a consequence, acquisition, spending money, is associated with positive emotional states. It follows from this that during times of emotional stress and anxiety there is an increased likelihood that money will be viewed as being more important psychologically, since it is something that has been associated with more congenial circumstances.

These ideas are presented in the form of a hypothesis; in spite of their tentative nature, however, one should be willing to entertain the possibility that some of the factors that contribute to the motivational importance of work incentives may be found in social events that are general in scope and are not part of the immediate work environment. The general drift and tenor of social-political events in the nation may create periods in which wages and material acquisition assume a high importance in the psychology of many individuals. These events create a background against which individuals experience the specific "in focus" happenings in their lives. Although one may not be able to trace a direct connection between community tensions and one's conduct, we should not let this fact lead us to ignore completely the potential influence of these sociological variables.

Wage Benefit Tradeoffs. Nealey and Goodale (1967) have used a slightly different approach in estimating the psychological importance of wage

incentives. In their study, blue-collar workers were given a list of seven benefits that all had equal monetary value. One item in the list was a wage increase; the other items involved time off from work. Each benefit was paired with every other benefit, and the workers were asked to choose the member of each pair they preferred. From these choices scale values can be computed for each item. Figure 7.1 shows the results of this scaling. Here we see that pay increases are well down on the scale, compared to benefits that would provide the worker with more time off from work.

There is another study in which Nealey used what he calls the game-board method (Nealey, 1964). In this approach each worker is given a hypothetical amount of money, and then is asked to "spend" this money on a set of benefits. It is possible to put all the money into a pay increase, or the worker can "buy" other kinds of benefits. Nealey reports the results of this approach when applied to a group of 132 male employees of the General Electric Company. In this instance, pay ranked third, behind increased sick leave (first) and extended vacations (second). The average amount invested in paycheck increases was only about 12

FIGURE 7.1 Relative Preference for Time-off Benefits and Pay

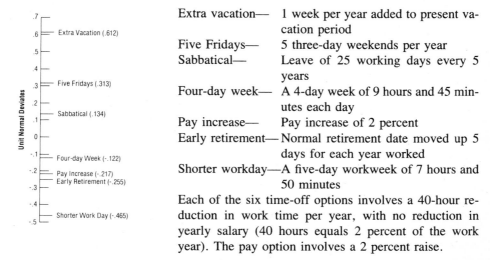

Extra vacation— 1 week per year added to present vacation period

Five Fridays— 5 three-day weekends per year

Sabbatical— Leave of 25 working days every 5 years

Four-day week— A 4-day week of 9 hours and 45 minutes each day

Pay increase— Pay increase of 2 percent

Early retirement— Normal retirement date moved up 5 days for each year worked

Shorter workday—A five-day workweek of 7 hours and 50 minutes

Each of the six time-off options involves a 40-hour reduction in work time per year, with no reduction in yearly salary (40 hours equals 2 percent of the work year). The pay option involves a 2 percent raise.

Source: Nealey, S. M. & Goodale, J. G. Worker preferences among time-off benefits and pay. *Journal of Applied Psychology*, 1967, **51,** 358. Copyright 1967 by the American Psychological Association. Published by permission.

percent, while over 30 percent of the money was spent for more sick leave and 22 percent was invested in longer vacations.

Factors Correlated with Perceived Importance of Pay

Not everyone sees pay in the same light; it is more important to some than to others. The extent to which a person sees pay as an important incentive seems to be a function of a number of variables, some of which are related to the person, some related to the job. For example, Nealey and Goodale (1967) report that the relative status of pay seems to change as a function of the worker's age, job type (white-collar or "physical" jobs), marital status, and number of children.

Sex. Sex is a variable that with some consistency has shown itself to be related to how much importance a person gives to wages (Jurgensen, 1978). Shapiro (1975), for instance, found that pay appeared to be the strongest job motivator for a group of male industrial workers, but for women the major determiners of work motivation were the level of responsibility associated with a job and job experience. Ronan and Organt (1973) report a study in which women, although receiving less pay than men, did not report pay to be a significant source of job dissatisfaction. Rosenberg (1957) and Herzberg et al. (1957) suggest that women find more motivational value in the social dimensions of work, whereas men have been found to lay greater emphasis on pay (Centers & Bugental, 1966, Gilmer, 1957).

Age. Age is another variable thought to influence the incentive value of wages, with the general drift of the data suggesting that older workers report that wages are less important. Why this is so is open to speculation. For many jobs, particularly those in the white-collar managerial areas, increasing age is associated with increasing pay (Ronan & Organt, 1973). As pay level increases, the psychological needs served by pay may be displaced by other need systems that are less well satisfied. As a consequence, work incentives other than pay may become more important in the eyes of the worker. Another related reason why older workers report that wages are not as important as other incentives is that wages, in the form of *direct pay,* can become less significant as a means for meeting needs as an individual grows older. With increasing age, health problems become more prominent, children leave home, and retirement approaches. As a result, there are job benefits other than direct pay that increase in attractiveness, since they are constructed to deal with these situations. Nealey (1964), for example, reports that in his sample of male industrial workers, pension benefits steadily increased in importance as the men advanced in age. For workers over fifty, pension benefits ranked first in the list of incentives.

Education. Education is another variable that is associated with the psychological importance of wage incentives. Jurgensen (1947, 1978) had applicants for jobs with the Minneapolis Gas Light Company fill out a job preference questionnaire that required them to rank ten working conditions according to their importance. Grouping applicants according to their education levels, Jurgensen found that with increasing education, pay moved up in the rankings. Troxell (1954) reports another study in which workers who had higher levels of education tended to place greater importance on wages.

What education has to do with the perceived importance of wages is a question that has no definite answer. There is evidence, however, that higher levels of schooling are associated with higher expectations regarding income (Penzer, 1969). With increased education the individual is more likely to perceive a career that is upwardly mobile, moving into higher levels of status and pay. It seems reasonable to predict that under these circumstances pay will be more important than it will be to an individual whose career expectations do not involve significantly increasing pay levels. Hence, the greater importance placed on wages by those who have greater amounts of schooling might be an expression of a belief that they have good access to higher pay levels.

Job Factors.　　Job factors also make a contribution to the perceived importance of financial incentives, one of the more significant factors being the actual level of pay the individual receives. Lawler and Porter (1963; 1966) report a study in which higher-paid managers were found to be not only more satisfied with their wages, but also that pay was a less important work incentive for them. Lawler and Porter suggest that as wage needs are satisfied, the relative importance of other work related incentives tends to increase. There are several other studies demonstrating that with increasing salaries, employees tend to be more satisfied with their pay (Schuster & Clark, 1970; Ronan & Organt, 1973). Higher levels of satisfaction with pay may lead employees to focus their concerns on other aspects of the incentive system, and perceive these other dimensions of work as being more important.

Before leaving this topic, it might be prudent to remember that the psychological importance of any incentive undergoes change from one period of time to the next. Just as the motivational value of food may change after we have just eaten a meal, so too does the relative importance of a job incentive change as a function of the extent to which the individual's immediate job situation is successful in satisfying one or another work-related need. At one time behavior may primarily be motivated by the worker's needs for security, and at another time financial needs may predominate. As a consequence, studies that produce a ranking of incentives should not be interpreted as suggesting that this list is fixed and stable. One should think of these ranks as estimates of the *average* potency of a given work incentive, and as reflections of the job conditions under which the individual typically works. These ranks may be interpreted as indicating that *on the average* a given person finds that one incentive carries higher motivational weight than another. Even though there may be instances when, let's say, wages play a central role in an individual's behavior, over the long term there may be other incentives that contribute more heavily to job motivation.

Factors Related to Actual Pay

What is it that determines the amount of money an individual is paid? Can we predict the wages a person receives from knowledge of such things as his level of education, age, and the level of his position in the organization? To what extent do the quality of work and the effort put into a job relate to the amount of pay an individual receives? Certainly there is a complex set of market factors that operate to determine the amount of an individual's wages. The availability of certain kinds of skills and the demand for them lie at the root of the wages paid for work. Apart from supply and demand, however, every organization maintains a unique set of values that contributes to wage differentials. Hence, in a given organization we may find that the pay differences found between blue- and white-collar wages are not related to the difficulty level or the technical content of the work, or to the learning time required to develop acceptable job skills. Rather, wage differences may be related more to the social status of a job or to the number of years of formal academic education received by those found in these positions (Gottfredson, 1977).

For managerial, white-collar jobs there seems to be good evidence indicating that the level of a job within the organization is a principal factor determining the amount of pay an individual receives. Employers often pay on the basis of the organizational status of a job; and even though there may be production jobs whose technical requirements and skill demands exceed those associated with management jobs, the pay scale is constructed to reflect the social position of the job in the organizational hierarchy. Lawler (1966b) collected data from three samples of managers employed by government agencies and four samples employed by private organizations. Information concerning each employee's seniority, educational attainment, and management level was obtained, together with the superior's ratings of the quality of job performance and how hard the individual worked. In both the government and private organizations the factor that correlated highest with the amount of money the individual received was the management level of the job. In both private and public work settings the factor that maintained the lowest correlation with pay received was the rating of the amount of effort the individual invested in the work (see Table 7.2). The quality of an individual's work also showed a very low correlation with pay in the private organizations, and virtually no correlation with pay in the government agencies. Hence, in these seven organizations, it appears that performance on the job, that is, the quality of work and how hard the individual works, does not maintain a very strong relationship with wages.

Lawler's study is not an isolated one. Ronan and Organt (1973) carried out a related study that analyzed almost nine thousand questionnaires that had been returned by the employees of a large organization. For management jobs, both job level and the amount of education turned out to be the best predictors of wages paid. Lawler and Porter (1966), in a study that involved over nineteen hundred managers who were members of the American Management Association, also found that management level was the best predictor of salary. Unlike the two previous investigations, however, this sample showed no relationship between education and the amount of money received as wages.

We tend to think of wages as compensation for job performance, and many believe that a fair wage system is one that is tied in with the efforts people invest in work and the quality of their performance. On the basis of the data just presented, it may be more accurate to say that we often pay individuals for the positions they hold rather than for the quality of their work. Along these lines, Siegel and Ghiselli (1971) report an interesting study that shows that traits related to management performance may change their relationship with pay as the age of the manager changes. Figure 7.2 summarizes Siegel and Ghiselli's efforts to correlate five aspects of managerial performance with the amount of pay received. These correlations

TABLE 7.2   Pearson Product-Moment Correlations between the Managers' Pay and Factors That Determine Pay

Factor	Actual pay	
	Private industry sample (N = 326)	Government sample (N = 327)
Seniority	−.17**	.21**
Education level	.50**	.23**
Management level	.58**	.60**
Quality of job performance[a]	.20**	.01
Effort expended[a]	.14*	.00

[a]Correlations computed separately for three management levels and then averaged.

*p < .05.

**p < .01.

Source: Lawler, E. E. Managers' attitudes toward how their pay is and should be determined. *Journal of Applied Psychology,* 1966, *50,* 273–279. Copyright 1966 by the American Psychological Association.

were computed separately for each of seven age categories, and the resulting coefficients were plotted to show the changing strength of these relationships from one age group to the next. Collected from a group of almost three hundred managers, the data reveal a rather consistent drop in the relationship between pay and intelligence, initiative, and self-assurance as age increases. In other words, the pay individuals in this sample received was more highly correlated with intelligence during the early stages of a career. As age increases, however, pay seems to lose steadily its positive association with how intelligent the manager is. For another variable, supervisory ability, it seems that the highest correlation with pay occurs during the middle segments of the work career, while at the later stages of work life, the relationship turned negative; that is, those who had higher levels of supervisory ability tended to be paid less than those whose abilities were not particularly strong in this area. The same negative relationships were found for each attribute when it was correlated with the pay these employees received during the later phases of their careers.

FIGURE 7.2 **The Correlation between Managerial Traits and Pay as a Function of Age**

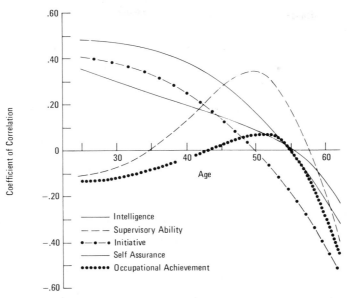

Source: Siegel, J. P. & Ghiselli, E. E. Managerial talent, pay and age. *Journal of Vocational Behavior,* 1971, *1,* 129–135. Copyright, 1971, Academic Press. Published by permission.

PAY—THEORY AND RESEARCH

Perceived Instrumentality of Work

One of the more important factors contributing to the motivational influence of pay is found in the worker's perception of the behaviors that lead to higher pay. Consider the motivational implications of going up to a worker and asking, "What do you have to do around here to make more money?" and receiving the answer, "You must work hard and work well." In this response there is a recognition that quality of work performance is seen as a path that leads to higher financial rewards, or in the words of the social scientist, work is perceived as being *instrumental* in producing wages. Hence, whether wages encourage higher levels and better quality of work depends in part on the workers' perception of pay-performance instrumentality. In addition, when we find workers who place high value on financial incentives and who function in a situation in which there are few barriers to productivity, then we should find that the financial incentive system has substantial impact on the performance of the individual employees.

Georgopolous, Mahoney, and Jones (1957), referring to these ideas as the "path-goal hypothesis," state, "If a worker sees high productivity as a path leading to the attainment of one or more of his personal goals, he will tend to be a high producer" (p. 346). Relying on blue-collar workers' responses to questionnaires that asked for their perceptions of path-goal relationships, these authors found that high producers were more likely to say that in the long run high production would help them make more money. High producers also tended to see high rates of production helping the individual to get along better with the work group. Low producers, on the other hand, did not see these relationships between performance and wages.

Vroom's Expectancy Theory. Victor Vroom (1964) is one of several theorists who have constructed motivational models that involve an individual's perception of the connection that exists betwen actions and outcomes. Vroom maintains that the motivational influences, called forces, that lead an individual to perform a given act are the algebraic sum (Σ) of the valences of all outcomes multiplied by the individual's expectation that the act will lead to these outcomes. In equation form the model reads:

$$F_i = \left[\Sigma(E_{ij}V_j) \right],$$

where F_i can be thought of as the intensity of the motivation the individual experiences; Σ refers to summing the terms inside the parentheses; E_{ij} refers to an individual's expectation that a particular act, i, will lead to an particular outcome, j; and V_j refers to the valence the individual attaches to the outcomes that follow an act. Valence refers to the individual's *anticipated satisfaction* received from an outcome.

An example might serve to clarify this model. Suppose worker A believes that quality performance will lead to his receiving higher pay, being recognized by management, and better job security. Suppose worker A also places a high valence on these outcomes—that is, anticipates that they will be satisfying to him. Worker A will then be well motivated to turn out high quality work. Worker B, on the other hand, places equally high valence on these rewards, but does not expect them to result from quality work (E_{ij} in his equation would carry low value). Under these circumstances, worker B will not be as highly motivated as A. Suppose worker C expects quality work to lead to the three rewards, but does not place high value on them (V_j is low). In this instance worker C will also not be as highly motivated as A. From these examples we can see that worker motivation, according to Vroom, is estimated by *multiplying* what a worker expects to receive from his performance by how highly he values these outcomes.

Vroom sees the motivational forces that operate in a work situation in terms of the worker's anticipation of outcomes which themselves are seen as serving as satisfiers or dissatisfiers. The motivation to work and be productive, therefore, derives from the worker's understanding of the psychological consequences of productivity and the probability that these consequences will occur.

The Porter-Lawler Model. Georgopoulus et al. (1957) and Vroom (1964) are not the only theorists who have drawn on ideas pertaining to the expectations of positive and negative outcomes. Porter and Lawler (1968) have developed a model that is an extension and elaboration of Vroom's position. This model includes, among other things, another set of expectations—workers' beliefs concerning the likelihood that they will be able to perform at a given level. Workers may find themselves in situations in which all the outcomes and instrumentalities associated with a given level of performance may clearly be seen. If, however, they believe there is a low probability that they can muster and sustain the effort required to achieve this level of performance, then the motivational impact of these outcomes will be reduced significantly.

One way of looking at this extension of Vroom's model is to recognize that Porter and Lawler have analyzed Vroom's expectancy term (E) into two separate components. One of these (E_1) refers to the perceived likelihood that an individual will be able, or willing, to achieve the level of performance required to reach a goal. This expectation may be formed out of the person's perception of his or her talents and energies. For instance, the performance route that leads to many highly prized goals may be crystal clear, but the expectation that one possesses the ability to reach these goals is often highly uncertain. Low E_1 expectations may also originate in the work situation, which might be the case in a "dead-end" job that does not provide an individual with the opportunity to display those behaviors that are valued in the organization. For example, the stenographer in the secretarial pool may possess all sorts of high-level competencies, but the job situation in which she operates prevents her from drawing on these talents. A third source of low E_1 expectancies might arise when a worker is unwilling to mobilize the effort needed to achieve a given level of performance. In each of these three instances, expectations that a given outcome is available would be low.

A second expectancy component (E_2) involves the perceived likelihood that a given kind of performance will lead to the desired incentive. It is this aspect of the general expectancy concept that is implied when one speaks of the perceived instrumentality of job performance. Taking these two expectancy components together, the equation that expresses the motivational force operating in a given situation now becomes:

$$F_i = \left[\Sigma(E_1 \cdot E_2)_{ij} V_j \right].$$

Notice that E_1 and E_2 combine by multiplying. In other words, Vroom's term, E_{ij}, is the product of these two separate expectancy components. Multiplying these two terms together implies that they are not independent; the value of one influences the contribution of the other. Therefore, if either one of these expectancies is low, the product is low, thus indicating a low general expectancy that the incentive is available.

Research. In a later chapter we will consider the influence of work group pressures on the level of productivity. Under this topic there is a whole set of studies that document the contribution of worker expectations to the motivational climate of work (cf. Roethlisberger & Dickson, 1939; Roy, 1952; Dalton, 1948). In many of these instances the workers' expectations led them to anticipate that a whole range of negative consequences would result from high rates of productivity. For example, rather than higher pay, workers reported that high rates of production led to an increase in the standards of work. High performance levels, therefore, were seen as being instrumental in raising production standards, and in such situations there were group pressures against high production.

Differences in Pay-Performance Instrumentalities

As might be expected, workers do not all agree on the factors that are instrumental in determining the level of their pay. Furthermore, differences in these perceptions have been shown to relate to certain characteristics of the workers themselves. Schuster and Clark (1970), for example, asked 575 white-collar, professional employees to indicate what they believed to be the factors that were instrumental in determining the level of the wages they received. These workers were arranged in groups according to their educational level, age, actual salary, and their performance level as rated by superiors. The results showed that perceived instrumentalities changed as a function of the worker's status on each of these four factors. For instance, higher-rated, better-paid, older workers who had lower education saw that work effort, production rate, and work quality were instrumental in determining wages. Younger, better-educated, more poorly paid, and lower rated workers reported that factors other than performance were instrumental in determing wages. Table 7.3 summarizes the patterns of instrumentalities that were obtained from the study. Notice that workers tended to see instrumentalities that were in agreement with their own strengths. For instance, highly rated workers tended to see performance as being important in determining pay. Those with higher levels of education saw scarcity of skills as being important; those who received high pay saw job responsibility and administrative skill as being important instrumentalities. There are exceptions to this trend in the table, but in general it would appear that the perception of instrumentality is to some extent related to the individuals' perception of their own strengths and weaknesses. This is probably true when it comes to a worker's perception of the factors that *should* be instrumental in determining the level of wages received.

Support for this hypothesis can be found in the study reported by Lawler (1966b) that was carried out in government and private organizations.

TABLE 7.3   Perceived Pay Determiners by Performance Level, Educational Level, Pay Level and Age

Pay Determiner	Performance Level	Educational Level	Pay Level	Age
Company Service	Inconclusive	Inconclusive	Inconclusive	Most important to younger
Education, Training and Experience	Inconclusive	Inconclusive	Inconclusive	Most important to older
Administrative Skill	Inconclusive	Inconclusive	Most important to higher paid	Most important to older
Job Responsibility and Pressure	Most important to good performers	Most important to less educated	Most important to higher paid	Most important to older
Work Quality	Most important to good performers	Most important to less educated	Most important to higher paid	Most important to older
Productivity	Most important to good performers	Most important to less educated	Most important to higher paid	Most important to older
Scarcity of Skills	Most important to poorer performers	Most important to more highly educated	Inconclusive	Inconclusive
Contribution to Technical Knowledge	Most important to poorer performers	Most important to less educated	Most important to lower paid	Most important to older
Start Salary	Most important to poorer performers	Most important to more highly educated	Most important to lower paid	Most important to younger
Effort Expended	Most important to good performers	Most important to less educated	Most important to higher paid	Most important to younger
Economic Factors	Most important to poorer performers	Most important to more highly educated	Most important to lower paid	Most important to younger
Supervisor	Most important to good performers	Inconclusive	Most important to higher paid	Inconclusive

Source: Schuster, J. R., and Clark, B. Individual differences related to feelings toward pay. *Personnel Psychology*, 1970, *23*, 591–604. Copyright 1970 by Personnel Psychology. Published by permission.

Groups of managers were asked to report how important a set of factors was in determining the pay individuals received. They were next asked to report their beliefs concerning how important each of these factors *should be,* and then to rate themselves on each of the factors.

Table 7.4 summarizes the relationship observed. From these data it is apparent that these managers felt that wages should be determined by those factors on which they rated themselves most highly.

Therefore, when we hear workers lamenting the fact that certain aspects of performance do not contribute significantly to the wages that are paid, they are likely to be telling us as much about how they view their own strengths as about real deficiencies in the wage program.

Pay and Intrinsic Work Motivation

As we have just seen, there is experimental evidence suggesting that pay best motivates work when workers perceive a connection between their performance and how much they are paid. There are, however, other sources of motivation that con-

TABLE 7.4   Correlations between Managers' Self-Ratings on Each Factor and Their Attitudes toward How Important the Factor Is and Should Be in Determining Their Pay

Factor	Is determined		Should be determined	
	Private industry sample	Government sample	Private industry sample	Government sample
Seniority	.09	−.09	.30**	.32**
Education and experience	.18**	.13	.27**	.26**
Responsibility level	.23**	.09	.30**	.36**
Quality of performance	.13*	.16*	.31**	.40**
Productivity	.14*	.29**	.42**	.40**
Effort expended	.29**	.31**	.45**	.46**
Scarcity of skills	.39**	.32**	.48**	.45**

* $p < .05$.
** $p < .01$.

Source: Lawler, E. E. Managers' attitudes toward how their pay is and should be determined. *Journal of Applied Psychology*, 1966, *50*, 273–279. Copyright 1966 by the American Psychological Association. Published by permission.

tribute to job performance, one being the satisfaction the worker derives from the job itself; in other words, the motivation that is intrinsic to the task. Deci (1975) maintains that intrinsically motivated activities have goals that are inherent in the task itself. As a general rule, these goals are sought because their attainment leads the individual to feel more competent and self-determining. Deci identifies two kinds of intrinsically motivated behavior. In one, individuals engage in certain activities in order to increase the level of stimulation to which they are exposed. Drumming on the desk top in a quiet room, singing to oneself when alone, studying with the radio playing, may all represent types of behaviors that seek to increase the amount of sensory input one receives. A second type of intrinsic motivation involves behaviors that attempt to meet a challenge or reduce some incongruity that the individual faces. The hobbyist trying to meet a personal challenge as he builds a model ship to demanding specifications, the avocational reader seeking to gain new insights into the workings of things that go on around him—both engage in tasks that are intrinsically rewarding.

There is little room for doubt that there are as-

pects of many jobs that may be inherently satisfying to the worker, but there is a question concerning the manner in which these internal incentives combine with incentives, like pay, that are external to the job. Deci (1972, 1975) argues that when a person engages in a task that is motivated by intrinsic rewards, and when an external source of motivation such as pay is then introduced, the level of intrinsic motivation is subsequently reduced. The reason for this is that by introducing external incentives, one tends to change the worker's perception of the *locus of causality* that is present in the task situation. By locus of causality is meant the individual's beliefs regarding the location of the agents responsible for generating the rewards that serve to motivate—that is, cause—that individual's behavior. An intrinsically motivated task is one in which important incentives are to be found *within* the activities that make up the task. Rewards are internal to the individual; that is, when engaged in the task the individual feels more competent and more self-determining. In essence, the locus of the rewards individuals receive is found within themselves. When pay is introduced into the task situation, particularly if the pay is dependent on behavior, the individual perceives that the locus of causality has changed; it has become external. The worker begins to respond to rewards that are manipulated by an external system, and as a consequence, the level of intrinsic motivation is reduced.

Although Deci and his associates have carried out a number of studies that bear on these ideas, the experiment we will take up (Deci, 1971) is a field study that was carried out in a real-life work situation. The setting for the experiment was a campus newspaper for which two separate staffs published a Tuesday and a Friday edition. During the study one staff served as an experimental group, the other a control group. The job studied involved writing headlines for the newspaper, and during four periods lasting several weeks each, production records were collected for each worker. The major difference between the experimental and control groups was that during the second period, lasting three weeks, the subjects in the experimental group were paid 50 cents for each headline they wrote. They were told that their pay represented an effort to spend surplus funds before the semester ended, and that they would no longer be paid when the funds were exhausted. During the third period the experimental group worked for no pay, just as they had done during the first period, and just as the control group did for all periods. Finally there was a fourth period, lasting the first two weeks of a new semester, which began five weeks after the close of the third experimental period. In this period no pay was received by either group.

The results of the study indicated that there were no differences between control and experimental groups during the first two periods; during the third and fourth periods, however—that is, during the periods following the withdrawal of pay—the experimental group began to work at a significantly slower rate than the control groups. Hence, after pay was terminated the production of the work group slowed significantly relative to the production of the group that had never received payment. Deci claims that this difference in production rates reflects the fact that the introduction

of pay changed the subjects' perceptions of the locus of causation from internal to external. External rewards reduced the level of intrinsic motivation; when pay was terminated, workers performed at a lower rate, since they were now functioning under a reduced level of intrinsic motivation.

Critical Evaluation.   Experiments like this one by Deci touched off a flurry of research activity that attempted to test the contention that under certain circumstances external rewards reduce the level of intrinsic motivation. Some of the arguments surrounding these studies involved criticism of the methodological aspects of Deci's research, and many of these are too detailed or complex to consider here. It should be mentioned, however, that a number of these critical views have not themselves held up under research evaluation (Pritchard, Campbell, & Campbell, 1977). In one study that seems to call Deci's work into serious question, Farr, Vance, and McIntyre (1977) reanalyzed the data from some of Deci's studies, using statistical procedures that were thought to be more appropriate. The new analysis tended *not to support* Deci's theory. Hence, Farr et al. (1977) contended that had Deci used methods of analysis that were more appropriate, he would not have been able to generate the support he did obtain for his theoretical model. Until these methodological difficulties can be resolved, one must view the experimental support for Deci's theory with some caution, but the question is still an open one requiring more research.

Doubtless the relationship between intrinsic and extrinsic motivation is a complicated one, and Deci's theory probably represents only a first approximation to an answer. For example, there is a good likelihood that the effect of an extrinsic motivator like pay depends on whether it is viewed as being equitable by the worker. Heslin and Blake (1969) report that when individuals see themselves as undercompensated by their wages, they often seek additional sources of satisfaction within the task itself. In these instances, financial incentives *enhance* the motivation that is intrinsic to the task.

Furthermore, whether pay is perceived as being intrinsic or extrinsic to the work probably varies from task to task and from individual to individual. Along these lines, Kruglanski et al. (1975) present evidence suggesting that when pay is seen as an inherent part of the task (for example, payoffs in a slot machine, piece-rate pay), the presence of financial incentives enhances task motivation. When, on the other hand, pay is seen as an external consequence of the task, then the presence of pay tends to reduce intrinsic motivation.

We need much more experimental support before we can invest any high level of confidence in Deci's hypotheses, but these ideas do represent an interesting and important point of view regarding the manner in which various sources of work incentives combine. To the extent that Deci's thinking is correct, we might conclude that an inordinate emphasis placed on wages would tend to rob work of its intrinsic interest and enjoyment. As a consequence, we might find that job motivation is not as high under these conditions as in work situations where wages are not given the same level of emphasis and importance. Therefore, there is a cost associated with relying on financial incentives, or any other external reward for that matter, to motivate work performance. That cost is in the diminished motivation the worker derives from the work.

Relative Pay—Wage Comparisons

The literature indicates that individuals' expectations regarding the consequences of their work activities are an important factor influencing the motivational climate of work. Motivation to work is assumed to be highest when workers believe that their productivity will lead to rewards that they

value. The magnitude of the reward, however, its *valence* in Vroom's terms, is a factor that has not yet received the attention it deserves. A worker may clearly see the path-goal relation between work and pay, and yet believe that the amount of pay received is grossly inadequate. In such circumstances, the "rewards" of work may serve to inhibit production rather than stimulate higher levels of output. Roy (1952) describes a work situation in which piece rates that were considered too low by the work group resulted in a substantial retardation of productivity. Path-goal connections, therefore, are not the only factors determining the incentive value of wages. The amount of pay is, obviously, an important consideration.

In considering the motivational implications associated with the size of the paycheck, many researchers have placed emphasis on the relative amount of the wage, rather than on its absolute amount. The valence of pay seems to be related significantly to workers' perceptions of their pay compared to the pay received by others. It is important to know whether workers see their pay as fair or unfair relative to the wages received by others. Variations in these perceptions can produce different effects on workers who are all receiving the same amount of pay for the work they do.

Patchen's Model. Patchen (1961) says that the psychological value of pay is a function of a comparison that workers make between the pay they receive and the pay received by others. In addition, this comparison involves those aspects of the jobs that are thought to be responsible for the wages paid. For instance, two jobs may be compared in the light of their education requirements, job pressures, skill demands, and the like. Two ratios are then formed:

$$\frac{\text{My pay}}{\text{His (their) pay}} \quad \text{compared to} \quad \frac{\text{My position on job aspects that are the basis for wages paid}}{\text{His (their) position on job aspects that are the basis for wages paid}}$$

When the ratio on the left is substantially smaller than the one on the right, then the individual is dissatisfied with his wages.

Let's take an example. Worker A finds that worker B receives the same wages. In considering those aspects of both jobs that he believes are the basis for pay, however, worker A perceives that his job requires more skill and exposes him to greater job pressures than does B's job. Hence, the two sides of the comparison, that is, the two ratios, do not form an equality. Job wages and job dimensions do not, in Patchen's terms, maintain a consonant relationship for the two jobs, and as a consequence, worker A sees his wages as being unsatisfactory.

Patchen's model is of interest because it introduces us to some of the central ideas that theorists have employed to deal with the motivational significance of pay. Fundamental to these theories is the notion that the psychological importance of pay depends upon some type of comparison that is made between different rates of pay. Another basic consideration involves an evaluation of pay in terms of some nonmonetary criterion. For example, pay may be evaluated in the light of a person's performance or in terms of the requirements of a job. From this system of comparisons there emerges a perception of value or fairness, and it is this perception that largely determines the motivational impact of a particular wage. In a theory presented by Jaques (1961) these comparisons involve a consideration of how closely an individual's job performance is monitored by superiors. In a theory developed by Adams (1963), subjective input-outcome ratios, which express a type of costs-benefits appraisal, are important factors determining the psychological importance of pay incentives.

Jaques's Time-Span of Discretion. In dealing with ideas like Patchen's, one must recognize that the choice of wage comparisons—that is, the jobs considered and the job dimensions chosen for consideration, are in large measure a matter of personal choice. Elliott Jaques (1961) suggests that one important factor that may be brought into the perception of the fairness of a wage is what he calls the *time-span of discretion*. In defining this concept, Jaques draws a distinction between aspects of a work role that are prescribed by a superior and aspects that are left to the worker's discretion. He also identifies what he calls *marginally*

substandard discretion. This refers to discretionary choices that result in outcomes that are just outside the limits of being acceptable. The time-span of discretion is "the period of time during which marginally substandard discretion could be exercised in a role before information about the accumulating substandard work would become available to the manager in charge of the role" (Jaques, 1961, p. 99). Jobs vary widely in their time-span of discretion, and Jaques maintains that this property of the job plays a significant part in determining people's perception of what constitutes a fair wage for the work. As the time-span of discretion increases, the wage payment perceived to be fair also increases. In other words, one of the characteristics of jobs generally thought to command high wages is a longer time-span during which substandard judgment will go unnoticed by a superior.

Jaques (1956, 1961, 1970) carried out studies whose results indicate that the time-span of discretion correlates with the management level occupied by a given job. As might be expected, time-spans tend to be longer for jobs at higher levels in the organization. He also found that the time-span of discretion correlates with the estimates people make of the salaries they consider fair for the work being done. In Jaques's words, "members whose work carried the same maximum time-span of discretion, whatever their field of work, were found to state—with only slight variations—the same salary as being a fair return . . . for the work they were doing" (Jaques, 1956, p. 45). Hence, Jaques's results suggest that individuals can use information concerning the time-span of discretion as a basis for deciding what constitutes fair pay for a job. Furthermore, Jaques claims that there is widespread agreement among people concerning fair pay, and paying an individual at a rate that is consistent with these standards of pay leads the worker to be satisfied with the wages received. Payment outside of the range considered fair produces a negative psychological reaction, the intensity of which is proportionate to the discrepancy between the actual pay and fair pay.

Adams's Principle of Equity. The psychological consequences of wages depend, in some large measure, on how workers perceive the money they receive and the efforts they invest in the job. It also makes a lot of sense to argue that the extent to which a wage motivates work behavior depends on whether or not the worker sees the wage as being fair. Undoubtedly, one dimension of this perception involves norms that the worker has developed for what constitutes an equitable salary. Norms of this sort probably include workers' assessments of the pay and working conditions associated with their own jobs, as well as assessments of the pay and working conditions found in other jobs. Therefore, comparisons within and between jobs serve as the basis for determining the equity of pay. Both Patchen and Jaques have thought along these lines, as have Sayles (1958) and Homans (1961). It is J. S. Adams, however, who has presented these ideas in a theoretical model that has received the greatest amount of attention; therefore, we will look more carefully at this interesting and important approach to the study of financial incentives.

Adams (1963, 1965) sees each worker as being in an exchange situation, one facet of which involves those things that the worker invests in his job. Skills, education, job training, seniority, time, and effort represent some of the resources each worker puts into a job. On the other side of the exchange, the job generates certain outcomes: some as a direct consequence of the worker's performance, others as a result of sets of rules, regulations, and organizational arrangements. Social status, work associates, fringe benefits, task satisfaction, and, of course, wages can serve as outcome variables.

In determining the fairness of the pay received, the individual engages in a kind of psychological auditing of the two sides of this exchange, considering inputs and outcomes and then calculating a ratio that expresses the relationship between the two. The elements that enter into these calculations are determined subjectively; that is, the input-outcome ratio that the worker associates with the job contains elements that are selected solely on the basis of what that worker considers relevant and proper. Two workers, holding the same job and receiving identical wages, may perceive ratios of input and outcome that are considerably different from each other. Each may take a somewhat different set of factors into consideration; and common factors may receive different weights.

Whether a work incentive is considered equitable does not depend on the absolute value of an input-outcome ratio, but rather is the result of a comparison of the individual's ratio with those calculated for other positions. Whenever the input-outcome ratio is perceived as not equal to the ratio computed for another position, then a condition of inequity exists. Depending on the degree of this imbalance, the individual initiates behaviors that attempt to reduce or eliminate this condition. Adams (1965, p. 280) represents inequity in the following manner:

$$\frac{O_p}{I_p} \neq \frac{O_a}{I_a}.$$

This inequality includes both the situation in which the person, *p*, sees that his ratio is smaller than the one calculated for individual, *a*:

$$\frac{O_p}{I_p} < \frac{O_a}{I_a},$$

and the situation in which *p* sees that his ratio is larger than that of *a*:

$$\frac{O_p}{I_p} > \frac{O_a}{I_a}.$$

Hence, inequity can exist whenever individuals perceive that they are either undercompensated or overcompensated. Inequity is present, therefore, in those instances in which individuals believe that their input-outcome ratio is unequal to a ratio computed for some other position. Adams maintains that when workers believe they are in inequitous situations, they experience tension, the magnitude of which is related to the degree of inequity. This tension state motivates the individual to take some sort of action that will eliminate or reduce the inequity. Workers, therefore, are motivated to maintain an equitable relationship between the inputs and outcomes of their jobs and the input-outcome exchanges they believe to exist in other jobs. Inequity refers to a set of beliefs held by a worker that leads to an increase in motivation. Equity theory, therefore, is a motivational theory, according to which the sources of motivation are found in the cognitions of the workers. As the motivational level increases, there is an increased likelihood that one may see behavioral signs of this inequity. The nature of the action taken in response to this heightened level of drive depends on the characteristics of the situation, the personality of the worker, and the worker's previous experience with similar circumstances.

Reactions to Wage Inequities

Many alternative courses of action are open to workers who find themselves in inequitous situations. Job inputs may be modified in order to readjust the input-outcome equation. Workers, for example, may reduce or increase their level of productivity or may alter the time and effort put into the job. The literature is filled with reports of workers placing restrictions on their productivity as a result of a belief that they are unfairly compensated, and later on we will consider studies in which increased productivity appears to result from a belief that the pay represents overcompensation.

There are instances in which a condition of equity can be restored by changing the outcomes that an individual obtains from work. For example, workers who see themselves as being unfairly paid may compensate by adopting dishonest work practices. The level of pilferage in work situations is often found to be quite high (Zeitlin, 1971), and although many motives may underlie such activities, perceived wage inequities may be one of them. Another alternative might consist of efforts to increase the social status or security of a job. Attempts by school teachers, a group underpaid by tradition, to maintain the social prestige and job

security of their profession may be interpreted in equity terms. Often, being frustrated in their efforts to obtain a wage that is fair among the ranks of professionals, teachers invest heavily in efforts to strengthen the institution of academic tenure that provides them with considerable job security.

Individuals may respond to a condition of inequity by restructuring the elements that entered into the input-outcome ratios that are compared. In other words, they can look at their jobs, and the jobs of others, in a new light. Inputs and outcomes can be adjusted cognitively so as to balance the ratios being compared. A worker who learns that similar jobs receive considerably more pay in another division of the company may adjust this apparent inequity by increasing the value placed on the congenial surrounding of the job, or by increasing the perceived input of the other jobs through a sharpened recognition of higher pressures placed on people in these positions. Although the truth of the matter may be that this worker is, in fact, receiving far less for the same amount and type of work, according to his adjusted calculations, he is being fairly paid.

Adams (1965) mentions other adjustments to inequity. The worker may leave the job if wage inequities are unacceptable. The worker may change the jobs that are used as a basis of comparison. There is an almost limitless variety of alternatives that may be adopted by workers who are faced with the belief that they are not receiving equitable distributions of incentives, and much research will be needed before we will be in a position to predict which one will be adopted in a given situation. Nevertheless, the central fact remains that the Principle of Equity states that when faced with inequity, the individual experiences an increase in the level of motivation which tends to direct behavior toward the reduction of this condition.

Research Findings

The research dealing with equity theory has tended to concentrate on four questions. One concerns the different motivational consequences of inequity when pay is computed either on an hourly basis or on a piece-rate schedule. A second deals with the effects of overcompensation and undercompensation. A third concerns the output measures observed, that is, quantity or quality of production. And a fourth concerns the methods used to generate the inequity conditions. Adams's theory has stimulated a very large number of research studies, and only a representative set of investigations will be presented in the following sections. These studies take up the four issues mentioned above, and as a group they represent some of the more interesting work done in this area.

Hourly Overcompensation.   One of the earliest studies in this area is an investigation carried out by Adams and Rosenbaum (1962), in which an inequity condition was established through the use of instructions that informed a group of subjects they were being overcompensated relative to the skills and experiences they were bringing to the job. The procedure followed was something like this.

A group of college students were hired through a placement office to work as interviewers at the rate of $3.50 an hour. As the students reported for the hiring interview, they were randomly assigned to an overcompensated condition or an equity condition. In the overcompensation condition, the person doing the hiring looked over the background information that had been supplied by the applicant. Then the applicant was told:

> You don't have nearly enough experience in interviewing or survey work of the kind we are engaged in here. I specifically asked the Placement Service to refer only people with that kind of experience. . . . I can't understand how such a slip-up could have occurred. . . . I guess I'll have to hire you anyway, but *please* pay close attention to the instructions I will give you. . . . Since I'm going to hire you, I'll just have to pay you at the rate we advertised, that is, $3.50 an hour. (Adams & Rosenbaum, 1962, p. 163)

The students in the equity conditions were told that they were fully qualified for the work they were about to do, and that the $3.50 was "standard for work of this kind performed by people with your qualifications'' (p. 163).

Equity theory predicted that these instructions left the overcompensated group facing a job in which their input, that is, training and experience, did not justify the outcomes that would be received—$3.50 an hour. To adjust this inequity it was predicted that subjects would increase their inputs, that they would produce at a higher rate than would those in the equity condition.

As predicted, the results of this study indicated that the subjects who were working under the overcompensation conditions tended to complete more interviews than did those who had been told that they were well qualified for the job. Adams interprets this difference as reflecting the motivational impact of the inequity conditions that led the overcompensated group to increase their input—that is, rate of production—in order to adjust for the overpayment they were receiving.

Much of Adams's early work deals with a situation like the one employed in the study described above. Employees paid on an hourly wage schedule are observed in a task for which they are overcompensated. Workers cannot adjust for this inequity by lowering their pay, since their wages are fixed and independent of performance; as a consequence, equity theory predicts they will increase their rate of production in order to attain a more equitable input-outcome balance. As we have just seen, this prediction was borne out in the Adams and Rosenbaum experiment, and subsequent to this study there followed a series of reports that have supplied further confirmation for this prediction (Lawler et al., 1968; Goodman & Friedmen, 1968; Weiner, 1970; Wood & Lawler, 1970). Hence, there appears to be reasonably good support for Adams's contention that overcompensated employees paid by the hour will tend to show an increase in rates of output.

Hourly Undercompensation.   Equity theory would predict that in the absence of more acceptable alternatives, low levels of performance will be generated by an hourly wage seen by workers to be undercompensating, and this is, in fact, what

Pritchard, Dunnette, and Jorgenson (1972) report in a study using college student employees. Other studies by Heslin and Blake (1969), however, and by Valenzi and Andrews (1971), failed to find any production differences between equity groups and groups that were underpaid. It would appear, therefore, that Adams's predictions concerning the effects of hourly undercompensation have not received consistent experimental support.

Of course, perceived inequity can result in adjustments to the input-outcome ratio in some fashion other than through a change in production. For instance, a person believing that his hourly salary is too low can quit, and this is, in fact, what happened in the Valenzi and Andrews study. In this case, eight out of eleven underpaid hourly workers either quit their jobs or admitted that they thought about quitting. Hence, the fact that wage inequities do not result in significant changes in production does not necessarily invalidate Adams's ideas. Workers may draw on behavioral alternatives other than production activities in order to set what they see as an unfair input-outcome in an equitable balance.

Piece Rate.   One of the more intriguing predictions that can be derived from equity theory concerns the consequences of overcompensation when the pay plan is a piece-rate system rather than the salary system that was observed in the Adams and Rosenbaum (1962) study. Equity theory predicts that when overcompensated and paid by the piece, workers will tend to produce at a *lower rate* than will individuals for whom the pay per unit produced is thought to be equitable. Overcompensated piece-rate workers tend to find themselves in a situation wherein the inequity of pay is increasingly aggravated with each unit produced. Higher and higher rates of production will result in an increase in the magnitude of inequity; hence, there will be motivational influences operating that will act to retard rates of output.

There is another alternative that may operate to decrease production; workers may attempt to reduce the level of inequity by increasing their personal investment in the production of each unit completed. In other words, it is predicted that ov-

ercompensated piecework will lead to an improvement in the *quality* of the production turned out. This attention to quality would, however, lengthen the amount of time invested in each unit, and as a result there would be a decrease in the *quantity* of output. Hence, when working under a condition of overcompensated piecework, Adams predicts a drop in the quantity of output, but an increase in the quality of work.

Since many of the studies that concern piece rates include both over- and undercompensation conditions, we will deal with these two situations in this section, and in doing so we will find that there seems to be rather good support for Adams's position. Adams and Jacobsen (1964), for instance, hired 60 college students to carry out a proofreading task in which instructions informed one group they were to be overpaid, relative to their ability and experience. A second group was informed that they were qualified to receive the standard rate, while a third group was informed that since they lacked the qualifications and experience required by the job, they would be hired at a rate that was one-third below the standard rate. This latter condition was thought to approximate an equity situation, since the lack of worker qualifications (input) was accompanied by a reduction in the piece rate (outcome). The results of this study confirmed predictions; that is, the overcompensated group proofed significantly *fewer* pages of a *higher quality* than did the two equity groups. No significant differences existed between the qualified group and the unqualified reduced-rate group.

Support for equity theory can also be found in studies by Wood and Lawler (1970) and Garland (1973), but perhaps one of the more interesting sets of findings comes from a study by Andrews (1967). Here, in addition to the usual three piece-rate conditions—over, under and equitable compensation—Andrews classified his subjects on the basis of the highest rate of pay they had received on jobs held in the past. It seems reasonable to believe that people's perception of the equity of their present wage is influenced by the level of wages received on previous jobs. Intuition might lead one to predict that the highest levels of work

**TABLE 7.5   Quantity of Work as a Function of Assigned
Piece Rate and Previous Wage Experience**

Previous high wage per hour	15¢ per piece (n = 32)	20¢ per piece (n = 32)	30¢ per piece (n = 32)	Row average
$2.25 or more (n = 25)	23.7	18.2	19.6	21.0
$1.60 to $2.20 (n = 46)	22.2	20.3	17.0	20.0
$1.55 or less (n = 25)	16.7	15.9	15.1	16.0
Column average	21.1	18.9	17.7	19.2

Source: Andrews, I. R. Wage inequity and job performance. *Journal of Applied Psychology,* 1967, *51,* 39–45. Copyright 1967 by the American Psychological Association. Published by permission.

motivation would be expected for the individual who is presently receiving high pay but who had received only low wages in the past. Equity theory, however, would predict just the opposite for this individual. From this point of view, every overcompensated unit produced increases feelings of inequity, and this effect is accentuated for workers who previously have never worked for high wages.

Table 7.5 shows the results of the experiment conducted by Andrews (1967). Pilot research done prior to this experiment indicated that the 20¢ per piece was judged to be an equitable wage for the work done; hence, the 15¢ rate represented undercompensation, and the 30¢ rate overcompensation for the work. The rows in the table identify groups that varied according to the highest amount of pay ever received on previous jobs. As predicted, Andrews found that the *highest* rates of productivity were found in groups that had received the *lowest* pay per unit produced, while the *lowest* amount of output came from the subjects who had received the *highest* pay per unit. Furthermore, these results are magnified when one takes level by previous pay into consideration. For example, the subjects who produced at the highest rate were those who were paid the least per unit and who had reported having made relatively high wages on one of their previous jobs. Table 7.5 shows that the group with the smallest output was the one paid at the highest piece rate, whose best previous salary had been

relatively low. Hence, a combination of low rates paid to individuals who previously held jobs that paid high wages appeared to be the incentive condition associated with relatively high levels of productivity.

The Andrews study not only provides interesting and important confirmation for equity theory; it also demonstrates the complexity of this whole wage incentive question. It seems that the incentive value of a particular pay rate is a function of a complicated cognitive assessment of wages that is carried out by the worker. In making this evaluation, the worker may draw on a broad range of sources, one of which concerns the amount of pay received in the past. Previous pay contributes to workers' responses to their current rates, and, at least according to equity theory, high rates of output should be found in situations that on the basis of intuition seem to provide relatively unattractive pay situations, that is, low unit pay, high previous pay. It appears, therefore, that common sense may not always be a valid source of insight into the incentive value of the wages paid to people for the work they do.

What is Manipulated in Equity Research?

One of the most persistent questions raised about equity research has concerned the methods used to establish the condition in which individuals believe they are overcompensated. One approach that has been frequently employed tells job applicants that their training and experience do not satisfy the requirements for the job. Then these persons are hired and paid the going rate for the job. Under these circumstances the individuals are led to believe that their pay exceeds the rate their qualifications would justify, and as a consequence they perceive that they are in an overcompensation condition.

Lawler (1968) contends that the instructions used in studies like those reported by Adams and his associates do not actually exert their principal influence on individuals' perception of their pay. Rather, instructions such as these exert their most potent influence on how individuals see someone else's view of them. When job interviewers tell applicants that they don't have the training or experience to justify the pay they will be receiving, it might be reasonable to suspect that the applicants' self-concepts have just been challenged. Rather than manipulating how the applicants view their pay, experiences such as these influence applicants' feelings of self-worth, and to the extent that this is true, high rates of performance represent a means whereby individuals can demonstrate their competence. Production, therefore, leads to higher levels of self-esteem, and higher rates of production do not necessarily reflect the push of wage incentives.

Several studies (Lawler, 1968, Evans & Molinari, 1970) have attempted to observe workers in a situation in which overcompensation does not imply that the worker is unqualified. Lawler (1968), for example, compared two overcompensated groups with an equity group. In one of these groups, subjects were told that their overcompensation was a function of their own inadequate qualifications; in the other group, overcompensation was a function of the pay requirements of a research grant. Hence, for subjects in this second group, overpayment was the result of contract requirements rather than a reflection of their lack of qualifications. Lawler predicted that when overcompensation was not accompanied by an attack on the individual's self-esteem, production would

be no different than what would be observed in the equity group, and this is, in fact, what did occur. Subjects who were overpaid by circumstances produced at about the same rate as those subjects who saw their pay as being equitable.

In a study that gives us some insight into the nature of the beliefs generated by Adams's overcompensation instructions, Andrews and Valenzi (1970) asked a group of subjects to role-play a situation in which they would apply for a job after being told they were unqualified to receive the wages that would be paid. In responding to this role a large majority reacted in terms of their self-images as workers, while none reacted to the situation in terms of the wages they were to receive. In other words, when given information suggesting they were unqualified to receive a given wage, subjects seemed to focus their attention on themselves rather than on the wages. Hence, it would appear that the methods frequently used to create the cognition of overcompensation do not have their principal psychological impact on subjects' beliefs about their wages, but rather seem to influence subjects' concern with themselves.

At present we must withhold final judgment concerning the effects of hourly overcompensation; the research literature is too cloudy to reveal any clear sense of direction. Perhaps in a real job situation the belief that one is overpaid relative to one's qualifications is not an event that occurs with high frequency. In most work situations the worker is aware that management has agreed to the wages that are paid; hence, there is good reason to suspect that the company sees the wages as being equitable. Under these circumstances it shouldn't be too difficult for workers to adjust their perceptions to fit those of their employers. Therefore, the motivational pressures that might temporarily arise from a suspicion that one is overcompensated would tend to encourage the worker to alter the way pay is perceived rather than result in significant changes in performance. Of course, there may be times when overcompensation does lead to changes in output, but these conditions may be difficult to maintain for any length of time in a laboratory setting.

Evaluation. These studies point to the methodological difficulties one finds associated with Adams's Principle of Equity. Surely Adams's work has given rise to an outpouring of research concerning the motivational influence of financial incentives and a renewed interest in this general area of work incentives. Research has left, however, a rather cloudy picture of the equity principle. Whether this situation is a reflection of some inaccuracies in Adams's ideas, or whether it is an indication of the problems involved in translating his ideas into experimental procedures, is a matter yet to be resolved. Cognitive theories such as this require that the experimenter establish the desired mental state in the subjects—for example, overcompensation—while at the same time placing the subjects in a task situation where they tend to adjust to this state by modifying their performance in a fashion that can be observed and measured. This is a difficult goal to accomplish.

Finally, there is research that suggests that one must proceed cautiously in assuming that any particular aspect of work will be perceived as an outcome or an input factor. Tornow and Dunnette (1970) for example, contend that individuals differ with regard to their perception of the input-outcome dimensions of the task. Two people approaching the same task may perceive a particular job dimension in entirely different ways. One may see it as an input factor, the other as an outcome. The hard work and effort required by a job may be seen by one person as a personal demand imposed by the task. Another person, considering the same job aspect, may see this as a source of challenge and stimulation. For the first person work effort is seen as a job input; for the second it is seen as a job outcome. Tornow and Dunnette (1970) present research evidence suggesting that people may vary in their tendencies to see certain job dimensions as input or outcome factors. There is also a possibility that these tendencies have a certain amount of stability; that is, a given person may generally tend to look at work dimensions of a certain type as inputs rather than outcomes. Hence, the effects of wage inequity depend on whether the individual perceives certain other aspects of the work as being inputs or outcomes. Tornow and Dunnette show that the effect of undercompensation tends to be greater for those who concentrate on job inputs. Although this does not invalidate the basic ideas of equity theory, these results do show that matters may be more complicated with regard to these perceptions than we had originally thought.

Equity in Wage Determination

The concept, equity, also applies to the values and attitudes of those persons responsible for setting wage rates. Equity theory suggests that managers would be expected to take their own salaries into consideration, using cognition of the input-outcome ratio associated with their own jobs as a factor that contributes to the calculation of a fair wage for another job. In one sense, then, the process of wage determination is one involving the distribution of pay among jobs, one of which is the individual's own. One objective of this distribution is to achieve a pay structure that both the manager and the worker see as being equitable.

In an attempt to look at certain aspects of this problem, Lane and Messé (1971, 1972) have carried out a group of studies that concern the distribution of pay incentives among people. In these studies individuals are asked to distribute, to themselves and one other, pay for a task they have performed. In carrying out this allocation a person can assign pay in such a way that it expresses one of three orientations. Allocators can maximize their own interests, they can maximize the interests of the other person, or they can strive to achieve some kind of equitable balance by taking into consideration the interests of both parties.

Relying on data generated by undergraduate students, Lane and Messé report that the most frequently used wage distribution was one that reflected the more equitable allocation of pay between the two persons. The next most used distributional strategy was one that maximized self-interest, with the altruistic distribution being used hardly at all—in only 6 out of a total of 558 distributions. An individual's tendency to adhere to an equity norm, however, is influenced by situational factors. For instance, in a public distribution of pay, as opposed to a private one, self-interest distributions occurred less frequently when the receiver was of the opposite sex. In situations in which allocator and receiver had different work inputs, equity norms seemed to depend on whether or not the receiver's inputs exceeded a certain threshold value. Allocators tended to give themselves as much pay as possible if they perceived that their partners had not worked hard enough to deserve more than a minimal rate. Once this threshold level was passed, then the distribution of wages tended to adhere to a norm of equity.

There is other evidence indicating there are significant differences among people who are asked to assign wages to others. These differences seem to be related to certain psychological characteristics of those who carry out the wage determination. Recall, for example, the study by Lawler (1966b) in which managers tended to indicate they felt that pay should be computed on the basis of factors that they saw themselves possessing in high amounts. Along related lines, Bass (1968) asked a large group of business college graduate students to make a set of salary recommendations for ten fictitious engineers who had just finished their first year with a company. Each engineer was described in terms of a different set of considerations, for example:

---

1. Al—an average producer
2. Bill—a very high performer
3. Irwin—has a boring, dull, and monotonous job
4. Jim—has a higher salary offer from a competitor

Measures of personal values and life goals were obtained for each allocator.

In examining the distribution of recommended raises, Bass found that the assignments that were made varied according to the recipient's ability, the work conditions, and the personal characteristics of the individual assigning the pay. Although each special circumstance surrounding a recipient's work was found to influence the raise to some extent, it was the recipient's performance level that seemed to be given the greatest consideration by those who allocated the raise monies. Wage distributions also varied as a function of the personal characteristics of the allocator; to illustrate, brighter and academically more successful subjects tended to recommend smaller raises than did those who were less able academically. Those whose primary life goals involved service tended to be more generous with raises, while those whose life goals focused on technical success were less so. Bass shows us that we might gain considerable insight into the factors that influence the setting of wages if we were to look at the personal values held by those who allocate the money.

Goodman (1975) has presented us with an interesting set of results that bear on this topic of wage determination. In this study Goodman asked a group of subjects to role-play a situation in which they were managers who were about to distribute wage increases to subordinates with high, average, and low performance. Before doing this, each "manager" was assigned to one of the following four input-outcome roles: a manager with low performance and low salary, with low performance and high salary, with high performance and low salary, or with high performance and high salary.

Goodman's results showed that managers' own input-outcome ratios appeared to be related to the decisions made regarding both the raises they are willing to distribute to people who differ in terms of their performance, and the total amount of money they are willing to spend on all raises. For example, the high-performance, fairly paid managers (high performance/high pay) drew the sharpest salary distinctions between high- and low-performing subordinates. The low-performance, fairly paid group (low performance/fair pay) tended to create smaller differentials between the raises given to the high- and low-performance subordinates. We see, then, in these results an indication that the pay received for the work an individual does is a factor that enters the picture when this individual is asked to assign wages to others. This suggests that within the work organization we should recognize the possibility that wages operate as an organization-wide system. Inequities that may be found at one level of the firm may well be found carrying over to influence the wage decisions that are made with regard to several levels of the organization. To find general wage dissatisfaction at one level of the organization, therefore, may signal trouble for the entire wage structure. This possibility should encourage us to invest more research effort in this important area of wage determination.

WAGE SATISFACTION

Wage satisfaction occurs whenever workers believe that their wages stand in an equitable relationship with the wages of others. Porter (1961) measures satisfaction with wages by asking employees how much pay there should be for their jobs and how much there is. Locke (1969) emphasizes the perceived discrepancy between what individuals want and what they receive. Satisfaction with wages, as with satisfaction with almost any aspect of work, is thought of in terms of discrepancies between a norm for what is desirable or fair and what actually exists.

In a later chapter the contribution of wages to general job satisfaction will be considered, so for the present we will confine our attention to studies that deal with workers' satisfaction with pay itself. In particular, we will try to answer the question, what are the variables that seem to contribute most heavily to workers' satisfaction with the pay they receive? Not unexpectedly, the variable that seems to contribute most to wage satisfaction is the amount of the actual wages the individual receives. Klein (1973), for instance, suggests that size of salary, size of salary increases, and timing of salary increases are important considerations and enter into an individual's experience of wage satisfaction. Ronan and Organt (1973) found that actual salary received was the principal determinant of

wage satisfaction among groups of management, salaried, and hourly employees. Two studies by Lawler and Porter (1963, 1966) have found a significant relationship between actual salary and reported satisfaction with pay, and there are other studies that corroborate these findings (for example, Andrews & Henry, 1963; Moore & Baron, 1973). Of course, when one moves up the salary scale, there are many other aspects of work that change as well. Job level, status, power, and autonomy are but a few of the important social psychological variables that may be expected to change with salary level. There is some evidence (Lawler and Porter, 1963, 1966), however, that the relationship between actual pay and satisfaction with pay remains about the same, even though these other variables are held constant.

It seems rather simple, but the literature gives considerable support to the conclusion that the more money workers make, the more satisfied they will be with their pay. Furthermore, there doesn't seem to be a whole lot of support for the often-made conjecture that after a raise, people gradually adapt to the higher salary and eventually little of the satisfaction remains from the time when the higher wage was first received. To be sure, there are other psychological factors that contribute to the individual's satisfaction with pay; the literature, however, seems to point quite clearly to the fact that within the range of salaries perceived to be equitable, the more money one makes, the more satisfaction there will be with pay.

The Utility of Wage Increases

Intuition would lead one to expect that the psychological consequences of a given wage increase would be influenced by an individual's current rate of pay. As a case in point, one might suspect that a $500-a-year increase would result in a smaller increment in pay satisfaction for a person earning $50,000 a year than it would for a person earning $5,000 a year. Economists speak of decreasing marginal utility to refer to the situation in which each added dollar has less value to the individual than the last dollar. Applying this concept to wage satisfaction, we would find that each dollar added to pay would result in an increment in satisfaction with the total wage, but the increase would be smaller for each dollar added. Under conditions of *decreasing marginal utility,* the plot of the relationship between satisfaction and pay increases would result in a nonlinear function that was ever increasing and negatively accelerated (see Figure 7.2). *Increasing marginal utility,* on the other hand, refers to the situation in which each added dollar produces a larger increase in satisfaction than the preceding dollar.

Equity theory suggests that a point would be reached where added pay increases would be seen as overcompensation, and as a consequence each dollar beyond this point would result in a reduction in the perceived value of the aggregate wage. To plot the relationship between satisfaction and raises, using an equity approach, one would find a function in which a point would be reached where the curve would begin to turn down. Beyond this point, each new dollar would result in a decreasing level of satisfaction (see Figure 7.3).

Another alternative would find a straight line describing this relationship. Here, for every dollar added to pay there would be a *constant increase* in the satisfaction experienced by the individual. A dollar added to the pay of the company president would have the same impact on feelings of wage satisfaction as would a dollar added to a rank-and-file production worker's pay.

These relationships between pay increases and satisfaction have been explored in a number of studies and, in general, no one function has been found to fit all situations. In one study, for example (Galanter, 1962, cited in Giles & Barrett, 1971), subjects were required to judge how much money would make them twice as happy as $10, $100, and $1,000. Results indicated that the subjects responded to wage increments according to a decreasing marginal-utility function. This type of function, however, was not observed in a study (Giles & Barrett, 1971) carried out on a group of 157 professional personnel who were asked to indicate the size of the merit increase they would consider to be fair for their next year's raise. Using this value as a standard, the subjects were then asked to judge the relative satisfaction they would

FIGURE 7.3   Four Possible Relationships between the Size of a Wage Increase and the Increase in Wage Satisfaction Experienced by a Worker

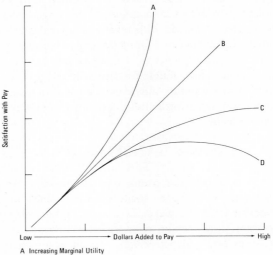

A   Increasing Marginal Utility
B   Linear Marginal Utility
C   Decreasing Marginal Utility
D   Equity Function

expect to receive from each of a set of alternative merit increases. The results of this study did not provide support for the decreasing marginal-utility concept. Rather, there seemed to be more evidence supporting an *increasing* marginal-utility function.

At first it might be difficult to imagine the psychological processes that would result in this type of increasing function. One possibility comes to mind. Think of the situation in which each added dollar is perceived as bringing the individual *closer* to a new standard of living. As a consequence of wage increases, there has been an upward revision of the individual's social and economic objectives. Now each dollar added to pay is a step toward these goals; each new dollar improves the probability of being able to adopt these new living standards. Hence, we might speculate that an increasing marginal-utility function can be expected whenever each added dollar is perceived as moving the individual *toward* a goal that has not yet been attained. Decreasing marginal-utility functions, on the other hand, can be expected whenever the individual psychologically focuses on a set of social and economic standards that have already largely been reached, and where current salary is seen in terms of maintenance of these standards. In these instances, added salary operates psychologically more as a surplus than as a step closer to a higher goal.

But not all of Giles and Barrett's subjects reacted to wage increases in a fashion consistent with an increasing marginal-utility function. For approximately 10 percent of the sample, merit increases did not continue to produce increasing levels of anticipated satisfaction. These subjects reached a point where larger raises resulted in increased worry concerning the consequences of overcompensation. One concern, for instance, was that higher and higher raises would result in increases in the expectations management would have regarding the individual's performance. The Giles and Barrett study, therefore, does not permit us to conclude that for every dollar in wage increments each individual would be expected to experience some sort of increase in wage satisfaction. A level can be reached where added dollars expose individuals to concerns regarding the security of their jobs and the performance level expected of them. At this point, added dollars bring decreasing wage satisfaction.

Looking back over the Galanter (1962) and the Giles and Barrett (1971) studies, we see that the subjective consequences of wage increases appear to change from one added dollar to the next. Whether this change is best described by a de-

creasing or an increasing marginal-utility curve appears to depend on situational circumstances. Furthermore, equity considerations probably place limits on the range of salary increases over which either the decreasing or the increasing functions seem to apply.

The Perception of Wage Increases

How large a raise in pay is necessary for an individual to perceive a salary adjustment that is psychologically meaningful? One might expect that the higher the salary level of the worker, the greater the size of the raise needed to produce a just noticeable increment in pay. Zedeck and Smith (1968) attempted to determine the size of raise needed for an individual to see it as being "just meaningful." Using a group of secretaries and a group of higher-paid junior executives, these authors confirmed the fact that the higher the pay, the more dollars it takes to produce a meaningful raise. Furthermore, they found a trend that suggested that a just noticeable change in pay was a constant percentage of the worker's current salary. In other words, regardless of individuals' salary level, their wages would have to be changed, say, 6 percent before they would report that the raise was meaningful. A person earning $300 per month would report that an $18 raise was a meaningful one, whereas a person earning $600 per month would require an increase of $36 for the raise to be seen as being meaningful.

In a related study Hinrichs (1969a) presented a group of 1500 white-collar employees with a set of fifteen monthly wage increases, ranging from $1.00 per month to $1000. Subjects were asked to sort these raises into the following five categories:

1. Extremely large increases in monthly salaries; I would be flabbergasted.
2. Large salary increases; I would be pleasantly surprised.
3. Neither large nor small increases; about average.
4. Small salary increases; I would be somewhat disappointed.
5. Just barely noticeable salary increases; I essentially would not view it as an increase at all.

Hinrichs predicted that the increment in wages that would be judged just noticeable would be a

constant proportion of the individual's current salary, and within a fairly broad range this is what

TABLE 7.6   Perceptions of "Just Barely Noticeable" Pay Increases as a Function of Present Pay

Current monthly salary (Dollars)	N	"Just barely noticeable" (versus "small") increases	
		X (Dollars)	Percent of current salary
Under 400[a]	18	18	5.1
400–499	96	19	4.2
500–599	107	20	3.7
600–699	95	21	3.3
700–799	113	25	3.3
800–899	122	27	3.2
900–1099	193	31	3.1
1100–1399	160	38	3.0
1400–2000	173	50	2.9
Over 2000[b]	34	56	2.2

[a]Midpoint assumed at $350.
[b]Midpoint assumed at $2500.
Source: Hinrichs, J. R. Correlates of employee evaluations of pay increases. *Journal of Applied Psychology,* 1969, *53,* 481–489 (p. 483). Copyright 1969 by the American Psychological Association. Reprinted by permission.

was observed. Consider Table 7.6 adapted from Hinrichs (1969a). Here we find the amount of money judged to be needed to differentiate a raise that was seen as being "just barely noticeable" from a raise that is seen as being "small."

Notice that as the current salary of the rater increases from under $400 per month to over $2,000, the amount of the raise separating these two categories shows a steady increase. When these values are expressed as a *percentage* of current salary, however, with few exceptions an increase amounting to about 3 percent is required to move a raise from the just noticeable category to the small category. Hence, Hinrich's predictions seem to be reasonable in the light of these results.

This is an interesting finding, since it tends to agree with what psychologists have often observed when people are asked to report on differences in the magnitude of sensory experiences. For instance, let's say a person is holding a 150-gram weight in his hand. How much do we have to increase this weight before a just noticeable change is experienced? The answer to this question is often found to depend on the magnitude of the weight that we start out with. In fact, the added weight required before the person can detect the change often is found to be a constant proportion of the starting weight. This relationship is referred to as Weber's Law (Guilford, 1954), and although this is not the appropriate place to consider this law in any detail, it is of considerable interest to learn that there is some reason to believe that the detection of wage increases may reflect the same principles as the detection of differences in a wide variety of stimulus magnitudes. All the studies in this area suggest that the methods of sensory psychology would be useful in the study of the psychological impact of different size raises that may be given for work.

Pay Dissatisfaction—Turnover

One of the correlates of dissatisfaction with wages seems to be found in a higher turnover rate. Finn and Lee (1972) split a group of 170 professional and scientific employees into two groups—those people felt that they were being fairly paid and those who felt they were not being fairly paid. The inequity group were found to be more responsive to a set of inducements (wage increases, more interesting work, and so on) that would be available to them if they were to consider changing their jobs. Hence, workers who were relatively dissatisfied with their wages showed evidence of a higher propensity to leave their jobs.

Pay also figures in turnover in a study by Ronan (1967), who analyzed exit interviews obtained from employees leaving a large manufacturing concern. He found that salary was the principle reason for leaving white-collar, administrative, and professional jobs, while job security was the major reason given for leaving blue-collar jobs. Smith and Kerr (1953; cited by Ronan, 1967) in a study that considered the content of exit interviews obtained from 48 different companies, found that pay was mentioned almost twice as often as any other factor as a reason for leaving a job. Finally, Valenzi and Andrews (1971) found that one consequence of an hourly underpayment situation was an increase in the number of employees who either quit their jobs or thought about quitting. Hence, there appears to be ample evidence that pay dissatisfaction can contribute to employee turnover. As this chapter has shown, however, this is not the only consequence of worker unhappiness about pay. It seems reasonable at this point to turn back to equity theory and conclude that wage dissatisfaction implies a heightened state of motivation that leads to behaviors the nature of which depends upon the alternatives the work situation makes available to the worker.

Wage Secrecy

It is not a rare event to find work organizations that give their employees little in the way of accurate information concerning wages. Often, secrecy about what people are being paid is considered to be an informal policy of the company. The motives underlying these practices are never clearly stated, but up and down the corporate corridor in many organizations it is considered bad form to discuss salaries. This topic resides within the domain of each individual's private affairs. The research literature on wages gives us substantial evidence, however, that the psychological impact of pay depends in large measure on the perception of pay rather than the actual monetary value of the paycheck. Often the motivational consequences of salary depend on the relationship of one salary to another. Hence, if workers do not have accurate information concerning wages, then they can construct their own set of beliefs and perceptions concerning the structure of the pay scale that operates in the organization. They draw on rumor, part truths, and the like to construct a pay scale, and as they talk with others who work with them, there may emerge an "accepted" wage structure that is generally recognized as being true and accurate, when in point of fact it is not. Psychologically this scale can assume real proportions, and to the extent to which people compute the equity of their salaries based on comparisons with this mythical structure, the organization may lose much of the motivational potential of its wage program.

Lawler (1965, 1967) has reported a number of studies that concern the motivational consequences of wage misperception. In most instances, the data were collected from companies that attempted to maintain complete secrecy concerning the wage structure. In each organization managers were asked to estimate the wages received by people working at the same level, as well as by people working one or two levels above or below. In addition, the manager's attitudes about pay and various aspects of work were obtained.

The results of these studies indicated that from a motivational point of view wage secrecy resulted in the worst possible distortion of the salary structure. First of all, managers did not have an accurate perception of the salaries being paid to others at all levels in the organization. The level of accuracy in most instances was rather low. In addition to this, the pattern of errors put the salary structure in a very poor light, since the managers tended to overestimate salaries of their peers and subordinates and underestimate the salaries received by those above them. In other words, they saw much less salary differentiation than actually existed. Furthermore, in instances in which peer salaries were overestimated and subordinate salaries were seen as being too close to their own, managers tended to express dissatisfaction with the pay they were receiving. As might be expected, managers who underestimated the pay of superiors one or two levels above were prone to say that promotion was not of great importance to them. Finally, managers who overestimated the pay of their peers tended to indicate that they put less effort into their work.

What Lawler's work has shown us is that pay secrecy can result in misperceptions of the wage scale that can have significant and negative consequences for work motivation. Pay dissatisfaction, a reduction in work effort, and a reduced interest in promotion may be the very high price an organization pays for a policy of secrecy surrounding the salaries that are paid.

One can question, however, whether the problem lies exclusively with a policy of wage secrecy. A study by Milkovich and Anderson (1972) casts some doubt on this possibility, since in a company where the wage policy was relatively open, managers were observed underestimating the pay of their superiors and overestimating peer and subordinate salaries. Perhaps the psychological equivalence of wage secrecy can occur in an organization that makes concerted efforts to provide open information about wage differentials. This happens whenever the level of mistrust of management reaches the point where workers begin to reject the accuracy of the information they receive. A policy of wage secrecy may *ensure* a distorted view of the company pay system, but an open wage policy coupled with a general lack of confidence in management can lead to the same consequences.

One can only guess why many companies continue to maintain secrecy regarding the wage system. A good possibility is that management wants to avoid what they expect to be a mountain of queries pouring in demanding to know "why Chadwick and Stephenson make more money than I." Perhaps it may be true that wherever an organization has a nonrational and arbitrary wage structure, the motivational costs of an open system might be much higher than the price paid for secrecy. The best of all possible solutions would seem to require a wage structure that is systematic and rational; where wage differentials do reflect differences in assignments and competencies. But these objectives are easier stated than achieved, since the ego-centered perceptions of differences between salaries may well place a "completely equitable" wage structure in the realm of fantasy. Hence, at this point we might best recognize this as an important problem that requires further discussion and research.

SUMMARY COMMENTS

It should be apparent by this time that wage incentives have received a large amount of research attention. Yet one can easily come away from this literature with the impression that many of the more important questions regarding the motivational implications of pay have not been adequately resolved. This is, in fact, quite true, and much remains to be done with regard to this aspect of work motivation. There is, however, a surprising amount of a general nature that we do know about wages. For example, there is good reason to believe that the motivational pushes and pulls of the paycheck do not exert a constant influence on a given individual. The motivational significance of pay varies from one period to the next. The motivational significance of pay also varies greatly between individuals. Furthermore, this variation does not occur randomly, but appears to be related to such factors as the sex of the worker, amount of education, age, and the amount of pay actually received.

Perceptual factors play a significant role in determining the motivational impact of pay. Although the objective level of an individual's pay cannot be ignored, the behavioral influence of wages depends on how people view their wages and upon a whole set of beliefs that they maintain about pay. Beliefs concerning the behaviors that are instrumental in determining the level of pay and beliefs concerning the usefulness of pay in achieving desired objectives also play an important role. Wage comparisons, the comparisons made by workers that contrast their salaries with those of others, also enter into the determination of the motivational impact of pay. The results of this kind of comparison lead the worker to beliefs concerning the equity of pay, and there is an abundance of research that tells us that when workers believe they are inequitably paid, there are likely to be motivational consequences that carry over into some aspect of job performance. We also know that the relationship between the cognition of inequity and job performance is not a simple one. For example, we cannot always assume that undercompensation will inevitably lead to a reduction in productivity. Finally, we know that when workers are kept in the dark about the wage structure of an organization, there is a good chance that they will concoct a structure of their own design that may very well be badly distorted.

There is one final aspect of pay that should be considered, since it has a bearing on much of the research that has been carried out; that is, in many work situations pay is a relatively constant event in the individual's work experience. For many workers, weeks and months may pass by before there is a change in the level of the paycheck; and within these periods, pay does not vary with the day-to-day variations in performance. In many instances, changes in pay level are experienced more or less at the same time by all the members of the work group, for example, as the result of a negotiation between management and union. Therefore, pay under many circumstances is most closely associated with organizational membership and employment status rather than with work effectiveness and efficiency. Hence, in the moment-to-moment affairs that go on in the workplace, pay might easily play the role of a background factor. By this is meant that from one moment to the next, workers tend to maintain a relatively low level of awareness regarding the financial incentives available to them. Pay as a motivational force, under these circumstances, tends to contribute to the psychological ambience of work rather than serving as a goal toward which a specific moment of work behavior is consciously directed.

Naturally, if asked, workers could comment on the connection, or lack of it, they see existing between their behavior and pay; there are probably many instances, however, in which pay is not consciously perceived as the most salient end result of behavior. It is probably in the social realm that we find incentives that are more focal. The social aspects of the workplace are constantly demanding that the individual respond, and in the social exchanges that take place between workers we find a dynamic system of incentives. Here we find a system of social rewards and punishments that tend to be more closely correlated with the variation that takes place in the individual's behavior. As a consequence, it might be reasonable to hypothesize that these incentives tend to play a more salient role in the day-to-day experiences of the worker. There are times when pay may emerge as the central motivational focus—for example, during times when promotions are made or when the individual looks for a new job—but by and large,

wages tend to be relatively stable dimensions of the work experience and quite often wages lie distant in time from the behaviors they are supposed to motivate. The fact that this is the case does not necessarily imply that pay carries less motivational force than the incentives found in social exchanges. Rather, financial incentives tend to operate as lower-order needs in the sense that Maslow (1943) uses the term. Maslow sees human needs being arranged in a hierarchy of potency. Compared to higher-order needs, a lower-order need is a motivational influence that is more essential to the individual's general well-being. Higher-order needs tend to exert more influence on behavior at times when lower-order needs are not active. Thus, during those times when pay and pay increases are far removed in time, behavior on the job tends to fall under the momentary control of other motivational influences. Pay tends to reward and compensate behavior that has taken place over a relatively long period of time. Payday, for instance, rarely occurs more than once a week, and merit increases in pay usually refer to the evaluation of performance that has taken place during months of work. Financial incentives, therefore, tend to vary with time units that are rather lengthy. The many incentives that occur in the social-political realm of the workplace tend to vary with smaller, momentary units of time.

In view of all this, it may be reasonable to think of pay as a motivational force that tends to influence the general approach workers take toward their jobs. For example, do workers value their jobs and think of them as long-term commitments, or do they approach the job as a temporary position that will serve until something better comes along. Pay, as it affects how individuals value their membership in a work organization, serves as a psychological influence that permeates all aspects of the work experience, but it might best be thought of as a motivational foundation on which rest the other incentives that play a more focal role in the moment-to-moment happenings of the workday.

8

The Rewards of Work—Job Satisfaction

Many contend that one of the more significant trends in work can be found in the growing number of individuals who want jobs that satisfy a broad set of personal objectives. With increasing frequency we read that people seek work that provides them with something more than just adequate wages and reasonable prospects for advancement. One version of this idea says that people want work that is socially meaningful, that makes a positive contribution to the community and leaves the world a better place. Another dimension of this theme maintains that people want work that is psychologically fulfilling, that permits personal growth and the utilization of individual talents. Along similar lines, others contend that people seek jobs in which the unique stamp of the individual is reflected in the work that is done—that is, jobs that permit the individual to achieve a clearly defined sense of identity.

General observation may suggest that there is some reason to believe that workers do apply these broader perspectives to the jobs they hold, yet all this kind of thinking may strike one as being unrealistic. There is still much work to be done that is of a routine and repetitive nature, and to think of a job solely in terms of a rich and rewarding career is to ignore the negative realities of the work world. By the same token, to think of work only in terms of a dreary commitment to toil and wage earning is equally shortsighted. Every job includes a range of positive as well as negative incentives; hence it is probably not unrealistic to think of jobs in terms of the moments of satisfaction and dissatisfaction the worker experiences. From this perspective, workers who tell us that they are satisfied with their jobs are probably telling us that the positive moments of their work experience in some way or another outweigh the negative ones.

In this chapter we will consider job satisfaction, its nature, its sources, and its motivational and performance consequences. Job satisfaction refers to individuals' affective reactions to the work they do and to the conditions under which the work is carried out. Job satisfaction concerns individuals' attitudes toward the job, and it includes their assessment of the separate components of the work as well as an overall evaluation of their job experiences. In reporting on job satisfaction, workers tell us something about the extent to which they like or dislike their work, and as a general rule we measure job satisfaction by asking individuals for a verbal report regarding their reaction to various facets of the job they hold.

There is no other area of the literature on work behavior that has received more attention than has job satisfaction. Estimates vary, but it is probably safe to say that well over five thousand articles have been published in the professional literature regarding this aspect of work. The size of the research literature testifies to the complexity of this behavior; job satisfaction has been found to relate to so many aspects of work that much research is necessary to map out these relationships. The size of the research literature also reflects the fact that data on job satisfaction tend to be relatively easy to collect. The questionnaire has been the principal instrument used to generate information on job satisfaction, and this technique, being less disruptive of ongoing work routines, provides the researcher with convenient access to industrial data.

The amount of the research literature requires that we impose limits on the scope of this discussion; hence, what we will set out to do in this chapter is to bring together a representative set of topics that have been considered in connection with job satisfaction, and we will begin by looking at some of the psychological processes that have been incorporated into the definition of the term.

A. BEHAVIORAL PROCESSES AND THEIR MEASUREMENT

There are many definitions of job satisfaction, and at present there does not appear to be any firm consensus among behavioral scientists regarding the meaning of the term. All definitions agree that job satisfaction involves some sort of appraisal of work experience, but a big problem seems to be that of deciding exactly what is evaluated when the worker makes this assessment. Some say that the evaluation deals with a worker's *expectations* regarding future job experiences, and others state that the evaluation refers to the extent to which the job *has fulfilled the needs of the individual.* Another approach draws a distinction between *needs* and *values,* maintaining that job satisfaction refers to the extent to which a job yields things that a worker values. *Equity* concepts seem to run through all these approaches, so one might define job satisfaction in terms of the extent to which a job generates a set of personal outcomes that are perceived as being fair.

Differences among these four approaches may strike one as being rather subtle, but they do refer to four different, although interrelated, behavioral processes. Let's look at each one to see how they are used in the job satisfaction literature.

Valence and Expectancy.   Valence and expectancy are concepts that have been used by Vroom (1964) to emphasize the fact that job satisfaction refers not only to an individual's reaction to job experiences that have already taken place but also to the anticipation of events that lie in the future. Vroom maintains that the meaning of job satisfaction can be found in his definition of the concept, valence. To Vroom, valence refers to people's affective reaction to the *anticipated consequences* of their behavior. It is a term that refers to individuals' *expectations* of what will happen to them as a consequence of a given action. When viewed in connection with job satisfaction, valence refers to workers' expectations regarding the kinds of rewards and punishments that might be applied to them on the job. In this sense, workers who are satisfied with their jobs are those who, when they think of the job, tend to anticipate outcomes which produce positive emotions. They think of the job as having good potential for making them feel good. Workers who are dissatisfied with the job are those who anticipate negative outcomes from their work. When these workers consider the future, they anticipate outcomes that will make them feel bad.

Need Fulfillment.   Porter (1962) defines job satisfaction in terms of the extent to which a job fulfills an individual's psychological needs. Job satisfaction is found on jobs on which there is little difference between the extent to which a worker thinks a particular need fulfilling condition should be present and the extent to which it is actually present in the job. As the discrepancy between *what is* and *what should be* increases, Porter infers that there is increasing job dissatisfaction. Hence, Porter approaches the definition of job satisfaction in terms of a worker's perception of deficiencies in need fulfillment that exist in the job environment.

Values.   Locke (1969, 1976) has drawn a distinction between need fulfillment and value attainment. He says that individuals often value things they do not need, and sometimes need what they do not value. At times, therefore, individuals' needs and their values do not completely coincide. To Locke, a need is an innate condition that is required by an individual in order to maintain physiological or psychological well-being. A value, on the other hand, is learned and is expressed in terms of something that is wanted or desired. Locke defines job satisfaction in terms of the pleasurable emotional states that result from the perception that a job permits the achievement of things an individual values highly. "Job satisfaction and dissatisfaction are a function of the perceived relationship between what one wants from one's job and what one perceives it as offering" (Locke, 1969, p. 316). The smaller the discrepancy between wants and outcomes, the higher the level of job satisfaction.

④ **Equity.** It is not difficult to find running through these approaches to job satisfaction concepts that are quite similar to those that are found in equity theory (see Chapter 7). When job satisfaction is defined in terms of a discrepancy between what one wants and what one receives, one is not too far away from defining job satisfaction in terms that are related to the concept of perceived fairness. From this point of view, therefore, job satisfaction refers to the extent to which a worker perceives a job as providing a distribution of outcomes that are seen as equitable.

Even though we find that job satisfaction has been defined in terms of four different psychological processes, there are common themes to be found in all of these approaches. One of these is that job satisfaction seems to involve an individual's perception of discrepancies that exist between what is desired and what is obtained. Whether this assessment involves needs or values, or whether it involves past experiences or the expectation of future conditions, shouldn't make a large difference. Needs and values are often, although not always, highly interrelated, and past job experiences are probably a good predictor of future expectation. As a consequence, we will settle on the following definition:

> Job satisfaction is evident to the extent that a worker perceives a job as being the source of positive feelings. These perceptions may include past, present, and anticipated experiences; workers' individual time frames determine the span of events that are included in their perceptions of the job.

Before leaving this question, it should be mentioned that regardless of the definition one may adopt, it must be recognized that job satisfaction should be thought of as a dynamic process. That is to say, job satisfaction concerns a set of affective reactions that show frequent change. Even though the procedures to measure it give us a set of numbers that appear to be fixed, we must remember that we are dealing with complicated emotional reactions that are in a state of constant change. From this point of view, measures of job satisfaction can be thought of both as a sample of the experiences one has on a job and as a sample of time.

Measurement of Job Satisfaction

There are several general approaches to the measurement of job satisfaction; but of the lot, the questionnaire is by far the most often used. As a rule, a series of written statements are presented to a worker, who is asked to react to each by choosing one of several response alternatives that are provided. Questionnaires differ widely in their construction (Edwards, 1957; Torgerson, 1958) and their content (Robinson, Athanasiou, & Head, 1969); and although the technical aspects of scale construction are beyond the scope of this text, we can nevertheless gain some idea about the measurement of job satisfaction by considering the content of the items that are included in scales of this sort.

The type of item that takes the most direct approach to measuring job satisfaction is the single, summary statement that asks the workers for an overall appraisal of the job. For example, an early scale by Hoppock (1935) contained the following item:

Choose one of the following statements which best tells how well you like your job.

1. I hate it.
2. I dislike it.
3. I don't like it.
4. I am indifferent to it.
5. I like it.
6. I am enthusiastic about it.
7. I love it.

In using items such as these, the researcher is assigning the entire task of evaluation to the respondents, who are left free to focus on any set of job experiences they may choose in order to arrive at an overall evaluation of their jobs. Not knowing what course a given worker may follow in reaching this kind of summary evaluation often leaves the researcher unsure about the structure and content of the measurement collected.

An alternative approach consists of breaking the job down into its various facets and presenting the worker with a questionnaire containing items that cover different aspects of the job. An example of this type scale is the *Job Descriptive Index* (Smith, Kendall, & Hulin, 1969), which contains groups of items that deal with five categories: the work itself, supervision, work associates, pay, and promotion. An example of the items tapping supervision appears below:

Supervision (Subjects answer, Yes, No, or ?)
Asks my advice   _____
Praises good work   _____
Stubborn   _____

The scale aids the respondent in breaking the job down into five categories, and to this extent it does provide a bit more direction to those who respond to it. The respondent still faces the problem of deciding when a particular item is, or is not, descriptive of the job experience, but judgment problems of this or a similar type are found in connection with much psychological measurement. The Job Descriptive Index (JDI) has been well received by researchers, and the instrument appears to have been constructed in a highly competent fashion.

Lyman Porter (1961; 1962; 1963a, b, c), in a series of studies dealing with satisfaction in management positions, has suggested that the measurement of satisfaction be approached by considering the extent to which the individual reports deficiencies in the job's ability to fulfill certain psychological needs. In doing this, he presents the subject with a set of statements that concern five categories of need: security needs, social needs, esteem needs, autonomy needs, and self-actualization needs. Each item is followed by three questions, one dealing with how much of a particular condition is there now, how much of the condition should there be, and how important is the condition to the individual. Reacting to the question "how much," the respondent is given a seven-step scale that allows him to express a judgment in degrees rather than in terms of the "Yes, No, and ?" categories used by the *Job Descriptive Index*. An example of an item from Porter's scale appears below:

The feeling of worthwhile accomplishment in my management position.

(a) How much is there now?
(min) 1 2 3 4 5 6 7 (max)
(b) How much should there be?
(min) 1 2 3 4 5 6 7 (max)
(c) How important is this to me?
(min) 1 2 3 4 5 6 7 (max)

A higher rating on response line (b) than on response line (a) is taken to indicate that the individual experiences a deficiency in the extent to which the job satisfies this need. Separate need deficiency scores are computed for each of the five categories.

There is no general consensus in the field concerning the most acceptable questionnaire approach to use in the measurement of job satisfaction. There does seem to be a general tendency, however, for those who survey nationwide samples to use a few relatively general statements that are open ended, while those who confine their research to more narrowly based samples tend to use

Table 8.1   Methods of Combining Facets of Job Satisfaction

JS = Σ	(JFS)	[1]
JS = Σ	(Importance × JFS)	[2]
JS = Σ	(Is Now)	[3]
JS = Σ	(Importance × Is Now)	[4]
JS = Σ	(Should Be—Is Now)	[5]
JS = Σ	(Importance × (Should Be—Is Now))	[6]
JS = Σ	(Would Like—Is Now)	[7]
JS = Σ	(Importance × (Would Like—Is Now))	[8]
JS = Σ	(Importance—Is Now)	[9]

JS = **Overall Job Satisfaction**
Σ = **Sum Over Job Facets**
JFS = **Satisfaction with a Job Facet**

Source: Wanous, J. P., & Lawler, E. E. Measurement and meaning of job satisfaction. *Journal of Applied Psychology*, 1972, *56*, 95–105.

instruments that include a larger number of questions that tap more specific facets of job satisfaction. In either case, not all the measurement problems have been solved, and they represent a major area of continuing concern for those who are interested in this aspect of worker behavior.

Combining Job Facet Scores

Porter's approach to measurement brings us to another aspect of the job satisfaction question, and that is a consideration of the different approaches taken in combining the various facets of the job that enter into the assessment of overall satisfaction. Wanous and Lawler (1972) have considered this question, and have found that there are a number of different ways that have been used in the research literature to combine these job elements. Furthermore, these different approaches do not always give you the same results. Table 8.1, derived from Wanous and Lawler's work, summarizes the techniques that have been used. Each equation represents a different method of computing job satisfaction scores from a questionnaire. Equation 5, for example, represents Porter's approach, in which workers provide two judgments for each item: how much is there now and how much should there be? Subtracting the two and summing

over all job facets yields a score that expresses the worker's overall job satisfaction. Equation 6 expresses the same concept, except in this instance each difference is weighted by the worker's judgment regarding the importance of the job facet.

Each equation in Table 8.1 shows us a different definition of the manner in which job facets combine to yield an overall evaluation of the job. In a study that asked telephone workers to rate various aspects of their jobs, Wanous and Lawler (1972) computed estimates of job satisfaction from each of nine equations, and they found that different equations led to different results. For example, their results suggested that if we were to ask workers to directly rate their level of job satisfaction, we might get results that differed from a situation in which we compute the difference between their ratings of how much of a given condition there should be and how much there is now. Wanous and Lawler suggest that all these equations represent valid definitions of job satisfaction, but each reflects one of the different kinds of feelings people may hold about their jobs. People can and do think directly about job satisfaction, but they also think about separate facets of the job, and what is and what should be. There is not, therefore, one approach to job satisfaction, but several, each giving us a somewhat different view of this complicated aspect of work behavior. Furthermore, there doesn't seem to be any one best way of measuring job satisfaction; hence, one equation can not be recommended over another. There are several routes to the quantification of job satisfaction, and each route can lead us to a different vantage point in looking at workers' assessments of the work they do.

THE STRUCTURE OF JOB SATISFACTION

To ask workers for an overall evaluation of a job is to ask them to sort through a very complicated set of job facets and come up with some type of summary statement. Wages, working conditions, fringe benefits, supervision, company policy, and work associates are but some of the categories that can be subjected to separate evaluation. There is, however, a limit to the complexity with which one may deal, so it is quite probable that when people evaluate their jobs, they do not consider every facet of their work experience. We have already found Porter suggesting that we should think of five facets of job satisfaction. Smith agrees with Porter on the number, but not the content of the job facets that require consideration.

Many studies have attempted to describe the categories in the job-satisfaction domain. A number of these investigations used a complicated statistical technique called *factor analysis* to achieve their objective. Briefly, factor analysis is a procedure that examines the interrelationships between events in order to determine the number and nature of the measurement dimensions that seem to be functioning. For example, one might refer to an oil painting as being beautiful, and discover upon analysis that what is meant by beauty involves the individual's reaction to the painting's color, form, size, and texture. Hence, in this case, beauty is an attribute of the painting that emerges from a combination of four basic factors found in the work of art.

When applied to a worker's appraisal of a job, factor analysis has been used to determine the number of job facets that enter into the domain of job satisfaction. One important question to be raised is whether there is a common thread running through a worker's reaction to the many facets of work. For example, if workers like their work duties, is there a a good chance that they will also like their supervisors? If all job facets are related to all others, then we may say there is a *general factor* underlying job satisfaction.

Wherry (1954, 1958) factor analyzed a scale that was developed by *Science Research Associates* (Ash, 1954) and he concludes that job satisfaction consists of a general factor that cuts across all aspects of work, and five other factors that are more or less confined to a particular aspect of work: financial incentives, working conditions, supervision, management, and personnel development. Roach (1958) also obtained a general factor

from an analysis of a 62 item questionnaire. He also observed ten other factors of a more specific nature. Bledsoe and Brown (1977) found only a general factor in their analysis of job satisfaction expressed by school personnel.

The presence of a general factor indicates that it is reasonable to think of a common influence running through a worker's evaluation of the job; yet not all factor-analytic studies have been able to demonstrate a general factor. Hinrichs (1968) factor analyzed a large set of items and found nine factors, but none of these could be described as a general factor. Finally, Smith, Kendall, and Hulin (1969), in the work that led to the construction of the *Job Descriptive Index,* reported five dimensions of job satisfaction, none of which could be considered a general factor. A good picture of the nature of the job facets that have been associated with the measurement of job satisfaction may be found in Table 8.2. The table shows factors that were obtained by Tuttle, Gould, and Hazel (1975) from a review of six relatively recent factor analyses of job satisfaction data. The number beside each entry represents the number of analyses that reported the presence of the factor. Notice the two most frequently cited dimensions of satisfaction— the work itself and financial incentives.

Perhaps the most we can say about the structure of job satisfaction is that it seems to vary with a number of conditions. Variations in the measurement instrument, the jobs observed, and the workers involved all seem to yield a different view of this aspect of a worker's reaction to a job. One thing is clear from Table 8.2; the job-satisfaction concept refers to behaviors that are multidimensional in their structure. Other studies reporting a general factor suggest that it might sometimes be realistic to think of job satisfaction as an overall, summary evaluation of an individual's job.

Motivation-Hygiene Theory of Job Satisfaction

Without question, during the past two decades the most prominent point of view regarding the nature and structure of job satisfaction is found in

Table 8.2　Listing of Job Satisfaction Dimensions Obtained from Six Studies[a]

Dimension	Frequency[b]
Work Itself or Intrinsic Job Satisfaction	9
Pay, Compensation, Benefits	6
Job-Work Demands, Work Load	5
Co-Workers and Associates	5
Social Status and Prestige	5
Security	5
Pride, Identification Relations with Company	5
Future Opportunity, Advancement, Self-Fulfillment	4
Anxiety, Pressure, Obstacles	4
Supervisor-Employee Relations	4
Independence and Creativity	3
Responsibility, Participation in Decision Making	3
Growth, Development, Progress	3
Communication and Being Informed	3
Recognition and Self-Esteem	3
Working Conditions, Physical Surroundings	2
Competency of Supervisor	2
Helping Others	2
Confidence in Management and Company	2
Exert Control over Others	2
Effective Management Policy and Procedure	1
Evaluation	1
Concern for Individuals	1
Development of Friendship	1

Source: Adapted from Tuttle, T. C., Gould, R. B., and Hazel, J. T. *Dimensions of job satisfaction.* U.S. Air Force, 1975.
[a]Studies surveyed: Ash (1954); Hinrichs (1968); Johnson (1955); Porter (1961); Roach (1958); and Weiss et al. (1967).
[b]Some factors from the studies were applicable to two or more dimenisons.

a theory presented by Herzberg, Mausner, and Snyderman (1959) (Herzberg, 1966). As it stands today, this theory shows the scars of extensive experimental evaluation, nevertheless, it still represents an interesting set of ideas concerning this important aspect of work behavior. The ideas found in Herzberg's theory are interesting from several points of view. First, they stem from a measurement technique that does not rely on the conventional questionnaire approach. Second, these ideas, when they were first presented, represented a rather unconventional view of the structure of the attitudes workers hold toward their jobs.

Methods.　With regard to the first point, the measurement procedures, Herzberg et al. (1959) have adopted a technique that was first developed

to collect merit evaluations on workers. Called the *Critical Incidents Technique* (Flanagan, 1954), this procedure asks workers to think of a time in the past when they felt especially good about their jobs. Workers are asked to focus their attention on past events that involve some objective happening that had an identifiable beginning and ending. They are then asked to describe the *factors* that they believe were associated with their postive *attitudes*. These factors may concern things like promotion, a pay raise, or any other specific happening that the workers believe to be related to the positive attitude they had experienced. Finally, the workers are asked to describe their understanding of the *effects* of these factors and attitudes. They are asked, for example, to relate how a particular incident carried over to affect their performance on the job.

After the individual furnishes information concerning positive job incidents, he is asked to relate incidents that involve exceptionally negative experiences. In doing so, the worker describes the factors felt to be critical to these negative feelings. We have, therefore, two sets of narratives; one dealing with job satisfaction, the other concerning the experience of job dissatisfaction. Data collection involves a relatively unstructured interview procedure, the scoring of which requires an analysis of the content of the narrative in order to determine the nature of the factors that are associated with positive and negative job experiences. The purpose of this technique is not to measure the degree of job satisfaction, but rather to determine the job conditions that appear to be present at the time job satisfaction or dissatisfaction is expressed.

Experimental Findings. Herzberg reports a study in which a group of engineers and accountants were asked to recall positive and negative critical incidents. An analysis of these interviews revealed that the job factors reported to be associated with periods of satisfaction were not the same set of factors as those involved with negative job experiences. Figure 8.1 summarizes the frequency with which various job factors were associated with satisfying and dissatisfying incidents. Notice that five factors seem to stand out with high frequency when the workers were discussing satisfying episodes. Achievement, recognition, the work itself, responsibility, and advancement themes seemed to have occurred with significantly higher frequency in those incidents where the worker was experiencing positive job attitudes. When analyzing the incidents that produced negative attitudes, these factors were mentioned with substantially lower frequency. On these negative occasions a different set of factors were identified: company policy and administration, the technical and interpersonal aspects of supervision, working conditions, interpersonal relations with peers, and the worker's personal life.

These results indicate to Herzberg that the roots

Figure 8.1

Factors Frequently Identified as Sources of Work Satisfaction and Dissatisfaction[1] (in order of frequency)

JOB SATISFACTION
1. Job Achievement
2. Recognition for Work Done
3. Job Duties and Work Activities
4. Job Responsibilities
5. Promotion and Job Advancement
6. Personal Growth

JOB DISSATISFACTION
1. Organizational Policies and Administration
2. Organizational Leadership
3. Relations with Work Associates
4. The Conditions of Work
5. Pay*
6. Social Position
7. Job Security

*Pay is primarily thought to be a source of job dissatisfaction, but it sometimes operates as a source of work satisfaction, especially as it functions to reflect management's recognition of effective job performance.

[1]Although this general pattern of satisfiers and dissatisfiers emerged from Herzberg's early study of engineers and accountants, Figure 8.1 is actually a theoretical summary of organizational profiles gathered in a number of studies carried out between 1959 and 1974 (Herzberg, 1976).

of job satisfaction and job dissatisfaction are found within different areas of work. In terms of their origins, positive and negative job experiences appear to be the result of distinct and independent facets of work. Traditionally, job satisfaction and dissatisfaction were thought to be opposite ends of a single scale; therefore, if an event produces dissatisfaction it was thought to move the individual down this scale away from the satisfaction end. Herzberg's results suggest, however, that *two scales* are necessary to represent positive and negative job experiences (see Figure 8.2). Both scales refer to the factor frequency; both begin at a point of attitude neutrality, but one scale represents satisfaction and the other dissatisfaction. Furthermore, each scale draws on a separate set of job factors. In other words, some areas of work have little to do with feelings of satisfaction; other areas have little bearing on feelings of dissatisfaction.

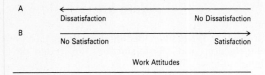

Figure 8.2 Job motivators and hygiene factors are thought to operate along two separate scales. Motivators generate responses that fall along scale B, and they tend to originate in events associated with the content of work. Hygiene factors may generate responses that fall along scale A. These responses tend to originate in events that form the environment of work.

Hence, Herzberg disputes the traditional idea that job dissatisfaction stems chiefly from work situations in which the usual sources of job satisfaction are absent. Rather, when reporting satisfaction, workers tend to be telling us of the presence of a particular set of conditions that lead to satisfaction. When they tell us about job dissatisfaction, they tend not to be reporting the absence of these satisfiers, but the presence of other factors that are associated with negative attitudes.

Herzberg maintains that satisfiers tend to be found in those aspects of the job that are intrinsic to the work itself. They define the *content* of the work, and it is in the performance of the job duties that the worker is most likely to find experiences that are satisfying. These job duties are, however, embedded in a social *context* that includes rules, supervisory practices, and a host of interpersonal relations. It is these context factors that seem to contribute most to the experience of job dissatisfaction. Satisfiers are called *motivators;* they lie within the work and encourage high performance. Dissatisfiers are called hygiene factors, since it is within these conditions of work that we find the conditions that produce negative job attitudes.

Herzberg (1966) is convinced that these two sets of factors reflect a basic dichotomy that exists in the need systems of human beings. One system concerns the motivational processes that are involved in personal growth, the other system involves the avoidance of unpleasant experiences. At work, individuals seem to find greatest opportunity to experience personal growth in the set of activities that define the content of the job. The negative experiences tend to be found in the social-environment surroundings within which the job duties are carried out.

Comment. Herzberg's work has stimulated much comment and a considerable amount of research activity and there has been much criticism of the theory, both with regard to the basic adequacy of its ideas (Farr, 1977) and the nature of the experimental procedures that have been used in its formulation. One vein of criticism holds that the theory is inconsistent with what we know about the sources of human motives. To suggest that certain factors operate in only one direction—that is, lead to satisfaction—seems to ignore the complicated nature of human motivation. For example, Locke (1976) points out that it is a well-known fact that lack of self-esteem (a motivator in Herzberg's theory) is a primary contributor to the unhappiness expressed by many who are seen by clinical psychologists. At the same time, an increment in self-esteem is often found to be a source of considerable personal satisfaction. Hence, self-esteem, or the lack of it, may function as both a satisfier or a dissatisfier.

Schneider and Locke (1971) observed that the distinction Herzberg made between motivators and hygiene factors seemed to parallel a distinction between what they call *events* and *agents*. An event is a happening that is the consequence of the action of some agent, and Herzberg's motivators tend to be events, and his hygiene factors tend to refer to agents. Schneider and Locke argue that achievement, recognition, work, responsibility, and advancement (all motivators) are usually thought of as outcomes of an event, while hygiene factors—supervision, company peers, working conditions, and the individuals themselves—all tend to be the agents whose actions lead to the outcomes that are listed as motivators.

Locke (1976) points out that Herzberg's results suggest that when describing a negtive critical incident, workers tend to focus on the agent that produces these unpleasant emotions; when describing a positive incident, they may focus on the outcome. Vroom (1964) has interpreted Herzberg's results in a somewhat similar fashion. Here Vroom concerns himself with the characteristics of the agent. He contends that when people describe incidents in which outcomes are positive, they tend to identify themselves as the agents. When describing incidents that lead to negative outcomes, they tend to identify agents that are external to themselves. As a consequence, when Herzberg asked workers to describe satisfying and dissatisfying job incidents, two separate lists of factors appeared in their narratives. Rather than identifying two separate and independent sources of positive and negative affect, however, the two lists are the result of defense mechanisms that lead the worker to take credit for satisfying outcomes and identify an external agent, for example, supervisor, for negative outcomes.

Experimental Work

Research efforts to evaluate Herzberg's theory have yielded an irregular pattern of support. Herzberg (1966), for example, reviewed ten studies in this area, and concluded that of 108 predictions made from the theory, less than 3 percent were contradicted by the research findings. House and Wigdor (1967), on the other hand, conclude that the motivator-hygiene theory has not been able to generate convincing experimental support. These authors reviewed 31 studies, concluding that these research findings indicate that Herzberg's model is an oversimplification of the sources of satisfaction and dissatisfaction found in the environment of work. That this is the case, in large measure, stems from the fact that a number of studies suggest that any single job facet, for example, recognition, does not consistently serve as a satisfier or a dissatisfier. Under some circumstances a factor may serve as a source of satisfaction; under other circumstances it may serve as a dissatisfier. As an example, several studies (Centers and Bugental, 1966; Friedlander, 1966a; Locke, 1973; Harris and Locke, 1974) have shown white-collar/blue-collar differences in the functioning of these factors. In the Harris and Locke (1973) study, for instance, it was reported that white-collar employees were more likely to derive *both* satisfaction

and dissatisfaction from Herzberg's motivator factors. Blue-collar workers, on the other hand, seemed to experience both satisfaction and dissatisfaction from their involvement with hygiene factors. Starcevich (1972) has reported similar results in a study in which three levels of white-collar employees reported that job-content factors were relatively more important than job-context factors in causing both satisfying and dissatisfying work incidents.

Not only does collar color play a role in determining what aspects of work satisfies or dissatisfies, but Saleh and Singh (1973) report that under certain circumstances, social background variables influence this relationship. With a group of lower-paid workers, these authors report that the perceived importance of content factors was higher for workers whose fathers held higher-status positions. There is also evidence suggesting that whether a factor operates as a satisfier or a dissatisfier depends on the age of the worker (Friedlander, 1966a; Wernimont, 1966), the sex of the worker (Centers & Bugental, 1966), and the worker's educational level (Singh & Baumgartel, 1966).

Personality variables have also been shown to play a role in mediating the relationship between job factors and the worker's experience of satisfaction and dissatisfaction (Gruenfeld & Weissenberg, 1970; Evans, 1973). Gruenfeld and Weissenberg (1970) divided a sample of supervisory personnel into field-independent and field-dependent groups. Field-independent persons are thought to be better able to respond to their experiences in an analytical fashion, being capable of perceiving parts of an event rather than responding to the event only as a whole. These individuals are usually less concerned with the social aspects of their world, and they show a greater concern for task accomplishment. Field-dependent persons tend to view things more as wholes, being less capable of analyzing their experience. They tend to react to global impressions of the events that go on around them.

Gruenfeld and Weissenberg found that the field-dependent supervisors who reported satisfaction with the content of their jobs also reported satisfaction with the context factors of their work. Those who reported dissatisfaction with the content of their work also reported dissatisfaction with context factors. Furthermore, both sets of factors correlated significantly with measures of overall job satisfaction. For the field-independent supervisors, those purportedly having higher capability for analytical perception, content and context factors tended to be independent of one another as sources of job satisfaction. Also, only the content factors seemed to be related to their overall estimates of job satisfaction. Hence, the independence that Herzberg observed between job content and context factors appeared to Gruenfeld and Weissenberg to be dependent on the personality characteristics of the supervisor.

Finally, organizational factors have been found to influence whether or not a particular facet of work contributes to an individual's feeling of job satisfaction. Soliman (1970), for example, finds that in an organization in which workers report many different kinds of needs being satisfied, job content factors seem to become a more important source of job satisfaction. In work environments in which many kinds of needs are not satisfied, job context factors become more powerful sources of job satisfaction.

Conclusions.   There seems to be enough research of the type presented above to warrant a conclusion that Herzberg's satisfiers and dissatisfiers do not operate in quite as simple a fashion as the theory suggests. The data do not permit us to say that job satisfaction usually derives from the content of work tasks and that dissatisfaction is generated by the events that surround these tasks. Rather, the studies indicate that the affective role played by any set of job dimensions quite clearly depends on a whole host of psychological and sociological variables. At present we have identified a number of variables that seem to influence the contribution made by various job facets to the worker's emotional reaction to a job. Personality, job level, age, sex, educational level, organizational characteristics, and the worker's social origins have all been shown to play a role. Whether an aspect of a job leads to job satisfac-

tion, therefore, depends on the status of these variables. As a result, in thinking about job satisfaction we have to consider things that are found both on and off the job; we have to think of differences between people as well as differences in the content of jobs and the social conditions that define the environment of work.

In spite of the difficulties encountered by Herzberg's theory, his ideas do represent an interesting outline for future research. The work that has been done in response to this theory, while pointing up shortcomings, provides us with valuable information that contributes to our understanding of the shifting patterns of job facets that contribute to the satisfaction and dissatisfaction people obtain from their jobs.

The Opponent-Process Theory

Herzberg's theory is primarily concerned with the sources of job satisfaction and dissatisfaction, but it tells us little about the nature of the affective reactions that are associated with these two psychological states. As a consequence, the theory is of little value to one who is interested in such things as how these emotional reactions change over time. For example, a worker receives a pay increase and the first paycheck containing the raise produces a highly positive reaction. This same pay rate will, however, be in effect over the entire year, and it is unlikely that the worker's reaction to it will remain the same as time progresses. Some would expect an upward adjustment in the worker's "standard of living" to reflect the newly acquired income. What was a desired luxury before the raise becomes a standard aspect of one's life after the raise has been in effect for some time. Hence, a significant positive emotion on the day of the raise becomes a neutral or indifferent reaction as the weeks pass.

A similar set of changes may take place when an individual is exposed repeatedly to negative events. Here, situations that initially resulted in a negative emotion will eventually produce a neutral response. From this one can see that an adjustment may occur to both positive and negative experiences, and the direction of change seems to be toward emotional neutrality. Furthermore, there is no reason to suspect that a person's affective reactions to events occurring in one area of life differ from those occurring in another area. As a result, it is reasonable to expect that the positive and negative emotions involved in job satisfaction and dissatisfaction will also tend to move, over time, toward a neutral or indifference level.

Landy (1978) has suggested that the *opponent-process theory of motivation* (Solomon & Corbit, 1974) be extended to account for the affective reactions that are involved in job satisfaction and dissatisfaction. This theory contends that feelings of pleasure and displeasure tend to undergo change, as an individual is repeatedly brought into contact with the circumstances that give rise to these reactions. Furthermore, the theory maintains that the changes taking place are the same regardless of whether the reactions are affectively positive or negative. These changes take place as the result of the following two processes:

1. An emotional arousal or excitatory mechanism that is triggered by an event taking place in the person's life. This emotional response is called the primary process, and it can be a positive or negative feeling.

2. An inhibitory process that is triggered by the primary process. This inhibitory mechanism counteracts (opposes) the positive or negative feelings that make up the primary process.

The main function of this opponent process is to maintain an individual's general emotional tone at a point that hovers around emotional neutrality. Hence, such emotional reaction, whether pleasurable or unpleasant, tends to give rise to an opposing mechanism; and the net result of this opponent process is to move the individual's affective reaction toward neutrality.

When applied to job satisfaction and dissatisfaction, the opponent-process theory explains the often-noticed tendency for employees to change their emotional reactions to some aspect of a job as they acquire additional experience with it. For example, the theory predicts that the importance an individual attaches to a reward will diminish as a function of the number of times the incentive has been received in the past. The theory also predicts a different pattern of affective reactions to intrinsic and extrinsic job factors. Consider, for instance, an extrinsic factor like an award for high performance. Here the presentation of the award initially brings forth a positive reaction. During repeated presentations of the award—the employee wins the plaque several times—there will be a growth in the influence of the opponent process, and this will result in a weakening of the positive reaction until the point is reached where the presentation of the award will evoke only a neutral response.

Now we come to a complication. Landy (1978) assumes that the positive reaction to the presentation of the award (the primary process) disappears rather rapidly, while the opponent process (displeasure) tends to be active for a longer period of time after the award has been given. Hence, while the positive emotion would move toward neutrality, the negative process would continue to grow *and operate during the award's absence.* The growth of this opposing process would increase each time the award was given, and we would find the employee responding more negatively to the work situation when the award was absent—that is, when he didn't win the award. This award, therefore, would then be functioning in a manner that is consistent with Herzberg's prediction for an extrinsic job factor. The award would evoke a neutral response when presented or a negative emotion when absent. In other words, this extrinsic factor would not contribute to an expression of job satisfaction, but it could contribute to an expression of job dissatisfaction.

To explain the role of intrinsic factors in job satisfaction, Landy assumes that many factors of this sort produce a negative emotional response when they are initially presented. For example, a person is given added responsibilities (an intrinsic job factor), but the initial reaction to these new assignments is apprehension or anxiety. It is only *after* these responsibilities have been successfully met that the individual responds positively. According to the opponent-process theory, the initial negative emotions set off an opposing process that tends to move these reactions toward neutrality; the positive aftereffects will continue to appear, however, and will eventually be seen in the individual's positive reaction to this aspect of the job. Hence, as Herzberg would predict, intrinsic job factors are associated with a range of emotional reactions that extend from neutral to positive, but they are not usually associated with dissatisfaction.

Comment.   It is too early to pass judgment on the opponent-process theory. Its usefulness in accounting for job-satisfaction phenomena has yet to be tested adequately, but there are conceptual problems that lead one to take a cautious view of the model. For example, the model puts great emphasis on the onset and termination of the emotion-arousing stimulus; the primary process begins at onset and disappears on termination of the stimulus. It is very difficult, however, to estimate the onset and termination of many sources of work motivation. Where is the onset of a pay raise? Does it begin when employees hear through the grapevine that raises are going to be large this year? Some, on hearing this, may begin extending their credit purchases in anticipation of the raise. Does it begin when employees are officially notified or when they actually receive the money in their paychecks? When does this event terminate? The reverberations of a pay increase can extend over a long period of time and appear in a wide variety of activities. A verbal commendation may distribute its psychological influence over a short segment of time; a reprimand may set up a variety of defensive behaviors that extend their influence over a long period of time that is filled with a complicated set of positive and negative events.

Complications such as these might require that the theory be extended to deal with these time considerations. The theory also might have to cope with the fact that a given reward can give rise to both positive and negative primary process, and now we are into some complicated algebra of emotional interaction. The model does, however,

take up some of the important questions concerning the changes that take place in affective responses, and in this sense it provides us with a new perspective on emotional adaptation to the motivational influences that operate in a work setting.

INCIDENCE OF JOB SATISFACTION

There appears to be a growing conviction in some quarters that people are becoming increasingly dissatisfied with the jobs they hold. Significant segments of the labor force have been identified as having to face problems at work that deprive them of much that might be meaningful and satisfying. Blue-collar workers, women, ethnic and racial minorities, young workers, and old workers have all been seen as facing a large number of negative experiences. Many culprits have been identified as the causes of these problems; technology, rising expectations, affluence, and accelerating social changes have all stood accused. The list is a long one, but implicit in much of this concern over the quality of working life is the belief that jobs do exist, or can be developed, that can provide the individual with a working environment that is psychologically wholesome. In a later chapter we will deal with some of these issues more fully, when the effects of technological change are taken up, but for the moment the questions that will be of primary concern to us deal with the extent to which workers report that they are satisfied or dissatisfied with the work they do. Specifically, we want to ask whether there is a substantial amount of evidence suggesting that large numbers of people express generally negative attitudes toward their jobs, and whether it is accurate to say that there is broad-scale discontentment with work in major segments of the labor market. Finally, we will be interested in whether there has been any indication that the level of job satisfaction, or dissatisfaction, has been changing over the past years.

There are bothersome time considerations, which at first glance cast doubt on the utility of questions concerning the level of work satisfaction in the country. Social change is real and constant, and data collected today may not apply to the social circumstances of tomorrow. As a consequence, perhaps the best that can be done is to describe the status of workers' attitudes in the recent past and conjecture about the present. This is probably true, but the use of past conditions to describe the present is aided by the fact that social change, rather than arbitrary and abrupt, tends to be regular and continuous. Social *trends,* such as the increasing level of education or the introduction of technology, involve step-by-step changes, not random and unpredictable swings. Hence, the working conditions that are found one year in large measure establish limits for the changes that may take place in the next. Nevertheless, the changing conditions of work require us to interpret job satisfaction data with caution, but the absence of evidence reflecting abrupt, new directions in working conditions will permit us to apply these data to the present.

Evidence

In spite of claims to the contrary (Sheppard & Herrick, 1972), the evidence available dealing with the incidence of job satisfaction indicates that most workers are moderately well satisfied with the jobs they hold. Furthermore, there is no substantial evidence that the level of job satisfaction has been declining during the past decade or so. Often, when asked directly whether or not they are satisfied with their jobs, an overwhelming majority of workers report that they generally feel positive about the work they do (Gallup, 1973). Quinn and Shepard (1974) report the results of a nationwide survey of employed persons in which the following question was asked: "All in all, how satisfied would you say you are with your job—very satisfied, somewhat satisfied, not too satisfied, or not satisfied at all?"

Almost 90 percent of the sample answered that they were either somewhat or very satisfied with their jobs. To be sure, 51 percent of the sample reported that their present jobs were not the kind they would *"most like"* to have, but the fact that

workers' jobs do not conform to their highest aspirations for congenial work does not justify the conclusion that they are unhappy with work. Robert Kahn (1972) gives us a good perspective on this question when he reviews almost two thousand job-satisfaction surveys, which reveal that relatively few workers think of themselves as being extremely satisfied with their jobs. Even fewer report that they are extremely dissatisfied. The typical response seems to come from workers who are moderately satisfied with the jobs they hold.

The one job setting that has been most frequently cited as leading to a high incidence of job dissatisfaction is the automobile assembly line. It is in this type of automated job that work specialization and machine pacing are found in their most advanced forms. Yet, even with work of this sort there is evidence that a large majority of the workers report they are generally satisfied with their jobs. Form (1973b), for example, has studied the attitudes of automobile workers in four countries (the United States, Italy, Argentina, and India) and found that a large majority (see Table 8.3) reported that they were satisfied with their jobs. Job satisfaction did vary with the skill level of the job, with higher levels of skill being associated with a higher incidence of job satisfaction. Even with those automobile workers, however, whose jobs required the lowest level of skill, 71 percent still said they were generally satisfied with their jobs.

There have been studies of selected populations that have shown a slight trend toward decreasing

TABLE 8.3   Job Satisfaction of American Automobile Workers by Skill Level (in percent)

Skill Level	Satisfied with Job
Unskilled	71
Semiskilled	85
Skilled	93
Total	84

Source: Form, W. H. Auto workers and their machines: A study of work, factory, and job satisfaction in four countries. *Social Forces,* 1973, *52,* 1-15(b). Copyright © The University of North Carolina Press

FIGURE 8.3   Percentage of "Satisfied" Workers, 1958–1973, Based on Seven National Surveys

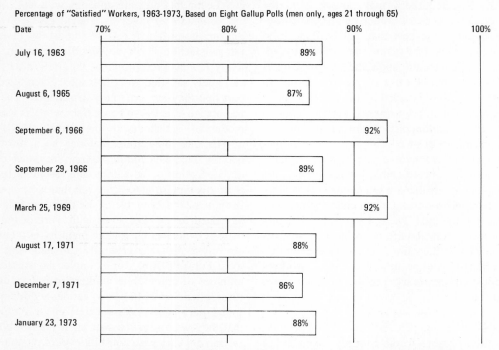

Percentage of "Satisfied" Workers, 1963-1973, Based on Eight Gallup Polls (men only, ages 21 through 65)

Note: This figures is based on the eight Gallup polls described in appendix A. The dates correspond to those printed on Gallup's questionnaires and are reportedly field dates of the polls. "Don't know" answers were excluded from the percentage bases.

job satisfaction over the past ten or more years (Smith, Roberts & Hulin, 1976; Smith, Scott, & Hulin, 1977), but in general there is no reason to believe that during the past several decades there has been a major shift in the character of workers' attitudes toward their jobs.

Other Indexes of Job Satisfaction.   Apart from the direct approach, which involves asking workers how well they like their jobs, there are other indicators that might be used to gauge the level of satisfaction with work. For example, one might argue that if there has been a growing trend in worker dissatisfaction, this condition would be reflected in the turnover rates that might have been noted among workers during the past years. Armknecht and Early (1972) report for the *Monthly Labor Review* that the changes in quit rate (that is, the rate at which workers voluntarily leave

their jobs) that have taken place over the past twenty years have shown no trend that implies a steadily rising job dissatisfaction. More recent data (U.S. Department of Labor, 1976) confirm these results, and Organ (1977) presents evidence to indicate that whatever national trend there may be can be explained by the entrance of an increasing number of young workers into the labor force. Furthermore, the same conclusion can be drawn from a study of the rate of unscheduled absences from work. Table 8.4 from Hedges (1975) shows a fairly steady rate of both full-week and part-week absences from work between 1967 and 1974. Hedges, comparing the 1972 and 1974 statistics, finds no change in absence rates across industries, occupations, and between the sexes. Related to this, there has been a steady increase in the participation rates in the labor market as a whole. That is to say, as a percentage of the population,

TABLE 8.4   Wage and Salary Workers on Unscheduled Absence from Work, 1957–74
(numbers in thousands)

Year	All workers	Absent the entire week[1]		Workers on full-time schedules	Absent part of the week	
		Number	Rate[2]		Number	Rate[2]
1967	62,881	1354	2.2	51,817	2015	3.9
1968	64,601	1468	2.3	52,888	2147	4.1
1969	66,701	1575	2.4	54,144	2199	4.1
1970	67,691	1674	2.5	54,253	2275	4.2
1971	68,209	1666	2.4	54,360	2343	4.3
1972	70,727	1660	2.3	56,498	2435	4.3
1973	73,451	1719	2.3	58,645	2563	4.4
1974	74,933	1774	2.4	59,240	2494	4.2

[1]Data on full-week absences are not available separately for workers on full-time schedules.
[2]Number per 100 workers absent in an average week.
Note: Data exclude agricultural and private-household workers. Because of rounding, sums of individual items may not equal totals.
Source: Hedges, J. N. Unscheduled absences from work—an update. *Monthly Labor Review,* 1975, *98,* 36–38.

a growing number of people have been entering the labor market.

Of course all these indicators reflect economic as well as psychological influences, but keeping this in mind, it would still seem that if there had been a linear growth in job discontentment, these psychological changes would have shown themselves in turnover rates, participation rates, and in the incidence of absenteeism. This has not been the case.

Trends.   Neither survey results nor statistical indicators show clear trends that indicate increasing job dissatisfaction. The *Survey Research Center* has reported trend data from nationwide studies of the quality of the working conditions in the United States, taken in 1969 and then again in 1973 (Seashore, 1972; Quinn & Shepard, 1974). If any trend is evident at all in expressions of overall satisfaction, the trend would suggest improving attitudes, and along the same lines, many statistical indicators have not shown evidence of a trend in worker discontentment. There may be one exception, however, and that is found in the increasing level of work stoppages in the past decade. Idle time due to strike activity doubled between 1961–1965

and 1966–1971 (Wool, 1973); the first half of the decade of the 1970s, however, has produced an interruption of this trend, so even these statistics do not provide consistent support to those who see progressive increases in worker discontent.

Conclusions.   In the face of the evidence one should restrain a gloomy outlook regarding any general increase in the level of job dissatisfaction. After making this statement, however, one should not conclude that job satisfaction-dissatisfaction is not a significant problem. Rarely does survey evidence suggest that the number of dissatisfied workers is less than 10 percent of those responding, and with a labor market close to 100 million, it is apparent that we are talking about a sizeable group.

CORRELATES OF JOB SATISFACTION—PERSONAL FACTORS

Since job satisfaction is a very general concept that potentially involves every facet of a job, it is not surprising to learn that there are few work-related variables that have not at one time or another been shown to correlate with it. Work, organizational, psychological, and demographic variables have all shown themselves to be related to workers' affective reactions to their jobs; in many instances, however, the correlations reported have been relatively weak ones. In this section we will present a selective review of these findings, concentrating on those variables found within the indivdual and the individual's background. These are some of the more important factors that have been used to identify the "pockets" of job dissatisfaction that have been found in the labor force. In considering these factors, therefore, we can think of ourselves as looking into some of the more significant correlates of worker discontentment.

Age and Tenure

One of the more consistent findings has been that there is a positive relationship between job satisfaction and age. Older workers seem to report higher levels of job satisfaction than do younger ones (Quinn & Shepard, 1974; Carrell and Elbert, 1974). Table 8.5, taken from a study of aging done by Siassi, Crocetti, and Spiro (1975), shows the results of a survey of 558 New Jersey factory workers and their employed spouses. Notice the large percent of workers reporting that they are satisfied with their jobs, but also notice the steady increase in the percentage of satisfied workers as age increases. Hence, it would appear that with increasing age there is an improvement in the worker's adjustment to the job. But the matter is not as simple as it first appears, since when age is permitted to increase, job tenure also tends to vary. As a result, the job-satisfaction/age relationship may in fact be a reflection of a tenure/job-satisfaction relationship. With increasing tenure on a job, individuals have a better chance to adjust to the work, and probably are making higher salaries. It may be, therefore, that it is increasing tenure rather than aging that leads to improved job satisfaction.

A number of studies have tried to separate these two variables, with the result that age and tenure do seem to operate as separate, and in some instances, contrary variables. Wall (1972), for example, studied a group of British workers em-

TABLE 8.5 Self-Reported Job Satisfaction among a Sample of Factory Workers and Their Employed Spouses (in percent)

	Age				
	Under 29	30-39	40-49	50-59	60 +
Satisfied	77.3	88.9	90.7	90.9	97.3
Not Satisfied	22.7	11.1	9.3	9.1	2.7

Source: Siassi, I., Crocetti, G., & Spiro, H. P. Emotional health, life and job satisfaction in aging workers. *Industrial Gerontology*, 1975, *2*, 289–296.

ployed in a chemical factory, and found that improvement in job satisfaction was observed only when *both* age and tenure were permitted to vary. When one or the other was held constant while the second varied, there was no significant relationship with job satisfaction. Gibson and Klein (1970), on the other hand, found that the two variables related to job satisfaction in opposite directions. Job satisfaction *improved* with *age* in this sample of blue-collar workers, but job satisfaction *declined* significantly with *tenure* throughout the worker's first twelve years of service on the job. Finally, in some cases it is likely that only certain dimensions of job satisfaction improve with age. For example, Schwab and Heneman (1977) report the results of a survey carried out in one organization, in which the only improvement in job attitudes with age occurred with respect to workers' satisfaction with the work itself.

We find, therefore, considerable consistency in the relationship between work satisfaction and age. As people grow older, they tend to report increasing satisfaction with at least some aspects of their jobs. No answer is available regarding why this relationship exists. Gibson and Klein (1970) suggest that older people maintain a different relationship with authority than do younger people. This operates in two directions; older people may relate to authority figures differently, and authority figures may relate to older workers differently.

Tenure does not appear to hold the same consistency in its relationship with job satisfaction. The psychological consequences of increasing service in a given job are probably more dependent on the characteristics of the work situation. Hence, in considering this variable of tenure, one must be more careful to attend to the specifics of the job situation.

Sex

In spite of the fact that women receive less pay for work similar to that done by men, and in spite of the fact that occupational sex typing often denies women many desirable jobs, there is no consistent evidence that women differ from men in job satisfaction. The 1969 quality of employment survey (Sheppard & Herrick, 1972; Quinn & Sheppard, 1974) shows a significant difference in job satisfaction, favoring men, but this difference disappeared in the 1973 survey. At present, therefore, there is not enough information available to draw even the most tentative conclusions regarding the relationship between the sex of the worker and job satisfaction.

Race

Exposed to high rates of unemployment, low pay, and low-status jobs, black workers often express high levels of dissatisfaction with their work. The 1969 *Survey of Employment Quality,* for example, found that black workers were twice as likely as whites to express feelings of job discontentment. For both groups, but particularly for the black workers, it was the younger worker who showed the highest incidence of dissatisfaction. With increasing age, both groups reported lower frequencies of dissatisfaction, but for those workers 44 years or older, fewer blacks than whites said they were dissatisfied with their jobs. In spite of this sharp drop in job discontentment as the middle years were reached, however, there were still twice as many black workers who reported dissatisfaction with life as there were black workers reporting job dissatisfaction. This difference between life and job satisfaction was not reported by the white workers. These findings seem to suggest that white workers experience greater conti-

nuity in their lives as they move from a work to a nonwork setting. In spite of the many employment difficulties they face, black workers often find in work a comparative haven from the housing, neighborhood, and the broader problems they must face. When the quality of employment survey was repeated in 1974, black workers again showed higher levels of job dissatisfaction. The gap between black and white groups was the same for both periods.

We know relatively little about the reasons for this discontentment among black workers. One might argue that the reasons are obvious, being found in the patterns of job discrimination that have victimized the black worker for decades. Doubtless this is a major contributing factor, yet *Work in America* (1973) reports that the deepest expression of work dissatisfaction is not found among blue-collar blacks in low-skill jobs, but among black workers in middle-ranked, white-collar jobs. Sheppard and Herrick (1972) report similar results from survey data, when they find that the incidence of job dissatisfaction among black workers does not appear to change significantly as a function of the level of income they receive. Workers in relatively high-paying jobs expressed as much job dissatisfaction as those on lower-paying jobs. We are facing a complicated question, for which at present there is need for considerably more information, but at this time it does seem relatively safe to say that in the work force as a whole job dissatisfaction does appear more frequently among black workers.

Education

In a previous chapter we have seen that there appears to be a negative relationship between education and satisfaction with pay. Klein and Maher (1966) suggest that this may be a function of differences in expectations regarding pay, with better-educated workers possessing higher expectations regarding what they could be making on another job. The available evidence, however, indicates that there is a *positive* relationship between overall measures of job satisfaction and education. Both the 1969 and 1973 surveys of employment quality found a progression in job-satisfaction scores as one moves up the education ladder. Hence, when job satisfaction is viewed as a general summary evaluation of a job, higher levels of education seem to improve the likelihood that a worker will respond positively to the global aspects of work. Satisfaction with pay, only one facet of global job satisfaction, tends to decrease with higher levels of education.

As with all relationships of this variety, it is often difficult to identify the reasons why two variables vary together. Certainly in this instance one may argue that with increasing education one may acquire information, attitudes, and values that are useful in adjusting to the work setting. Then too, higher levels of education often give the individual access to the more congenial jobs, and there are probably a dozen other factors that directly or indirectly contribute to the positive relationship between job satisfaction and education. At this point we can conclude only that in many samples this relationship exists, and then await further evidence that may throw additional light on the specific nature of this association.

Blue-Collar, White-Collar

The ''blue-collar blues'' is a term that reflects the belief that in blue-collar segments of the work force lie some of the most aggrieved pockets of discontentment with work. Sheppard and Herrick (1972) report that it is during the middle years of work life that blue-collar workers seem to express the highest frequency of job dissatisfaction as compared to white-collar groups. These authors attribute this to the fact that it is generally during these middle years that the blue-collar worker experiences the greatest pressures on an income that has little chance for significant improvement. Therefore, much of their dissatisfaction stems from financial sources, and when economic pressures lift during their later years, differences between blue- and white-collar groups virtually disappear.

Occupational Level

One of the more consistent relationships found in this area shows that job satisfaction tends to increase as one moves up the hierarchy of jobs that have been ranked according to social prestige. We have already seen in Chapter 6 that the social status of an occupation does relate in a positive direction to measures of job satisfaction (Kornhauser, 1965; Inkeles, 1960). The quality of employment surveys lend more recent evidence of this relationship. Here overall job satisfaction scores seem to be higher for jobs that have higher social status, but there were exceptions; for example, private-household workers showed relatively high levels of job satisfaction.

Rural-Urban Background

There is some evidence indicating that social origin is a factor that contributes to workers' evaluation of their jobs. Blood and Hulin (1967; Hulin & Blood, 1968), for example, contend that workers coming from rural backgrounds have a higher incidence of job satisfaction than workers who have an urban background. Rural workers are thought to invest higher values in the work itself, whereas urban workers tend to look at their jobs primarily as a means of making money. As a result, rural workers are seen as being more responsive to the content of their jobs and being better satisfied with jobs that involve more complex duties and a greater variety of experiences (Turner & Lawrence, 1965). But in spite of research evidence supporting this idea, there are other studies that suggest one should use caution in adopting such a viewpoint as a general principle. Fossum (1974), for example, did an experiment in a laboratory setting, in which college students from urban and rural backgrounds were hired to perform a task that was dull and repetitive. His results indicated that when compared to urban subjects, rural subjects were more satisfied with the task and the pay they received.

Shepard (1970), studying workers raised in rural and urban environments, reports no difference between the two groups in their reactions to jobs that are less complex and more narrowly specialized. Therefore, we are at a choice point with regard to this relationship between the worker's social origins and job satisfaction. There appears to be no simple principle that can be used to predict rural-urban differences in job satisfaction. Perhaps Schuler (1973) has an idea that can give us a more useful perspective on this question. He suggests that urban-rural influences on job satisfaction should appear most clearly when workers' early social environments are different from the social settings in which their present jobs are found. When the social environment of childhood matches the social environment of work, the individual should report higher levels of job satisfaction. Hence, the most dissatisfied workers should be found among persons raised in a rural setting who are now holding jobs in an urban setting, or among those raised in an urban environment who are now working in a rural setting.

Comment. The studies mentioned above demonstrate that the level of job satisfaction does change in conjunction with certain background variables, but the relationship between these variables tends to be complex. Further, when only a single background factor is considered, its relation with job satisfaction tends to be rather weak. That this is the case points to the complicated structure of the concept of job satisfaction and the structure of its measurement. When we ask workers to evaluate their reactions to a job, we are asking them to process a huge amount of information. Job satisfaction, therefore, reflects a composite of many different work experiences; and as a consequence, there is a good probability that it will overlap to some extent many aspects of an individual's life.

There is another idea that might be used to explain this long list of weak associations, and the best way to present it is to refer to a study done by Jury et al. (1971). These authors studied relationships between workers' perceptions of job satisfaction and demographic characteristics such as sex, age, education, tenure, and management level. Over eleven hundred subjects employed in six companies participated in the study, the results of which showed that only certain facets of job satisfaction seemed to vary as a function of background variables. More specifically, Jury et al. found that the aspects of job satisfaction that concern financial compensation and the individual's progress and development in the job do not seem to change very much with variation in worker background. Satisfaction with the organizational facets of a job, such as superior-subordinate relationships and company policy, did vary according to the background of the worker. Hence, the way workers perceive those aspects of a job that directly relate to themselves and their careers seems to vary less as a function of age, sex, education, and so on; how the worker sees the contribution of organizational variables seems to vary more as a function of these background factors. The low correlations found between demographic variables and *overall* job satisfaction, therefore, may point to the fact that only certain aspects of job satisfaction vary along with background factors; other facets remain relatively constant over differences in background conditions.

SITUATIONAL FACTORS

We now come to face directly the important questions of what it is that leads to job satisfaction, and of what the performance consequences of these job attitudes are. Actually, the preceding pages contain much information bearing on the factors that result in job satisfaction. For example, Herzberg would probably argue that job satisfaction is most likely to be the result of job conditions that permit the worker to experience some sense of self-actualization. Lofquist and Dawis, Porter, Holland, and many others might talk about the extent to which a job is capable of fulfilling certain psychological needs, where a key consideration is to be found in the adequacy of the fit between job and individual. Then we could run down a long list of correlational studies in which variables such as age, tenure, education, and job status have been found to be associated with a worker's affective reaction to a job.

Work Roles

A work organization can be thought of as consisting of a large number of work roles. Work roles refer to consistent patterns of activities that identify what an individual does in an organization. One of the more important work roles can be found in the set of duties assigned to a given job. Here we are talking about the content of an individual's job—the activities that are required of the worker by the job. Apart from these formal work tasks, there are other work roles that identify the part played by an individual in the social relations that take place on the job. For example, one worker may play an important role in the informal communications that pass up and down the organization's grapevine. Another worker may be found serving a status-maintenance role by doing certain things that support the status relationships that exist among members of the organization. A supervisor may assume a role that reinforces the authority and discipline systems operating within the organization. In this instance, the adoption of this role by one supervisor may permit other managers to adopt a warmer, more considerate role, since they can always draw on the other supervisor's disciplinarian behaviors when circumstances warrant. The school principal may often be found serving such a role.

Several aspects of the work role have received a lot of attention in connection with their relationship to job satisfaction. Both *role ambiguity* and *role conflict,* for example, have been found to be factors that contribute to feelings of job discontentment. A worker experiences role ambiguity during those times when certain aspects of a work role are not clearly defined. In these instances the worker is uncertain about what is expected. Disagreement between a worker and a supervisor concerning the responsibility for a particular function constitutes one form of role ambiguity. Uncertainty regarding the amount of authority held by a worker may constitute another.

At other times a worker may be faced with a conflict between roles. For example, an individual may hold a job in which incompatible sets of expectations are imposed. Loyalty to one's immediate boss may come into conflict with the worker's commitment to the welfare of the organization or with the best interests of the customer. Role conflict may stem from numerous work ac-

tivities, but whatever its source, there is general agreement that it, along with role ambiguity, constitutes one of the more important sources of job dissatisfaction.

In their extensive study of organizational stress, Kahn et al. (1964) found evidence indicating that role conflict and role ambiguity tend to occur independently of each other. A job situation that creates one condition for the worker is not likely to create the other. The influence of the two conditions tends to be similar, however, in the sense that both are correlated with the worker's emotional reaction to the job. As work-role ambiguity and conflict increase, job tensions and job dissatisfaction tend to increase as well.

Subsequent research (for example, Miles, 1975; Maher & Piersol, 1970) has, by and large, tended to support the contention that negative relationships exist among work-role ambiguity, conflict, and job satisfaction. This more recent research reveals, however, that these relationships are not to be found in every job situation (Tosi & Tosi, 1970; Tosi, 1971; House & Rizzo, 1972; Hamner & Tosi, 1974). Furthermore, the relationship seems to vary as a function of several conditions. For instance, Hamner and Tosi (1974) and Schuler (1975) show that at higher levels of organizational management, role ambiguity seems to have a more negative relationship with measures of job satisfaction than does role conflict. Conversely, at lower levels role conflict tends to bear a more negative relationship with workers' reports of job satisfaction. Some argue that these results reflect the different nature of the work found at higher and lower levels of the organization. At higher levels, individuals are faced with a greater variety of unstructured situations that are central to the problem-solving tasks dealt with on a daily basis. At the same time, persons in these higher positions have greater power to deal with whatever role conflicts they may face. As a consequence, role ambiguity becomes a more important contributor to job dissatisfaction, while role conflict is of less significance, since it can be more easily dealt with.

Keller (1975) maintains that role conflict and ambiguity correlate differently with different facets of job satisfaction. For many jobs the principal source of role conflict is found in a worker's relationship with the supervisor and with the incentive systems under the boss's control. Role ambiguity, on the other hand, tends to originate in the duties of the job and in the problem-solving situations created by the job. As a consequence, one should find that role ambiguity maintains a negative relationship with satisfaction with the work itself, while role conflict should lead to dissatisfaction with supervision and other context factors. Others (Organ & Greene, 1974; Lyons, 1971) argue that work-role difficulties relate to job satisfaction as a function of the personality of the worker. For example, Lyons (1971) finds that role clarity relates to job satisfaction only for those who possess a high need for clarity. In other instances satisfaction with certain types of supervision has been shown to be related to personality factors. It is apparent, then, that even though role deficiencies may contribute to job satisfaction-dissatisfaction, these factors do not operate alone. Their relationship with job satisfaction seems to change as a function of job and organizational variables, as well as with factors associated with the personality of the worker.

Causal Relations. Implicit in many discussions regarding the contribution of work roles to job satisfaction is the assumption that role ambiguity and conflict are, in themselves, a source of psychological difficulty, and that they lead directly to feelings of job dissatisfaction. There is some evidence, however, (Greene, 1972; Greene & Organ, 1973) that indicates that role difficulties serve as only one link in a chain of factors that lead to job dis-

contentment. For example, a worker on a job in which there is little role ambiguity is in a better position to comply with the requirements and expectations of the job; the work roles are clearly defined. In complying with the requirements of work, the worker tends to exhibit behaviors that are more likely to be rewarded, and increased satisfaction is experienced as a consequence of the rewards received. Figure 8.4 (Greene & Organ, 1973) illustrates this causal relation in which role clarity leads to compliance, which in turn leads to performance that is rewarded. It is the improvement in the rewards received by the worker that results in an improvement in job satisfaction.

Organizational Variables

Efforts have been made to investigate whether the social structure of a work organization has an influence on the level of job satisfaction. Organizational structure—size, number of management levels, centralization of control, and so on—is the social framework within which work activity takes place. The size of the organization, for example, has a bearing on the level of work specialization or the social distances between people. The number of layers of management has a direct bearing on the nature and efficiency of work communication. Hence, when we consider the structure of organizations, we are dealing with properties that have a direct relationship with the experiences of the people who work within these settings. Therefore, it doesn't seem unreasonable to expect job satisfaction to vary as a function of the structure of an organization. Dawis et al. (1974), for instance, look at the structure of the organization in terms of its impact on the system of reinforcements

FIGURE 8.4   A Model of the Relationship of Role Accuracy to Satisfaction

Source: Greene, C. N., & Organ, D. W. An evaluation of causal models linking the received role with job satisfaction. *Administrative Science Quarterly*, 1973, *18*, 93–103. Copyright 1973 Administrative Science Quarterly.

(that is, rewards and punishments) that are employed in connection with working. Changes in the structure of a work organization are thought of in terms of changes taking place in this system of reinforcement. Along related lines, Smart (1975) has shown that for different organizational environments, there are differences in the pattern of the job facets that enter a worker's overall evaluation of the job. In other words, the dimensions of the work contributing to general job satisfaction seem to change as a function of the characteristics of the organizational environment.

Porter and Lawler (1965) have looked into the studies relating organizational structure to worker attitudes and have found that of seven organizational properties considered, five seem to have a relationship with job satisfaction. As an example, higher levels of management seem to have higher levels of job satisfaction than do lower management levels, and line management tend to be more satisfied than managers in staff positions. The size of the work group appears to influence levels of job satisfaction, with small work-group units being associated with higher levels of satisfaction. Porter and Lawler (1965) suggest that large subunits lead to lower group cohesiveness, higher levels of work specialization, and a deterioration of communication. These conditions lead both to lower levels of job satisfaction and to an increase in turnover, absenteeism, and labor strife. Interestingly, there appears to be no simple relationship between the number of layers of management and job satisfaction. What evidence there is (Porter & Lawler, 1964; Porter & Siegel, 1965) suggests that a flat organizational structure (few layers of management) seems to be associated with better job attitudes in small organizations. In large work organizations the results have not shown much consistency.

Comment. In considering the relationship between organizational variables and job satisfaction, one must bear in mind that objective job characteristics do not always correspond with job characteristics as they are perceived. Attempts to correlate objective organizational variables with measures of job satisfaction may not, therefore, take these subjective "revisions" into consideration. The weak associations that have been reported between organizational structures and job satisfaction may reflect the fact that objective rather than subjective measures of organizational characteristics have been used.

Studies of this sort may also neglect to consider the possibility that workers can improve their satisfaction with a job by altering the way they look at their work. Hence, workers in jobs that are badly managed and poorly paid may still have high satisfaction because they overlook these negative aspects and focus on a challenging set of job duties and interesting work associates. Positioned between job conditions and a worker's reaction to them are these perceptual factors that can make an objectively negative situation appear more positive to the individual worker (Salancik & Pfeffer, 1977).

Organizational Climate

Apart from the actual structure of a work organization, there are the individuals' perceptions of the social environment in which they work. The overall impressions the worker forms about an organization have been referred to as the *organizational climate* of work (Lyon & Ivancevich, 1974; Schneider & Snyder, 1975). This concept refers to an individual's global impressions of the organization, and it is the *evaluation* of these general perceptions that is involved in the concept of job satisfaction. The organizational climate may be thought of as a perceptual background against which the worker views the specific happenings of work. It refers to an individual's general perceptual orientation toward the social environment of work.

There have been a number of studies showing that these global perceptions do correlate with job satisfaction. Taylor and Bowers (1972), using methods that permit the inference of causation, found that organizational climate seems to be one of the factors that serve as causes of job satisfaction. Other studies (for example, La Follette & Sims, 1975; Lawler, Hall, & Oldham, 1974;

Gavin & Howe, 1975) have found a relationship between the worker's generalized perception of the organization and measures of job satisfaction. Work settings that were seen as having a more clearly defined and efficient structure, structures that produced an equitable reward system along with low amounts of management interference, pride in work, and organizational loyalty, were found to be associated with higher levels of job satisfaction.

As yet there is no clear picture of the manner in which organizational climate contributes to job satisfaction. There is one piece of evidence (Pritchard & Karasick, 1973) that suggests that this climate has more influence on job satisfaction than it does on job performance, but at present it would be unwise to conclude that job performance is unrelated to the concept. The best we can do is repeat Lawler, Hall, and Oldham's (1974) hypothesis, which identifies organizational climate as a perceptual factor that intervenes between the work environment, job attitudes, and performance. It is a complicated construct, but it may well prove to be a reasonable description of the manner in which workers often view their jobs. The general impression, the global overview of one's job and work organization, can serve as a kind of perceptual filter that influences significantly the individual's interpretation and evaluation of the specific events that take place. The concept of organizational climate refers to this generalized perception of the work environment, and it is a psychologically meaningful concept that warrants increased attention regarding its relationships with other variables.

JOB SATISFACTION AND NEED FULFILLMENT

One of the most widely held theories of job satisfaction contends that individuals experience satisfaction with work to the extent that their jobs are able to meet their psychological needs. Satisfaction is the result of need gratification, and job dissatisfaction occurs whenever the gratification of an ongoing need is frustrated (Wolf, 1970). As a rule, this approach adopts Maslow's need hierarchy theory (Maslow, 1954), arguing that an individual's needs can be ranked in an order ranging from low (basic physiological needs) to high (need for achievement and self-actualization). Lower-order needs are psychologically more potent than higher-order ones, but as these lower-order needs are fulfilled, motivational influences shift to the higher-order needs, which begin to play an active role in motivating the individual.

Job satisfaction is experienced whenever job-related events result in gratification of needs that are active. An individual whose lower-order needs are not fulfilled will be satisfied by job experiences that meet these needs. An individual whose lower-order needs have been fulfilled will experience job satisfaction from those aspects of work that tend to gratify higher-order needs. Often, writers trace lower-order need gratification to what Herzberg calls the context factors in work. Gratification of higher-order needs is often associated with the content factors of work (Neeley, 1973; Orpen & Pinshaw, 1975).

Congruence between an individual's needs and the facets of jobs that potentially can gratify these needs is a basic ingredient that contributes to job satisfaction, and several important theories of work behavior utilize this idea to explain and predict a worker's reaction to the job. The *Theory of Work Adjustment* (Dawis, Lofquist, & Weiss, 1968; Lofquist & Dawis, 1975) is one such theory. We have already considered this theory in Chapter 6, so a very brief sketch of its main points should be sufficient here. From the point of view of this theory, work adjustment is inferred from two primary conditions—worker satisfactoriness and satisfaction. Satisfactoriness refers to the quality of an individual's performance, and it is the result of the congruence that exists between a worker's abilities and the ability requirements of the job. Satisfaction with a job derives from the correspondence between the kinds of rewards that are provided by the work and the vocational needs of the worker. Each job presents the worker with a unique pattern of needs that potentially may be fulfilled in the work environment. Satisfaction with work, therefore, can be expected in a situation in which there is a congenial matching of a worker's vocational needs with the various facets of the incentive system.

Holland's Theory of Careers

Probably the most influential theory of occupational choice has been one developed by John L. Holland (1966; 1973). By and large this theory is thought of as being most relevant to those engaged in vocational counseling, but it does deal with the concept of job satisfaction. We will ignore the counseling implications and focus only on the one aspect that relates to job satisfaction. Holland's theory uses a *congruity model,* stating that job satisfaction is most likely to be found in work situations in which the personality characteristics of the individual are congruent with the characteristics of the work environment. Essentially there are six broad personality types:

> *The Realistic Type*—Has preference for activities which involve an ordered and systematic manipulation of objects, tools, machines and animals. This type tends to acquire skills of a manual, electrical, mechanical, agricultural and technical nature. They usually do not develop high competency in educational and social areas of skill.
>
> *The Investigative Type*—Has preferences for activities that concern observational, systematic, symbolic and creative undertakings often in the areas of science and culture. These preferences often lead the individual to develop high competence in science and mathematics, and to have lower competencies in social and persuasive areas.
>
> *The Artistic Type*—Has preference for ambiguous, free, unsystematic activities which involve the manipulation of words, pictorial, musical, or physical things in order to create art forms. These preferences lead to the development of competencies in music, art, drama, language and writing, and to a deficit in clerical or business systems competencies.
>
> *The Social Type*—Has preference for activities

which involve interacting with others in order to train, develop, cure or enlighten. These preferences lead to the development of human relations competencies and to a deficit in manual and technical competencies.

> *The Enterprising Type*—Has preferences for activities that involve the manipulation of others to achieve organizational objectives or economic gain. Tends to have competencies in interpersonal, persuasive and leadership behaviors, and a deficit in scientific competencies.
>
> *The Conventional Type*—Has preference for activities that are ordered and systematic and involve the keeping of data or records, organizing materials, operating business machines and data processing. Tends to have high competencies in clerical, computational and business systems areas. Tends to have little artistic competence. (Holland, 1973, pp. 14–18)

Few if any people have personalities that can adequately be described by a single type; therefore personality patterns are constructed by combining different subsets of the six types. Some of these patterns are made up of types that are more closely related to each other than are others, and in these instances Holland refers to personality *consistency*. A consistent pattern, for example, may combine artistic and social types, while an inconsistent pattern may find conventional and artistic types combining.

Work environments can also be described in terms of these six types, but in this instance each type refers to the demands made on the worker's behavioral resources and the various opportunities that are available. People seek out jobs that enable them to express their personalities and draw on their most abundant behavioral resources. For example, realistic personality types seek out job environments that permit them to draw on their mechanical and technical abilities. Through selective recruitment, various job environments also seek out individuals who ''fit in.'' What results is a complicated system of selective sorting of people among jobs. As a consequence of this selectivity, each environment is dominated by a particular personality type, and each occupation, by virtue of the people it attracts and the work demands made on them, confronts individual workers with a characteristic set of problems, opportunities, and behavioral requirements.

A congruent relationship between an individual's personality and a work environment leads to improved prospects for job satisfaction. A person is in a congruent work setting when that setting produces exposure to people whose values, abilities, and commitments are similar to that person's own. This fit, however, is not conceived as an all-or-none arrangement in which the worker's personality must achieve an exact fit with the environment before the worker can experience satisfaction with the job. Rather, there are varying degrees of congruence, which lead to varying degrees of job satisfaction.

The degree of person-environment congruence is represented by a hexagon, the corners of which identify a personality style (see Figure 8.5). The shorter the distance between two positions on the hexagon, the greater the consistency between personality types. Likewise, when used to represent *both* personality types and work environment types, the shorter the distance between positions, the greater the *congruence* between person and occupation. As an example, a social person will find an artistic or enterprising work environment more satisfying than a realistic or investigative environment.

Holland's theory is much more detailed than the above discussion reflects; we have presented only a general summary of his main ideas. The point can be made, however, that Holland's Theory of Careers is another model that defines job satisfaction in terms of the extent to which a work situation has within it opportunities and requirements that fulfill the psychological needs of the worker. This is an idea that one can find running throughout much of the literature on work behavior (for example, Roe, 1956), but rather than consider the work of other writers, which largely duplicates the ideas already discussed, let's turn now to the research that has been conducted to evaluate this point of view.

FIGURE 8.5   A Hexagonal Model for Defining the Psychological Resemblances among Types and Environments

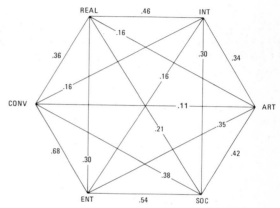

Source: Holland, J. L., et al. An empirical occupational classification derived from a theory of personality and intended for practice and research—ACT research report no. 29. Iowa City: The American College Testing Program, 1969, p. 4. Copyright 1969 by the American College Testing Program. All rights reserved. Reprinted with permission.

Research Evidence

The best series of studies dealing with the relationship between need fulfillment and work satisfaction has been reported by Lofquist and Dawis (1969, 1975) in conjunction with their theory of work adjustment. In all, twenty work groups representing a variety of occupations were studied. Measures of an individual's vocational needs were taken, together with a measurement of the incentives found on the job. The extent to which these two measures corresponded—that is, the extent to which the job contained incentives that corresponded with the worker's needs—was found to correlate significantly with measures of satisfaction in fourteen of the twenty work settings. Lofquist and Dawis (1975) report that under certain conditions their theory permits them to accurately predict worker satisfaction for seven out of every ten workers.

More recent work has tended to support the need-fulfillment theory, although some believe the model has not been adequately tested (Salancik & Pfeffer, 1977). Pinto and Davis (1974) identified different need types among a group of managers, each of whom was given a set of scales that measured different facets of job satisfaction. The study indicated that need type played a role in determining the facets of the job that entered an individual's overall evaluation of the job held. For one need type, for example, satisfaction with career progress, promotion bases, and supervisory competence contributed heavily to overall job satisfaction. For a second need type, overall satisfaction was more influenced by satisfaction with work challenge, supervisory competence, and promotion practices. For still other need types, ability utilization contributed to overall feelings of job satisfaction. Orpen and Pinshaw (1975) were able to show a relationship between need fulfillment and overall job satisfaction in a group of 100 insurance clerks, but these authors were unable to demonstrate that need fulfillment in a specific area related to satisfaction with a *related* facet of the job. Another study by Lacey (1971) failed to show that a worker's perception of a job's ability to satisfy a particular need was related to the satisfaction the worker expressed in that need area.

In general, therefore, there seems to be a reasonable amount of evidence supporting the contention that overall job satisfaction arises from those situations in which the job permits the worker to satisfy psychological needs. Job-facet satisfaction, however,—that is, the satisfaction reported for a specific facet of a job—has not been shown to relate to a worker's reports of the extent to which needs in that particular area have been fulfilled. We are, therefore, in a position to define job satisfaction in terms of some concept of overall need fulfillment, but at the present time the research literature does not permit us to demonstrate a clear one-to-one relationship between the individual facets of job satisfaction and the corresponding facets of need fulfillment.

Job Satisfaction and Life Adjustment

Since a job often requires such a large investment of an individual's personal resources, it seems reasonable to suppose that there must be a correlation between the extent to which workers are satisfied with their jobs and their general psychological adjustment. In all probability, this relationship is a reciprocal one. That is to say, psychological problems in nonwork areas of life influence an individual's adjustment to work, and problems originating at work influence adjustment to nonwork situations.

In general, two ideas have been advanced to deal with this relationship. One of these, called the *compensation hypothesis,* states that dissatisfaction with work leads the individual to search out compensating sources of gratification in nonwork areas. If this is the case, then we should find that those who are dissatisfied with work report higher levels of satisfaction with other areas of their lives. The second idea, called the *generalization hypothesis,* contends that a poor adjustment to work tends to undermine an individual's efforts to adapt to other aspects of life. In other words, there occurs a generalization of discontent, with those who express job dissatisfaction tending to report higher levels of discontentment with the nonwork components of their lives.

By and large, the predominance of the evidence seems to suggest that the generalization hypothesis is the better statement of the relationship between job satisfaction and life satisfaction. For example, Kornhauser (1965), in his widely cited study of automobile workers, provides us with some support for this point of view. In this study, he reports that workers who say thay are dissatisfied with their jobs also indicate that they are generally dissatisfied with their lives. In fact, to some moderate degree, Kornhauser found that there was a general interdependence among all measures of satisfaction. He measured satisfaction in five areas—job, life, family and home, leisure time, and community—finding positive correlations among all of them. Kornhauser favors the interpretation that job dissatisfaction spills over to influence the individual's adjustment to other areas of life, although he recognizes that these influences probably move in both directions.

A more recent study by Cammann et al. (1975) has also reported that job satisfaction seems to relate to a worker's adjustment to a variety of areas of life. In this study, intercorrelations between workers' job-related attitudes revealed what Cammann et al. called a *"satisfaction cluster."* This cluster involves workers' satisfaction with the job, feelings of self-esteem, job-related moods, satisfaction with life in general, and the predisposition to quit the job. Job satisfaction tended to accompany positive attitudes in all other areas in the cluster, showing what appears to be a continuity in these areas of adjustment.

Iris and Barrett (1972) have obtained evidence that also supports the generalization hypothesis. In this study two groups of foremen took part, one group being seen by management as a problem group that had low morale. The second group was seen as a nonproblem group that had higher morale than the first. Both groups were given questionnaires that measured satisfaction with different facets of their jobs and satisfaction with different facets of their nonwork lives. The results indicated that the high-morale group scored significantly higher on every facet of the job-satisfaction scale. Furthermore, this group scored higher than the low-morale group on every facet of the life-satisfaction scale.

Gechman and Weiner (1975), studying a group of 54 women school teachers, report a moderately high correlation between job satisfaction and a measure of mental health. Those teachers who had high job satisfaction were also found to be psychologically better adjusted.

Finally, Langner and Michael (1963) in their midtown Manhattan study, conclude that the work sphere is very important in its influence on mental health. They report that measures obtained from a "work worries" factor were their best predictors of the presence of mental disturbances. As the frequency of work worries increased, there was an increase in the risk of mental problems.

Kasl (1973), reviewing the literature concerning mental health and the work environment, concludes that the correlation between job satisfaction and personal happiness tends to be moderately high and rather consistently positive. Furthermore, there is no convincing evidence indicating that a lack of satisfaction in one area of life is compensated for by heightened satisfaction in some other area. The generalization hypothesis, therefore, seems to give us the best perspective concerning the relationship between job satisfaction and the individual's satisfaction with other areas of life.

JOB SATISFACTION AND PERFORMANCE

One usually thinks of job satisfaction as the *consequence* of events associated with a particular work environment and with the personality characteristics of the individual worker. From this perspective, job satisfaction is the outcome of a congenial fit between work and worker; job dissatisfaction, on the other hand, is an undesirable consequence of job conditions that cause poor work adjustment. In this sense, job satisfaction and dissatisfaction occur at the end of a psychological sequence, and they are thought of as being outcomes rather than causes. It takes little thought, however, to recognize that the end of one event usually serves as a stimulus that leads to another. It follows from this that job satisfaction and dissatisfaction can also be thought of as psychological conditions that influence subsequent behaviors, and a reasonable assumption would seem to be that job satisfaction and dissatisfaction function as motivational conditions that carry over to influence the performance of individuals.

In keeping with this point of view, one often hears statements to the effect that a satisfied worker is a productive worker—that is, that one of the to-be-expected consequences of high job satisfaction is high levels of productive efficiency. Job dissatisfaction, on the other hand, is often linked with high rates of absenteeism, turnover, grievances, and low production quantity and quality. Hence, the central objective of many personnel programs is to improve conditions of worker satisfaction, since it is assumed that with rising levels of job morale, there will follow an improvement in worker productivity, a reduction in turnover and absences, and a general improvement in the functional efficiency of the work organization.

Turnover and Absences

There seem to be fairly clear and consistent relationships among job satisfaction, turnover, and absences from work. Porter and Steers (1973) have reviewed much of the research that has been done concerning these relationships, and the evidence points quite clearly to the conclusion that both turnover rates and absenteeism increase as job satisfaction decreases. Hence it appears that the unhappy worker tends to withdraw from work, by staying away from the job, by taking days off, or by quitting. Thomas Lyons (1972) reports an interesting set of results that suggest that absences and turnover should be thought of as a sequence of adjustments made to job dissatisfaction, rather than two independent alternatives that are available to discontented workers. In all samples studied by Lyons, workers who eventually quit their jobs had a higher absentee record than did workers who remained. Waters and Roach (1971) report similar findings in a study of women employees in an insurance company. It would seem, therefore, that job dissatisfaction first leads to an increased rate of absences, and then the worker leaves the job altogether. In a similar vein, Fleishman and Harris (1962) report evidence suggesting that grievances seem to precede turnover; hence, although the evidence is not complete, we can hypothesize that job dissatisfaction, if it persists over an extended period, sets up a sequence of adjustments that begin with heightened grievances, increased absences, and finally resignation. Of course, as Seashore (1973) points out, job dissatisfaction does not lead only to adjustment patterns that are to be considered negative. Job dissatisfaction can lead to forms of adjustment that are positive in their effects on workers and on the organizations for which they work. For instance, there is always the possibility

that dissatisfied workers will work hard in an effort to improve their relations with a boss who is the principal source of their discontentment.

Porter and Steers (1973) find that not only do measures of overall satisfaction correlate negatively with turnover and absences, but measures of the individual facets of job dissatisfaction seem to hold a similar relationship with turnover and absence data. For example, studies have shown that dissatisfaction with pay and promotion opportunities is related to withdrawal from work. Dissatisfaction with supervision, work associates, and job content have all been shown to relate to turnover and absenteeism. Hence, on the basis of the research evidence, job satisfaction and many of its separate components appear to be motivational conditions that contribute to the probability that workers will leave or remain on the job.

There is one caution that should be taken into consideration before conclusions regarding these relationships are too firmly drawn. In a study replicated across both organizations and time periods, Waters and Roach (1973) found that only a small number of attitudinal measures were consistent predictors of turnover and absences. Many of the attitude measures that predicted withdrawal behavior in one period, or in one organization, failed to predict significantly when applied to another time period or another organization. Of course we must balance this caution with the knowledge that there have been many separate studies, done in a wide variety of work settings and at widely different times, that have shown job attitudes to be significant predictors of withdrawal behavior. The Waters and Roach study does signal us that studies dealing with these relationships should plan for some sort of replication in order to check on the consistency of their findings.

Finally, while acknowledging the relationship between job satisfaction and turnover, one should not assume that there are no other job attitudes that can predict this kind of behavior more closely. Workers' statements concerning their intentions to remain with an organization have been shown to be better predictors of turnover (Mobley, Horner,

& Hollingsworth, 1978; Waters & Roach, 1979). Koch and Steers (1978) have found that measures of job *attachment* predicted employee turnover more accurately than did job satisfaction measures. Job attachment refers to an individual's identification with the work and the stated intention to avoid seeking alternative employment. It is interesting that job attachment appeared to be more strongly related to characteristics associated with the individual (age, education) whereas job satisfaction was more closely related to the characteristics of the job. All this suggests that the factors contributing to employee turnover are to be found in both individual and job characteristics, with some possibility that individual factors play the more substantial role.

Satisfaction and Productivity

The consistency found in the results of studies dealing with job satisfaction and withdrawal behaviors has not been duplicated by studies concerned with job satisfaction and productivity. At present, after many efforts to investigate this relationship, the best we can say is that the relationship between job attitudes and worker production levels is not a simple one. For many years much of the thinking done on this subject was significantly influenced by a review of the literature done by Brayfield and Crockett (1955) who concluded:

> It appears that there is little evidence in the available literature that employee attitudes of the type usually measured in a morale survey bear any simple—or, for that matter, appreciable relationship to performance on the job. (p. 408)

In a later review of this area, Vroom (1964) concluded that the relationship between work satisfaction and performance tended to be positive (high satisfaction associated with higher levels of production), but the strength of this relationship was consistently quite low.

Locke (1976) in a more recent analysis of the literature in this area, has concluded:

> Just as reviews of the literature have shown

consistently that job satisfaction is related to absences and turnover, they have been equally consistent in showing negligible relationships between satisfaction and level of performance or productivity. (p. 1332)

There seems, therefore, to be no substantial body of information indicating that the *direct* relationship between job satisfaction and productivity is anything but a modest one. Yet the psychologist has become involved with a "chicken-or-the-egg" question regarding which factor serves as the cause and which the effect. At one time it was generally felt that a "good" human relations program directly led to higher levels of morale and then to higher levels of production efficiency. As research evidence began to accumulate, however, it became clear that this hypothesis did not seem to account for much that was observed by the researcher. Current thought seems to be leaning in the direction of job performance serving as a condition that causes job satisfaction or dissatisfaction, rather than being a response to the worker's satisfaction with the job.

Perhaps the most widely quoted statement of this point of view is found in a model presented by Porter and Lawler (1968), which attempts to tie together worker attitudes and performance. Reference to Figure 8.6 finds a schematic representation of the basic ideas contained in this point of view.

One of the most appealing aspects of this model is that it takes the form of a behavioral loop, with job satisfaction serving as both the end point of one cycle of events and a contributor to the beginning point for the next. In this respect, therefore, job satisfaction is represented as *both* a cause and effect; it is both the result of job performance and a contributor to job performance. In the Porter-Lawler model, job satisfaction is linked to productivity whenever the system of rewards reinforces high levels of performance. In this sense, then, job satisfaction is a response to the advent of a reward or is the result of an expectation of a reward that will eventually follow high-level productivity.

FIGURE 8.6   The Porter and Lawler Model

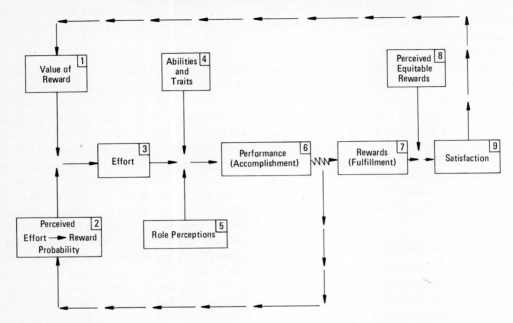

This model was originally developed to deal with the effects of managerial attitudes on managers' performance. The model has been extended to deal with a wide range of work situations.

Source: Porter, L. W., and Lawler, E. E. *Managerial attitudes and performance.* Homewood, Ill.: Richard D. Irwin, 1968, p. 17. Copyright, 1968 Richard D. Irwin, Inc.

Let's look at this model and briefly consider its terms. We begin with element 1, value of reward, which is the relative attractiveness of the possible consequences of different levels of performance. This is a perceptual variable, referring to the worker's perception (expectation) of the outcome that will follow as the result of performance. The second variable (2), perceived effort-reward probability, refers to the worker's expectation that certain amounts of effort will be followed by certain levels of reward. Here Porter and Lawler tell us that we are dealing with the worker's perception of the probability that performance will be instrumental in obtaining reward. Another element of this variable consists of the worker's perception of the probability that investment of effort will be successful in generating the rewarded types of performance.

These two variables contribute to the motivational condition called effort (3). Here the model considers how hard the worker tries to perform. Effort combines with the worker's abilities (4) and the worker's perception of work roles (5) to produce a certain level of performance (6). Work role refers to an individual's perception and understanding of the expectations others have regarding his or her behavior in the work setting.

As Figure 8.6 indicates, the performance element (6) refers to the individual's actual accomplishments; it is this aspect of behavior that is the end result of effort, ability, and role perception. To the extent that performance leads to reward (7), or is perceived as leading to reward, there is a loop in the model that feeds back to influence subsequent performance. The reward involved, on the other hand, is itself subject to an evaluation (8), in that it is compared with the amount of reward the individual believes *should* be received for a given level of performance. Finally, satisfaction (9) stems from those circumstances in which the worker perceives that the rewards received meet or exceed the reward levels thought to be equitable. Hence, we find in the Porter-Lawler model the concept of satisfaction being equated with the individual's perception of the extent to which rewards received correspond to the level of reward thought to be equitable. Satisfaction does *not* necessarily correspond directly to the amount of reward actually received; it is the worker's perception of the reward that is important.

While being mindful of the feedback components of the model—that is, satisfaction looping back to serve as a factor contributing to later performance, Porter and Lawler hypothesize that worker performance tends to have a more direct effect on satisfaction than satisfaction has on performance. Hence, we find job satisfaction assuming an influence on job performance, while at the same time it reflects an outcome of job performance. The model also shows us that the relationship between satisfaction and performance is more direct in one direction than the other. As an outcome, satisfaction follows performance, being mediated only by the reward system. As a cause, satisfaction is shown functioning along with a larger set of variables.

Recent studies (Siegel & Bowen, 1971; Greene, 1973; Sheridan & Slocum, 1975) have been able to show that job satisfaction should be thought of more as an outcome of job performance than as a psychological antecedent of job performance. Using special statistical procedures that permit one to estimate the direction of causation in a relationship between two variables, these studies give reasonable support to the Porter-Lawler hypothesis. It seems reasonable, therefore, to think of job satisfaction in motivational terms, but in doing so emphasis should be placed on its role as an outcome variable. Job satisfaction appears to be a reward for the kind and level of performance that is tied in with the organization's system of incentives, and although it functions primarily as an

outcome variable, the expectation that high performance will lead to rewards, thence to a state of satisfaction, can also serve as a motivational force that encourages high levels of productivity in the future.

CONCLUDING COMMENTS

In many respects job satisfaction is an unwieldy concept. James Taylor (1977) calls it an embarrassing ambiguity. It refers to a broad range of work experiences, it involves complicated perceptual and motivational behaviors, and its status changes from person to person and from one time interval to the next. The concept confronts the social scientist with measurement problems that are formidable, and furthermore, job satisfaction scales have not shown themselves to be highly predictive of job performance. As a consequence, it is often tempting to suggest that we narrow our attention and focus on the more specific attitudes toward particular facets of the work.

Yet in spite of the many problems, the concept has figured in literally thousands of experimental studies of work behavior. In large measure, all this activity testifies that psychologists tend to look at job satisfaction as a basic motivational process that plays a role in an individual's adjustment to virtually every phase of the job; it also can be one of the more significant rewards in an individual's life.

The job-satisfaction literature provides us with a good example of the application of behavioral research methods to a problem that is currently regarded as a socially important one. Concern with job satisfaction has been growing over the recent past, in part as a function of our general interest in matters bearing on the quality of life, in part as the result of a rapidly changing technology that is seen as a factor that has been robbing work of much of its psychological value. A main concern here is with the content of the work people do. Many think of work as a potentially rich source of psychological fulfillment, and believe that with proper knowledge we will be able to construct jobs that do meet these important objectives. Emphasis is placed on what may be called the engineering aspects of job design. Although few would deny that proper selection, placement, and training are factors of some considerable significance, it is in the performance requirements of the job, the eight-hour-a-day duties, that one finds many of the major influences contributing to job satisfaction. By restructuring the content of work, it is assumed that job satisfaction will show its most significant improvement.

The research literature indicates that measures of job satisfaction tend to correlate with a large variety of work-related and demographic variables; the magnitude of these coefficients tends to be rather low, however, and their value is dependent upon the presence or absence of other mediating variables. Job satisfaction has been shown to relate consistently with only certain aspects of employee performance. With good regularity, research has shown a relationship between job attitudes and decisions to remain or leave a job. With equally good consistency, research has revealed low or insignificant relationships between job satisfaction and productivity. Perhaps this disappointing relationship between satisfaction and productivity reflects the fact that in many employment situations, reward systems are not tied in with production be-

haviors. Within broad limits, it is often the case that the rewards of employment are not contingent on how hard or how effectively an individual works. Lawler (1966), for example, found that in seven work settings, ratings of performance quality and the amount of effort expended correlated very low with the pay workers actually receive. The availability of rewards, an important ingredient in job satisfaction, is often not perceived by workers as being related to productivity; hence, productivity and job satisfaction are often found to maintain a modest relationship with each other. In situations in which rewards are tied in with productivity, job satisfaction should correlate more highly with production levels (Cherrington, Reitz, & Scott, 1971; Kesselman, Wood, and Hagen, 1974). We need much more research on this question before we can draw any definitive conclusions. Over the years research has led us to revise the questions being asked regarding the relationship between satisfaction and performance. At one time the question raised was a general one—what is the relationship between job satisfaction and employee productivity? Now the question is, under what circumstances can we expect to find a relationship between these two variables?

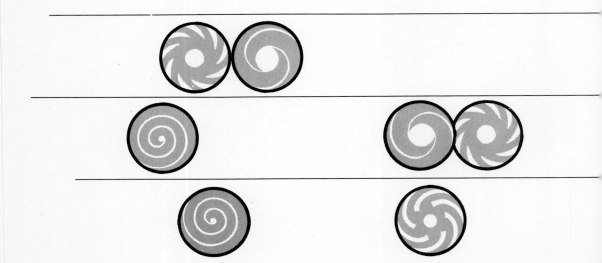

3

THE SOCIAL CONDITIONS OF WORK

9

The Social Environment of Work: Models of Social Behavior

If one were to take time to listen to workers talking about their jobs, it would become evident that work is an activity that is closely bound up with social relationships. Doing work, to one degree or another, involves interacting with other people, and oftentimes these social dimensions of the job can assume an importance to the individual that transcends the work activities themselves.

The social relations that surround work are organized according to some set of plans, and in most situations one can see many levels of social organization, beginning with interactions between two people and extending up to include the entire work enterprise itself. Over the years social scientists have been actively interested in these social structures, but until the recent past their attention has been focused largely on the simpler facets of social systems. Particular attention has been given to the immediate work group, and in a later chapter we will review some of the information that has been gathered regarding its role. Recently, however, there has been a growing interest in the more complicated social structures that are found in the work setting, and considerable progress has been made in extending our thinking to include these larger units.

Of course, as one's interests move away from the simpler social units, new problems begin to appear. Rigorous research methods are much more difficult when one is attempting to study variables that encompass an entire industrial organization. For example, the isolation and control of variables that is possible in a laboratory setting is often an impossibility in studies of this sort. Furthermore, it is sometimes difficult to identify organizational variables that have the same meaning as one moves from company to company or from one department to the next in the same organization.

In attempting to study the work organization, the social scientist must make some sort of commitment to the level of analysis that will be used. Simply put, the level of analysis refers to the size and complexity of the units that are manipulated by the research. Should the approach be one that attempts to vary factors that are properties of the organization as a whole, or should it manipulate variables associated with small social units? Does one approach the complex business organization, for example, by observing the workings of its individual departments? How much information can be gathered about the behavior of departments by observing the interactions among pairs of workers?

The answer to this question is that each level

of analysis provides us with partial information. There are tradeoffs; the more direct our approach to the study of large social units, the more difficulty is involved in constructing satisfactory measurement and experimental procedures. Observing smaller units, on the other hand, eases certain of these research problems, but leads to results that must be generalized to the organization as a whole. Recognizing these problems, social scientists have drawn on a number of theoretical approaches that serve to orient their thinking about these issues. In the present chapter an attempt will be made to present a representative cross-section of the ideas that have been developed to advance our understanding of complex social behavior.

In this chapter we will concentrate our attention on several of the theoretical models that have been developed to deal with organizational behavior. Progress in the more theoretical areas appears to have outstripped our ability to accumulate good, substantial, research information concerning the behavioral consequences of many organizational variables. Furthermore, these models will give a good picture of the kinds of ideas that are being manipulated by those who are interested in complex organizations, and will permit us to evaluate the amount of progress that has been made in their thinking.

Perhaps a good place to begin this discussion is to consider a model that describes organizational characteristics shared by a large number of business enterprises. This model refers to a bureaucratic structure, and it will be assumed that such an organizational configuration is the modal type found in the field of work. By modal is meant that which occurs most frequently, and the bureaucratic model is selected since it probably is the best description of the organizational arrangements found most often in the social structure of governmental and business concerns. Although it is recognized that all work environments are not bureaucratic, this model will introduce us to a way of thinking about organizational structures, and at the same time it will provide us with a framework of ideas that can be used in viewing work organizations.

THE BUREAUCRATIC WORK ORGANIZATION

In common usage, the term bureaucracy has been equated with red tape, administrative indifference, and organizational inefficiency. The general understanding is that the concept most accurately applies to all that is frustrating in an individual's dealings with a large and impersonal organization. Often the term is used as an explanation for why things don't work, and the word "bureaucrat" is frequently equated with mindless and rule-ridden incompetence.

The social scientist, on the other hand, uses the term to describe a set of structural characteristics found in many large and complex organizations; and although it is often the case that these organizations are beset with problems, the diagnosis and correction of such difficulties are not satisfied by labeling them bureaucratic. For the moment we must try to keep separate the structural attributes of an organization from its functional aspects, and consider only those relatively fixed patterns of intergroup relationships that will define our use of the term bureaucracy. It is essential that one give thought to the characteristics of this type of organization, because so many of our social institutions are constructed along these lines. Bureaucracy is a fundamental concept in the study of social organization; it is a beginning point for those who wish to embark on any consideration of complex organizations.

Bureaucratic Structures

Perhaps the most fundamental property of a bureaucratic work organization can be found in the high degree of compartmentalization of the work that is done. Planned specialization, the assignment of a narrow set of duties to a given department or a single position, creates a social system in which the completion of the overall work mission requires that many separate activities be integrated into a final product or service. Specialization is expressed in a social structure that has been broken up into a number of departments or offices, each of which assumes responsibility for some part of the organization's work objective. Work duties and authority are assigned to these offices and not directly to those workers who occupy a particular office. Personnel can change and the activities of an office remain unchanged. In addition, the duties and responsibilities of the department tend to remain relatively stable over time.

Contrast, for example, the relatively fixed responsibilities of an accounting section in a large corporation, or a segment on an automobile assembly line, with the changing work activities observed in a small job-shop where "everybody just pitches in and does whatever is needed." In the former instance we see what Weber (1946) refers to as fixed jurisdictional areas, while in the latter instance we find work jurisdictions rather ill defined and fluid. For the model bureaucratic organization, then, we find work being specialized and assigned to agencies and departments that have fixed jurisdictional boundaries. We must think of the *degree* of bureaucratization in terms of the extent to which the total work process has undergone a process of subdivision and specialization. To obtain a first-hand impression of the compartmentalization of activities found in this type of social organization, one need only look at the organization chart of a large government enterprise. Divisions, subsidiaries, departments, and offices all form a picture of a complex process that has been analyzed into a series of interrelated tasks (see Figure 9.1).

Hierarchy.   The bureaucratic model has a vertical dimension. In moving up this dimension, one moves among departments that possess increasing power, authority, span of control, and social prestige. This hierarchy refers to the ascending levels of management that are found in every organization. Although management authority may, to some extent, be influenced by the personal characteristics of the individual officeholder, it is the office itself that confers power to the incumbent.

Furthermore, positions on this vertical scale are assigned through a system of appointments that are made by those higher up in the organization. Exceptions are found, of course, at some levels of government agencies where Civil Service and merit-system rules apply; in many instances, however, promotion up the organizational ranks is not made on the basis of qualifying examinations or elections, but by officials who occupy positions higher in the hierarchy. Hence, to the extent that promotion carries with it attractive incentives, interpersonal relationships with those above is an important and at times dominant social influence operating within the bureaucracy.

Authority.   The nature of bureaucratic authority is a particularly interesting aspect of the system. Weber (cf. Etzioni, 1961) recognizes three broad types of authority. *Legal authority* stems from rules or regulations that are enacted to govern the affairs of an organization. Within the organization certain members are given the authority to interpret and enforce these rules by virtue of the position to which they have been assigned. *Traditional authority* refers to social positions stemming from long-standing practices and understandings, which, although not usually codified, dictate the distribution of authority. Finally, there is *charismatic authority,* which derives from the personal characteristics of the indivdual. Competency level may be considered a facet of this type of authority, where high levels of knowledge and skill command obedience of those who do not possess these attributes but who are in some fashion dependent on them. To the extent that competency is a qualification for an office that itself holds certain kinds of legal authority, we can see the close relationship that sometimes exists between charismatic and legally constituted authority.

Space does not permit a lengthy discussion of the factors that enter into each of these three types of authority. Needless to say, the sources of authority stem from a variety of factors. For the present, however, and as a first approximation to a general position, we will contend that the ultimate basis for authority in a business or industrial enterprise derives from the fact of ownership. The

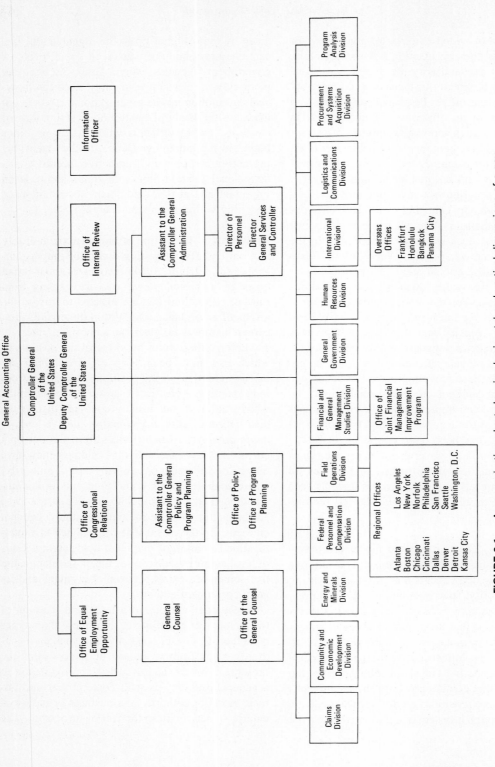

FIGURE 9.1. An organization chart showing horizontal and vertical dimensions of a government agency. Although this chart does not give a detailed breakdown of the authority (vertical) levels of the agency, it does reflect the complex degree of work specialization that is characteristic of an organization of this type.

Source: *U.S. Government Manual 1979–1980.* Office of the Federal Register, National Archives and Records Service, 1979.

authority of the officeholder, therefore, can be traced back to the general authority legally possessed by those persons or institutions who own the corporation. This point of view does not deny the existence of other sources of corporate authority; it merely places emphasis on the prerogatives and sanctions of ownership that serve as a social foundation on which are built systems of authority that operate up and down the vertical dimensions of the business firm. Some may challenge the equity of these values, but that task does not fall within our immediate jurisdiction. The question is a complicated one, and we are merely setting it aside with the general suggestion that private property and all the traditions, laws, and regulations surrounding it serve as the ultimate base for much authority that is exercised within a work setting.

Rationality. If specialization and hierarchy are thought of as the primary structural dimensions of a bureaucratic organization, then rationality may be considered its principal psychological characteristic. By rationality is meant the application of objective reasoning to the solution of organizational problems. The outcomes of this approach are sets of rules, policies, plans, and written procedures that govern the affairs of the bureaucracy in a manner that is calculated to achieve efficiency. Rules establish production standards, employment conditions, marketing procedures, jurisdictional boundaries, wage structures—the entire range of affairs that occur within the organization. Behavior is regulated by rules, and the individual case is decided on the basis of how these rules are interpreted and applied. Mastery of the rules is a condition of officeholding, and their interpretation and implementation are assigned to departments situated at all levels of the organizational hierarchy. Rational solutions to problems are sought; objective, hence impersonal, regulations are established, which identify the range of official options available to those who administer the rules. Individuals and programs are evaluated on the basis of abstract statistics that summarize, sometimes deficiently, the work that is done.

The impersonality of this system of rules lies at the heart of organizational ethics. Objective rules, administered impartially, represent one of the bureaucracy's principal claims to equity, although there are doubtless many instances where this claim may be challenged. It is within the social framework defined by these rules that the individual worker is confronted with those things that give the bureaucratic organization its peculiar psychological climate. Perhaps the most salient dimension of this climate is its impersonal nature. A single event with its individual set of particulars may often be stripped of its unique character and dealt with as it fits a set of rules that have been established to govern general categories of events. Complicating or extenuating circumstances are often ignored, since to take them into consideration would move supervisors beyond the limits of legally constituted authority, that is, rules, and involve them in decisions that could be challenged on their seemingly biased and arbitrary nature. This could call the legitimacy of the entire system into question and generate organizational stress. Hence, we see that one aspect of the bureaucratic manager's job lies in the skillful utilization of rules to meet the exigencies of organizational affairs without stressing the structure of the bureaucracy. Decisions must be based on rules; special cases and exceptions must be avoided if at all possible.

Whenever the existing rules yield solutions that are not generally acceptable or that produce internal strain, then new rules are constructed to deal with future events. Hence, the growth in a system of bureaucratic rules is in part stimulated by organizational stresses; human relationships and the conditions of work are governed by a changing system of regulations, the maintenance of which defines one of the principal duties of the manager.

Oligarchy. Even though successive layers of a complex bureaucracy possess what appears to be increasing amounts of power and authority, as a general rule real power tends to be concentrated in the hands of a relatively few individuals who occupy positions at the top of the organization. Some contend that this oligarchical distribution of power and control is an inevitable consequence of many of the things—such as organization size, social complexity, and technology—that have been identified as conditions that give rise to bureaucratic structures. Although each organization has its own unique distribution of power and authority, in each bureaucracy one typically finds that the levers of control tend to be concentrated in particular offices and usually these offices are situated at or near the top of the structure.

Presthus (1962) contends that within this oligarchical structure one may frequently find what appear to be democratic procedures, and the signs of a broad delegation of authority and power. Conferences and meetings held for the purpose of decision making give the impression that within the organization the management function has a broad base and that policy formation is a process that is widely shared. One may find, however, that in many areas of organization activity, delegation and the sharing of influence are more apparent than real, and that democratic forms and practices are manipulated to achieve a tight oligarchical control.

Control of a large organization may, in large measure, be vested in a single office, and the influence of the single, powerful officeholder may be found throughout the length and breadth of the enterprise. A case in point may be found in a study by Baumhart (1968), which surveyed over fifteen hundred businessmen regarding problems of business ethics. The study concludes that in many instances the ethical climate of a company is the "lengthened shadow" of the chief officer whose ethical standards and practices serve as a model for many who hold offices below his. Here Baumhart gives us evidence of the substantial influence that may be exerted on large organizations by a single person who holds a position of power and influence.

Regardless of the specific nature of the distribution of authority and power, however, one should recognize that within the typical bureaucratic work organization, the property of oligarchy is often an important characteristic of the social environment. Oligarchy, together with specialization, hierarchy, authority, and rationality, serves

as the central property of our bureaucratic model, and it is this model that will serve as our starting point as we continue to consider the social settings of work and worker behavior.

Contributing Conditions

There are several factors associated with the appearance of a bureaucratic social structure. Although some writers may view one or more of these as properties of the structure itself, we will consider them as factors that create the conditions within which bureaucratic structures most readily form.

Size. The first of these conditions is the size of the work organization, defined here as the number of employees on the personnel rolls. As a general rule, as the size of an organization increases, one can more clearly see the structural outlines of a bureaucracy. This is so because increasing size tends to encourage the multiplication of the departments and offices that constitute the organization. As the structure becomes more complex and specialized, there is an increased need for management control and administration. All these things are characteristic of the bureaucracy; hence we can conclude that bureaucracies tend to be an expression of organizations that are large in size.

Current information indicates that it is reasonable to view the large industrial organization as the modal environment setting within which work is carried out. For example, a survey of the 500 largest industrial organizations in the United States (*Fortune,* 1979) revealed that these corporations accounted for approximately 65 percent of all industrial employment. In other words, if we were randomly to select an individual whose job is in the industrial sector of the economy, the chances are about two in three that the job would be with one of these 500 work organizations.

What does this mean in terms of organization size? Just how large are these firms? To get some idea of this, let us consider a fictitious worker who joins the firm ranked in the middle of this group, when rank is based on number of employees. In this instance we would find that our worker has become one of almost 17,000 employees in a corporation whose total assets exceed $400,000,000 and whose sales for a single year pass the $600,000,000 figure. If our imaginary worker were to quit this job and move to the nation's largest employer, we would now find him as a single entry on an employment roll containing 840,000 names.

Hence, within this one major sector of the labor force we see that a substantial proportion of all employees carry out their job duties in organizations that hire large numbers of workers and control substantial economic resources. The size of these organizations suggests that it would be impossible for a single individual to be acquainted with all, or even a sizable proportion, of the members. As a result of this, acquaintanceship and friendship are usually confined to relatively small groups; and beyond these circles, social influences of an impersonal nature form a real and important part of the individual's work experience. One dimension of this impersonality is a set of rules that has been constructed to govern these more distant social relationships, and correlated with all this is an organizational structure that tends to be bureaucratic in form.

Technology. Technology is another factor that encourages the development of a bureaucratic organization. Often correlated with organization size, high levels of scientific and engineering technology point to work processes that for many employees are more complex. As a consequence, job duties demand from some employees higher levels of knowledge and technical skill, while at the same time the complexity of the job denies many employees a comprehensive grasp of much that enters the entire work process. Work organizations become stratified along technical lines, and at lower levels there is a tendency for work to become specialized and highly compartmentalized. Here again we have conditions that are associated with a bureaucratic structure.

Geography. If technology encourages bureaucratization of the work, so too does the geographic dispersal of employees. When we find workers in plants and divisions located in scattered parts of the country, we find a condition that requires a more elaborate coordination of work. Rules, written procedures, and policy statements must be constructed in order to integrate the efforts of separate divisions. Higher levels of administration emerge to direct the activities of these agencies, and once again we find the structural details of the bureaucratic model beginning to emerge.

Other Factors. Large size, sophisticated technology, and geographic dispersal of members all tend to create conditions that influence the degree of bureaucratization of work organizations. Doubtless, there are other factors that influence the formation of bureaucratic structures. Some have suggested that prosperity may encourage the growth of departments in an organization, since the flourishing corporation may more willingly expand into activities that under leaner times would be seen as nonessential. Then too, the growth and increasing complexity of governmental regulations may create pressures that result in the expansion of corporate departments and an increase in the employment of specialists.

Whatever the underlying conditions, however, one should recognize that a bureaucratic structure should be viewed as the result of an organization's efforts to solve problems and cope with pressures. To look at the process of bureaucratization as some form of social perversity is certainly not warranted, even though many social and psychological problems may, in fact, emerge from the bureaucracy's inability to deal effectively with the individual worker. The bureaucratic model is, above all, a fundamental form of social organization that might be thought of as the modal social setting for work. To study the characteristics of this type of social organization, therefore, provides an individual with a realistic vantage point from which to consider problems surrounding work and worker behavior.

THE ORGANIZATION AS A DYNAMIC SYSTEM

The characteristics of work bureaucracies that have just been considered should be seen as a set of highly abstract, general properties that form the framework within which the structural details of each individual work organization are found. Furthermore, one must not look at work organizations as institutions whose social structures are static and unchanging; rather, it is better to consider them as complex and dynamic social systems that are undergoing constant change. The bureaucratic model tends to lead one to ignore many of the shifting patterns of social relationships that characterize an organization's efforts to adapt to changing problems and objectives. In attempting to come to grips with its problems an organization undergoes continuing change in much the same fashion that we find individuals trying to adjust to the changing social and physical environments they encounter. For the complex organization, the forces of change may at times be traced to external affairs. At other times, however, we find that the more substantial sources of change reside within the organization in the form of power struggles, technological developments, political infighting, and the like. The organization must maintain the resiliency to meet these changing conditions brought on by both internal and external pressures, and it is this type of problem that has occupied the attention of a large number of theorists.

It would be impossible to give even glancing recognition to the many writers who have contributed to the theoretical developments in this area; in what follows, however, an attempt will be made to outline some of the more prominent theories that have been developed to account for the many aspects of organization dynamics. In doing so the only claim made is that the ideas in these models represent basic concepts that occur again and again in the theoretical literature in this area.

The Systems Approach

To deal with the bureaucracy as a social *system* requires one to pay attention to the organization as a whole rather than looking at it in terms of its individual parts. According to this approach, there are properties of every social system that are lost whenever one looks separately at the many subdivisions that make it up. It is in the *pattern of interrelationships* that exists among the individual units that certain important organizational properties are found. Power, for example, is a concept that is pertinent to any consideration of organizational activity, yet one can obtain a satisfactory impression of this social force only when one considers both ends of a relationship between people or groups. The fact that a manager issues a directive to subordinates does not, in itself, indicate power. Power can be inferred, however, from the compliance of the subordinates and from the extent to which the manager's superiors support the directive. Power is inferred not only from the nature of the action that is initiated, but also from the characteristics of the behavior of those who respond to this initiative. From this perspective, power is an attribute that is observed only in the interrelationships among the separate parts of a social system, not readily observed when one considers the individual units that are involved in this type of social interaction.

Ideas such as this occur in many areas of the behavioral sciences. For example, people report that they recognize a melody, yet find that what they hear as a tune is not dependent upon the individual musical notes, since the same melody is heard when played in a different key that utilizes a completely different set of notes. The melody, therefore, emerges as a consequence of the pattern of interrelationships that exists among the notes, not as a property of one particular set of musical elements.

The systems approach can be found in much of the theoretical work that has been done on complex organizations. The ideas associated with this point of view are very fundamental, best described as a set of basic assumptions upon which many of our theories regarding the dynamic qualities of work organizations rest. These concepts are quite abstract, referring to the most general properties of organizational activity. As a consequence, upon first being exposed to the systems approach, many may raise questions about its usefulness in dealing with real events. Bear in mind, however, that systems theory serves to establish a global framework within which the more specific aspects of organizational activity may be observed. These abstract ideas are an implicit part of many of the theories that have been developed to deal with more specific types of organizational dynamics.

Equilibrium. The idea that the organization should be viewed as a system in a state of equilibrium is another concept involved in the thinking of many organizational theorists. This line of thought holds that the organization possesses social mechanisms that are geared to maintain standardized practices and values that have evolved over time. Whenever something happens to change the established ways of doing things, these social mechanisms begin to operate in an effort to regulate change and restore conditions to their former state. The resistance to many types of change widely observed in work organizations is a reflection of these equilibrium tendencies, which many theorists see as a fundamental property of complex work organizations.

As an illustration of this concept, a research group has led a ''live-and-let-live'' existence for a number of years. Productivity has been moderately low with only a few members actively pursuing meaningful projects. Yet the group has evolved a set of practices in which no pressure is put on the nonproductive members and high status is afforded the productive ones. This situation has existed in a state of equilibrium for some time, as the productive researchers refrain from challenging the unproductive ones, and the unproductive members willingly testify to the high quality of their colleagues' research. A new member enters the group and challenges this system by accusing some researchers of inactivity. Social equilibrium has been disturbed, and the group mobilizes its energies to re-establish a cordial and secure working climate. The recalcitrant member is isolated socially and this aggravates his hostility toward the group. His complaints become more frequent and

strident, and the group undertakes an effort to convince the supervisor that pathological motives underlie these outbursts. The supervisor, although recognizing the validity of the new member's accusations, does not wish to enter into a confrontation with the entire group. As a consequence, the supervisor accepts the group's interpretation of the complaining member's behavior and begins to discourage its continuation. Isolated and insecure, the new member asks for a transfer, and the group resumes its previous practices.

Coalitions. The organization is often viewed as a series of coalitions that exist among people who maintain a network of alliances, working agreements, and shared strategies. From this perspective the firm is perceived as a system of interpersonal attractions, friendship groupings, and patterns of cooperation and competition. To understand the dynamics of organizational behavior from this point of view, one must understand the variables that bring people together into cooperating groups and competing factions. There are several models of social behavior that have been developed to deal with these issues, and the ones we will consider are those that may be extended to include the workings of large complex work organizations. From the perspective of these models, large organizations are extensions of the social systems that may be viewed within the boundaries of the smaller groups that make up the firm. Understanding the social dynamics of these smaller units, therefore, moves us closer to an understanding of the behavior of the entire organization.

Katz and Kahn's approach. We can find a useful example of the systems approach in the work of Katz and Kahn (1978) who have analyzed the systems characteristics of large organizations. To these authors, the dynamics of organizational activity are seen as a system that involves a complicated exchange of energy. Energy is defined here in terms of a broad set of influences that range from company profits, through authority and role expectations, to factors associated with the job satisfaction of the individual worker. Organizational activity consists of a series of energy exchanges that are cyclical in nature, with the organization functioning as a system in which various forms of energy inputs are acquired and transformed into units of energy outputs. Associated with this system are feedback mechanisms whereby the energy obtained from the output system is translated into new forms of energy input, which reactivates the system and causes the cycle to begin again.

The most obvious example of this system can be found in the production cycle. Here raw materials (inputs) are transformed by the production efforts of labor (input) into manufactured goods (output), the sale of which generates funds (output), which are employed to purchase more raw materials, and the cycle repeats itself.

Open and Closed Systems.   Katz and Kahn lay great emphasis on the openness of these social systems, and they make a distinction between certain kinds of closed systems that are found in the physical sciences and the open-systems ideas that are used by social scientists. In a closed system there are internal influences at work that move the system to an end point where it ceases to operate; the system tends to run down. The open system, on the other hand, does not reach this terminal point, since it acquires new sources of energy from the external environment. Communication with external sources of energy, therefore, is the basic factor that differentiates the open from the closed system, and the consequences of openness is a system that tends to maintain its activity for relatively long periods of time.

Entropy, the process that leads a closed system to its terminal stage of inaction, is a property found in all systems; as a part of all open social systems, however, there are processes that tend to counter these forces of entropy. Katz and Kahn refer to these restoring tendencies of open systems as the property of *negentropy*. A principal source of negentropy, therefore, is found in the ability of the system to transform output energies into new forms of input energies that reactivate the system, thereby initiating a new activity cycle.

Hence, Katz and Kahn see the most abstract dimensions of social organizations as cyclic systems of energy exchanges, which begin with the acquisition of energy inputs that are transformed into energy outputs that are exported to the external environment. Environmental influences react to the output and new sources of energic input are generated. As the end point is approached, the chain of events will repeat itself, triggered by input energies that have been obtained from the output. For an example from a relatively simple social system, office gossip about an event involving an employee will lose its energy (interest value) with the passage of time. Katz and Kahn would say entropy has brought the process to a terminal point. If, however, this gossip leads to a negative outburst from the employee, the communication system will be re-energized and the gossiping will continue.

Dynamic Homeostasis.   Finally, Katz and Kahn contend that in order to maintain its functional effectiveness, each organization must include a negative feedback mechanism that provides the system with information concerning things that produce deviations from desired courses of action. These negative feedback systems help maintain the organization in what Katz and Kahn call a state of *dynamic homeostasis*. By this they mean that some level of constancy is established in the process of energy exchange, such that the ratio of energy input to output tends to be maintained at a steady value. Of course the system changes, and the steady state undergoes modification, however the system may strive to maintain a controlled and orderly rate of growth and change, and at any one time the system is under the influence of the feedback systems, which resist influences that tend to disturb the stable balance of energy exchange that is characteristic of the particular organization.

We see, then, in the writings of Katz and Kahn an approach to organizations that is highly abstract; to a certain degree, however, the nature of organizational dynamics is such that more concrete models may be inappropriate. According to these authors, an organization is a social system that is not defined by physical structures, but instead is observed as a patterning of events that recur with some regularity and according to some plan. Although activities are patterned and cyclical, they are much more variable than are those one usually associates with biological and physical systems. As a consequence, organizational models must consider these properties by being highly general in their approach.

The Organization as a Political System

An interesting point of view concerning social systems has been suggested by the economist, Kenneth E. Boulding, in his discussion of the theory of the firm (1960). Boulding states that in many respects complex organizations operate in a fashion that parallels the actions of political parties and legislative bodies. For example, within the large bureaucratized work organization one typically finds such things as functions that are in competition with each other, coalitions being formed, power of one sort or another being utilized, and compromises being struck. In short, one finds patterns of interpersonal and intergroup relations that might best be described as political.

The advantages associated with viewing a work organization as a political system is as much a matter of emphasis as it is a matter of substance; and although it probably doesn't offer much in the way of new insights into the dynamics of organizational activities, one tends to see from this perspective certain significant aspects of social affairs that other points of view may overlook. For instance, this point of view lays emphasis on the competitive character of much organizational activity. Competition lies at the heart of political relationships, and it is within the day-to-day affairs of the large industrial organization that one sees a broad range of competitive relationships that operate as part of the internal and external affairs of the firm.

A major point of focus for these competitive activities is the authority system of the organization. Individuals and groups compete in order to maintain or improve relationships with those who possess authority over the affairs of the organization. With this authority goes power, and to see the organization as a political system is to see the significance of power in governing the behaviors of those who occupy leadership positions in the bureaucracy. Power refers to a person's or a group's access to sanctions, allegiances, and resources. It refers to the direct or indirect control of valued incentives. As a consequence of power, one can see the impact of a person's actions in the reaction of others. Hence, power is a social force that operates to influence behavior and intergroup activities. To view a work organization as a political system leads one to emphasize the role of the power relationships that form an important part of organizational activities.

The political perspective also leads one to place emphasis on the social mechanisms of *reciprocity*. Reciprocity implies that a give and take is required in relationships between people and groups. It recognizes that social relationships are bidirectional in that the exchanges of behavior that take place within the organization often involve costs and benefits for both parties participating in an event. Finally, *compromise* is an adjunctive dimension of reciprocity. That is to say, in the stable organization where the balance of forces is well understood, the outcome of most social activities must be represented for each party as a list of costs and gains; no one overwhelms another, and as a result the outcome leaves the system in a state that is still operative.

A political approach to organizational activity encourages one to recognize that in their own right political considerations become an important part of the life of the organization. Political activities do not pursue exclusively self-serving objectives, but there are many times when they are calculated to serve an individual's or the group's social position in the firm. One should recognize that the nature of much work is such that it generates no tangible output that can be objectively evaluated. Job performance often is evaluated solely by subjective judgments, and in situations like this, a person's status in a system of interpersonal relationships becomes a vital factor in job security.

We are now talking about a setting in which political activities assume an important role.

The Economic Model

As the last section illustrated, the social scientist often finds advantages in building theoretical models that are based on analogies. Hence, we have seen the dynamics of complex organizations viewed in terms of political processes that are analogous to those found in party and governmental organizations. Now we take up an approach to complex organizations that utilizes a marketplace analogy to deal with systems of social relationships.

We can find an interesting beginning point for this approach in the writings of George Homans (1950, 1958, 1961), who has applied what is now referred to as exchange theory to the social relationships that are found within small groups. According to Homans, interaction between persons is seen as being analogous to an exchange of goods that carry with them some value. When thought of in terms of a single pair of interacting persons, a behavioral exchange is seen as a type of psychological marketplace in which events—that is, behaviors—that have a value are interchanged in the course of two people trying to make a behavioral accommodation with one another.

According to exchange theory, a fundamental consideration governing interpersonal and intergroup relations is found in the anticipation of reward or benefit. Individuals entering a social exchange draw on the behaviors they calculate will yield the highest return. The rewards sought vary widely, some being found in the consequences of an action, others being an integral part of an activity that is engaged in for its own sake. Whichever may be the case, social behaviors of even the most casual sort are seen as efforts to secure a psychologically desirable objective. Not everything in the exchange is gain, however, since obtaining a reward often requires that a cost be incurred by both parties involved in the social interchange. As a consequence, individuals enter into social relations both in anticipation of rewards and in anticipation of costs, and the social behav-

iors that emerge from these situations represent an attempt to achieve the greatest level of reward commensurate with the costs surrounding such activity.

A simple example may be found in an instance in which an officer of an organization meets a subordinate in the hallway. The subordinate smiles and speaks in a respectful and deferential manner, thus signalling that he acknowledges the superior's higher status. Here, at this point, a social interaction is initiated with an investment by the subordinate, and this is followed by a social gain; that is, the officer returns the subordinate's greeting with a casual and friendly gesture. Authority has thus been acknowledged in an exchange that has netted the subordinate an increment in feelings of security. Both parties have invested psychological capital in the episode, both have derived an element of profit, and a balanced accommodation has been made.

Stable Social Relationships.   One interesting aspect of Homan's theory concerns the manner in which it deals with social relationships that have formed stable patterns. Recurrent social behaviors are often the result of sets of rules that impose external limits on the actions of people. There are other instances, however, in which stable patterns of behavior emerge more or less spontaneously from interaction among people. With regard to this latter form of behavior, Homans contends that stable and recurrent social conduct comes from situations in which the exchanges that take place fall within a range of profits (that is, gains minus costs) that is considered acceptable to the participants. Upon confronting the same situation, similar behaviors will again occur whenever past events lead both parties to anticipate consequences that fall within an acceptable range of profits. Under these circumstances, the exchange processes tend to work toward a state of equilibrium. Eventually, there emerge from this interchange of costs and benefits stable patterns of social activity that become recognized as aspects of an organization's structure.

Social Exchange in Complex Organizations

Blau (1964) has extended the exchange-theory model in order to deal with the social activities that are observed in complex organizations. He contends that although the social behaviors found in both simple and complex groups follow the same general principles as those presented by Homans, there is one important distinction that must be drawn between the two situations. For small groups, called microstructures, social behavior is best described in terms of the relationships that exist between individuals. On the other hand, if one considers complex organizations, called macrostructures, one finds that the most important units that determine the structure of these systems are themselves social groups. Hence with macrostructures, smaller groups, not separate individuals, make up the basic units that give the organization its structural characteristics. Furthermore, it is in the dynamics of intergroup relations that the important dimensions of organizational behavior are to be found. As a result, group consensus and shared ideas become important factors in directing the activities that occur between these groups. In other words, there are sets of standards that are generally shared by group members that serve to govern the exchanges that take place among the groups that make up the complex organization. These standards frequently concern values that enter into the assessment of the gains and losses that result when one group interacts with another. In addition, the processes of intergroup relations follow the same basic principles and they stabilize around the same general points of equilibrium as was the case when social relations considered were between pairs of individuals.

Authority.   One cannot deal with the day-to-day activities of a complex organization without giving some attention to the role of authority, for it is power and status anxiety that serve as important motivational forces governing the social behaviors that take place on many jobs. Blau adapts exchange-theory ideas to this problem of determining the factors that underlie legitimate authority, and he comes to the conclusion that authority is built on a set of *obligations* that are jointly shared by the members of the group.

Blau maintains that associated with each position of formal authority there is control over certain incentives that are valued by subordinates. The officeholder can distribute these incentives, thereby accumulating credits that operate as obligations for the favors rendered. Perquisites of one sort or another, delivered to subordinates, increase their indebtedness to the officeholder, and serve as a basis for a set of obligations that lead them to submit to the officeholder's directives. Blau argues, however, that legitimate authority does not stem from the individual obligations that exist between the officeholder and the individual subordinate. Rather, legitimate authority derives from those obligations that are assumed by the *group* of subordinates, and it develops out of those instances in which the officeholder issues behavioral credits that serve the collective interest of the group. In these instances, joint obligations are established, and over time these obligations are incorporated into a set of collectively held norms that require compliance to the leadership influence of the officeholder. These collective norms are adopted by individuals and are seen by them as their own individual standards. Then, as with other such standards of social behavior, these standards are enforced through a system of social pressures that are brought to bear on group members to encourage conformity. Hence, authority is a social influence that comes out of sets of mutually held obligations to a leader. These obligations are part of an exchange that is made with a leader who supplies the group with certain kinds of highly valued incentives.

Cooperation and Compliance Models

One doesn't have to look very closely at the things that go on in a complex organization to gain an impression of the psychological importance of authority and power. Visit the conference room where subordinates gather to report to their superiors, or listen in on conversations over coffee or at lunch, and the psychological presence of authority and power will often be in evidence. In fact, for many who work, the most compelling dimension of organizational life is found in the sets of interpersonal relationships that revolve around those who hold positions of power and authority in the organization.

Much that has been written about complex organizations deals with the nature and functions of these social influences. Power and authority are frequently defined in terms of a person's access to and control of those incentives that are valued by the members of the organization. It is in the manipulation of such things as wages, promotions, and the like that one identifies the nature and extent of power and authority and their influence over the behavior of others. Control of valued incentives implies control over the affairs of others, and one may profitably study organizational power from the vantage of this system of rewards.

On the other hand, rather than looking at power and authority in terms of the behavior of those who control the incentive system, we may obtain another perspective by considering the pattern of reactions of those toward whom authority is directed. Obviously, it would be shortsighted to ignore one or the other pole of the relationship between those who lead and those who are led. In the theories that follow, however, we will see that the emphasis is placed on the behaviors of those who comply with the actions of those who are in positions of authority. We have already considered one point of view that has dealt with aspects of this relationship. In the last section we found the exchange theorists explaining legitimate authority in terms of sets of obligations that are collectively accepted by the group. Now we will look at two theories that treat the authority system in a somewhat similar fashion.

Barnard's Cooperative Organization. The first of these two approaches is found in the work of Chester I. Barnard, whose book, *The Functions of the Executive* (1938), is viewed by many schol-

ars as an important and seminal contribution to the study of organizational dynamics. In this book, Barnard contends that the basic components of a complex organization are found in a system of communication, a set of common purposes, and in a general willingness on the part of the employees to serve these common objectives. In this latter instance, Barnard stresses the need for cooperative efforts that are directed toward organizational, as distinct from personal, goals. In the efficient and effective organization, individuals must be *willing* to participate in efforts that do not necessarily have immediate or direct implications for their own personal goals. Barnard sees this cooperative orientation requiring individuals to understand and accept the objectives of the firm, and to display in their behavior a general recognition that the health and prosperity of the firm is a condition that is essential for their own personal well-being.

Commitment to the group along with an element of self-denial are, in Barnard's mind, essential to the survival of the organization and to the welfare of its individual members. The organization is first and foremost a cooperative enterprise whose purposes and objectives are generally endorsed by its members. Barnard believes, however, that this cooperative orientation is not established or maintained apart from an individual's self-interest. On the contrary, the purposes of the organization have no compelling meaning to individuals unless they can see that the attainment of these objectives will be instrumental in ultimately reaching some of their own desired goals. A person's willingness to cooperate is the end product of a personal accounting of both the burdens and rewards connected with a given activity. According to Barnard, cooperative effort is the net effect of the positive inducements balanced against the sacrifices involved. The net satisfactions associated with a given action are compared to those afforded by the alternatives that are available, and the *decision to cooperate* in corporate activities usually occurs whenever these comparisons favor such a course of action.

Since cooperation is a keystone of the organization's activities, Barnard builds his theory of authority on subordinates' *conscious consent* to follow the leadership directives of their superiors. There can be no authority that endures over time

without there being a general willingness to follow, and this agreement to accept the directives of the leader requires that four conditions be present:

1. the subordinate can and does understand the communication coming from the authority figure,
2. the subordinate believes that the directive is not incompatible with what he believes to be the organization's objectives,

3. the subordinate accepts the directive as being consistent with his own personal objectives, and
4. the subordinate has the ability to comply with the directive. (Barnard, 1938, p. 165)

Barnard points out that there is no better-established principle of organizational authority than one that requires those in positions of leadership to refrain from issuing orders that cannot, or will not, be obeyed without question. This necessitates that leaders be aware of followership tolerance of their directives. In this regard, he postulates that within each subordinate there is a *zone of indifference* that identifies leadership directives that will be obeyed without question. Within this hypothetical range, one finds a distribution of orders that are acceptable to the subordinate, but outside this zone lie orders that are reacted to with considerable reluctance, or that are disobeyed completely. The width of this zone of indifference is primarily a function of the distribution and the sum of positive and negative incentives that are associated with the subordinate's membership in the organization. If positive inducements predominate and membership results in considerable satisfaction, the zone of indifference will be rather wide. In those instances where organizational membership involves a considerable burden, then this zone of compliance will tend to be relatively narrow.

Individual zones of indifference do, after time, become incorporated into a system of norms that is shared by the group. Furthermore, Barnard points out that among those who find advantages from their membership in the organization, there is a general norm of compliance to authority, since to ignore authority is to weaken the organization. As a consequence, groups generate social pressures that are directed at members who show resistance to the leadership directives of those who occupy positions of authority.

Barnard is rather severe on those who fail to cooperate with organizational authority:

If objective authority is flouted for arbitrary or merely temperamental reasons, if, in other words, there is a deliberate attempt to twist an organization requirement to personal advantage, rather than to safeguard a substantial personal interest, then there is a deliberate attack on the organization itself. To remain outside an organization is not necessarily to be more than not friendly or not interested. To fail in an obligation intentionally is an act of hostility. This no organization can permit; and it must respond with punitive action if it can. . . . (Barnard, 1938, p. 171)

Most members comply with the directives of the superior. To disregard these communications frequently means to accept the personal responsibility for whatever action is taken. It is often more secure to consent to the directive, thereby letting the superior retain responsibility for the success or failure of the venture. Finally, Barnard contends that those in authority must exercise care to ensure that only acceptable directives are given; hence, we see forces at work on both ends of the authority-subordinate relationship that increase the probability that the dynamics of organizational behavior are generally cooperative.

Etzioni's Model.   Bear in mind that the term, organizational dynamics, refers to the changing, day-to-day activities that take place among the people and groups who work in the organization. These dynamics can be viewed from a number of different perspectives, but at present we are considering them in terms of how individuals react to the power influences that operate within the firm. Barnard lays emphasis on willingness to cooperate in achieving the aims and objectives of the enterprise. A second model, by Etzioni (1961), deals with the various patterns of compliance behaviors that occur in response to authority and power.

Etzioni, like Barnard, sees compliance as the central property of the behaviors one observes in complex organizations, and he uses different patterns of compliance to develop a scheme whereby organizations may be classified and compared. Compliance patterns are identified on a grid that

has two dimensions (see Table 9.1). The nine cells constructed by combinations of these two dimensions identify the kind of compliance behaviors that are characteristic of different social environments.

Power. Let's begin by considering the three kinds of power that enter the scheme. Power is defined in terms of an individual's ability to induce or influence another person to carry out directives. Etzioni differentiates three types of power on the basis of the means employed to influence another person:

1. Coercive power—influence that stems from the use of threats of one sort or another
2. Remunerative power—influence that is the consequence of the control of material rewards
3. Normative power—influence based on the manipulation of awards and symbols that indicate prestige, and power based on the positive responses and support of others

Within the dynamics of a given organization, one would most likely find all three types of power being utilized; in each instance, however, a single type tends to be the dominant means of influencing members.

Involvement. Etzioni deals with organizational involvement in terms of a scale that varies as a continuum. He marks out three zones on the scale. *Alienative involvement* is negative in its character, reflecting aggression, competition and mistrust. *Moral involvement* refers to the region of highest positive commitment, and it is most usually an expression of an individual's allegiance to values and standards that serve constructive objectives. *Calculative involvement* tends to be more rational, less emotional, and it often concerns matters that serve the immediate self-interest of the member.

Etzioni uses the term involvement to refer to the psychological bond that links the person to an organization. For example, calculative involvement refers to the worker who defines membership in a firm strictly in terms of self-interest. Such things as career progress, income, recognition, and

so on, are the primary reasons for a worker's affiliation with the firm. Moral involvement, on the other hand, refers to membership that is explainable in terms of an individual's moral goals. In this case, one sees membership in the organization as a means of achieving highly constructive objectives. Alienative involvement concerns membership linkages that serve aggressive or hostile objectives.

It is possible that any type of involvement can occur in organizations that rely on any of the three types of power, and Table 9.1 represents the nine combinations of power and involvement that are possible. Each cell in the table describes a different pattern of social interaction that is characteristic of a given organization. In broad terms, each cell refers to the dominant type of social behavior found within the firm, and Etzioni refers to each type as a pattern of compliance.

Kinds of Compliance. As shown in Table 9.1, Etzioni draws a distinction between congruent and noncongruent patterns of compliance. The congruent cases are those that are found in the three

TABLE 9.1   Types of Organizational Compliance

		Kinds of Involvement		
		Alienative	Calculative	Moral
Kinds of Power	Coercive	1	2	3
	Remunerative	4	5	6
	Normative	7	8	9

Cells 1, 5, and 9 represent combinations of involvement and power that are considered to be congruent. Cells 2, 3, 4, 6, 7 and 8 represent combinations that are thought to be incongruent; hence, they occur with lower frequency.
Source: Etzioni, A. *A Comparative analysis of complex organizations.* New York: Free Press, 1961. Copyright © 1961 by The Free Press of Glencoe, Inc.

cells along the major diagonal (cells 1, 5, and 9). These are the three types of compliance behaviors one finds most frequently in large organizations. Etzioni contends that this is so because these patterns are the most effective in terms of their performance efficiency. Since organizations are under considerable pressure to operate efficiently, the three combinations of power and involvement tend to be encouraged. The six incongruent types can and do occur, and their occurrence often reflects the fact that organizations are not able to control completely the types of power that are utilized within the system, nor can they control completely the level of member involvement. The latter is especially true with members who are found in the lower levels of the organization's hierarchy. For these workers, the range of organizational rewards tends to be narrow; hence inducements for involvement are not always effective.

The Dynamic Hypothesis.   The major component of Etzioni's theory is embodied in what he calls a dynamic hypothesis. This hypothesis contends that organizations generate a considerable amount of pressure to resist the emergence of incongruent patterns of compliance and encourage types of compliance that are congruent. This implies that the means drawn on by an organization to generate power and influence determine the pattern of organizational behavior that one observes taking place within the establishment. Certain types of organizations tend to draw on one type of power, and as a consequence we find a particular congruent style of compliance behaviors operating

inside these settings (see Table 9.2 below). Another organization employs different means of generating social power, and as a result, different kinds of psychological involvement are observed.

Different types of organizations (for example, blue-collar industries, prisons, religious groups) display different patterns of organizational compliance. If an organization tends to rely on remunerative incentives to influence its members, as is the case with most work organizations, then the social forces in these settings tend to encourage calculative types of member involvement. This means that Etzioni would expect to find worker involvement, particularly among rank-and-file employees, to be of rather low intensity. Universities are prone to display patterns of compliance that are congruent with the use of normative power. Hence, the power systems that operate within a given organization create social forces that predispose organizational behaviors that are congruent with the methods used to influence people. This, according to Etzioni, is the central principle governing organizational dynamics.

Decision-Making Models

There are a number of strategies one might follow in developing a theory of organizational dynamics. One of these is to adopt a social analogy that is thought to contain many of the more important aspects of behavior that are observed operating in the complex organization. Representative of this approach are Boulding's political model and Homans's economic model. Another approach is found in the models that focus on a

TABLE 9.2   Classification of Complex Organizations According to Congruent Patterns of Compliance

Compliance Pattern

Predominantly Coercive—Alienative
  Concentration camps
  Prisons (most)
  Correctional "institutions" (large majority)
  Custodial mental hospitals
  Prisoner-of-war camps
  Relocation centers
  Coercive unions
Predominantly Remunerative—Calculative
  Blue-collar industries and blue-collar divisions in other industries
  White-collar industries and white-collar divisions in other industries (normative compliance is a secondary pattern)
  Business unions (normative compliance is a secondary pattern)
  Farmers' organizations (normative compliance is a secondary pattern)
  Peacetime military organizations (coercive compliance is a secondary pattern)
Predominantly Normative—Moral
  Religious organizations
  Ideological political organizations
  General hospitals
  Colleges and universities
  Social unions

Adapted from: Etzioni, A. *A comparative analysis of complex organizations.* New York: Free Press, 1961.

particular dimension of social behavior, contending that this behavior is the focal point around which all forms of organizational activity revolve. To account for the workings of this focal dimension, therefore, is equivalent to understanding the basic essentials of organizational behaviors. To illustrate this approach we have considered models that focus on power and authority as the dominant social process found in all organizational activities. This approach was taken by Barnard and Etzioni in models that placed emphasis on cooperation and compliance.

Simon's Administrative Man. Now we will consider an approach that focuses on the decision-making functions of management. There has been much work done on this topic, but the writings of Herbert A. Simon (1947, 1957) appear to give us the closest approximation to the conditions one might find in an ongoing work environment. Simon sees the central character of organizational

activities in terms of the decision-making role management plays in meeting their job responsibilities. In taking this approach, he draws a distinction between what he calls *economic man* and *administrative man.* These two terms refer to different kinds of decision-making situations, each one identified by the amount and type of information that is available. Economic man functions in an organizational setting in which all the alternatives that are relevant to a decision are clearly evident and well within his grasp. Furthermore, associated with each alternative solution is a set of consequences that are both clearly evident and exhaustive of all outcomes that can take place.

Some models of economic man have him dealing with situations in which the alternative solutions and their outcomes are linked together with certainty; each solution invariably leads to a specified outcome. There are also models that see the relationship between alternative solutions and consequences in probability terms. A given solution to a problem generates a certain probability that a particular outcome will occur. Simon (1957a) refers to these latter models as *risk theories*. Finally, there are models of managerial decision making that see the manager being unable to link known probabilities to each outcome. It is this type of model that one encounters most frequently in the writings of those who deal with *game theory* (Taylor, 1965). In this case, two or more parties enter into a competitive situation in which the strategy of the opponent introduces a considerable element of uncertainty to the problem that the decision maker must face.

In situations like those described above, Simon maintains that the decision maker engages in what might be described as *objective rationality*. Here economic man can clearly express a preference for the outcomes that are linked to these alternative solutions, and the decision made under these circumstances is the one that achieves some optimum set of outcomes. The solution chosen is the one that leads to the consequences that are most preferred under the circumstances.

Simon argues that decision-making models of this sort are inappropriate when used to deal with the dynamics of real-life organizational behaviors. Their most apparent deficiency is found in their requirement that the individual be aware of all alternative solutions and all of the consequences that may follow each alternative. Further, in many instances these models require that the individual be knowledgeable of the probabilities that connect solutions and outcomes. Simon sees many of the problems facing managers being so complicated that they prohibit the manager from considering, or even being aware of, many of the alternative solutions that are available. Also, there is often no way the manager can anticipate the full range of outcomes that may occur if a given solution is chosen.

Administrative man functions in this organizational world where the outlines of problems and solutions are not sharply drawn, and as a consequence we find that his behavior takes on characteristics that reflect this lack of definition. In this situation the administrator adopts different criteria

for selecting a solution to the decision-making problems he faces. For example, rather than striving for an optimum set of outcomes, the manager adopts alternative solutions until he finds one that yields an outcome that falls within a range of acceptable consequences. In other words, the process of decision making is directed toward what Simon calls, *satisficing*—that is, selecting an alternative whose consequences are satisfying, even though it may not be the best possible outcome.

Here we see the dynamics of organizational decision making being directed by a strategy that differs from the objective rationality that characterizes the economic-man model. Under these circumstances problem solving tends to follow the strategy of what Simon calls *bounded rationality*. It is here that problem solvers come to grips with fragments of complex problems, without a clear image of solutions and outcomes, adopting solutions that satisfice rather than optimize the utility of an outcome. Within this setting are boundaries that limit the rational choices that can be made. Rationality is bounded by the fact that the manager must adopt a model that is an incomplete and simplified version of the problem. March and Simon (1958) call this simplified model the manager's "definition of the situation." This term refers to how the manager perceives the problem: the elements that are considered, the elements that are ignored. When facing new problems a definition of the situation must first be constructed, and this requires a search for alternative approaches to the solution of the problem. When, however, the problem is one that has been dealt with before, much of this search activity is not necessary and previously used definitions of the situation are invoked. In these circumstances, the organization proceeds to follow a programmed response. These established procedures are called *performance programs,* and March and Simon contend that these routinized responses account for a large portion of all organizational behaviors.

Organizational structure consists, in large measure, of these performance programs. Since the major part of the problems faced by an organization come from circumstances that have occurred many times in the past, most organizational behavior involves playing out these established programs. As these problem-solving routines become stabilized and become a permanent part of the organization's routines, they take on structural properties and become an integral part of the social structure of the organization.

The Simon model is one that sees organizational structure and function emerging out of human problem-solving activities. This approach places emphasis on the ambiguities surrounding the problems that are faced, and it places the manager in a setting where uncertainty is a real part of the problem. In these circumstances, the manager is often forced to establish a view of the situation that is incomplete and simplified. This is the way the organization sees the problem, and the behaviors that follow reflect this viewpoint. Interorganizational differences in structure and dynamics reflect different definitions of the situation. Managers in one organization may use a different model of a problem situation than do managers in another company. Hence, both company-to-company differences and the internal dynamics of a single organization can be considered in terms of how problems are defined by those seeking solutions.

A Small-Group Model

The complex work organization is an intricate network of interpersonal relations. The small group plays an important role in this system, for at the center of organizational activity is a set of social behaviors that take place within and between small groups. An understanding of the actions of these small social units is essential to an understanding of the dynamics of large organizations. In attempting to explain these events, one might draw on the entire field of social psychology, but for the present we will consider the work of George Homans (1958, 1961), since it represents an important contribution to our understanding of small-group behavior.

Homans begins his analysis by identifying what he considers to be the fundamental units of social behavior, which he calls *activities, interactions,* and *sentiments.* The term activity is used to refer to the things people do. The concept of interaction refers to the patterns of association that occur among people. It deals with instances in which one person makes social contact with another; it does not, however, consider the activities that occur. The third elementary unit of social behavior, sentiments, concerns the affective dimensions of behavior. In this class of events Homans puts motivational states of all sorts, as well as emotions and attitudes. An important kind of sentiment is the liking of one person for another.

Homans contends that in observing social behavior one typically finds relationships existing among the three classes of elements. Changes taking place in one kind of element frequently are accompanied by changes in another element of social behavior. For example, whenever activities are changed, there is often a change in the pattern of interaction among the group members. A case in point may be found in the literature on automation, where changes in the methods of doing the work frequently lead to changes in the patterns of social interaction. Consider the social consequences of assembly-line work. Here modification of job activities has resulted in a considerable reduction in the number of social contacts workers have with each other (Walker & Guest, 1952; Chadwick-Jones, 1969). Changes in activities, therefore, lead to changes in interactions.

Internal and External Systems. Homans draws a distinction between what he calls internal and external social systems. The external system refers to the behaviors that enable the group to cope with the demands of its environment, while the internal system deals with those aspects of group behavior that involve the members' expressions of sentiment toward one another.

A number of hypotheses are developed to deal with the dynamics of the behaviors taking place within this internal system. For example, there is an important set that concerns the relationship between social interactions and the sentiments group members hold toward one another. Quoting from Homans (1950, p. 111–113),

1. Persons who interact frequently with one another tend to like one another.
2. If the frequency of interaction between two or more persons increases, the degree of their liking for one another will increase, and vice versa.
3. If interactions between members of a group are frequent in the external system, sentiments of liking will grow up between them, and these sentiments will lead in turn to further interactions, over and above the interactions of the external system.
4. A decrease in the frequency of interaction between the members of a group and outsiders, accompanied by an increase in the strength of their negative sentiments toward outsiders, will increase the frequency of interaction and the strength of positive sentiments among the members of the group, and vice versa.

We find in these principles, a social psychology of the small group that focuses on a general theory of interpersonal attraction. We also find a set of relationships that are reciprocal in the sense that changes in one element, interactions, produces changes in another element, sentiments. With Homans's theory, one approaches organizational behavior from a perspective that considers the feelings that develop between the members of the firm. Knowledge of the activities and interactions that occur permit one to draw inferences about the feelings people have toward one another; and in doing so, an important fact of organizational life is taken into consideration.

Social Equilibrium. Social equilibrium refers to the tendency for a group to maintain the behavior of its members within a range of acceptable conduct. Behaviors that depart from this range are met with pressures that attempt to direct actions back into an acceptable range. Often the concept of equilibrium is used to deal with the general resistance to change that is found in many groups.

The relationship between the elements of Homans's theory are seen as operating within a system of equilibrium. He contends that a social system is in equilibrium when changes that occur in one set of elements (activities, interactions, and sentiments) result in changes in the others. Not only do changes in one facet of social behavior tend to be accompanied by changes in another, but these variations sometimes operate in a compensating fashion. Hence, the amount of change in one system is related to the extent of change in the other, and the system of social behavior remains in a state of balance. Compensating changes tend to keep the group operating within a range of social behavior that the members consider to be acceptable. When these balancing mechanisms are functioning, then the group is seen functioning in a stable social system. When they do not, there is much more variety in the behavior of the group, and behavior is less predictable.

A major contribution of Homans's theory is that it encourages us to look at organizational dynamics from a broad perspective that includes not only what individuals do, but also the patterns of social interaction and the sentiments they hold for one another. The process of social equilibrium is viewed in this context and is not narrowly confined to the activities of the work group. It involves social interactions and sentiments as well. Like many theories of social behavior, Homans's work awaits considerable progress in the development of effective research strategies that will give us good experimental access to these ideas. The theory does, however, provide us with a conceptual framework that presents an interesting orientation to the study of the small groups that make up the social fabric of the complex organization.

Organization Design and the Environment

Many believe that both the structure of a complex organization and the behavior of its members are influenced by the environmental setting within which the organization functions. Furthermore, in a large, complex organization, these environmental forces do not operate uniformly across all parts of the firm. Rather, the various subdivisions of the firm are exposed to different environments, and as a result their structure will vary to reflect the different influences. Hence, as one moves from one department to another, one is likely to find variation in organizational structure, and to the extent that these structures influence behavior, one will also observe different patterns of behavior.

Ideas like these play an important role in a theoretical model that has been developed by Lawrence and Lorsch (1969, 1970). This model has been constructed from a detailed analysis of a series of case studies taken from firms doing business in several industries. Hence, although not a product of experimentation, it has been developed from observations taken from the operation of a number of large business organizations.

Lawrence and Lorsch maintain that the general environments within which business firms conduct their operations can be analyzed according to three subenvironments. For example, the *market subenvironment* is the setting within which marketing functions are carried out. Within the *scientific subenvironment* the organization's research and development subdivisions are found, and within the *technical-economic subenvironment* the firm's production operations are carried out. Each of these subenvironments may be described in terms of three dimensions, and it is variation in the pattern of these dimensions that will lead to the emergence of different organizational structures. The three dimensions are:

1. The rate with which conditions change over time
2. The degree of certainty that exists regarding information pertaining to the organization's activities
3. The time required to obtain feedback concerning the consequences of a decision

Each department of a firm is organized to cope with the influence of its own subenvironment, and these environmental influences can be classified according to the above three considerations. For example, the marketing subdivisions will organize to meet the configuration of these three dimensions as they function within the market subenvironment. The three dimensions may operate in a different fashion within the technical-economic subenvironment; and as a consequence, the production subdivisions of the firm will be organized in response to these influences.

Differentiation.   When they consider the organizational structure of a firm, Lawrence and Lorsch place emphasis on the concept of differentiation. This refers to the degree to which the organization has been broken up into departmental units—and correspondingly, the degree of specialization of function that is found. As the level of differentiation increases, there is predicted a corresponding change in the pattern of behaviors observed in the organization. For example, persons working in a highly differentiated subdivision tend to be more task-oriented than person-oriented.

They tend to deal with their work in smaller units of time, and be less involved with the overall goals of the organization. With respect to this latter consideration, Lawrence and Lorsch hypothesize that "the members of a subsystem will develop a primary concern with the goals of coping with their particular subenvironment" (Lawrence & Lorsch, 1969, p. 8). Hence, as organizational differentiation increases, members would be expected to become more involved with the specialized subsystem of the firm and lower their commitment to the organization as a whole.

Integration.   Integration is defined as the process of achieving unity among the subdivisions of the firm. Lawrence and Lorsch predict that the degree of integration required for effective organizational performance is a function of the extent to which the organization has undergone differentiation. Usually it is believed that the achievement of integration is essentially a management function. It is the principal job of the manager to coordinate the activities of the subdivisions of the firm, although Lawrence and Lorsch contend that there are other integrating systems in the firm. For example, there are a number of "voluntary" activities that occur at all levels of the plant that serve to unify the efforts of the various departments. In environments that require both a high level of differentiation and integration, management is often not able to meet the demand for coordination of subsystem activities. As a result, integrative mechanisms will voluntarily develop within the firm. Furthermore, in environments that require a high degree of integration among departments, effective organizational performance requires both a high level of structural differentiation and a high degree of task integration.

Research. Organizations operating in the same business environment are found to vary both in their organizational structure and in the effectiveness with which they conduct their affairs. Lawrence and Lorsch (1967) studied six such organizations functioning in the chemical-processing industry, where the major problem facing each was the development of new products for an industry that was constantly coping with rapid change. Measures were developed to obtain information concerning the level of differentiation and integration characteristic of each firm, and a number of indexes were developed to measure the business effectiveness of each company. Table 9.3 shows the relationships observed among differentiation, integration, and performance effectiveness. Notice that Lawrence and Lorsch's predictions were borne out with respect to the two most and the least effective organization in the group. High integration

and high differentiation in the rapidly changing, highly technical chemical-processing industry was accompanied by high levels of organizational effectiveness. Low levels of integration and differentiation, however, were found in the lowest-performing firm, although there was one low-performing organization that was highly differentiated, while low in integration.

These findings appear to support Lawrence and Lorsch's contention that the environments within which an organization functions impose certain structural and management requirements on the firm. In the case of the six companies operating in the same industry—hence, in the same business environment—high levels of organizational differentiation and managerial integration were associated with high levels of performance effectiveness. Companies that did not adapt to the requirements of their environments (for example, the low differentiation and integration organization) did not display evidence of performance effectiveness that was as high as the companies that had achieved a more satisfactory level of environmental adaptation. Hence, the Lawrence and Lorsch approach finds the influence of a particular social structure to vary as a function of situational conditions. Effective organizational performance requires an appropriate match of structure, management function, and environmental requirements, and no one organizational structure is uniformly effective across all environmental conditions.

TABLE 9.3 Organizational Differentiation, Integration, and Performance

Company	Differentiation	Integration	Performance Effectiveness
I	High	High	High
II	High	High	High
III	Low	High	Medium
IV	High	Low	Medium
V	High	Low	Low
VI	Low	Low	Low

Adapted from: Lawrence, P. R., & Lorsch, J. W. *Developing organizations.* Reading, Mass.: Addison-Wesley, 1969.

CONCLUDING COMMENTS

In this chapter we have been considering theoretical ideas that deal with the social environment of complex organizations. We have done so because it is within social structures such as these that one finds the modal social setting for work. When the question is asked, where does one find work behavior, we have answered that most typically, one finds work being carried out within a social environment that is complex and bureaucratic. Work specialization, social stratification, the impersonal aspects of rules, and the concentration of power within a relatively few offices are all social conditions that one frequently finds surrounding the duties that constitute people's jobs.

Obviously, wide variation is found among the social conditions of work, but the bureaucratic model provides a broad outline within which we may organize our approach to the study of work behavior. Furthermore, some social scientists believe that in the context of these bureaucratic organizations are found many of the important influences that significantly influence the development of the adult personality, and that underlie certain psychological problems identified with contemporary work roles. Robert Presthus (1962), for example, sees in the modern work-bureaucracy sets of psychological pressures that tend to stifle individuality and creativity, while at the same time they encourage behaviors that are conforming and lacking in genuine friendship qualities. He sees large numbers of individuals adapting to these conditions through a pattern of indifference to work, which tends to focus an individual's principal psychological investments in those areas of life that are not directly work-related.

Along a similar vein, Merton (1957) argues that the bureaucracy's need to maintain efficiency and rationality leads it to strive for a high degree of reliability and conformity in the behavior of its members. To achieve these behavioral objectives, bureaucratic organizations mobilize social pressures along with a broad range of other incentives in order to encourage sets of values and attitudes that support these conforming tendencies, many

times to the point where human variability is reduced and organizational behavior is rigid and unspontaneous. Situations arise wherein conformity to rules becomes an end in itself, and under these circumstances Gouldner (1954) maintains that workers have little incentive to perform at a level that is much beyond that which minimally satisfies the rules that govern organizational conduct.

Argyris (1957, 1964) stipulates that formal bureaucratic structures tend to establish work requirements that counter higher human motives such as needs for self-esteem and achievement. Under these circumstances, Argyris sees workers demonstrating increased submissiveness and a sense of powerlessness over those aspects of work that involve them.

There seems to be little doubt that structural factors such as organizational size (Indik, 1963, 1965), the degree of centralization, steepness of status gradations, and number of organizational levels do influence worker behavior (Porter & Lawler, 1965). The relationships that have been demonstrated with these variables have been relatively weak, however, leaving room for substantial influences that may reside in nonstructural sources. To see the bureaucratic social structure as an unequivocal source of psychological problems requires that one go beyond the available evidence. Nevertheless, one may legitimately think about problems related to organizational structures, but in doing so it may be desirable to bear in mind that some of the characteristics of a bureaucracy may well be inevitable consequences of the nature of the work, the level of technology employed, and the characteristics of the workers who carry out the job duties.

When we turn to the dynamics of behavior observed within the large organization we find a range of theoretical models that attempt to deal with these complicated events, although there is considerable variation in the approaches taken. For instance, the systems concept is a central idea in much of this thinking. In this approach the behaviors one observes among the members or small groups that make up these organizations are dealt with as if they formed a complicated network of social relationships. Forces applied to one area of this system cannot be dealt with as an event narrowly confined to one part of the organization, but must be seen as an influence affecting the entire system.

Relating to the systems approach is the concept of social equilibrium that is found in several of the models that have been considered. Here we find the notion that pressures for change tend to elicit behaviors that are directed toward maintaining some desirable and preexisting state. The maintenance of this state is a factor that enters into the directions group members will take when confronted by the forces of change. Social equilibrium, as it is most frequently conceived, is not a static condition but an inertial force that operates to hold in check pressures that would tend to disturb and disrupt the social adjustments that previously had been made by the members of a group. Hence, we should not think of the concept as a static balance of social-psychological forces, but rather as a continuing process of social adjustment with a tendency to move toward a state that has not yet been reached and that is considered to be desirable by the group. What usually emerges from this interplay of social forces is an accommodation of the past with the present, and this in turn serves as a new point of departure.

Perhaps the most persistent thread running through these models of organizational behavior is one that deals with the consequences of social action. Although the concept appears in a variety of forms, the general idea maintains that the outcomes of social action, or the anticipation of these outcomes, is a powerful factor in determining the nature and direction of behavior. Behaviors leading to psychologically rewarding consequences tend to persist and enter the individual's or group's repertoire of responses used to cope with social demands. Behaviors that exact an unacceptable cost or lead to psychologically negative consequences tend not to be used to cope with social pressures.

Since the outcomes of most social behaviors usually contain both positive and negative elements, some type of reward-cost assessment is usually seen entering into the subjective appraisal of these behavioral consequences. We find this theme running from the loosely structured system of Barnard's cooperation model to the more systematic approach of Homans and Simon. And although on the surface this idea seems both obvious and simple, it is probably safe to say that no other idea has played a more important role in psychological theorizing or has been more useful in dealing with a broad range of social and psychological phenomena. The consequences of action or the anticipation of consequences is a primary determinant of group dynamics, and group behavior tends to crystallize around actions and social relationships that yield a positive cost-reward outcome. Outcomes that tend to increase the likelihood of the recurrence of certain responses are said to be positively reinforcing, and it is through the selective presentation of reinforcers that behaviors are shaped and stabilized into enduring patterns of action.

One remaining comment regarding these models of organizational dynamics: although considerable progress has been made in the development of these social theories, at present they appear to be best able to deal with the social dynamics of small groups. In some instances, the concepts developed for small experimental groups suggest direct extensions to groups of the order of complexity that one meets in an industrial work setting. At the moment, however, we have only the broad outlines of this extension, and many problems remain to be solved before we can deal with these larger units with any degree of precision. Furthermore, associated with all these positions there are fundamental measurement problems that beg for solution. For example, the measurement of psychological costs and rewards has proven to be an extremely difficult one for the social scientist. Another concerns the fact that the extent to which an event is a cost or a reward is, in most instances, dependent upon the past experiences of the individual. It is difficult to think of a material reward, for instance, that carries with it the same reinforcing value for every individual. For example, we considered financial incentives in a previous chapter, and it was here that we ran into numerous examples that pointed to wide individual differences in the reward value connected with pay. How do we explain such variation among people? The answer is complex, but the solution lies to a great extent in the past history of the individual. To recapture the past we must either rely on memory, and this presents obvious difficulties, or be able to manipulate the present with considerable facility. This also is often difficult, particularly when our interests lie in the dynamics of an ongoing business organization that may be reluctant to accept certain kinds of experimental intrusions.

10
Organizational Communications

Complex work requires complex communications, and in large industrial enterprises one can find elaborate communication networks that give direction and organization to the work performed. Subordinates receive directives from superiors, policies are announced, an enormous variety of problems are solved, work orders processed, government regulations considered, and the grapevine fills the workplace with rumors. This is the kind of activity that characterizes the workday, and running through all of this are systems of information exchange that keep the organization and its personnel moving toward their objectives.

Although there are some important exceptions (when a worker exchanges information with a machine), communications tend to be social phenomena. They involve an exchange of behavior between people and groups, and it is in the communications process that one finds many important social relationships that are involved in the performance of work. When studying communications, therefore, one is viewing social behavior that has been analyzed according to such elements as sender, message, channel, and receiver. Hence, the study of organizational communications gives us not only information about the exchange of messages but also about the full range of social activities that make up the environment of work.

Usually there is an organized aspect to the communications that take place in a work setting. One

type, *formal communications,* is thoroughly planned and disseminated along well-established channels. Rules specify much of its content, form, and direction, as, for example, in the case of the many personnel forms, work orders, and reports that move through a company. Other communications are *informal,* involving more spontaneous social interactions generated by the immediate work situation. Of course, it is not uncommon for both types of communication to be taking place at the same time. During a planned meeting of management personnel, for instance, problem-solving messages may be tempered by informal "sociability messages" that are employed to create a climate of interpersonal warmth among the participants (Sypher, 1977). Whether, however, one observes formal or informal communications, there tends to be a form or patterning in the interpersonal and intergroup contacts that take place. As a result, we can think of the communications process in terms of the concept of structure. That is, in considering who communicates with whom, we often find that it is possible to diagram the pattern of interactions that are taking place. It is this pattern of interaction that identifies the structure of a communications system. When we find that this pattern of message exchange repeats itself and persists over time, we refer to it as a communications network.

It may be the case, for example, that when certain types of information are passed through the organization, messages are not freely exchanged among all members. Some workers may only receive messages, while others may be found both receiving and sending messages. In this instance we would say that one channel of communication is unidirectional and the other is multidirectional. In other instances certain members of a group may exercise a certain amount of control over who receives a message and the general content of the message sent. Information may flow directly between workers; in other instances information may pass through an intermediary who receives and sends messages to group members who do not communicate directly with one another. In short, we often find that the elements of a communication system—senders, receivers, and channels—form a structure that involves a number of stations (persons) and a set of channels (routes) over which communications flow. Certain basic network types have been recognized, and there has been considerable progress made in studying their operational characteristics and efficiency.

In this chapter we will consider a number of issues relating to the communications that take place in a work organization. Our first concern will be to take up some of the work that has been done to create and study communication networks in a laboratory. Not only will we consider the nature of these basic networks, but we will also look into how these systems operate to achieve efficiency in problem solving. For example, does a particular network of communications function with equal effectiveness in all kinds of work situations? Do communication systems show flexibility in the sense that they change their structure as a group acquires experience with a task or when a task changes in its complexity? What about the communications that take place between groups? We often observe that one work group is itself a part of a larger work group, and that many communication episodes taking place in large organizations involve groups that are *embedded* in other groups. Can these events be studied in a laboratory?

The study of communications has not been confined to the laboratory. Much of what we know about this complicated process has been obtained from ongoing industrial settings, and it has been here that we have collected information concerning the functioning of that fascinating informal network known as the grapevine. A veritable avalanche of messages circulate throughout a work organization, containing information about the personal lives of work associates, workers' perceptions of company politics, rumors, gossip, and insights into future plans and programs. The organization is alive with interest concerning the people who make up the work force and the political systems of work—power relationships, alliances, competitions, and conflicts. The grapevine is a dynamic channel of communication regarding these very important social relationships that enter into the psychological climate of work. In this chapter we will consider these kinds of communications, which play such an important role in the relationships between people. It is in this system that one can see the complicated skein of interpersonal relationships that serve as the social context within which work tasks are embedded.

Finally, we will take up the possible uses of communication feedback as a tool for organizational change and development. An organization is internally complex and dynamic (changing) and it exists in a larger social environment that is itself complicated and dynamic. An important job of the manager is to bring together information concerning how the organization is functioning under the changing demands resulting from market conditions, growth, government regulations, and the like. Communications about many aspects of the organization can be brought together and used as an agent for change, and formal programs using communication feedback have been set up to serve as a tool for directing and coordinating these changes. One important program of this type involves the use of employee-attitude surveys as a source of communication feedback used in organizational change and development.

Before we consider these programs and other studies of communication in ongoing work situations, we should begin by considering communication systems in their most basic structural forms. In the laboratory, conditions can be constructed that reproduce the structures of different communication networks, and by changing certain aspects of these structures we can observe their influence on the effectiveness of group performance.

LABORATORY STUDIES

Early theoretical work by Bavelas (1948, 1950) and experiments by Leavitt (1951) and Christie, Luce, and Macy (1952) have provided us with a set of concepts and procedures making it possible to bring basic communication networks into the laboratory. These networks can be set up in such a way as to simulate the communication systems that are found operating in a real-life work organization. Problems are presented to the subjects who are asked to assume the roles of various department members in a large corporation. The communications task is, therefore, a representation of the kind of information exchange that takes place at work, but in this case it is observed under the tighter controls of a laboratory.

Although there have been a number of variations on the early experimental approaches, the basic procedure has a group of subjects seated at a round table on which partitions have been constructed so that members can not see one another. In the center of the table a box, in which slots have been cut, forms the hub of the apparatus through which members communicate with each other by exchanging written messages. By opening and closing some of these slots, the experimenter can construct network structures, permitting some members to communicate with some but not other members of the network. In the figure below (Figure 10.1) we have diagrammed some of the more common networks that have been studied in the laboratory. In this figure the circles represent members of the network and the connecting lines represent the channels of communication that are available to each person. Arrows, when indicated, show the direction of information flow. When not indicated, messages flow over the channel in both directions.

In the network labeled WHEEL we have a communication system in which a central position

FIGURE 10.1 Communication Networks Used in Experimental Studies.

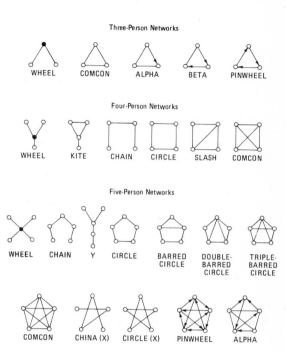

Dots represent positions, lines represent communication channels, and arrows represent one-way channels. It will be noted that the same label is used for similar networks for groups of different sizes.

Source: Shaw, M. E. Communication networks. In L. Berkowitz (Ed.), *Advances in experimental social psychology, vol. 1.* New York: Academic Press, 1964.

(black circle) can communicate directly with each other position; however, all remaining stations can communicate with each other only through this central person. In the CHAIN network, two of the positions, the ones at either end, can communicate with each other only through three intermediaries. The CHAIN, when compared with the WHEEL, is structurally less *centralized*. By this is meant that in the WHEEL network there is an individual in a strategic position, through whom much of the communication must pass. In the CHAIN no one position is as highly centralized, even though at each end there are peripheral positions that are more remote from other stations. In the COMCON network, no one position is *structurally* more central than others since every member can communicate with every other member.

When seeing such terms as WHEEL, CHAIN, and COMCON one should not conclude that one is dealing with abstractions that have little contact with reality. Actually, these networks can be found in ongoing work organizations, although as they are studied in the laboratory, they usually involve fewer members than may occur at work. For example, the WHEEL network is found in instances in which a single communication station serves as a central hub through which all other members must communicate. One instance of this arrangement can be found at a taxi service where drivers stationed in mobile units communicate with customers through a central dispatcher. A CHAIN network may be found in military and industrial organizations where messages move up and down the ranks (for example, the sergeant talks to the lieutenant who talks to the captain, and so on). The COMCON network may be found operating around the table during a conference. Here everyone has access to all others, and no one member serves as a conduit through which conversations pass. This same conference can transform into a WHEEL network under the influence of an autocratic discussion leader who discourages direct conversations among the members of the group.

Other examples could be found, but the point worth noting is that the network types studied in the laboratory may be thought of as elemental examples of the kind of interactions found when people communicate with each other in real work settings. The different kinds of communication networks are formed as the result of a number of influences, perhaps the most basic of which is that they reflect the interaction of people who are involved with common objectives. The specific structure of the network may indicate the nature of the task, authority differences, variation in knowledge or skill, company rules that specify

who communicates with whom, and friendship groupings. These networks sometimes endure over long periods of time; some others are more temporary arrangements. Within any large organization one may find a wide variety of networks, and any given worker may participate in a number of them, each of which has a different structure.

Network Structures and Communication Processes

A basic question is whether the structure of a communication network exerts a significant influence on the group interactions involved in the exchange of information (O'Reilly & Roberts, 1977). This question concerns not only the efficiency of the system but also patterns of social organization—groups that evolve when people attempt to communicate with each other. For example, what kind of leadership organization might we expect from persons who are functioning within a highly centralized communication system, like the WHEEL, as compared to a more decentralized arrangement like the CIRCLE? Then we might ask about the reports people make concerning the amount of satisfaction they experience while working within one or another of these networks. In short, we are asking whether it is reasonable to expect that there are differences in efficiency, satisfaction, and social interaction associated with the structure of a communications network.

We will consider only a few of the pioneering studies that have dealt with the basic characteristics of communication systems. In one of these studies, Bavelas (1950) reports on an experiment that involved only two network patterns, the five-person CIRCLE and CHAIN (see Figure 10.1). Subjects in these networks were each given a card containing five of a set of six possible symbols that were contained on a master list. One symbol was common to all cards. The group's task was to determine this common symbol, with members communicating with each other by passing messages back and forth according to the restrictions imposed by the structure of the network.

Perhaps the most significant finding of this study was Bavelas's demonstration that certain aspects of group behavior and performance efficiency appeared to be associated with the structure of the network over which messages were passed. For instance, more errors occurred in the CIRCLE than in the CHAIN, and there seemed to be a consistent pattern of leadership emerging from the CHAIN—the member in the central position usually emerged as the leader. There was no consistent pattern of leadership observed among people operating in the CIRCLE network.

Leavitt (1951), in a study employing a similar task with four five-person networks (CIRCLE, CHAIN, Y, and WHEEL), again reports systematic relationships between network structure and the behavior of group members. For example, as was the case with Bavelas's study, the CIRCLE network appeared to yield the highest number of errors, the CHAIN and the WHEEL produced about the same intermediate number of errors, and the Y proved to be the most accurate. Expressions of satisfaction, measured by questionnaires, appeared to be highest for the CIRCLE and lowest for the WHEEL. Hence, although the CIRCLE network seemed to generate a high number of errors, morale among the members of this network tended to be higher than that observed in the more accurate WHEEL structure.

In analyzing his data, Leavitt reported finding that the person who occupied the more central positions in the network seemed to play a dominant role in the communication process, and to some extent seemed to solve the problems with greater efficiency. Hence, Leavitt reports that some communication networks function more effectively than do others, and that there appear to be systematic differences in the communications role played by members who occupy different positions in the network structures. For instance, members who hold positions in the center of the CHAIN, WHEEL, and Y networks tend to serve as conduits through which information was passed and decisions made and sent back to the peripheral members of the group. In these positions, the members exert considerable power and leadership.

Mediating Factors. Shaw (1964) analyzed the outcome of several studies that were carried out subsequent to the early work of Bavelas and Leavitt. Although the essential character of these studies remains about the same, additional variables were incorporated into the design of these later experiments. One of the variables is the complexity of the task undertaken by a network. Table 10.1 below, taken from Shaw (1964), summarizes the results of this work. The pattern of these results seems to suggest quite clearly that the complexity of the problem is one of the variables that determine what goes on within the different networks. Look, for example, at the time required for solution and the errors committed. In both instances, although there were exceptions to the trend, the centralized systems of communication functioned more effectively when the group was involved in the solution of a relatively simple problem, whereas greater effectiveness is in evidence for the decentralized networks in those instances in which the groups were involved in the solution of a more complex problem. With good consistency, and for both simple and complex problems, subjects seem to report higher satisfaction with their experiences with the decentralized networks.

Independence and Saturation. Shaw draws on two basic concepts to explain the results of these studies. The first concept, *independence,* refers to a position's "answer getting" potential, to the degree of freedom that a person has to function within the group. The central person in the WHEEL, for example, may be found to experience a greater degree of independence than those who occupy peripheral positions, since there is available a wider range of discretionary options that result from the fact that all information funnels through that position and decisions tend to originate in that position. Peripheral positions, on the other hand, are dependent on the actions of the central member, and as a consequence they experience less independence. Shaw suggests that independence may have a greater bearing on member satisfaction than on performance; it also influences the member's willingness to perform.

TABLE 10.1　Number of Comparisons Showing Differences between Centralized (WHEEL, CHAIN, Y) and Decentralized (CIRCLE, COMCON) Networks as a Function of Task Complexity

	Simple problems[a]	Complex problems[b]	Total
Time			
Centralized faster	14	0	14
Decentralized faster	4	18	22
Messages			
Centralized sent more	0	1	1
Decentralized sent more	18	17	35
Errors			
Centralized made more	0	6	6
Decentralized made more	9	1	10
No difference	1	3	4
Satisfaction			
Centralized higher	1	1	2
Decentralized higher	7	10	17

[a]Simple problems: symbol-, number-, and color-identification tasks.
[b]Complex problems: arithmetic, word arrangement, sentence construction, and discussion problems.
Source: Shaw, M. E. Communication networks. In L. Berkowitz (Ed.), *Advances in experimental social psychology*, vol. 1. New York: Academic Press, 1964.

The second concept, *saturation,* refers to the "sum of the input and output requirements placed on a position." Two kinds of saturation are recognized: "channel saturation," the number of channels with which a position must deal, and "message unit saturation," the number of messages that pass through a position. Shaw contends that group effectiveness in a problem-solving task varies inversely with saturation. As the number of messages passing through each position increases, there is a decrease in the efficiency of the group's performance.

By employing these two concepts Shaw attempts to explain why the central network seems to function more efficiently when the task is a simple one, but tends to be less efficient when task complexity increases. He sees task complexity having little influence on independence, but a substantial influence on saturation. As task complexity increases, the demands placed on each network position tend to increase. Nowhere are these increasing demands more likely to reach or exceed a saturation point than in the central positions of a centralized network. As this occurs, the effectiveness of the entire group decreases, since these

central positions play such a vital role in the problem-solving process. In the decentralized network, on the other hand, a greater latitude of operation is available both to cope with increasing task complexity and to avoid the saturation of any one position. In this case, saturation of one position can be compensated for by shifting the overload to another position.

Organizational Implications

We see in the results of these studies principles that may be useful in dealing with communications in large work organizations. The findings suggest, for example, that it may be poor strategy to vest a heavy responsibility for communication and problem solving in a single position in the work group. This is particularly true if the centralization of communication is made fixed by sets of formal rules that prevent the system from adjusting to changing demands. Channel flexibility would appear to be a desirable objective, with a centralized and even autocratic network functioning when problems are routine and simple, but giving way to a more decentralized network when problem magnitude and complexity increase. In other words, for certain problems the supervisor may be given a central position in the development of solutions. For other more difficult problems, a broader base of employee involvement may be called on by restructuring the communication channels along more decentralized lines.

Network Changes during Problem Solving

The lines of communication established by the network structure do provide a group with some flexibility in the operation of the system. For instance, Bavelas (1950) presents diagrams that describe two of the operating alternatives that a group may adopt while solving problems within the structure of the CHAIN network. In diagram A, below, messages (solid lines) pass along the CHAIN from one end to the other while decisions (dashed lines) pass back in the reverse order. In diagram B, messages move from both ends to the central position, then decisions are sent out from this position to both ends. Hence, we see that operational possibilities are not completely fixed by a given network structure.

As a group attempts to complete a task, one might expect that the operational procedures that are adopted will tend to move toward those actions that tend to satisfy the immediate needs of the group. It would be unrealistic to believe that groups do not modify their operational procedures in order to achieve a more efficient system of communication. Either under the direct molding influence of the rewards that are generated by efficient functioning or through conscious planning activities, groups attempt to develop the communication procedures that are the most effective within the

limitations of the network structure imposed on them by sets of organizational rules.

Experiments by Guetzkow and his associates (Guetzkow and Simon, 1955; Guetzkow and Dill, 1957) have attempted to study directly the process of organizational change that takes place within a communication network as a group attempts to solve problems. In these studies, the WHEEL, CIRCLE, and COMCON (see Figure 10.1) networks were employed in problem-solving tasks that required five-man groups to find a common symbol. Each group was presented with twenty tasks, with each solution being followed by an intertrial interval of two minutes, in which the members could exchange messages concerning matters of organization and operation. It was the outcome of these organization periods that was of primary interest.

The results of these studies reveal that the three networks did differ significantly with respect to their efficiency in solving problems. As in several other studies, the WHEEL appeared to provide the most effective communications network. Differences in efficiency were attributed, however, to the fact that the networks differed with regard to how they organized during the problem-solving sessions. For example, all 15 WHEEL groups developed quite rapidly into efficient two-level hierarchies (see Figure 10.3). In this kind of organization, four members send information to the fifth, who in turn returns answers to all members. By the end of the twentieth problem, 17 of the 20 COMCON groups had organized themselves into the two-level hierarchy for the purpose of information exchange, but only 11 of these 17 used the same organization for returning solutions to the members. Finally, only 10 of 21 CIRCLE groups developed a hierarchical organization to send out answers, but of these 10, only 3 developed a hierarchical arrangement to gather information. Furthermore, those groups that did not develop a hierarchy organization tended to remain "primitive" in the sense that they did not develop much specialization in the membership. Many members continued to retain both information- and answer-sending roles, and this interfered with efficiency.

FIGURE 10.2

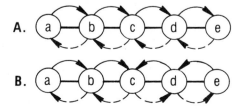

FIGURE 10.3   Patterns of Hierarchical Organization

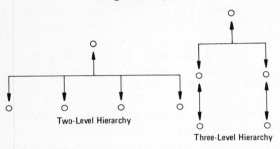

Two-Level Hierarchy

Three-Level Hierarchy

Perhaps the most interesting finding was that differences in operating effectiveness disappeared when only the network groups that had evolved hierarchical organization were compared. Recall that previous studies had indicated that the WHEEL was a more efficient network than the CIRCLE for the simple type of problems considered in the present study. The present findings would suggest, however, that the relative efficiency of a network may be a function of the fact that networks differ in the amount of difficulty people have in developing efficient operating schemes while working on a given type of problem. The CIRCLE, for instance, may appear to be less efficient than the WHEEL because CIRCLE networks have greater difficulty establishing a hierarchical organization.

Some indirect support for this hypothesis may be found in the fact that significantly more organizing messages were exchanged in the groups functioning in the CIRCLE and COMCON networks as compared to the WHEEL. However, although these networks sent many more organizing messages, they generally failed to organize effectively.

These studies suggest that the behavior significance of different communication networks may lie in the opportunities they provide group members to adapt their operating procedures to fit the requirements of the situation. The dynamic qualities of communication systems relate in part to the efforts made by a group to evolve a set of practices that will improve the effectiveness of problem solving. No matter what the nature of the structural

characteristics, groups have options for organizing their exchange of messages; they may find, however, that they face more difficulties in organizing while functioning within some networks than in others.

Organizational Implications.   An organization that installs communication systems that are difficult to change and adapt to the demands of new situations is probably operating under a handicap. Often this rigidity stems from a leadership that is unwilling to relinquish its dominant role in a communication network, since to control the passage of information is often an index of power, security, and status. Furthermore, since communication effectiveness will improve to the extent that group members have had experience with different kinds of networks, managers should give workers opportunity to play different roles in problem-solving and information-exchange situations. Perhaps what this suggests is the kind of broad-based participation that is often advocated by those who study supervisory leadership. Whatever advantages there are in democratic styles of leadership may stem from a leader's willingness to permit followers to acquire skill and experience in a variety of communication roles. What emerges from this is a more flexible and adaptable problem-solving group that shows less resistance to change and higher levels of operating efficiency.

Organizational Embeddedness.   Much of what we know about communication networks comes from the study of groups functioning in social isolation. Yet the realities of the large work organization typically find groups functioning in a social system made up of other groups; hence, members deal with communication channels that are both internal and external to their own immediate group. Recall Blau's (1964) contention that it is in intergroup relationships that the most important aspects of organizational behavior are to be found. If this be the case, then the literature on communication nets should be reexamined to determine whether our knowledge of communication in microstructures (Blau's term for isolated groups) is applicable to communication in macrostructures (Blau's term for intergroup processes).

Cohen and his associates (Cohen, Robinson, & Edwards, 1969) have given us an interesting look at communication in macrostructures in an experiment in which each group was "embedded" in a larger group. Each subgroup worked on part of a rather involved problem that was the responsibility of the larger group. As a consequence, these subgroups were required to interact with one another in order to meet the objectives of the larger organization. Subgroups were structured in the WHEEL and COMCON networks.

The results of this study indicate that in more complex organizations members of subgroups will orient themselves externally whenever internal network restrictions limit internal communication. The greater restriction found in the WHEEL, for example, appears to have encouraged members to go outside their group in order to exchange information with members of other groups. Recall that many studies of isolated groups concluded that the centralized system tended to be more efficient than the decentralized networks. Not so when Cohen et al. (1969) studied embedded groups. In this instance, the centralized networks did produce correct solutions to problems; they tended to do so, however, at the cost of efficiency. Moving outside one's subgroup required that more messages be exchanged, and this tended to reduce the efficiency of problem solution.

This study gives us a look at communication in a setting that approximates the conditions found in large industrial organizations. The information that it provides suggests that we might profitably broaden our gaze and study groups that function within a communication system that provides opportunities for individuals to move outside their immediate social groups. After all, people at work usually do have this option available to them. Consider, for instance, the grapevine that one finds in most work settings. Here we see a complex and highly efficient network of communications that plays important roles in the total communication process that goes on in an organization. One of these roles is to serve as an alternative channel whenever other networks fail to function effectively.

FIELD STUDIES OF ORGANIZATIONAL COMMUNICATIONS

Informal Communication Networks

The distinction drawn between formal and informal communication systems is often difficult to apply in a real-life work situation. Formal systems are planned in terms of the content of their messages, the channels that operate, and their purposes. Usually, they are part of the written operating rules of the organization. Scheduled meetings, production summaries, performance reports, and executive memos that circulate from office to office are but a few of the formal networks that are found in a workplace. Informal systems, on the other hand, are usually not the result of planning, nor are their channels and purposes prescribed by written documents. They can, however, sometimes function with the regularity of the formal system, and often both systems are found operating side by side. As a consequence, it is frequently impossible to separate the two.

The term "grapevine" is used to describe informal communications in order to signify both that this system branches out to encompass the entire organization, and that the information passing along its channels tends to spread with impressive efficiency. Grapevine is also a term associated with gossip, half-truths, and rumor. It is often thought of as a network where the more rigorous tests of reasonableness and reliability do not apply. Yet the research that has been done on this system indicates that these impressions are not always accurate. For example, the network is not completely spontaneous, and there is no convincing evidence that the system is more subject to error than some of the formal networks. Furthermore, the speed with which it functions has been found to vary with such things as whether information is passing up or down the hierarchy.

Davis's Study.   Davis (1953) reports an interesting investigation of a grapevine that he observed in a moderate-sized factory. His method was to trace the paths of information by asking recipients how they first learned of a piece of news. From this he could analyze the operation of this informal system and diagram how these channels worked. One of the many interesting observations Davis makes is that the major direction taken by certain kinds of information was not *within* the four major departments that made up the organization (production, sales, finance, and office), but between them. As an example, an executive in a production department with news of general interest was more likely to share it with someone in, say, the sales department than with another person in the production division. We see in this particular grapevine system the notion of group embeddedness operating in a significant fashion. Work groups do, in fact, function with other groups, and all communication options do not lie within the network established by the worker's immediate group. Many of the more active channels of communication extend beyond the immediate boundaries of the work group to involve the members of other units of the organization.

The grapevine is also capable of disseminating information at an impressively rapid rate. For instance, Davis reports that within three hours after its arrival, almost one-half of the entire management group knew of the birth of a child into the family of one of the executives. Furthermore, Davis found that information tends to be passed through this network in a reasonably selective and responsible fashion. There was observed a sense of propriety, governing who received certain kinds of information. The grapevine should not be thought of as a system that involves only indiscriminate gossip. Also, the grapevine system was found to operate mostly at the workplace, even though many managers had ample opportunity to exchange information with each other outside the plant.

It is Davis's contention that the volume of information found in the grapevine is directly correlated with the amount of activity one finds in the formal channels of communication. In fact, in many instances, the speed and efficiency of the grapevine encouraged the formal system to serve as a certifying source for the information already passed along through the unofficial channels. In all probability, there is enough distortion of information found in most grapevine systems to make one of the important roles played by the formal system "setting the record straight" regarding what is and what is not valid information passing through the informal system. To the extent that the formal system must assume this function, we can find a reason for the relationship between the volume of activity in the two channels; an active grapevine is often observed operating alongside an active formal system of communication. Some instances have been reported, however, where the level of activity in the two systems is independent (Marrett, Hage, and Aiken, 1975).

Before leaving this topic, it is interesting to note that for most pieces of information, only a few individuals function as transmitting agents; most members merely receive the information and do not pass it along the system. Davis reports on one incident in which news of a resignation was received by 81 percent of the management group, yet only 11 percent of this group participated in passing the news along. Hence, rather than a chainlike network where information is passed from one person to the next in a straight-line fashion, we see a cluster network emerging, in which a minority of transmitting individuals communicate with clusters of recipients who in turn do not pass the information along. With different items of information, however, those who previously had served as transmitters assumed the role of recipients, while former recipients took over the transmission role. In line with this, Davis reports no evidence that any one small group consistently served in the role of transmitter; rather, communication roles changed with the information that was being circulated.

Sutton and Porter's Study. Sutton and Porter (1968) have attempted to study the grapevine in a manner quite similar to Davis's approach. In this study the paths followed by nine items of information were traced as they passed through a work organization. Three types of communication roles were identified. One included persons who did not receive information about these issues 50 percent of the time; these individuals were labeled *isolates.* *Dead-enders* were people who received information and did not pass it on to others, and *liaisons* both received information and passed it on to others.

Consistent with Davis's findings, Sutton and Porter report that comparatively few workers (10 percent) served as liaison members, 33 percent served as isolates, and 57 percent were dead-enders. It is interesting to note that 100 percent of the people in supervisory positions served a liaison function. Unlike Davis's results, however, the most active channels of communication tended to be located within rather than between functional groupings. Sutton and Porter suggest that this might stem from the fact that the major portion of their sample were nonmanagement personnel who could move around the plant less freely than the exclusively management sample in the Davis study. Therefore, the results of these two studies show us that there may be important differences in the functioning of grapevine systems that operate at different levels of a complex work organization. At rank-and-file levels the grapevine may be more active among members of the same work unit, whereas at management levels the system may show considerable activity across work units.

Communication in Organizational Hierarchies

As we have just seen, a good share of the communication that goes on in a complex work organization occurs between, rather than within, groups. In many instances information channels move across groups that differ according to status and power positions in the formal organization. In passing between persons who hold different status positions, communications take on a different character, since a new set of functions is being served. We are now talking about the exchange of messages between those who lead and those who follow.

Research dealing with communication along the vertical dimension of a work organization suggests that the predominant direction of activity is downward and horizontal (Dubin & Spray, 1964). This is particularly true with the types of messages that fill the company grapevine. Here relatively little information flows upward to the executive levels of the organization, in the sense that the number of separate messages flowing upward tends to be small. Wickesberg (1968) has reported a survey concerning this network in which 91 managers and nonmanagers kept daily records of their communication activities. The results of this survey indicate that when a message deals with "scuttlebutt," there is a significant difference in the pattern of activities of managers and nonmanagers. It seems that a much higher percentage of managers pass this type of information along diagonal channels, that is, to organizational units and status levels different from their own in the organization. Nonmanagers tended to send the overwhelming portion of this type of communication along horizontal channels; they send comparatively little up or down the chain of command.

The observation that much organizational communication goes to peers and subordinates rather than upward to superiors does not mean that the higher levels are poorly informed; just the contrary. Davis (1953) in his field study of informal communication systems, reports that higher-level executives tended to have more information concerning work-day events than did even those in the formal organization structure who were closer to these happenings. Whenever something did happen at the lower levels, information tended to follow an efficient and direct line up to the highest levels of the company; then the dissemination processes started downward and horizontally, and most members of the organization received their information from this channel.

We need more information bearing on this finding of Davis's, since it may well point to an important characteristic of certain types of communication that go on in work organizations. The possibility exists that in the informal channels the upward flow of communication is quite efficient in the sense that messages get up to the top by passing rather rapidly through relatively few hands. Here the "chain of command" is short-circuited, with intermediary levels being bypassed as subordinates communicate directly with upper levels. Counting the number of messages exchanged in this channel might give the impression that this upward flow is relatively insignificant. On the way down, however, a more active process is observed, with many receiving information from those above and from peers. Here we find many messages being exchanged, but much of the activity follows the receipt of information by the upper levels of the organization who serve as initiators in the downward flow (Sutton & Porter, 1968).

Power, Prestige, and Communication.   At the present time it would be quite hazardous to conclude that the downward or horizontal channels of communication are always the more active ones in work organizations. The studies cited above merely point to this possibility existing in certain settings and with certain types of information. One must not overlook, however, the upward movement of messages in complex organizations, since there is a considerable body of evidence pointing to the psychological importance of these channels. Much industrial communication is significant to the careers of those involved in the exchange of messages, and this is nowhere more apparent than in the channels that run up and down the chain of command.

Many writers (Ackoff, 1967; O'Reilly & Roberts, 1974) have pointed to the existence of selective and distorting factors operating within the vertical dimension of an organization, and Kelley (1951) suggests that in some instances the passage of information up the organization represents a form of behavior that serves as a substitute for real upward mobility by those who desire to move up in the establishment but who have low prospects for real locomotion. Here the exchange of messages with higher levels creates the illusion of status, and this in itself may be a rewarding activity. Cohen (1958) finds that low-status members who have no chance of upward mobility send upward different types of messages than those who do have some prospects for mobility. Here the mobile group was found to send significantly longer messages than the nonmobiles, and the content of these communications dealt predominantly with work-related matters. Nonmobile persons tended to send significantly more irrelevant messages upward. In the case of the former group, therefore, we see messages that probably are constructed to enhance career objectives, while with the latter group we find in the non-task-related messages attempts to create general impressions of social intimacy. When observed within a work group, messages of this latter type are likely to be designed to create the impression of status in the eyes of members of a peer group, rather than actually moving the sender into higher levels of formal status.

There are other studies that suggest status differences may serve as a barrier to communications (Hurwitz, Zander, & Hymovitch, 1960; Barnlund & Harland, 1963), with those occupying high-status positions communicating infrequently with those below, and those below tending to send a large portion of their messages up toward their more prestigious associates. Allen and Cohen (1969) for example, report on a study that was carried out in a research and development organization, using groups of Ph.D. and non-Ph.D. technicians. Observing the flow of both technical communications and social exchanges, these authors report that the predominant flow of activity appeared to be in the upward and horizontal directions. Ph.D.'s were found to communicate quite actively among themselves; however, they infrequently discussed technical matters, or even socialized, with the non-Ph.D.'s below them. Interestingly, these non-Ph.D.'s did not reciprocate in kind, but tended to channel the bulk of their *communications and social exchanges* upward to the higher status Ph.D. groups; the members of this group scarcely ever socialized with one another. Ph.D.'s directed 94 percent of their social exchanges to other Ph.D.'s, while the non-Ph.D. group directed only 36 percent of their social interactions toward their own group.

Communication between individuals who occupy different status positions often involves attempts to manage the impression that each wishes to create in the eyes of the other. The content of the message, as well as the style with which it is delivered, is often calculated to achieve a number of objectives, only some of which are seen in the overt reasons for communicating. Under these conditions there is an increased likelihood that the accuracy of communication will decline. Distortion of communication can be costly to an organization, and there have been a number of research efforts made to study the accuracy of information exchange in networks that move across different levels of an organization.

Accuracy of Communication in Hierarchies. People who work in large organizations frequently find themselves confronted with a dilemma concerning their role in the communication system, and the problems faced are most critical when they deal with information that is passed up and down the chain of command. For instance, recognizing their responsibility to be accurate in sending information up to their superiors, subordinates are sometimes faced with the threat of passing up messages that may reflect unfavorably on their job performance (Rosen & Tesser, 1970). While coping with this threat, the lower-status person must strike a balance between sending information that assures the superior that the subordinate is reasonably competent while at the same time not offering a challenge to the superior's position. The superior, on the other hand, must learn to deal with communications in this channel in such a way as to maintain his own status while not becoming unapproachable to his followers, on whom he is dependent for accurate information (Jones, Gergen, & Jones, 1963). The manager must also learn how to filter and interpret information from below that he knows is often distorted and highly colored (Sussman, 1974).

Viewed from this perspective, the communi-

cations process becomes one of striking some sort of compromise among the many objectives and requirements of the system, and under these circumstances one may wonder how much accuracy is sacrificed in the name of career considerations. There have been numerous studies reported in the research literature dealing with the variables that influence the content and accuracy of communications as they are passed up to positions of higher power and status. Frequently in these studies the accuracy of communications is inferred from the amount of agreement that is found among superiors and subordinates concerning aspects of work. Hence, we must rely on indirect evidence to obtain a glimpse of the filtering and distortion that many associate with communication in the chain of command.

A case in point is a study by Read (1962), carried out with 104 second- and third-level managers employed in three large industrial organizations. Accuracy of upward communication was measured in terms of the degree of agreement between superior and subordinate pairs concerning the amount of difficulty encountered by the subordinate in dealing with a set of industrial problems. On the basis of the hypothesis that an individual's desires for promotion and higher status influence the accuracy of the information he passes up to his superiors, Read separated the second-level managers into two groups that differed in terms of the strength of their aspirations to improve their positions in the organization. Finally, Read obtained a measure of the subordinates' trust in their superiors' motives concerning the subordinate's careers and status in the organization, and a measure of the subordinates' perception of their superiors' influence over certain aspects of the subordinates' careers.

Read reports that subordinates who expressed the greatest aspirations for career mobility tended to be less accurate in their communications with their superiors. Here we see the role of personal motives entering into the upward channels of communication that operate in work organizations. Every message in this system involves multiple objectives, not all of which ensure the highest accuracy and efficiency in the exchange of information between positions in the chain of command. Read also reports, however, that this distortion drops considerably when subordinates have trust and confidence in the motives of their supervisors. Hence, we find that an element of trust will help to insulate upward communications from the distorting influences of career ambitions. It is only when the subordiante does not have confidence in the superior that the subordinate's motives appear to exert a distorting influence on upward communication.

Athanassiades (1971) speaks in similar terms when he discusses a study on the distortion of upward communication. He concludes that this process of distortion is a systematic one in the sense that workers *intentionally* revise the information they send up to their bosses, and in doing so they see this as being consistent with their self-interests. In addition to supporting Read's findings concerning the role that career ambitions play in distorting upward communications, Athanassiades reports that problems of distortion are greatest when the level of employee insecurity is high. Hence, career aspirations, feelings of insecurity, confidence in leadership, and doubtless other motivational factors enter into the communication processes that one finds in large work organizations.

The content of the message moving up the chain of command has also been shown to influence the accuracy of communication. Maier et al. (1961) have shown that when messages deal with the content of a subordinate's job, communication accuracy appears to be quite high. When superiors and subordinates, however, send messages relating to obstacles that interfere with the subordinates' performance, then accuracy drops off considerably. It is probably this area of interaction that holds the greater day-to-day threat for the subordinate, and the low rate of accuracy reflects, in part, the efforts of the subordinate to cope with this threat.

Comment.   This entire set of studies points to the fact that organizational communications are complicated processes influenced by a large set of variables that range from those found in the structural characteristics of a network to the motives and aspirations of the communicators. Communications that operate in places of work are complex and dynamic social-psychological systems. As such, they are influenced by a range of variables that enter into virtually all phases of human relationships. For example, the trust that is shared between people, the extent to which a person receives support from a group, and the general cohesiveness of a group are but a few of the interpersonal influences that have been found to affect the accurate and open flow of information among people (O'Reilly & Roberts, 1974; O'Keefe, Kernaghan, & Rubenstein, 1975; O'Reilly, 1977).

We have given primary emphasis to communications flowing up the organizational hierarchy, but we mustn't overlook a parallel set of filtering and distorting processes that operate in the downward direction (Davis, 1968). In fact, what we find in this whole process of organizational communication is a complicated system of social exchange, only one dimension of which is the transmission of information concerning the objective conditions of work tasks. There is evidence, for instance (Julian, 1966), that communications are sometimes used as a source of psychological currency which is exchanged for the cooperation of those who are in a subordinate position. Cooperative acts are rewarded by the superior who delivers certain types of valued information to the subordinate. Information of this sort can be used by the subordinate to enhance his status among his peers who are encouraged to interpret his possession of information as the mark of a close relationship with management.

Signaling

In the day-to-day relationships between superiors and subordinates we find behaviors reflecting what Jones, Gergen, and Jones (1963) refer to as the tactics of ingratiation. Here we are talking about intricate and sometimes rather subtle sets of signals made by superiors and subordinates that serve to communicate the fact that a party acknowledges the norms of the social system and intends to abide by the rules governing status relationships. These signals take on many forms and serve many purposes, but their role in the status system is quite interesting. For example, in the myriad of small happenings taking place during the day, patterns of deference may be observed in the relations between superiors and subordinates—seemingly insignificant instances in which one member defers to the behavior of another, and in doing so signals acknowledgement of a status difference that exists between them. These tactics of ingratiation involve such matters as who passes through a door first, who seats himself first and in what position around a table, who defers to whom whenever two people begin talking simultaneously. There are many other examples of this type of behavior that one may cite; for example, one aspect of this conduct that has been studied is the use of forms of address between persons of different status. Several studies (Brown & Ford, 1961; Slobin, Miller, & Porter, 1968) have found that a difference in status is often signaled by a person in a low status who uses both title and last name when conversing with a superior. The superior, on the other hand, uses the person's first name. In conversations with peers, however, the subordinate may, in referring to the same superior, use the first name to imply a closer relationship and hence a closer personal association.

Along similar lines, Jones, Gergen, and Jones (1963) report that high-status members of a group tended to conform less than low-status members on matters of opinion that concerned the group's task. Modesty was also called for when high-status members were encouraged to personally acknowledge their own accomplishments. Of course, the low-status members played the role of pointing out these accomplishments that the high-status member modestly dismissed. Low-status members tended to flatter themselves more on matters that were unimportant to the group's activities.

Signals go in both directions, with the superior at times communicating social intimacy and at times signaling social distance. One might think of this behavior functioning as a kind of probe whereby status relationships are tested and checked out. There are times when one of the purposes served by a manager's conduct is to provide subordinates with the opportunity to engage in behaviors that signal loyalty and deference. The meeting, called for no significant purpose, attended faithfully by subordinates who show interest and active involvement, may serve as a case in point. Here superiors may be probing the system of status differentials while the subordinates' behaviors signal their role in it.

There is great need for additional research in this area before we can arrive at a more clearly defined picture of this type of informal communication. But it is quite probable that it is in this area of organizational behavior that many of the social skills essential for upward mobility are to be found. In a later chapter the literature dealing with the movement of people up into executive positions in large industrial organizations will be considered. It will be found that social and personality skills seem to play a crucial role in shaping the career patterns of upwardly mobile executives. It is suggested here that one of the more salient dimensions of these social behaviors can be observed in the individual's mastery of this set of social signals that we have been calling tactics of ingratiation.

COMMUNICATION FEEDBACK

During the course of work, individuals and groups receive information concerning the effectiveness of their performance. This type of communication may come directly from the work, as is the case when workers become aware that they have successfully completed a unit of production; it may be fed back in the form of a company report; or a worker may receive information during a conference with a superior. No matter what its form, it is probably safe to conclude that this type of communication feedback plays an important role in almost every facet of work behavior (see Chapter 4).

Basically, feedback involves the transmission

of information that has some bearing on previous performance. This type of communication does not necessarily involve evaluation, but it often does provide information concerning the adequacy of past performance. Ilgen, Fisher, and Taylor (1979) have analyzed feedback mechanisms with regard to the basic constituents of the communications process: sender, message, and recipient, and have found that each of these elements is capable of influencing the behavioral consequences of feedback. For example, it is not just the content of the message that determines the significance of this kind of communication. Variables associated with the sender also play a role in determining whether a message exerts a significant influence on the recipient. The credibility of the sender has been found to be an important consideration, with highly credible senders tending to transmit more influential messages. Although there are probably other factors associated with the term, credibility is largely determined by the perceived expertise of the sender coupled with power over the rewards and punishments that are important to the recipient. As a general rule, the impact of a feedback message is enhanced when the sender is perceived as being a credible source of information. Hence, the mail-room clerk may not serve as a credible source of feedback when he compliments the vice-president on the good job she is doing. The behavioral impact of a similar message coming from the company president might be quite substantial.

Generally speaking, feedback, or knowledge of results as it is sometimes called, serves several basic psychological functions that have been shown to have considerable influence over the learning of new behaviors and the retention of those already acquired. This stems from the fact that information of this sort is often associated with the many systems of rewards and punishments that are found in the work setting. The salesman who receives feedback concerning the outcome of a successful road trip and the machinist who receives knowledge concerning an excessively high number of rejected units of production have both been exposed to information that has a bearing on the likelihood that they will share in some of the incentives found in the work organization. We can, therefore, think of performance feedback as serving as a type of reinforcement in the sense that this term is used by psychologists to refer to events that increase or decrease the likelihood that a given response will appear. Information feedback that points to performance that is successful will, in all probability, increase the prospects that the behaviors involved will persist in the future. Information indicating unacceptable performance will decrease the probability that the behaviors involved will reappear under similar circumstances. Hence, one function of performance feedback is to serve as information having positive or negative reinforcing properties.

Along similar lines, knowledge of results serves to provide workers with information that gives direction to their behavior. Positive or negative results, when fed back to employees, inform them whether it is advisable to persist in a given set of responses or to seek new behaviors that might yield more desirable outcomes. Here we see the cognitive aspects of feedback, in the sense that this information system is used as an aid in the selection of behaviors that are employed to achieve a certain work objective. Vroom (1964) refers to this as the cue function of performance feedback.

Finally, McGehee and Thayer (1961) maintain that knowledge of results plays an important role in motivating the worker. Citing a program involved with the training of life insurance salesmen in how to conduct an interview, these authors contend that trainees receiving knowledge of the results of their interviewing efforts displayed a general picture of higher motivation than did trainees who received no such feedback. Likert (1961) and Bass (1966) also recognize the motivational consequences of this type of communication, as does Vroom (1964) who cites a number of early laboratory studies that indicate heightened performance under feedback in tasks on which there were limited opportunities for new learning. The fact that subjects had overlearned the task suggests that the heightened performance associated with knowledge of results points to heightened motivational states.

Feedback and Social Behaviors. As might be expected, communications concerning the effectiveness of work performance have been shown to influence a variety of social behaviors. For example, when the supervisor informs subordinates that their work has been below standard this message affects not only future performance but also supervisor-subordinate relationships. A salesperson's status in the group changes when the yearly sales figures are posted at the office. Management's announcement that an engineering department has been recognized for outstanding performance increases the competition this department receives from other engineering groups in the firm.

Feedback messages impact not only on production activities, but also serve to influence the social relations that occur at work. Karabenick and Meisels (1972) report that individuals were observed standing at a greater distance from the members of their group following messages indicating failing performance. Butler and Jaffee (1974) cite evidence indicating that the content of leaders' verbal behavior varies as a function of the feedback they receive regarding their own performance. Finally, Leavitt and Mueller (1951), observing subjects operating in a communications task, report that unrestricted feedback improves the accuracy of the interpersonal communications that take place within a group.

This latter finding illustrates an important point about the communications process: the effectiveness of communications can change as a group acquires more experience with a task. Furthermore, abundant feedback concerning the effectiveness of job performance can work to improve the communication process itself. Leavitt and Mueller (1951) suggest that unrestricted feedback permits the members of a group to learn a mutual language that aids in their efforts to exchange information and ideas. With feedback, group members seem to develop more efficient means of communicating with each other. As a consequence, one sees improvement in the general level of group performance. Along similar lines, Pryer and Bass (1959) maintain that another possible consequence of feedback is that it improves a group's approach to

problem solving. Group members will tend to adopt those problem-solving strategies resulting in positive feedback, so apart from learning the content of a task, groups guided by feedback systems can learn to employ the most effective approaches to a task. One aspect of this might involve the identification of group members who are the most effective in their performance. Feedback concerning the performance of individual group members could well result in a group delegating more power to those who are best able to cope with the problem. In doing so, the group will find that it has significantly improved its effectiveness. Hence, feedback in these instances involves a group learning how to learn.

So we see that the communication of knowledge of the consequences of performance is a factor that has been shown to operate in shaping behavior in abroad range of social situations. In addition to training performance and production rates, feedback messages can influence social distance, leadership behavior, and a host of other social activities that surround the work that is done in an organization. Communication is a complex process that is learned by both individuals and groups; and like most other complicated activities, the learning of communication skills is aided by the presence of feedback mechanisms that transmit information regarding the effectiveness of performance.

Survey Feedback and Organizational Change

It might be of interest to look at how some of these feedback concepts have been extended to deal with efforts to exert influence on the activities not of an individual, but on the general pattern of performance that one finds in large organizations. In doing so, we will be looking into a rather general process called organizational intervention, which refers to any of a large variety of efforts to enter an ongoing organization with the purpose of offering help (Argyris, 1970). As a central ingredient of this intervention, there is an attempt to collect valid information that is used to give direction and impetus to changes that might take place. Those involved in these activities are frequently called change agents.

A change agent, or interventionist, serves an important role by assembling information and placing it before the members of an organization in such a form that they can use it in planning changes that eventually might be introduced. This interventionist is often an outside expert, but at times one may find a member of the organization serving in this capacity. Argyris (1970) points out that change is not the primary objective of the interventionist, but rather his goal is to put the members of the organization in a position in which they can make decisions regarding future courses of action. In this context then, a major aspect of the interventionist's responsibility is found in the development of valid information and the feedback of this information to the members of the organization.

In considering organizational intervention one must not lose sight of the fact that these efforts involve a variety of communication procedures used to bring about change or improve the quality of decision making in the firm. In a large business organization problems often arise out of activities that extend beyond the limits of the communication channels available to any one division. As a consequence, every unit in the entire organization may be functioning with only partial information bearing on the nature and causes of these difficulties. In this setting the organizational interventionist attempts to obtain information that arches the entire social system, and in feeding this information back to its members, may be giving them a view of the problem that is more complete than that previously available. The foundation of these procedures is a communication system that assembles and disseminates information for the use of those who are making decisions or solving problems. In drawing on the services of the interventionist, therefore, the organization is often opening up a new channel of communication that is global in its scope and capable of carrying messages that normally do not move through the channels that already exist. Being new routes for information, the channels created by the organizational interventionist may also be comparatively free from the kind of distortion that was discussed in previous sections of this chapter.

One source of information that has received considerable attention in connection with this process of organizational development is the survey of the attitudes and opinions of the members of a work group. Here, under standardized procedures, a series of carefully constructed questionnaire items are administered to the members of the organization, and the information obtained from their responses serves as one basis for planning the changes that are introduced in the work situation.

Dimensions of Survey Feedback

Actually, we may think of the process of survey feedback as involving three types of activities (Miles et al., 1969). As a first step, data are generated by scales that have been developed to tap activities found within the system under observation. It is generally recommended that members of the organization contribute to the development of the survey instrument. The survey usually deals with the participants' perceptions of the events and situations that are found in the work setting. For example, organization members could be asked for their views concerning the nature of the problems besetting the firm, and the possible solutions that might be applied to the problem areas.

As a second step in this process of survey feedback, the data are tabulated for each individual work group and for the combinations of groups that make up the various functional units of the organization. Data summaries are also presented for the organization as a whole. Miles et al. (1969) talk about "work families," that is, groups reporting to a common supervisor. Bowers and Franklin (1972) talk about a "waterfall" pattern of communication in which feedback is presented in some detail to higher-authority groups before moving down to groups lower in the organizational hierarchy. Obviously, each situation may recommend a different pattern of communication; the process typically begins, however, with a consideration of the tabulated results of the questionnaire. In the setting of a meeting or series of group meetings group members draw heavily on their own experiences, norms, and understandings to deal with the information summaries that are developed from the survey data.

The third phase of the feedback system is what Miles et al. (1969) refer to as processes analysis. Here, during the interaction that takes place among organization members, there begin to develop the complex processes of problem solving and decision making. Guided by the data, which many times focus attention of the participants on certain aspects of a problem (Neff, 1965), there appears a growing commitment to seek new solutions to problems through efforts to develop the organization so that the modified social system can better deal with the difficulties it confronts.

There is no narrow prescription that an organization may follow in attempting to use information systems to deal with the problems of change; each situation requires a certain amount of improvisation so that the unique needs of the organization can be met. The systematic use of survey feedback procedures has, however, been shown to have considerable influence in efforts to improve the effectiveness of complex work organizations, and the industrial survey should be thought of as an important component of the communication system that operates within the firm.

The Inter-Company Longitudinal Study

Work done at the University of Michigan's Institute for Social Research (Bowers, 1973) gives us some useful information concerning the effects of survey feedback on the process of organizational development. This project, called the Inter-Company Longitudinal Study, which involved over 14,000 employees in 23 organizations representing a broad variety of industrial enterprises, provides us with data bearing on the effectiveness of survey feedback. The project will also give us further insight into several techniques of organizational intervention, since one aspect of the study involved a comparison among intervention methods.

The basic question raised by this project was

whether several intervention techniques were differentially effective in producing changes in organizational functioning. The plan for research involved a before-and-after design. In each of 23 organizations a questionnaire was administered on two occasions, separated, in most instances, by an interval of one year. During the period between the two testings, intervention procedures were employed with members of the organization. Before-and-after comparisons of questionnaire responses gave information concerning the effects of the intervention procedure, and comparison across organizations exposed to different intervention techniques gave information concerning their relative effectiveness as change-inducing procedures.

Intervention Techniques. Let's consider the intervention techniques studied before we take up the areas measured by the items of the questionnaire. We have already indicated that survey feedback represented one of the developmental procedures investigated. Within each company in which survey feedback was employed as the primary source of intervention, supervisors received tabulations of the questionnaire data obtained from their own subordinates along with materials that assisted them in the interpretation of this information. A technical expert consulted with each supervisor regarding the information and arranged a time for a meeting in which subordinates could be informed of the results and meaning of the survey procedure.

A second intervention procedure, called *interpersonal process consultation,* involves the change agent in an attempt to develop within the work group a capacity for constructing and carrying out their own program for change. The focus here is on the process of change, and efforts are taken by the interventionist to encourage the group to develop procedures that will serve them as the vehicle for change.

A third type of intervention studied, called *task process consultation,* deals with task objectives and the interpersonal relations that are associated with them. Here the change agent consults with supervisory personnel concerning group objectives

TABLE 10.2   Summary of Content and Reliability of 16 Indexes of
The Survey of Organizations Questionnaire

Area-Measure	Description	Number of Items	Internal Consistency Reliability Coefficient
Organizational Climate			
Human Resources Primacy	Whether the climate indicates that people, their talents, skills, and motivation are considered to be one of the organization's most important assets.	3	.80
Communication Flow	Whether information flows effectively upward, downward, and laterally in the organization.	3	.78
Motivational Climate	Whether conditions and relationships in the environment are generally encouraging or discouraging to effective work.	3	.80
Decision-Making Practices	How decisions are made in the organization: whether they are made effectively, at the right levels, and based upon all the available information.	4	.79
Technological Readiness	Whether the equipment and resources are up to date, efficient, and well maintained.	2	.58
Lower-Level Influence	Whether lowest-level supervisors and employees feel they have influence on what goes on in their department.	2	.70
Managerial Leadership			
Support	Behavior toward subordinates that lets them know they are worthwhile persons doing useful work.	3	.94
Interaction Facilitation	Team building, behavior that encourages subordinates to develop close, cooperative working relationships with one another.	2	.89
Goal Emphasis	Behavior that stimulates a contagious enthusiasm for doing a good job (*not* pressure).	2	.85
Work Facilitation	Behavior that removes roadblocks to doing a good job.	3	.88
Peer Leadership			
Support	Behavior by subordinates toward one another that enhances their mutual feeling of being worthwhile persons doing useful work.	3	.87
Interaction Facilitation	Behavior by subordinates toward one another that encourages the development of close, cooperative working relationships.	3	.90

TABLE 10.2 (*Continued*)

Area-Measure	Description	Number of Items	Internal Consistency Reliability Coefficient
Goal Emphasis	Behavior by subordinates toward one another that stimulates a mutually contagious enthusiasm for doing a good job.	2	.70
Work Facilitation	Behavior that is mutually helpful; helping each other remove roadblocks to doing a good job.	3	.89
Group Process	How the group functions; does it plan and coordinate its efforts, make decisions and solve problems, know how to do its job, share information; is it motivated to meet its objectives, is it adaptable, is there confidence and trust among its members?	7	.94
Satisfaction	Whether employees are satisfied with economic and related rewards, adequacy of their immediate supervisor, effectiveness of the organization, compatibility with fellow employees, present and future progress within the organization, and their job as a whole.	7	.87

Source: Bowers, D. G. OD techniques and their results in 23 organizations: The Michigan ICL study. *Journal of Applied Behavioral Science*, 1973, *9*, 21–43. Copyright 1973, NTL Institute, reprinted by permission.

and future courses of action. Planning focuses on end points and the routes group members may adopt in order to achieve these objectives.

A fourth intervention procedure involved in the project consisted of a series of *laboratory training* exercises. Here groups were brought together, usually at a site removed from the workplace, and put through what might be called an interpersonal relations laboratory. Discussion periods, problem-solving exercises, and the like were carried out, with the principal focus on the social and emotional aspects of group interaction.

Finally, more for control purposes than anything else, a data handbook procedure was followed in a few groups. In these instances, questionnaire results were simply tabulated and returned to supervisors with no attempt to encourage groups to come together in order to discuss these procedures and results. Further, in a few ad-

ditional organizations, there was nothing done that could be described as a true intervention procedure.

The Questionnaire. Before turning to the results of this study, we should look at the questionnaire that served as the measure of organizational functioning. This instrument, called the *Survey of Organizations* questionnaire, had been developed over a number of years and as the result of several studies (Taylor & Bowers, 1972). The instrument yields 16 indexes, each reflecting a different aspect of organizational activity. Statistical analyses of these scores suggested that the 16 measures appeared to cluster together to provide information on five major aspects of organizational activity. Table 10.2, reproduced from Bowers (1973), describes the 16 indexes that are arranged in the five dimensions. Bowers contends that scores on these

16 indexes may be interpreted as indicating levels of organizational effectiveness, and it was the purpose of this series of studies to determine whether significant changes in these scores could be associated with the methods of organizational intervention that were carried out in the 23 organizations that participated in the project.

The effectiveness with which these various intervention procedures produced changes in organizational effectiveness was considered in terms of the organizational system as a whole, and in terms of what the Michigan group calls "capstone groups," the groups at the upper echelons of the management hierarchy. Analysis of before-and-after scores on the *Survey of Organizations* revealed that without question, survey feedback appeared to be the most influential means of improving the functional effectiveness of organizations. Of the 16 separate indexes on the questionnaire, 11 showed significant improvement for the whole system, following the initiation of the feedback procedures. Furthermore, for both the capstone groups and the system as a whole, none of the measures taken showed negative changes after feedback procedures were introduced.

This was not the case for all methods of intervention, however, since a substantial number of negative changes were observed in conjunction with the laboratory training programs. Here, after introducing these laboratory exercises, there were significant negative changes noted in the organizational climate for both the capstone groups and the organization as a whole. In addition, at the level of managerial and peer-group leadership there was observed a decline in the degree to which individuals supported each other while functioning in the work setting. Also, after this type of intervention there was observed a significant decline in measured job satisfaction in the system as a whole. Finally, there were some positive changes observed in connection with the use of laboratory training intervention techniques. There seemed to be, for example, an improvement in the planning and decision-making activities of groups at all levels, and motivation to meet objectives seemed to increase after this type of intervention.

Interpersonal process consultation presented a generally positive impression as an intervention procedure, but the impact of these procedures was not quite as clear as that associated with the communications feedback. Positive changes here tended to be found in the managerial and peer-group leadership areas. Finally, task process consultation showed five negative changes for the whole system, while registering two positive changes for the capstone groups; negative changes were found in the area of organizational climate for the system as a whole.

While admitting that we have given only a sketchy outline of a rather involved research project, there are still several general conclusions that may be drawn from the results of this study. First of all, it appears that planned efforts to improve the effectiveness of complex work organizations can succeed in achieving positive gains. Although not all intervention procedures would appear to be equally effective, it is in the company's communication system that we find what seems to be a promising approach to organizational development. In this regard, the Michigan studies point quite clearly to some sort of communication feedback system in which the perceptions, attitudes, and beliefs of organization members are surveyed, analyzed, and used as a basis for organizational development. Furthermore, of the intervention procedures considered, feedback systems appeared to be those most closely associated with substantial improvements in the organizational climate of work. By this is meant that survey-feedback procedures seemed to be linked with improvements in such things as motivational climate, decision-making practices, human relations awareness, and other factors that enter into the social environment in which work groups function. In an earlier study Baumgartel (1959) came to a similar conclusion in evaluating a feedback program that had been installed in an electric utility company.

Finally, we can see from the results of the Michigan studies that it is quite possible for intervention procedures to be associated with organizational changes that are not desired. Task process consultation, for example, was found to be linked to a reduction in the emphasis placed on human relations in the workplace. Consequently, one must exercise caution in attempting to intervene in the ongoing affairs of a work organization. But once having said this, there is still reason for considerable optimism for those who deal with the constructive development of work environments. No detailed directions are presently available, but when dealing with problems of organizational development, a change agent would be wise to look to the communication system as an area of activity that could have a constructive influence on change within the organization, and although it is not without risks (Brumback, 1972; Connolly & Miklausich, 1978), survey-feedback procedures might be a good place to begin a program of organizational development.

One final comment might be made before bringing this topic to a close. This is that organizational intervention and development may be viewed in ways other than from a communications perspective. Organizational development refers to a large set of procedures that may be drawn on to deal with a variety of management problems. Efforts to modify the structural dimensions of the firm, the development of new problem-solving mechanisms, setting up organizational objectives, and evaluation procedures are all important parts of this general area. Each involves a complex set of planning, information-gathering, and decision-making activities, but at the foundation of the system lie the fundamental communication processes that are characteristic of all social systems. Thinking of organizational development in terms of communication systems is, therefore, a realistic way of approaching these complicated management activities.

CONCLUDING COMMENTS

Little goes on in a work setting that does not involve the communication process in one form or another. As a consequence, the material presented in this chapter might best be thought of as an important component that runs through most, if not all, that takes place during the workday. Ranging from the reams of forms and reports that circulate throughout a large organization to the feedback workers receive from their jobs as they move through one cycle of work, the study of organizational behavior requires that one consider the complex systems of information exchange that operate on the job.

Our review of research has pointed to a number of important concepts that have been found useful in dealing with communciations behavior. For example, research results indicate that the structure of a communications network is an important factor in determining how it functions. The nature and number of channels, whether the network is centralized or decentralized, the extent to which positions are independent, and the extent to which channels are saturated with messages, all have been shown to contribute to the functioning of these systems. In addition, task-related factors have been shown to influence the communications system by playing a role in determining how these structural properties affect the exchange of messages. Complex tasks, for instance, seem to require a network that is decentralized in its structure, while routine and relatively simple tasks seem to flourish when carried out in a centralized structure.

Studies of communication in groups embedded in larger organizations have widened our view of information exchange systems. Groups functioning within larger groups have options available to them that are not present in the traditional experiments that study communication in isolated groups. Network restrictions encountered in their own immediate work groups often lead workers to plug in to channels that extend outside to other groups in the organization. What we have learned about the company grapevine may illustrate this point. Here we found that much of the information that passes through this system tends to cut across work-group lines. Whatever the reason for this, it is clear from the research that in the informal network of message exchange, intergroup communications channels are active and important aspects of organizational life.

In a similar vein, we have considered the channels of communication that pass up and down the chain of command. Here we found that when dealing with "scuttlebutt," the most active channels seem to run in a horizontal and downward direction. When operating in an organization in which there is a centralized power structure, however, and with information that is technical in nature, upward channels may become quite active.

Finally, we have seen how the communication system can serve as an influential source of reinforcement in shaping and maintaining worker behavior. The feedback of information concerning performance effectiveness has been shown to in-fluence the behavior of individuals, work groups, and entire organizations. Along this line, research has demonstrated that a survey of workers' attitudes and beliefs can, when fed back in an appropriate fashion, serve as a useful tool in efforts to introduce change in the work organization.

The broad scope of this topic prevents us from making any sweeping conclusions regarding the communications process. Much work remains to be done before a comprehensive picture can be drawn. In carrying out this work we will be making a significant contribution to our understanding of individual and organizational behavior.

11
The Work Group

As a general rule, group membership is a necessary condition of work, and it is within the work group that one finds many of the important influences that contribute to the behavior of the individual worker. Actually, a job requires the worker to assume a role in a number of interrelated groups. Company, division, section, department, and the immediate work crew all have the worker's name on their rosters, and each presents a set of conditions and demands to which the worker must react. There are times when these multiple memberships lead to problems; in most instances, however, these groups help to regulate the workday so that it proceeds in an orderly fashion.

If one observes people at work, one finds that there are many aspects of the daily routine that are shared by all the members of a work group. At the beginning of each morning workers can often predict with considerable accuracy not only the kind of work task they will perform but also many of their social interactions and nonwork activities. Not only do the job and work rules contribute to the orderliness and regularity of the workday, but it is from the work group itself that much of this routine arises. People interact, and from these relationships emerge ways of doing things that become established parts of the workday, and in large measure the extent to which individuals are liked, trusted, and supported by their fellow workers is a function of the extent to which they adopt these group practices.

There are many social functions served by the work group apart from those directly related to getting the work done. Obviously, social contact is an important part of work, and within the work group are found many of the more significant associations and friendships that enter into an individual's adult life. Actually, we should differentiate the two social groupings found at work that Warr and Wall (1975) call *task groups* and *sentient groups*. A task group is a collection of people who are brought together by the demands of the work task. The roles assumed by the members are often a direct reflection of the different facets of the job to be done. Sometimes the task group is referred to as a *formal group*.

A sentient group usually forms around nonwork activities, and its membership is an expression of people choosing one another on the basis of the feelings they have toward each other. Different roles emerge as the result of one individual's needs and abilities interacting with the needs and abilities of another. As a result, the structure and activities of these groups depends on the particular set of people who constitute its members. The structure and activities of a task group, on the other hand, is a reflection of the work that is being done. Members may leave, others may enter, and the basic social dimensions of the group remain relatively unchanged, since they are linked to the characteristics of the job duties.

Every worker maintains membership in both task and sentient groups, and within each we find another major social function being carried out. This is the development of standards of performance and deportment that govern the worker's behavior. At times the standards held by sentient and task groups are compatible with each other; at times they are in conflict, and this situation has generated a large amount of research activity that has appeared in the experimental literature.

In the present chapter we will consider three aspects of the work group that have received considerable attention in the research literature. The first concerns the development and maintenance of group standards that govern worker conduct and productivity. In dealing with this topic, special attention will be given to the operation of these standards as they regulate the level and style of productivity that is characteristic of the work group.

A second topic deals with some of the factors that determine the degree of influence a group exerts on its members. Generally speaking, it is both the structure of the group and the personality and background of its individual members that are the principal factors underlying the level of group influence. Finally, the third topic involves the concept of social deviance. Although one may find widespread conformity to group standards, it is not unlikely that a work group will contain members whose behavior deviates from the established rules of conduct. In some instances a work group will tolerate departures from their standards; in other instances, the deviant will come under strong group pressures. The present chapter will consider the conditions under which group tolerance and rejection occur.

Basically, the chapter will attempt to study the role of the work group in establishing the conditions under which people work. The group is an important source of support and security for the individual; for management it is a force that must be reckoned with, since it exerts a significant influence on its members. Effective personnel management requires knowledge of both individual and group, and it is the relationship between the two that will be the principal concern of this chapter.

WORK-GROUP NORMS

The concept of group norm was first introduced when we considered theories of organizational behavior. Recall the discussion of Homans's social interaction model, where a group norm was de-

fined as a standard of conduct that is held by the members of a group. It is against this standard that the behavior of the individual group member is compared and evaluated. In a certain sense a norm represents a set of general understandings held by group members concerning what they should and should not do. Norms vary in the amount of control they exert over the behavior of individual members, but in general one can obtain considerable insight into the behavior of groups by acquiring information concerning the norms that exist, the origin of these norms, and the mechanisms that are used to maintain them.

The industrial studies that have dealt with social norms have tended to concentrate on the influence of the work group in regulating production rates. A particularly interesting aspect of this research is found in work groups with established production standards that function to lower production rates well below the standards set by management. In several of these studies, worker restriction of production was observed in jobs for which there was a wage incentive available for higher output; hence, in these instances the social pressures that led to output restrictions worked at cross-purposes with a wage incentive that was intended to encourage high levels of productivity.

The purpose of reviewing these studies is not merely to demonstrate that work groups do, in fact, hold back on their rates of productivity. The evidence available suggests that this is a rather commonplace occurrence. What is important, however, is that one becomes aware of the variety of methods groups employ to achieve their work objectives, and the complicated social mechanisms they adopt to enforce commpliance with their standards. The organization, the job, and the composition of the work group all combine to create a situation from which workers develop the specific mechanisms of social control. Using the situation that is at hand, the work group improvises the manner in which the behavior of the members is regulated. Hence, all work groups impose standards of conduct on their members; it is the mechanics of doing this that varies widely from one group to the next.

The studies we will consider will also demonstrate that although work groups may invest considerable energy in maintaining production standards, they also develop parallel procedures for regulating a whole variety of social behaviors that take place on the job. At times these regulations appear to the outsider as being rather petty and functionless, but the studies to be reviewed suggest that these norms do serve important psychological and social purposes, and that members of work groups often give evidence that the control of these seemingly insignificant behaviors is of high importance to the well-being of the group.

The Hawthorne Studies

One of the most widely cited and influential studies of work-group norms is found in an extensive program of research that was carried out at the Hawthorne Works of the Western Electric Company (Roethlisberger & Dickson, 1939). The studies extended over a period of five years (1927–1932) beginning with observations of only five workers, but eventually including as many as 20,000 employees before the project was brought to an end. These studies have great historical significance for the study of industrial behavior, since they represent one of the earlier experimental efforts to inquire into the dynamics of productive behavior. Further, they represented a turning point of sorts for the study of industrial behavior, since they are an early instance of investigators' awareness of the broad range of social and emotional factors that contribute to the determination of worker behavior.

The Bank Wiring Room Studies

No attempt will be made to summarize the entire set of studies that make up this series; only one, the Bank Wiring Room study, has direct relevance to our discussion of work group norms. This was a study of a group of workers engaged in the assembly of complicated electrical switches that were incorporated into sets of office communication equiment. Basically the job consisted of three steps: banks of terminals were wired, then soldered, and finally inspected. For each phase of the process there was a separate job specialty, and the group involved was composed of fourteen men—nine wiremen, three soldermen, and two inspectors. During one cycle of the work wiremen stood before workbenches on which were placed banks of electrical terminals. The wiremen would make the prescribed mechanical connections by binding wires to the 200 terminals that made up what was referred to as "an equipment." After the wiremen had completed their work on one level of an equipment, they would switch over to work on a second, while the soldermen followed them up and made the wired terminals permanent. Finally, the inspectors would examine the work, using an electrical device that would signal when a circuit was malfunctioning.

The pay system in operation was constructed to encourage high levels of production. Essentially, the plan was a complicated group-bonus system in which a production standard was set up and the workers received additional pay for units completed beyond the standard. The added incentive pay generated by each worker was pooled and evenly divided among all members of the group. Production rates falling below the company standard received a guaranteed salary, but, of course, contributed nothing to the group bonus pool.

The Procedure. The Bank Wiring Room study was an interesting one in the sense that it made no effort to manipulate variables found in the work setting. Rather, the study relied exclusively on direct observation of a work group that was carrying out its normal job responsibilities and was located in a special work room. For the purposes of the study the work group was removed from its usual work station and placed in a special test room that contained all the technical facilities necessary to carry out the job. In this room better control of the workday could be achieved, and it gave an observer better opportunity to record the events that took place.

This observer was present in the room at all times, and during a period of seven months he maintained extensive records regarding the activities of the fourteen men who were members of the work group. For example, an important kind of data involved production rates. Two sources of output information were used, the first consisting of readings of the actual number of units produced during the morning and afternoon work spells. The observer obtained these data for each wireman after the work group had left the room for lunch or home. Workers had no knowledge that this information was being collected. These objective output records were supplemented by another set of production figures that were supplied by the wiremen themselves, who reported to the foreman the number of terminals they had wired during the course of the day. These reports, together with the records kept by the observer, constituted two views of the level of production achieved by each worker. It was in the comparison between actual production and reported production that some interesting observations concerning the operation of group production norms were obtained.

Production records provided only one kind of data for the study; the observer kept notes concerning the significant events that took place during each day. In addition to these daily records, all men were interviewed several times before they were introduced to the test room and again during the period of the study. Hence, it is apparent that just this single phase of the Hawthorne plant's experiments generated an impressive amount of information regarding the job activities of the small work group that was under observation.

The Results.   One of the interesting aspects of the Bank Wiring Room study concerned the level of production that was maintained by the work group. Specifically, there appeared to be evidence indicating that the members of the group were consciously restricting production output. In point of fact, there was a veritable mountain of data suggesting that during the typical workday the group completed considerably fewer terminals than were required by the official work standard that had been set up by the engineering department.

That there were two production standards was a fact that was known to all, workers and supervisors alike, and interview records as well as conversations recorded in the test room revealed that the men talked openly about a group-supported production norm that was at variance with the

standard (called the bogey) that had been established by the engineers. It was this group-generated output norm that appeared to be controlling the work rates. Furthermore, although there seemed to be some confusion in the thinking of the group regarding the level of the official standard (7312 terminals per day), there was little confusion among the men concerning the standard of 6600 terminals that the group had adopted as a production norm for a day's work. The unofficial rate standard, therefore, was clearly understood and of primary importance in controlling the output of the group.

The idea that there was a level of production that constituted a reasonable day's work was supported by yet another idea that held that violation of this standard would result in negative consequences for the members of the work group. The members of the group believed that the piece rate would be cut, the bogey raised, jobs eliminated, or that the supervisor might bawl out the slower men, if workers disregarded the output standards that the group had established. Not all men gave the same reason for maintaining the 6600 standard, but there seemed to be good agreement that repeated violation of this work rule would result in dire consequences for the members of the group.

Quotes from interviews illustrate some of the thinking underlying a work standard that most agreed represented a substantial restriction on a rate of production that might reasonably be expected from this group.

For example:

Int: "You say there is no incentive to turn out more work. If all of you did more work, wouldn't you make more money?"

W_4: "No we wouldn't. They told us that down there one time. You know, the supervisors came around and told us that very thing, that if we turn out more work we would make more money, but we can't see it that way. Probably what would happen is that our bogey would be raised, and then we would just be turning out more work for the same money. I can't see that" (Roethlisberger & Dickson, 1939, p. 418.)

This and other comments clearly point to the fact that the members of the work group were consciously aware of the rate standard that had been set up by the members. It was also widely recognized that it was quite possible for many workers to exceed this 6600-unit norm. Furthermore, the interview records revealed that the work group had developed a rationalization that attempted to justify their restricted production rates, and by and large the basis for this rationalization was to be found in certain fears and apprehensions concerning the consequences of exceeding this standard.

Demand for Straight-Line Production Curves. In conjunction with group efforts to maintain a level of production that was considered reasonable and secure, there was yet another idea frequently expressed by the members of the work group. This was that production records should show consistency from week to week. Although there were differences among the men in their production output, it was generally thought that it would be unwise for an individual to show great fluctuations in production from one week to the next. Such variation, it was thought, might call attention to the higher rates and cause the supervisor to put pressures on workers to achieve these hgher levels more consistently. As a consequence, the group maintained still another production standard, and this one was for the maintenance of a straight line production curve. A plot of reported production curves for the nine wiremen revealed that, with few exceptions, there was little variation in average hourly output from week to week during the course of the study. Reference to Figure 11.1, taken from Roethlisberger and Dickson (1939), gives a picture of the week-to-week trends in reported production throughout the course of the study. When viewed over the entire period of the study, there was no noticeable trend, either upward or down, in the reported production curves. If one were to try to fit a mathematical function to these data, a straight line with zero slope would appear to be the most appropriate representation of the production curves observed. Hence, two important production norms were found governing the work activities of the test room group: one standard

regulating the amount of production, the other controlling the consistency of production rates.

Group Enforcement. What the observer was seeing in this small work group was an elaborate system of social control that functioned to regulate the amount that was produced and the consistency of production rates. Underlying this system was a set of beliefs that predicted negative consequences to all who violated the production norms of the group. Some ideas that entered into these belief systems had little basis in fact; for example, there was little substance to the belief that increased production would result in an increase in the bogey or a loss of wages. There was one aspect of this belief system that was essentially true, however, and this involved the prediction that individuals who consistently violated group norms would call down upon themselves all manner of group pressures. The truth of the matter was that the group did maintain an elaborate system of enforcement in which a miscreant would become the target of some not too subtle forms of group disapproval. As might be expected, verbal abuse was commonly used to control the behavior of the members. Wiremen 2 and 6, for example, were usually highest in production rates, and in response to this were given names such as "runt," "cyclone," and "slave." Another source of aversive control was found in a game that the group played, called "binging," which consisted of punching a man in the upper part of the arm as hard as one could. The unwritten rules of this game required that the man accept this form of aggression as a game rather than as a serious attack. It was "all in good fun," but the probability of becoming the recipient of such aggression was strongly correlated with an individual worker's violation of one of the standards established by the group. The following incident reflects the use of binging to control production:

W_8: (To W_6) "Why don't you quit work? Let's see, this is your thirty-fifth row today. What are you going to do with them all?"

W_6: "What do you care? It's to your advantage if I work isn't it?"

FIGURE 11.1   Reported Average Hourly Output Per Week for Base Period and Test Room Period.

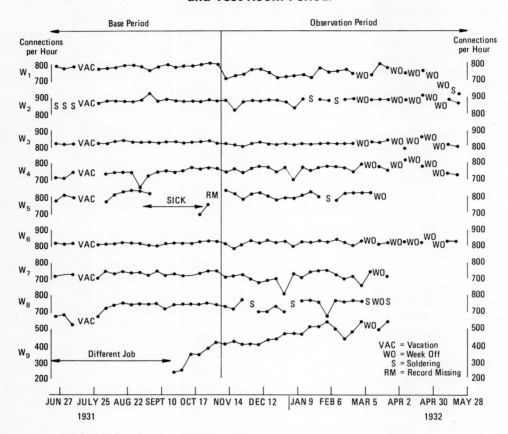

The records for the base period were collected during the weeks preceding the introduction of the work group into the test room.

Source: Roethlisberger, F. J., & Dickson, W. J. *Management and the worker.* Cambridge, Mass.: Harvard University Press, 1939, p. 424. Copyright, 1939 Harvard University Press.

W_8: "Yeah, but the way you're working you'll get stuck with them."

W_6: "Don't worry about that. I'll take care of it. You're getting paid by the sets I turn out. That's all you should worry about."

W_8: "If you don't quit work I'll bing you." (W_8 struck W_6 and finally chased him around the room.)

Obs: (A few minutes later) "What's the matter, W_6, won't he let you work?"

W_6: "No. I'm all through though. I've got enough done." (He then went over and helped another wireman.) (p. 422)

We see in this incident a mechanism of group control in the form of a hostile game, the rules of which had been laid down by the workers. This game was just one of the many social mechanisms the workers employed to enforce compliance with the standard they had adopted to limit production. Although the same production standard applied to every individual in the Bank Wiring Room, variation in enforcement procedures were observed among different clusters of workers. Hence, the uniformity found in the group's commitment to production levels might, to the casual observer, be obscured by the variety of techniques that were drawn on to enlist compliance.

Control of the Daily Routine. It would be an error to think that the norms established in the test room dealt only with job duties and production. Actually, what was seen during the period of observation was an extensive set of unwritten rules that served to regulate behaviors of the work group in many aspects of its daily activities. There were numerous events routinely occurring in the shop that pointed to the existence of a broad range of behavioral standards that served to regulate the workday and generate patterns of interpersonal relationships that were stable and predictable.

As an example, there was a general understanding concerning who would leave the shop each day to purchase lunches for the members of the group at a nearby lunch counter. This was a low-status task and it was always carried out by soldermen, who were seen as occupying a position of somewhat lower status than the wiremen. The person who got the lunches was given the title "lunch boy," and it was a task that frequently netted the one who performed it considerable kidding from the rest of the group. That the social implications of this job were generally understood by the group is illustrated in an instance in which one of the wiremen went about collecting the money for the lunches. He was immediately subjected to pressures from the group. "Look who's getting the lunches today" was broadcast over the shop. The wireman turned the money over to a solderman who went out and bought the lunches.

The regulation of the windows in the shop was also under some informal control. As a general rule the wireman located nearest a window saw the window as his own, and controversies would arise if someone violated this understanding. The following episode illustrates this:

W_6 had his window open and W_5 closed it.
W_6: "You leave that window open. I want some fresh air in here."
W_5: "It's too cold. I want it closed."
W_6: "You take care of your window. This one

is mine and if I open it, it's going to stay open." (p. 502)

An argument ensued in which W_6 threatened to punch W_5 in the nose, at which point W_5 let the window alone.

We have already mentioned one "game," binging, that was played in the test room, but in addition to this there were a large variety of play activities that had been incorporated into the workday. For example, there was daily betting on horse races, in which members of the test room would pool small amounts to place on the "Test Room Horse." In addition to this there was a whole set of gambling activities, ranging from pitching pennies to participating in baseball pools. The games were governed by sets of rules, and there was a fairly stable pattern of participation in these events; some workers rarely joined in these games, while others participated on a regular basis.

In considering patterns of participation, the observers noted that there were two groups active in these affairs, and that each group participated to the exclusion of the other. One group accounted for all the gambling activities that went on in the shop, while all the binging went on in the second group. Both groups purchased candy from the company store, but they made their purchases separately, they tended to buy different kinds of candy, and they rarely shared their purchases with members of the other group.

Informal Social Structures. The fact that participation in these play activities was not shared by everyone in the group of fourteen workers points to a general social condition that was found in the Bank Wiring Room. This was that, in fact, not one but two sentient groups were functioning in this room. If one looked at the company organization chart, one would have found evidence for only one task group; in many of the day-to-day activities, however, the presence of two social cliques was clearly in evidence. One of these groups, Clique A, was located toward the front of the workroom; the other, Clique B, was found in the back. For each clique there were sets of social norms controlling member behavior. In some instances these norms were peculiar to one clique; in other instances both shared similar norms. For example, Clique B fooled around more and engaged in binging games, they traded jobs among themselves more often (an activity that was illegal), and argued more about the windows. Members of Clique A thought of themselves as being somewhat superior to Clique B. Conversation, thought to be of a more serious nature, accounted for more of Clique A's time, and on occasion there was some friction between the two groups as a result of the horsing around that went on in group B.

Before proceeding further, it should be pointed out that not all workers in the Bank Wiring Room were members of these cliques. In point of fact, four workers did not play an active role in either group, and it was toward these individuals that many of the antagonisms of the day were directed. In addition, a plot of the friendships that existed in the workroom revealed that these workers were isolated and had few if any friends in the shop. Friendships tended to be confined to members of the same clique, and the antagonisms that operated in the room seemed to emanate from Clique B and be directed toward those individuals who did not maintain any strong friendships.

To one degree or another, members of both cliques and the isolates tended to adhere to certain norms that were held in common by all. All tended to agree, for instance, that workers should not turn out too much work, that they should not inform on their fellow workers, and that they should not show in their conduct an attitude of social superiority. All members endorsed certain ideas concerning the consequences of norm transgression, and all showed considerable knowledge of the social norms that operated in all phases of the activities that took place in the workroom.

Hence, we see that within what, on the surface of things, appeared to be a relatively uncomplicated group of fourteen workers, there were levels of social organization that were reflected in every phase of the daily routine. On each level there were sets of norms that governed the behavior of

the members, and at each level there was a different pattern of membership. In some instances the entire group of fourteen functioned as a unit; in other instances two distinct cliques were observed, and there were one-to-one personal relationships that also reflected the presence of social norms operating at this dyadic level. Social circles thus formed within social circles, and within each, sets of informal rules would emerge to control the behavior of the members. The Bank Wiring Room study, therefore, is in large measure a description of an elaborate system of social control, which extended far beyond those activities that directly contribute to work output. This system involved shared understandings as to what constituted acceptable conduct, and associated with these guidelines were sets of rational arguments that justified the behaviors they encouraged. The arguments dealt not only with the fairness of the norms, but also contained predictions concerning the consequences that might be expected if one were to violate group norms. In many instances these anticipated consequences were, in fact, real, since there was a system of enforcement that was maintained by these workers whose objective was to protect the orderliness and stability of social relations. Social transgressions that threatened the established patterns of work provoked antagonisms and the threat of social ostracism; compliance with the social norms tended to ensure that individuals would receive their share of the social amenities that the group had to offer. In short, the Hawthorne studies succeeded in demonstrating the complexity of the social environment of work and confirmed that much of what is seen in worker behavior can be understood only from a knowledge of these social influences.

Although the Hawthorne studies were among the early efforts to study the social components of work, there have been a number of subsequent reports that have extended many of the observations reported from the test room. Perhaps one of the most frequently cited reports of this nature is the "participant observer" study that was carried out by Roy (1952, 1953). A participant-observer study is one in which the investigator plays an active role as a member of the group whose affairs are being observed. In many instances, the other members of the group are unaware of the investigator's efforts to collect observations without disclosing intentions to collect scientific information regarding group actions. The Hawthorne studies were not of this type, since the observer did not assume the role of a worker but remained outside the work group as a nonparticipant observer.

Production Norms in a Machine Shop

The significance of this set of observations lies in the fact that Roy found a work group that maintained two production standards. One of these was similar to the norm found operating in the Bank Wiring Room, in that it placed an upper limit on the amount produced during the day. The second norm dictated extremely low production rates whenever workers believed that the company wage incentives were unfairly established.

For this study Roy took a job as a radial drill operator in the machine shop of a steel-processing plant, and during the ten months he was employed, he kept detailed records of the events that took place in the work group to which he was assigned. Of particular interest to him were the output norms that functioned in this group. In studying these production standards Roy kept careful records of his own output, maintaining that these data gave a representative reflection of the general approach to work that he observed in the entire group. In addition to information bearing on production, notes were kept on conversations and happenings in the shop. The job Roy held was in a shop in which changing production orders meant that the men periodically had to change the product they were turning out. Before each new job was begun, the Methods Department carried out a time study for the purpose of establishing a new standard. Once established, the standard identified a level of production at or below which the men received a guaranteed salary, called the base rate. If an individual's output exceeded this standard, there was a bonus that was calculated on a piece-rate basis; therefore, a critical factor determining a worker's

pay would be the level at which the production standard was set. It was in connection with this official standard that group production norms were established, and in many instances Roy observed, "the work group was applying a heavy foot to the production brake, day in and day out" (Roy, 1952, p. 430).

Referring to his own output, Roy found that a plot of work records resulted in a bimodal distribution of production. That is to say, there were two predominant rates of work, one that was considerably below the official standard, and one that was considerably above. Associated with each rate was a group-supported norm that resulted in the substantial restriction of production that Roy observed in his own performance. For the faster rate there was a norm that functioned to set a maximum on the amount an individual produced during the day. This norm, referred to as a "quota restriction," operated on jobs for which the standard was low enough that operators could exceed it by considerable amounts. In these instances the group held to a norm that set an upper limit on the amount that a worker produced. When this level was reached, the worker simply stopped work and engaged in some other type of activity.

Quota restriction was a production norm that was similar to the one observed operating in the Bank Wiring Room, in that an upper limit functioned to control the amount produced during the day. As with the Bank Wiring Room norm, quota restriction was accompanied by a set of rationalizations that justified the maintenance of this norm. A conversation between Roy and another worker (Starkey) illustrates this point:

> R: ". . . what do you suppose would happen if I turned in $1.50 an hour on these pump bodies?"
>
> S: "Turned in? You mean if you actually did the work and turned it in!"
>
> R: "I mean if I actually did the work and turned it in. They'd have to pay, wouldn't they? Isn't that the agreement?"
>
> S: "Yes! They'd pay me—once! Don't you know that if I turned in $1.50 an hour on these pump bodies tonight, the whole God-

damned Methods Department would be down here tomorrow? And they'd retime this job so quick it would make your head swim! And when they retimed it, they'd cut the price in half! And I'd be working for 85 cents an hour instead of $1.25." (Roy, 1952, p. 433)

To give some idea of the amount of time wasted on jobs for which quota restriction was in force, Roy presents the following evidence. During the ten-month period in which he kept records, he was assigned 75 different piece-rate jobs, and of these his output reached the official standard on only 31. Of these 31 jobs, there were 20 on which Roy could have produced beyond the group quota, and Table 11.1, adapted from Roy (1952, p. 434), summarizes the results of quota restriction on the output and earnings of these 20 jobs. As can be seen, the impact of these output norms was substantial. Roy wasted 36.4 per cent of the total time that he spent on these jobs, and as a consequence he lost $601.25 in earnings while he was making $983.18. On one of the jobs he actually wasted more time than he spent working.

Goldbricking. As was previously indicated, a second production norm was found operating in the work group. This norm dealt with those jobs on which the workers believed they could not make substantial bonus earnings without exerting an excessive amount of effort. When given these jobs, called "stinkers," the men would work at rates that were substantially below the level considered standard by the Methods Department. Roy applied the term "goldbricking" to this kind of sluggish work rate. The rule that operated was this: if a worker, exerting a reasonable amount of effort, could not make $1.00 per hour—that is, exceed the $.85 base rate by $.15—then the bonus incentive was considered not to be worth the effort. In these instances the worker would adopt a work rate that was considerably below one-half the rate considered standard by the Engineering Department. This low level of production would be maintained until the job was completed or until the standard was lowered.

TABLE 11.1 Time Losses on Twenty Jobs on which Quota Restriction Was Enforced

Job	Total Hours on the Job	Total Wasted Time (In Hours)
1	157.9	57.8
2	120.5	31.6
3	111.0	56.9
4	94.4	43.7
5	75.8	21.8
6	46.0	16.7
7	37.7	12.3
8	28.5	10.7
9	24.0	7.2
10	19.3	8.4
11	18.0	3.4
12	14.9	2.0
13	9.6	3.5
14	7.0	2.8
15	6.7	2.3
16	4.5	2.3
17	4.3	1.4
18	4.1	1.0
19	1.5	0.5
20	0.8	0.3
Total	**786.5** (98.3 days)	**286.0** (35.75 days)

Adapted from Roy, D. Quota restriction and goldbricking in a machine shop. *American Journal of Sociology*, 1952, *57*, 427–442. Copyright, 1952 The University of Chicago Press.

That this type of work slowdown was practiced openly is illustrated by notes from Roy's diary, which described an extended argument between several operators and the Methods Department regarding the standard that had been set on the machining of hinge bases.

Joe Mucha drilled 36 of the bases (... $8.80 per 100) today. "The most I'll ever do until they retime this job is 40," he said. "Do you know what they expect us to do? Why, I wouldn't bust my ass to do 50 for $8.00, when day rate is almost that!" (p. 437)

And at another time, Roy noted:

McCann said that Starkey was arguing all day over the price of the hinge bases. The methods men maintain that they can't raise the price because the jacks that the parts go onto sell for $14.00 apiece. They plan to retool the job and lower the price. According to McCann, Jack told them that if he didn't get a decent price he was going to make out on the job but scrap every one of the pieces.

"Jack fights it out with them," said McCann. "He'll stay right with the machine and argue. I get disgusted and walk away." (p. 438)

Observations such as these illustrate an often-reported finding that group norms that restrict rates of output function quite openly in the work setting. The members of this group were frequently found discussing these restrictions and at times these discussions included representatives of management. Furthermore, not only were these production restrictions practiced openly, the amount of time wasted during these episodes was considerable. With one job, for example, 3.5 production hours were wasted each day, with a corresponding loss in wages of $.55 per hour.

Comment. We find in Roy's work experience another illustration of group restriction of productivity. As was the case in the Bank Wiring Room, a work group had established sets of rules governing the output performance of each worker, and the net result of these rules was to encourage large amounts of wasted time. It is impressive to see that in this one shop workers frequently wasted one-third or more of the entire work day. Reference to Table 11.1 shows that for one set of 20 jobs Roy had worked 98.3 days, and during this period his wasted time accounted for 35.75 days of nonproduction activities. Roughly speaking then, for every three months spent on these jobs, Roy took more than one month's paid vacation.

Banana Time

The Bank Wiring Room study showed us that it is not just production behaviors that come under the influence of work-group norms; a variety of daily events are regulated by informal rules that give the day's activities a routine and orderly character. Along the same lines, Roy (1960) has reported another participant-observer experiment in which his principal concern was a set of highly developed daily routines that were improvised by a work group in order to combat the deadly sameness of a job that was dull and unchallenging. In this instance the monotony of a repetitive task, carried out by a small group of workers, was dealt with by developing a series of almost standardized games and conversational themes that occurred at regular times during the workday. This is a type of activity that will give us a different view of group norms. Now we will see a work group developing standards of conduct that, at first glance, appear frivolous. We will learn, however, that this type of routinized social interaction can become an important part of the workday, serving both to stave off the boredom of the job and to provide a psychologically secure set of social diversions that are in themselves a source of satisfaction.

This study is an important one, not only because it provides an interesting illustration of a group's efforts to come to grips with an empty job, but because it also provides us with a clear illustration of the fact that the individual segments of the workday are tied together in a psychological system. Disruption of one segment of this system can lead to a generalized disruption that spreads across the entire workday. In this regard, then, we will see in the Roy study that the adjustment a work group makes to a job situation can be viewed as a social-psychological system that operates in state of balance. If this balance is disturbed, then the entire system may be disrupted and attempts to reestablish the previous stable state will follow.

The Job. Our illustration of these points is set in a barren room, isolated from the rest of the plant, where Roy joined three other machine operators who worked at a dull, repetitive job that extended across a twelve-hour workday. These operators ran "clicking machines" that stamped plastic sheets into various shapes. The job required the worker to insert the plastic sheet into a die and punch the clicker, remove the stamped piece, insert another, punch, and repeat the cycle over and over again. A principle source of variety in this job was found in changing the color of the plastic sheets that were stamped.

Games.   Roy's diary reports that the first twelve-hour stint on this job was an extremely difficult one, and during the initial few days on the job, fatigue, coupled with the boring routine of the work, made him entertain thoughts of quitting. During these early days, Roy found himself searching out ways for combating the emptiness of his work by inserting some kind of meaning into the dull task that repeated itself throughout the long day. One solution to the difficulty consisted of making a game out of the insignificant little segments of his job. By manipulating such things as the color of the materials worked on and variations in the shapes that were stamped, Roy managed to fabricate a series of short-term production goals, the attainment of which would be rewarded with a change in activity.

As time passed and he became more proficient at his work, Roy gradually became aware of a series of gamelike activities that were carried out by the other members of the work group. These activities took place at regular times during the day, and they came to assume an important part of Roy's work experience. Let's rely on Roy's description of some of these games:

Ike would regularly switch off the power at Sammy's machine whenever Sammy made a trip to the lavatory or the drinking fountain. Correlatively, Sammy invariably fell victim to the plot by making an attempt to operate his clicking hammer after returning to the shop. And, as the simple pattern went, this blind stumbling into the trap was always followed by indignation and reproach from Sammy, smirking satisfaction from Ike, and mild paternal scolding from George. My interest in this procedure was at first confined to wondering when Ike would weary of his tedious joke or when Sammy would learn to check his power switch before trying his hammer.

But, as I began to pay closer attention, as I began to develop familiarity with the communi-

cation system, the disconnected became connected, the nonsense made sense, the obscure became clear, and the silly actually funny. (Roy, 1960, p. 161)

Minor dramas such as this dotted the workday and as time passed, Roy gradually became a willing participant in these affairs, which he had first viewed as being ridiculous. As an example, the group had their "times" which consisted of a cessation of work and a brief, standardized social interlude. Roy describes one of these:

My attention was first drawn to this time business during my first week of employment when I was encouraged to join in the sharing of two peaches. It was Sammy who provided the peaches; he drew them from his lunch box after making the announcement, "Peach time!" On this first occasion I refused the proffered fruit, but thereafter regularly consumed my half peach. Sammy continued to provide the peaches and to make the "Peach time!" announcement, although there were days when Ike would remind him that it was peach time, urging him to hurry up with the midmorning snack. Ike invariably complained about the quality of the fruit, and his companions fed the fires of continued banter between peach donor and critical recipient. . . .

Banana time followed peach time by approximately an hour. Sammy again provided the refreshments, namely, one banana. There was, however, no four-way sharing of Sammy's banana. Ike would gulp it down by himself after surreptitiously extracting it from Sammy's lunch box, kept on a shelf behind Sammy's work station. Each morning after making the snatch, Ike would call out, "Banana time!" and proceed to down his prize while Sammy made futile protests and denunciations. George would join in with mild remonstrances, sometimes scolding Sammy for making such a fuss. The banana was one which Sammy brought for his own consumption at lunch time; he never did get to eat his banana, but kept bringing one for lunch. At first this daily theft startled and amazed me. *Then I grew to look forward to the daily seizure and the verbal interaction which followed.* (Roy, 1960, p. 162, italics added)

There followed a series of other "times," window time, pickup time, fish time, and coke time, all of which followed similar routinized courses, each unfolding as a pleasant interlude in the otherwise bleak world of the clicking machines. Each episode followed what appeared to be almost prearranged lines, and the regularity of form and substance of these times confirmed the existence of conduct norms that the group upheld with considerable persistence.

Conversational Themes. The standardization of the workday that Roy noted among the clicking machine operators included sets of conversational themes that made up an important part of the social exchanges that took place. Topics of conversation would recur again and again over the weeks, forming well-defined ways by which the members of the work group related to each other. Some of these themes were of a serious nature, but much of this type of interaction involved the members of the group kidding each other. Again we cite Roy's diary.

> Kidding themes were usually started by George or Ike, and Sammy was usually the butt of the joke. . . . Sammy received occasional calls from his wife, and his claim that these calls were requests to shop for groceries on the way home were greeted with feigned disbelief. Sammy was ribbed for being closely watched, bossed, and henpecked by his wife, and the expression, "Are you a man or a mouse?" became an echolalic utterance, used both in and out of the original context. (Roy, 1960, p. 163)

Roy became an object of one of these themes when he mentioned one day that he owned two acres of land. The group began to elaborate on a joking theme that involved Roy's "farm," and as time progressed, this two-acre holding became stocked with all the appurtenances of a major agricultural enterprise.

There were serious conversational themes that occurred regularly; these involved reminiscences of past hardships, discussions of Roy's future, and conversations regarding family problems. One of these conversational themes, "the professor theme," played an important role in the disruption of the congenial flow of social interchanges that took place in the group one day. Quoting from Roy's account of this theme,

> George's daughter . . . had married the son of a professor who instructed in one of the local colleges. The professor theme was not in the strictest sense a conversation piece; when the subject came up, George did all the talking. The two Jewish operatives remained silent as they listened with deep respect, if not actual awe, to George's accounts of the Big Wedding which, including wedding pictures, entailed an expense of $1,000. It was a monologue, but there was listening, there was communication, the sacred communication of a temple, when George told of going for Sunday afternoon walks on the Midway with the professor, or of joining the professor for a Sunday dinner. (Roy, 1960, p. 164)

Disruption of Group Norms. One day, at Roy's instigation, one of the members of the group jokingly proclaimed that the professor of George's narrative was in reality a faculty member in a barber college located in one of the lesser sections of town. This assault on this most valued theme resulted in an immediate and strained termination of much of the social interplay that normally took place during the day. There was no conversation at lunch. Fish time was terminated, George did not drink his coke at coke time, and the general flow of conversational banter came to a virtual standstill. The entire social fabric had been placed under severe strain and the small group worked in silence for the remainder of the day.

For days the entire daily routine was disrupted. Arguments erupted, workers criticized one another, no one sang, but then, after thirteen days of these strained relationships, a shift occurred in the pattern of interaction. Gradually the old banter began to reappear, friendly conversations emerged, and traditional themes were again a topic of discussion. Finally, the "times" were reintroduced. The work group had gradually adjusted to their social plight, and life in the clicking room reverted to a condition that was almost as it had been in the past. There was one exception; the professor theme never reentered the conversation of the group.

Comment. We see in this series of happenings a system of well-established social relations come under the impact of a challenge to one of the norms that controlled the conversational activities of the group. The professor theme, prior to its disruption, had a stable structure with social roles being adopted by the members of the group in patterns that were persistent and predictable. The abrupt collapse of these roles meant not only the cessation of the one theme but a general revision of the social relations found in the entire range of group activities. That the group eventually reestablished the old relationships represents an often-cited tendency for groups to maintain a stable set of social experiences. Furthermore, in a situation where group membership is a necessary condition of work, and where the work provides little but fatigue and monotony, the conditions are set for the group to reinstitute those social mechanisms that served them so well in the past. In this respect the Roy study is an interesting and valuable illustration of the dynamics of work-group social adjustment.

Facilitative Effects of Group Norms

Thus far we have seen work-group norms that functioned to restrict production in situations in which there were financial incentives available for increased productivity. Now we look at a situation in which group norms functioned to increase rates of performance in a situation where there was no financial incentive tied to higher rates of work.

Doyle P. Johnson (1974) reports on another participant-observer-type study in which for fifteen months he held a job in the Sanitation Department of a large food corporation. Working as a member of a twelve-man group that was responsible for cleaning all the food-processing equipment during the 9:30 p.m. to 6:00 a.m. shift, Johnson reports on the operation of work-group norms in a plant that had been recently built and for a group that had been recently hired.

Two types of tasks were performed by the group, B jobs and C jobs, and these were distinguished by the fact that the C jobs carried higher prestige and pay. Although the basic operation performed on both jobs was washing pipes and equipment, C jobs required workers to disassemble and reassemble equipment, while B jobs did not. Since the members of the work group had all been recently hired, Johnson noted that there was little initial difference in the level of proficiency the workers had for the jobs to which they were assigned. As a result, the social structure that first formed revolved around such things as personality characteristics, background similarities, and nonwork social position. As an example, some of the members had been in the military service, which gave a common thread of experience around which conversations and eventual friendships could form.

As time passed and the men developed skill on their jobs, differences in speed and work proficiency became an important factor in determining an individual's status in the group. Fast workers were awarded positions of higher prestige and the quality of a worker's performance became a factor that influenced an individual's social ranking. Norms that encouraged fast work emerged and negative sanctions were developed that were used against those individuals who were careless with their work or who were slow in finishing an assignment. Fast work was rewarded by free time at the end of the work shift in which the worker could relax. It was generally understood that there was a certain amount of work to be done during a shift, and when this was completed, workers were free to pursue their own interests. Workers who managed to complete their assignments before the end of the shift would put pressures on those still working; and although the same workers didn't always finish first, there was a noticeable tendency for certain workers to have more free time than others, and it was these men who held higher status in the group. Hence, we see in this work situation the operation of norms that encouraged high rates of productivity, and a status system, maintained informally by the work group, that ranked workers as a function of how fast they completed their work.

It is interesting to note that these status rankings seemed to appear in many of the social activities that took place in the shop. For example, Johnson observed that the order in which workers left the shop for lunch or for a work break often was correlated with these status factors. Remember, the C jobs generally carried the higher status, and it was the highest-ranking, that is, the fastest workers on these C jobs who would leave the work area first, followed by the slower B workers. During work breaks, C workers tended to sit together and talk. They sat on benches that were located in the break area, while the B workers sat on the floor outside the break area. Hence, job status, in part a function of work rate, appeared to influence the composition and behavior of the friendship groups that were observed in the work setting. This is a finding that was also observed in the Hawthorne studies.

Work Changes.   There came a time when the group was compelled to face two major changes in their work. First, an engineering study revealed that substantial amounts of time were being wasted in nonproductive activities at the end of the workday. As a result, the foreman began to assign additional tasks to those who completed their regular assignments before the end of the shift. Furthermore, in the eyes of the workers, these extra tasks were more like the lower-status jobs that were usually carried out by the B workers. Hence, apart from the increased workloads that the entire group shared, now the faster C job workers were "rewarded" for rapid performance with an assignment that placed them in a lower-status position. This meant that the higher-status members of the work group had to carry the highest cost for this change in work assignments.

Another disruption of the status hierarchy occurred as the result of technological changes. New techniques developed by the Quality Control Department led to the elimination of many of the more skilled tasks that had been performed by the C workers. As a consequence, jobs that previously had been handled by B workers were now shared by both groups. Also, changes in work technology tended to break up work teams, since jobs that

previously had been two-man assignments were now carried out by a single employee.

Norm Revision.   We saw in the clicking-room study a work group faced with events that threatened the existing social equilibrium in a work group. In that case the forces of disruption were internal to the group, and for a while they resulted in the suspension of much of the cordial interaction that characterized the day. In the present case we find a work group confronting changes that are imposed by external sources, and as might be expected, the group modified many of the social relationships that previously had been established. Johnson reports that soon after these changes were introduced, there was a noticeable drop in group morale. Complaints were frequent, and the workers quickly came to the conclusion that the new work rules and revised technology were quite unfair to the members of the group. Next, there appeared a revision of the relative status of certain jobs as the result of the C workers' "discovery" that some of the tasks the B group performed, tasks that C workers now carried out, required higher levels of skill than had been previously thought.

Perhaps the most fundamental adjustment made to the changes in the work was found in a new norm that the group began to develop. This new standard required that the workers pace themselves in such a way that their regularly assigned duties would fill up the entire eight-hour work shift. In this fashion workers could avoid what they saw as unfair and demeaning job assignments that awaited an early finish. Norms, which at one time encouraged rapid work, were thus transformed into a set of group standards that encouraged group restriction of productivity, and the status system that operated in the work group now became associated with different aspects of work behavior. Under the new standards both the very fast and the very slow workers were held in positions of low prestige, while employees who could maintain a steady pace and fill up the entire work spell with their regularly assigned duties were granted the highest social rank. As time progressed, these new norms began to stabilize and the group eventually established new ways of adjusting to the work. This was true not only with regard to production, but also with regard to the pattern of informal social interaction that took place among the workers. For example, much of the fooling around was gone from the day, and Johnson reports that the group appeared to lose some of its solidarity. Less frequently would one find the entire group involved in a conversation, but rather conversations now more likely included only pairs of workers. In general, there was less evidence that individual workers received much satisfaction from the socializing that took place in the shop.

Stability and social equilibrium had thus been disturbed by a set of influences that was external to the group. This was followed by lowered morale and a period in which complaints were frequently raised. New norms emerged, and a revised pattern of production and social behaviors began to stabilize. A cycle had been completed, with the work group now in a new state of social equilibrium.

THE SOCIAL SETTING OF WORK

The preceding studies have presented a picture of the social complexity of work, and they all confirm a statement that was made at the beginning of this chapter: namely, to understand worker behavior one must have information concerning the social setting within which individuals function. The literature points quite clearly to the fact that it is among the social interactions that take place within a work group that many of the most powerful factors influencing production rates are to be found. Furthermore, it is within this social realm that one may also find some of the more important factors that serve as sources of satisfaction for the worker. For example, we have seen that work groups elaborate on the daily routine that is thrust upon them by the duties of the jobs they hold. An internal social system is established, which involves status rankings, friendships, games, and other diversions that better enable the worker to face the routines of work. The workday is thereby enriched by congenial social interactions. As a rule these events take place in stable patterns, and this fact tends to make for a less threatening social environment. Recurring patterns of social relations give individuals a sense of structure that better enables them to predict the events of the day. Under circumstances such as these they understand what they are supposed to do and how they should deal with certain things that come up. As a consequence, this system of behavioral norms provides the worker with a base of psychological security.

But we have found that whatever psychological security there is in these standardized practices is sometimes purchased at the cost of a reduction in wages. The Hawthorne Studies were one of the earliest demonstrations of the fact that group production norms can result in a reduction in the pay received by the individual worker. Roy's experiences in the machine shop is another illustration of a substantial decrease in pay that was the consequence of group work standards. Results such as these certainly suggest that it would be inappropriate to think of the motives of workers solely in economic terms. The workers' apparent willingness to curtail their economic objectives in order to comply with a group's production standards indicates that a number of motivational influences may be operating to result in the output rates that are observed.

Workers' Objectives

What are some of the objectives that lead workers to hold back production and take a cut in pay in doing so? Obviously, there is no one answer to this question; every work situation will present the observer with a unique pattern of factors. We can, however, consider some of the reasons suggested by researchers who have studied the question.

Reduced Competition. One of the reasons workers may have for maintaining restrictive output norms is to level group performance, and in doing so, reduce the threat that might arise if their work rate varied widely. When the members of a work group agree to abide by restrictive production norms, then the magnitude of the differences in output rates is reduced. All workers agree to produce about the same each day, and this decision, in essence, represents an agreement not to compete with each other in terms of output. The potential threat of competition is thus reduced, or at least displaced to other aspects of worker relations where outcomes are less important.

Congenial Social Relations. Output restriction may be perpetuated by a desire on the part of workers to maintain congenial social relations. To uphold restrictive output standards requires an elaborate system of cooperation among the members of a work team, and the need for cooperation in this area of work-group activity may generalize to influence the general level of cordial relations that exists among the members of the group.

Often there is an element of risk in carrying out restrictive work rates; and even if the fact that this collective action reduces the risk to the individual, there is a sharing of a common adversary that may increase the positive bonds between workers. Management, in the person of foreman or methods engineer, stands as an advocate of a higher output standard, the enforcement of which generates external pressures that may result in increased group cohesiveness.

Fear of Rate Cutting. Perhaps the most frequently cited motive underlying restrictive production norms is the fear that workers have of an upward adjustment of the official work standards (Roethlisberger & Dickson, 1939; Roy, 1952; Hickson, 1961). A related worry concerns the fear that high rates of production will jeopardize the job security of the group members. Often these concerns find their substantiation in the myths and folklore of the work group, with older workers telling the new ones about episodes from the past in which wages were cut or jobs lost as a consequence of too rapid a work rate.

Hickson (1961) reports an incident in which group concern over official output standards led to production restrictions; in this instance, however, he could find no significant evidence suggesting any distrust of management or fear that the rates might be deliberately reduced. What appeared to be at the foundation of these restrictive norms was a feeling of uncertainty regarding the accuracy of time-study methods. The members of this work group were apparently aware of the many subjective elements that entered into the methods used to determine the official rates. As a consequence, they were unwilling to take a chance that their wages would be depressed by an error in time study; thus they informally adhered to an upper limit on the amount they would produce.

The Effort Bargain. It is quite possible that employees hold to an idea that expresses what they consider to be a "fair day's work." This concept arises through some type of informal, and purely subjective, analysis of the investment of energy and personal skills required by the work and the rewards available to those who carry out the job. The standard that is arrived at through informal group interaction represents what Behrend (1957) calls an *effort bargain*. This bargain reflects a group consensus regarding an equitable exchange of effort for reward. The work situation, thus, does not become one of gross exploitation, but one in which a fair and reasonable exchange of labor for wages takes place. Whatever discrepancy exists between the official and the informal output standards, therefore, represents the results of two different methods for arriving at a definition of the effort bargain. Management uses the systematic procedures of the engineer; rank-and-file workers rely on the informal dynamics of social interaction.

Enjoyment of Free Time. In many of the studies that have been done on worker restriction of production it is reported that one of the consequences of lower output norms is an increase in the amount of free time available to the employee (for example, Roy, 1952; Johnson, 1974). It is not unusual to find this free time filled with gamelike activities that apparently provide an enjoyable social diversion from the routines of work.

Restrictive Norms and Aggression against Management. Roy's experience in a machine shop revealed that quota restriction can also serve as an expression of worker antagonism toward management. Slowing down or shutting down early was, according to Roy, a means of getting back at the foreman for those times in which he put pressures on the members of the group. To violate what a foreman often sees as the necessity of maintaining the appearance of productivity was a means whereby the group could retaliate for unwanted supervisory pressures. Hence, quota restriction can be used as a collective weapon to counter the abusive use of supervisory power.

The Return Potential Model

The above by no means exhausts the list of motives that might be found underlying the production norms that operate in a given work group; many possibilities exist. Furthermore, it is probably safe to assume that in any given instance there is a multiple set of motives behind the work levels maintained by a work group. The situation is a complicated one, and to understand the psychological and social variables involved in a group's output standards requires much more information than is usually available to the casual observer. Such things as the history of the work group, the technical details of the job, the background and personality of the members, and the characteristics of supervision must be understood before even the most careful inferences can be drawn regarding the motives that lead a work group to restrict production. But even though we may be uncertain about the motives involved, there are ways of thinking about social norms that improve our understanding of this important aspect of group functioning. What is needed is a general framework of ideas that will permit us to think about group norms as they are found in a wide range of circumstances.

The framework we will adopt is called the *Return Potential Model,* presented by Jackson (1965, 1966). This model deals with social norms in terms of a potential distribution of approval and disapproval expressed by the members of a group in response to the conduct of an individual member. In considering this model, we start off thinking about the various response alternatives that are available to an individual when confronted with a specific situation. For instance, we can think of the alternative work rates that a worker may adopt

in performing the job. Let's say that these alternatives are ordered along the scale that serves as the baseline for Figure 11.2. Along the vertical scale, one finds a distribution running from high disapproval, through indifference, to high approval. This scale represents the range of reactions a work group may make to the behavior of the individual member. Now we have a system wherein for each possible output rate there is an estimate of the potential level of approval that the worker may receive from the group. The curve drawn in Figure 11.2 represents the relationship that exists between these two scales and depicts the return potential for approval and disapproval associated with the range of production rates that a worker might maintain. The shape of this curve will change to reflect the characteristics of the social situation at hand; and by analyzing certain as-

FIGURE 11.2   The Return Potential Model.

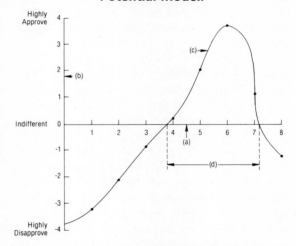

Schematic diagram showing the *Return Potential Model* for representing norms. (a) A behavior dimension; (b) an evaluation dimension; (c) a return potential curve, showing the distribution of approval-disapproval among members of a group over the whole range of behavior; (d) the range of tolerable or approved behavior.

This figure is reproduced from the Fifty-ninth Yearbook of the National Society for the Study of Education, with the permission of the Society.

pects of this figure, we can gain insight into some of the more interesting and significant properties of social norms.

Point of Maximum Return (PMR). The highest point on the return potential curve refers to what may be thought of as the ideal behavior for a given situation. This point on the curve shows the behavior that receives the highest approval from the group. In a work setting, for example, we might find that the individual who consistently produces at one particular rate has the greatest potential for receiving other workers' approval. Rates that lie away from this ideal value net an individual varying degrees of approval, and if one's work rate lies too far from the PMR, one is exposed to the disapproval of the group. This curve tells us, therefore, that a norm refers to a range of behaviors, not a single highly approved response to a situation. Although there may be a single high point on the curve, around this point there is usually a range of behaviors that evoke positive responses of varying degrees. Beyond this range we find a set of response alternatives that produce group reactions of disapproval. To describe the normative influences functioning in, say, a production situation requires that we deal with group standards in terms of two separate ranges, one involving a set of alternative responses from an individual worker, the other a range of evaluative reactions from the work group.

Range of Tolerable Behavior (RTB). In addition to the point of maximum return, the return potential curve will provide information on the range of tolerable behaviors. This refers to those behaviors that give rise to some degree of approval from the group. It is possible that the width of this range may be found to relate to the amount of pressure being exerted on the group by external agents. And in a similar vein, the width of this range may relate to the level of anxiety found among the group members. With increasing external pressures and with rising levels of anxiety, one may discover that the width of this range of tolerable behaviors begins to narrow.

Intensity. Another interesting property of a social-norm system is its *intensity*. Here we are referring to the amplitude of the return potential curve along its entire width. The amplitude of the curve serves as an indication of the intensity of group reaction to the set of behavioral alternatives that fall under the jurisdiction of group control. Return potential curves that associate high approval or disapproval with a wide range of response alternatives depict a normative system that is highly important to a particular group. In this case there are many behaviors that produce intense reactions from the group. Jackson (1966) suggests that the intensity of a norm be gauged by computing the average absolute level of approval-disapproval for all positions on the behavior scale.

Potential Return Difference. The algebraic sum of the evaluative reactions groups make to the various response alternatives is used to compute what Jackson calls the *potential return difference* (PRD). Here we move along the baseline, summing *separately* the positive and negative values on the vertical scale. The two sums are then subtracted and the PRD assumes either a positive or a negative value. Our concern is whether a group tends to employ positive or negative sanctions to enforce norm compliance. When positive, the PRD refers to a normative system that places emphasis on rewards as a means of controlling member behaviors. A negative PRD indicates a normative system that relies on punishment to bring the behaviors of the group members into line. Jackson (1966, p. 40) maintains that positive PRD indexes, when found in many different situations, indicate that normative control occurs in a climate that is generally tolerant and supportive, whereas a large number of negative PRDs suggest that the general situation is restrictive and punitive in its nature.

Crystallization. It is possible to plot a return potential curve for each member of a group, and the extent that these curves are similar is the extent to which there exists a consensus regarding the norm system. Jackson uses the term ''crystallization'' to refer to the amount of agreement there is in a group, regarding the characteristics of a social norm. In our examination of the research literature, for example, we found in the Bank Wiring Room study what appeared to be high crystallization of the norms governing production standards. In this work environment, interviewers and observers alike reported widespread agreement among the members of the work group concerning the 6600-unit standard that was used to define a fair day's work. With regard to other norms—for example, games—there appeared to be less crystallization, as there were strains between the two cliques regarding the appropriateness of certain types of activities. Jackson contends that agreement among group members regarding norm systems is a factor that is involved with the integration of a social system, and in instances in which this integration is high, there is a good potential for social control. This would especially be the case when high intensity is found along with high crystallization; a group reacts strongly to the behavior of its members, and there is general agreement concerning their response to a particular action. In such a setting, group influence will be quite high.

Utility of the Model

The Return Potential Model gives us a broad framework within which we can measure and describe some of the more important properties of a system of social norms. The model also provides us with a method whereby the ideas it expresses can be translated into observations that are measurable. Furthermore, the methods suggested by this model are comparatively simple, straightforward, and applicable to a wide range of social situations. The ability to deal with a wide range of happenings and the availability of methods that enable one to measure these events are two important properties of a scientific theory. The Return Potential Model, possessing both of these attributes, provides us with a useful tool for dealing with the social standards that contribute to the direction and control of group behavior.

The basic methodological requirement of the model is that one secure judgments from group members concerning the probability of approval or disapproval one might expect from the group when they are confronted with the behavioral alternative that might be adopted by an individual member. A plot of these judgments over a range of behavior alternatives and a description of the form of the resulting curve are the principal ingredients from which descriptions of the norm system are drawn. Each social situation would be expected to yield a somewhat different curve. For example, production norms might give rise to a curve that differs from one describing the characteristics of the norms governing social status among the members of a work group. The Return Potential Model gives us a means whereby we can describe in quantitative terms the changing properties of social norms from one work situation to the next.

CONFORMITY TO GROUP NORMS

Factors in Conformity to Group Pressures

There are individual differences in sensitivity to group influence, and we will now consider some of the factors that have been studied with regard to conformity to group norms.

Personality Factors. The research literature suggests that there are certain personality characteristics that predispose an individual to conform to the norms of a group. Although the influence of any one of these factors may, at times, be substantial, one should not think about these variables without being aware of the contribution made by the social situation within which the person is functioning. A given personality trait may be associated with a tendency to conform under one set of circumstances and not under another. Hence, one must not be led into the belief that conformity to social pressures always appears in the form of a highly generalized personality attribute that is independent of the social environment.

Bearing this point in mind, we find that a number of studies have reported that a tendency to conform to social pressures seems to be associated with the general level of emotional adjustment of the individual. For example, one experiment (Levine et al., 1954) compared the responses of psychiatric and medical patients to a situation that placed them under social pressures. Frequently in experiments such as this it is found that behavior tends to converge toward a group norm (Sherif, 1935, 1936); in the present instance, however, there was no tendency noted among the neurotic subjects to converge around some group norm. Such a tendency was, however, observed in the groups made up of patients not receiving psychiatric treatment. Hence, the results of this study suggest that neurotic subjects are less influenced by group pressures. Similar results are reported in studies by Cervin (1955, 1956), in which subjects who scored high on scales measuring emotional stability were less likely to change their opinions in the face of group pressures than were subjects whose scores on the test indicated higher emotional stability. Perhaps emotional difficulties tend to involve individuals with their own problems to such an extent that they are distracted from the social events that go on around them. As a consequence, the neurotic individual may be less receptive to social pressures.

If there are any personality variables that have a relationship with conformity to group pressures, then such characteristics as submissiveness and dependency would seem to be likely candidates. Kagan and Mussen (1956) observed that when exposed to group pressures, subjects who had high dependency scores on a projective test tended to yield more frequently to majority opinion. Other studies (Helson et al., 1956; Gage, Leavitt, & Stone, 1957) indicate that it is within this general area of dependency and submissiveness that one can find personality influences that relate to tendencies for individuals to conform to group pressures. Then there is evidence (Moeller & Applezweig, 1957) suggesting that high tendencies to conform are found among individuals who display high social-approval and low self-approval motivation, and among individuals who show low need for achievement (Krebs, 1958; Marlowe, 1959). We could continue to add to the list of attributes found to be associated with social conformity—for example, self-confidence (Coleman, Blake, & Mouton, 1958; Mausner & Bloch, 1957), authoritarianism (Berkowitz & Lundy, 1957), conservatism (Rambo & Finney, 1974), need for affiliation (Sistrunk & McDavid, 1965; McGehee & Teevan, 1967)—but the main point is served when one realizes that there are personality variables that enter into the operation of group norms and contribute to determining the patterning of conformity behaviors observed in the affairs of the group. These personality factors, however, probably enter into this process while interacting with other variables, some of which are other personality factors (Samelson, 1957), some of which are characteristics of the situation itself (Kaplan, 1961), and some of which concern the characteristics of the individuals who serve as the source of influence (Berkowitz & Lundy, 1957; Wagner, 1975; Markey, 1973; Krivonos, Byrne, & Friedrich, 1976). Hence, the study of social norms involves the entire range of social-psychological influences.

Status and Conformity

One of the more interesting questions regarding the influence of a social group concerns the role of status in contributing to an individual's susceptibility to social pressures. Specifically the question is, who conforms most to the norms of the group? Is it the high-status member who stands to lose a great deal in the face of group disapproval, or is it the low-status member who holds a relatively weak and insecure position in the group? One could probably develop convincing arguments for either alternative, so under these circumstances it might be best to turn to the research literature. In doing so, however, we find that no clear-cut answer seems to be available. In fact, there is research support for each of the several arguments that one could advance; hence once again we find that a question posed regarding the functioning of a single variable leads us to see that other factors enter into the picture to influence the relationships observed.

Kelley and Shapiro (1954), for example, report on a study in which group pressures encouraged individuals to report incorrect solutions to a judgment task. In this instance, the tendency to conform was most evident among those who maintained low status in the group. Sundby (1962), on the other hand, cites results that suggest that high-status persons are more susceptible to group pressures, and then there are several studies (Dittes & Kelley, 1956; Harvey & Consalvi, 1960) reporting that it is among those who hold second rank in a group that the highest levels of conformity are found.

All of these results, when viewed singly, make sense. With regard to the low-status person, for example, we might suspect that low status is associated with high social strivings that encourage the individual to be more sensitive and responsive to group influences. Fenchel, Monderer, and Hartley (1951) cite a study in which college students who estimated that their status was low showed higher strivings for social status than did those who estimated that they possessed high status. With regard to the high-status position, we might argue the high-status person, being in a more visible position, tends to incur more intense pressure when deviating from group norms, and Alvarez (1968) has presented evidence indicating that this may be the case, especially when the individual is functioning in a group that has experienced low levels of success. Finally, with regard to persons in the second rank, we might argue that they should be more responsive to social influences, since being so close to a position of highest status tends to make the leadership role seem more available; hence its pull is greater and the incentive to conform is much higher.

Homans (1961) suggests that the relationship between social status and susceptibility to group pressures may be described by an inverted-U-shaped function—that is, both the high-status and the low-status members showing a tendency to deviate from group norms more than do members who maintain middle status. The member low in status has little in the way of social position to lose, and as a consequence, negative group sanctions do not represent substantial costs. High-status members, on the other hand, are often expected

to assume a leadership function that requires them to innovate and strike out in new directions. These tend to be high-risk behaviors, and if one is not successful, high status insulates one from group reaction. As a consequence, Homans maintains that it is the member of intermediate status who should display the greatest sensitivity to groups' standards of conduct.

Looking back both at Homans's ideas and the research that has been cited, we see that there appears to be support for several alternatives. In fact, it seems that on one occasion or another, a high tendency to conform may be found at almost any position along a scale of social status. Here we are faced with a situation that is not an unusual one for those who read the literature in the social sciences. A question is raised concerning the behavioral influence of a single variable, and there seems to be research support for several different answers. Under these circumstances, what is the appropriate explanation for this apparent confusion in the research findings? Perhaps the best single answer requires one to adopt a contingency model that contains a set of variables interacting to form a pattern of influence. The effect of one variable, for example, social status, may be dependent upon the level of one or more additional variables. To study the influence of a single variable over its entire range, as well as in conjunction with the range of the other variable with which it interacts, often requires an extensive series of research efforts. Hence research progress is often painfully slow, and the literature becomes filled with what appears to be contradictory evidence. These contradictions often are an expression of the interaction between variables involved. We probably found an illustration of this point when we inquired into the relationship between social status and the individual's responsiveness to group norms.

Group Reaction to Deviance

The field studies we have considered provide ample information concerning the reaction of work groups to those members whose behavior deviates from group norms. The general finding is that groups tend to direct aversive pressures against those who do not comply with the standards of conduct that have been adopted. It seems quite reasonable to suspect, however, that not all members of a group will share the same consequence if they deviate from group norms. Social status would certainly be one factor to consider. Hollander (1958, 1960, 1961, 1964) suggests that as individuals acquire status in a group they also acquire a certain kind of social resource that they can count on to mitigate the group's response to their deviant ways. He reasons that the positive feelings a group has for any member is a direct function of the status of the individual, and that these favorable perceptions are thought of in terms of a set of credits that the individual may draw on to avoid negative reactions to deviance. Hollander calls these resources *idiosyncratic credits* and he sees in their accumulation a sort of fund, the expenditure of which permits the member to engage in behaviors that are divergent from the norms of the group. He suggests that there is a linear relationship between idiosyncratic credits and social status. As a consequence, the response of the group to occasional deviance would be expected to be more severe when the member involved is of low status, hence possessing fewer idiosyncratic credits. Of course anyone may overspend these credits either by too frequently engaging in idiosyncratic conduct or by violating a social norm that is very highly valued by the group. Hollander contends that affiliation with the group is brought to an end whenever one exhausts one's reserve of idiosyncratic credits. Hence, the fact that an individual is a member of the group implies that that person maintains some reserve, and as a consequence, along with all other members, maintains the potential of deviating from the norms that are held by the group. This point of view, therefore, recognizes that the potential for norm violation is held by all members of the group, but this potential is not the same for every member; it varies with social status.

It stands to reason that any factor that contributes to an individual's status in a group should influence the group's reaction to deviant behaviors. For example, an individual's general level of competence in areas of activity that are important to the group should contribute to status position and hence to the accumulation of idiosyncratic credits. Furthermore, for two persons of equal competence, the person with the longest group membership should have had greater opportunity to gather together a larger reserve of credits; therefore that member, rather than the newcomer, should be exposed to less negative pressure for deviant behavior.

Both of these predictions have received confirmation. For instance, in one study Hollander (1960) found that when competence is equivalent, persons who deviate from group norms early in the course of their affiliation are less likely to receive the support of the members than do persons whose nonconformity occurs after they have maintained a longer membership in the group. In another study (Hollander, 1961), nonconforming actions received less disapproval when the act was carried out by a member of higher competence, and in still another study (Pepitone, 1958) it is reported that the higher a group member's status, the greater is the tendency for others to attribute good intentions to both positive and negative acts. Furthermore, Pepitone finds that groups tend to see negative acts of high-status members as being more justified.

Hence, the research evidence available suggests that social status and factors contributing to it make a contribution to determining who conforms to group norms and the reactions of the group toward the member who engages in deviant behaviors. But here again we must point out that other factors influence this relationship. We had previously cited a study by Alvarez (1968) in which group members assigned greater esteem to high-status members than to low after they were involved in deviant behaviors. This relationship, however, held only for groups that had been previously successful. For groups that had experienced low levels of success, the high-status member loses greater esteem after he is involved in deviant conduct. So once again we see one variable, group success, mediating the influence of another variable, social status. It would appear that before being able to make a statement about status and susceptibility to group influences, one would have to have knowledge of the extent to which the group has been functioning successfully.

Institutionalized Deviance.   Dentler and Erikson (1959) contend that deviation from group norms is a function of both the personality of the individual and the characteristics of the group as a whole. Concerning this latter consideration, the authors contend that deviance, rather than being universally unacceptable to the members of the group, sometimes serves ends that are considered desirable. As a consequence, groups are often found in the act of encouraging and reinforcing certain kinds of deviant behavior.

The deviant serves the members by creating contrasts which accent both group norms and the reward system. Dentler and Erikson (1959) argue that contrasts are necessary for the maintenance of group norms, since these standards become most sharply focused when someone violates them. As a consequence, groups maintain their standards by balancing deviance and conformity, and both processes tend to become an institutionalized facet of group activity—that is, become a part of the group's routine. With regard to the reward system, Dentler and Erikson suggest that the fact that some members receive larger rewards than others confirms the vitality and meaning of the incentive system. This is so because the behavioral contrasts created by the deviant behavior correlate with the contrasts in the distribution of rewards. This correlation between conformity and reward adds meaning and validity to the incentive system. Finally, Dentler and Erikson argue that because the deviant does serve a worthwhile purpose, the group will tend to resist actions that would result in the rejection of the deviant. Hence, coping with deviance becomes a part of a group's efforts to sustain standards of conduct, and is often made to strike a balance between the group's needs for con-

formity and the activities that diverge from the norms of the group.

Group Cohesiveness and Group Influence

The results of Alvarez's study suggest that in addition to individual variables, there are characteristics of the group as a whole that also contribute to the extent to which the group is influential in shaping the conduct of its members. Group cohesiveness is one such variable, although as with other group characteristics, it is not an easy concept to translate into measurement. The definition of cohesiveness usually reflects one or both of two related ideas. First, cohesiveness refers to the extent to which individuals are attracted to the group and have a feeling of liking for the members. From this perspective, then, group cohesiveness concerns the extent to which members like each other and express behaviors that indicate a network of interpersonal attraction shared by the group members. Related to this point of view is the definition of cohesiveness that emphasizes the extent to which the individual members value the various rewards that are available to those who operate within the group. A cost-reward concept is appropriate here, with group cohesiveness being a direct function of the extent to which group members believe that the rewards of group membership exceed the cost of belonging.

In a study that involved over 225 work groups in a large company engaged in the manufacture of heavy machinery, Seashore (1954) reports that he observed little relationship between measures of work-group cohesiveness and actual levels of production. On the average, highly cohesive groups appeared to be no more productive than were groups of low cohesion. Seashore found, however, that there was much greater variation in production rates in the low-cohesion groups. In terms of production rates, the high-cohesion groups were more homogeneous than were the members of the low-cohesion work groups. Hence cohesiveness, measured in terms of attraction to the group, was found to relate to the *variation* in rates of production found within work groups; there was less variation in production in groups in which members expressed high attraction. Interestingly, however, Seashore reports that variation of production rates *between* work groups was greater for those groups that showed evidence of high levels of cohesiveness. Highly cohesive groups varied more among themselves than did low-cohesion groups, with the high groups showing both high and low rates of production, whereas the low-cohesion groups tended to show average production rates that were more moderate.

What do Seashore's results tell us about the operation of production norms in a work group? Perhaps we might infer that attraction to a group and a feeling of belonging is associated with an individual's acceptance of many of the norms that the group maintains. Affiliation with a work group in which the individual feels a general liking for the members implies that the individual is willing to abide by the norms that govern the conduct of the group. A group that is cohesive, therefore, is one for which there is a high generalized level of compliance with the group's standards. In the terms of the Return Potential Model, group cohesiveness refers to a situation in which there is a high level of norm crystallization.

Since, however, groups vary in the norms they maintain, and are subjected to varying levels of external pressures, one should expect to find considerable group-to-group variation in production norms. This would be particularly true for highly cohesive groups where all members would tend to cluster around the established norm. Hence, cohesiveness does not necessarily suggest high or low productivity. Rather, it suggests that members will show a widely shared allegiance to the work standards of the group.

Cohesiveness and Member Similarity. Group cohesiveness is also facilitated in those instances in which the members of a work group share similar needs, attitudes, and personality characteristics (Krivonos, Byrne, & Friedrich, 1976; Terborg, Castore, & DeNinno, 1976). Members who hold similar attributes are often able to establish congenial working relationships that lead to a more highly developed team spirit. Some (Wirich, 1958) argue that *need complementarity* is another important factor that determines interpersonal attraction, hence heightened group cohesiveness. Need complementarity is found, for example, when one member of a pair possesses a strong need to control the environment, while the other member has a need to submit to external influences. In the ongoing realities of work organizations it happens infrequently that teams are built by systematic efforts to bring together complementary need structures, but on an informal basis the importance of psychological compatibility is widely recognized by managers who strive to move up in the ranks those individuals who "fit in" with members of a management group.

Cohesiveness and External Pressures. Cohesiveness may stem from sources that are external to the group, as might be the case in situations in which management exerts pressures on a group for increased productivity. In these instances, group members may band together in a cohesive structure in order to provide mutual security and resistance to these external influences. There are numerous studies that bear on this situation. Zimbardo and Fromica (1963), for example, found that persons functioning under stress tend to prefer to be with others who share these emotions. There is also a study by Mulder and Stemerding (1963) that shows the effects of external stresses on the tendency of people to cluster in cohesive groups. In this study, groups of shopkeepers, when exposed to the threat of increased competition, showed heightened attraction to a newly formed trade association. Hence, in looking for factors that influence the cohesiveness of groups, one should look outside as well as inside the group.

Cohesiveness and the Nature of Group Norms. Schachter et al. (1951) maintain that whether cohesiveness facilitates a group's efforts to influence productivity depends upon whether group pressures are directed toward increasing or decreasing output. They created a production situation in a laboratory in which members of high- or low-cohesion groups were exposed to what they thought were group pressures to change their rates of production. Some group members were exposed to positive induction—messages that indicated that the other group members wanted them to increase their production; some to negative induction—messages asking them to slow down. The purpose of the study was to determine the effects of positive and negative induction on high- and low-cohesion groups, and the results indicated that when group pressures called for increased production there was no difference in the responses. Both groups increased their output. When group pressures counseled a slowdown, however, highly cohesive groups tended to reduce their rate of work more than did the low-cohesion groups.

These results suggest that the effectiveness of pressures to *increase* production rates does not depend upon the internal cohesion of the group. This might result from the members seeing pressures of this sort as coming from sources that are external to the group. An individual being encouraged to increase production is receiving pressures that are compatible with the interests of external authority, that is, management. When, on the other hand, a group pressures an individual to hold back on production, it encourages action that is contrary to the interests of external authority. There is a risk involved in abiding by these restrictive norms, but this risk is less threatening in a group that is bound together in a cohesive structure. There is greater security associated with lower production rates when the work group bands together for protection. Hence, there is probably an increased chance that cohesiveness is a factor influencing the potency of group standards only when they are directed toward a restriction of productivity.

Groupthink and Institutional Deviance

We should not leave this discussion of the work group without acknowledging the fact that not all

forms of compliance are beneficial to group effectiveness. Janis (1972), for example, finds that within certain highly cohesive groups there arise psychological forces that serve to undermine the group's ability to deal with complexity and to develop effective solutions to the problems the members confront. He applies the term "groupthink" to these circumstances, and about this condition he states:

> I use the term "groupthink" as a quick and easy way to refer to a mode of thinking that people engage in when they are deeply involved in a cohesive in-group, when members' strivings for unanimity override their motivation to realistically appraise alternative courses of action. . . . Groupthink refers to a deterioration of mental efficiency, reality testing, and moral judgment that results from in-group pressures. (Janis, 1972, p. 9)

At times groups can invest too heavily in trying to maintain unanimous commitment to standards of thought and conduct. Amiability and goodwill become the dominant concern of the group, with the result that decisions are predicated more on an effort to maintain an internal climate of harmony and camaraderie than they are on getting the work done and seeing that the best solutions are obtained. Janis contends (1972, p. 9):

> The central theme of my analysis can be summarized in this generalization: The more amiability and esprit de corps among the members of a policy making in-group, the greater is the danger that independent critical thinking will be replaced by groupthink, which is likely to result in irrational and dehumanizing actions directed against out-groups.

Janis recognizes two primary conditions that increase the likelihood that groupthink occurs. The first involves high levels of group cohesiveness, which becomes a group goal in and of itself. The second is found wherever these cohesive groups become insulated from new and different ideas that originate outside the group. The group often is found developing attitudes that prevent the intrusion of different points of view, and in the absence of these cross-pressures, there occurs the conviction that the group is infallibly correct and morally superior. Janis (1972, pp. 197–198) includes the following as symptoms of groupthink behavior:

1. an illusion of invulnerability, shared by most or all the members which creates excessive optimism and encourages taking extreme risks;
2. collective efforts to rationalize in order to discount warnings which might lead the members to reconsider their assumptions before they recommit themselves to their past policy decisions;
3. an unquestioned belief in the group's inherent morality, inclining the members to ignore the ethical or moral consequences of their decisions;
4. direct pressure on any member who expresses strong arguments against any of the group's stereotypes, illusions, or commitments, making clear that this type of dissent is contrary to what is expected of all loyal members;
5. self-censorship of deviations from the apparent group consensus, reflecting each member's inclination to minimize to himself the importance of his doubts and counterarguments;
6. a shared illusion of unanimity concerning judgments conforming to the majority view (partly resulting from self-censorship of deviations, augmented by the false assumption that silence means consent);
7. the emergence of self-appointed mindguards—members who protect the group from adverse information that might shatter their shared complacency about the effectiveness and morality of their decisions.

SUMMARY COMMENTS

The research that has been cited in the present chapter points to the fact that there are normative influences residing in a work group that play a significant role in shaping and directing the behaviors of the individual members. Although these factors can be thought of as part of the individual psychology of each member, the origin and maintenance of these influences are best thought of in terms of the group as a whole. The purposes they serve are many, but of primary importance is the fact that social norms function to bring order and regularity into the daily affairs of the group; and although within each day there are unique and unpredictable happenings, one of the functions of social norms is to keep the variety of work experiences within limits that permit workers to make a satisfactory psychological adjustment to their jobs. All individuals have a substantial investment in the mechanisms that regularize the interpersonal relations that take place in their jobs. Social norms serve this purpose by providing a standard of conduct to which each worker may refer in adopting a particular mode of behaving. As we have seen,

workers typically have considerable knowledge of these norms, and it is important that they do, since such information is essential to a congenial social adjustment to one's job. Each work group has within its control many psychological incentives that can be quite important to the individual worker. Our examination of the research literature has shown us that conformity to group norms is a factor contributing to an individual's prospects of receiving a reasonable share of these incentives.

One of the inducements to conform lies in the fact that social norms tend to place the individual worker in a job environment in which the things that happen are predictable. Knowledge of norms that govern group behavior enables individuals to more accurately anticipate the social consequences of their and others' behaviors. The workers in the Bank Wiring Room knew quite well that certain kinds of social pressures awaited them if they consistently ignored the production quotas that the group maintained. The men with whom Roy worked in the clicking room knew their "dramatic" roles whenever it was banana time.

One must not carry away the impression that in each work group there is unswerving conformity to a single behavioral standard. The Return Potential Model tells us that in many social situations there is a range of behaviors that receive the approval of the group, and within most groups one will find workers whose behavior lies outside this range. Hence, the pattern of social adjustment found in most work groups extends through a zone of conformity and beyond to an area of deviance.

Most would agree that a worker's lack of responsiveness to group norms carries with it psychological and social costs. In some instances, past performance coupled with status put an individual in a position to "afford" these costs. In this regard, each member of the group has a "deviancy account" from which credits that purchase tolerance for norm violations may be withdrawn. There are instances, however, when a commitment to cordial group relations discourages all forms of dissent and deviance. Unanimity becomes an important end in itself, and the normal range of internal checks and balances that come from different points of view cease to function in group actions. Under these circumstances a group becomes less able to view problems and solutions from a number of different perspectives. As a result, it becomes less adaptive to changing conditions and much of the group's vitality and flexibility are lost. Some argue (Presthus, 1964) that all groups and organizations should consciously maintain vigilant support for a climate of open dissent, lest groupthink become established as the dominant psychology of the group.

12

Union Membership

No discussion of the social environment of work can be considered complete without some attention being paid to the labor union. Although not found in every work organization, labor unions are an important part of the job environment for a large number of workers. Even when they are absent from a particular setting, unions still represent a highly visible, and at times controversial, part of the worker's broad picture of work.

We often view the labor union as an organization that represents workers in situations in which their interests come into conflict with the interests of management. From this perspective we think of the union playing the role of an advocate in the competitive relationship that exists between worker and management. Labor relations, grievances, negotiations, arbitration, and strikes are all terms that surround this view, and it is this aspect of union activity that tends to generate the most controversy. It is not difficult to find people, professionals and laymen alike, who can be divided into pro and con factions on these issues.

There is another view of the union, however, which does not enter our thinking quite as prominently but which, in terms of the quality of the individual's work life, may be just as important as negotiations, contracts, and disputes. This aspect concerns the fact that the labor union is a social organization that is found within the general setting of an individual's job. The union is a part of the social environment of work; it is a social reality to which the worker must make some kind of adjustment. It is one of the facets of the job that can provide the worker with a sense of status and security; it serves as a channel through which a worker may voice resentments and hostilities toward management. The union provides information on a wide variety of work-related and political matters; it is a bureaucratic agency, complete with rules and regulations by which the worker must abide. In short, the union is part of the individual's total work experience. Roles in the union, the level of involvement in its affairs, perceptions of its role and function, and the use of its resources to achieve personal objectives are all real and important aspects of an individual's work life. We find wide individual differences in the manner in which workers react to this facet of their job experience.

This chapter will try to answer questions concerning the labor union, viewed from the perspective of the individual member. For example, an attempt will be made to describe the different roles workers may adopt in connection with their membership in the union. To what extent does the worker participate in the affairs of the union, does he attend the union meetings, is he aware of the policies and actions of the organization, does he vote in union elections? How does he see the union, does he approve of its leadership and tactics, does he support its political activities? Why does he join in the first place? These are the kinds of questions that will be taken up by the present chapter, and in doing so emphasis will be placed on the psychological implications of union membership. Relatively little attention will be paid to such matters as labor law, labor economics, and the history of the union movement.

The chapter will also attempt to look at several facets of the psychology of union-management relations. Recognizing that the relationship between the two groups is a fundamentally competitive one, we will try to deal with labor relations from the viewpoint of the individual worker. Such questions as the extent to which the worker identifies with the union or management will be taken up. To what extent workers are willing to strike, and to what extent they see the union as an extension of their own hostilities toward management are questions that will be considered in the light of the social science literature.

GENERAL CHARACTERISTICS

Before we take up these issues, however, it might be useful to begin with a consideration of some of the general background characteristics of unions and their members. As we will see, membership in labor organizations tends to be most heavily concentrated in certain segments of the labor force; union members do not make up a representative cross-section of all workers. Hence, before we begin our discussion of the individual union member, it might be prudent to consider some of the general characteristics of the groups of workers who do affiliate with these organizations.

Extent of Union Membership

Many seem to have the impression that the majority of people in the labor force are members of labor unions. Especially when thinking about blue-collar jobs, it is frequently assumed that the typical worker is a member of a union. The fact of the matter is, however, that union membership constitutes a minority of not only the total labor force, but of the blue-collar sector as well. Consider Table 12.1, which shows for the years 1958–1978 union membership in absolute numbers and as a percent of the nonagricultural labor force.[1] [2] Throughout this period, union membership has never accounted for more than one-third of the total number of people employed, and over this fourteen-year period there has been a rather steady decline in the percentage of the labor force that affiliates with a union or an employee association.[3] During 1958 approximately one in three workers was a union member; by 1974, however, this figure had dropped to about one in four.

It is impossible to explain completely this drop in the percentage of membership, but one of the more interesting contributors to this trend is doubtless found in the changing structure of the occupational fields that make up the labor market. Economic and technological changes have resulted in significant changes in the kinds of work people do. For instance, there has been a steady increase in the number of managerial and professional jobs, a substantial increase in the number of white-collar and service jobs, and a major growth in the number of jobs held by state and federal employees. It is in these areas of employment that the success of union organizing efforts has been low. As a consequence, as the growth of these kinds of jobs has continued to account for a disproportionate part of the growth of the total labor force, there have resulted the trends represented in Table 12.1—a steady increase in the *number* of union members and a steady decrease in their *proportion* of the labor force.

---

[1]The statistics reported here and elsewhere in this section are, unless noted otherwise, obtained from the *Directory of National Unions and Employee Associations 1975*. U.S. Department of Labor, Bureau of Labor Statistics, 1977, Bulletin 1937.

[2]Total labor force includes employed and unemployed workers, self-employed, members of the Armed Forces, and others. The nonagricultural labor force excludes members of the Armed Forces, unemployed, self-employed, domestic servants, agricultural workers, proprietors, and unpaid family workers.

[3]Employee associations include professional organizations and state employee associations that engage in collective bargaining activities. Examples are The National Education Association, National Football League Players Association, American Association of University Professors.

TABLE 12.1 National Union and Employee Association Membership as a Proportion of Labor Force and Nonagricultural Employment, 1958–78 (Numbers in Thousands)

Year	Member-ship excluding Canada	Total labor force		Employees in nonagricultural establishments	
		Number	Percent members	Number	Percent members
Unions and associations:					
1968	20,721	82,272	25.2	67,951	30.5
1969	20,776	84,240	24.7	70,442	29.5
1970	21,248	85,903	24.7	70,920	30.0
1971	21,327	86,929	24.5	71,222	29.9
1972	21,657	88,991	24.3	73,714	29.4
1973	22,276	91,040	24.5	76,896	29.0
1974	22,809	93,240	24.5	78,413	29.1
1975	22,361	94,793	23.6	77,364	28.9
1976	22,662	96,917	23.4	80,048	28.3
1977	22,456	99,534	22.6	82,423	27.2
1978	22,880	102,537	22.3	84,446	27.1
Unions:					
1958	17,029	70,275	24.2	51,363	33.2
1959	17,117	70,921	24.1	53,313	32.1
1960	17,049	72,142	23.6	54,234	31.4
1961	16,303	73,031	22.3	54,042	30.2
1962	16,586	73,442	22.6	55,596	29.8
1963	16,524	74,571	22.2	56,702	29.1
1964	16,841	75,830	22.2	58,331	28.9
1965	17,299	77,178	22.4	60,815	28.4
1966	17,940	78,893	22.7	63,955	28.1
1967	18,367	80,793	22.7	65,857	27.9
1968	18,916	82,272	23.0	67,951	27.8
1969	19,036	84,240	22.6	70,442	27.0
1970	19,381	85,903	22.6	70,920	27.3
1971	19,211	86,929	22.1	71,222	27.0
1972	19,435	88,991	21.8	73,714	26.4
1973	19,851	91,040	21.8	76,896	25.8
1974	20,199	93,240	21.7	78,413	25.8
1975	19,553	94,793	20.6	77,364	25.3
1976	19,634	96,917	20.3	80,048	24.5
1977	19,902	99,534	20.0	82,423	24.1
1978	20,246	102,537	19.7	84,446	24.0

Source: Department of Labor, *Directory of National Unions and Employee Associations 1980.* Washington, D.C.: Government Printing Office.

We see, therefore, that in terms of percentages, labor-union members represent a sizable *minority* of the people who are employed. Approximately three of every four workers in the nonagricultural labor force are *not* affiliated with a labor organization; in spite of their minority status, however, labor unions still represent well over 20 million jobholders.

TABLE 12.2 Distribution of Membership of National Unions by State and as a Proportion of Employees in Nonagricultural Establishments, 1976 and 1978

| | Membership (thousands) | | | | Total union membership as a percent of employees in nonagricultural establishments | | | |
State	1976	1976 rank	1978[1]	1978 rank	1976 (revised)	1976 rank	1978	1978 rank
All States	19,874	—	20,459	—	24.9	—	23.6	—
Alabama[2]	229	23	257	22	19.0	25	19.2	25
Alaska	50	43	43	46	29.1	13	26.2	13
Arizona[2]	117	32	122	30	15.4	35	13.8	37
Arkansas[2]	102	34	109	33	15.5	34	15.0	33
California	2148	2	2184	2	26.3	14	23.7	17
Colorado	175	27	172	27	17.4	31	15.2	32
Connecticut	309	17	296	18	24.9	18	21.9	22
Delaware	49	44	52	43	20.7	24	21.0	23
Florida[2]	365	16	367	16	13.1	44	11.7	46
Georgia[2]	261	20	271	20	14.2	38	13.6	38
Hawaii	129	29	120	31	36.9	3	32.1	6
Idaho	41	46	47	45	14.1	39	14.3	36
Illinois	1451	4	1497	4	31.8	8	31.5	7
Indiana	621	8	643	8	30.7	11	29.3	10
Iowa[2]	192	26	212	26	18.5	27	19.2	26
Kansas[2]	125	31	117	32	15.0	37	12.8	42
Kentucky	275	19	274	19	24.7	19	22.4	21
Louisiana[2]	213	25	227	24	16.2	32	16.0	30
Maine	67	40	74	39	17.9	29	18.3	27
Maryland-District of Columbia	440	14	458	14	21.2	23	21.0	24
Massachusetts	570	10	611	9	24.6	21	24.5	14
Michigan	1165	6	1223	6	35.7	5	34.6	3
Minnesota	385	15	411	15	25.3	15	24.4	15
Mississippi[2]	87	35	103	35	12.0	47	12.7	44
Missouri	572	9	578	10	31.8	7	30.0	8
Montana	60	42	67	41	23.9	22	24.1	16
Nebraska[2]	87	35	92	36	15.2	36	15.3	31
Nevada[2]	69	38	80	37	24.7	20	22.9	20
New Hampshire	43	45	48	44	13.7	40	13.2	40
New Jersey	697	7	683	7	25.3	16	23.0	19
New Mexico	73	37	54	42	18.7	26	12.1	45
New York	2515	1	2753	1	37.1	2	39.2	1
North Carolina[2]	141	28	147	28	6.8	49	6.5	50
North Dakota[2]	26	48	34	47	12.1	45	14.6	35
Ohio	1289	5	1294	5	31.5	9	29.5	9
Oklahoma	126	30	138	29	13.5	42	13.4	39
Oregon	221	24	232	23	25.2	17	23.1	18
Pennsylvania	1642	3	1595	3	36.4	4	34.2	4
Rhode Island	114	33	108	34	31.1	10	27.1	12
South Carolina[2]	68	39	76	38	6.6	50	6.7	49

TABLE 12.2 (*Continued*)

State	Membership (thousands)				Total union membership as a percent of employees in nonagricultural establishments			
	1976	1976 rank	1978[1]	1978 rank	1976 (revised)	1976 rank	1978	1978 rank
South Dakota[2]	21	50	24	50	9.6	48	10.3	48
Tennessee[2]	288	18	303	17	18.3	28	17.7	28
Texas[2]	563	11	575	11	12.0	46	11.0	47
Utah[2]	62	41	68	40	13.4	43	12.9	41
Vermont	30	47	33	48	17.8	30	17.4	29
Virginia[2]	252	21	258	21	13.6	41	12.7	43
Washington	453	13	496	18	35.3	6	33.1	5
West Virginia	232	22	226	25	38.9	1	36.8	2
Wisconsin	506	12	522	12	29.3	12	27.8	11
Wyoming[2]	25	49	28	49	16.0	33	14.9	34
Membership not classifiable[3]	133	—	60	—	—	—	—	—

[1]Based on reports from 125 national unions and estimates for 49. Also included are local unions directly affiliated with the AFL-CIO and members in single-firm and local unaffiliated unions.

[2]Has right-to-work law.

[3]Includes local unions directly affiliated with the AFL-CIO.

NOTE: Because of rounding, sums of individual items may not equal totals. Dashes indicate no data in category.

Source: Department of Labor *Directory of National Unions and Employee Associations 1980*. Washington, D.C.: Government Printing Office, 1980.

Distribution of Union Members

By States. There are regions in the country in which membership in labor unions is very high, and there are regions in which a relatively small number of workers affiliate with the union. As might be expected, large numbers of union workers are concentrated in those states that have the largest number of people employed in nonagricultural jobs. In 1978, for example, six states (New York, California, Pennsylvania, Illinois, Ohio, and Michigan) accounted for over one-half of all union members (see Table 12.2). These rankings, however, do not give us a good picture of the extent to which unions have been successful in organizing a large percentage of a state's labor force. For instance, Michigan is ranked third in the nation in the percentage of its labor force affiliated with a union (34.6 percent). West Virginia with 36.8 percent ranks second and New York with 39.2 percent ranks first. North Carolina (6.5 percent), South Carolina (6.7 percent) and South Dakota (10.3 percent) are the three states with the smallest portion of union membership in their labor force.

By Industry. The Bureau of Labor Statistics (1974) has made estimates of the extent of union organization in thirty-five industry classifications. These data reveal that the degree to which unions have been successful in their organizational efforts varies widely from one industry to the next (see Table 12.3). Among the industries reporting the highest percentage of union membership are transportation, construction, and transportation equipment. Union organization in these instances has reached 75 percent or better of all workers employed. The railroad industry is the most highly organized, with approximately 80 percent of the workers affiliated with a union. In the automobile

TABLE 12.3   Industry Groups Arranged according to Percent of Union Membership

| | Percent of Union Membership | | |
75 percent and over	50 percent to less than 75 percent	25 percent to less than 50 percent	Less than 25 percent
1. Transportation	7. Primary metals	19. Printing publishing	26. Nonmanufacturing
2. Construction	8. Food and kindred products	20. Leather	27. Textile mill products
3. Ordnance	9. Mining	21. Furniture	28. Government
4. Paper	10. Apparel	22. Electric gas utilities	29. Instruments
5. Electrical equipment	11. Tobacco manufacturing	23. Machinery	30. Service
6. Transportation equipment	12. Petroleum	24. Chemicals	31. Local government
	13. Manufacturing	25. Lumber	32. State government
	14. Fabricated metals		33. Trade
	15. Telephone and telegraph		34. Agriculture and fishing
	16. Stone, clay and glass products		35. Finance
	17. Federal Government		
	18. Rubber		

Source: Department of Labor, *Director of National Unions and Employee Associations 1977*. Washington, D.C.: Government Printing Office.

industry about 60 percent of all employees are union members. At the low end of the scale are found government, service, textile, and agricultural industries. Here the extent of union organization is less than 25 percent. In textiles unionization accounts for only 10 percent of those employed.

By Union.   Just as union membership is concentrated in certain regions and industries, so too we find that union membership is concentrated in a comparatively few large labor organizations. In 1974, for instance, 16 union organizations (less than 10 percent of the total number) enrolled 12.8 million members. This number represents about 60 percent of all union members. Hence, 60 percent of the 20 million union members were represented by a comparative handful of labor organizations, while at the other end of the scale there were 82 unions (out of a total of 177) whose combined membership accounted for only 2.2 percent of the national total.

We see from these figures that affiliation with a labor organization typically brings the worker into membership with a large and socially complex entity. This fact, together with the fact that employment tends to be concentrated in a relatively few large business enterprises (see Chapter 6) lends support to the hypothesis that the social environment of work often places the worker in a position that is psychologically distant from the policy-making centers that play a major role in shaping the conditions under which the work is performed. Furthermore, the size and complexity (that is, the psychological distance) of both union and management are important variables that determine the nature of the worker's psychological commitment to the job.

Characteristics of Union Members

It is interesting to note that people who are members of labor unions are in several respects not representative of a broad cross-section of the workers who make up the national labor force. For example, a disproportionate number of union members are men (see Table 12.4). A 1978 survey (Department of Labor, 1980) found that while men constituted 58 percent of the labor force, they accounted for almost 76 percent of the union membership. Union members also tend to be concentrated in blue-collar sectors of the job market. As a case in point, in 1970 nearly 40 percent of all blue-collar workers were found to be union members, while at the same time only about 17 percent of all white-collar workers were affiliated with unions (see Table 12.5).

In addition to the fact that union membership is concentrated among blue-collar workers, union

TABLE 12.4   Membership of Women in National Unions and Employee Associations, Selected Years, 1954–78

Year	Number of women members (thousands)	Percent of total membership
Unions and associations	5398	23.9
1970	5736	24.9
1972	6038	25.0
1974	6857	28.1
1978		
Unions		
1954	2950	16.6
1956	3400	18.6
1958	3274	18.2
1960	3304	18.3
1962	3272	18.6
1964	3413	19.0
1966	3689	19.3
1968	3940	19.5
1970	4282	20.7
1972	4524	21.7
1974	4600	21.3
1976	4648	22.0
1978	5267	24.2

Source: Department of Labor, *Directory of National Unions and Employee Associations 1980.* Washington, D.C.: Government Printing Office.

TABLE 12.5   White-Collar Membership of National Unions and Employee Associations, Selected Years, 1956–78

Year	Number of white-collar members (thousands)	Percent of total membership
Unions and associations	4917	21.8
1970	5202	22.6
1972	5881	24.3
1974	6296	25.8
1978		
Unions		
1956	2463	13.6
1958	2184	12.2
1960	2192	12.2
1962	2285	13.0
1964	2585	14.4
1966	2810	14.7
1968	3176	15.7
1970	3353	16.2
1972	3434	16.5
1974	3762	17.4
1976	4068	19.3
1978	4067	18.7

Source: Department of Labor, *Directory of National Unions and Employee Associations 1980.* Washington, D.C.: Government Printing Office.

employees also tend to be somewhat older than those who are not members. In the Department of Labor survey, the median age of union workers was found to be 41 years, while the median age for people not affiliated with a union was 36. Furthermore, union members have been found to have educational levels that are higher than those of comparable workers who are not members. Bok and Dunlop (1970) report that 44 percent of union members who were heads of households had received some high school education, while the comparable figure for nonunion workers was only 32 percent. This relation was reversed, however, at the higher levels of education; it was found that only 1.4 percent of the heads of families who were union members had received college degrees while

11.4 percent of the nonunion family heads had graduated from college.

Income.   Bok and Dunlop also report that union members tend to fall in the middle ranges of the income distribution, while nonunion members tend to be found at either very low salary positions or at the other, high end of the income range. In 1970, union members who worked in full-time, year-round jobs had median earnings that were about $100 a month higher than their nonunion counterparts. This difference was primarily due to the wage advantages maintained by union blue-collar workers over their nonunion counterparts, where the difference was almost $2,000 per year. Within the blue-collar job classifications the widest margin of wage difference was found between union and nonunion craftsmen working in construction; here union workers received a median wage that was 40 percent higher than that of nonunion craftsmen.

Nonunion workers tended to be found in heaviest concentrations at the two ends of the income distribution. For example, as compared to 11 percent of the union workers, 25 percent of the nonunion workers made less than $5,000 a year in 1970. At the upper end of the wage scale, however, only 5 percent of the union workers made $15,000 or more, while 11 percent of the nonunion workers reached this level. Hence, union membership carries with it the implication of a middle wage range, with nonunion workers concentrating at the high and the low end of the wage scale.

Summary Comment

Concentration is the word that best applies to the distribution of many of the factors that are associated with union membership. Union membership tends to be associated with individuals who are concentrated in certain sectors of the country, in certain industries, and even in a relatively small number of labor organizations. Union membership tends to be disproportionately high among men, among individuals who hold blue-collar jobs, and among those whose earnings place them somewhere in the middle of the wage distribution. In

talking about the social psychology of union membership, therefore, we are in fact dealing with a group that in many respects is not generally representative of the broad range of jobs and workers that make up the labor market. We are talking about a group that tends to be concentrated in urban areas and that tends to contribute large numbers to what we may think of as the lower-middle and middle-middle classes of the American social structure. We are, however, talking about a group that does account for over 20 million jobs; a group whose social, political, and economic influence is substantial in shaping the conditions under which many other people work.

WHY PEOPLE JOIN UNIONS

It is quite widely believed that people who join labor unions are motivated by the negative feelings they have toward management. Fear of management power, job insecurity, and hostility toward employers are often considered to be important motivators underlying an individual's decision to affiliate with a union. In some cases this point of view is undoubtedly correct, but in others the decision to join the union does not involve a negative orientation toward the company or management. Instead, the decision to join a union often involves a number of considerations, some carrying more weight than others (Schriesheim, 1978). For example, in a great number of instances the decision to join a labor union is part of a larger decision made by the individual to accept employment with a particular organization. This is the case because in many places of work there exists a union-shop agreement that requires union membership as a condition of employment (see Table 12.6). In these instances, individuals wishing to retain their jobs with the company must join the union within a designated period of time after their initial employment (Cook et al., 1978).

It is extremely difficult to obtain a precise estimate of the prevalence of these kinds of contract requirements; the Bureau of Labor Statistics (1975), however, has reported the results of a review of over 1500 bargaining agreements, which

TABLE 12.6   Major Kinds of Union Security Provisions

1. A *union shop* requires all employees to become members of the union within a specified time after being hired and to remain members of the union as a condition of employment.
2. A *modified union shop* is the same as a union shop except that certain employees may be exempted—for example, those already employed at the time the provision was negotiated who had not as yet joined the union.
3. An *agency shop* requires all employees in the bargaining unit who do not join the union to pay a fixed amount monthly, usually the equivalent of union dues, as a condition of employment, to help defray the union's expenses in acting as bargaining agent.
4. *Maintenance of membership* describes an arrangement whereby employees who are members of the union at the time the agreement is negotiated or who voluntarily join subsequently, must maintain their membership, usually for the duration of the agreement, as a condition of continued employment.
5. *Sole bargaining agent* describes the arrangement whereby the union is recognized as the exclusive bargaining agent for all employees, union and nonunion, in the bargaining unit, but union membership is not required as a condition of employment.

Source: *Characteristics of Major Collective Bargaining Agreements July 1974.* U.S. Department of Labor, Bureau of Labor Statistics, Bulletin 1888, 1975.
Some contracts contain combinations of these provisions.

sheds some light on this matter. It was found that approximately 68 percent of all contracts reviewed included a provision establishing a union shop or a modified union shop. From this we can see that in many instances there is a compulsory aspect associated with union membership. Even in those instances in which the worker is compelled to join, however, he may do so with the conviction that his membership is right and desirable. An early study by Seidman et al. (1951), for example, found that even in instances in which workers join a union in response to external pressures, they do so with some degree of conviction that this is a proper course of action. Hence, even though it must be acknowledged that union membership is often a condition of employment, one must not assume that this situation is usually responsible for compelling large numbers of workers to join against their wishes.

Pay and Working Conditions

A variety of reasons lead to the decision to join a labor union, and at present the weight of the evidence suggests that dissatisfaction with the job is the most potent factor underlying a worker's willingness to affiliate with a union (Getman, Goldberg, & Herman, 1976; Hamner & Smith, 1978; Schriesheim, 1978; Bigoness, 1978). It also seems that a negative attitude toward pay is one of the more important dimensions of this general dissatisfaction that leads to union membership. For example, Schriesheim (1978) studied a group of production workers who were participating in a union representation election. He distributed a set of job-satisfaction scales that measured eight dimensions of job attitudes. Four of these dimensions referred to economic facets, and four dealt with noneconomic aspects of work. Two other scales measured the workers' attitudes toward unions in general and toward the local that was involved in the election. Estimates were made of the relationship between all scales and the workers' votes in the certification election. Significant relationships were obtained for all but two attitude dimensions (satisfaction with job variety and creativity), but the most substantial relationships observed were those involving dissatisfaction with the economic aspects of the job. Voting for the union was also strongly related to the workers' attitudes toward unions in general and toward the local involved in the election.

Bigoness (1978) carried out a study relating job and union attitudes held by a group of faculty members at a New England university. As was the case with the blue-collar workers studied by Schriesheim (1978), the strongest single predictor of the professors' attitudes toward collective bargaining was dissatisfaction with pay. As was also the case in the blue-collar sample, attitudes toward unions was significantly related to a wide variety of job-attitude variables; dissatisfaction with pay, promotion opportunities, and supervision, however, seemed to contribute most to the attitudes that were held toward the union.

A final study is one reported by Hamner and Smith (1978) who collected information on job and union attitudes from 250 groups of sales personnel. Here again the degree of dissatisfaction expressed by workers appeared to be related to the degree to which they became involved in union activities. In this sample, however, dissatisfaction with supervision emerged as the most important factor underlying union activities.

If one were to respond to the question, why do workers join unions, it would be quite reasonable to answer that they do so for many reasons, the most significant one being dissatisfaction with some aspect of the job. In general, the expectation that union membership will result in improved working conditions and better pay is a factor that undoubtedly plays an important role in a worker's decision to join. In connection with this, workers often look at union membership as giving them some influence in controlling the benefits they receive from their work. Union membership, therefore, can give workers a sense of participation and control over the conditions under which they work (Sayles & Strauss, 1953; Stagner, 1956; Duffy, 1960). As a consequence, individual members may see the union as an organization that enhances their status, while at the same time providing them with the security that comes from having influence in important areas of the job.

Social Pressures

Social pressures of one sort or another often are found as reasons underlying a worker's decision to join a union (Seidman et al., 1951). Workers whose parents had expressed positive sentiments toward unions have been found to be more willing to join. Social pressure from work associates, even to the extent of joining merely because others have

done so, is a factor that has been found to influence decisions to accept membership in unions. Past experience with other jobs and with other labor unions is another reason that is sometimes given for joining a union (Husaini & Geschwender, 1968).

General Social Attitudes

Even attitudes of a very general nature have been found to be related to the decision to join a union. For example, Husaini and Geschwender (1968) report that political liberals tend to be more favorably disposed to joining, and Bass and Mitchell (1976) have found that the individual's belief in the inherent fairness of people relates to the worker's disposition toward the union. In this latter study, those who tended to reject the idea that there is a sense of fairness possessed by most people expressed more positive attitudes toward collective bargaining as a procedure that should enter into employer-employee relationships. Along similar lines, Messick (1973, 1974) presents a mathematical model that predicts a high likelihood that workers will join unions when considerations of their own self-interests are coupled with certain levels of concern for the welfare of the group.

These studies show us that the decision to join a labor union may very well be correlated with sets of beliefs and attitudes that extend well beyond the confines of the individual's work experience. Willingness to join is probably most likely when the decision is consonant with the broad range of social and political convictions held by the individual. It seems reasonable to think that there are social beliefs that can more easily accommodate the worker's membership in the union. There are also belief structures with which the reality of union membership does not comfortably fit.

Defensive Motives

Workers join unions for defensive purposes. Fear and mistrust of management may lead a worker to seek the security of union membership. The worker may see the union as a source of protection for the job, and general job dissatisfaction has been found to be a factor that enters into a worker's decision to affiliate with the labor organization. Bass and Mitchell (1976) found that workers who were dissatisfied with their jobs were more likely to endorse the need for collective bargaining in labor-management relationships. The union grievance procedure can also be seen as a mechanism that insulates the worker from the pressures of arbitrary and unfair supervision (Duffy, 1960). Workers sometimes see union membership in broad sociological terms. For example, ideologies that deal with social classes—''big shots'' versus ''the little guy''—can be found serving as considerations underlying the decision to join a union.

Summary Comments

Seidman et al. (1951) summarize their study of why workers join unions by concluding that the reasons behind such decisions are varied and complex. They found workers joining local unions with feelings ranging from high enthusiasm to negativity. The reasons for joining did not fit comfortably into neat little categories, but were found to reflect the individual circumstances that surround a worker's life. If one were forced to speculate about the reasons most often involved in the decision to join a union, the need for job protection and improved economic benefits, coupled with the compulsory aspects of the union shop, would probably be found near the top of the list. There is need for further research before we will be in a position to understand why one worker adopts a given pattern of reasons for joining a union, while another worker, functioning in the same situation, adopts an alternative set of reasons. The key is doubtless to be found in workers' perceptions of the work situation and their positions in it. Self-interest is a potent factor, and Cook et al. (1979) suggest that affiliation with a union is an expression of an individual's assessment of the circumstances surrounding the job and the contribution the union might make in achieving personal objectives. Gordon et al. (1980) report a study in which a scale measuring commitment to the union was subjected to a factor analysis. This analysis revealed that workers who expressed the greatest

loyalty to the union perceived that there were substantial personal gains to be achieved from joining the union. They also expressed pride in the union's record of accomplishments in contributing to the workers' welfare, and saw their decision to join their local to be a smart move. Future attempts to study the reasons why workers join unions would profit from taking these perceptual factors into consideration.

WHY WORKERS DO NOT JOIN UNIONS

In the absence of reasons for affiliating with a union, workers do not necessarily refuse to join. Rather, it is when they have specific reasons for not affiliating that they refuse to join. We can examine this assertion more closely by looking at some of the research that has been done on this question in areas of the labor market that currently have been showing greatest resistance to unionization. In general, it has been in the white-collar segments of the labor force, and more specifically in professional and technical jobs, that unions have encountered considerable resistance to their organizing efforts. It is here that we will look for reasons why workers refuse to join unions, although we must recognize that a different picture might emerge if we were to study other segments of the labor force.

Status Inconsistency

Professional workers often view union membership as being inconsistent with the status afforded them by their jobs. Their rejection of a union is an expression of the belief that membership will bring them into an organization that represents workers who hold positions of lower status. As a consequence, they may see union membership requiring that they lose a certain amount of social prestige, and if this cost is too high, they will refuse to join.

For example, a professional engineer, although not recognized as a member of management, holds a position that is closely identified with management. The fact that a large number of people tend to look at the engineer's job in this way provides the engineer with a source of considerable status and self-esteem. To affiliate with a labor union under these circumstances might be viewed as moving the engineer's job outside this traditional, management-related role, bringing with it a loss of status (Goldstein, 1955; Kuhn, 1963; Strauss, 1964). Social costs of this sort may discourage the engineer from joining a labor union; the same engineer, however, may join a professional engineering association that engages in many of the same activities as the union and feel no status inconsistency whatsoever.

Identification with Management

Related to the status implications of union membership, identification with management is probably a factor that plays a significant role in decisions that are made not to join a labor union. In these instances the labor union, which is usually associated with rank-and-file employees, is seen as an organization whose actions and objectives are not wholly compatible with those thought to be characteristic of managers. The strike or work slowdown, for instance, is a form of action that is seen as being inappropriate by those who are psychologically allied with management. For a group of workers to withhold their services from an employer is perceived as being incompatible with the norms of conduct that operate in management circles.

Identification with management is particularly important among white-collar workers who, when thinking of career prospects, often see upward mobility primarily through management channels. Hence, considerations of self-interest lead white-collar workers to identify with those whose ranks they aspire to join. Under these circumstances white-collar workers may see union membership as not fitting in with their career objectives.

Individual versus Collective Bargaining

Some workers may perceive their job situations in a way that makes collective bargaining appear to be the best means for achieving their personal objectives. Feelings of powerlessness, management indifference, or timidity may convince some workers that group bargaining might be more effective than trying to negotiate with an employer as an individual. Others may see advantages to individual negotiations in which wages, promotions, and working conditions are worked out between each individual worker and manager.

This latter perspective is probably more characteristic of individuals who occupy jobs that are largely scientific and technical in their content, although certain levels of management may also show preference for individual bargaining. In these instances, the employee often sees meritorious performance and individual achievement as factors that improve a person's bargaining position. Job mobility—that is, the threat of taking a position with a different firm, is also seen as a lever that may be used as a bargaining chip in these individual negotiations. Also contributing to this preference for individual bargaining is the kind of training professionals receive. For the long periods of their lives during which they were being trained, professionals operated in a system that relied exclusively on individual performance as the basis for distributing rewards. School grades, graduate school stipends, academic awards, and the like are all rewards that reflect individual merit. Having been successful at school, technical and professional workers continue to endorse incentive systems that are based on individual merit. Union approaches to reward distribution, on the other hand, tend to focus on collective systems. Contract settlements tend to cover collections of people and often fail to differentiate individuals on the basis of performance. As a consequence, highly trained managers, technicians, or scientists are often not attracted to collective-bargaining procedures; in fact, they may see them as being irrelevant to their careers. For reasons such as these, they may decide not to join a union.

Union Approach to Problem Solving

There is a related consideration that some say discourages white-collar workers from seeking union membership: that by training and experience, individuals in professional and technical jobs tend to approach a wide range of problem-solving activities from a rational perspective. In keeping with this, these workers believe the decisions concerning wages and working conditions should be sought through discussion and reason. Facts should be mustered to support requests for improved wages, and the resolution of these issues should parallel solutions of technical and business problems; they should be rational. From this perspective, an emotionally colored strike action is seen as a fundamentally irrational, hence unacceptable, method for settling disputes. From this perspective, therefore, union membership holds with it the threat that the individual may be propelled into a confrontation with authority in a situation more highly charged with emotion than with reason.

WORKERS' ATTITUDES TOWARD UNIONS

Although the literature does not permit us to make a final statement concerning why workers do, or do not, join labor unions, we should accept the fact that large numbers do join and are subsequently compelled to make some sort of adjustment to the organization. Once a member, the worker's perceptions and attitudes must be shaped to fit the experience with the union. The mere fact of joining would seem to imply that at least initially workers bring with them positive feelings toward the union; their affiliation brings them into a potential conflict situation, however, since they also have employee status with the management group that hired them. On first impression, one might conclude that such circumstances place the worker at a choice point. Unions and management, as they are often seen, maintain a competitive relationship with each other, and employees who are members of both organizations may find themselves being forced to choose sides between the two. Certainly both groups make an effort to secure the loyalties of the worker, and on the basis of these considerations it would seem reasonable

to expect that workers would have to join one group at the cost of rejecting the other. To the extent that this is true, one would find a negative correlation between the attitudes workers hold toward labor unions and management. A negative correlation would indicate that workers who had favorable attitudes toward one group would tend to have unfavorable attitudes toward the other. For instance, pro-union workers would be expected to possess negative attitudes toward management.

Dual Allegiance

In much of the research that has been done, a positive rather than a negative correlation has been found to describe the relationship between union and management attitudes held by workers. What this indicates is that workers who express positive sentiments toward their labor union also tend to express positive sentiments toward their management group. The converse is also implied by these positive correlations; negative attitudes toward labor unions are associated with negative attitudes toward management.

Findings of this sort have given rise to a term *dual allegiance,* which has been used to describe the tendency for union and management attitudes to vary together in a positive fashion. The concept of allegiance, as it is used in this context, indicates that the attitudes involved are not of the type that are highly charged emotionally. In terms of its emotional implications, allegiance is a less intense concept than identification and loyalty. These latter terms express a certain level of emotional attachment to a group. A person who identifies with a group, for example, is thought to have made an ego investment in its affairs. In this case, the person's emotions tend to rise and fall with the successes and failures of the group. Allegiance, on the other hand, is a term that refers to an understanding and a general acceptance of the worthwhile nature of an organization, its activities and purposes. When applied to union-management affairs, allegiance refers to the worker's recognition that the groups serve a worthwhile purpose and that they are important to the welfare of the worker. Dual allegiance, therefore, refers to a belief held by a worker that both union and management are basically constructive agencies that are essential to the achievement of the worker's goals.

Research Support. Numerous studies have given support to the dual-allegiance concept. Katz (1949), for example, cites results from a survey of the attitudes of automobile workers that indicates that these workers saw a harmonious relationship between union and management. The large majority saw both union and management working together, each having the welfare of the other as part of its objectives. Stagner (1954, 1956) carried out a study in which employees in eight companies were interviewed regarding their attitudes toward various aspects of their work experience. In each plant, rank-and-file workers who expressed positive attitudes toward management tended to express positive attitudes toward their union. Biles (1974) presents a study of white-collar public employees in which evidence of dual allegiance was displayed by 61 percent of the employees; Gordon et al. (1980) report similar results.

Purcell (1960) found evidence for dual allegiance in studies carried out in three meat-packing plants that differed markedly in the history of their labor-management relations. In one of the plants studied by Purcell, the interviews obtained were taken during a time of labor unrest and strike activity. Even under these stressful circumstances, dual allegiance was observed in the attitudes of the union members. In another study, Dean (1954a) reports evidence of dual allegiance even in a plant in which there was a history of intense union-management conflict, marked by two long and bitter strikes within a twelve-year period.

These studies, and there are others reporting similar results, illustrate the broad range of circumstances that have provided evidence for the validity of the dual-allegiance concept. This is not to say that all employees display this kind of consistency in their attitudes; for example, 5 percent of Biles's sample showed unilateral allegiance to either management or labor. The weight of the evidence, however, suggests that union membership and positive attitudes toward the labor organization do not necessarily imply negative attitudes toward the company and its management. On the contrary, the weight of the data suggest that those who are positively disposed toward their union tend to have similar attitudes toward their employers.

Mediating Variables. At this point it should be pointed out that although there is little question concerning the legitimacy of the dual-allegiance phenomenon, it is not found in every work situation. The nature of the *relationship* between union and management attitudes has been found to vary as a function of the presence or absence of certain other variables. Dean (1954a), for example, found little evidence of dual allegiance among a group of active union participants who were employed at a plant having a history of poor labor-management relations. Dean concludes that dual allegiance appears to change as a function of at least two variables: the nature of the relationship existing between union and management at a given plant, and the extent to which employees participate in union meetings. Biles (1974) finds that the union members who perceived that there was a harmonious relationship existing between labor and management were the ones who tended to show evidence of dual allegiance. The same study also showed dual allegiance increasing with age, tenure with the company, and length of membership in the union.

Hence, like most other relationships that are found in the work environment, dual allegiance changes its character in response to the influence of other work- and employee-related variables. The social scientist would say that the positive relationship observed between union and management attitudes is mediated by other variables that are associated with the worker and the workplace. Yet, while keeping this latter point in mind, we should acknowledge that the research literature has been able to demonstrate the presence of dual allegiance in a wide variety of work settings.

Why Dual Allegiance?

We must speculate about the reasons for the widespread appearance of a positive relationship between labor and management attitudes. Apparently, when workers join a union they usually are not compelled to choose sides; rather, they construct attitudes toward both organizations that are quite consistent and harmonious. Stagner (1954) talks about an attitudinal climate embracing both union and management that leads workers to perceive both groups in a similar fashion. The origins of this climate are difficult to identify, but we might hypothesize that one factor contributing to its formation is found in the size and complexity of both organizations. In Chapter 9, where we considered the social setting of work, it was pointed out that a sizeable portion of the labor force works for large companies that have thousands of workers on their payrolls. In the beginning of the present chapter it was shown that a large percentage of union workers are members of labor organizations that enroll thousands of members. Large companies and large unions tend to create a social climate that gives both organizations the appearance of being psychologically distant from the individual worker. Under these circumstances, workers often feel that the real power-holding layers of both groups reside at social levels that are far removed from their own. The ''big shots'' in both company and union may be glimpsed on television or seen in newspapers, but they are rarely if ever present in an immediate social sense. As a consequence, both company and management are viewed as sources of distant authority over which the worker has little control. Under these circumstances it is often difficult to identify with either group. Workers do, however, have an overall evaluation of their jobs, and it is this global assessment of the total job that underlies their attitude toward both groups.

There is a related consideration that might be drawn on to explain the appearance of dual allegiance. This is that many workers display a comparatively high level of apathy toward both the affairs of the union and the actions of their company. As we shall see in the next section, many union members are relatively apathetic toward their union, and their rate of participation in its affairs and the amount of knowledge they have concerning union programs is very low. Hence, in talking about membership in both union and management, one often finds oneself talking about levels of affiliation and commitment that are relatively weak. Of course, crises can arise that tend to heighten an individual's psychological attachment to one or both of the groups, but these crises are rare. Hence, in the day-to-day experience of work many workers maintain a benign and relatively nondiscriminating set of attitudes toward both the union and their company. Rather than choosing sides, they look at both union and management through similar sets of attitudes.

WORKERS VIEW THEIR UNIONS

One may ask more interesting questions about workers' perceptions of their unions than whether their attitudes are positive or negative. This matter can be dealt with rather easily, for although there are wide individual differences, it seems that the majority of union members are favorably disposed toward their unions as organizations. Workers may, at times, show exasperation with their locals or with the policies of the union leadership, but by and large, workers as a group seem to hold relatively positive attitudes toward their own unions and toward the union movement in general.

It is interesting to note that workers tend to view their unions primarily in terms of a relatively narrow set of considerations. Of the many dimensions of labor organizations that may be the subject of workers' attitudes, their sentiments often crystallize around issues that relate to their immediate experience. Matters relating to their self-interests, ''bread and butter'' considerations such as wages, security, fringe benefits, and working conditions, are the items on which workers' attitudes tend to focus. In responding to the wide range of union issues that are remote from the individual's direct experience, (for example, jurisdictional matters, labor legislation) workers often show indifference and low levels of knowledge (*Monthly Labor Review*, 1966).

Uphoff and Dunnette (1956) surveyed a large group of union members and found that a large majority expressed quite positive attitudes toward the union's role in improving wages and providing job protection. When questioned, however, about their attitudes toward such things as the union's involvement in hiring new workers, matters of labor law, and union security provisions, there was a substantial drop in the level of positive support expressed.

Sayles and Strauss (1953) interviewed groups of union members and found that "almost every worker interviewed was convinced that the union was needed for protection against arbitrary management action and as an instrument for obtaining economic security" (p. 222). Members also showed overwhelming support for the union's economic activities, yet the level of emotional attachment to the union was found to be rather low. In other words, Sayles and Strauss found widespead evidence of union allegiance, but comparatively little evidence of union identificaiton. Rank-and-file affiliation tended to reflect a low level of psychological involvement. Workers were detached from the union in the sense that they did not have a high emotional commitment to the organization and its leadership. Although they intellectually recognized the important role played by the union in security wages and job protection, Sayles and Strauss found that workers' emotional investment in the organization was roughly comparable to that which they invested in such organizations as Blue Cross.

Worker attitudes often take on a self-serving appearance. For instance, a survey on the members of 16 unions located on the West Coast (*Monthly Labor Review*, 1966) revealed that a large majority of workers felt that their unions had succeeded in improving living standards and providing job security, fringe benefits, and improved working conditions. In spite of this, however, a majority of the members felt that the dues were too high and expressed reluctance to have their dues increased in order to strengthen the unions' ability to obtain improved benefits for the members.

This survey gives us a glimpse of the narrow range of commitments that can often be found linking the worker to the union. Concrete, bread-and-butter considerations relating directly to the worker's self-interest in wages and working conditions serve as a principal connection between worker and union. Apart from this, there is a broad list of union activities that tend to lie outside the attitudes and understandings of the members. Furthermore, there are instances in which member attitudes and interests are found to be contradictory to the objectives of union legislative and social programs. The West Coast survey, for example, found instances in which union policies regarding civil rights issues were counter to the attitudes held by large numbers of members. Along similar lines, Blume (1973) studied United Automobile Workers' (UAW) attitudes toward an open-housing ordinance in Toledo, Ohio, and found that although a majority of the members accepted their union's interest in this ordinance, only 39 percent were willing to support the union's point of view regarding this issue.

Chamberlain and Cullen (1971) point out that labor unions, being complex organizations, often face instances in which organizational interests conflict with the immediate interests of the individual member. Jurisdictional questions—for example, the range of jobs that fall under union control—may be of great concern to the union organization but be of little concern to the rank-and-file members who would prefer their union to concentrate on wages and working conditions.

Oftentimes the labor union is seen by the general public as an organization actively engaged in political affairs, yet there is evidence indicating that workers do not support political unionism as a primary function of their labor organizations. Form (1973a), in a study of union workers in four automobile plants located in different parts of the world, found that only a small minority of the members saw political action as one of the more important functions of the union. Rather consistently, higher wages and better working conditions were seen as the union's primary objectives. Hence, we see once again evidence of workers viewing their unions in relatively narrow terms, thinking of the organization mainly in terms of its contribution to their immediate experiences. Outside this sphere one finds union functions that are generally ignored by the typical rank-and-file member. It is in these areas that the union leader has extensive degrees of freedom to set policies and establish direction for union activities. The West Coast study (*Monthly Labor Review,* 1966) concludes:

> . . . Member interest and support on a specific issue declines as the issue gets more abstract or further removed from the place of work. There seems to be a firm relation between what members want and what the leadership does in the "bread and butter" areas, but on other issues—automation, support of candidates friendly to the union, and the like—much of the membership either does not understand or does not sympathize with the position of the union and its leadership. (p. 177)

Types of Union Members

If one were to study the characteristics of the members who make up a political party, one would find that there is a wide assortment of membership types. Ranging from the most apathetic to the office seeker and ideologue, membership in the party can assume many different forms. So it is with a labor union; type of membership in these organizations varies from one worker to the next. Seidman et al. (1951) interviewed the members of six local unions and found that they could discern seven different types of union memberships: the ideological unionist, the "good" union member, the loyal but critical worker, the crisis activist, the dually oriented member, the card carrier, and the unwilling unionist.

The Ideological Unionist. The ideological unionist is found among workers who see their membership in the union as an extension of certain beliefs that they hold regarding the social world in which they live. Often endorsing a liberal or left-

wing political ideology, this type of member sees management as a social group that carries out an exploitative role in its relations with workers. For these members, the union-management distinction is a reflection of a set of broader differences that separate the social classes into haves and have-nots. Seidman et al. report that the number of members of this type is very small, sometimes accounting for less than 2 percent of the membership.

The "Good" Union Member. In the "good" union member we also find the high degree of commitment and support found among the ideological types. Union membership is not, however, interpreted in terms of wider social concerns. The "good" union member supports the union fully and understands the need for union solidarity and union security, but does not see management as a social class bent on oppressing the working classes. Such members may be hostile toward their own management groups, but they tend not to generalize this hostility to management as a social class. This type of member sees the union as an organization that is working toward the improvement of working conditions. The "good" union member does not, as do his ideologue associates, see it as an instrument for broad social reform. Seidman et al. (1951) found that this type constitutes a small portion of the total membership, perhaps not exceeding 10 percent.

The Loyal but Critical Member. The loyal but critical union member tends to show the same support and commitment to the union organization that is evident among the first two types; these members do, however, express criticism of the union leaders who direct their own locals. They support union strike activities and may be found advocating militancy in union-management relationships, but they are also often found among the ranks of an opposing faction that challenges the leadership of the union officers.

The Crisis Activist. Normally inactive and apathetic to union affairs, crisis activists renew their commitment and involvement during times of crises. As a rule this type of member possesses little knowledge of union affairs, and maintains a rather poor attendance record at the union meetings; but during times of crises these members show themselves to be loyal supporters of the organization. Apart from these critical times, these members are found to be passive supporters of the union. Seidman et al. estimate that this type outnumbers all other types of member in many union locals.

The Dually Oriented Member. Dually oriented members give the union support on a wide range of issues, but they tend to view production and work efficiency matters from the perspective of management. They tend to see spheres of activity that fall solely within the jurisdiction of management. Matters concerning wages, job security, and the like are seen as falling within the joint purview of union and management. There are matters, however, relating to work efficiency, discipline, and production that these members view strictly from the management perspective.

The Card Carrier. In the so-called card-carrying members we find the completely indifferent unionist. Often membership is the result of wanting to belong to the work group; but having joined, these members are totally apathetic to the organization and its activities. Participation in union activities often awaits substantial pressures from work associates. These members are indifferent and uninformed.

The Unwilling Unionist. We find some union members who have been forced into the union against their will. Attitudinally, these members tend to be generally critical of the union and its leadership. Often they identify with management in labor disputes.

In all probability it would be impossible to find a single union member who represents one of these categories to the exclusion of all others. In representative union members we would probably find combinations of several of these types. But in each member one type might be more prominent than others. Like all typologies, these seven categories represent abstractions of behavior; their usefulness lies in providing us with a framework for viewing the different relationships workers maintain with their unions.

PARTICIPATION IN UNIONS

The rate of worker participation in union activities varies both with the nature of the activity and with the characteristics of the worker and work group. Consider, first, type of activity. It is not unusual to find relatively high levels of participation in such activities as voting in union elections, serving on picket lines, and paying union dues on a regular basis. On the other hand, it is also not unusual to find comparatively low levels of participation in such things as attendance at union meetings, and volunteering for service on union committees.

Attendance at union meetings has been used most frequently as an index of worker involvement in union affairs, and the evidence accumulated thus far seems to confirm Sayles and Strauss's (1953) contention that workers often show a relatively low level of psychological involvement in their labor organizations. For example, Seidman et al. (1951) found that in four of the six union locals studied, attendance at union meetings rarely exceeded 10 percent of the membership. Table 12.7, taken from Sayles and Strauss, shows the attendance figures that were obtained from a group of local unions during meetings in which no extraordinary events were scheduled. With the exception of a few relatively small locals, where attendance was between 25 and 33 percent of the membership, most locals could entice only 2–6 percent of their members to attend their meetings. Along the same lines, the Department of Labor study of West Coast unions (*Monthly Labor Review*, 1966) reported that the majority of the members who responded to a mail questionnaire had not attended any of the last six meetings held by their unions.

There are additional studies, but the weight of

TABLE 12.7   Attendance at Meetings in Locals Studied

Industry	Size of Local	Normal Attendance	
		(Actual Number)	(Percent of Membership)
Manufacturing	4000	30	1
Manufacturing	2000	40	2
Steel	1900	48	3
Utility (Production local)	1800	100	6
Automobile Assembly Plant	1800	35	2
Needle Trades (Italian local)	1800	35	2
Needle Trades (Operator's local)	1500	75	5
Automobile Assembly Plant	1100	70	6
Steel	900	35	4
Public Utility (White-collar)	850	40	5
Manufacturing	600	20	3
Foundry	600	30	5
Needle Trades (Pressers)	600	90	15
Needle Trades (Unskilled operators)	400	25	6
Needle Trades (Cutters)	400	80	20
Needle Trades (Skilled operators)	200	60	30
Insurance Workers	150	50	33
Clerical Workers	110	12	10
Public Utility (Engineers' local)	110	26	24

Source: Sayles, L. R., & Strauss, G. *The local union.* New York: Harper & Brothers, 1953, p. 173. Copyright, 1953 by L. R. Sayles and G. Strauss.

all the evidence is reflected in those that have already been cited; namely, with the exception of a relatively few local organizations, member participation in local union meetings tends to be rather low. Perhaps during times of crisis, attendance might improve, but even under some circumstances that might be thought to encourage attendance, membership participation has been found to be disappointingly low. For example Rogow (1968) cites an instance in which a union made a considerable effort to encourage attendance at meetings—for example, members were fined for nonattendance—and still membership turnout was around 50 percent, with participation stabilizing around 6 percent after the first six or seven meetings. Sayles and Strauss studied two other, older locals; except during the time of a wildcat strike or during a meeting when free beer and entertainment were provided, attendance at both of these locals rarely exceeded 6 percent of the membership.

Who Participates?

Attendance at union meetings tends to be selective; certain types of members seem to have higher rates of participation than do others, although one may find that these types vary from one local to the next. Several authors (Spinrad, 1960; Perline & Lorenz, 1970; Huszczo, 1975) have searched the literature for variables that seem to correlate with union participation, and have found that many factors contribute to workers' willingness to attend the meetings of their locals. Both organizational and personal factors seem to be involved. For example, attendance rates often are high in locals that operate in small plants having a relatively stable work force. Workers holding high-status, craft-type jobs seem to be more active in union affairs, as are workers who have jobs that tend to bring them into close contact with their work associates. Along similar lines, Dean (1954b) reports that union activists are more likely to associate after hours with their work associates, and Sayles and Strauss (1953) report that groups made up of workers who share many common attributes tend to have higher rates of union activism.

Older workers are often found attending union meetings more frequently than their younger workmates (*Monthly Labor Review,* 1966), and related to this, workers with longer tenure with a company seem to participate more in union affairs. There is evidence suggesting that union participation is greater among workers who express higher satisfaction with the jobs they hold (Huszczo, 1975), and Tannenbaum and Kahn (1958) were able to find little difference between high and low activists with regard to the amount of hostility they expressed toward management. Finally, there is some evidence suggesting that union activists do not perceive their careers as taking them into the ranks of management.

Why Do Workers Participate?

Hundreds of motives may be found as reasons why one individual or another becomes active in the affairs of the union. Personal ideologies, class consciousness, labor crises, economic interests, concern about job security, negative feelings toward management, work-group and family pressures are but a few of the individual factors that might be found behind a worker's level of participation. The studies that have been done in this area, however, suggest that there may be a general principle that can be applied to explain the motivation underlying participation in union activities. This principle, which should be put forward in the form of a tentative hypothesis, is that any factor that links workers' perceptions of their self-interests with union activity is a factor that may be related to participation. In other words, whenever workers perceive that active involvement in the union will prove to be instrumental in satisfying their psychological needs, there is a good likelihood that they will participate in union affairs. Factors that facilitate the development of this perceived instrumentality also will be found to be associated with participation rates.

In support of this hypothesis, Hagburg (1966)

reports a study that indicates that active union members tend to think of their organization as a source of primary satisfaction. Inactive members tend *not* to think of the union as an organization wherein they may satisfy many of their fundamental social needs. Inactive members often obtain satisfaction of this sort from their involvement with their families, church, or neighborhood, rather than in the union or in a work-related setting. Hagburg presents evidence indicating that active members report that their participation in the union gives them a sense of enjoyment, an opportunity for spontaneous expression, and a feeling of working with others toward a common goal. Large numbers of union activists, as compared with inactive members, report feelings of satisfaction obtained through helping others and feeling they are part of an important group. Union activists were also found to participate more than their inactive associates in fraternal and community organizations. Huszczo (1975) has also found that active union members are more active in community and political affairs.

Participation—A General Tendency. These findings are of considerable interest since they suggest that active involvement in union affairs may very well be a manifestation of a broader tendency that leads the individual to assume an active role in many areas of life. Participation in the union, therefore, is a reflection of this general tendency to participate in the affairs of all types of social organizations.

Evidence of a similar nature is available from the field of political behavior (Milbrath, 1965; Lipset, 1960). Here the data indicate that the individual who plays an active role in a political party tends to show higher levels of participation in a variety of social activities. Almond and Verba (1963), for example, have presented evidence supporting this contention. These authors even found that political activists were also more active in the decision making that went on in their families, jobs, and schools. Hence, in talking about the social activist, whether viewed from the perspective of union or political involvement, one may be speaking of a general tendency on the part of individuals to play active roles in the organizational affairs that enter their lives.

One of the important psychological factors underlying social activism is, perhaps, a dimension of the self-concepts that lead individuals to perceive that their own activities do have an important influence on the decisions that are made in even the largest and most complex social organizations. Perhaps this variety of ego orientation is found in individuals who are intellectually more involved with the events that go on around them. To perceive the connection between one's actions and the decisions and outcomes that occur in complicated social organizations may require relatively sophisticated ways of looking at social affairs. In keeping with this point of view, there is some evidence (Milbrath, 1965, p. 44 ff; Rambo, Jones, & Finney, 1973; Jones, Rambo & Finney, 1975) that suggests that participation rates in politics are higher for those who possess larger amounts of information concerning social-political affairs. This information provides a tool that may be used by individuals to tie together their own activities and the often distant outcomes of a complicated political process. These higher levels of information also reflect a more active intellectual involvement with the things going on in the world.

When we look at the studies dealing with union participation, there is some evidence that links information levels with participation rates, but this evidence is far from complete. The West Coast study (*Monthly Labor Review*, 1966), for example, reports that union activists indicated that they felt better informed about union programs than did the inactive members, and Lieberman (1954) reports that workers who eventually were elected to the position of shop steward reported that they had read the union contract more frequently than did workers who had not assumed this kind of position in the union.

Hence, we might tentatively conclude that participation in the affairs of the labor union is often a manifestation of a more general tendency to participate in social affairs, and that this general orientation to social action is related both to workers'

perceptions of the consequences of their participation and to the extent to which they are intellectually engaged with the social events which go on around him.

Union Democracy

Stagner (1956, p. 242) points out that unions are inherently democratic. By this he means that the structure of these organizations is such that power is intended to be concentrated in the hands of the rank-and-file members who elect leaders to represent them. From this perspective, therefore, union democracy is a manifestation of the social structure of the organization. By way of contrast, the structural characteristic of the business organization is inherently undemocratic, since the structure invests power most heavily in the upper levels of the firm where a relatively small number of people holding elite status are to be found. Of course, the process of delegation can permit the firm to function in a democratic fashion, just as a variety of factors can operate to prevent a union from functioning democratically. The basic social structure of the labor union, however, focuses power in the lower, membership layers of the organization; hence, an undemocratic union functions in a way that contradicts its social structure.

Unions vary widely in the extent to which the organization carries out its activities within a democratic framework. Worker apathy and noninvolvement are probably among the more significant factors that discourage effective democratic practices. With a membership that is largely indifferent to a broad range of issues and whose involvement with the organization is relatively weak, it sometimes happens that union leaders exercise an initiative that does not mirror the sentiments of the rank-and-file members. The same problems exist in many complex organizations: educational, governmental, scientific, and professional.

Organizational Variables. We have already considered some of the psychological variables underlying worker participation, but there are also factors associated with the union organization itself that seem to be related to member participation, and hence to union democracy.

One of the most successful efforts to study union democracy is a study carried out with the International Typographical Union by Lipset, Trow, and Coleman (1956). Here a number of social-organizational variables were identified as factors influencing the likelihood that the union would function democratically. For example, there seemed to be a relationship between the structural complexity of a labor union and the chances that it would operate in a democratic manner. As one might suspect, increasing complexity, especially in the form of increased bureaucratization, tends to reduce the chances of union democracy. Another structural property found to relate to union democracy is the extent to which local unions function autonomously with regard to the national union. Lipset et al. found that with greater autonomy came an increased chance that the local would function democratically.

Industry variables were also found to influence union democracy in that the more highly concentrated ownership was in an industry, the less the likelihood that unions would operate democratically. Furthermore, democratic practices were more likely to be found in instances in which the union maintained a secure relationship with management. Finally, occupational variables were also found to contribute to the prospect of union democracy. Unions representing groups that were rather homogeneous with regard to their occupational status had a greater chance of being democratic in their orientation.

It is apparent that there are a host of psychological and organizational variables that correlate with the extent to which a labor union functions in a democratic fashion. Many of the organizational variables seem to relate directly to the size and social complexity of the union, and as a general rule, as the size of the union increases and as its social structure becomes more complex, it becomes increasingly difficult to maintain democratic procedures. There are numerous reports in the literature showing that in the early years of a union member participation and involvement are

high. As the union matures, however, it tends to become increasingly bureaucratized, and democratic practices give way to worker apathy and oligarchic control (Stein, 1963). Hence, with time, organizations often become increasingly complicated in both their functions and their structures. These changes can have profound effects on the degree of democratic control.

Blum (1953) describes the weakening of a democratic climate in a local of the United Packinghouse Workers of America. In the early days of this local, days filled with hardship and crisis, union meetings were general meetings held for the rank-and-file membership. Union social structure was comparatively simple. As time progressed, however, the executive board organized the local into departments, which held separate meetings to consider specific aspects of union affairs. These first symptoms of bureaucratization gradually led to decreased member participation. Attendance at union meetings began to decline, until some years later not more than 100 out of a membership of about 4000 were usually found at a meeting.

Union democracy faces problems that are shared by many complex social groups. Many factors seem to contribute to these difficulties, but of particular significance is the changing organizational structure that contributes to the patterns of participation and the practices of decision making that are found in the group. The implications of this relationship between social structure and democratic practices is of great significance, not only to work-related groups but to all organizations that function in the society.

UNION LEADERSHIP

Compared with what is known about company executives (see Chapter 14), the research literature contains relatively little information regarding the psychological characteristics of those who hold leadership positions in labor unions. Information concerning the social origins and background of these individuals is also rather limited, compared with what is available concerning managers. Nevertheless, from the data that have been col-

TABLE 12.8   Numbers and Proportions of Full-Time Union Officers in Various Countries

Country	Total union membership	Total number full-time officers	Approximate ratio of officers to members
United States	18,000,000	60,000	1:300
Australia	2,400,000	2500–2750	1:900
Great Britain	8,000,000	4000	1:2000
Sweden	1,500,000	900	1:1700
Norway	500,000	240	1:2200
Denmark	775,000	1000	1:775

Source: Adapted from Lipset, S. M. Trade unions and social structure. *Industrial Relations*, 1962, 1(2), 89–110.

lected we can draw a sketch of the union leader and make some tentative comparisons with company officers. In doing so, however, we must bear in mind that around every statement that can be made there is a wide range of individual differences. As a result, we will be trying to describe what might be thought of as model or typical characteristics of union leaders. In drawing this picture we must avoid seeing this group as a homogeneous collection of people, all sharing the same backgrounds and psychological characteristics.

Leadership positions form a highly visible part of the social structure of the American labor organization. In part, the prominence of union leadership is a function of the fact that there seems to be a relatively large number of these positions. Lipset (1962), for example, finds that compared to unions in European countries (see Table 12.8), American unions have a much higher proportion of full-time officers. This abundance of leaders doubtless places the union official in a social setting in which there are a complex distribution of power and intricate channels of communication. The labor leader's position also can be described in terms of its political character. It is an elected position in which the incumbent periodically must run for reelection by the rank-and-file members. As an index of the level of political activity found in unions, Appelbaum (1966) reports that within one three-year period (1960–1962), about 40 percent of the 97 local unions that he surveyed re-

placed their presidents and 60 percent replaced their vice presidents. Of course, all this turnover cannot be attributed to the effects of internal struggles, but these data do show us that tenure in union leadership positions is oftentimes not very long. The data also suggest that in many unions there are frequent election campaigns, which doubtless involve factions and some degree of internal competition. Many valid parallels can be drawn between the position of the labor leader and the position held by an elected governmental official.

Background Characteristics

Bok and Dunlop (1970) found that a great majority of union leaders have moved up through the ranks of the workers whom the union represents. Selection of union leadership, therefore, tends to be an in-house affair, with comparatively few officers being recruited directly from college and university training programs. Furthermore, a small number of labor leaders come from families headed by fathers who have received at least one year of college education. Almost 50 percent of the management trainees come from homes in which the father has some college training.

As might be expected, Bogard (1960) found that a substantially higher percentage of the management trainees had received a college degree compared with the sample of union members. Bok and Dunlop (1970) report the results of a survey of union presidents, vice-presidents, and secretary-treasurers, which indicates that about half of this group had no more than a high school education, and 25 percent never graduated from high school. In comparison, a survey of business leaders (Brua, 1973) found that 83 percent of the presidents of large corporations had undergraduate degrees, while 42 percent had received some graduate training. Hence, the data available indicate that union leaders tend to differ from their management counterparts in terms of social class, background, and level of formal education. Union leaders, unlike business managers, come from blue-collar families and begin their work careers in blue-collar jobs. Movement into union positions is out of these jobs, rather than out of the colleges and universities that are the training grounds for young managers.

Personality Characteristics

In many respects the personality descriptions that have been made of people holding positions of union leadership seem to be comparable to those often made of persons who hold management positions. For instance, in a study of 20 union locals, Sayles and Strauss (1953) found that local leaders tended to be individuals whose behavior reflected high levels of activity and creative energy. In addition, like many management leaders, union officials were motivated by a need to achieve and accomplish worthwhile objectives. Also like managers, union leaders tended to commit themselves to hard work and long hours. As a consequence, they often reported that union activities affected many aspects of their nonwork life. Family relations were often burdened by the demands of the union position, but in spite of this the union leaders frequently indicated that they received considerable satisfaction from their union activities.

Bogard's study (1960), comparing union and management trainees, came up with a host of factors that suggest some basic personality differences between the two groups. Although the samples used were small and limited to a single work setting, Bogard found that prospective union officers tended to be more altruistic and less concerned about working on practical problems than were the group of management trainees. Union members were also less aggressive, tended to be less responsible, and displayed a pattern of interests similar to those found in people who deal with art, music, languages, and with other people. Management trainees, on the other hand, tended to express interests similar to those of people who deal with objects and with office records.

There is great need for additional information regarding the personality of labor leaders. Numerous studies have been carried out on management groups, but comparable efforts focused on union leaders have not been reported. While there is no reason to believe that startling contrasts will be found, only further empirical efforts will permit us to complete our comparison of the personality characteristics of those who enter the ranks of union and management leadership.

Perceptions and Attitudes

The psychological characteristics of union leaders that have received the most attention concern the value attitudes they hold and their perceptions of work-related issues. As a general rule, studies in this area compare union leaders with management personnel, the results indicating that in some respects there are interesting similarities between union and management leaders; in other respects there are differences.

Perception of Job Objectives. Union leaders tend to see their jobs in terms of objectives that are moralistic, service oriented, and idealistic (England, Agarwal, & Trerise, 1971; Won & Yamamura, 1968; Miller, 1966). Management leaders, on the other hand, are more likely to perceive the objectives of their jobs in terms of their own careers and in terms that are political and practical in their nature. To some extent these statements are in line with Bogard's report that union personnel tended to be more altruistic and less interested in practical problems than were management representatives. It should be recognized, however, that the manner in which job objectives are perceived is a reflection of both the realities of the job situation and the personal motives of the individual. Of course, there are also social pressures that operate to color a person's statements regarding job objectives, and we shouldn't overlook the possibility that these may have been at work in the present instances. It is probably much more acceptable for individuals in management positions to express profit and career objectives. The social norms that operate inside labor unions, on the other hand, probably encourage public commitments to service and social progress. To what extent these social pressures contribute to union and management leaders' statements of personal objectives is a matter that must be considered in interpreting the above results.

Self-Perceptions. In certain respects union leaders view themselves as being similar to their management counterparts. For example, Haire (1955) presented groups of union and management leaders with photographs of individuals who were described as being either union or management officials. When asked to assign behavior characteristics to these photographs, union officials tended to see managers as much like themselves. In considering a list of 290 personality traits, union officers chose only the term "dependable" to differentiate photographs of union and management personnel; all other terms were applied to the two groups with approximately equal frequency. Managers, on the other hand, seemed to draw a sharper distinction between photographs described as either union or management officials. Here managers saw union leaders as being more active, aggressive, argumentative, opinionated, outspoken, and persistent.[1]

When viewing their own capabilities, union officials have been found to express patterns of beliefs similar to those expressed by managers. For example, Miles and Ritchie (1968) found that union officers tend to rate themselves just as capable as the officers who are above them in the union. They see substantial differences, however, between their own capabilities and the capabilities of the rank-and-file members whom they represent; union officers tend to see themselves as being more capable. A similar pattern of perceptions has been obtained from a survey of management personnel (see Table 12.9); in fact, managers have been found to consistently overvalue their abilities

TABLE 12.9 Comparative Perceptions of Individuals' Capabilities in Various Organizations

	Average rating given for:			
Group	Rank and file	Level below respondents	Respondents' own level	Level above respondents
Union officials (N = 83)	2.9	4.4	5.8	5.9
Middle and upper level business managers (N = 215)	3.0	4.8	5.7	6.0
Public health administrators (N = 250)	3.7	4.9	5.6	5.9
Middle level managers in government Agency A (N = 35)	4.1	5.0	5.8	6.0
Middle level managers in government Agency G (N = 21)	3.5	4.9	5.9	6.2

Note: Cell entries represent ratings of capabilities; larger numbers represent high estimates of ability.
Source: Miles, R. E. & Ritchie, J. B. Leadership attitudes among union officials. *Industrial Relations*, 1968, 8(1), 108–117.

[1] Snyder and Hammer (1977) carried out a similar study that gave results that these authors say contradict Haire's findings; this later study, however, is reported in such a fashion as to make comparison with Haire's results impossible.

(Kidd & Morgan, 1969; Larwood & Whittaker, 1977) relative to others. Interestingly, both union and management officers expressed support for democratic practices, but both groups of leaders expressed doubts about the quality of their subordinates' judgment.

These perceptions tend to create problems for those who advocate the introduction of democratic practices in the workplace (Maier, 1963). It seems to be comparatively easy to convince leaders of the virtue of democracy, but a real problem emerges when attempts are made to translate these ideas into practices. Many times a significant impediment is found in a leader's lack of confidence in the judgment, motives, and competence of the followers. Whatever the reason for this belief, the results of the Miles and Ritchie (1968) studies show that this is a situation that is characteristic of union as well as management leadership.

Differences in Perception. As one might predict, it is in those areas where labor and management are in competition that the sharpest differences in perception have been observed between the two groups. At times these differences have involved aspects of interpersonal relations that are so basic that they point to the existence of fundamental obstacles to effective cooperation. For example, several studies (Weaver, 1958; Schwartz, Stark, & Schiffman, 1970) have reported differences between labor and management leaders in the meaning assigned to words they use to deal with industrial relations. Weaver (1958) talks about semantic barriers that stand between the two factions. In a study in which union and management officers expressed the meaning they gave to industrial concepts, it was found that management and labor officials clearly assigned different meanings to these terms. Not only did labor tend to assign more extreme meanings to the industrial relations terms, but there also seemed to be great agreement among the union leaders regarding the meaning of these words. On the basis of these results, Weaver concludes that semantic barriers are greater for labor than for management.

One must be cautious in drawing such sweeping conclusions, especially in the light of evidence that indicates that the situation may be more complex than this generalization implies. For example, Schwartz, Stark, and Schiffman (1970) find that these semantic barriers do not appear to be uniform across all levels of union or management. Greater differences in perception of the meaning of words were found to exist between shop stewards and first-line foremen. Although there were differences in perceived meaning found at higher levels, these were smaller than the differences found at those lower levels where employer and union have their most extensive set of day-to-day contacts.

No good estimate can be made of the extent to which these disparities in perception found at lower levels carry over to influence the psychological climate in which the higher policy-making and negotiating levels operate. The situation is further complicated by the fact that similar communication barriers operate within as well as between these organizations. In contrast to the Weaver study, the Schwartz et al. study (1970) reports that the meanings assigned to words varied much more among two levels of union officers than among two levels of management.

These studies cited above give us information that is of great potential value in understanding the functioning of complex organizations (see Chapter 9). To find basic differences in the use of words at different levels of an organization or between interacting organizations has broad significance for an understanding of the dynamics of organization performance. For example, such information may shed light on the nature of the patterns of cooperation and competition that are observed in the relations between labor and management groups. We need much more research in this interesting area of inquiry.

Perception of Workers' Needs. There is evidence in the research literature that indicates that management can at times be out of touch with the needs of their employees. In one study (Kahn, 1959), when asked to predict rank-and-file workers' perceptions of the importance of various needs, foremen were found to overestimate workers' interest in wages and underestimate their interest in nonfinancial incentives. Results such as these show us that those who manage incentive systems do not always have good understanding of the relative value of the rewards they control. But union leaders have been observed making similar errors. A number of studies (Lawler & Levin, 1968; Gluskinos & Kestleman, 1970; Howells & Brosnan, 1972) have indicated that at both the shop-steward and the local-official levels there are patterns of misperception similar to those found with managers—that is, overestimation of the importance of wages and underestimation of the workers' interest in nonfinancial incentives. As a specific example, Lawler and Levin (1968) asked a group of union officials to predict their members' preference for a group of ten job incentives. In doing so, the union leaders tended to overestimate the importance workers assigned to such things as a shorter workweek and wages, and underestimate their interest in vacation time, holidays, early retirement, and long-term disability pay. Of all the ten incentives, wages produced the greatest discrepancy between what the workers said they wanted and what the union leaders predicted they wanted. In view of the fact that the principal responsibility of union leadership is to represent the interests of the membership, it seems reasonable to assume that this group should possess better awareness of the interests of their constituents than a comparable group of managers. Yet the research literature casts doubt on this assumption.

One must not be led into concluding that either union officials or management leaders are completely out of touch with the expressed interests of their subordinates. By and large, the research indicates that both groups can predict with reasonable accuracy the expressed needs of the rank-and-file members. It is in the pattern of errors they make that one finds what appears to be shared misperceptions. Perhaps these perceptual problems stem from an assumption sometimes made by leaders that those in subordinate positions are in fact psychologically different from those in positions of leadership. As a case in point, industrial leaders, both managers and union officials, often acknowledge that they themselves place greater importance in nonfinancial incentives; yet, as we have seen, they still perceive that money rewards are the primary incentives for those below them in the organization.

Simple generalizations dealing with the union leader's perceptions of membership interest should not be made, because this apparently changes as a function of a number of factors. For instance, accuracy of perception has been found to vary widely from one company to the next (Howells & Brosnan, 1972). Furthermore, a given union leaders' perceptions may be more accurate for some groups than for others. Gluskinos and Kestleman (1970) present information that suggests that union leaders may not always achieve the same level of accuracy when they try to predict the interests of white-collar and blue-collar groups that make up their organizations. Doubtless other variables can be found that influence these perceptions; but whatever the complexity of these relationships, we see once again an interesting similarity between positions of leadership in both company and union.

UNION-MANAGEMENT RELATIONS

When one speaks of industrial relations one is usually thinking of the complicated procedures followed by unions and management to accommodate themselves to each other. Much has been written about this process; but of all the facets of intergroup behavior that have been studied, none has received more attention than the conflict that now and then occurs between the two groups. Contract demands, arbitration, grievances, and strikes have stirred up considerable interest among those who study labor relations. Surprisingly little attention has been given to the broad areas of cooperation that exist between the two groups.

Incidence of Industrial Conflict

In certain respects it is rather strange that so much attention has been given to the negative aspects of union-management affairs, since if one

TABLE 12.10   Labor-Management Unrest: Work Stoppages—1950 to 1976[1]

Year	Work Stoppages		Workers Involved		Worker-Days Idle During Year		
	Number	Average duration (calendar days)	Number[2] (1000)	Percent of total employed	Number (1000)	Percent of estimated working time	Per worker involved
1950	4843	19.2	2410	5.1	38,800	.33	16.1
1955	4320	18.5	2650	5.2	28,200	.22	10.7
1960	3333	23.4	1320	2.4	19,100	.14	14.5
1965	3963	25.0	1550	2.5	23,300	.15	15.1
1967	4595	22.8	2870	4.3	42,100	.25	14.7
1968	5045	24.5	2649	3.8	49,018	.28	18.5
1969	5700	22.5	2481	3.5	42,869	.24	17.3
1970	5716	25.0	3305	4.7	66,414	.37	20.1
1971	5138	27.0	3280	4.6	47,589	.26	14.5
1972	5010	24.0	1714	2.3	27,066	.15	15.8
1973	5353	24.0	2251	2.9	27,948	.14	12.4
1974	6074	27.1	2778	3.5	47,991	.24	17.3
1975	5031	26.8	1746	2.2	31,237	.16	17.9
1976	5648	28.0	2420	3.0	37,859	.19	13.6

[1]Prior to 1960, excludes Alaska and Hawaii. Excludes work stoppages involving fewer than six workers or lasting less than one day.

[2]Workers counted more than once if involved in more than one stoppage during the year.

Source: *Statistical Abstract of the United States.* U.S. Department of Commerce, Bureau of the Census, 1978.

were to look at the thousands of contacts that take place between the two parties, one would probably find that the overwhelming proportion of these interactions are harmonious and constructive. For example, during any one year only a very small portion of the total number of workdays are spent idle because of strike activities. As a usual rule, labor statistics indicate that only a small fraction of 1 percent of the work year is used up in labor disputes (see Table 12.10). Even these figures are somewhat misleading, because the incidence of strike activities is often found to be concentrated in certain industries, and in these industries strikes seem to occur only during certain phases of cycles that also include long periods of cooperation. Arthur Ross (1961) speaks of centers of conflict to express his finding that a large percentage of strike activity has been concentrated in a relatively few major industries, while many industries are characterized by long periods of labor-management peace.

Types of Union-Management Relations

Thus it appears that if one were to try to characterize the kind of relationships typically found between American labor and management groups it would be a mistake to describe them as being hostile and belligerent. To be sure, industrial relations in this country reflect a varying pattern of competition and cooperation. There are times when the balance between the two forces is altered and episodes of conflict appear, but by and large these relationships tend to be moderately cooperative and constructive.

A study by Derber, Chalmers, and Edelman (1962) can be cited as evidence. In this study an attempt was made to use a relatively sophisticated statistical technique known as factor analysis to describe the basic types of union-management relations that were found to exist in a sample of 37 work organizations. This analysis revealed that most of these relationships seem to fit one of three types; and of these three, one type (Type X) seems to describe the situation in a very large majority of instances. The Type X relationship (see Table 12.11) involves a situation in which the two parties maintain relatively friendly relationships with one another. While neither side is completely happy with its success in achieving its goals, neither shows major incompatibility in the goals it seeks. Here the union is willing to confine its attention to issues that bear directly on the work, and it makes little effort to influence financial, sales, and technical aspects of the company. As Derber et al. (1962) state,

> Perhaps the chief characteristics of Type X is its moderation and its spirit of give and take or willing compromise. The union is seen by both sides as a positive force in the establishment, but essentially in the role of a protective agent of the workers interests and not as a serious challenge to the managerial organization. (p. 268)

Two other types of labor management relation-ships were found among a minority of the 37 organizations, one type being called ''quiescent'' (Type C), the other called ''aggressive and resist-ant'' (Type A).

In a Type C relationship the union has a low influence, uses little pressure, and maintains favorable attitudes in a climate of friendliness. The Type A relationship is one in which the union exerts considerable influence in an unfriendly atmosphere in which there is the use of high amounts of pressure and frequent inability to negotiate without outside mediators. Observations of labor-management relations at these 37 companies, taken several years apart, revealed that there was very little shifting from one type to another. Hence, not only did this study reveal that an overwhelming number of labor-management relationships were relatively free from intense conflict, but that these relationships remained fairly stable over time.

Conflict Absorption

Why most labor-management relationships tend to be moderately harmonious is probably a function of a number of interrelated factors, one of

TABLE 12.11   Most Common Types of Union-Management Relationships

Dimensions of Union-Management Relationships	
I	Feelings about Joint Relationships—union-management feelings about working together.
II	Extent of Union Influence—scope of union vote in decision making.
III	Joint Problem Solving—exchange of information or consulting with each other on problems.
IV	Use of Pressure—use or threat of work stoppages to achieve objectives.

TYPE X RELATIONSHIP		TYPE C RELATIONSHIP		TYPE A RELATIONSHIP	
I	Moderate feelings	I	Favorable feelings	I	Unfavorable feelings
II	Moderate union influence	II	Low union influence	II	High union influence
III	Moderate joint problem solving	III	Little joint problem solving	III	Little joint problem solving
IV	Low use of pressure	IV	Low use of pressure	IV	High use of pressure

Adapted from Derber, M., Chalmers, W. E., & Edelman, M. T. Types and variants in local union management relationships. *Human Organizations,* 1962–1963, *21,* 264–271.

which being that in many areas the aspirations and objectives of both parties are mutually interdependent. To achieve many of their objectives management is dependent upon labor and labor is dependent upon management. But apart from sharing common objectives, union-management relations are often tempered by social mechanisms that permit organizations to absorb conflict in such a way that signs of stress are prevented from coming to the surface (Etzioni-Halevy, 1975).

Conflict is often a consequence of efforts to produce change, and when the changes sought are unacceptable to those who occupy positions of power, an organization will mobilize coping mechanisms to deal with this challenge. At times these mechanisms are directed toward suppressing conflict; counterthreats and intimidation may be used. Under other circumstances, the organization may adopt strategies that will permit at least the partial expression of conflict, while attempting to control its impact on the organization. At times like these, an organization will initiate techniques for coping with these threats in order to ensure that the changes that follow do not lead to fundamental alterations in the organization's structure or in its objectives. For example, promises to study a question, assignment of a disputed matter to a committee, partial concessions involving aspects of the demands that have no far-reaching effects, and statements of assurance that the demands are being considered, or are about to be dealt with, are but a few of the options available.

Efforts to absorb certain kinds of labor-management conflict may lead an organization to promote those individuals who are involved in the conflict. Schenkel, Dewire, and Ronan (1973) studied a group of 117 aerospace workers who had submitted three or more grievances within a five-year period. Characteristics of this group of chronic grievants were compared with a control sample of workers who had not submitted a grievance during this period. One interesting outcome of this comparison was that the chronic grievant was found to have been promoted with a significantly higher frequency than their nongrievant work associates. Lieberman (1954) reports a study

in which a large group of workers were observed for a period of a year, during which time some individuals were promoted to foreman and others to shop steward. Prior to their promotions these individuals were found to have expressed greater job discontentment than did their work associates who were not promoted.

These results suggest the ''squeaking wheel'' hypothesis—that organizations tend to absorb conflict by promoting those who are responsible for creating tensions. This also suggests that in studying labor-management relations one should be aware of the procedures employed to cope with worker discontentment before it reaches the stage of open conflict. The absence of a history of strikes and work stoppages in a particular organization may well reflect the fact that management has developed effective procedures for conflict absorption, as well as represent the fact that tensions and conflict may not be present in any form.

FACTORS UNDERLYING INDUSTRIAL CONFLICT

In spite of the fact that most labor-management relations are relatively harmonious, there still remains in the United States a level of industrial friction that makes this problem a significant one. In 1975, for example, there were 1.75 million workers involved in one of the over five thousand work stoppages that took place. Strike activity tends to be a more visible part of labor-management relationships in this country than it is in some other parts of the industrialized world. Ross and Hartman (1960) report that strikes in the United States and Canada occur with higher frequency than in Northern European countries. Furthermore, a strike tends to last longer in North America than in Northern Europe.

A long list of variables have been associated with the propensity for industrial conflict. Organizational factors such as union and plant size (Britt & Galle, 1972; Eisele, 1974) and stage of technological development (Woodward, 1965) are thought to be related to the incidence of industrial friction. Eisele (1974) found that with industries employing technologies other than mass production, it is in the medium-size plants that strike frequency is highest. In mass-production industries, however, it is the larger plants that seem to have higher strike frequency.

With all the many complicated organizational and economic variables that might be correlated with strike activity, no consistent picture emerges. Trends are evident, as, for example, the tendency for strike activity to be related to unemployment levels, but perhaps the closest one may get to a working hypothesis is to conclude that propensity to strike is increased by any condition that undermines the maintenance of harmonious human relationships. Poor leadership, ineffective communication, rapid and poorly managed change, and a variety of factors that produce insecurity all probably increase the likelihood of industrial conflict.

There is some evidence that the strike has many properties that makes it comparable to other forms of human conflict. Lammers (1969), for example, presents evidence suggesting that industrial strikes and military mutinies share many of the same determinants. Some social scientists (for example, Berkowitz, 1970) suggest that the presence of aggressive behaviors serves to increase the likelihood that others who observe these behaviors will also display some form of aggression. Aggression is thought to serve as a stimulus to further aggression; hence, there is a contagious aspect of belligerent behaviors, which in an industrial setting could translate everyday interpersonal frictions between individual workers and management into an increased likelihood of union strike action.

Worker's Social Location

Kerr and Siegel (1954) suggest that it is the worker's location in the society that influences a tendency to strike. For instance, in work settings where the worker is isolated from the main currents of society, there are factors that increase the tendencies to strike. Miners, longshoremen, and lumbermen are examples of workers who find themselves in communities that are relatively homogeneous in social composition and isolated from the broad cross-section of the society. Sharing similar community and work experiences, members of these groups also share common grievances. Without the internal checks and balances that might be supplied by others with different life experiences, the social conditions are conducive to an escalation of tensions until they appear in the form of open hostility, that is, a strike.

Other social factors mentioned by Kerr and Siegel include the relative absence of opportunity for vertical and horizontal mobility. In those instances in which workers are fixed in their current circumstances, with little chance to move up or out, the strike becomes an outlet for the accumulating tensions that develop on the job and is seen as a chance to improve one's social and occupational circumstances.

The nature of working conditions also serves to attract workers who have a certain propensity to strike. Kerr and Siegel maintain that work that is generally unpleasant and that requires relatively low levels of skill will attract workers whose social rearing make it more likely that they will look for action-oriented solutions to their problems.

Grievances

From one point of view, intergroup conflict is an expression of the accumulation of a large number of frustrations and tensions experienced by the members of a group. These may not be shared frustrations, as they originate in a variety of different experiences found on the job. These aggravations sum together in some fashion to form a general climate of human relations. Any one member of the work group may not be able to tell you in any convincing way why relations between labor and management are so poor. Vague claims that "they don't give a damn about us around here," serve as explanations for low morale, and when pressed for particulars, it is difficult to find two workers who will give the same reasons for the bad relations that exist.

Under these circumstances a strike is an expression of the coalescence of these individual tensions around a general issue that is shared by the members of the union. This issue is the "cause" of the strike only in terms of providing a rationale for actions that have their origins in a multitude of diverse aggravations. Hence, the day-to-day grievances that workers experience can, if given no outlet for expression or solution, create a psychological climate that is fertile ground for group hostility. The strike may be an expression of these hostilities, the point being that its causes are not to be found in specific conditions that are faced by all members of the group, but are found in a collection of separate experiences that are different for each worker.

Aggrieved Workers

It is in the individual grievance that one can find some of the elementary conditions that give rise to collective aggression. As a consequence, we might gain insight into the dynamics of union strike action by looking at the characteristics of those workers who submit grievances. Parnes (1956), in a study of the industrial strike, concludes that it is often the rank-and-file member who is more prone to be extreme in contract demands than the union leadership. As a result,

> . . . the function of the leadership is not to arouse the membership and to convince them of the righteousness of the demands, but rather to restrain the rank and file from pressing for terms which the leaders' wider experience and greater knowledge tell them are either unwise or indefensible. (Parnes, 1956, p. 61)

Ash (1970) studied grievances submitted over a five-year period by employees of a large work organization employing over ten thousand production and maintenance personnel. These grievances were broken down into *group grievances*—a complaint was raised by a group of workers—and *"name" grievances* where the grievant was an in-

dividual. All in all, 40 percent of the grievances were of the "name" type, but in those areas of the plant where grievance rate was highest, there was a much higher percentage of "name" grievances than there was in low grievance areas. Counter to the previous suggestion that grievance rate relates to strike activity, Ash was unable to find any relationship between the two. There was, however, a clear relationship between grievance rate and the work stoppages that were localized in a particular department. Here high grievance departments were more likely to be the ones involved in work stoppages.

To determine the characteristics of the high-grievance worker, Ash drew a sample of workers who had submitted a "name" grievance and compared them with a sample of workers who had not submitted a grievance. Surprisingly, few variables differentiated the two groups. Such factors as sex, marital status, education, and length of service failed to differentiate grievant from nongrievant. Three variables—age, race, and veteran status—were found to be significant indicators. Younger, white veterans seemed to submit a higher number of grievances, leading Ash to suggest that aggrieved workers were individuals who had not yet "settled down" compared to their nongrievant associates. Interestingly, in each year but one the mean earnings of the aggrieved worker were slightly higher than the mean wages of the nonaggrieved worker.

Ash's suggestion that the aggrieved worker had not yet settled down finds some support in a study by Schenkel, Dewire, and Ronan (1973). These researchers studied the characteristics of workers who over a five-year period submitted at least three grievances. Twenty-eight factors were studied, with six of these separating the chronic griever from a sample of nonaggrieved workers. Chronic grievers were

1. younger
2. younger at time of original hiring
3. more likely to be single
4. more likely to have moved into the state seeking work
5. reported to have performed in an unsatisfactory fashion in a previous job
6. found to have a much higher promotion rate on the present job

The worker who openly expresses grievances, therefore, may be an indivdiual who is unable to see that the job is "getting him anywhere." This, coupled with the belief that there is still good potential for moving on to other jobs, creates a set of psychological conditions that support open displays of discontentment and aggression toward management.

We need more information about the aggrieved worker. We also need more information concerning grievance rates and the propensity to strike. Does the grievance machinery serve as an outlet for some of the aggression and frustrations workers experience, or should we view these greivances as a barometer of the likelihood of union-sponsored work stoppages? Both perspectives are probably partially correct, and our task is to learn more about the circumstances in which the grievance serves to release negative energies and reduce the prospects of other forms of discontentment.

SUMMARY COMMENTS

Labor unions, like business firms, are complex organizations. As such, they share many characteristics with the business enterprise. There are, however, important differences, a principal one being found in the sources of the power the two organizations wield. Management organizations draw heavily on the concept of property for the power it employs, and as a consequence, primary authority is found in the ranks of the stockholders and their representatives, a board of directors. The labor union, on the other hand, draws its power from the membership whose interests it represents. For the union, power is calculated in terms of the size and cohesiveness of the membership, and the social-economic significance of the skills they possess. From this it can be seen that there is a basic difference in the *locus of power* found in business and labor organizations. Primary power tends to be found external to the people who make up the operational segments of the business firm, whereas the unions tend to draw on primary sources of power that are located within the operational divisions of the organization.

Responding to these organizational differences,

Munson (1965) comments that by being outside the business firm, stockholders do not weaken the effectiveness of a firm by ignoring its activities. Union power, on the other hand, is significantly weakened by a membership that is apathetic and indifferent. All this creates basically different psychological climates in the two organizations. For example, Stagner (1956) contends that the structure of the labor organization is inherently democratic in its character. The leader's role is a representative one, very similar to the role assumed by the political leader. In fact, a useful analogy can be constructed between the workings of a labor organization and a political party. Ranging from the types of membership roles found to the kinds of influence leaders may exert on the membership, there are many similarities that may be found existing between the two types of organizations. In any event, the analogy that can be drawn between unions and political parties is probably more satisfactory than is the one that could be constructed between parties and business firms.

Participation in the labor union is by and large a function of the extent to which the individual employee perceives personal interests tied up with the affairs of the union. Hence, in a climate of labor peace, there is little stimulus to encourge many workers to assume an active role in the union. This accentuates an impression that the typical member is indifferent and generally apathetic. Yet this conclusion may be based on the fact that labor-management relations are often quite tranquil and harmonious. In times of trouble, however, there is an awakening of membership involvement and an increase in rates of participation.

What does all this mean in terms of the question of the importance of union membership to the individual employee? Perhaps it tells us that for many workers the union is often viewed in relatively narrow terms. It is bread-and-butter issues like wages, fringe benefits, hours, and conditions of work that identify connections that tie worker to union. To the extent that these issues surface and begin to appeal to the worker's self-interests, the union membership presents a picture of active involvement. During those periods in which these issues assume background proportions, union involvement gives the appearance of indifference and detachment. For many workers, therefore, the union maintains a changing status. There are times in which the union functions as an element in the work experience that is perceived as being useful in achieving personal objectives; there are other times when the union assumes a background role and the worker adopts a role that is not well integrated with the activities of the union. One should think about the psychological involvement with a union in terms of a range of values rather than as a single level. Turning to the research literature, we find a picture of union participation that suggests a large group of indifferent and uninformed workers, but there is little information of a longitudinal type to indicate the extent to which this apathy gives way during times of threat and negotiation.

Workers hold a variety of attitudes toward their labor unions, but the research literature indicates that union membership, even if it involves active participation, does not necessarily imply a negtive attitude toward the company and its management. In many work situations employees seem to express the desire for a cooperative relationship between the two organizations, and they see that it is well within their best interests for the union not to set out to ruin the business firm. There is always room for competition between the two factions, but this competitive relationship operates within limits that are defined by shared interests. Hence, workers often acknowledge that both labor and management play constructive roles and are essential to their general welfare.

4
WORK
LEADERSHIP

13

Work Supervision

INTRODUCTION

Whether called foreman, department head, or manager, the person who serves in a supervisory position plays a significant role in the work people do. The supervisor serves many functions in the work group: evaluation, planning, decision making, technical consulting; but the essence of the job can be summarized in a single word, leadership. The supervisor is the formally established leader in the work group, and in this position often holds considerable power that stems from the control of many of the incentives that are of great importance to those who work. To one degree or another, supervisors administer the organization's incentive systems. They control or have significant input into the psychological positives and negatives of work. As a result, workers often report that their relations with their supervisors is a major source of concern for them. Recall that in Chapter 6 it was reported that workers often found their supervisors to be the cause of much of the tension and psychological conflict they experienced on the job. In Chapter 8 we found that a supervisor can at times be seen as a major source of job dissatisfaction.

But all is not negative. Supervisory practices have also been associated with high levels of morale and worker satisfaction, and high levels of production efficiency have been related to certain styles of supervisory behavior. Hence, whether one is thinking about the efficiency of a work group or the work experiences of a single worker, the behavior of the supervisor is an important element in many of the things that go on in a work environment.

In this chapter an attempt will be made to answer several questions regarding this important dimension of work. It is impossible, however, in a single chapter to consider all the issues that have been raised concerning industrial supervision; few areas have been given as much research attention. As a consequence, the discussion will be confined to a limited number of issues, with the hope that those selected will give a representative reflection of the status of the field.

Perhaps the most basic question concerning work supervision involves the research that has been done to describe the behaviors that are characteristic of different types of business and industrial supervision. What does a supervisor do and how can we categorize the various behavioral styles in which these activities are carried out? A related issue: if one were to attempt to measure varieties of supervisory leadership, along how many separate dimensions would one have to collect data? In other words, we would first like to know something about the structure of supervisory behavior, that is, the number and types of factors that make up this social process.

Another important consideration involves the performance consequences of different styles of supervisory leadership. It is often assumed that group effectiveness is a reflection of competent supervision. Certainly, supervisors are often rewarded for the high performance levels of their group. As a result, one may inquire about the styles of work leadership that have been associated with good group performance. Do workers produce more for one type of supervision than another? Is it possible that one style of supervision is equally effective in all work situations, or is it more likely that the most effective pattern of leadership varies from one setting to the next? In other words, is the effectiveness of any given style of supervision *contingent* upon the characteristics of the work environment?

Supervision, to be completely understood, must be viewed within its organizational context. One aspect of this involves the simple fact that most supervisors themselves have supervisors, and it is in this relationship that some of the important variables governing work leadership are to be found. The term, *supervisory climate,* is appropriate here. This term expresses the idea that there is a relationship between the kind of supervision one individual receives and the type given to those working at the next lowest level. Most often the implications drawn are that the type of supervision received is similar to the type given to subordinates. In dealing with this topic we will be discussing supervisory styles as an expression of a social system that is larger and more complicated than a single superior-subordinate pair. The primary question to be raised here concerns whether one must take larger segments of an organization into consideration in order to explain the appearance of the style of supervision found in a given work group.

Before taking up these questions, however, it would be profitable to consider briefly some ideas pertaining to the general nature of leadership behavior. After considering these general issues, we will then turn our attention to the work setting and deal with more specific issues relating to industrial supervision.

Leadership—Three Points of View

It is always difficult to develop a completely satisfactory classification of ideas, and the leadership area provides no exception to this problem. One can discern, however, three general approaches to the definition of leadership that appear in the thinking of those who study the topic.

Personality Traits. Perhaps one of the more direct ways of dealing with leadership is to consider it a component of the individual's personality. Actually, those who approach leadership from this perspective most often think of the concept as a higher-order dimension of the personality in the sense that it emerges from a particular pattern of more basic traits rather than being a fundamental trait in and of itself. From this point of view, leadership is an attribute of the person that is carried from one situation to the next. One often reads of individuals having "proven leadership capabilities," which is a phrase that implies a continuity of leadership competence across situations. We find the consequences of this outlook in many instances in which leadership roles, say in the government, are assigned to those who have been successful leaders in business and industry.

Efforts to identify the traits that are related to leadership have not gone without success. In fact, looking at studies of this type (Stogdill, 1974), the idea might cross one's mind that there appears to have been a bit too much success. One is struck by the long list of personal attributes that have at one time or another been found to be associated with leadership status. In an impressive summary of this work, Stogdill (1974, p. 74) identifies 43 traits found to be associated with some aspect of leadership. In this list, however, there are some variables that give indication of more substantial and consistent relationship with leadership than do others. Stogdill, commenting on these variables, writes,

> The leader is characterized by a strong drive for responsibility and task completion, vigor and persistence in pursuit of goals, venturesomeness and originality in problem solving, drive to exercise initiative in social situations, self-confidence and sense of personal identity, willingness to accept consequences of decision and action, readiness to absorb interpersonal stress, willingness to tolerate frustration and delay, ability to

influence other persons' behavior, and capacity to structure social interaction systems to the purpose at hand. (1974, p. 81)

Situations.   Although not many would deny the contribution that personality traits make to leadership behavior, there are those who place stronger emphasis on the demands of the situation in which the individual functions. This point of view holds that the social situation calls forth the behaviors needed to serve the leadership requirements of the group. Leadership is seen as part of a group's response to social circumstances; therefore, the particular style of leader behavior one observes is an expression of such things as the size, structure, and task objectives of the group.

These situational influences are most clearly evident when one considers leadership in an established organization. Here supervisors are appointed. They are appointed to an office that carries with it obligations, powers, and technical demands. Leadership, in such instances, is a formal job duty, and those who serve in this capacity are assigned to groups that are already formed and have established traditions and values. No doubt they are appointed to such positions because it is felt that they possess the wherewithal to succeed. Once in the formal supervisory role, however, the requirements of the work task and the characteristics of the social situation place substantial limits on the kinds of leader behavior that are acceptable. Leadership in these instances requires the individual to adopt the role that is appropriate to the setting. To understand leadership, then, one must look at these situational variables, for it is here that the dominant behavioral determinants are to be found.

Interaction.   Perhaps the most widely held theoretical perspective is one that sees personal traits interacting with the characteristics of the situation to produce a pattern of leadership. By interacting is meant that the effect a personal trait may have in shaping leadership patterns depends upon the situation being observed. By the same token, the influence of the social situation on leader behavior varies as a function of the personal traits of those who enter the situation.

One version of the interaction theme is that leaders emerge from the group as a function of their ability to contribute to the needs of the membership. Those who possess the personal traits best suited to achieve desirable results are the ones who play leadership roles. Whenever group objectives shift—that is, when the social situation changes— then a different pattern of traits becomes more functional, and as a consequence the pattern of leadership is altered.

This is the point of view that will be adopted in the present chapter, since it seems reasonable to envision some sort of interaction among variables as numerous and complex as those traits and situational factors that have been associated with the leadership role. Few behavioral variables are independent of the influence of some second variable; but over and above this consideration, the interactionist approach is more complete than either the trait or situationist point of view. Its advantage lies in the fact that it encourages one to think about the *separate effects* of both influences, but it also requires that we think about their *joint impact*. As a consequence, it leads one to view the leadership process as the result of *combinations* of variables. As these combinations change, so too will the leadership behavior observed.

WORK SUPERVISION

It's time to narrow our attention to the work environment. The study of business and industrial supervision has accounted for an impressive amount of the research that has been carried out on behavior in the work setting, and much energy has been directed toward the leadership role of the first-line foreman. That this is the case reflects the recognized importance of these first-line management positions. After all, it is at this juncture in the organizational structure that management and the worker come together. This is where management planning and policy are translated into the day-to-day activities that occur at the workplace.

The first two questions we might ask about industrial supervisors are—what do they do and how do they do it? With regard to the first, it is obvious that we are referring primarily to job duties. *What* the supervisor does is in large measure specified by the formal job duties associated with the position. As with all jobs, there is room for variation and interpretation, but in the main, what these supervisors do is prescribed by external demands placed on their behavior. *How* they go about their duties, although subject to some external constraint, is more likely to be a reflection of their skills in interpersonal affairs (Stogdill, Scott, & Jaynes, 1956).

The Job

The job of the first-line supervisor has much in common with the job of the business executive. Both often face a day segmented into many brief intervals of activity, which change frequently and involve a large number of social contacts. Guest (1956) reports a study in which 56 production foremen were observed during the course of an eight-hour work spell. He reports that on the average the activity of the foreman changed *every 48 seconds*. The work these foremen performed was described as involving a succession of interruptions, discontinuities, and an impressive variety of activities. Furthermore, output was the principal concern in a large number of these jobs. That is to say, planning, monitoring, training, and encouraging work activities of the group represent a substantial portion of the supervisor's concerns (Mandell & Duckworth, 1955, Guest, 1956).

The significance of this latter finding is of considerable interest, particularly when considered in the light of one of the main themes found in the literature on work supervision. The idea is often expressed that the principal part of the supervisor's job is not direct management of production activities, but rather in the area of human relations. The supervisor's job has as its primary concern the social and emotional components of the workplace. Furthermore, it is often assumed that if this human-relations aspect is carried out properly, con-

ditions are created for high levels of group efficiency. From this perspective, the foreman's job is to create a good psychological climate for work. Be this as it may, many industrial and business supervisors report, or are observed, investing relatively little of their time in these human-relations activities. Production, getting the work out, appears to be the category of performance that very often accounts for much of the supervisor's time and energy, and human relations may not receive the attention the literature often indicates it warrants. For example, in a study involving both blue- and white-collar foremen, Mandell and Duckworth (1955) found that personnel administration and human relations accounted for only 7 per cent of the supervisor's time and activities. Hence, when one refers to the job of the first-line foreman, it is not at all unlikely that the job is one focusing directly on the production activities of the work group.

As might be expected, however, there is tremendous variation in the work done at this level of an organization—variety from position to position, and from day to day within a single position. Kay and Meyer (1962) report that observations of 24 production foremen employed by General Electric revealed that the typical foreman does not spend most of the day following some preplanned schedule. Rather, the foreman receives a high volume of almost random inputs from a variety of different sources. The day, therefore, consists largely of reacting to these unplanned external events. Guest (1956) cites considerable variation among different foremen and on different days. Hence, looking at *average* amounts of time spent on various activities by the *typical* foreman might mislead one into overlooking the variation in work activities found at these supervisory positions.

Supervisory Job Types.   One of the best studies carried out in this area is a survey of 452 supervisory jobs in thirteen companies located in a number of different industries (Mahoney, Jerdee, & Carroll, 1965). Supervisory jobs ranging from foreman to department head were analyzed, and eight categories of activities were developed to describe the work that was being done:

1. *Planning*—Determining goals, policies, and courses of action. Work scheduling, budgeting, setting up procedures, setting goals or standards, preparing agendas, programming.
2. *Investigating*—Collecting and preparing information, usually in the form of records, reports, and accounts. Inventorying, measuring output, preparing financial statements, recordkeeping, performing research, job analysis.
3. *Coordinating*—Exchanging information with people in the organization other than subordinates in order to relate and adjust programs. Advising other departments, expediting, liaison with other managers, arranging meetings, informing superiors, seeking other departments' cooperation.
4. *Evaluating*—Assessment and appraisal of proposals or of reported or observed performance. Employee appraisals, judging output records, judging financial reports, product inspection, approving requests, judging proposals and suggestions.
5. *Supervising*—Directing, leading, and developing subordinates. Counseling subordinates, training subordinates, explaining work rules, assigning work, disciplining, handling complaints of subordinates.
6. *Staffing*—Maintaining the work force of a unit or of several units. College recruiting, employment interviewing, selecting employees, placing employees, promoting employees, transferring employees.
7. *Negotiating*—Purchasing, selling, or contracting for goods or services. Tax negotiations, contacting suppliers, dealing with sales representatives, advertising products, collective bargaining, selling to dealers or customers.
8. *Representing*—Advancing general organizational interests through speeches, consultation, and contacts with individuals or groups outside the organization. Public speeches, community drives, news releases, attending conventions, business club meetings. (Mahoney, Jerdee, & Carroll, 1965, p. 100)

Managers were asked to estimate the amount of time they typically allocated to the eight areas of activity; and although average times were computed for each area, relatively few of the individual jobs had patterns of activity that were like the average pattern. It was discovered, however, that these jobs could be grouped into job types. Eight job types were identified (see Table 13.1).

TABLE 13.1 Average Percentage Distribution of Time among Performance Functions within Job Types

Perfor-mance function	Job types								
	Plan-ners (N=89)	Investi-gators (N=35)	Coordi-nators (N=29)	Evalu-ators (N=19)	Super-visors (N=173)	Nego-tiators (N=22)	Gener-alists (N=56)	Multispe-cialists (N=29)	Total (N=452)
Planning	39	12	12	13	13	12	17	22	20
Investigating	10	44	9	8	8	9	13	14	13
Coordinating	13	12	39	13	11	9	17	18	15
Evaluating	10	9	10	35	10	8	14	16	13
Supervising	18	15	19	21	50	12	18	17	28
Staffing[1]	5	3	4	4	4	2	7	3	4
Negotiating	4	4	5	4	3	45	11	8	6
Representing	1	2	2	1	1	4	3	2	2
Total*	100	101	100	99	100	101	100	100	101

*Total may be more or less than 100 per cent due to rounding.
Source: Mahoney, T. A., Jerdee, T. H., & Carroll, S. J. The job(s) of management. *Industrial Relations*, 1965, *4*, 97–110.
[1]Entries omitted in original table with no explanation. They have been inserted by present author.

The jobs in six types tended to invest a high proportion of time in a single activity and relatively little time in other areas of activity. Two types, Generalist and Multispecialist, were defined in terms of several activity areas rather than a single prominent area.

Some job types occurred more frequently than others. Seventy-one per cent of all jobs (see Table 13.1) fell in the Supervisor, Planner, or Generalist categories, with the Supervisor type accounting for almost 40 per cent of the total. The proportion of jobs falling into each type, however, was not the same everywhere in the organization. Taking these 452 jobs and grouping them in three management levels, Mahoney et al. found that the distribution of job activities seemed to change from one level to the next. Figure 13.1 shows systematic changes in job types as one moves up the organization. Compared to higher levels of management, proportionately more first-line positions are of the Su-

pervisor type, whereas the Planner and Generalist types seem to increase considerably as one moves to the higher levels of management. Hence, the activities of managers change as a function of their level in the work organization. Yet, Mahoney and his associates report that running through all job types there seems to be a common core of activities that make the job of one manager overlap the jobs of most other managers. According to Mahoney et al., these common work activities account for approximately half of managerial performance. Beyond these common elements there are varying patterns of activities.

SUPERVISOR STYLES

Although the official duties of the supervisor's job are of considerable interest, it is often not so much what supervisors do as how they go about doing it that is important. As a consequence, the measurement and description of supervisory styles has received much attention from those who study work behavior.

Dimensions of Supervisory Leadership

Perhaps the best way to present the problem of determining the dimensional structure of supervision is to ask the question, how many separate scales would be needed to measure differences in supervisory styles? Consider asking this question with regard to the attribute of height. If we had two people in the room who were both exactly 69 inches tall, we would conclude that the two were identical with respect to this attribute. Here a single number contains all the information needed to describe a person's status on this attribute.

Consider being told that these same two persons have an I.Q. of 123 each. Can we conclude that both are identical in terms of their intellectual competence? Probably not, since it is quite possible that the two differ with respect to the pattern of intellectual strengths and weaknesses they possess. Here we find a measurement scale that yields a total score; we also find, however, that there are numerous patterns of test performance that will give the same total score. One of our hypothetical

FIGURE 13.1   Distribution of Assignments among Job Types at Each Organizational Level*

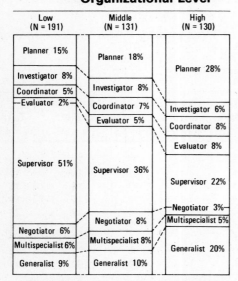

*Totals do not add up to 100 per cent because of rounding.

Source: Mahoney, T. A., Jerdee, T. H., & Carroll, S. J. The job(s) of management. *Industrial Relations*, 1965, *4*, 97–110.

persons might have, for example, performed quite poorly on questions dealing with numbers and arithmetic, while the second person might have shown weakness on vocabulary and verbal questions. Yet in spite of the fact that these differences existed, the two emerged from the test with the same total score. Situations like this suggest that the attribute being measured, in this case intelligence, is a complex one. It suggests that the concept exists as a *multidimensional attribute,* and that it is really a summary of several kinds of intellectual behaviors that combined into the I.Q. score.

Supervisory behavior, like intelligence, is usually thought of as being multidimensional; but unlike intelligence, its structure is often thought of as being relatively simple, consisting of but one or two dimensions. Of course, there are exceptions to be found where supervision is seen as being more complex; on balance, however, it seems reasonably accurate to state that when many social scientists think of supervisory leadership, they think of behavior that falls into two major categories. Whether these two categories refer to two independent dimensions or whether they can be represented as opposite ends of a single bipolar scale is a matter that is not always clearly delineated by theorists. This is not, however, a problem that is important at the moment. What is important is that one recognize that when they think of leader behavior, many theorists have two contrasting varieties of leadership in mind.

These two aspects of supervision have been given many different names — for example, democratic-autocratic, permissive-restrictive, employee-centered/production-centered, consideration-initiation of structure, participative-directive—and although distinctions can be drawn among them, there is still a basic idea running through the pairs (Stogdill, 1974). On the one hand we find supervision that is oriented toward work; on the other hand supervision that is people oriented. With the former style one sees an approach to supervision that is focused on production, consisting mainly of directing workers when and how to work, and concerned with the evaluation of work performance. With the latter style of supervision one finds

behavior that is human-relations oriented. In this instance there is a tendency on the part of the leader to permit participation in a variety of planning and decision-making activities. In this style of leadership there is an awareness of the social and emotional needs that are characteristic of the members of the work group.

It is probably quite true that differences in supervisory styles vary along more than just two dimensions. But it may be equally true that two dimensions, no matter what they are called, account for a substantial portion of the differences that are observed in leader behavior. Furthermore, the two-dimensional approach has played such a dominant role in the work that has been done in this area, it seems to be a reasonable starting place for any study of leader behavior.

Two Dimensions of Work Supervision

Perhaps one of the most widely quoted series of studies that have drawn on a two-dimensional concept of leadership was conducted at the Institute for Social Relations at the University of Michigan. The basic plan for many of these studies consisted of entering a work situation and identifying the most and the least effective work groups in the organization. Once these groups had been selected, the behavior of the supervisors was studied in an effort to detect the supervisory practices that differentiated the high-performance from the low-performance work groups.

These studies revealed that supervisors with the poorest records of group performance tended to concentrate their leadership efforts directly on the production activities of their subordinates (Katz, Maccoby, & Morse, 1950; Katz et al., 1951). Supervision tended to be close in the sense that the supervisor displayed an interest in seeing that the members of the work group were kept busy with a prescribed series of production tasks. Supervisors of this type were found to spend much time and energy at such things as trying to motivate people to produce, inspecting the work, and showing people how to achieve production objectives. This approach to work leadership was called *production centered.* In Likert's terms (Likert, 1961a) production-centered supervisors tend to base their approach to leadership on the following task and authority practices:

> 1. Break the total operation to be performed into its simple, component parts or tasks.
> 2. Develop the best way to perform each of the component parts.
> 3. Hire people with appropriate aptitudes and skills to perform each of these component tasks.
> 4. Train these people to do their respective tasks in the specified best way.
> 5. Provide supervision of such a kind that these employees perform their designated tasks using the specified procedure at an acceptable rate as determined by timing the job.
> 6. Where feasible, also, use incentives in the form of individual or group piece rates. (Likert, 1961a, p. 6)

In short, production-centered supervision tends to be rather narrow in its scope, dealing largely with those subordinate activities that are directly related to doing the work.

In contrast to production-centered supervision, the Michigan studies identified a second style, called employee-centered. Employee-centered supervisors tend to devote their attention to the human-relations aspects of the work situation. Rather than focusing attention on production activities, the employee-centered supervisor tends to adopt a general approach to supervision. Here an effort is made to first establish an awareness and understanding of work goals, and then to create a climate of freedom within which employees can do their jobs in the manner most acceptable to them. Likert (1961a, p. 8) quotes an employee-centered supervisor:

> My job is dealing with human beings rather than with the work. It doesn't matter if I have anything to do with the work or not. The chances are that people will do a better job if you are really taking an interest in them. Knowing the names is important and helps a lot, but it's not enough. You really have to know each individual well, know what his problems are. Most of the time I discuss matters with employees at their desks rather than in the office. Sometimes I sit on a waste paper basket or lean on the files. It's all very informal. People don't seem to like to come into the office to talk.

We will return to these studies later when we take up the effects of supervision on performance.

Ohio State Studies.   Another extensive series of studies of industrial supervision was carried out by the Personnel Research Board of Ohio State University. As a part of this series, a questionnaire, called the Supervisory Behavior Description, was developed (cf. Hemphill, 1950; Fleishman, Harris, & Burtt, 1955) to measure supervisory style. When applied to supervisors functioning in military and industrial settings, it was found that two important dimensions of leader behavior seemed to be at work. One dimension, Consideration of Others, refers to behavior that is "indicative of friendship, mutual trust, respect and a certain warmth between the leader and his group" (Fleishman, Harris, & Burtt, 1955, p. 27). A second dimension, Initiating Structure, refers to behavior of a supervisor that "organizes and defines the relationship between himself and the members of his group. [The supervisor] tends to define the role which he expects each member to assume, and endeavors to establish well-defined patterns of organization, channels of communication, and ways of getting the job done" (Fleishman, Harris, & Burtt, 1955, p. 27).

Supervisors thought to be high in Consideration tended to be described by the following kind of items on the Supervisory Behavior Description questionnaire:

1. He is friendly and can be easily approached.
2. He is willing to make changes.
3. He expresses appreciation when one of us does a good job.

4. He stresses the importance of high morale among those under him.

Supervisors thought to be high in Initiating Structure tended to be described by the following type of items:

---

1. He emphasizes meeting of deadlines.
2. He decides in detail what shall be done and how it shall be done.

3. He sees to it that people under him are working up to their limits.
4. He criticizes poor work.

The Ohio State group thought that these two dimensions of leader behavior were independent of one another; that is, a supervisors' status on one dimension was not related to status on the second.

Theory X and Theory Y. McGregor (1960) has presented some ideas concerning the nature of supervisory leadership that have been given a lot of attention. Here again one finds a two-dimensional approach to leadership embodied in what McGregor called Theory X and Theory Y. These theories deal with sets of assumptions that are thought to underlie two fundamentally different approaches to industrial supervision. Theory X refers to a set of assumptions concerning human nature that are thought to underlie styles of leadership that are directive and controlling. Theory Y refers to assumptions thought to underlie varieties of supervision that create working conditions in which there is an integration of the worker's personal goals with those of the organization.

Theory X is found in association with more traditional forms of supervision. The theory expresses the following three assumptions:

1. The average human being has an inherent dislike of work and will avoid it if he can.
2. Because of this human characteristic of dislike of work, most people must be coerced, controlled, directed, threatened with punishment to get them to put forth adequate effort toward the achievement of organizational objectives.
3. The average human being prefers to be directed, wishes to avoid responsibility, has relatively little ambition, wants security above all (McGregor, 1960, Ch. 4).

The assumptions contained in Theory Y perceive the individual worker exercising self-control and self-direction. These assumptions maintain:

1. The expenditure of physical and mental effort in work is as natural as play or rest.
2. External control and the threat of punishment are not the only means for bringing about effort toward organizational objectives. Man will exercise self-direction and self-control in the service of objectives to which he is committed.
3. Commitment to objectives is a function of the rewards associated with their achievement.
4. The average human being learns, under proper conditions, not only to accept but to seek responsibility.
5. The capacity to exercise a relatively high degree of imagination, ingenuity, and creativity in the solution of organizational problems is widely, not narrowly, distributed in the population.
6. Under the conditions of modern industrial life, the intellectual potentialities of the average human being are only partially utilized (McGregor, 1960, Ch. 4).

A given supervisor may not always be aware of the assumptions underlying his supervisory practices, but McGregor maintains that upon reflection and analysis, ideas such as these exist at the heart of the two basic varieties of supervision that are found in work situations.

The Managerial Grid. Blake and Mouton (1978) see supervisory behavior varying along two dimensions, one representing concern for production, the other representing concern for people. These two aspects of supervision are brought together to form the borders of a grid (see Fig. 13.2), the cells of which identify variations in supervisory practices. Since there are nine levels of concern for people and nine levels of production concern, the managerial grid contains 81 cells, each of which refers to a different supervisory style.

FIGURE 13.2 The New Managerial Grid

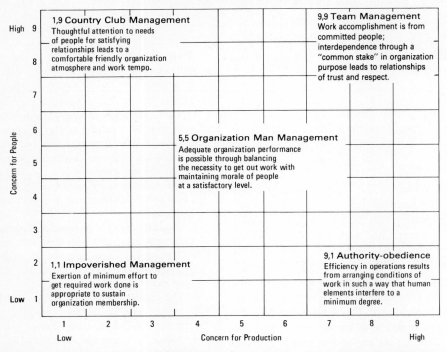

Source; Blake, R. R., & Mouton, J. S. *The new managerial grid.* Houston: Gulf, 1978, p. 11. Copyright © 1978, published by permission.

Blake and Mouton describe in some detail the supervisory practices found in the corners and in the center of the managerial grid. For example, at the top left-hand corner is found the 1,9 style. This combination represents an approach to supervision in which concern for production is low but concern for people is high. A 9,1 style reflects high production concern and low people concern. The following is a brief summary of the supervisory practices associated with five significant positions in the grid:

9,1 Supervision. The 9,1 style of supervision places major importance on work and job requirements. Subordinates tend to be viewed as instruments of production, and the control of the work group relies heavily on the use of authority and obedience. Workers are expected to show unswerving obedience to their supervisors. Little interest is expressed in the personal development of subordinates, and communication with them often consists of issuing orders and instructions that are accompanied by little in the way of explanation.

1,9 Supervision. The type of supervision expected from those with a 1,9 orientation tends to result in harmonious human relationships; the achievement of high levels of productivity, however, is unlikely. Supervision is directed toward winning the approval of the group. The supervisor attempts to gain control and give direction through gentle persuasion rather than by giving commands. Above all else, the supervisor tries to hold the affection of the subordinates, and every effort is made to avoid exerting pressures and disciplinary actions that will alienate the group. Cordiality is an important work norm. Conflict and disagreement, being violations of this norm, are avoided at virtually all cost.

1,1 Supervision. With the 1,1 orientation, supervision expresses little concern for either people or production. There is minimum contact between supervisor and worker with communication consisting mainly of passing messages along from one level to the next. Supervision is mainly interested in avoiding responsibility, and in McGregor's terms, supervision consists of "being present, yet absent."

5,5 Supervision. With the 5,5 orientation a balance is sought between people and production aspects of work. Communication is open and free, since it is assumed that people will work effectively if given reasons for doing so. Some emphasis is placed on production, but at the same time people are not disregarded. Direction and control are sought by attempting to motivate people and communicate with them. Orders are given, but never without explanations as to why they were issued.

9,9 Supervision. The 9,9 orientation leads to supervisory practices in which subordinates' needs for work involvement and commitment are well served. Supervision of this type encourages subordinates to draw on their creative talents in dealing with the work. As a consequence, there tends to be an integration of human goals and organizational goals. People and production are interconnected by shared goals. Supervisory direction and control rely heavily upon subordinates' participation and involvement in the planning of the work. Such participation leads to higher levels of subordinate commitment, which is the key to this type of supervisory control.

The managerial grid provides us with another example of the tendency of social scientists to view work supervision in terms of two basic dimensions. As a general rule, one of these dimensions deals with the supervisor's awareness of the social and psychological needs of subordinates. The other refers to those aspects of supervision that direct, structure, and generally emphasize production. As is evident from the managerial grid, these two dimensions can be used to generate a relatively large number of supervisory styles; but regardless of the number of combinations generated, the basic

structure of work leadership is often seen in terms of these two independent facets of behavior.

Other Views

Not everyone agrees with a two-dimensional model of supervisory behavior. Some maintain that in viewing supervision in terms of two dimensions, one is guilty of oversimplifying behaviors that are much more complicated. For example, in a later series of studies (Stogdill, Goode, & Day, 1962, 1963a, 1963b, 1964) by the Ohio State group, the data suggested that an adequate description of leader behavior required twelve, not two, categories (Stogdill, 1974).

> Representation—speaks and acts as representative of the group.
> Demand reconciliation—reconciles conflicting organizational demands and reduces disorder to system.
> Tolerance of uncertainty—is able to tolerate uncertainty and postponement without anxiety or upset.
> Persuasiveness—uses persuasion and argument effectively; exhibits strong convictions.
> Initiation of structure—clearly defines own role, and lets followers know what is expected.
> Tolerance of freedom—allows followers scope for initiative, decision, and action.
> Role retention—actively exercises leadership role rather than surrendering leadership to others.
> Consideration—regards the comfort, well-being, status, and contributions of followers.
> Production emphasis—applies pressure for productive output.
> Predictive accuracy—exhibits foresight and ability to predict outcomes accurately.
> Integration—maintains a closely knit organization; resolves intermember conflicts.
> Influence with superiors—maintains cordial relations with superiors; has influence with them; is striving for high status (Stogdill, 1974, p. 143).

A new version of the *Leader Behavior Description,* LBD—XII, was developed to measure these twelve facets of supervisory behavior, and subsequent research (cf. Stogdill, 1969) gave support to the argument that supervisory behavior can profitably be described in a way that is more complex than the earlier two-dimensional approach would suggest.

Along similar lines, Stogdill (1974) reviewed fifty-two studies, each of which used a complicated statistical procedure known as factor analysis to study the structure of leader behavior. He reports that the great majority of these studies identified not two but three or more dimensions. Factors that appeared most frequently are

Social nearness, friendliness
Technical skills
Task motivation and application
Group task supportiveness
Social and interpersonal skills
Leadership effectiveness and achievement
Emotional balance and control

All in all, twenty-six different dimensions were identified by at least three of the fifty-two studies surveyed. Hence, we see from this that the use of two dimensions to describe leader behavior is probably an oversimplification of the complex nature of this aspect of social behavior.

Using a different approach, Randle (1956) identified thirty characteristics of management performance, involving 1427 men at all positions above foreman who were found in twenty-five large companies. These men were interviewed, described by associates, their backgrounds and experience were analyzed, and they were given psychological tests. On the basis of the information collected, the following behavioral dimensions were found to enter into the descriptions that were obtained:

Characteristics of Management Performance

1. Position performance: How well the executive carries out the duties of his present job
2. Intellectual ability: Ability to solve problems, to adapt to new situations, to analyze and make judgments
3. Human relations skill: Ability to motivate people to get them to work together
4. Personal characteristics: The total of temperament or personality characteristics bearing on executive functioning

5. Technical knowledge: The knowledge of functional skills needed to carry out position requirements.
6. Breadth of knowledge: Range of interests; use of information and concepts from other related fields of knowledge
7. Planning: Looking ahead; developing programs and work schedules
8. Administration: Organizing own work and that of others; delegation, follow-up, control of position activities
9. Accomplishment: Effective use of time; amount of work produced
10. Quality: Accuracy and thoroughness; high standards
11. Dependability: Meets schedules and deadlines; adheres to instructions and policy
12. Acuteness: Mentally alert; understands instructions, explanations, unusual situations and circumstances quickly
13. Capacity: Mental depth and breadth; reservoir of mental ability
14. Flexibility: Adaptable; adjusts rapidly to changing conditions; copes with the unexpected
15. Analysis and judgment: Critical observer; breaks problem into components, weighs and relates; arrives at sound conclusions
16. Creativeness: Original ideas; inquiring mind; fresh approaches to problems
17. Verbal facility: Articulate, communicative; generally understood by persons at all levels
18. Socialness: Makes friends easily; works "comfortably" with others; has sincere interest in people
19. Acceptance: Gains confidence of others; earns respect
20. Sensitivity: Has a "feel" for people, recognizes their problems; quick to pick up "the way the wind is blowing"; is considerate of others
21. Leadership: Receives loyalty and cooperation from others; manages and motivates others to full effectiveness
22. Developing others: Develops competent successors and replacements
23. Motivation: Has well-planned goals; willingly assumes greater responsibilities; realistically ambitious
24. Attitude: Enthusiastic, constructive, optimistic, loyal; good orientation to company, position, and associates
25. Vision: Has foresight, sees new opportunities; appreciates, but not bound by, tradition or custom
26. Self-control: Calm and poised under pressure

27. Initiative: Self-starting; prompt to take hold of a problem; sees and acts on new opportunities
28. Drive: Works with energy; not easily discouraged; basic urge to get things done
29. Self-confidence: Assured bearing; inner security; self-reliant; takes new developments in stride
30. Objectivity: Has an open mind; keeps emotional or personal interests from influencing decisions (Randle, *Harvard Business Review,* 1956, *34,* 122–134).

There are pitfalls that one must avoid in dealing with structural questions such as this. Research results of the type presented here can easily be misconstrued to read that the structure of supervisory behavior, whatever it may be, is fixed and unchanging. More likely, supervisory behavior is not only multidimensional but also dynamic in its structure. That is to say, this complex pattern of behavior undergoes change over time. These changing patterns of behavior are probably traceable to the fact that individuals learn and continually modify their behavior to the events around them. Furthermore, the job situation is under constant pressure to change, and this encourages varying styles of supervisory performance.

The value of the studies that have been carried out on this subject lies in the fact they show that in any given situation it seems to be possible to describe supervisory practices in terms of a limited number of dimensions. Supervision is, therefore, not so complex that it defies behavioral description. It would appear unwise, however, to commit oneself rigidly to one fixed set of behavioral dimensions. While acknowledging this, one must also recognize that the two-dimensional approach—for example, production-centered, employee-centered—does involve important components of behavior, components that have been given considerable research support. As a result, our review of the research literature will reflect this emphasis.

LEADERSHIP AND PERFORMANCE

The point has been reached where we should ask how these different styles of supervision influence the behavior of others. Surely it is reasonable to expect that worker performance and job satisfaction will be significantly influenced by the type of supervision given. If this be the case, then one may ask, what is the best type of supervision? Can one best ensure that production schedules are met and work groups operate at an acceptable level of efficiency by having supervisors who give close and continuing attention to the work? Or should the supervisor focus on the social and motivational dimensions of the workplace and give workers broad freedom in carrying out the job assignment? Under what type of supervision do workers report greater feelings of job satisfaction? In short, what we want to know is how different types of supervision impact on people at work.

The Michigan Studies

We have already made reference to a series of studies carried out by a research team at the Institute for Social Research (Likert, 1961a). The general approach followed in this series was to locate pairs of work groups engaged in the same activities, with one group of the pair having a record of consistently high production and the other group having a history of low production. Supervisors in each group were interviewed about their job behavior and work attitudes. Nonsupervisory personnel were interviewed about the supervision they received and their attitudes toward the work. A variety of work situations were studied: clerical workers, railroad track gangs, automobile workers, and groups employed by an electric utility. From these studies emerged results that were thought to represent important principles relating supervisory behaviors to group productivity. One important aspect of this principle concerned the differentiation of the supervisory role.

Differentiation of Supervisory Role. The Michigan studies suggested that supervisors who lead high-producing groups seem to play a role that is much different from the work role maintained by the other members of the group. They seem to invest considerably more time in activities that are supervisory in nature and less time in doing the same kind of work as the rank and file.

Planning work accounts for a considerable portion of the activities of supervisors in high-producing groups; also, they seem to spend more time on interpersonal relations than do their counterparts who lead low-production groups. These low-producing supervisors are found investing more time in functions that are the same as those carried out by rank-and-file members. They tend to take a more active role in actually doing the work that is done by their subordinates. Table 13.2 presents data collected from three markedly different work situations that were observed by the Michigan group. We see that with good consistency supervisors of high-production groups spent more time in supervising than did those who led lower-pro-

duction sections (Kahn & Katz, 1960). Effective supervision, therefore, would appear to involve sets of behaviors that are clearly differentiated from the behaviors required of the rank-and-file employees who are responsible for production.

Closeness of Supervision.   Closeness of supervision refers to the extent to which supervisors delegate authority to those working under them. Close supervision, as contrasted with general supervision, tends to check up on those who do the work and place limits on workers' freedom to carry out the job in their own fashion. The Michigan group reports that high-producing groups tend to be led by supervisors who give general rather than

TABLE 13.2   Relation of Time Spent in Supervision of Section Productivity
(Sections in an insurance company; section gangs on a railroad;
work groups in a tractor factory)

Questions:
Insurance company—"What proportion of your time is given to supervisory matters? What proportion to other duties?"
Railroad—"How much of your time do you usually spend in supervising, and how much in straight production work?"
Tractor factory—"How much of your time do you usually spend in supervising the men, and how much in other things like planning the work, making out reports, and dealing with people outside your section?"

Section Productivity	50% or more of Time Spent in Supervising	Less than 50% of Time Spent in Supervising	Not Ascertained, or Can't Separate Functions (%)	Total	N
Insurance Company					
High	75	17	8	100	12
Low	33	59	8	100	12
Railroad					
High	55	31	14	100	36
Low	25	61	14	100	36
Tractor factory					
97-101%	69	31	0	100	52
91- 96%	59	41	0	100	71
86- 90%	48	52	0	100	89
80- 85%	41	59	0	100	69
50- 79%	54	46	0	100	35

Source: Kahn, R. L. & Katz, D. Leadership practices in relation to productivity and morale. In D. Cartwright and A. Zander *Group dynamics—research and theory*. Evanston, Ill.: Row Peterson 1960. Copyright 1960, Row Peterson.

close supervision. Low-producing supervisors tend to check up on their subordinates more frequently, and give people less opportunity to set their own pace in doing the job. In a number of instances general supervision was also associated with higher levels of morale.

Employee versus Production Orientation. The production-centered supervisor tends to view employees as instruments that get the work done, while the employee-centered supervisor recognizes the broad range of social and emotional needs that employees possess. Employee-centered supervisors offer subordinates supportive relationships and take interest in their subordinates as people. The Michigan studies present considerable evidence suggesting that high-producing work groups are found being led by supervisors who are employee rather than production centered.

These studies have had a significant effect on much of the thinking that has gone on about industrial supervision. They, along with several other classic studies—for example, the Hawthorne Studies—have played an important part in the development of the human-relations approach to industrial management. Implicit in this approach is the assumption that styles of supervision that reflect certain basic principles of human relations will result in higher levels of worker performance. These principles place emphasis on the motivational climate of work, and it is thought that the human-relations-oriented supervisor creates the motivational conditions that encourage workers to achieve higher levels of performance efficiency. Styles of work leadership that narrowly concentrate on production are seen as being deficient in the sense that they ignore the important motivational role of the supervisor. The Michigan studies suggest that "good human relations" involve supervision that is general rather than close, that is employee centered rather than production centered, and involve a supervisory role that is considerably different form the role of the rank-and-file worker.

Other Studies. A study (Kay & Meyer, 1962) conducted at the General Electric Company gives

some good support to this point of view. From a total set of 120 foremen, two groups were selected, one made up of the 12 foremen rated highest by their superiors and subordinates, and the other composed of the 12 foremen receiving the lowest ratings. The results revealed that the higher-rated foremen tended to be less production oriented, gave general rather than close supervision, and spent more time in planning for work than playing a production role similar to that of their subordinates.

Indik, Georgopolous, and Seashore (1961), observing supervisory behavior in a large package-delivery organization, found that high work-group performance was positively related to open channels of communication between workers and foremen, a relatively high level of subordinate satisfaction with the supervisor's attempt to support the members of the work group, and a high level of influence, shared by supervisors and subordinates, concerning the affairs of the group.

Andrew L. Comrey and his associates (cf. Comrey, Pfiffner, & Beem, 1952; Comrey, High, & Wilson, 1955) have reported a series of studies that tend to support the human-relations approach to work supervision. In one (Comrey et al., 1955) it was found that for a group of supervisors working in the aircraft industry there was a significant positive relationship between human-relations variables and work-group productivity. In another study done with groups of forest rangers (Comrey et al., 1952), it was reported that supervisors of highly rated districts were likely to be more democratic with their assitants, more sympathetic with subordinates in dealing with their personal problems, and more willing to share information with those who worked under them.

There are other studies that show a positive link between a supervisor's human-relations orientation and the work effectiveness of the group; the studies cited above, however, drawn from a wide range of working situations, demonstrate that the connection between supervisory practices and productivity has been demonstrated in numerous instances. On the other hand, we should not leave this discussion without recognizing that studies have been conducted that yielded negative support for certain aspects of this human-relations point of view. Hise (1968) reports the results of a laboratory study that suggests that close supervision may have a positive effect on group productivity. Andrews and Farris (1967) studied supervisory practices in groups of scientists, and found that supervisors who were high in human-relations orientation tended to be found leading teams of researchers who were least innovative in their work. Finally, Fiedler (1960; Fiedler & Mahar, 1979) in a series of studies we will consider in more detail later, reports that effective work performance is sometimes observed in groups led by supervisors who are psychologically distant from their subordinates; much depends on the nature of the leadership situation.

We see, therefore, that the human-relations approach to work supervision has received only mixed support in the research literature. Yet, on balance, there is enough support for this point of view to warrant continued interest in it. We will find, as this chapter progresses, that no single approach to leadership is universally effective. Whether one or another type of supervisory practice is effective depends on many variables, some of which are found in the work group and in the general work situation. Before we pursue this idea further, however, we should look at another, but related aspect of the human-relations approach to supervision.

Democratic Participation in Supervision

Although the distinction between democratic and autocratic supervision probably involves some of the same ideas that differentiate employee-centered and production-centered supervision, there is a difference in emphasis that makes it reasonable to treat the two sets separately. Basically, democratic supervisory practices encourage work-group members to play an active role in determining the conditions of work. The democratic supervisor shares power and authority with those who are in lower positions. One important aspect of this involves the delegation of decision-making activities to the subordinate members of a group. In these instances, decisions that are in the supervisor's jurisdiction are shared with subordinates who participate in the solutions of problems. Democratic practices, therefore, give workers a say in how the work should be done and the conditions under which it is to be carried out. With autocratic styles of supervision, decision-making activities remain with the leader, who shows reluctance to share these functions with subordinates.

There were a number of early studies reporting that a democratic approach to supervision resulted in desirable group consequences. For example, studies by Lewin and his associates (Lewin, 1947; Lippitt & White, 1947) demonstrated that group members who were given opportunity to participate in decision making were more likely to translate final decisions into practice, required less constant supervision, and were more innovative in their work. But in spite of these early results, the intervening years have provided only mixed support for the contention that democratic supervision leads to higher levels of group performance. In some instances this has been true; in other instances, it has not.

The problem is that the performance consequences of participation seems to be contingent upon other factors found in the work environment. For instance, some suggest that the personality characteristics of subordinates is one of the factors that determines the consequences of participation. Vroom (1960) maintains that under participatory forms of supervision one would expect higher gains in production from subordinates who have strong independence needs and who are nonauthoritarian. This seems to be a reasonable prediction, and there is considerable support for it, but there are also other studies (Tosi, 1970; Abdel-Halim & Rowland, 1976) that have failed to report positive results. Perhaps the effects of supervisory styles depend upon the mediation of not one variable but *patterns* of variables, some of which are found in the psychological makeup of subordinates, some residing in the work itself.

Goal Setting. There are still others (Likert, 1961b) who contend that participation by subordinates leads to substantial performance benefits in instances in which goals are being established. Usually three approaches to goal setting are considered. In one of these goals are assigned to subordinates by their superiors. A second approach involves the group members, who participate in establishing work goals; and in a third approach little is done to define a goal beyond the supervisor encouraging the group members to "do their best."

A study by Latham, Mitchell, and Dossett (1978) reported that democratically led groups of technical workers set higher goals for themselves than did groups that were directly assigned their work objectives. A subsequent study by the same authors (Dossett, Latham, & Mitchell, 1979), carried out with female clerical workers, found no difference between participation groups and groups for whom work goals were unilaterally assigned by the supervisor. The "do your best" approach to goal setting did, however, result in lower levels of performance. Ivancevich (1977) reports similar findings.

Comment.   Numerous studies have attempted to describe the relationship that exists between different approaches to supervision and levels of group performance. A particular point of interest concerns the consequences of democratic practices on group productivity and goal setting, and thus far research has failed to provide us with unequivocal support for a positive relationship. Perhaps the difficulty lies in the fact that many of the studies have not been designed to deal with the complex relationships that exist between these variables. The impact of supervisory styles on performance depends on a list of variables that is probably quite long—such as the education and background of the subordinates (Latham & Yukl, 1975), personality variables, task variables, and a number of variables that reflect the social structure of the group. In the light of these possibilities, it is probably much more fruitful to think of adapting supervision to the requirements of a given situation, or molding the situation to fit the characteristics of the available supervisory personnel. It does not seem warranted, on the other hand, to make generalized predictions that a specific approach to supervision will invariably lead to improved group performance. The situation appears to be much more complicated than that.

One final note concerning participatory supervision: there is evidence indicating that in spite of the high value placed on democratic supervision by classic management theory, these practices are not particularly popular among those who manage (Brown, 1977; Buchholz, 1977). Managers often think of supervision in authoritarian terms. Jago (1977) does report, however, that at higher levels of management, individuals tend to be more favorably disposed toward using democratic procedures, but this in part is a function of the fact that shared decision making is a more appropriate activity at these supper levels.

Democratic Decision Making and Reactions to Change.   There is one aspect of democratic supervision that seems to receive a reasonable amount of research support. That is, in instances in which changes are being introduced into the work situation, democratically oriented decision making seems to be helpful in overcoming resistance to change and encouraging group members to give their support to the changes that are being made. When workers participate in the development of policies and practices that represent changes in the methods and conditions of work, there often seems to be greater acceptance of the change.

An experiment by Coch and French (1948) will illustrate this point. Carried out in a plant involved in the manufacture of wearing apparel, the study involved four work groups in jobs that exposed workers to both frequent changes in the methods of work and transfers to other jobs. Interviews with workers who had been exposed to job changes revealed a pattern of negative attitudes toward the work, resentment against management, and a significant increase in the number who decided to quit.

One of the four work groups, a control group, followed the usual routine when change was introduced into the work. For workers in this group, the production department first modified the job and set a new standard of production. A meeting of the employees was then called in order to notify them of the change and answer any questions. After the meeting the group returned to their work stations and the change was introduced. In the first of three experimental groups, experimental group 1, the workers were called together and told of the need for making changes in the work. Next, a small group of "special" operators were chosen to participate in a training session in which there were opportunities to make suggestions concerning the new job. The new job was then presented to the entire group during a second meeting and the special operators served to train the other operators on the new job. The second and third experimental groups followed the same procedures as the first, except that instead of choosing a small group of special operators to represent them in making decisions regarding the change, all members participated in these decision-making and training activities.

Figure 13.3 summarizes the results of this experiment, and it shows quite clearly that worker participation in the planning for change does result in improved performance. For instance, the figure shows that after the changes were introduced into the work there was little change in the production efficiency of the control group. Furthermore, members of this group showed signs of considerable resistance to the changes that were taking place. There were signs of aggression toward management, deliberate restriction of production, and a general lack of cooperation with the supervisor. Also, within the first forty days after the change, 17 per cent of the group had quit their jobs.

The results were more promising for the groups that participated in formulating work changes. For the group having representatives participate in the decision making (experimental group 1), there was an initial drop in production after the change was introduced, but production again reached a standard rate fourteen days later. During this time there were no quits, and the climate of attitudes in the group was one of cooperation and permissiveness. The remaining two experimental groups were the ones in which all members participated in planning the changes that were made. For both these

groups production rates recovered much faster than was the case for experimental group 1, and by the end of the forty-day period both groups were producing at a rate that was about 14 per cent higher than their prechange level. There were no quits during the period of observation, and the attitudinal climate remained positive.

Over the years, the Coch and French study has been cited again and again to illustrate the effectiveness of group participation in introducing change in the workplace. It is often argued that the effectiveness of democratic supervision is found in the fact that when individuals participate in decision making they tend to become ego involved with the outcomes. Being able to see a reflection of one's self in the work increases the motivational appeal of work and increases the likelihood that the individual will support whatever procedures are agreed upon. Hence, democratic supervision rests on a basic psychological principle that predicts a heightened commitment to work when individuals are given opportunity to incorporate their sense of self in the work that is done.

Maier's Research. Over the years N. R. F. Maier has been involved in research dealing with creativity and problem solving (Maier, 1952, 1963, 1970), and it is his contention that democratic leadership creates a climate in which groups can more effectively deal with problem solving. Democratic leadership tends to upgrade the quality of the solutions generated by the group. This is obviously an important stipulation, since intuition leads many to assume that by broadening the base of participation the quality of a problem's solution would suffer. From this perspective the solution of problems should rest in the hands of those best able to cope with them, and it is in the leadership ranks that these talents are most often found. Yet Maier presents evidence (Maier, 1950; Maier & Solem, 1952) that indicates that when groups are skillfully led, member participation in problem solving enhances solution quality.

Skillful leadership, according to Maier, is not something that happens spontaneously only as a consequence of the psychological makeup of a su-

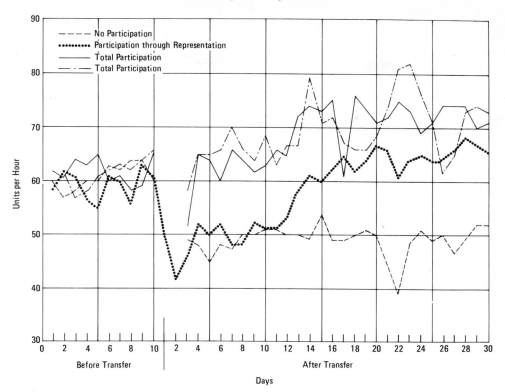

FIGURE 13.3   The effects of participation in decisions to change work methods. The curve shows a sharp drop in production rates for the group that had no participation in planning for change. The group having representative participation shows an initial drop in productivity followed by a gradual recovery. The two groups having complete participation show rapid recovery followed by a sustained improvement in production rates.

Source: Coch, L., & French, J. R. P. Overcoming resistance to change. *Human Relations*, 1948, *1*, 512-532.

pervisor. Whether supervisors rely on democratic procedures depends both on giving them the freedom to do so and the training to develop the appropriate techniques. Without these conditions, attempts at democratic leadership are not always successful (Maier, 1968; Maier & Thurber, 1969). Hence, from this perspective, effective leadership draws on the tools of democratic supervision that can be acquired through appropriate training.

Performance Consequences of Initiating Structure and Consideration

In discussing two-dimensional models of supervisory behavior, we mentioned the work that

was done at Ohio State University in which two facets of supervision were designated "initiation of structure" and "consideration." Fleishman and Peters (1962, p. 130) define the two dimensions:

Initiating Structure: Reflects the extent to which an individual is likely to define and structure his role and those of his subordinates toward goal attainment. A high score on this dimension characterizes individuals who play a more active role in directing group activities through planning, communicating information, scheduling, trying out new ideas, etc.

Consideration: Reflects the extent to which an individual is likely to have job relationships characterized by mutual trust, respect for subordinates' ideas, and consideration of their feelings. A high score is indicative of a climate of good rapport and two-way communication. A low score indicates that the supervisor is likely to be more impersonal in his relations with group members.

Stogdill (1974) reviewed a large number of studies that attempted to determine the production and job-satisfaction consequences of these two dimensions. He concluded that "group productivity is somewhat more highly related to structure than to consideration" (p. 395). Satisfaction with work, on the other hand, seemed to be more closely associated with the consideration dimension. Stogdill suggested that the most effective leaders tend to impose high structure on their groups, while at the same time dealing with the members in a highly considerate fashion. We obtain from this the idea that effective supervision requires a highly active involvement in the major facets of the leadership function. Technical knowledge, organizing talent, and interpersonal skill combine to yield good work supervision. To be sure, shortcomings in one or another facet of the effective supervisor's role may appear more prominently in certain aspects of work-group behavior. Low levels of initiation of structure, for example, may lead to lower rates of production (Gilmore, Beehr, & Richter, 1979), but it is probably true that competent supervision is an expression of an active commitment to every aspect of the supervisor's role.

SUPERVISION—A CONTINGENCY APPROACH

It seems quite clear from the preceding sections that the relationship between supervisory behavior and work-group performance rests on a number of contingencies. For example, within the social environment of work one may find numerous variables that alter the relationship between a particular style of supervision and the productivity of a work group. Therefore, in response to the question, what style of supervision is most desirable from the standpoint of group performance, the answer

must be that it depends on the nature of the work situation.

The approaches to business and industrial supervision that we have thus far considered have all been forced to acknowledge this contingency problem, but it is now time to consider an approach to leadership that formally takes these contingency factors into consideration. This theory incorporates the traditional view that classifies leadership styles according to polar type, *task motivated* and *relationship motivated* (Fiedler & Mahar, 1979). The principal problem considered by this model is how these two types of leadership influence group performance when this influence is viewed across a variety of different work situations.

Fiedler's Contingency Model of Leadership

The work of Fred E. Fiedler (1964; 1967; Fiedler & Chemers, 1974; Fiedler & Mahar, 1979) is important because it represents an integrated series of studies that have systematically explored the question of supervisory effectiveness. Furthermore, Fiedler has made an effort to develop a system by which certain properties of the leadership situation can be measured and described. In a certain sense, he has made a beginning effort to develop a taxonomy of the social situations in which leadership behavior is observed. His theory, therefore, places us in a better position to deal with the situational contingencies that enter the relationship between supervisory practices and group performance.

Situational Dimensions. Fiedler classifies leadership situations along three dimensions, each of which can take on one of two values. The first, and perhaps the most important situational dimension is found in the interpersonal relationships that exist between the leader and the members of the group. This aspect of the leadership situation, called leader-member relationships, relates to the extent to which leaders and members like and trust each other, and two approaches have been used to measure this factor. One method employs sociometric techniques. Here members are asked to do such things as choose people with whom they would like to work, and the extent to which the leader is chosen is used as a measure of the leader's relationship with the group. A second pro-

cedure asks leaders and members to describe each other, using a series of bipolar scales of the type presented below:

Cooperative	__:__:__:__:__:__:__:__ : Uncooperative
	1 2 3 4 5 6 7 8
Supportive	__:__:__:__:__:__:__:__ : Unsupportive.
	1 2 3 4 5 6 7 8

Groups are ordered according to their scores on these kinds of measures, and high- and low-scoring groups are chosen to define leadership situations that have good or poor *leader-member relationships*.

The second situational dimension is called *task structure*. Fiedler, drawing on a system developed by Shaw (1963), defines task structure in terms of four properties:

1. Goal clarity—the degree to which job requirements have been stated clearly and are known by the members of the work group
2. Goal-path multiplicity—the extent to which alternative routes to job completion are available to workers; the number of ways of doing a job or solving a problem.

3. Decision verifiability—the degree to which the "correctness" of work done or decisions made can be ascertained. Are procedures clearly available for evaluating the "right or wrong" aspects of a decision or solution to a problem?
4. Decision specificity—the degree to which there is more than one correct solution to a problem

Task structure is measured by having judges rate jobs on these components.

Position power is the third component that Fiedler takes into consideration in identifying a leadership situation. In large measure this dimension concerns the extent to which a job position

gives the supervisor access to the many positive and negative incentives that operate in work environments. Fiedler (1972) suggests the use of a checklist, devised by Hunt (1967) to determine power position. The following represents some of the items included in this scale:

1. Can the supervisor recommend subordinate rewards and punishments to his boss?

2. Can the supervisor punish or reward subordinates on his own?

Evaluating each of these three components of the leadership situation in terms of two possible levels

results in a conceptual scheme that involves the eight categories shown in Figure 13.4 below:

FIGURE 13.4 Leadership Components Evaluation

	I	II	III	IV	V	VI	VII	VIII
Leader-Member Relations	Good				Poor			
Task Structure	High		Low		High		Low	
Position Power	Strong	Weak	Strong	Weak	Strong	Weak	Strong	Weak

Source: Fiedler, F. E., & Chemers, M. M. *Leadership and effective management.* Glenview, Ill.: Scott, Foresman, 1974. Copyright 1974, published by permission.

The Least Preferred Coworker (LPC)

The measure of supervisory behavior in Fiedler's system is one that derives from what he calls the Least Preferred Coworker (LPC) method. Figure 13.5 taken from Fiedler (1967) describes the LPC procedure. Subjects are asked to think of individuals with whom they have worked, and then select one person considered to be least preferred. This person is then described, using the bipolar scales in Figure 13.5. Positive terms, those referring to favorable human characteristics, are given the largest scores; hence a person who scores high on the LPC method is an individual who tends to describe the least preferred coworker in terms that are positive and complimentary. Those who make a low score tend to describe the least preferred

Pleasant	___ : ___ : ___ : ___ : ___ : ___ : ___ : ___ : Unpleasant
	8 7 6 5 4 3 2 1
Friendly	___ : ___ : ___ : ___ : ___ : ___ : ___ : ___ : Unfriendly
	8 7 6 5 4 3 2 1
Rejecting	___ : ___ : ___ : ___ : ___ : ___ : ___ : ___ : Accepting
	8 7 6 5 4 3 2 1
Helpful	___ : ___ : ___ : ___ : ___ : ___ : ___ : ___ : Frustrating
	8 7 6 5 4 3 2 1
Unenthusiastic	___ : ___ : ___ : ___ : ___ : ___ : ___ : ___ : Enthusiastic
	8 7 6 5 4 3 2 1
Tense	___ : ___ : ___ : ___ : ___ : ___ : ___ : ___ : Relaxed
	8 7 6 5 4 3 2 1
Distant	___ : ___ : ___ : ___ : ___ : ___ : ___ : ___ : Close
	8 7 6 5 4 3 2 1
Cold	___ : ___ : ___ : ___ : ___ : ___ : ___ : ___ : Warm
	8 7 6 5 4 3 2 1
Cooperative	___ : ___ : ___ : ___ : ___ : ___ : ___ : ___ : Uncooperative
	8 7 6 5 4 3 2 1
Supportive	___ : ___ : ___ : ___ : ___ : ___ : ___ : ___ : Hostile
	8 7 6 5 4 3 2 1
Boring	___ : ___ : ___ : ___ : ___ : ___ : ___ : ___ : Interesting
	8 7 6 5 4 3 2 1
Quarrelsome	___ : ___ : ___ : ___ : ___ : ___ : ___ : ___ : Harmonious
	8 7 6 5 4 3 2 1
Self-assured	___ : ___ : ___ : ___ : ___ : ___ : ___ : ___ : Hesitant
	8 7 6 5 4 3 2 1
Efficient	___ : ___ : ___ : ___ : ___ : ___ : ___ : ___ : Inefficient
	8 7 6 5 4 3 2 1
Gloomy	___ : ___ : ___ : ___ : ___ : ___ : ___ : ___ : Cheerful
	8 7 6 5 4 3 2 1
Open	___ : ___ : ___ : ___ : ___ : ___ : ___ : ___ : Guarded
	8 7 6 5 4 3 2 1

Figure 13.5 Think of the Person with Whom You Can Work Least Well. He May Be Someone You Work with Now, or He May Be Someone You Knew in the Past. He Does Not Have to Be the Person You Like Least Well, But Should Be the Person with Whom You Had the Most Difficulty in Getting a Job Done. Describe This Person as He Appears to You.

Source: Fielder, F. E. *A theory of leadership effectiveness.* New York: McGraw-Hill, 1967, p. 41. Copyright, 1967, used with the permission of the McGraw-Hill Book Company.

coworker in negative and generally uncomplimentary terms.

There appears to have been some confusion in the literature regarding the behavioral implications of high and low LPC scores. Many have concluded that the high LPC score is found in an individual who places high value on social relations. The low-LPC-scoring person is often thought to be an individual who, when in a leadership role, places emphasis on task completion. Fiedler (1972), however, maintains that this interpretation of the LPC score, while not completely incorrect, does represent something of an oversimplification of the meaning of the score. The behavioral implications of a high or low score depend on situational characteristics, particularly the level of stress or threat found in the leadership setting. Fiedler (1972) gathers together a goodly amount of evidence indicating that when functioning in a situation where there are low levels of threat and stress, the high LPC leaders tend to be task oriented, while the low LPC leader tends to focus on interpersonal relations. These behavioral tendencies seem to reverse themselves when leadership behavior is observed in a high-stress and threatening situation. Now low-LPC-scoring supervisors tend to behave in a task-oriented fashion, while the high LPC supervisor is found behaving in a relationship oriented manner. Although Fiedler distinguishes between two basic supervisory styles, task oriented and people oriented, he suggests that one may realistically expect to find both orientations operating in a single person. Whether one or the other orientation is observed depends upon the characteristics of the social situation in which the person functions.

Leadership Effectiveness of High and Low LPC Supervisors

There are other situational aspects of Fiedler's work, for not only does the situation determine the behavioral style of high and low LPC supervisors;

it also influences their relative effectiveness as leaders. Fiedler reports the results of efforts to correlate LPC scores with measures of group effectiveness in over 800 interacting groups. These were groups in which the members had to coordinate and integrate their activities in order to achieve a common group objective. Basketball teams, for example, were chosen for study, as were policy-making groups and land-survey teams. Military groups and a variety of experimentally assembled groups were also included in this program of research. These groups were ordered according to what Fiedler considers their degree of favorableness. Favorableness refers to the extent to which a situation provides a leader opportunity to satisfy important needs and is free from stress and threat. Assuming leader-member relations is the most important component of favorableness, followed by task structure, and then leader power; Fiedler arranges eight leadership situations in the fashion found in Figure 13.6. This figure summarizes the relationships he observed between LPC and group performance over the many groups included in this series of studies. For each situation he computes a correlations coefficient describing this relationship.[1] The dashed center line represents no relationship between LPC and group performance. Points above the line represent settings in which groups functioning under high LPC supervisors performed better than those under low LPC supervisors. The points falling below the dashed line refer to instances in which low LPC supervisors were found to be leading higher-performance groups than were high LPC supervisors.

From this figure it is apparent that the effectiveness of the supervisor, measured in terms of the level of group performance, is not solely a function of leadership style. Situational factors seem to play a role in mediating the relationship between style and performance. It would appear that when the situation is favorable to the leader

---

[1]For the purpose at hand, we may define these correlation coefficients in terms of the strength and direction of the relationships between LPC and group performance. Positive coefficients refer to high LPC scores being found with high performance. A negative coefficient refers to a relation in which low LPC supervisors are found leading high-performance groups. The magnitude of the coefficient expresses the strength of the relationship observed.

FIGURE 13.6 **Correlations between Leaders' LPC Scores and Group Effectiveness Plotted for Each Cell.**

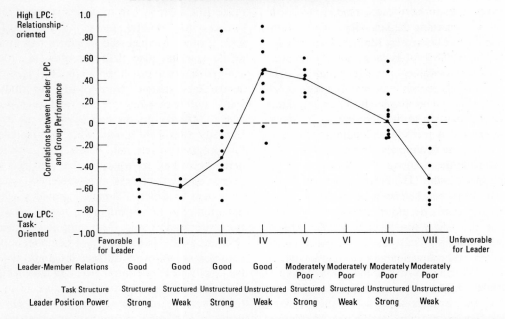

Source: Fiedler, F. E. *A theory of effective leadership.* New York: McGraw-Hill, 1967, p. 146. Copyright, 1967, used with the permission of the McGraw-Hill Book Company.

or when it is highly unfavorable, high levels of group performance tend to be found under low LPC supervisors. In group situations that are intermediate in favorableness, it seems to be the high LPC supervisor who is found leading the high-performance groups.

We find in Fiedler's results clear indication of an interaction between supervisory styles and the characteristics of the leadership situation. First, the social situation is found interacting with personality factors to produce different leadership styles within the same supervisor. Unfavorable situations tend to produce a social-relationship orientation in the low LPC individual, while a favorable leadership setting tends to produce a task orientation in the low LPC individual. Next, we find an interaction between the situation and the relative effectiveness of a given supervisory style. In an unfavorable and in a moderately favorable leadership situation, a relationship orientation tends to be found associated with high levels of group performance. In a favorable situation, a task orien-

tation seems to be most effective in encouraging high performance.

The net result of Fiedler's work, therefore, is to counsel caution to those who might prescribe a particular brand of supervision for all work settings. Such an approach represents an oversimplification of the relationships that have been observed when situational factors have been permitted to vary. As with most work-related behavior, a realistic understanding of industrial supervision will not be available to those who do not take into consideration the interaction between the psychological characteristics of the individual and the surrounding social circumstances. These interactions play a fundamental role in Fiedler's model of supervisory leadership.

Supervisory Styles— Situational Determinants

Thus far our primary concern has been with the fact that a given style of supervision is not equally effective in all work situations. Now we will consider in more detail the possibility that supervisors may display different patterns of leadership as they move from one situation to the next. Could, for example, a supervisor exhibit democratic supervisory behaviors in one work setting and autocratic behaviors in another? Supervisory style is unquestionably an expression of the personality and the social skills of the individual, but it is also quite clear that many individuals show considerable flexibility in adapting to the demands of different social situations. A part of this flexibility involves changes in a leader's supervisory practices to meet the demands of the situation.

Recall that Fiedler (1972) has shown that high LPC supervisors may be task oriented in some situations and people oriented in others, and there is a fairly large amount of additional evidence suggesting that supervisors do modify their leadership styles to reflect the characteristics of the situation. One might ask, however, what the situational factors are that have been found to influence the style of supervision displayed by a given leader. Farris (1969) and Farris and Lim (1969) have presented evidence that indicates that work-group productivity exerts a significant influence on the style of supervision. Thus, if supervisors move between groups that maintain different levels of production efficiency, their supervisory practices may change in response to these differences in group competence.

Lowin and Craig (1968) have shown that the perceived competency of the subordinate influences the pattern of supervisory practices. In this study, subjects who had been hired for a supervisory job were exposed to a subordinate who was in reality a confederate of the experimenter. In some instances the subordinate was described to the subject as being incompetent, in other instances the subordinate was described as being competent. There followed a series of preplanned incidents to which the supervisor had to react. For example, in an incident designed to test for closeness of supervision, the subordinate would bring some completed work to the supervisor and say, ''I'm finished doing the first batch of these. Man, there are still a lot of them to do yet. I guess I'll take a break now and read a magazine.'' The con-

federate would record the response of the supervisor to this incident.

The results of this experiment showed that supervisors rather consistently gave closer supervision to incompetent subordinates. Furthermore, managers of highly competent subordinates initiated less structure than did those who supervised subordinates seen as being less competent. Finally, supervisors of highly competent subordinates seemed to display patterns of leadership that were higher in consideration than did supervisors of low-competence subordinates.

We find, then, in these studies an interaction between group production efficiency and the particular pattern of work leadership that emerges. High-production groups seem to create a social climate that encourages a different style of supervision than do low-production groups. But there is yet another side to this interactive relationship between supervision and performance. Several studies (Berlew & Hall, 1966; Stedry & Kay, 1966; Korman, 1971) have produced evidence that a leader's expectations of competence in subordinates tends itself to be a factor that influences the subordinate's level of performance. Leader expectancies of high performance tend, in some fashion, to be communicated to subordinates, and this in turn is associated with higher levels of actual performance. Leader expectations of incompetence tend to be related to lower levels of performance. Hence, subordinates seem to behave in a fashion that is consistent with the expectations of their leaders. We see from the research that there are aspects of group performance that influence the style of leadership, and there are aspects of leadership that influence the performance of the group. We find, therefore, in the leadership situation a classic example of behavioral interaction.

Personality of Group Members. Previously we found that the personality of the leader is a factor that contributes to the style of leadership employed. Now we will discover that the personality of the follower may also contribute to determining the style of leadership one finds operating in a work group. Haythorn and his associates (1956b), for example, report that different styles of leadership are observed in groups whose subordinates are authoritarians, as compared with groups made up of subordinates who are equalitarians. In another study (Haythorn et al., 1956a), evidence is presented indicating that the behavior of a leader appears to be a function of the personality of the followers, while at the same time, the behavior of the followers appears to be related to the personality of the leader.

Along similar lines, group-member preferences for various leadership styles have also been shown to be a function of the personality characteristics of the members. Sanford (1951), for example, reports that group members who were authoritarians tended to prefer a directive style of supervision. These members described a "good" leader as an individual who has power and personal strength. Nonauthoritarian members, on the other hand, tended to prefer leadership that was more responsive to people. They thought of the "good" leader as one whose behavior is guided by the needs of the followers.

Leadership Climate.   One of the more important situational factors that influences supervisory style is the type of leadership a given supervisor receives from above. To meet the expectations of a highly authoritarian general foreman, for example, a foreman might have to engage in supervisory practices that are themselves authoritarian. Those who supervise persons who in turn supervise others may value more highly patterns of supervision that are consonant with their own. Hence, in their supervisory efforts they may establish a social climate that encourages certain kinds of supervision and discourages others.

A relationship between adjacent levels of supervision was noted in several of the Michigan studies. For instance, Katz, Maccoby, and Morse (1950) reported a significant relationship between the amount of pressure supervisors receive from above and the amount of pressure they direct toward their own groups. Fleishman, Harris and Burtt (1955) report that foremen working under supervisors who were high in consideration tended to be described by their workers as also being high

in consideration. The same sort of relationship was observed with the initiating-structure dimension. As a consequence, we find a pattern of supervision given that reflects the pattern of supervision received. Supervisors of work groups may very well exhibit a tendency to lead their subordinates as they themselves are led.

Rambo (1958) carried out a study of supervisory practices in a large automobile manufacturing plant. Looking at leadership behavior of adjacent ranks of middle managers, he found that assistant superintendents whose leadership style was high in initiation of structure tended to have general foremen serving under them who also imposed high structure on their subordinates. Assistant superintendents low in structure had general foremen who were also low in structure.

These studies suggest that some of the situational factors that contribute to determining the kind of supervisory practices used with a given work group are to be found in the pattern of supervision taking place in higher reaches of the chain of command, the style of supervision received contributing to the style of supervision given. This leadership climate may at times be found pervading the entire work organization, creating a degree of consistency in the supervisory practices found in the various departments in the firm. In an experiment that used simulated work groups, Litwin and Stringer (1968) found that the supervisory style of the chief officer has widespread effects in shaping the general work climate of the organization. Hence in every sense of the word, supervisory leadership is a situational phenomenon. It both establishes a social climate within which other levels of leadership take place and reflects the influence of other leadership jurisdictions in the organization.

Comment.   Bringing all these studies together, we assemble evidence that a contingency model of work leadership appears to provide the most accurate picture of the processes that give rise to differences in supervisory styles. Factors within the supervisor and factors within the work situation interact together to produce influences that result in a particular brand of supervision. The social circumstances of work help to determine the type of supervision given, but then the type of supervision given shapes the social circumstances of work. The task remaining for those who study industrial supervision is to describe in more complete detail the nature of these interactions. For the present, however, one should recognize the risk involved in assuming that a given supervisor is democratic or autocratic in all supervisory practices. Supervisory style varies within a given leader, changing to meet the demands of the situation that is at hand. The effective leader may be the individual who has a broad range of supervisory options available to handle different job situations. Naturally, these alternative practices should be applied in an appropriate fashion. At a later point in the chapter, we will consider the Vroom and Yetton model, which will offer recommendations regarding what is and what is not a feasible leadership style for a given situation.

The Supervisor's Motivational Role

As pointed out previously, the supervisor of a work group plays a significant role in the distribution of the rewards and punishments of work. The supervisor is often in a position to influence who is rewarded (or punished), what aspect of performance is rewarded, and the value of the rewards that are distributed. The supervisor can also function to clarify the kind of behavior that leads a worker to a valued goal. Finally, through their efforts to remove obstacles and pitfalls, supervisors can make the work itself more satisfying. The supervisor's function derives much of its power and significance from its relationship to the incentive system, and as a consequence, work supervisors play an important motivational role. It is with regard to this function that the path-goal theory of leader effectiveness has been developed (House, 1971).

In outline form, the path-goal theory of leadership identifies the motivational role of the leader in terms of

1. The leader's function in delivering and withholding rewards and punishments for task-related successes and failures
2. The leader's role in clarifying the paths of these incentives
3. The leader's efforts to make the paths to a goal more satisfying

A number of predictions can be generated from this model. For example, the leader can enhance the motivational climate of work by clearly defining the routes one may follow to achieve desired goals. Hence, in cases where job duties are ambiguous, there should be a positive relationship between the extent to which the supervisor initiates task-relevant structure and the extent to which workers perform well and are satisfied with the job. When the task is well defined, high levels of initiation of structure will be unsatisfying to subordinates.

In instances in which the work done by a group is ambiguous and also requires interdependent action from the members, a leader high in Consideration will encourage social support and friendliness among the members. The work will, therefore, become more satisfying. Human relations activities tend to compensate for certain deficiencies in the job. For instance, the more satisfying the task in itself, the less the significance of Consideration behaviors in generating satisfaction and effective performance. For unsatisfying tasks, Consideration will tend to compensate and be more important in improving satisfaction and performance.

The path-goal theory of leadership has stimulated a considerable amount of research that has been directed at testing its many hypotheses. The results of this research activity have given the theory only partial support (Schriesheim & Von Glinow, 1977; Downey, Sheridan, & Slocum, 1976), but for the moment the importance of this theory to our study of work behavior is found in the fact that it broadens the view of leadership to include the important role the leader plays in the administration of the incentives systems that surround the job and its social environment.

A NORMATIVE MODEL

Vroom and Yetton (1973; Vroom, 1976a) have developed a model that formally recognizes the situational factors found operating in group problem-solving settings. The model is called a normative one, since it leads to recommendations for the style of leadership that *should* be adopted in a given situation. At its present stage of development, the model lacks a rigorous methodology whereby its parameters may be identified and measured. It does provide, however, a valuable conceptual framework for dealing with group problem-solving situations; but for the present one must be patient while waiting for new methodologies with which to implement these ideas. Space does not permit a complete presentation of the model; therefore only an outline will be developed to represent the basic ideas of this approach.

Essentially, the model serves as an aid in the identification of different types of group problem-solving situations and as a means for prescribing the styles of leadership considered feasible for each situation. Three sets of parameters are important, the first of which involves a classification of leadership methods. Ranging from completely autocratic to broadly democratic, there are five general patterns of decision-making leadership, which vary in terms of the extent to which subordinates are given opportunity to participate in decision making. These methods are presented and described in Table 13.3.

A second major component of the model involves criteria that may be used to consider the effectiveness of the decisions generated in any situation. These criteria include the quality of the decision, subordinates' acceptance of the decision

TABLE 13.3   A Taxonomy of Leadership Methods

Leadership method	Characteristics
A-I	You solve the problem or make the decision yourself using information available to you at that time.
A-II	You obtain necessary information from subordinates, then decide on the solution yourself. You may or may not tell subordinates what the problem is in getting information from them. The role played by your subordinates in making the decision is clearly one of providing the necessary information to you, rather than generating or evaluating alternative solutions.
C-I	You share the problem with relevant subordinates individually, getting their ideas and suggestions without bringing them together as a group. Then *you* make the decision, which may or may not reflect your subordinates' influence.
C-II	You share the problem with your subordinates as a group, collectively obtaining their ideas and suggestions. Then you make the decision, which may or may not reflect your subordinates' influence.
G-II	You share the problem with your subordinates as a group. Together you generate and evaluate alternatives and attempt to reach agreement (consensus) on a solution. Your role is much like a chairman. You do not try to influence the group to adopt "your" solution and you are willing to accept and implement any solution which has the support of the entire group.

Source: Vroom, V. H., & Yetton, P. W. *Leadership and decision making.* Pittsburgh: University of Pittsburgh Press, 1973, p. 13. Copyright © 1973 by University of Pittsburgh Press, published by permission.

or their willingness to follow through on the decision, and the amount of time needed to arrive at a solution. Vroom and Yetton have developed a set of seven rules that can be used to determine the leadership styles considered inappropriate for a given type of problem situation. These rules are presented in Table 13.4.

TABLE 13.4   Rules Governing Feasibility of Leadership Styles

1. *The leader-information rule*
   When the quality of the decision is important and the leader lacks the information or ability to solve the problem alone, then leader style A-I (see Table 13.3) is not appropriate.
2. *The goal-congruence rule*
   If the quality of the decision is important, but if the subordinates will not attempt to achieve the organization's goals when they try to solve the problem, then G-II is not feasible leadership style.
3. *The unstructured-problem rule*
   When the quality of the decision is important and the problem is unstructured, while at the same time the leader lacks the ability or the information needed to solve the problem by himself, the method for solving the problem should give subordinates who do have the necessary information an opportunity to interact with one another. This situation eliminates A-I, A-II and C-I from the appropriate styles of leadership.
4. *The acceptance rule*
   If the acceptance of a solution by subordinates is important and there is uncertainty regarding the acceptance of an autocratic decision, then methods A-I and A-II are eliminated from the feasible set.
5. *The conflict rule*
   If group acceptance of a solution is important,

and if an autocratic decision will not be accepted, and if there is a likelihood of disagreement among those subordinates who attempt to solve the problem, the method of leadership should permit the disagreeing parties to resolve their differences and give them complete knowledge of the problem. Under these conditions, leadership methods A-I, A-II and C-I are not feasible.
6. *The fairness rule*
   If group acceptance is important but the quality of the decision is unimportant, the method of leadership should permit subordinates to interact and negotiate over what is a fair solution. If under these conditions it is uncertain whether an autocratic decision will be accepted, then leader styles A-I, A-II, C-I, and C-II are eliminated from the feasible set.
7. *The acceptance-priority rule*
   If acceptance of the solution is important, not certain to result from an autocratic decision, and if subordinates are willing to strive for the organization's goals in working out a solution, then leadership methods that provide equal partnership without threatening solution quality are desirable, since they result in greater acceptance. Therefore, leadership methods A-I, A-II, C-I and C-II are not feasible.

Source: Vroom, V. H., & Yetton, P. W. *Leadership and decision making,* 1973. Copyright © 1973 by University of Pittsburgh Press, published by permission.

The third component of the model involves a set of basic properties that identify different kinds of problem-solving situations. These properties can most easily be presented as a set of seven questions, presented in Figure 13.7. Although each property exists as a continuous scale, Vroom and Yetton often deal with them in a two-category, yes-no fashion. With seven characteristics, each found in either one of two categories, there are 2^7 = 128 possible combinations of situational properties. Since many of these combinations are quite improbable, however, for example, a "no" answer to both questions A and B (see Figure 13.7), Vroom and Yetton have identified thirteen problem-solving situations for which they make recommendations regarding the appropriate styles of leadership.

Answering these seven questions leads one to the type of problem situation that is present. In Figure 13.7 the route described by each pattern of yes-no answers directs one to a leadership method recommended for that problem situation. At the extreme right in Figure 13.7, at the end of each path, are the symbols identifying the problem situation and the leadership types considered feasible for each. Beneath the branching network of paths, identifying the letters at the top of the figure are the seven questions the answers to which determine the path that is followed. Each box in the figure identifies a point in the sequence at which either a yes or no answer must be given to the question represented by the letter at the top of the figure. For instance, the first box refers to question A. If the answer to this question is "no," one

Question

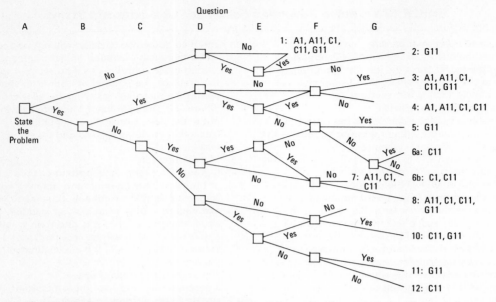

A. Is there a quality requirement such that one solution is likely to be more rational than another?
B. Do I have sufficient info to make a high quality decision?
C. Is the problem structured?
D. Is acceptance of decision by subordinates critical to effective implementation?
E. If I were to make the decision by myself, is it reasonably certain that it would be acceptec by my subordinates?
F. Do subordinates share the organizational goals to be attained in solving this problem?
G. Is conflict among subordinates likely in preferred solutions?

FIGURE 13.7. Decision-process flow chart for group problems. Seven questions (A through G) are asked about the decision-making situation. The answer to each (Yes or No) determines the branch of the flow chart that is followed. For example, the first question (A) states, is the quality requirement such that one solution is likely to be more rational than another? If the answer to this is Yes, then one follows the Yes branch to question B. If the answer is No, then one follows the No branch to question D. The flow chart leads to the right-hand side, where leadership behaviors appropriate for a decision-making situation are identified.

Source: Vroom, V. H. *Leadership.* In M. D. Dunnette (Ed.). *Handbook of industrial and organizational psychology.*
Boston: Houghton-Mifflin Co. Copyright 1976 by Houghton-Mifflin Co.

moves up following the line labeled ''no'' to the box under question D. If the answer to question D is also ''no,'' this terminates the path, and problem situation type 1 has been identified, for which leadership styles, A-I, A-II, C-I, C-II, and G-II are considered feasible.

In instances in which several styles are feasible, additional considerations are suggested for choosing among them. For example, one possibility is to choose the style that requires the smallest investment in time. The order of alternatives in Fig-

ure 13.7, starting with the one at the right of each path, is in terms of what Vroom and Yetton call the ''minimize man-hours'' criterion. According to this criterion, whenever a problem situation leads to more than one feasible style, *the more authoritarian the style the more it is to be preferred.* Other possibilities exist; alternatives could be arranged according to their long-range effectiveness or according to their short-term impact. But the main point is, that regardless of the ordering of the alternatives on each line of the model, the Vroom and Yetton approach ties together supervisory style with the characteristics of the decision-making situation.

Research Studies. Vroom and Yetton (1973) have employed their model in several interesting studies of supervisory leadership. In one, a set of case studies was prepared to express the various decision-making situations included in the model. Large number of managers were then asked to read these case studies and choose the leadership approach they would use to deal with each. In Vroom and Yetton's words, the results indicated:

> To be sure there were differences *among* managers in their general tendencies to utilize participative methods as opposed to autocratic ones. . . . These differences in behavior between managers, however, were small in comparison with differences within managers. On the standardized problems, no manager has indicated that he would use the same decision process on all problems or decisions, and most use all five methods under some circumstances. (Vroom, 1976a, p. 1545)

The major variation in the use of leadership methods was found, therefore, within managers as they moved from one problem situation to another. Some managers used participative methods more frequently than others, but the variation between managers was about one-third the amount of the variation in methods used by the individual manager. In a subsequent test of the model, Vroom and Jago (1978) reported that the relationship between a manager's behavior and the quality of the decisions made was consistent with the recommendations that can be obtained from the model.

Interestingly, managers seem to differ in the rules they use to guide their selection of leadership styles. For instance, Vroom and Yetton report that any two managers who use a participatory style with about the same frequency still may be found applying this style to a different set of situations. One manager may encourage participation in situations in which the quality of the decision is of little importance; another may be more likely to employ this approach to situations in which group acceptance is the principle concern. But whatever the specific rule, this observation suggests that such things as the work situation, the problem, the manager's leadership skills, personality, and past experience interact in some complicated manner to produce a set of behavioral rules that determine how the manager selects a supervisory style for a given occasion. The nature of these rules and their origin are not clearly understood, and this represents some of the more important work left undone in this area of work leadership.

Vertical Dyad Linkages

Most theories of leadership have not left room for the variations in behavior one can often observe as a leader comes into contact with the individual members of a work group. These theories leave one with the impression that leaders, functioning within a given situation, will display a rather uniform pattern of behavior as they interact with each individual member. Doubtless there are common elements that run through a leader's interactions with the different members of a group, but there are also differences, and these differences in leader behavior have been ignored by most theorists. One would probably be hard pressed to find anyone in this area who would deny the existence of this within-group variation in leadership style, but from the perspective of the available theories, leaders are most often described as pursuing a uniform pattern of behavior in their dealings with the group as a whole and with the individual members.

The vertical-dyad-linkage approach (Dansereau, Graen, & Haga, 1975; Graen, 1976) views leader behavior as a complex distribution of responses that can vary as the superior interacts with different subordinates in the group. This approach also recognizes that the members of a work group are not uniform with respect to their interactions with the leader. Rather, individuals approach their leaders from different social-psychological positions in the group and enter into exchange relationships with the leaders who, in turn, modify their behavior in a manner consistent with this exchange. It is from this exchange that a pattern of leader-follower behavior emerges.

Exchange.　The concept of exchange was first discussed in Chapter 9. Briefly, this concept views the relationship between a dyad (a pair of interacting persons) in terms of a marketplace model where each member of the pair possesses resources valued by the other. The behavior patterns that emerge are those that result in a mutually acceptable exchange of these resources. For example, a subordinate may display strong loyalty to the position or person of the leader, who in exchange provides the subordinate with a considerate and nonthreatening set of working relations. Withdrawal of this loyal followership will lead to a revision of the exchange, in which the superior may be less considerate of the subordinate's wishes.

VDL and ALS.　The vertical-dyad-linkage (VDL) approach does not describe leader behavior by computing an average leadership style (ALS) that is applied to all leader-follower dyads in a group. Rather, each leader-follower dyad (vertical dyad) is viewed as a separate unit of observation. These dyads are ordered according to some aspect of leader behavior, and these ordered dyads are related to some performance measure—for example, turnover (Dansereau, Cashman, & Graen, 1973). Hence, the VDL approach focuses on the changing pattern of leader behavior that might be observed within a group, whereas the ALS approach tends to collect leader behavior averages for each of a number of groups and to subject these averages to intercomparisons.

Leadership and Supervision.　The leader's role in a dyadic relationship is described in terms of two concepts that are very similar to those that have been used to identify different varieties of leader behavior. The VDL approach makes a distinction between the techniques of *leadership* and those of *supervision*. When engaging in supervision, superiors place heavy reliance on the formal sources of power and influence that are associated with the office they hold in the organization. In drawing on these sources of formal authority, a superior is more likely to deal with subordinates in an impersonal manner, as if they were "a part in a complex machine."

In using leadership techniques, the superior approaches each member of the group and seeks out an interpersonal accommodation that is satisfactory to both members of the dyad. Simply put, the superior's behavior acknowledges the individual differences that exist in the group. Influence, under these circumstances, derives from the personal investments each member of a dyad has in the exchange relationship that has been established.

Research.　The vertical-linkage concept actually represents an alternative approach to the study of leader behavior. Unlike the more traditional approach that utilizes average leadership behavior, this approach employs the dyad as its primary unit of analysis; and it views the relationship between leader and follower from the perspective of an exchange model in which the outcome of these systems of exchange is a set of social roles that describes the relationship between two people. One study by Graen and Schiemann (1978) will be used to illustrate the general nature of this approach. Our primary interest with this study concerns the procedures followed, although some reference will be made to the findings of the experiment.

The hypothesis studied in this experiment was that the extent to which a leader and a member agree with each other regarding the meaning of certain aspects of the job will be influenced by the quality of their interpersonal relationships. A high-quality dyad was defined as a relationship between a leader and a follower that is characterized by reciprocal influence (that is, mutual deference and sensitivity), mutual trust, respect, and liking for one another, and sharing a common fate. A low-quality relationship involves a one-directional influence going downward from the superior to the subordinate, in a situation where interactions are defined by work rules and other organizational regulations. In this latter relationship superiors serve as "overseers" in their relations with subordinates.

In the experiment, Graen and Schiemann identified groups of leader-follower dyads that maintained high-, middle- and low-quality relationships, and then determined the extent to which the members of these dyads agreed with each other on a number of issues. These issues involved the severity of job problems faced by the subordinate and the extent to which the leader was sensitive to the subordinate's job and supported the subordinate. To illustrate, low-level agreement might occur in situations in which superiors believe they are giving their subordinates strong support, but the subordinates report that they detect little support from their leaders.

Graen and Schiemann contend that previous research efforts have shown that there is often little agreement between superiors and subordinates with regard to work-related issues of the sort studied in their investigation. These previous studies, however, had used the average-leadership approach, and these averages have tended to obscure this relationship. Using the dyadic aproach, this study was able to show that the amount of agreement between leader and member varied with the quality of the exchange relationship that existed between them. Hence, the failure of previous research to generate similar results is, according to Graen and Schiemann, the consequence of the unit of observation employed, that is, group averages. The use of dyadic units permitted this relationship to be observed.

This experiment by Graen and Schiemann illustrates that by adopting the dyad rather than the entire work group as the unit of observation, it is possible to demonstrate relationships that are otherwise obscure. When the group as a whole is used as the unit, and leadership is described in terms of an average response that the leader makes to the individual members, variation from one dyad to the next is treated as error. Obviously, this is not an appropriate designation. Leader behavior does, as the Graen and Schiemann experiment demonstrates, vary from one dyad to the next within a work group. In large measure this variation attests to the fact that group members are not identical with regard to a wide range of social and psychological variables. The fact that these differences

influence the behavior of a leader is something that should be studied and understood, and not treated as an unexplained source of error in our observation.

SUMMARY COMMENTS

Over the years the topic of supervisory leadership has received considerable attention in the social science literature. This high level of research activity testifies to our recognition of the importance of the leadership role in the effective functioning of work organizations. In addition, most recognize the potent psychological impact work supervisors have on those who work under them. In carrying out this research, three points of view regarding the basic characteristics of leadership behavior seem to be in evidence. In some instances leadership has been thought of as a dimension of the personality structure of the individual. From this perspective, leadership potential is viewed as an attribute that individuals carry with them from one situation to the next. Another point of view has it that leadership is a product of the social demands of the situation. Leadership is seen as a response to the requirements of the social setting, and it is within this social environment that we can find the major forces that determine who will lead and how the leadership role will be carried out. A third point of view sees leadership as the result of an interaction between psychological and situation variables. It is not one set of influences or the other, operating alone, but the *combination* of factors that produces the type of leadership observed. It would seem that at the present time this interactionist approach is a dominant one in the thinking of those who study work behavior.

In this chapter we have been focusing on the job and social role of the work-group supervisor. In doing this we have been concerned with what these people do and how they do it. With regard to the first consideration, the job of the work-group supervisor has many things in common with the job of the higher-level executive. As is the case when we study the executive, supervisors have jobs that confront them with a day that is constantly changing. Their primary concern seems to be with the work itself, that is, getting the work out. Human-relations activities, although given great emphasis in the personnel administration literature, often receive a relatively minor investment of the supervisor's time.

When it comes to thinking about different styles of supervision, we find that many social scientists use a model that involves two contrasting types of leader behavior. Although given a variety of names—for example, democratic-autocratic, employee centered/production centered, and so on—the basic idea is that one style of behavior gives major attention to the people who carry out the work and the other style stresses the work itself.

Efforts made to determine whether one or the other of these approaches to supervision results in higher levels of work-group efficiency have met with mixed success. For example, in some instances democratic supervision has been associated with high rates of productivity, but then in other instances an autocratic leader seemed to be able to achieve higher levels of group output. The resolution of this inconsistency seems most likely to be found in an approach like Fiedler's, which stresses the importance of the interaction between psychological and situation variables. It is Fiedler's contention that the impact of a certain style of supervisor behavior on the productive efforts of a group is a function of the nature of the leader's relation with the group, leader power, and the degree of structure in the work. In an approach that parallels Fiedler's, Vroom and Yetton maintain that whether one should use an autocratic or a democratic approach to group problem solving depends in large measure on the nature of the task the group confronts.

There seem to be many factors that contribute to determining the style of supervision one sees in a work situation. Research has shown that such things as the personality and skill of the leader, the personality characteristics and general competence of group members, and the general organizational climate of leadership are factors that interact to produce different supervisory styles. There is also evidence of considerable variation in style within a single leader. Leaders tend to draw

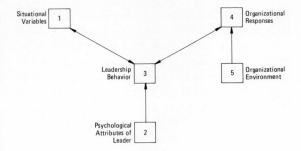

FIGURE 13.8 Schematic representation of variables that enter leadership research. The direction with which one variable influences another is indicated by the arrows. Hence, variables in the work situation 1 influences leader behavior 3, but leader behavior also influences many of the variables in the work situation. One could make all arrows bidirectional, but relationships depicted represent those most commonly studied in leadership research.

on different supervisory styles in different situations. Hence, leaders of work groups follow certain rules that govern whether they will draw on one or another style of supervisory behavior, and there appears to be a spread of individual differences in these rules.

We find, therefore, that like most complex social behaviors, supervisory leadership is best thought of in terms of the interaction between sets of psychological variables. A good summary of these relationships is presented in Figure 13.8 adapted from Vroom (1976a). Here leadership behavior 3 is represented as the product of situational variables 1 and the psychological characteristics of the leader 2. The organizational response to different leadership styles 4 is mediated by the larger environmental context within which the organization operates 5. Hence, leader behavior is an element in a complicated skein of interacting variables that reside in both the psychology and sociology of the work situation. Social scientists are beginning to incorporate these more complex relationships into the research that is being carried out, and as a consequence, there is good reason to be optimistic about the future growth in our understanding of this important type of work behavior.

14
The Business Executive

There is an abiding and pervasive commitment to success and upward mobility in the culture of the United States. The social order is thought of as a system that provides a broad range of opportunities within the reach of all who apply themselves to the rigors of study and the discipline of hard work. To be somebody, to prosper in comparison to preceding generations, is not a distant hope in the national psyche, but rather an expectation held to be the birthright of virtually every citizen who looks for opportunities.

The business executive symbolizes much that is involved in this American love affair with success, and in this role are found many of the social goals that have such high appeal to so many. Executives occupy a position of high prestige, and once having attained this lofty station, assume a leadership role that at times extends far beyond the jurisdiction of the business firm. They lead philanthropic drives, they serve on the governing boards of cultural and educational agencies, and their judgment and leadership are frequently recruited for the highest levels of government. The American business leader is, in fact, a most interesting and influential person.

It is not glamor alone, however, that attracts us to the business leader. There are many more compelling aspects of the role that warrant our attention, not the least of which is the substantial amount of power these leaders often possess. Consider for a moment their control of resources. The principal officers of many American business enterprises direct organizations whose financial resources exceed the governmental budgets of many nations in the world. But let us look closer to home

to get some idea of the magnitude of the resources manipulated by these industrial organizations (Dictionary of 500 Largest Corporations, 1977). If one were to rank American industrial organizations according to their 1976 sales and then select the corporation ranked twenty-fifth in this list, one would have identified an organization whose sales for a single year exceeded the governmental tax revenues of all but eight states in the United States. The largest corporation reported sales that exceeded the tax revenues of the state of California (the richest state) by a factor of two and a half.

It is power, then, that makes the study of American business executives an important undertaking. But apart from their power, business executives play a role that makes our concern with them even more relevant to the study of work. This role is a policy-making one that in some major measure determines the conditions under which employees of these large organizations work. Baumhart (1968), in a study of business ethics, concludes that the ethical standards one finds operating in a large corporation reflect the lengthened shadow of its principal officer. The chief officer exerts an influence on the company's ethical practices that extends throughout the entire organization. In a similar fashion, top executives establish rules governing working conditions that affect every member of the firm. In addition, executives' style of work, their commitment, drive, values, and expectations, serve as potent models that contribute significantly to the general psychological climate of work. As a consequence, the role and characteristics of business leaders are factors that figure prominently in determining the social conditions under which people work, the type of projects they undertake, and in some instances the style they employ in completing their job assignments. Therefore, to understand the social dynamics of complex work organizations, it is important that one consider the significant role played by these business leaders.

Not surprisingly, there has been an active research literature dealing with the business leader. Some of this work has been conducted to provide information that might contribute to the selection and training of persons who might occupy these positions. But much that has been reported merely reflects a lively curiosity about those who direct the affairs of large corporations. A major question deals with the personality characteristics of these individuals. Are there, in fact, personality traits that have been found to warrant the stereotypic images widely held about business executives? What can we say regarding the general pattern of their careers? How and where do they enter the labor market; then how do they move up the chain of command? How long does it take them to reach the top? What are some of the factors that seem to correlate with the career pattern they display?

These and other questions will be the concern of the present chapter, but before we look into some of the psychological characteristics of the business elite, let's look more closely at the jobs they hold and try to get a picture of the work they do. A number of investigators have attempted to collect observations regarding the work activities of business leaders, and it is with these studies that we begin.

THE EXECUTIVE'S JOB

The nature of the manager's work, dealing as it does with such things as planning, decision making, and leadership, is difficult to describe in satisfactory detail; also the work has a nonroutine character that makes its description troublesome. Finally, it is particularly difficult to describe the content of managers' jobs, since there is often no clear-cut production unit resulting from their activities. We can, however, attempt to describe

managers' jobs in terms of the kinds of demands placed on them and the organizational roles they are expected to play. In doing so, however, we must face the obvious fact that executives do not all carry out the same duties. Nevertheless, several investigators have attempted to develop a general description of this kind of work from a study of the schedule of activities that fill the executive's day, and it is from these sources that we can try to piece together a picture of the job of the business manager.

Hours Worked

One of the things most frequently reported about the executive's job is the long hours required. Research results suggest that it is not unusual to find business executives spending sixty or more hours each week on their jobs, and many report that there are periods during the year when work requires a complete commitment of their waking hours. Recall the study by Heckscher and DeGrazia (1959) cited in Chapter 5. Here a mail questionnaire received from over thirteen hundred business executives indicated that their workweek was averaging fifty-five hours. Carlson (1951), in a widely cited study of Swedish executives, reports that the workday for this group consistently exceeded eight hours, and Sheikh (1966) indicates that over two-thirds of the 132 executives surveyed in his study were spending more than fifty hours each week on their jobs. Finally, Heidrick and Struggles (1977) have conducted a survey of 342 presidents of the largest corporations in America. As a part of this survey, executives were asked to estimate the number of hours spent each week on the job, and their replies showed that 90 percent devoted fifty or more hours to their jobs, while 50 percent invested sixty or more hours.

Yet in spite of the long hours invested in their work, many executives report feeling that they do not have enough time to complete all they would like or all that is expected of them. Sheikh reports that 80 percent of all executives in his study felt that they were hurried in their jobs, and 72 percent indicated that they often felt that time was scarce and that they frequently seemed to be working at

FIGURE 14.1   A Statistical Composite of the Typical Chief Executive Officer of the Country's Largest Business Organizations

The position	The person
Title Chairman and chief executive officer; selected primarily through initiative of predecessor	**Age:** 56
Compensation: $285,000 salary and bonus Stock options Automobile, club and extraordinary insurance	**Marital Status:** Married to first spouse **Religion:** Protestant
Workload: 50 to 59 hours devoted to business weekly 3 corporate directorships	**Education:** Graduate degree **Career Path:** Three full-time employers Primary functional experience in sales/marketing 22.5 years with present company 7.9 years as chief executive officer
Board Relations: Directors more involved in corporate affairs, particularly senior officer compensation and nomination of board members	**Career Satisfaction:** Believes that CEOs enjoy their work more than executives at other levels Believes his business career has been more satisfying than nonbusiness pursuits would have been
Changing role: Government regulation has the greatest impact Ability to project the corporation's public image now vital	**Successor selection:** Has identified possible successors to the board

Note: The 1000 largest industrials and 300 largest banking, diversified financial, life insurance, retailing, transportation and utility companies, as ranked by *Fortune,* were surveyed. CEOs were all male; 554 returned the questionnaire.
Source: *Profile of a chief executive officer,* Heidrick and Struggles, Inc., 1980.

a high pace. Furthermore, a large majority of this sample reported that their workday frequently did not proceed according to an orderly plan.

Varied Activities

The long hours and high pace speak of a day that is filled with many activities. Executives often tell of days in which they are occupied with a seemingly endless variety of activities, many of which involve contacts with other people. For example, Henry Mintzberg (1973) reports the results of a series of observations made on five chief officers over a one-week period. The workload was impressive; on the average, each executive processed thirty-six pieces of mail every day, participated in eight meetings, had five telephone calls, and took one tour. There usually is little free time;

executives, during the infrequent periods when they are alone in their offices, are constantly interrupted by others. Carlson (1951) reports instances in which the average time period when the executive is alone is only eight minutes.

Social Contacts

The typical day is filled with a large variety of brief social contacts. Burns (1954) reports a study in which executives were found to be spending 80 percent of their workdays talking to others. Kelly (1964) found another group of executives spending two-thirds of their time in conversation with other people. Although there are meetings and conferences lasting a half-hour or more, much of the executive's time is spent in a series of very short encounters that last only a few minutes. Mintzberg

(1973), for example, found that half of all an executive's activities lasted less than nine minutes. It is apparent, then, that a fast-changing pace of this sort does not encourage a meditative approach to planning and policy formation. In fact, Mintzberg suggests that executives tend to prefer this type of rapidly changing activity, participating in tasks that are of short duration and becoming involved in affairs that are action oriented rather than contemplative. They prefer issues that are current, questions that deal with concrete matters, and programs that are directed toward getting things done. Mintzberg reports that executives tend to show a strong preference for communications that are verbal rather than written, with two-thirds of all their social contacts being either by telephone or through unscheduled face-to-face meetings. In short, the tempo of the executive position and the nature of the communications received tend to foster a work setting that is varied, rapidly changing, and highly social. It is a job that often prevents extensive study and leisurely contemplation of the problems to be faced.

We must not overlook the many formal meetings and conferences in which the executive participates. Because of their duration they are fewer in number than the unscheduled contacts referred to above, but Mintzberg reports that planned meetings account for almost half of the executive's time. Many of these meetings are ceremonial, since the executive represents the firm at a large number of civic and professional affairs. Mintzberg's data indicate that the scheduled meeting is frequently used when large amounts of information are to be transmitted and when strategy making or negotiations are to be undertaken.

Summing Up

We find the executive's job, therefore, involving a wide variety of personal contacts. Executives are truly social animals who live in an electric, fast-paced world of conversation, where brief social encounters and lengthier formal meetings occupy much of the day-to-day activity. They are infrequently alone, being sought out by large num-

bers of subordinates who exchange information with them during the brief exchanges that mark the day. They often have little time to think and reflect, and the large amount of reading that awaits their attention many times is carried home to be considered in the evening. Considering the scope of their responsibilities and the consequences of their official actions, some might at times wish that their jobs would provide more time for deep concentration and reflection, and that they would have greater opportunity for thought and study. When this time is not available, the executive is often forced to rely on information summaries that are provided by assistants and technical specialists who have given matters more thorough consideration. In short, the executive is often required to delegate many important aspects of decision making (for instance, the collection of information) to others whose jobs permit more detailed consideration of a problem. But whatever one's personal inclination in this regard, the job requires that the business executive confront a tremendously complex set of problems and personal demands that change frequently and demand a substantial investment of thought, energies, and judgment.

BACKGROUND OF BUSINESS EXECUTIVES

In his discussion of the large bureaucratic organization, Robert Presthus (1962) says that the promotions of individuals up the leadership hierarchy is often the consequence of a process of cooptation. That is, those who hold positions of power and influence choose their own successors. Under such circumstances, one might be led to expect that this system of executive mobility would reflect regularities and biases that restrict promotion opportunities for some and enhance them for others. If this is true, then one may ask what variables seem to facilitate promotion into higher levels of management. What are the characteristics of those who emerge as successful candidates for positions among the business elite?

Social origins

Over the years there have been several attempts to study the background of those who occupy positions of executive prominence. Earlier studies (Taussig & Joslyn, 1932; Warner & Low, 1947; Rogoff, 1953) concluded that opportunities for upward mobility were decreasing and that business prominence was increasingly restricted to a select group. By looking at the social class of the father and that of his sons, these investigators were able to gauge the amount of social mobility that was experienced by different social groups. The general finding was that the children of the socially privileged tended to rise to positions of business leadership, while the children of those in lower social strata were not well represented among the ranks of the executive group.

Perhaps one of the more ambitious studies of this type is one conducted in the 1950s at the University of Chicago (Warner & Abegglen, 1955a, 1955b). Relying on a rather elaborate questionnaire, Warner and Abegglen contacted a large number of individuals who occupied the highest

positions in the largest business firms in America. By collecting information on the occupation of each executive's father, it was possible to make an assessment of the social origins of this group of business leaders. As was the case with the earlier studies, Warner and Abegglen found that some social groups were overrepresented in the sample, while other groups were underrepresented. For example, business executives and business owners accounted for only 4 percent of the total male population of the United States in 1920, yet 31 percent of the group of business executives studied (1952) had fathers whose occupations were in this category. Conversely, unskilled and semiskilled laborers made up 31 percent of the male population in 1920, but this group contributed only 5 percent of the 1952 generation of business leaders. The sons of business executives and owners are said to be overrepresented (by a ratio of 7.75), while the sons of laborers are underrepresented (by a ratio of .16) in the 1952 sample of the business elite. Table 14.1 summarizes the findings, which indicate that certain occupational backgrounds tend to contribute a disproportionately high number of in-

TABLE 14.1 Occupational Distribution of the Fathers of Business Leaders and of the U.S. Male Adult Population for 1920

Occupation	Percentage of Fathers of 1952 Business Leaders	Percentage of Total U.S. Male Adult Population in 1920	Ratio
Unskilled or semiskilled laborer	5	31	.16
Skilled laborer	10	16	.63
Owner of small business	18	5	3.60
Clerk or salesman	8	10	.80
Foreman	3	2	1.33
Minor or major executive: owner of large business	31	4	7.75
Professional man	14	4	3.50
Farm laborer	0	7	0.00
Farm tenant or owner	9	20	.45
Other occupations	2	1	2.00
Total	100	100	

Source: Warner, W. L. & Abegglen, J. C. *Occupational mobility in American business and industry.* Minneapolis: University of Minnesota Press, 1955, p. 40. Copyright © 1955 by the University of Minnesota Press.

dividuals to the executive class, and that others—for example, farm tenant or owner—had contributed many fewer executives than their numbers in the population would predict. It is quite apparent from these data that business executives come from social backgrounds that represent the upper middle and upper classes of the population. Hence, it would seem that large numbers of business leaders come from backgrounds that are privileged in the sense that the occupations of their fathers put their families well above average in social position and income. Sturdivant and Adler (1976), in a study of top executives, estimate that only 3 percent of their sample came from social backgrounds that could be described as being poor.

Education

As might be expected of a group coming from high social origins, a large majority of executives go to college and many go on to graduate school. In one study Brua (1973) reports that in the United States 83 percent of the presidents of large corporations have undergraduate degrees and 42 percent have done some postgraduate work, with 36 percent of them earning an advanced degree. Brua also found that at the undergraduate level, science and engineering degrees accounted for the largest group of college graduates, while at the postgraduate level almost half did their work in law and 25 percent studied business administration. Sturdivant and Adler (1976) estimate that 7 percent of the top executives in the nation have Ph.D. degrees.

We see that the education of the business executive is often a technical one, and it would appear that top management officers tend to be educated at a level that is considerably above that found in the general population (see Figure 14.2). Warner and Abegglen (1955a) see this as an indication that the business leader in America represents a professional class that requires for admission high levels of post-high-school education. According to these authors, it is education that provides what they call "the royal road to success," a route that individuals of low social origin must follow if they aspire to move up in the hierarchy of business leadership.

Education seems to relate closely to the age at which an individual achieves executive prominence. Of course as one changes the educational level of a sample, other factors vary as well, but as a general rule, increasing education is accompanied by increasing age of entry into career positions and decreasing number of years required to achieve an executive position. Warner and Abegglen found, for example, that executives who completed only high school tended to enter business when they were about nineteen and moved into executive positions about twenty-eight years later. Executives who completed postgraduate work entered business when they were twenty-three and achieved executive status twenty years later. Doubtless, the social status of the executive's family background varies along with the educational level, thus confounding two important variables. Although links of this type between variables make for difficulty in interpreting the findings, it is evident that as the number of years of education increases, the years taken to reach the top executive positions decrease.

Summing Up

We see, then that the backgrounds of individuals in high executive positions do not reflect a representative cross-section of the population. There seem to be selective factors at work that relate to the movement of people up the organization. The middle and upper middle classes seem to contribute more than their share to the ranks of the business elite, as do certain regions of the country—the Middle Atlantic and New England states. The executive elite also appear to be privileged with regard to the amount of education they have received, and as a group we find them to be predominantly in the middle and later years of their lives. Although there are, at times, attempts made to surround business leadership with a youthful image, it is not unusual to find lower and upper management ranks separated by a generation of time.

CAREER PATTERNS

In attempting to describe the patterns of vertical movement found in the work histories of high-

FIGURE 14.2 Educational Background of Chief Executive Officers (CEOs)

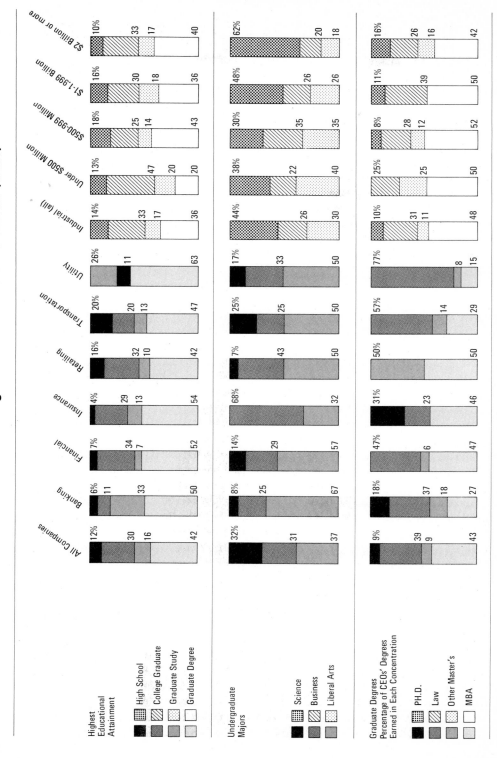

Source: *Profile of a chief executive officer.* Heidrick and Struggles, Inc., 1977

TABLE 14.2   Career Sequence of 1952 Business Leaders (percent)

Occupation of Business Leader	First Occupation	Five Years Later	Ten Years Later	Fifteen Years Later
Unskilled or semiskilled laborer	11	1	0	0
Skilled laborer	3	2	1	0
Clerk or retail salesman	34	15	4	1
Salesman	9	10	4	2
Foreman	1	4	3	1
Minor executive	9	35	43	25
Major executive	1	6	26	57
Business owner	1	2	3	3
Engineer	9	8	4	3
Lawyer	6	5	4	3*
Other profession	9	8	6	4
Military career	2	2	1	1
Government service	1	1	1	0
Training program	3	0	0	0
Other occupation	1	1	0	0
Total	100	100	100	100

Source: Warner, W. L., & Abegglen, J. C. *Occupational mobility in American business and industry.* Minneapolis: University of Minnesota Press, 1955, p. 116.

level executives, one turns to the research literature, only to find that relatively little has been done with regard to this question. Much of the work in this area concerns the factors that seem to facilitate a person's movement up the organization and the personal attributes sought after by companies searching for executive personnel. We will look at this literature a bit later on, but first let us consider the studies that have attempted to describe the sequence of jobs held by individuals who have moved up to the top of large organizations. Where do we find executives starting their careers and what routes do they follow in their climb to positions of high leadership?

Warner and Abegglen (1955a, 1955b) attacked the question of career patterns directly when they asked the executives in their study to report on the jobs they held at five-year intervals across their careers. From these data (see Table 14.2) they found that at the beginning of their careers a majority (52 percent) held white-collar jobs, with the designations "clerk" and "salesperson" accounting for the largest category of first employment (43 percent). Technical and professional jobs accounted for another 24 percent of the first jobs. Five years later, only 25 percent of the group still

held jobs as clerks and salespersons; now 35 percent had minor executive positions. During this same interval there was relatively little change in the percentage employed in technical and professional jobs (21 percent). Five years later only 8 percent of the entire sample held clerking and selling jobs, whereas 69 percent had assumed some level of executive position. During this same period, however, 14 percent of the sample were still engaged in technical and professional undertakings. Hence, it appears that engineers, lawyers, accountants, and the like retain for a longer part of their careers an identification with their technical specialties, while those who begin their work careers in other types of white-collar jobs move more rapidly into general supervisory positions. This does not imply that technically oriented individuals are retarded by their specialties, just that it is later in their careers that they move away from the area of their technical training and assume a role in general supervision.

Heidrick and Struggles (1972) report that the executives included in their sample tended to enter business from colleges and universities, and the institutions most heavily represented were those that maintained reputations for academic strength (see Table 14.3). Members of this sample also reported that the area of their most extensive experience was in general administration (27.6 percent) and marketing (23.3 percent). About 20 percent reported that their most extensive experience was obtained in technical and scientific positions, while experience in manufacturing jobs accounted for less than 7 percent of the reports.

It is often said that the individual who is upwardly mobile is also horizontally mobile. That is to say, the person who eventually reaches the higher levels of management more frequently moves from one employer to the next. Not so, according to the Heidrick and Struggles data, which show that three of every four executives in their sample had previously had no more than two employers. Along similar lines, prior to their appointment, company presidents usually had accumulated considerable tenure with the organization they then led. The Heidrick and Struggles survey shows that over 60 percent of their sample had been employed with their present companies sixteen years or more, and almost one in four reported that they had served their companies for thirty-one

or more years. Although the data indicate a recent trend toward increased job mobility among the executive group, still one gets a picture of a group whose employment history has been relatively stable over the years.

Summarizing, then, we find that the career patterns that have been identified by research find large numbers of executives leaving college upon graduation to enter the work force in white-collar and technical jobs. For those who begin their careers in technical jobs, there is a longer period of employment before they find themselves in positions of general management. For that large group of persons who begin in clerical and sales jobs, a major shift to minor executive status appears after the first five years of employment. By the time ten years have elapsed after the individual's first full-time job, the major career directions have been determined. Over 70 percent of the Warner and Abegglen sample had by this time moved into management positions. This group, along with those still found in technical jobs, accounted for over 85 percent of the group that eventually made it to the top of the business ladder. The remaining

TABLE 14.3   Schools Granting Most Degrees to Presidents of America's Business Elite

School	Total Number of Degrees	Number of Bachelor's Degrees	Number of Graduate Degrees
Harvard	50	8	42
Yale	30	24	6
University of Michigan	20	9	11
Stanford	20	11	9
Princeton	18	16	2
MIT	16	6	10
University of Illinois	13	10	3
Northwestern	13	8	5
University of Minnesota	12	6	6
University of Pennsylvania	12	7	5
Columbia	11	6	5
Carnegie-Mellon	10	6	4
University of Chicago	10	4	6
New York University	10	4	6
University of Virginia	10	6	4
Purdue	9	9	0
Cornell	6	4	2
University of Iowa	6	3	3
University of Texas	6	6	0
Penn State	6	5	1

Source: Heidrick & Struggles, Inc. *Profile of a president.* Chicago, Ill.: Heidrick & Struggles, Inc., 1972.

15 percent were scattered over a variety of positions at the end of ten years.

Factors Affecting Executive Promotion

It has already been pointed out that social origins and education are factors that have been found to relate to an individual's movement up through the management ranks. Scofield (1956) contends that the business advantages of a college education involve not just a narrow set of formal skills acquired during the college years; rather, the college degree identifies individuals who are likely to possess acceptable values, personality characteristics, and social skills. As a consequence, they are sought by corporations and placed in positions in the organization that serve as training ground for the upwardly mobile in the firm. Possessing the college degree suggests to employers that the individual may have those communication skills that are a requisite to a successful management career. Executive positions are primarily social in their character, and as a consequence, effective written and verbal communication are essential skills that one must possess in order to maintain a viable management career. Possession of the college degree improves the likelihood that the individual has developed these skills to an acceptable level.

Scofield suggests that we do not think too narrowly about the vocational implications of the college degree. Granted, there are management positions that do demand a high level of technical expertise that can be obtained only through formal education. There are other management positions, however, whose technical content does not draw directly on college-taught skills. Dalton (1959), for example, found that in one group of 226 managers, 62 percent held positions whose duties did not relate to the formal education they had received. Dalton comments on the ''unofficial requirements for success'' that often play a major role in the promotion of executives. His study revealed that along with education, such factors as membership in lodges and social clubs, national origin, and political affiliation were factors that seemed to correlate with management position. He sees promotion as an important event in the internal politics of the firm. Loyalty to those already in power is an important consideration when new members are brought into the circle of leadership. The searching out of people who share similar views with those presently in office sometimes leads the older executives to advance those whose education, social origin, and affiliations are compatible with their own.

After an extensive series of preliminary observations and interviews with business leaders on the West Coast, Reed Powell (1963) constructed a detailed questionnaire tapping managers' perceptions of the workings of the promotion system that operated within their organizations. Two hundred forty executives participated in this survey, and from their responses Powell identified sets of factors that these managers thought played an influential role in determining the promotability of the individual. Some of these factors are within the scope of an individual's control, while others in large measure were not. Listed below are some of the factors Powell's subjects indicated helped an individual in the promotion system:

1. A participant in nonpartisan civic, charitable, and professional organizations
2. A Republican, member of the Chamber of Commerce
3. Helped socially by a wife who fits in and who is accepted
4. Effective in informal social relations with superiors
5. A member of a reputable social club
6. Ambitious and loyal to the company
7. Holds a college degree
8. An effective decision maker
9. An outstanding performer
10. White, Anglo-Saxon
11. Tall, clean-cut, properly dressed
12. A capable leader
13. A social drinker
14. Lucky

These factors have not been listed in order of importance, and the last one, luck, acknowledges that even though an individual may possess all the attributes thought desirable in a manager, there is still an element of being in the right place at the right time that contributes to the career success of each management employee.

Coates and Pellegrin (1956) contend that an executive's progress is greatly influenced by one's definition of the situation. What is meant here is that how executives see their job situations is an important factor in determining how far they will rise in the firm. A series of interviews with mobile and nonmobile management people revealed that those who moved up in the organization saw real opportunities in their work situations, whereas those whose careers were not upward bound tended to see themselves in situations that did not involve these kinds of opportunities. To a certain degree these mobile and nonmobile careers reflect what Coates and Pellegrin call a self-fulfilling prophecy; the individual's perception of the work situation leads to behaviors that confirm these perceptions. For example, the worker who sees little opportunity for promotion in the job tends to draw on behaviors that are consistent with that point of view. It is this type of behavior that retards the individual's chances of promotion; hence the prophecy is fulfilled. On the other hand, the person who sees good promotion chances in the job initiates behaviors that are consistent with this perspective, and these behaviors improve the individual's chances for promotion.

Bowman (1964) surveyed almost 2000 businessmen, two-thirds of whom were in top or upper middle management positions, concerning their views on the characteristics of the promotable executive. Of the sixty factors included in the questionnaire, nine were identified by over 90 percent of the respondents as being helpful in furthering an executive's upward mobility. With the exception of having a college education and presenting a good appearance, these factors (see Table 14.4) relate to what may be called job performance. A high level of drive coupled with an ability to deal effectively with people were seen as crucial to the executive's image of success.

TABLE 14.4   Qualities Judged as Positive Factors in Executive Promotion by More Than 90 Percent of the Almost 2000 Executives Surveyed by Bowman

Qualities	Percent Responding
1. **Ability to communicate**	94.7
2. **Ambition and drive**	93.5
3. **College education**	93.4
4. **Making sound decisions**	93.1
5. **Self-confidence**	92.3
6. **Good appearance**	92.3
7. **Getting things done with people**	91.5
8. **Capacity for hard work**	91.2
9. **Responsibility and conscientiousness**	91.2

Adapted from Bowman, G. W. What helps or harms promotability? *Harvard Business Review*, 1964, *42*(1), 6–26. Copyright © 1955 by the President and Fellows of Harvard College, all rights reserved.

With regard to job performance, Berlew and Hall (1966) report a study in which significant relationships were found between what companies expect of managers and their performance effectiveness on the job. Individuals who were placed in the most demanding jobs tended to be more effective and successful than were those placed in less demanding positions. An interesting aspect of these results is that this relationship between job demands and work effectiveness appeared during the very first year the person was on the job. This led Berlew and Hall to suggest that it is during the early stages of employment that managers develop approaches to work that carry on through their career. Job expectations also seem to play something of a role in shaping these approaches to work. Hence, career patterns may be laid down during the very first year on the job, and these patterns are shaped by the expectations the company imposes on the person as well as the manner in which the individual responds to these early expectations.

Hence, we find that the list of factors perceived to be important to an executive's upward mobility is rather long. Warner and Abegglen (1955a, 1955b) see social origin and education as critical factors, Powell (1963) includes in his list membership in certain organizations, Coates and Pellegrin (1956) stress the way the executive perceives the job situation, Bowman (1964) mentions interpersonal competence, and Berlew and Hall (1966) emphasize early job expectations. Possibly there is an element of truth in each point of view, but whatever the case, it does seem apparent that the image of the upwardly mobile business person is a rather complicated one.

Perhaps one can gain some insight into the factors that seem to be associated with success in business organizations by looking at the research that has been done in an attempt to predict performance in executive positions. We might argue that those variables shown to relate to successful performance in management positions are the ones that we should include in our picture of the factors that are important in shaping the career patterns of managers.

Predicting Management Success

Intelligence.   Mental ability is the first attribute that comes to mind when one thinks about business success. The problem-solving and decision-making activities typically associated with the executive's job suggest that these positions call for a high level of intellectual ability. Yet when one looks at the research reports, there is little consistent evidence that intelligence tests are useful in predicting executive job performance. Granted, tests of this sort have shown some predictive strength in several studies (Laurent, 1962; Grant, 1965; Bentz, 1968; Grimsley & Jarrett, 1973), but in the main, tests of intellectual abilities have not correlated highly with executive performance.

This does not necessarily mean that high mental ability is unimportant to managerial performance. Korman (1968) suggests that one factor that lowers the predictive capabilities of mental-ability tests may well be that high-level management personnel have already undergone a considerable amount of preselection, which has resulted in the screening out of those less intellectually able. As a consequence, most of those who reach the executive level possess relatively high amounts of intellectual ability; hence, whether a person succeeds or

fails in these positions is a function of other factors. We have seen, for example, that much recruitment of executive talent takes place among those who have successfully completed a college education, and by the time these individuals reach middle and upper management positions, they have been well sifted out according to their general intellectual competence. A study of business executives by Piotrowski (1964) gives some support to this contention. In dealing with a sample of 110 presidents and vice-presidents of large corporations, Piotrowski found that the range of *Weschler Adult Intelligence Scale* I.Q.'s was 116 to 150, with a mean of 133. This is quite impressive; the mean I.Q. places the average executive in this sample in the upper 2 percent of the general population in general intelligence. Hence, the inability of intelligence tests to predict executive performance may be an indication of the fact that executives as a group have come through a screening process that tends to eliminate those who are intellectually less able to cope with the demands of the job.

Personality and Interest Factors.   No other psychological variables have received more attention in connection with executive behavior than have those relating to personality. Yet, in the studies that have attempted to predict executive performance through personality scales there has been only modest success. One notable exception to this is found in a series of studies (Bentz, 1968) carried out at Sears, which attempted to predict executive performance from a battery of psychological tests. In a number of these studies personality variables were found to relate to the effectiveness with which executives carried out their jobs. Variables like sociability, social leadership, dominance, self-confidence, and general activity were found to relate to the measures of management success that were used. As with measures of intellectual ability, however, single personality scores did not yield high levels of predictability.

The same tale may be told with regard to scores derived from tests that measure interest patterns. Basically a measure of motivation, the interest inventory attempts to assess the areas of activity in which individuals find the highest satisfaction and in which they are able to maintain relatively long periods of attention. Korman (1968), in his review of studies that have attempted to predict management success, finds that interest inventories appear to present a rather dismal view of predictive accuracy. Hence we again find that the use of single-test predictors yields relatively low levels of prediction when they are applied to the task of anticipating managerial success.

Confounding Factors. Why should this be? The types of tests we have just considered represent very basic and major components of human behavior: intelligence, personality, and interest areas. Furthermore, there are probably no other areas of psychological measurement that have received more research attention than have these three. Why then should we find that these tests do not yield high levels of prediction when they are applied to the problem of managerial performance?

Several factors contribute to this difficulty, one of which has already been mentioned with regard to the use of mental-ability tests. The process of recruiting, selecting, training, and promoting managerial personnel can be thought of as a complicated screening system that tends to do much of the work that tests are asked to do. To evaluate a test requires that we have a measure of executive performance, but obviously we cannot obtain a satisfactory performance measure until the individual has passed through this elaborate screening system and has been assigned to an executive position. At this point, when we ask tests to differentiate people who have already been screened, the tests are given a much more difficult task than they would have faced had all the prior screening not taken place.

Other factors that might be mentioned include the difficulty of obtaining a satisfactory measure of executive performance. Consider for a moment the problem of evaluating the productivity of a machine operator. Here, a carefully collected sample of production units may give us a relatively direct estimation of the worker's effectiveness. For the executive job, however, the task of developing a satisfactory measure of productivity is much more difficult. Here we find a job that deals with problem solution, decision making, and judgment, and rarely if ever are there concrete outcomes that represent the end product of these activities. Hence, we must rely on less objective standards by which to evaluate the executive's job performance, and in doing so we measure with less accuracy and, as a consequence, with less predictability.

Finally, the job of the executive is extremely complex. It is a job that draws on a broad range of human talents and abilities. Consequently, to expect a single human attribute to account for a major portion of this complicated task is perhaps asking too much. The answer would seem to lie, then, in the use not of single tests but combinations of tests, each of which accounts for a different facet of executive performance, although any one of them may not account for a major portion of the executive's behavior.

This, in fact, is the case, and it is when batteries of tests are used rather than single tests that we find levels of predictive accuracy that are quite useful. The Sears study (Bentz, 1968), for example, reports impressively high correlations between measures of executive performance and a battery of tests that includes intelligence, personality, and interest tests, along with instruments that simulate real-life problem-solving situations. Grimsley and Jarrett (1973) reported that batteries of personality and mental-ability tests yielded levels of prediction that were also quite high. Therefore, by combining tests that tap different facets of executive performance it is possible at times to predict success in management jobs with a level of accuracy that is equal to that reported by similar attempts to predict performance in rank-and-file positions.

The Assessment Center. One interesting approach to predicting executive performance is the assessment center (Bray & Grant, 1966; Hinrichs, 1969; Byham, 1971). The typical assessment center is located in an attractive setting away from the job. A small group of promising managers is taken there and asked to participate in a series of activities thought to be useful in identifying prospective executives. Figure 14.3, taken from Byham (1971), describes the schedule of activities followed in a typical two-day assessment-center program. At all stages of the program, participants are observed by a team of assessors who, when the program closes, meet for several days to pool their observations and develop evaluation reports. These reports often include an assessment of ex-

ecutive potential, an evaluation of strengths and weaknesses, and a prescription relating to areas of future training that might be appropriate for each participant.

There are several studies available that indicate that the assessment center can provide useful information relating to management potential. Bray and Grant (1966) report on an instance in which an assessment-center program conducted by AT&T successfully identified a high percentage of

FIGURE 14.3   Two-Day Assessment-Center Program

DAY 1

Orientation Meeting

Management Game—"Conglomerate." Forming different types of conglomerates is the goal, with four-man teams of participants bartering companies to achieve their planned result. Teams set their own acquisition objectives and must plan and organize to meet them.

Background Interview—A 1½ hour interview conducted by an assessor.

Group Discussion—"Management Problems." Four short cases calling for various forms of management judgment are presented to groups of four participants. In one hour the group, acting as consultants, must resolve the cases and submit its recommendation in writing.

Individual Fact-Finding and Decision-Making Exercise—"The Research Budget." The participant is told that he has just taken over as division manager. He is given a brief description of an incident in which his predecessor has recently turned down a request for funds to continue a research project. The research director is appealing for a reversal of the decision. The participant is given 15 minutes to ask questions to dig out the facts of the case. Following this fact-finding period, he must present his decision orally with supporting reasoning and defend it under challenge.

DAY 2

In-Basket Exercise—"Section Manager's In-Basket." The contents of a section manager's in-basket are simulated. The participant is instructed to go through the contents, solving problems, answering questions, delegating, organizing, scheduling, and planning, just as he might do if he were promoted suddenly to the position. An assessor reviews the contents of the completed in-basket and conducts a one-hour interview with the participant to gain further information.

Assigned Role Leaderless Group Discussion—"Compensation Committee." The Compensation Committee is meeting to allocate $8,000 in discretionary salary increases among six supervisory and managerial employees. Each member of the committee (participants) represents a department of the company and is instructed to "do the best he can" for the employee from his department.

Analysis, Presentation, and Group Discussion—"The Pretzel Factory." This financial analysis problem has the participant role-play a consultant called in to advise Carl Flowers of the C. F. Pretzel Company on two problems: What to do about a division of the company that has continually lost money, and whether the corporation should expand. Participants are given data on the company and are asked to recommend appropriate courses of action. They make their recommendation in a seven-minute presentation after which they are formed into a group to come up with a single set of recommendations.

Final Announcements

Source: Byham, W. C. The assessment center as an aid in management development. *Training and Development Journal*, 1971, *25*, 10–22. Copyright 1971 by the American Society for Training and Development, Inc.

individuals who, within a period of several years following their participation in the center, were promoted to higher management positions.

The principal strength of the assessment-center approach to management appraisal is found in the focus it places on social behaviors. We have already described the substantial social requirements of the executive's job, and basically, the assessment center is a place where social behaviors are observed and evaluated as the individual grapples with business-related problems. Hinrichs (1969) reports data suggesting that more conventional, and less costly, management appraisal systems may be able to provide information that parallels that obtained from these complicated situational tests. His study of an assessment-center program at IBM suggests that a careful review of personnel records may provide information concerning management potential that is similar to that obtained from the situational exercises carried out in the assessment center.

But our purpose here is not to evaluate assessment centers; rather, we seek to gain insight into the characteristics that identify successful managers. Experience with the assessment-center approach would seem to suggest that it is in the social sphere that we should look to identify behaviors that are critical to effective executive performance. In particular, the aspects of behavior that relate to the individual's active and aggressive participation in interpersonal relations seem to be important dimensions of management effectiveness (Hinrichs, 1969). Furthermore, decision-making style and administrative effectiveness are also behavior components that are accessible through assessment-center procedures, and that seem to relate to performance in an executive position. Finally, the assessment center provides information regarding the individual's response to social stress. This is an area of performance that would appear to be an important ingredient in determining the success with which the executive carries out the duties of the job, but at the present time there is little firm evidence that this aspect of assessment-center performance relates closely to the measures of executive effectiveness that have been used.

PERSONALITY CHARACTERISTICS OF BUSINESS LEADERS

In reading about the behavior of people in high executive positions one is often struck by the dynamic character of their style. The elan, social aggressiveness, and high levels of self-confidence that are often attributed to executives' activities suggest that they possess personality and motivational characteristics that are well structured and interesting. We have already considered the role of personality factors as predictors of executive success, and have found that when used in conjunction with a battery of psychological tests, personality measures do, in fact, contribute significantly to the prediction of management performance. Now we will take up studies of a more descriptive nature, which have attempted to present a picture of the personality characteristics that are most typical of those in executive positions. In considering these studies, one should realize that they all recognize the wide range of individual differences found among executives; obviously, business leaders are not all alike in personality structure. What these studies try to do is present a picture of the modal executive. As a consequence, they give us a picture of business leadership that is characteristic of many, not all, who hold these positions of corporate management.

The Need for Achievement

Research reported by W. E. Henry (1949) is a good place to begin our study of the personality of the business executive. This is probably the most frequently cited work in this area, and it has served as a point of departure for several investigations. In this study Henry administered a series of personality tests and short, undirected interviews to a group of successful business executives. These individuals were managers in positions of high responsibility, for whom there was general acknowledgment that their careers still held good prospects for further promotion. When they were asked to make up themes describing a series of pictures they had been shown, the stories constructed frequently involved people getting things done, achieving their objectives, or being thwarted in their attempts to do so. Henry interpreted these stories as reflecting a strong need for achievement, which he saw as a central part of the executive's personality makeup. The need for achievement (McClelland, 1961) is often thought of as one of the more potent motives that underlie social behavior. It is defined as a drive to reach a desired level of success in carrying out a task, and psychologists have been able to show that this drive is associated with many aspects of performance effectiveness.

Henry reports that for his group of successful executives, the drive to achieve did not focus on the consequences of achievement. The rewards and recognition one might receive as the result of hard work, although important, were not the principal components of this high-achievement drive. Rather, the primary investment appeared to be in the act of achieving itself. Getting things done, seeing one's hard work result in the successful completion of a task, is what appeared to lie at the foundation of the high-achievement needs expressed by this group of executives.

Henry's study does not represent an isolated set of results, for several other studies have reported similar findings. Veroff et al. (1960) found, for example, that compared to individuals in lower-status occupations, business managers displayed a higher need for achievement, and Meyer, Walker, and Sitivin (1961) have reported similar results in comparing groups of managers with groups of technical specialists. Cummin (1967), studying a sample of executives divided into successful and nonsuccessful groups on the basis of their income, reports that successful executives tend to show high need for achievement along with a high need for power.

On the basis of these results is it safe to characterize business managers as ambitious individuals? Probably yes, in the sense that this ambition is expressed as a commitment to advancement to positions that provide the manager with a broader field in which to satisfy the need to accomplish difficult goals. In adopting this point of view, however, one should not assume that the typical business executive is insensitive to financial and social rewards. This is not true, but the research does suggest that the business manager tends to be a person whose behavior reflects a strong commitment to getting things done, and this in and of itself is a fundamental component of the personality structure. Furthermore, there is evidence that this strong achievement need is not something that appears during the later years of the work career; rather, it is a characteristic that has been visible even during teenage years (Warner & Abegglen, 1955a).

The Need for Power

McClelland and Burnham (1976) argue that the nature of the achievement motive is such that it is not a major contributor to management effectiveness. They contend that a high-achievement drive leads individuals to seek accomplishments that can be carried out by themselves; it also requires frequent feedback concerning the effectiveness of performance. Neither of these conditions is characteristic of the typical executive's job. In the first place, executives tend to achieve their objectives through the efforts of others. Second, the feedback they receive is often infrequent and vague. As a consequence, high-achievement individuals would probably find the executive job quite uncongenial and would not be particularly effective, if they were placed in such a position.

McClelland contends that a principal motivational factor underlying executive behavior is a high need for power. In this context, he uses the concept of power in terms of having available the resources needed to influence other people. The need for power is a desire to have impact, to be strong and influential (McClelland, 1975; McClelland & Burnham, 1976), but this drive for power does not have self-enhancement as its primary objective. Rather, the effective executive's power motivation is restrained and inhibited, directed toward strengthening the organization. Hence, McClelland distinguishes between varieties of power motives, and it is those motives that are more altruistic that are of major importance to the behavior of the business executive. Finally, as a part of this general motivational pattern, McClelland contends that the effective executive does not show a high need for affiliation. That is to say, these executives do not require that they be liked by other people. They are able to deal with issues without being tangled up in the complications of the need to be liked.

In a project that measured the motivational scores of over fifty management personnel from a large company, McClelland & Burnham, (1976) found that over 70 percent of all executives scored high in the need for power. In addition, when the departments managed by these individuals were divided into high- and low-morale groups, it was discovered that the high-morale units were led by managers who scored very high on the need-for-power scale and relatively low in the need for affiliation. Hence, McClelland observed that effective managerial performance shows a high need for *institutional power,* coupled with low levels of interest in being liked by others. As a result, he emphasizes that the executive role involves the individual in a job that requires constant concern with social influence. In exerting this influence, however, the manager may draw on a number of different behavioral styles. In the majority of cases in which the executive appeared to be effective, this style was democratic in its form. Hence, one must recognize that in talking about power motivation, McClelland is not discussing a drive for personal power that will be used for self-aggrandizement. Rather, the power motive is a drive for social influence that expresses itself in democratic forms; the executive is more concerned with meeting organizational objectives than with being liked by those involved with the work.

Comment.   These are interesting results, and they represent an important extension of the traditional idea that the major source of motivational energy for company executives stems from a high-achievement need. Power is a visible and salient dimension of the executive's job, but this power is a social force that is needed to get things done. Furthermore, many social scientists who talk about executive achievement drives are careful to point out that this drive to achieve is not usually directed toward self-aggrandizement. Rather, it is a direct expression of the need to achieve for the sake of achievement. Recall that W. E. Henry (1949) reported that the executive's drive to achieve does not emphasize the personal consequences of achievement. It is instead, a direct expression of a drive to get things completed, and this drive is characteristic of the individual's life style from early years on. It is, therefore, reasonable to think about executive motivation in terms of a strong achievement drive coupled with a strong commitment to a necessary condition for achievement— the power needed to achieve one's objectives. Finally, it is probably not a difficult feat for the individual executive to perceive that the achievement of others is in reality a manifestation of the executive's effective leadership and influence. In short, it may be quite easy to interpret group accomplishments in terms of one's own personal achievement that stems from the effective use of the primary instruments of work, other people. There is need for more information regarding how executives view the achievements of their subordinates. How frequently, and under what conditions, do they interpret subordinate achievement as a manifestation of their own talents and influence?

Self-Concept.   How do business leaders see themselves? What is the nature of their self-concept? Henry (1949) maintains that successful leaders tend to display a strong self structure. By this he means that they tend not to deceive themselves regarding who they are and where they are going. This sense of self and direction tends to be strongly constituted, not easily disturbed by outside influences, and is often supported by a strategy of some sort that involves the means to achieve one's objectives. Coupled with this is a strong reality orientation that leads the executive to focus on things that are immediate and practical rather than distant and visionary. As a group, they also tend to display high confidence in their abilities (Larwood & Whittaker, 1977).

There is a possibility, however, that these self-conceptions may not always be accurate. For example, Rosen (1959) reports that many executives show a relative lack of insight into themselves and their motives, and a tendency to avoid deep self-analysis. Along these lines, Rosen reports that there is a reluctance on the part of many highly placed managers to try to see any connection between childhood experiences and relationships and their present behavior. Hence, there is the possibility that business leaders often present a picture of a strongly constituted and clearly held self-concept that tends to have a somewhat surface quality, beneath which the manager is reluctant to explore. We need more data in order to examine this hypothesis more carefully.

Fear of Failure.   In spite of the many facets of personality that reflect strength and commitment, Henry reports that underlying all this is a strong fear of failure. This seems to be a reasonable finding from a group of individuals who, with respect to their careers, tend to maintain few terminal goals. In achieving one objective highly mobile managers often continue to seek another still more difficult, and there is no vision of a point at which these strivings for higher position will be brought to an end. All this places an individual in a situation where personal risks are high and the consequences of failure may be psychologically disastrous. Thus, Henry finds a fear of losing one's grip and failing underlying a personality structure that otherwise suggests a person who is active and assertive.

Miner and Culver (1955) administered a personality scale to a group of executives and compared their responses to those of two control groups, one consisting of college professors and the other including persons from a wide variety of occupations from all parts of the country. In comparing groups it was found that the executives expressed anxiety concerning illness or injury with higher frequency, leading Miner and Culver to suggest that this apprehension was related to the same pervasive fear of failure noted by Henry. These authors see a fear of failure and a fear of the incapacities of illness and injury as stemming from the same psychological sources.

Warner, et al. (1963), in their study of executives in the federal service, found that these leaders often see themselves living in a high-pressure world filled with authority figures and demands that originate in many different places. Although they look positively at authority figures, conflicts do arise and the threat of failure is perceived as being ever-present. This concern about the prospects of failure can create considerable anxiety for the executive, and this is a type of apprehension that is often difficult to cope with.

Social Relations.   Henry's data indicate that business executives tend to relate to their superiors with a sense of personal attachment. Liking for one's superiors may not be an essential ingredient in the makeup of the successful executive, but a clear recognition of the career advantages to be found in their relationships with their superiors is found in many who hold positions of business leadership. While identifying with their superiors, however, successful executives tend to interact with their own subordinates in a fashion that is detached and impersonal. Subordinates are, in Henry's words, ''doers of work.'' They are elements in the career strivings of managers; and although managers tend to treat them in a constructive manner, they still do not show the strong attachment and identification they display to their superiors. The executives studied by Fisher (1976) did not appear to have much interest in being thought of as ''nice guys.'' Friendly relations with others was not an area of life that was of great concern to these successful business leaders. Jennings (1971) suggests that the mobile executive tends to look at work associates as important parameters in a career strategy that is calculated to move the individual upward.

Hence, we might describe the social relations found among high corporate leaders in utilitarian terms rather than in terms of friendship patterns; but in doing this, we should recognize the range of individual and situational differences that exist. For example, Coleman (1970) describes a group of successful executives in the farm-equipment industry as being trusting, free of jealousy, shy, and good team players. Rawls and Rawls (1968), on the other hand, describe a group of successful executives in a utility company as being competitive, manipulative, and opportunistic in dealing with others.

Pruden's Study. Pruden (1973) maintains that there are three basic patterns of the adjustment managers make to the social requirements of the large bureaucratic organization. Drawing on a model presented by Presthus (1962), Pruden presents evidence suggesting that managers tend to fit one of three categories that describe their efforts to adapt to the social system of work. The first type, called the upward-mobile, involves the kind of behaviors characteristic of those we have been describing as successful executives. These individuals tend to see those in authority as constructive influences whose conduct serves as a model and whose career success is greatly admired. Individuals in this category tend to adopt uncritically the rules that govern the organization. Loyalty to the system and to those who administer it is a highly developed characteristic of the upward-mobile person.

A second type, the indifferent, refers to individuals who see the central components of their lives as lying outside the work setting. These are persons who have been more or less turned off by the requirements of the job, and as a consequence, they tend to reject the status and financial rewards

that it holds out to those who display more interest in their work. These are "eight to fivers," whose careers have little promise for upward movement. The third group, the ambivalents, consists of persons who can not accept the authoritarian aspects of the organization, but who, for one reason or another, are unable to reject the rewards that it offers the loyalist. The ambivalent experiences great problems in trying to relate to authority figures, and is often found challenging the rationality of a system that depends on rules that are justified on authoritarian principles.

Pruden (1973) identified five variables that can be used to differentiate individuals who fall in one or the other of Presthus's categories, and Table 14.5 summarizes the pattern that is characteristic of each type. There are several terms in the table that may require interpretation before we consider the results of a study that was done to evaluate this model. For instance, Alienation (Blauner, 1964) refers to the extent to which individuals feel estranged from some significant aspect of their lives. Alienated persons would tend to report such things as feeling that the job was meaningless or that they had little power in dealing with the important elements of the job. Cosmopolitanism (Gouldner, 1958a, 1958b) refers to a set of attitudes that vary between two poles. At one pole there are local attitudes found in individuals who identify with the values, beliefs, and practices that operate in their own work organizations, whereas the cos-

TABLE 14.5   Ideal and Actual Patterns of Accommodation for Upward Mobiles, Indifferents, and Ambivalents

Variable	Ideal Patterns			Observed Patterns		
	Upward Mobiles	Indifferents	Ambivalents	Upward Mobiles	Indifferents	Ambivalents
Job Satisfaction	High	High	Low	High	High	Low
Career Anchorage	High	Low	Medium	High	Low	Medium
Alienation	Low	Medium	High	Low	Medium	High
Cosmopolitanism	Low	Medium	High	Low	High	Medium
Organization Rank	High	Low	Medium	High	Low	High

Source: Pruden, H. O. The upward mobile, indifferent and ambivalent typology of managers. *Academy of Management Journal*, 1973, *16*, 454–464. Copyright 1973 by the Academy of Management.

mopolitan tends to identify with the values, beliefs, and practices that are found in groups outside the work organization. Cosmopolitan research scientists, for example, may more closely identify with their professional organizations than with the companies that employ them. Career Anchorage refers to an idea developed by Tausky and Dubin (1965) that concerns the point of reference individuals use to evaluate past career successes and frame their aspirations for future achievement. Pruden uses "high career anchorage" to refer to persons who consider their careers in terms of some future peak level of occupational success toward which they strive. A low-anchorage orientation describes persons who see their careers in terms of the mobility that has already been experienced since their entry into the work world. Hence, one orientation, high anchorage, perceives a career in terms of upward progress yet to be made, whereas the other orientation perceives the career in terms of progress already made.

Pruden administered to a large group of management persons a battery of scales that measured each of the five variables represented in Table 14.5. For each of Presthus's three types he predicted the pattern of scores one would expect from these five scales. (These patterns are presented in Table 14.5 under the column headed "Ideal Patterns.") Applying special statistical procedures to the data, he found that he could construct three distinct groups of managers on the basis of the pattern of the scores they made, and by comparing these "obtained patterns" with the "ideal patterns," Pruden found that his managers tended to fall into groups that were very similar to those talked about by Presthus. This, of course, gives Presthus's ideas some welcomed support, but for our purposes it indicates that it might be useful to think of management people as adapting to the social demands of their work in these three general ways. A single view of the business leader as an individual who is upwardly mobile in Presthus's terms may be accurate for many, but Pruden's data suggest that one should be prepared to find, among the ranks of management, individuals who represent the indifferent and the ambivalent types. The

hard-driving team player may be found most frequently in the ranks of business managers, but the eight-to-fiver and the nonauthoritarian were both well represented in Pruden's sample of managers.

Machiavellianism. Immersion in an active and competitive social world, linked with a persistent ambition to get ahead, is likely to encourage behaviors that are Machiavellian. From the perspective of the more popular descriptions of the executive type, it is very easy to include in this image tendencies to be devious, narrowly self-serving, and manipulative. Yet Gemmill and Heisler (1972) report that they could find no relationship between upward mobility and Machiavellian orientation. Apparently, according to their data, the manipulator, the individual who maintains shifting personal loyalty to ideology and principle, does not enjoy greater occupational bouyancy than does the individual whose management career is non-Machiavellian. The Machiavellian does, however, report higher levels of job strain in the form of tensions and anxieties, and also lower levels of satisfaction with work, than does the executive who less frequently adopts a Machiavellian posture. Hence, we must reserve judgment regarding this aspect of the business leader's approach to social relations until more data are available. On the one hand, many of the characteristics frequently associated with the executive would lead one to think of them as being manipulative and opportunistic. On the other hand, Gemmill and Heisler's study indicates that this inference may well be a false one.

MANAGEMENT MOTIVATION AND JOB SATISFACTION

A question of some interest to those who study work is whether there are motivational differences between persons at different levels of management. More specifically, what personal goals do people in high management positions seek, and how do these goals differ from those held by others in lower positions? A related question concerns the reports of job satisfaction one obtains from individuals located in different positions up and down the organizational ladder. This involves not only whether executives report more or less satisfaction with work, but how they differ from others with respect to the sources of job satisfaction and dissatisfaction.

We have already seen that the need for achievement appears to figure prominently in the motivational system of the upwardly mobile executive. Also, a strong commitment to work and social assertiveness seem to describe the drive underlying much executive performance. In view of this, one may wonder whether these patterns of motivation change as a manager moves up in the organization. Do the demands of each successive level require that the manager draw on different sources of motivation and strive for different goals? From what we know about the changing role requirements of management positions that are found at different levels, it does not appear to be completely unreasonable to expect that executives' personal goals will change as they go from one management level to the next. Yet the studies that deal directly with this question do not give us a great deal of support for this point of view.

Rosen and Weaver (1960), for example, attempted to determine what managers want from their work, and whether these goals change as one moves up the company hierarchy. They administered a questionnaire to four levels of management personnel in a large company. This questionnaire asked individuals to report how important various aspects of the work were to them, and on the basis of the responses to this instrument, Rosen and Weaver concluded that the men in the four managerial levels assess the importance of job conditions in much the same manner. These researchers suggest that one can legitimately talk about management as a relatively cohesive class of persons who share common motives regarding what they want from their jobs. They further contend that as one moves from level to level in the organization, little variation may be expected in the pattern of motives that underlie the work behaviors observed.

A different view emerges, however, when one looks at the extent to which levels of management are able to satisfy these motives. Rosen (1961)

asked the same sample of executives the extent to which a set of desirable working conditions existed in different management levels. Now we find that differences do begin to appear among the four management levels. In general, those in lower positions reported that there were fewer rewards available to them in their work environments than were reported by those in higher management positions. Hence, managers appeared to vary but little in their perceptions of working conditions thought to be desirable, but managers at different levels did differ with regard to the rewards they saw as being available to them.

Along similar lines, Porter has reported two studies (1961, 1962) in which he asked groups of managers to report on their perceptions of deficiencies in opportunity for need satisfaction in their jobs. In one study (1962) he asked questions of this sort of almost two thousand managers who were classified into five levels, ranging from first-line supervisor to president. Across each level he further classified his respondents into four age groups. In both studies his results indicated that as one moves down the management hierarchy there appears to be an increase in the reports of deficiencies in opportunity to fulfill psychological needs. This finding was particularly evident when managers were considering the need for esteem, autonomy, and self-actualization. These findings, when viewed along with Rosen's, suggest that as individuals move up the organizational hierarchy, there is a good likelihood that they will find themselves in jobs that are psychologically more congenial. On the other hand, Porter (1963a,b), like Weaver and Rosen, found substantially less variation among organizational levels with respect to managers' reports on the personal importance of certain needs. When considering social needs and needs for security and esteem, individuals at five different management levels seemed to agree on the relative importance of these needs. Greater importance, however, was attached to the need for self-actualization and the need for autonomy by individuals found at higher levels of management. Therefore, on the basis of these studies we might speculate that individuals found in management positions do tend to be somewhat homogeneous in terms of the psychological needs they see as being important to them. Although Porter noted some variation when he compared first-line supervisors with company presidents, there still seems to be considerable agreement among managers with re-gard to what they see as being psychologically im-portant. When one passes from one level of the organization to the next, however, there appears to be considerable variation in the extent to which individuals report that their needs are being met adequately. The higher the management position, the greater the prospects that it contains working conditions that are satisfying.

Little is known about how men and women ex-ecutives differ in motivational characteristics. Studies of work incentives have shown that there are sex differences in how people evaluate the im-portance of rewards, but most of these studies have been carried out with production workers. The problems in doing research on this subject are ob-vious; there are too few women in executive po-sitions. We are fortunate in having one study by Herrick (1973) in which men and women execu-tives in governmental jobs were compared in terms of their perceptions of need deficiencies. The re-sults of this study indicate that although there were some small differences noted between the two groups, by and large, men and women executives presented quite similar reports. In a related study, Morrison and Sebold (1974), after comparing women executives and nonexecutives, concluded that the motives that appeared to be prominent in the lives of the women executives were similar to those found in studies of male executives. There-fore, in talking about the motivational character-istics of high-level management personnel, sex does not seem to be a factor that substantially in-fluences the general pattern of motives found to be underlying job behaviors. Since this literature is not very extensive, however, we should withhold making a firm commitment to this position until more research has been reported.

Executive Roles

Thus far we have been concentrating on the personality characteristics and motives of those who hold high management positions, and without question these variables do play an important part in determining the style of leadership observed. It is apparent, however, that managers do not adopt an approach to their jobs solely on the basis of their own psychological makeup. The entire social group—subordinates, peers, and superiors—con-tributes a significant source of influence that shapes the behaviors found in a management po-sition. All expect the leader to carry out certain functions. Many expect the leader to perform these functions in a fashion deemed appropriate for that position. Organizations maintain norms that reg-ulate the conduct of the principal officers, and these normative influences must be taken into con-sideration by anyone studying business leadership.

There is not much information available con-cerning these social expectations as they apply to high-ranking officers. There is one report, how-ever, that sheds some interesting light on this sub-ject. DeSola-Pool (1964), in a study of business activities in organizations involved in international trade, surveyed over nine hundred top business executives in order to obtain a picture of the kind of activities they carried out on their jobs. In plan-ning this study, DeSola-Pool and her associates anticipated that these business activities would be correlated with such conventional variables as the age, education, political affiliation, and personal-ity of the executive officer. DeSola-Pool states, however, "All these variables turned out to have some significance in the study. But in sheer mag-nitude they were all swamped by another variable . . . the man's role as head of the firm" (DeSola-Pool, 1964, p. 148). In other words, the manner in which the executives approached their jobs was to some small extent related to their social back-ground, education, and psychological makeup. The activities of these officers could best be pre-dicted, however, from knowledge of the firm's definition of their jobs and the role they were ex-pected to play as head of the organization. Differ-ences reflecting psychological and social back-ground were found, but a more significant determinant of the executive's activities was a role that originated in the expectations of other mem-bers of the firm.

For example, an executive's foreign travel, both for business and recreation, was not highly related to education, income, or attitudes. Rather, junkets abroad were taken because of business demands and *because status considerations required them.* When it came time for vacationing, excursions abroad were considered the thing to do for an individual in a position of such high status. According to DeSola-Pool, the fact that a person was the head of a firm told much more about the kind of behavior that would be displayed than did any of the background and personality measures that were available on this leader.

We need much more work in this area; not that there is a paucity of research dealing with role concepts and group norms, but there is disappointingly little available concerning the roles and role expectations of persons in high management positions. We must understand better the circle of social influences that surround those who lead, and put ourselves in a position to calculate the extent of the demands and restrictions these place on behavior. Until we do, our understanding of the business leader will be incomplete.

Executive Stress

There is a popular belief that the jobs of company executives expose them to high levels of stress. Both in the jobs themselves and in the personality of the individuals who are attracted to these positions factors that create high tensions can be found. Schoonmaker (1969) sees interpersonal conflict and competition as a significant source of tension in the executive's job environment. To some major degree the social climate found in many management groups is one that involves people in competition for scarce resources. For example, E. E. Jennings (1971) argues that as a group, executives display a keen interest in upward mobility. Promotion into positions of higher power and prominence is a focal point of the career strategy pursued by large numbers of executives, and this drive for mobility underlies the high commitment to hard work and long hours that is frequently characteristic of this group. To move up in the organization becomes an end in itself, but the consequence of this orientation is to create a social climate in which executives are thrown into competition with each other for the small number of positions at the top of each organization.

Since promotion requires the support of others, interpersonal relations become vitally important to the career aspirations of the upward-bound manager. Social contacts, whether with peers or superiors, assume an intensely functional character as they enter into these mobility strategies, and in day-to-day affairs aspiring executives become extremely sensitive to the social feedback they receive concerning their standing in this competition. There is relatively little reliability, however, in the feedback from work associates. One day the cues appear to be positive, the next day doubts are raised. This is a situation in which stress and anxiety are likely happenings.

The conditions that give rise to work-related tensions are frequently described in terms of role concepts. Role overload, as an example, refers to a situation in which the individual is faced with tasks too numerous to complete in the time available. The separate obligations may be well within the person's general range of competence, but their excessive number confronts the individual with work that is always incomplete. This is a complaint often heard from individuals who occupy positions of executive prominence.

Other role difficulties have been studied in connection with the appearance of psychological stress. Role conflict, a situation where a person is faced with contradictory and incompatible obligations, has been correlated with reports of tension (Kahn, 1974). Role ambiguity, a discrepancy between the amount of information needed and the amount available to do a job, has also been shown to relate to psychological tensions. Finally, role responsibility, that is, accountability for other people's welfare, has been shown to be linked with such stress-induced disorders as peptic ulcer, high blood pressure, and diabetes (Cobb, 1974).

Executives and Stress Symptoms

At the beginning of the chapter we described the job conditions found to be characteristic of high management positions. From these descriptions it is easy to see that the work of the business manager involves all the role overload, responsibility, and so on that studies have linked to stress symptoms. Hence, we might expect to find a high incidence of stress-related disorders among executives. Yet there is no clear evidence that this is the case. Flemming (1962), for example, reports two studies performed at Du Pont, both of which discovered no significant differences between executives and nonexecutives in the incidence of stress-related disorders such as ulcers and high blood pressure. McLean (1960) contends that there is no substantial evidence indicating that executives suffer a higher incidence of emotional illness, in spite of the fact that the manager's job contains many factors that are stressful. We have previously presented evidence (Rosen, 1961; Porter, 1962) that suggests that higher levels of management report greater job satisfaction, and we can even find evidence that executives as a group tend to live longer than individuals in the general population (Metropolitan Life Insurance, 1974).

Hence, although they may be exposed to considerable stress, business executives do not appear to present a picture of an inordinately high level of stress-related symptoms. McLean (1960) maintains that persons in higher positions are better able to cope with the stresses and strains of work than those at lower occupational positions. French (1974) suggests that job pressures translate into stress reactions mainly when there is an absence of fit between the individual and the job, and presents some research evidence that supports this point of view. As a consequence, job pressures alone do not ensure the development of tension states. Rather, job pressures taken together with the abilities and personality of the jobholder create the conditions that produce stress reactions. French also maintains that the interconnections among job conditions, personal characteristics, and psychological stress are often very specific in nature. By this he means that a specific personality structure interacting with a particular condition of job pressure produces a specific variety of stress. To understand the stresses and tension experienced by those in executive positions, one must consider both the sources of pressures and the personality and competencies of the jobholder.

We need much more information before we can draw any significant generalization regarding executive stress, but for the moment we can set aside the popular notions that the life of the business executive is beset by tensions and anxieties that exceed those of other jobholders. There is no question but that there are real and substantial pressures found in the work that executives do, but for reasons that have not been completely determined, business managers do not present us with a picture of being burdened with great psychological stress. If anything, they are healthier and more satisfied with their work than are those below them, and in what appears to be an added reward for their success, they tend to outlive those who serve under them.

SUMMARY COMMENTS

In considering the business executive we found an active and rather extensive literature on the subject, but in most instances the amount of research available on any one question is not adequate to permit any firm conclusions. From this literature it is clear, however, that the positions held by many high-level management persons are fundamentally social-political in their nature. High-level managers tend to operate in an intensely social world that requires persuasion, decision making, delegation, negotiating, rewarding, dominating, and a long list of other social skills to deal with the tangle of interpersonal relations that make up a large portion of their day. The job often consists of a series of relatively brief social encounters, and at not too infrequent times executives report that their jobs permit insufficient time for reading and contemplation. Often there are not enough hours in the day to complete all that is expected of them.

It is the substantial social aspects of this work that seem to figure into the recruitment, selection, and training of individuals who move up through the organization to high management positions. Executive ranks tend to be filled primarily by individuals who have middle-class, white-collar social origins. Educational attainment is usually quite high, and many enter the middle stages of their careers before they emerge at or near the top of the organization. Their promotion involves job performance, but since job performance is so heavily weighted with social competencies, personality factors and personal values can have a significant influence on the movement of people up the organization. Among other factors sometimes mentioned as influencing the individual's chances of promotion to executive position are social origin and education. Some authors lay emphasis on interpersonal competence, while others say much depends on the way the budding manager looks at his job. Also, some acknowledge the role luck plays in career success. But whatever the combination of factors involved, one should always take into consideration the broader dynamics of the organization in which the manager works. The transfer of power in an organization is of such obvious importance to all who work there that the promotional system must be viewed as an operation that takes into consideration more than a fit between job duties and an aspirant's abilities.

The personality characteristics popularly associated with people in executive positions give emphasis to a dynamic and assertive style of behavior, and to some considerable extent these conceptions are supported by the research literature. For instance, there seems to be some good evidence that a high need for achievement is one personality dimension of the typical business leader. Jennings (1972) even contends that the business executive is "mastered by a single force." By this he refers to a strong drive to achieve through involvement in increasingly challenging tasks. Many, however, see underlying an exterior that appears to be strong and self-confident an undercurrent of anxiety that originates in a generalized fear of failure that many executives possess.

The so-called higher needs (Maslow, 1943) are often thought of as being of greater psychological importance to those in executive positions. A striving to maintain a competent grasp on the things that go on around them and an effort to engage in tasks that provide the individual with a sense of fulfillment are considered to be important sources of motivation. Self-actualization is the term probably used most frequently to describe a complex of motives that appear to underlie much executive performance. And although no one would deny the motivational importance of pay and social status, still many see executive motivation as more significantly influenced by these higher-psychological-need systems.

Finally, although all would admit that the business executive's job can, at times, place a person under considerable pressure, there seems to be no convincing evidence that these pressures typically result in emotional difficulties or psychosomatic disorders. What evidence there is suggests that executives report greater need fulfillment and higher job satisfaction than do those lower in the organization. As a group they tend to be relatively healthy, and to live longer than the average person in the population.

Little has been said in this chapter concerning the general process of leadership. Obviously, leadership is a central obligation of the business executive; the literature on this topic is so extensive (cf. Stogdill, 1974), however, that a separate chapter has been presented dealing with the business and industrial aspects of this process.

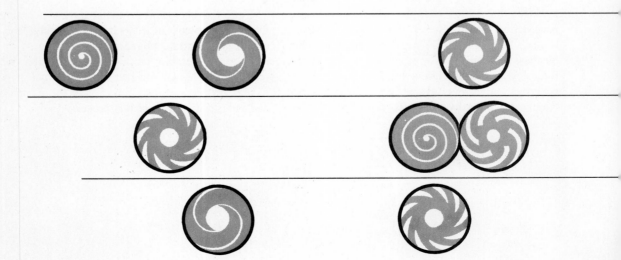

5
CHANGING CONDITIONS OF WORK

15
Work and Technological Change

The high rates of change to which modern societies have been exposed is a fact of living that has received considerable attention in the social science literature. Social analysts find themselves seeking terms that can adequately express the compelling, and at times psychologically costly, demands that are placed on the individual by conditions that are always in a state of transition. Revolutionary is the term most frequently applied to the process of change, and shock is a term often used to describe its impact on the individual.

The factors underlying social change have always been quite difficult to isolate. Some variables seem to function as both causes and effects, and their complex nature makes it difficult to subject them to experimental tests. Population growth, mass urbanization, changing patterns of poverty and wealth are just a few of the more significant factors involved in this changing social world. Of all the agents of change, however, none is recognized as being more potent than the rapidly expanding progress that has been taking place in science and technology. Scientific and technological innovations have had great impact on virtually every facet of society, and this is never more true than when one is considering the conditions under which people work.

As the result of technological advancement, much (although by no means all) of the drudgery of work has been eliminated. The machine has assumed much of the responsibility for the stooping, digging, carrying, and lifting that had been a burdensome part of many jobs. Product quality, a consideration that was traditionally associated with craftsmanship, now is often sought in a set of engineering specifications that build quality into the performance of a machine. A growing number of people now find themselves monitoring the work of a machine rather than carrying out the work themselves, and many problems that previously had given work a significant mental component now are solved by electronic devices that require only a relatively simple manipulation of controls.

Technological innovation has changed the structure of the labor force, just as it has altered the content of individual jobs. For example, in 1960, of those individuals classified as "professional, technical, and kindred" workers, fewer than 2 in 1000 were computer specialists. In 1970 approximately 24 in every 1000 were computer specialists. Between 1960 and 1970 there was a 246 percent increase in systems analysts and an almost 6000 percent increase in the number of clerical workers who operate computers and their related equipment (Dicesare, 1975). Rezler (1969) points out that of the 21,741 jobs included in the 1965 edition of the *Dictionary of Occupational Titles,* 6432 were not in the earlier 1949 edition. The new fourth edition (U.S. Government Printing Office, 1977) contains 2100 new jobs, but 3500 old jobs disappeared from the occupational rolls.

We see, then, that the structure of the job market has been undergoing significant alteration; old jobs have been eliminated, new jobs have been created, and existing jobs have been modified, all in response to a changing technology.

In this chapter we will try to deal briefly with the employment consequences of technological change, but of primary concern to us will be the social and psychological implications of these changes. Technology has generated influences to which large numbers of employed persons have had to adjust. The insecurities of unemployment, the uncertainties of adapting to new work requirements, the need for retraining, and the fear of obsolescence have all become a real part of an increasing number of work careers. Today, it would be unwise for a person to embark on a new work career without anticipating the necessity of making a significant adjustment, at one time or another, to the changes brought about by technological innovations.

There is another aspect of technological change that we will consider, and that is the very significant transformations that have been taking place in the content of jobs. Great concern has been expressed that technology has been restructuring jobs and robbing them of much of the content that previously gave the individual meaningful and challenging work. Job specialization of the type characterized by assembly-line operations, endless hours of monitoring the control panels of highly automated equipment, machine-tending chores, all represent work that is often seen as being psychologically unrewarding. In contrast to the creation of jobs that are psychologically empty, technology has also required from some workers more complicated understandings and knowledge. Engineering requirements have become more complicated and demanding, maintenance jobs have increased in numbers and in their technical requirements, and along with all this, there has occurred what is reported to be a polarization of workers into large groups of low-status, semiskilled operatives and smaller groups of high-status technical elites. Hence, we can see that the implications of technological change are extensive, ranging from problems of unemployment and employee obsolescence, through a whole catalog of psychological considerations, to modifications in the social structure of the work environment. It is the purpose of this present chapter to look into the research literature to learn something about the social and psychological consequences of changes that are introduced into the work environment by technological innovation.

TECHNOLOGY AND THE LABOR FORCE

It is a very difficult task to isolate the effects of technological change on conditions of work. Usually, when new technological procedures and equipment are introduced, there are other changes being made in the work at the same time. Bright (1958), for example, found that when a company invests in new automatic equipment, it often changes some aspect of the product being made, and as a consequence, it is impossible to separate out the effects of the new technology from the effects resulting from changes in product design. For similar reasons the employment consequences of new technologies are difficult to isolate. Some argue that technical innovation has resulted in loss of jobs and a substantial displacement of workers to other positions. Others argue that new technology creates job opportunities and should be viewed as a positive influence on the level of employment. There are aspects of each argument that are probably correct, but since we are usually not able to separate the effects of technological change from other changes taking place in the economy, it is impossible to bring these two arguments to final resolution.

The best we can do for the moment is to look at some of the more significant changes that have been taking place in the structure of the job market and assume that these changes do, to some degree or other, reflect the influence of technological innovation. This assumption seems reasonable in view of the fact that the motive frequently found underlying management's decision to install new automated equipment deals directly with the cost and availability of labor. As a case in point, Bright (1958) reports that a principal motive behind the introduction of new technology is found in management's interest in reducing labor costs and increasing the efficiency of production. In these instances the connection between technology and the number of people employed is a direct one. Whenever production efficiency increases and is not accompanied by a comparable increase in the demand for a product, then there is a reduced need for workers.

Production Efficiency and Employment Levels

Over the years there have been impressive achievements in improving the production efficiency of workers. Productivity, measured in terms of output per hour worked, grew at a rate of 3 percent per year from 1947 to 1973 (Kutscher, Mark, & Norsworthy, 1977), and in some industries these increases in efficiency have been accompanied by a reduction in the number of persons employed. A dramatic case in point is found in coal mining. Over the years the coal industry has made substantial investments in new techniques that have integrated the cutting and loading of coal into one continuous procedure that requires considerably less labor. As a consequence of these innovations, 1947 production levels could be achieved in 1961 with 54 percent fewer workers. In one area, bituminous coal mining, employment rolls decreased from 426,000 in 1947 to 145,000 in 1961 (U.S. Department of Labor, 1963), a drop of two-thirds in the number of workers employed.

Agriculture offers us another example of an industry in which there has been a steady decline in the number employed, accompanied by an impressive increase in the level of production; railroads have reported similar experiences. One could cite other examples, but the main point is that throughout the past several decades a number of industries have experienced a drop in the number of workers employed, accompanied by an increase in the amount of goods produced. Of course, there are many factors that have combined to create these conditions, but in spite of this, it is reasonably safe to argue that in a large number of these industries technology has made a substantial contribution to improved production efficiency.

Changes in Occupational Groupings

Perhaps the best view of the changes that are taking place in the occupational structure of the job market can be gained from looking at the shifting percentages of workers in the major occupational groupings. A comparison of 1960 and 1970 data reveals that the occupational structure of the labor market has been tending in the direction of a significant increase in the number of persons employed in white-collar jobs (see Table 15.1). White-collar employment during this period rose to account for almost 46 percent of the labor force, while there was a 3 percent drop in blue-collar employment and a drop of over 3 percent in the number of farm workers. During the years following 1970 white-collar employment continued to increase until today one out of every two persons employed works in a white-collar job.

The Service Sector.   One of the most significant changes that has taken place in the structure of occupational fields is found in the substantial increase in the number of people employed in service-dispensing, as opposed to production-generating, positions. If one were to trace the growth in the number of service jobs found in such areas as transportation, public utilities, finance, insurance, travel, entertainment, health, and education, one would find that this segment of the labor force has increased in size until at present more than half of all people employed can be classified in one or another of these service categories. Over the years, therefore, we find that work has shifted in its characteristics from an activity with the central focus on the production of goods to an activity with the delivery of services as the modal concern.

A Post-industrial Society

The sociologist Daniel Bell (1973) maintains that the emergence of this large service sector re-

TABLE 15.1   Percentage Distribution of Employment, by Major
Occupational Group, 1960 and 1970

Occupational Group	1960	1970
Total	100.0	100.0
White-collar workers	40.8	45.6
Professional, technical, and kindred workers	10.8	14.0
Managers and administrators, except farm	3.7	7.9
Salesworkers	7.2	6.8
Clerical and kindred workers	14.1	16.9
Blue-collar workers	36.5	33.4
Craft and kindred workers	13.8	12.9
Operatives, except transport	13.6	12.7
Transport equipment operatives	3.9	3.6
Laborers, except farm	5.1	4.2
Farm workers	6.2	2.9
Farmers and farm managers	3.9	1.7
Farm laborers and supervisors	2.3	1.2
Service workers	11.6	11.8
Service workers, except private household	8.9	10.4
Private household workers	2.7	1.4

NOTE: Percentages do not add to total because "occupation not reported" cases were excluded.

From Dicesare, C. B. Changes in the occupational structure of U.S. jobs. *Monthly Labor Review*, 1975, 98(3), 24–34.

flects the fact that the United States is fast becoming what he calls a *post-industrial society*. Bell identifies three stages in the social-technical evolution of social systems. The earliest stage, the *pre-industrial society*, is characterized by a labor force involved primarily in harvesting the basic raw materials that are required for life. In such societies the bulk of the labor force is engaged in agriculture, fishing, mining, and forestry. Production efficiency tends to be quite low, in part as the result of a technology that relies on human energy to achieve production objectives.

An *industrial society* is one in which the principal concern of the labor force is with the production of goods. Manufacturing is a central activity. In this social setting the machine, powered by nonhuman energy, is an expression of a technology that is geared to achieve efficient production. Here one finds bureaucratic organizations engaging in the coordination of production activities that become increasingly specialized as the machine technology seeks to achieve higher and higher levels of efficiency.

The *post-industrial society* represents a third stage, which emerges from an increasingly more sophisticated technology. It emerges, in part, as a function of a more efficient system of production that is capable of meeting a society's needs for goods, while at the same time requiring a decreasing amount of human labor. As this scientific and technical development continues, the service sector begins to account for a growing portion of the available resources; and knowledge, rather than human energy, becomes a central requirement of work. A growing group of technically educated elites assumes a central role in the economic and political life of the society, and problem solving and planning become a critical and high-status activity. Efficiency is achieved through the coordination of the activities of people, rather than the functioning of machines, and highly specialized groups of professionals are brought under a system of bureaucratic control.

It is Bell's thesis that developments in science and technology are producing profound changes in the pattern of work, both in terms of where people work and the kind of work they do. The emergence of the post-industrial society represents a fundamental structural change that will have significant influence, both on social institutions and on the life style of each individual. At work, traditional production skills that involve physical dexterity and practical knowledge will give way to an emphasis on knowledge of a more abstract and theoretical nature. Higher-order problem solving—that is, the development of problem-solving systems of the type found in computer programs, operations research, and decision-making models—will draw on workers' ability to deal with concepts that are abstract and difficult. Finally, and perhaps most significant of all, mental work, an area of human activity that traditionally has been carried out in a free and unstructured climate, will be performed by groups operating within the constraints of bureaucratic organizations. The intellectual freedom that has been considered an essential condition for creative mental work will be increasingly controlled by organizational rules.

Occupational Mobility

Paralleling this picture of change in the occupational structure of the labor market is another picture that suggests a dramatic shift in the occupational mobility of the American labor force. Sommers and Eck (1977) analyzed data from the 1970 Census and discovered that almost one-third (32.2 percent) of the persons working in 1965 had changed to a new *occupation* by 1970. Bear in mind that this means that within a five-year period one-third of the labor force made a change that involved moving to a new occupational category, not just changing jobs and taking on similar duties with a new employer. During this period, out of all the reasons for an individual's separation from a job, occupational transfer accounted for the largest number. Transfers into new occupations also accounted for more people entering a particular occupation than did new labor-force entrants. Of the workers responding in 1965, only 44.8 percent were still holding jobs in the same occupation when they participated in the 1970 census.

All this indicates that the area of our lives that is occupied by work has been subject to the same kinds of substantial changes that have occurred in other aspects of social living. The Sommers and Eck data also indicate that these changes cannot be explained solely in terms of the entry of a new generation of employees who are coming into the labor force with different kinds of education, training, and career aspirations. Rather, these data indicate that the experienced work force is demonstrating a very high rate of mid-career occupational mobility. To what extent these data reflect efforts to improve one's job by changing occupations, to what extent they reflect discontentment with jobs, or to what extent they indicate the influence of a changing technology that is displacing workers into new occupations are questions that cannot be answered. But regardless of the pattern of causes, these employment statistics suggest that for a growing number of workers, a work career includes a change in occupational classification.

Psychological Consequences

The psychological impact of a job change, let alone a change in occupation, is difficult to measure. Intuition tells us, however, that such a move often requires a major psychological readjustment, and there is some experimental evidence that tends to substantiate this. Holmes and Masuda (1973) report a study in which subjects were asked to rate the psychological impact of a variety of changes they had experienced. Marriage served as a reference point, being given a change score of 50, and other changes were given ratings in relation to this reference point. Table 15.2 shows the ratings given to a list of life changes. Notice that "change to a different line of work" was judged as having an impact on people that is quite similar to that experienced with the death of a close friend. Occupational change was rated as having greater psychological significance than such things as trouble with one's boss, death of a close friend, the foreclosure of a mortgage, and a son or daughter leaving home.

In a series of related studies, Paykel and his associates (Paykel, 1969; Paykel, 1973) interviewed a group of people suffering from acute psychological depression and another group drawn from the general population who were free from these symptoms. Each person was asked to relate happenings that took place in their lives, depressive subjects being asked to describe the events that took place six months prior to the beginning of their depression, the other subjects describing events taking place during the six months prior to the interview. These interviews indicated that change of all varieties was a factor found more

TABLE 15.2   Social Readjustment Rating Scale

Rank	Life event	Mean Value
1	Death of spouse	100
2	Divorce	73
3	Marital separation	65
4	Jail term	63
5	Death of close family member	63
6	Personal injury or illness	53
7	Marriage	50
8	Fired at work	47
9	Marital reconciliation	45
10	Retirement	45
11	Change in health of family member	44
12	Pregnancy	40
13	Sexual difficulties	39
14	Gain of new family member	39
15	Business readjustment	39
16	Change in financial state	38
17	Death of close friend	37
18	Change to different line of work	36
19	Change in number of arguments with spouse	35
20	Mortgage of over $10,000	31
21	Foreclosure of mortgage or loan	30
22	Change in responsibilities at work	29
23	Son or daughter leaving home	29
24	Trouble with in-laws	29
25	Outstanding personal achievement	28
26	Wife begin or stop work	26
27	Begin or end school	26
28	Change in living conditions	25
29	Revision of personal habits	24
30	Trouble with boss	23
31	Change in work hours or conditions	20
32	Change in residence	20
33	Change in schools	20
34	Change in recreation	19
35	Change in church activities	19
36	Change in social acitvities	18
37	Mortgage or loan less than $10,000	17
38	Change in sleeping habits	16
39	Change in number of family get-togethers	15
40	Change in eating habits	15
41	Vacation	13
42	Christmas	12
43	Minor violations of the law	11

From Holmes and Rahe, 1967, Table 3, p. 216. In J. P. Scott & E. C. Senay, *Separation and depression.* Washington, D.C.: American Association for the Advancement of Science, 1973. Copyright 1973 by the American Association for the Advancement of Science.

frequently in the lives of the depressed individuals than in the lives of those who were not burdened with these problems. Two of the areas of highest incidence were "start of a new type of work" and "change in work conditions." Hence, these results give us some insight into the possible psychological costs that are associated with the changes that take place in the vocational areas of an individual's life. The rapid rate with which people seem to be changing jobs may exact a high cost in terms of their emotional adjustment; therefore, we might measure some of the cost of technological change from this perspective.

Job Displacement and Unemployment

One of the major concerns surrounding technological change has been its effects on the level of unemployment. Numerous writers have voiced apprehension regarding the possibility that new technology creates a general reduction in the need for workers. A related concern is found in the belief that changes taking place in the technology of work are raising the level of skills required to hold a job. It is felt by some that technology tends to increase the skill demands of many jobs, thus creating a condition that is virtually insoluble for less able workers. As automatic equipment displaces these unskilled workers, there are fewer jobs remaining in the labor market that they can satisfactorily fill. As a result, there will be a growing number of people who are not just unemployed, but who are, in fact, unemployable. Hence, we find that we must deal with two questions, one concerning the changes in skill demands brought on by technology, and a related second question concerning the effects of technological innovation on the levels of employment-unemployment found in the labor market.

Macroeconomic Changes in Employment

On the highest macroeconomic level we find that the labor market has been growing over the years, not only in terms of the absolute number of people employed but also in terms of the percentage of the population holding jobs. For example,

the U.S. Department of Labor (1977; Young, 1979) reports data that show a steady rise in the percentage of the noninstitutional population in the labor force. In 1947 about 59 percent of the population was found in the labor force, in 1969 about 61 percent, and in 1977 this figure had risen to 68 percent. As the years progress, therefore, the labor market seems to be taking in an increasing proportion of the population. Hence, over years that have witnessed a significant rise in the introduction of new work technology, there has been an overall increase in the rate of participation in work. Yet, with the exception of a few years (mainly those during which the United States was involved in the Korean and Vietnam Wars), unemployment has varied between 5 and 8 percent of the labor force (U.S. Department of Labor, 1977).

In considering the impact of technological change on unemployment, one must distinguish between the general level of unemployment found nationally and the *displacement* of particular workers employed at specific locations. Concerning national levels of unemployment, there are probably few who would argue that the introduction of sophisticated technological equipment has resulted in a general and sustained rise in the levels of joblessness. There is, however, a considerable amount of evidence suggesting that in a variety of ways the introduction of new equipment does result in the displacement of workers. By this is meant that the advent of new production equipment does force some workers to transfer to new jobs, either within their present places of employment or to new jobs with different employers. The changing structure of the occupational field reflects the kind of employment shifts that are most clearly tied to a changing technology. We have already considered some aspects of this displacement on a national, macroeconomic level and found a significant increase in white-collar (particularly science, engineering, and professional) jobs and decreasing percentages in blue-collar and agricultural jobs. Related to these changes is the great increase in the number of jobs that are found in the service sector of the job market. In general, the shift has been from jobs involved with production of goods to jobs involved with the delivery of services.

Microeconomic Changes in Employment

Lying beneath the surface of national and industry averages, which express general levels of employment, is a dynamic local labor market where people move into and out of jobs. Researchers who have narrowed their attention to individual work organizations have found that the impact of technological innovation has been much more complicated than one might suspect at first glance, and no single pattern of employment shifts has emerged from these studies. For instance, Sheppard and Stern (1957) report an instance in which a major reduction in employment levels occurred as the result of an automotive plant's decision to automate its stamping process. Bright (1958), on the other hand, reports an instance in which another automobile company reported a sizable increase in employment, following substantial investments in new technology.

In some instances the immediate impact of automation may be masked by other factors. Often companies will make some effort to absorb workers who have been dislocated from their old jobs by transferring them to new positions in the organization, and as a result, levels of employment do not drop. At times new technology is a response to the need to expand production capacity, and at times the new equipment represents the company's move into a new product line. Time variables must be taken into consideration. The building of new, more advanced facilities may result in the eventual closing down of older facilities that are located in other communities (Mann & Hoffman, 1960), thereby resulting in a geographic displacement of whatever unemployment effects may be attributed to the new equipment. There are other instances in which there are no immediate changes in employment levels, but future needs for labor may be significantly altered. Hence, technological change may result in any one of a complex pattern of reverberations that can be direct or indirect, immediate or deferred, local or distant. Probably the best approximation to a general conclusion can be found only if one recognizes that the introduction

TABLE 15.3 Types of Factors Influencing Employment Opportunities in Automated Plants

Tending to Reduce Employment

  Increased productivity of automation
  Consolidation of production facilities
  More efficient layout and workplace arrangement
  Substitution of new equipment for old
  Product redesign for simplicity
  Shift from departmental to line production
  Mechanization of formerly manual operations

Tending to Increase Employment

  Increased demand
  Addition of new production facilities
  Addition of new product
  Introduction of more complex product
  Union regulations on working conditions
  Increased need for maintenance and support services
  Management desire to upgrade quality, improve working conditions, and provide better housekeeping

Adapted from Bright, J. *Automation and management.* Boston: Harvard University Press, 1958. Copyright 1958 by the President and Fellows of Harvard College. All rights reserved.

of new work technology has *both* employment-reducing and employment-increasing effects that often operate in different configurations at different times within a single plant. The net employment results of these influences depend upon the particular pattern of factors that are found in a given instance (see Table 15.3).

Comments

Dislocation, displacement, and reassignment are the terms that seem to be most descriptive of the impact of technology on the labor market. Although there is no conclusive evidence regarding technology's contribution to general levels of employment or unemployment, the introduction of more advanced equipment has been associated with a shifting about of the labor force, either in terms of people occupying new jobs or in terms of their adaptation to jobs whose content has been significantly modified. Over the years there have been significant changes in the number of workers found in many job categories. Some jobs have virtually disappeared from the labor scene either as a direct or as an indirect result of technological innovation, but to one degree or another, these changes have been balanced by the creation of new job categories that have grown out of new technology.

Following Blau and Duncan (1967), we might identify shifts in employment levels in terms of whether they have occurred predominantly within or between generations. *Intragenerational* shifts refer to changes in job classifications that take place *within* an individual's work career. *Intergenerational* shifts refer to the movement of new workers toward or away from a particular line of work. For example, fields like sales or clerical work have changed their employment levels over the past several decades, following a pattern of mobility in which at some intermediate point in their careers more people leave the clerical field than move into it. Hence, there is a net intragenerational loss. On the other hand, the number of new workers coming into the clerical field has exceeded this intragenerational loss; the growth in the number of clerical workers, therefore, is primarily a result of this large inflow of new workers entering the field (an intergenerational increase).

Other occupations have changed in size primarily as the result of intragenerational movement. The ranks of managers and officials, for example, tend to receive a large inflow of people who are changing positions during some intermediate phase of their careers. Relatively few people enter the labor market for their first jobs in these fields; hence, growth in this area is described as being intragenerational. Blau and Duncan have described several different patterns of occupational mobility; and although the relative contribution of technology to these different patterns of movement has not been determined, these ideas suggest a framework for studying the social mobility impact of technological innovations.

The record seems clear on one point. Technological innovation has been a factor that has had a significant effect on the fluidity of certain occupational fields. Work careers seem to involve increasingly more mobility in the sense that workers more frequently pursue careers that involve movement across jobs and across different occupations. Although some of this movement is an expression of individual efforts to improve job positions, some is a function of technological change. To the extent to which this is true, we hypothesize that a work career carries with it increasing psychological costs. The need to adjust to changing job conditions and uncertainties regarding the future nature of one's job create psychological conditions that make higher demands on the worker's adaptive resources.

PSYCHOLOGICAL CONSEQUENCES OF TECHNOLOGICAL CHANGE

Much has been written about the human consequences of technological change. Opinions have been mixed as to whether the net impact of these innovations has improved or impaired the psychological climate of work; and as the research literature stands now, there is little possibility of resolving this question. There are trends, however, and it is to them that we now turn.

Tensions and Anxiety

One idea that has come up time and time again in this area is the notion that technological change has increased the psychological tensions that surround work. Most agree that improved technology has relieved the individual of much of the physical drudgery of work, but some maintain (cf. Frankenhaeuser, 1977) that there remains an emotional residue that becomes more visible and may even be enhanced by the requirements of the new equipment. Concern regarding the human consequences of work technology has been widely expressed in Scandinavian countries, where legislative action has been taken to proscribe conditions of work thought to be psychologically harmful. For example, the Norwegian Work Environment Act requires that steps be taken to ensure:

1. that the work pace not be controlled by machines or assembly lines
2. that menial repetitive tasks be avoided
3. that the employee is enabled to develop self-determination and vocational responsibility
4. that piece rates are avoided on jobs where this may be detrimental to safety (Gardell, 1977)

Specialization of work, a restriction of the scope of the worker's activities to a smaller segment of the total production process, has received particular attention as a negative influence on workers' job experiences. Yet when we look at case histories that describe the introduction of new technologies into the workplace, we find that the data seem unable to confirm these suspicions. What the data do suggest is that workers possess considerable capability for adapting to changing working conditions. The anticipation of change often has been found to cause people to become anxious; but after the change has been implemented, workers tend to make reasonably good adjustments. This is not to say that new technology does not ever increase the pressures and tensions of work. The initial period after installation is often a time when reactions are most negative, but if the observation period is permitted to continue, it is often found that job attitudes improve markedly.

A case in point is found in a study by Walker (1957), which describes the broad range of changes associated with building a new automated seamless pipe mill and closing an older mill that had produced the same pipe, using less automated methods. In discussing workers' adjustment to the new mill, Walker reports that the workers feared their new jobs at first, but later began to express considerable satisfaction with the new procedures. It is of interest to note that the factors of the new jobs that were initially disliked were some of the same factors that the workers liked most after they had had opportunity to adjust to the modified working conditions.

Bright (1958), in a study that concerned the impact of technology in thirteen different plants, reports that although there were some plants in which workers expressed fear in anticipation of the new equipment, in most instances workers eventually made a positive adjustment to the job. In a few instances, however, continued worker anxiety expressed itself in the form of hostility and aggression toward both management and the work.

Machine-Paced Jobs. More persistent negative reactions sometimes develop in situations where the pace of work comes under mechanical control. Conveyor belts, assembly-line types of transfer, tend to lead workers to report nervousness and emotional strain. For instance, Walker and Guest (1952), in a study of a newly built automobile assembly line, found that mechanical pacing was one of the most frequently cited reasons for disliking work. Faunce (in Jacobson & Roucek, 1959) and Blauner (1964) report observing the same kind of reactions in their studies of assembly-line work, and Mann and Hoffman (1960) observed that the increase in work interdependency found in a newly automated power plant increased the workers' feelings of nervousness. In this latter instance, the employees stated that since so many other jobs were dependent on theirs, the consequences of any errors they might commit were much more threatening.

There are a number of psychological problems associated with machine-paced jobs. For instance, a line that moves across work stations at a constant rate does not allow for individual differences in ability and motivation. Production curves for any one person tend not to be perfectly consistent from one day to the next or from one segment of the work spell to the next. As a result, lines moving at a constant speed often expose workers to work rates that may on any given day be too fast or too slow. Walker and Guest (1952) report auto assembly workers talking about working themselves into a hole. By this they mean finishing one unit late in a cycle and as a result having less time to complete the next unit. After this happens a few times these deficits build up, leaving less and less time to complete each unit, until the point is reached where workers find themselves "fighting the line" in order to keep up with the pace.

Case studies concerning work that is not machine paced often report a variation in work tempos within as well as among workers. For instance, workers have frequently been observed putting aside completed work to turn in on some later day, thereby giving themselves an occasional day in which production demands are eased. Along similar lines, case studies have frequently observed workers restricting the amount of work they do during the day. On machine-paced jobs, these options are not available to the workers. As a consequence, they lose control over one of the more significant aspects of their work, and their negative attitudes often reflect this lack of control.

Positive Consequences

In contrast, there is considerable evidence of instances in which automation has been associated with improved worker attitudes toward their jobs. Form (1969), in a study of automobile assembly plants situated in four distinctly different cultures (United States, India, Italy, Argentina), observed positive job attitudes in at least 75 percent of the employees. Both Walker (1957) and Chadwick-Jones (1969) studied the impact of automation in steel-processing plants, and both found workers reporting that they preferred their new jobs in the automated plant to their old jobs in the nonautomated mill. Daniel (1969) reports favorable attitudes from a group of British workers who were subjected to substantial changes in their jobs as a result of technological innovation.

Mueller's Study. Mueller (1969) attempted to assess the impact of technological advances in a study that involved a sample of 2662 employees, selected so as to be representative of the U.S. labor force. Workers were interviewed in their homes, using interview schedules that asked respondents to describe their current work situations and any changes they had experienced during the previous five years in the machinery they used. After describing these changes, workers were asked about their reactions to the new working conditions.

In summarizing her findings, Mueller states: "Throughout this analysis it appears, in the view of the workers affected, [that] changes in machine technology tend to make jobs more interesting and more demanding in the non-physical sense. It also appears that jobs which become more demanding tend to become more satisfying" (Mueller, 1969, p. 108). On the whole, Mueller observed an increase in worker expressions of job satisfaction as the result of changes in machine technology. When the change in machinery was also accompanied by a change to a different job, an even greater proportion reported an improvement in job satisfaction (see Table 15.4).

TABLE 15.4   Change in Job Satisfaction over the Past Five Years among Workers Changing Jobs and/or Machines (percent)

Change in Satisfaction	All	Same Job for Past 5 Years		Different Job	
		Machine Change	No Machine Change	Machine Change	No Machine Change
More	51	58	40	67	64
Same	34	34	45	16	20
Less	9	8	9	11	9
Not Ascertained	6	0	6	6	7

Adapted from Mueller, E. *Technological advance in an expanding economy.* Ann Arbor: Institute for Social Relations, University of Michigan, 1969. Copyright, 1969 by the University of Michigan Press.

What was it about the changes the new machinery brought to the job that was correlated with improvements in workers' attitudes? For a large number of employees new machinery brought changes in the immediate content of the work they were doing. For instance, many reported that their jobs now required more skill, provided greater opportunity to learn new things, provided increased opportunity to plan, use judgment and personal initiative, and gave them increased opportunity to organize and influence their work. A majority (60 percent of those who did not change jobs and 75 percent of those who did) reported higher interest in the work after the introduction of the new machinery. Technology appeared to make jobs more demanding, to require more of the worker, and it was this aspect of technology's impact that was underlying the positive shifts that took place in the worker's orientation to the job.

It would seem, therefore, that we should recognize that the impact of technological change is not universally negative. Both positive and negative consequences should probably be anticipated in every case, and we should think about these outcomes in terms of a balance sheet of some sort. Mueller found, for example, that in addition to the positive changes described above, in about one-half of the cases the introduction of new machinery required workers to perform at a higher rate of speed. In dealing with the individual case, it is probably more accurate to keep these individual consequences separated and not try to combine them into an overall measure. In doing this we are more likely to avoid the pitfall of universally condemning or commending the mark that technological change leaves on the work that we do.

Technology and Skill Demands

It seems quite reasonable to assume that by incorporating more advanced scientific and engineering concepts into work, we have placed even greater demands on a worker's knowledge and skill. Hence, as the process of technological advancement continues, we might be led to assume that work will become more and more complex in terms of what it requires us to know and the skills it demands that we possess.

When one looks at the evidence supporting this point of view, there seems to be a reasonable amount of support for the general case. That is to say, if one were to consider the labor market as a whole, there seems to have been an upgrading of the skill demands made by jobs during the past few decades. For example, Mueller's work shows us that technological change often results in workers reporting an increase in the level of skill required by their jobs. In this nationwide sample, over one-half of those who experienced change in machinery also reported an increase in the skill level of their jobs. Bear in mind, however, that it is this increase in the skill content of a job that is frequently cited as a reason for improved worker satisfaction.

Scoville's Study. Scoville (1969) reports a valuable study that bears on the overall change in work skill levels between 1940 and 1970. Although these data reflect the influence of several variables, the impact of technological change on skill levels is undeniably important. Scoville suggests a system for classifying jobs according to their level of complexity. Factors considered are estimates of the general and specific training required, and the aptitudes, interests, temperaments, and working conditions that are necessary for the worker to be an average performer on the job. Five levels of complexity are considered.

Referring to these five categories, Scoville maintains that over the years there has been a marked increase in the general level of complexity of the jobs found in the labor market. Table 15.5 shows the distribution of jobs among the five levels for data collected for 1940, 1950, and 1960, and projections that were computed for the 1970s. Notice, for example, the steady increase in the percentage of jobs found at the most complex levels (Levels I and II), and the declining percentage of jobs found at the lowest levels of complexity (Levels IV and V). But in spite of this increase in the number of higher-level jobs, Wool (1976) reports labor-market projections that indicate a future surplus of workers available for these kinds of positions and an undersupply of workers available for lower-level jobs.

TABLE 15.5 United States: Job-Content Level (percent)

Level	1940	1950	1960	1970
I	6.1	6.8	8.7	9.4
II	9.6	11.5	14.2	16.1
III	28.5	32.5	34.2	34.7
IV	24.5	20.8	17.0	15.8
V	31.6	28.4	25.9	24.0

From Scoville, J. G. *The job content of the U.S. economy, 1940–1970.* New York: McGraw-Hill, 1969, page 54. Copyright 1969 by the McGraw-Hill Book Company.

Skill Reduction. Even though there has been a general increase in the level of skill required by work, this trend is not evident in all instances in which automation has been introduced into the work environment. For example, approximately 10 percent of Mueller's sample reported a drop in skill demands that was associated with the introduction of new machinery. A not unusual pattern of results is one that finds technology upgrading the skill demands made in some jobs, while at the same time reducing the skill level of others. The Bright (1958) study, for example, found that the introduction of automated equipment often led to a modest downgrading of the skill requirements of operators' jobs. To operate the new equipment did not usually require increased skill, although it sometimes broadened the scope of workers' responsibilities by giving them control over a wider span of the production process. Substantial upgrading in skill was observed, however, in jobs that supported the production jobs. Jobs involved with the maintenance of the automatic equipment, for instance, were often upgraded by the increasing sophistication of the new machinery. Machine design and construction jobs also tended to upgrade skill demands in response to technological innovation.

Qualitative Changes. Walker's study of an automated steel mill led him to conclude that in many instances the new technology did not require an increase of skill, but rather required the worker to draw on different *kinds* of skills. For example, the

new jobs exposed workers to tasks that demanded constant monitoring of the equipment; hence vigilance became an important requirement. In fact, it is not uncommon to find that technological change results in a reduction of the job's physical skills while at the same time the mental content of the work is increased. As a consequence, it is oftentimes very difficult to decide whether the general level of skill required by the job has been increased or decreased. Perhaps a more accurate statement for these instances would be that the new equipment requires a different configuration of skills.

EDP and Skill Demands

One type of automation that has received as much attention as any other involves the introduction of the computer into office situations. A review of the studies in this area reveals that electronic data processing (EDP) equipment has had a profound effect on the nature of office work. Jobs have been eliminated (for example, file clerk), jobs have been created (for example, keypunch operator) and the content of many jobs has been substantially changed. Shepard (1971) contends that the effects of EDP should be considered separately for jobs that are serviced by computers and for jobs that are directly involved with the actual operation of the computer. In offices, computers tend to reduce the degree of specialization, that is, the division of labor, in areas that depend on the output of the computer. Jobs that are low-skill and routine, like file clerk, tend to be eliminated by the introduction of EDP, while remaining jobs are broadened to include a wider range of responsibilities. In general, studies have found that clerical jobs tend to be upgraded in areas that are directly affected by the computer.

Within the data-processing unit, however, Shepard finds significant trends toward increasing job specialization. Many who are responsible for the operation of the computer, as well as those on support equipment such as those who operate data-entry equipment, report the work to be dull and routine. Hoos (1960, 1961), in a two-year study of nineteen organizations that had recently introduced EDP, found the job of keypunch operator to be a dead-end position, requiring low-grade skills for work that is simple, repetitious, and monotonous. In addition, she reports that the nature of data-preparation tasks is such that it is relatively easy to apply output measurements to the work. As a consequence, this kind of office work is amenable to the kind of production-room thinking that is usually found in factory work. Work in these essentially clerical settings has been taking on many characteristics of the assembly line. Hoos refers to these work environments as "paper processing factories."

Other jobs directly associated with EDP require very high levels of skill. Hoos talks about elitist groups who surround EDP units. Programmers and systems analysts, for example, bring with them a high level of skill that sets them apart from many of their work cohorts. Shepard (1971) recognizes the high level of skill required by computer "software" functions that are involved in the development, change, and operation of the computer. Yet, in office settings, the *net* impact of EDP on employees working directly in the computer unit is often only a slight increase in skill levels. Perhaps the best study available in this area is one reported by Crossman and Laner (1969) who studied eighteen cases in which the computer was applied to a variety of commercial and production-control processes. This study is of importance because the authors develop a methodology for measuring the skill level required of those working as either direct labor (those directly involved in a work process) or indirect labor (those who, like supervisors and maintenance personnel, are involved in support roles). In a banking situation that involved the processing of checks, Crossman and Laner found that the introduction of EDP raised the skill level of direct labor by a slight amount, but it significantly increased the skill level of those providing indirect labor. This corresponds with Shepard's observations concerning the impact of EDP in clerical settings. To complicate the picture, however, Crossman and Laner report that in the majority of the cases studied they found that technological change increased the direct skill requirements and decreased the indirect skill requirements. It seems clear that there are job variables

not yet accounted for that mediate the skill-demand implications of EDP. Apparently, technology does change the skill mix one finds in white-collar settings, but the nature of these changes and the variables leading to them are matters that will require further research.

Comment

In answer to the question, has technological change resulted in an upgrading of the skill requirements for work, one would have to give a qualified yes. Overall, the net effect of advanced technology has been to increase the level of knowledge—and to some extent the level of skill—necessary to hold a job. This is not to say that the rate of movement is outstripping the growing supply of qualified labor. Rather, there is some evidence available (Wool, 1976; Abramson, 1975) that suggests that there is an oversupply of trained people waiting for these higher-level jobs. As an example, Abramson (1975) projects a tragic oversupply of Ph.D.s that will be available for scientific and professional jobs during the period 1972–1985 (see Table 15.6). He estimates that for 187,400 job openings requiring this advanced degree, there will be a supply of 583,400 individuals with the degree, seeking these positions. Hence, there is indication that whatever the upgrading of skill demands taking place, it may well have produced a substantial overreaction from agencies involved in training. To the extent to which this oversupply exists, we can expect a growing source of frustration that will be experienced by a large group of well-trained job aspirants, entering a labor market in search of challenging and rewarding jobs that are not available in adequate numbers. The broad social and psychological implications of this abundance of trained labor are beyond the scope of the present discussion, but one must keep these problems in mind when thinking of the consequences of advancing technology.

Beneath the general increase in skill demand, however, lies a complicated pattern of more specific changes in the characteristics of work. In many instances technology has eliminated some low-skill jobs, but it has also created others. Technology has narrowed the content of some jobs,

**TABLE 15.6   Supply of and Demand for Ph.D.s, 1985
(in thousands)**

Field	New Supply, 1972–85	Openings, 1972–85	Difference
All fields	583.4	187.4	396.0
Engineering and natural science	224.4	105.6	118.8
Engineering	50.3	33.3	17.0
Physical Science	60.3	37.1	23.2
Chemistry	25.8	19.6	6.2
Physics	19.9	9.7	10.2
Life Science	92.2	26.0	66.2
Mathematics	21.6	9.3	12.3
Social science and psychology	101.6	32.1	69.5
Psychology	37.7	15.0	22.7
Arts and humanities	79.6	15.7	63.9
Education	148.8	28.9	119.9
Business and commerce	19.2	1.7	17.5
Other fields	9.7	3.4	6.3

Note: Because of rounding, sums of individual items may not equal totals.

From Abramson, E. W. Projected demand for and supply of Ph.D. manpower, 1972–1985. *Monthly Labor Review*, 1975, *98*, 52–53.

requiring an increased division of labor, while at other times technological change has reduced the division of labor and broadened the range of the worker's responsibilities. To anticipate the consequence of an advancing work technology in any one work situation requires detailed knowledge of the man-machine systems that are a part of the work process. In looking for the consequences of these changes it is better to approach the task expecting a redistribution of skills, rather than a simple upward or downward movement in the skill content of work. Qualitative shifts are also well within the range of possibility. Technological change not only produces vertical changes in skill demand, but workers find themselves doing qualitatively different things as the result of the introduction of new equipment.

TECHNOLOGY AND ALIENATION

In spite of the objective data, which show positive as well as negative consequences of technological change, there are many who have expressed great concern, sometimes bordering on alarm, regarding the undesirable social and psychological impact of new technology. Phrases such as "blue-collar blues" and "white-collar woes" have been coined, giving an impression that the incidence of worker discontentment is spreading and approaching crisis proportions. Individual cases are often cited that testify to the erosive effect new equipment has on the content of jobs. One such case that has received a lot of attention concerns the personnel problems that occurred in 1972 at the Lordstown plant of the General Motors Corporation (Gibbons, 1972; Widick, 1973). This incident is often seen as a prime illustration of the widespread employee discontentment that can be associated with the technology of the assembly line.

The Lordstown Plant

The Lordstown plant was constructed in the late 1960s by General Motors to assemble the Vega automobile. At the time, this was GM's most modern assembly facility, and it incorporated in its design and engineering the most advanced production techniques. One of its most impressive characteristics was its efficiency of production. As a rule, automobile assembly lines are constructed to produce at a rate of 55 to 65 cars an hour, but the Lordstown plant was constructed for a 100-car-an-hour rate of production.

The work force was young, highly paid, and given rather lengthy and regularly scheduled rest breaks, both in the mornings and the afternoons. The employee support facilities were modern and attractive, and efforts were taken to make the plant an agreeable place to work. Yet the work itself was of the type typically found on assembly lines. Operators had small, well-defined units of work to perform, the work was routine and repetitive; and in what proved to be a major source of job discontentment, the jobs had been engineered so as to reduce to 36 seconds the average time for completing one cycle of work. In other words, on the average, an operator completed his work on a car every 36 seconds, then moved on to the next car and repeated the same work cycle over again.

Workers' Response. For a time the assembly line appeared to be functioning as management and engineers had planned, but soon production problems began to mount. Cars that failed to meet quality standards began to pile up; absenteeism increased, reaching a level of 13 percent on some Fridays. A new management group was brought in, who quickly began to reorganize the plant. Some of the early moves involved eliminating 300 jobs from the line, stronger enforcement of work rules, and training foremen in an effort to improve their human-relations skills. Shortly thereafter grievance rates shot up, to the point where in one period, from October 1971 to February 1972, a total of 5000 grievances were filed. Production quality suffered, as the workers failed to install some parts on every car. Paint was scratched, bodies dented, and keys were snapped off in ignition and trunk locks. Sabotage and inefficiency became such a problem that the 2000-car repair area filled up at times and an entire work shift would have to be sent home to enable repair crews to catch up and reduce the inventory of defective cars. Finally a strike was called, the major issues of which were

not pay and fringe benefits, but the job duties themselves and the pace of the work.

The Lordstown incident is often cited as evidence that workers are becoming more concerned about the content of the jobs they perform. The fact that the Lordstown employees were quite young is also used as evidence that there has been a significant change in the values of today's workers, which require that work involve tasks that are not tiring, tedious, and dull. The high pace and work specialization that result from new technologies are considered unacceptable to this group of youthful workers, and the high absentee rate at Lordstown testifies that these workers view their time as being more valuable than the money that could be earned by spending the missed day on an empty job.

There were many factors underlying the Lordstown situation: management decisions, work-rate increases, the background characteristics of the work force. A significant factor contributing to many of these problems, however, was thought to be a modern technology that was geared to engineering efficiency and not to human needs. In response, there was an outpouring of grievances, absenteeism, sabotage and finally a strike.

Alienation

In dealing with workers' negative reactions to technological change, social scientists have often drawn on a term that was used by Marx to describe the principal psychological consequences of an economic system that denies workers ownership of the means of production. *Alienation* refers to a feeling of detachment from the things that go on around one. As currently used to deal with work environments, alienation implies that there is an element of estrangement and rejection in the relationship between an individual and the work, a low level of involvement and a general lack of concern with the work, coupled with a feeling that somehow or other the job does not fit well with the individual's self concept. The term is often thought of as having four dimensions, which are used both to identify the sources of alienation and to describe the different facets of an individual's psychological reactions. These dimensions concern feelings of powerlessness, lack of purpose, estrangement from social groups, and belief that the work does not contribute to feelings of self-esteem. Some (Kanungo, 1979) treat alienation as one end of a scale that has job involvement (see Chapter 5) at the other end.

Powerlessness. This dimension of alienation concerns the belief that one does not have an acceptable amount of influence and control over the things that enter the work. Consider, for example, the traditional image of the craftsman. Here we find a worker under whose jurisdiction falls the control of the style and quality of work, the pace of work, the order of steps followed to complete many parts of a task, and, in large measure, the evaluation of the finished product. The craftsman is not totally immune from the forces of the marketplace or from the direction of an employer, but in this type of work we expect to find a sense of autonomy and control over the process of work that is usually absent in, let's say, the modern assembly line.

The size of the work organization is another factor that can contribute to a sense of powerlessness. Here, decision-making and policy-forming centers are distant from the worker; management and union alike are viewed as being remote from the individual worker. Another factor contributing to a feeling of powerlessness is the extent to which the job duties confine the individual to a particular place and prevent movement from one location to another.

Meaninglessness. Meaninglessness is a dimension of alienation found when workers cannot perceive a significant connection between what they do and something that is considered important and valuable. A major source of meaninglessness is work specialization. Involvement with only a small segment of a complicated task makes it quite easy for the worker to lose sight of the fact that that particular job is a part of a significant outcome. Repetition, doing the same thing over and over again, often creates conditions that make it

difficult for workers to maintain a belief that the job is in fact a meaningful task. Working within the framework of bureaucratic rules, workers may lose sight of the connection between the quality of their work and the distribution of rewards; and working in a large and complicated organization sometimes discourages the notion that the work has some bearing on the overall mission of the firm.

There are certain aspects of a sophisticated technology that may encourage a sense of meaninglessness in work (Hart, 1953). This stems from the fact that as equipment and processes become more complicated, an increasing number of workers do not fully understand the work process they control. An operator may understand the input side of the work cycle, know the steps that must be followed to activate the equipment, and be directly aware of the outcome of the cycle, but the intervening steps that are automatically carried out by the equipment may be a veritable mystery. The initial response to such technological advances may produce a reaction of wonder and satisfaction, but prolonged exposure to such a task may cause the worker to see the job as quite meaningless.

Social Isolation

By social isolation we mean that the worker feels no sense of membership in the work community. The worker finds no reason for identification with the work group, the union, the company, or the industry. As a result, such workers function in an environment where group norms, if they exist in any clear form, appear not to coincide with personal standards of conduct, and they are led to conclude that they are living in a world of which they are not a part. The technology of assembly-line work, for example, has been accused of weakening the structure of the work group. The spacing of workers in a straight line places limitations on group interaction, and team work is less evident than is the work of the single individual.

Chadwick-Jones (1969) describes the impact of new technology in weakening the work group in a situation in which workers were being transfered to a new, automated rolling mill. In the old mill, the work was done by teams and involved six jobs, all differing in both skill and status. When the new mill opened, most of the employees were assigned to monitoring tasks. Status differentials were leveled and the satisfaction many obtained from being members of a work team was significantly lowered.

Self-Estrangement

Self-estrangement, literally, means detachment from the self, and it is a consequence of other forms of work alienation. Workers on jobs that are meaningless, in situations where they lack power and feel isolation from social groups, find themselves in jobs that compel them to generate behaviors that are neither satisfying nor personally justifiable. Continued exposure to the job enmeshes workers in a routine of activities that evoke their *own disapproval*—disapproval of the self, a sense of detachment, a day-in-and-day-out routine that is unrewarding and empty. Such workers see themselves as objects that are constantly compelled to react to the demands of an unpleasant set of job duties, and their awareness of more satisfying alternatives leads them to disapprove of their own behavior. Hence, there is a feeling of detachment from the self, a sense of self-alienation. Work becomes a means to an end rather than a source of fulfillment. Under these circumstances, workers adopt an instrumental orientation to work, oftentimes viewing work strictly in terms of the wages it produces.

Blauner's Thesis

One of the more influential discussions of the relationship between technological change and worker alienation can be found in a study by Robert Blauner (1964). In considering the changing nature of work, Blauner sees a historical progression of technology, beginning with traditional, craft-dominated industries and reaching its highest advancement in the continuous-process technologies, where much of the production is under the control of completely automatic equipment. Petroleum refining, chemical manufacturing, and the rolling of sheet steel are examples of continuous-process technologies. Here workers have little direct contact with the product, their jobs being to monitor the operation of the automated equipment that does the work.

In craft-oriented work, Blauner finds workers deriving considerable self-esteem and status from the highly developed skills they bring to the job. Tools and equipment, although they may be sophisticated, are usually under the skillful control of the craftsman. In completely automated work, on the other hand, skill demands can be quite low, but in compensation for this, workers often find themselves with increased responsibilities for expensive equipment and for large segments of a complex production process. As a consequence, they can draw on these new and expanded responsibilities to give their work importance and status. Hence, at both the craft and automation ends of the evolutionary process, Blauner sees workers in jobs that provide considerable opportunity for maintaining a sense of self-respect and dignity. Alienation on these jobs tends to be low.

In the transitional phases of the evolution from craft to automation, mechanization and job specialization tend to dominate these intermediate phases of technical progress. It is with work such as this that the erosion of skill becomes most acute. Blauner refers to the process in which craft-level skills are broken down into a number of narrowly specialized jobs as *deskillization*.

To Blauner, alienation can be traced to the design of a job, which in large measure is defined in terms of the duties required of the workers. Job design is significantly influenced by the type of technology employed; hence feelings of alienation are a reflection of the level of technology. At present, Blauner sees America as being well along in the intermediate stages of technological development. Further automation will tend to eliminate low-skill machine tending and assembly-line jobs, while it creates jobs that require either high levels of engineering and maintenance skills or high levels of worker responsibility. Historically, as we have progressed from craft to automated work, alienation has followed an inverted U-shaped course. If the future leads to expanded employment of automated equipment, Blauner anticipates a decline in the feelings of alienation that workers experience on their jobs.

Research Evidence

Blauner's theory concerning the relationship between technology and worker alienation has been endorsed by a number of authors who have contributed research support for this point of view. Both Faunce (1965) and Fullan (1970), for example, think of technological advancement in terms quite similar to Blauner's. Fullan (1970) identifies three types of industrial technology: the craft system, mass production, and continuous-process technology. Faunce, like Blauner, classifies industrial technology in three stages of development: a handicraft stage, a mechanization stage, and the automatic production-control stage. Each stage is characterized by a different set of relationships between worker and machine and between worker and the social groups that define the social environment of work. Faunce maintains that in both factory and office highly automated production systems do tend to create conditions in which alienation is low. Fullan reports a survey of a large number of Canadian workers employed in five printing firms (craft industry), two automobile plants (mass production), and five companies in the oil-processing industry (continuous process). Fullan's main concern is with the extent to which the three types of technology are significantly related to workers' perceptions of their levels of integration with four aspects of the work organization: work associates, supervisors, the status structure, and labor-management relations. Integration refers to the extent to which workers see themselves as being a part of the social activities that go on in the organization. Lack of integration reflects the extent to which people are isolated from each other or the extent to which they are in conflict with one another.

In general, Fullan found that workers involved in highly automated technology showed considerably higher levels of integration with work than did workers employed in mass-production industries. Craft workers tended to fall between these

two groups. Hence, to a major degree the Fullan study gives support to Blauner's theory concerning the relationship between work technology and feelings of alienation.

Functional Specialization and Alienation. The dimension of job design that has been most closely linked to feelings of job discontentment and worker alienation is the degree of *functional specialization* of the work routine. By functional specialization is meant the extent to which a set of duties has been broken down into a number of narrow jobs, each assigned to a different employee. The automobile assembly line is a prime example of functional specialization. With specialization comes increased meaninglessness, and with the machine pacing often associated with this type of work, there exist conditions that lead to a sense of powerlessness.

Blue-Collar Work. Jon Shepard (1969) reports a study that confirms the contention that functional specialization of the type found on automobile assembly lines does tend to be associated with worker alienation. Three groups of workers were involved in the study: automation workers who monitored control rooms in oil refineries, craftsmen from automobile assembly-line maintenance crews, and automobile assemblers. A strong positive relationship was observed between functional specialization and reports of powerlessness. Reports of powerlessness were rather few from craftsmen whose jobs involved the smallest degree of specialization, while at the highest level of specialization, assemblers, a high incidence of powerlessness (93 percent) was observed. On two related dimensions, meaninglessness and perceived autonomy-responsibility in work, assemblers continued to report more alienation than the craft workers. The monitor group were intermediate to the craftsmen and assemblers in powerlessness and autonomy-responsibility. They did display, however, the lowest incidence of perceived meaninglessness in work. Shepard offers no explanation for this finding.

The Shepard study indicates that variation in

worker alienation has been observed across jobs within a single industry as well as across industries, as the Blauner (1964) and Fullan (1970) studies have also indicated.

White-Collar Work.   Similar results have been observed in a white-collar setting. Kirsch and Lengermann (1971) report a study carried out with three types of bank employees: computer personnel, clerical workers, and machine operators. Responding to questionnaires, these employees clearly showed distinct differences in objective conditions of alienation among the three types of jobs. What this means is that computer personnel reported fewer job characteristics that led to feelings of powerlessness, meaninglessness and lack of promotional opportunities. Machine operators (keypunch operators, proofreaders and card-sort operators) described many conditions that were alienating, and clerical workers (clerks, clerk-typists, clerk-bookkeepers) fell in the middle. Correlated rather strongly with these differences in exposure to alienating job conditions were workers' reports concerning feelings of self-estrangement (see Table 15.7). Only 4 percent of the computer programmers and systems analysts reported high levels of self-estrangement; 48 percent of the clerical workers and 64 percent of the office-machine operators did so. Hence, in white-collar settings we find that the objective working conditions that are usually thought to produce alienation do, in fact, appear to be linked with workers' feelings of self-estrangement.

There are other studies (Shepard, 1977) that either directly or indirectly lend support to Blauner's thesis that work technology creates conditions that give rise to feelings of discontentment and psychological detachment from work and its social setting. Furthermore, there seems to be reasonably good evidence that job specialization, the narrowing of job duties for the purpose of increased efficiency, tends to be a prime suspect as a factor contributing to these negative worker reactions. As with most areas of inquiry dealing with matters of work, however, there are some who contest this point of view and bring forward experimental evidence supporting their contention.

TABLE 15.7   Extent of Alienating Work Conditions and Self-Estrangement among Three Groups of Bank Workers

Self-Estrangement Score	Conditions of Work Alienation		
	LO Computer Personnel	MED Clerical Workers	HI Machine Operators
Low	60%	29	18
Medium	36	23	18
High	4	48	64

Adapted from Kirsch, B. A., & Lengermann, J. J. An empirical test of Robert Blauner's ideas on alienation in work as applied to different type jobs in a white-collar setting. *Sociology and Social Research*, 1971, *56*, p. 188. Copyright 1971 by Sociology and Social Research.

Contrary Evidence

Blauner (1964) maintains that automated technology of the kind found in continuous-process industries creates working conditions that reduce worker alienation. For instance, such work often provides the worker with the opportunity to move about the workplace during the day, gives the worker freedom to regulate the pace of work, and provides some opportunity to control the quantity and quality of work. These are thought to be objective conditions of a job that lead to low feelings of worker discontentment. Yet Sussman (1972) has reported a study of a group of continuous-process jobs that indicates that in many instances automation does *not* create the job conditions usually associated with low levels of alienation. Sussman suggests that other, nontechnical characteristics of automotive jobs, such as pay and status differentials, contribute substantially to workers' feelings of involvement-alienation. To attribute workers' subjective reactions to their work solely to the impact of technology is, according to Sussman, to deal with a complicated matter in an overly simplistic fashion.

Goldthorpe (1966), observing British auto-assembly-line workers, provides us with a contrary *interpretation* for the often noted high levels of alienation found in these work settings. His data agree with those of Blauner (1964), Chinoy (1955), Walker and Guest (1952), and others, when he reports that the assemblers in his sample derived very little satisfaction from the duties of their jobs. Reports of monotony were high, workers complained about the fast work pace, and many found their jobs physically tiring. Approximately two-thirds indicated a preference for some other job, mainly a job that was away from the moving line. Yet workers appeared to show integration with their jobs. To a major extent, the link that integrated the worker with the job was found in the economic rewards the job offered, together with the fact that the paycheck was seen as being a relatively secure one. Hence, workers saw their jobs on the assembly lines in an instrumental fashion. Work was perceived primarily as a means to an economic end, rather than as a source of self-fulfillment.

Many social scientists argue that work that is psychologically unfulfilling encourages workers to develop an instrumental orientation in which work becomes merely a means to an end, rather than a rewarding end in itself. Goldthorpe argues, however, that even though these instrumental orientations are frequently viewed as symptomatic of high self-estrangement, in his study these attitudes were not the result of the technological conditions of work. Rather, these workers were *attracted* to this type of work by their interest in high salaries. Their interest in wages was not, therefore, the consequence of assembly-line work, but their reason for seeking out this kind of work in the first place.

Walker and Guest (1952), in their study of American assembly-line operators, and Inkson and Simpson (1975), in their study of New Zealand assembly-line workers, report that the availability of good wages played a significant motivational role in psychologically integrating workers to monotonous jobs. Goldthorpe (1966) makes the interesting point that the roots of alienating work should be sought out not only with reference to the technology of work but also in the deep social currents that give rise to a strong interest in economic gain at the expense of any self-fulfillment that may be experienced through work.

Form (1972, 1973), in his cross-cultural study of assembly-line workers, found that routine and monotony on the job are often not seen as reasons

TABLE 15.8   Responses to Question: What Do You Most Dislike about Your Job?

Job Attributes	Oldsmobile
Nothing	18
Monotony, lack of power and responsibility	20
Pace of work, machine problems	—
Working and physical conditions	30
Other*	31
Total	99
N =	(247)

*Five percent concerned with low pay and lack of advancement.

Source: Form, W. H. Auto workers and their machines. *Social Forces*, 1973, *52*, 1–15. Copyright © 1973 The University of North Carolina Press.

for disliking the work (see Table 15.8). Over and above this, he reports that the majority of American assembly-line workers in his sample saw office work as being more monotonous than factory work. Furthermore, a substantial majority of this sample indicated that they were satisfied with their jobs, and that monotony and lack of job control was not a major complaint.

Comment

The impact of technology on working conditions and on workers' attitudes is an extremely difficult subject to research. The topic leads to questions that are difficult to translate into an experimental design that meets the standards of rigorous research. Technology is a variable not easily manipulated or measured. At present, the literature does suggest that certain kinds of work in the highly mechanized segments of the job market frequently generate feelings of monotony and discontentment, but we have also found reports that suggest that these consequences are far from universal. There is also reasonably clear evidence that certain types of advanced automation create job situations in which worker alienation is relatively low, but there are also data indicating that this type of automation can create jobs that are every bit as dull and routine as those found on an assembly line.

There is one important question that has received little attention in the research literature, and that concerns the long-term consequences of a worker's exposure to a job that is dull and unchallenging. Obviously, there are wide individual differences in adjustment to such situations, and Stagner (1974) gives us some data suggesting that with increasing age, fewer and fewer workers are found on assembly-line jobs. There appears to be a continuing sorting of workers taking place after they are hired and placed on the line; and with increasing seniority, older workers seem to drop off the line by quitting, retiring early, or taking other jobs in the plant. In many instances, therefore, assembly-line work is work that is carried out by younger workers. Two implications can be drawn from this. First, the problems often associated with this type of technology may be confused with the problems young workers have in adjusting to work and to the early phases of a work career. Kornhauser's (1965) finding that job satisfaction appears to improve with age among assembly-line personnel is in line with this hypothesis. Second, and related to the first hypothesis, there is a selective attrition on the line, in which older, dissatisfied workers are permitted by their seniority to seek alternative positions and their places are filled by younger workers; hence, the long-term impact of psychologically unfulfilling work is to encourage a worker to seek out different types of work whenever seniority or economic circumstances permit.

Finally, we must bear in mind Goldthorpe's (1966) suggestion that the interest in financial incentives often found in this type of work may not be the consequence of the design of a job, but the reflection of a set of worker orientations that develop before a worker takes a job and that play a role in leading the worker to seek out that kind of work.

JOB ENRICHMENT

Many believe that some of the highest psychological costs of technological change can be attributed to a trend toward increased job simplification and work specialization. There have been many instances, in both office and factory, in which new equipment has created jobs that have a relatively restricted range of duties and that require workers to draw on narrow sets of skills and activities. Since the psychological consequences of work of this sort are thought to be boredom, alienation, and lack of self-fulfillment, there have been numerous suggestions made to redesign jobs to encompass a broader range of duties and involve the worker in a richer set of experiences.

Job enrichment is a term used to refer to a variety of efforts to expand and improve the content of jobs. It is difficult to arrive at a satisfactory definition of the term, because it relates to such a broad range of job-design changes. As a consequence, research on job enrichment, like research on technological change, focuses not on a restricted set of influences but on a complicated variety of changes that have been made in the structure of jobs. Looking over the literature in this area, one finds that definitions typically recognize two dimensions of change, horizontal and vertical, that enter into the meaning of the concept. Horizontal changes refer to the expansion of job duties to include both a greater number and a wider variety of activities. Production jobs, for example, may be broadened to place within a worker's jurisdiction many additional components of the production process. In addition, workers may also be given responsibility for setting up and maintaining their equipment, they may be assigned the responsibility of inspecting and evaluating the work done, or they may be required to repair production units not meeting quality standards. Job-design changes of this sort are sometimes referred to as job enlargement.

Vertical changes are often thought of in terms that are quite similar to those one finds associated with employee participation in decision making. This dimension of job enrichment, therefore, involves workers in the planning and control of the work activities that are being carried out. Hence, job enrichment is a concept that involves workers in a broad range of production and decision-making activities. Advocates of these programs maintain that the consequences to be expected from this type of job redesign can be found in improved worker performance and in a reduction of the negative attitudes that have often been observed on jobs that involve a restricted set of duties and limited employee control over the work process.

Case Studies

Many efforts to evaluate the effect of job enrichment have been presented in the form of case studies summarizing the experience of a single company that experimented with such a program. By and large, the results of these case studies indicate that job enrichment does lead to desirable human consequences. *Work in America* (1973), a government report on contemporary work problems, lists and summarizes twenty-seven reports from which the human consequences of job enrichment can be evaluated. In each instance, the result of job redesign was an improvement in some aspect of people's reaction to their work. Morale and job satisfaction were found to improve in some instances, turnover and absences declined in oth-

ers, and improved commitment to work and company was reported in other cases.

Several authors (Hulin and Blood, 1968; Cummings, Molloy, & Glen, 1977) are critical of many of the studies in this area, citing their lack of experimental rigor and objectivity. These authors are probably correct in raising this point, but we should not ignore this impressive group of instances that point to improved employee response to enriched jobs. Neither should we conclude that the effects of job enrichment are uniformly positive (Frank & Hackman, 1975). Of course, there are a multitude of organizational changes that might be called job enrichment, and it would be naive indeed to expect all of them to lead to the same employee consequences. The pattern of research findings that have thus far been reported, however, seem to indicate generally positive outcomes associated with efforts to enrich work (Hackman, 1977).

Hackman and Oldham (1976) list five characteristics of jobs that lead to improved motivation and higher levels of performance and satisfaction:

1. *Skill variety*—the range of activities included in a job, which draw on different skills
2. *Task identity*—the extent to which a worker completes an entire unit of production rather than producing only a part of the total product
3. *Task significance*—the degree to which the job

makes a contribution or has an impact on people
4. *Autonomy*—the degree to which the job provides freedom and decision making in scheduling the work and selecting the procedures used
5. *Feedback*—the availability of information regarding the effectiveness of the worker's performance

To say that jobs possessing these characteristics will lead to positive employee reactions is one thing, but to be able to specify the specific nature of these reactions is another, requiring knowledge of the individual situation. For example, Umstat, Bell, and Mitchell (1976) report on a job-enrichment experiment that resulted in a substantial improvement in job satisfaction, but no appreciable change in production levels. Locke, Sirota, and Wolfson (1977) report on an enrichment program that led to improved production and reduced absences and turnover; yet there was no significant improvement in employee attitudes. In all cases it

is easy to provide reasons for a particular outcome *after* the data have been collected, but to predict the pattern of employees' reactions to a given enrichment program is beyond our immediate capabilities. Generally, the large majority of job-enrichment studies report that programs of this type make a positive contribution to working conditions, but whether production quantity, quality, or any of a variety of worker attitudes are affected depends upon factors found in each situation. Finally, the success of job-enrichment programs depends not only on the changes that are made in the various facets of the job, but also on the social and psychological characteristics of the workers who are exposed to these changes.

The Role of Workers' Attitudes. Lawler (1969) argues that job-enrichment programs can be expected to affect employees' level of work motivation only when the design changes increase workers' expectancies that the job provides a route to highly valued outcomes. It is the higher-order needs that are most directly linked to the design structure of the job. The duties and responsibilities of work are closely tied in with the prospects that workers will experience a sense of achievement, self-esteem, and fulfillment from the work they do. These needs are not uniformly potent for all workers, and it is in the background and experience of the individual that we find the factors that determine the importance of these higher-order needs. Hence, job-design characteristics interact with the needs of the worker to determine whether job enrichment leads to a more positive worker reaction.

Lawler suggests there are job characteristics that are important in leading workers to expect that the work will appeal to their higher-order needs. First, workers must have a source of performance feedback that gives information concerning the success and failure of their work. Second, their jobs must be seen by workers as requiring them to draw on skills that they value highly; and third, their jobs should give workers a feeling of autonomy in that they have a high degree of control over their work goals and work pace.

Since satisfaction of the higher-order needs seems to revolve around workers' beliefs that they are performing their jobs well, Lawler maintains that the behavioral effects of job enrichment should most clearly be seen in the quality of the worker's performance. The quantity of work done is not as closely or consistently associated with workers' beliefs that they are performing well. Hence, they anticipate that job-enrichment programs will have a tendency to lead primarily to improved quality in job performance, although quantity may improve as well. This is, in fact, what Lawler finds when he searches the literature

on these programs. He cites ten studies dealing with job-enrichment efforts, and in each instance the results reported show an improvement in work quality; in four cases, higher levels of production output were observed. We need more work regarding this hypothesis, but for the moment it would seem worthwhile to continue to look for the effects of job-enrichment programs in those criteria of work performance that reflect some aspect of quality. This, of course, does not rule out the possibility that other aspects of employee behavior will also respond to job enrichment efforts.

Employee Background and Job Enrichment

It is quite unlikely that the design of a job will carry the same psychological implications for every worker. Workers coming from a variety of social backgrounds, bringing with them different orientations toward work, would be expected to react differently to the content of their jobs. Several studies that substantiate this expectation have been reported. Turner and Lawrence (1965), for example, carried out a study in which an attempt was made to describe the relationship between the level of job complexity and workers' performance and attitudes. Anticipating that both performance and attitudes would show signs of decline as job duties became increasingly simpler, Turner and Lawrence found that this expectation was confirmed only when they considered job attendance. Here, in a large sample (n = 403) of employees holding forty-seven different jobs in eleven different industries, workers on relatively simple duties tended to absent themselves more from work than did workers engaged in a more complicated set of job duties. When relationships involving worker attitudes were studied, on the other hand, no significant results were obtained that stood up across all work situations. What Turner and Lawrence did find, however, was that in those situations where workers came from small towns, the relationship between job content and attitudes was as anticipated—that is, the more complex the job duties, the more positive the workers' attitudes. In those instances in which workers came from urban settings, there was found to be a negative relationship between task variety and job attitudes; that is, on jobs whose duties provided more variety, urban workers tended to have lower job satisfaction. Similar relationships were found between job satisfaction and the number of people with whom the worker interacted. Urban workers whose jobs required them to interact with a large number of people tended to have more negative job attitudes.

We see in the Turner and Lawrence data some evidence that the content of work, that is, the level and variety of work experience, maintained different relationships with workers' attitudes as a function of the socio-geographic background of the workers. The impact of job-design factors was not the same on workers coming from an urban setting as on workers coming from small towns. When one attempts to explain these relationships, one must fall back on speculation. Turner and Lawrence, along with others (for example, Hulin and Blood, 1968), speculate that workers from small towns and rural settings tend to have what these authors see as middle-class work values. Urban workers do not have a strong commitment to these norms, and as a consequence, intrinsic characteristics of work are less highly valued by workers coming from such social backgrounds.

Comment

To see urban workers as a group that tends to reject the idea that commitment to hard work will lead to certain personal and social advantages probably has as many pitfalls as does the notion that job-design factors affect all workers in a similar fashion. Yet these background variables cannot be ignored and should be considered when dealing with this question of the effects of job enrichment. There is a string of studies (Kennedy & O'Neill, 1958; Kilbridge, 1961; Turner & Miclette, 1962; Form, 1973) in which workers located in urban settings showed no negative reaction to highly specialized jobs possessing narrow and simplified job duties. There are other studies (see Hulin and Blood, 1968) that suggest that workers from rural backgrounds do react more favorably to more complex job duties. Hence, we must keep all these studies in mind when we think about the prospects of job-enlargement programs. Programs of this sort have been effective in a number of work situations, but to expect them to yield positive results when applied to all segments of the work force may be, in the light of the evidence, quite unrealistic.

TECHNOLOGY AND SOCIAL ORGANIZATION

Thus far we have been considering what are essentially the psychological implications of a changing technology. Our primary concern has been with the impact of technical innovation on the individual worker. Now we will consider briefly the effects of technology on social structures, paying particular attention to the relationship between technology and the formal social characteristics of the work organization. In doing so we will give only passing recognition to the many case studies that have demonstrated a variety of changes occurring in the social dynamics of the work group as the result of the introduction of new equipment and procedures. Chadwick-Jones (1969), for example, cites evidence that the opening of a new continuous-process rolling mill significantly affected the social aspects of work. The new technology tended to disband the small, socially stratified work teams that formerly carried out the rolling operations. Not only did this result in a loss of status for some workers who had high-status positions in these teams, but workers lamented the loss of a sense of camaraderie that had existed among the members of the work group.

Walker and Guest (1952) refer to the social costs of the straight-line spacing of workers along the assembly line, which tends to encourage the formation of loosely knit work groups. Spacing people in a straight line results in each member interacting with a different set of associates, those on either side. Under these circumstances each worker interacts with a unique set of neighboring work stations, and as a consequence this arrangement makes it difficult for work groups to develop cohesive properties.

There are other case studies that describe the social impact of technological change on the small work group (Baumgartel & Goldstein, 1961; Mann & Hoffman, 1960), but little progress has been made in incorporating these findings into a set of general principles. This case-study literature is quite clear in demonstrating that technological innovations can have significant consequences for the social climate that operates within the work group, but at present this literature does not permit us to draw more specific generalizations.

Woodward's Study

Some attempts have been made to develop some general principles concerning the effects of technology on the social structure of large and complex organizations. Perhaps the most influential of these attempts can be found in the work of Joan Woodward (1965), who studied this problem in a survey of 100 British industrial organizations. In this study firms were classified on the basis of the size of their production runs, and this factor was used as a measure of the level of technology characteristic of the company under consideration. Eleven categories were used, ranging from production runs composed of individual units or small batches (for example, custom-made products, small batches made to customer's order), through large-batch mass-production runs (large runs of standardized units), to continuous-process production (as in the chemical and petroleum industries). Unit production was viewed as the least advanced technologically and continuous-process procedures were considered the most advanced.

Woodward reports finding that companies with similar production systems also had similar organizational structures. For instance, moving from the technically least advanced to the most advanced production systems, there seemed to be a corresponding increase in the number of management levels found in departments that were directly involved with production. Technology also related to the span of control of the firm's chief executive. In unit-production firms the number of people directly responsible to the chief executive tended to be much smaller than the number in continuous-process industries. The ratio of managers to total personnel also changed with different stages of production technology; firms with more advanced technology had a much higher proportion of management personnel. Other structural factors rose to a peak in the middle of the technical scale, dropping off to a low value at either end. For example, the average number of workers supervised by first-line foremen reached a peak in mass-production industries. Foremen in unit-production and continuous-process technologies controlled relatively small numbers of employees.

There were other variables that the Woodward study associated with the level of technology, but the main point to take away from this research is that certain structural characteristics of work organizations appear to reflect the kind of technology employed in getting the work done. As Perrow (1967) points out, technology defines, to a very large degree, the kind of work that is done in an organization, and it is certainly not unrealistic to expect that the nature of this work exerts a major influence on the pattern of interpersonal relationships that go on. As these patterns stabilize and become fixed by formal rules and policies, we begin to think of them in terms of a discernible structure. Technology makes a significant contribution to this structure, and this is what the Woodward study demonstrates.

Since the Woodward study a number of attempts have been made to shed additional light on this question concerning the extent to which technology affects the structure of a work organization. Hage and Aiken (1969), for example, found a significant relationship between routineness of work and the extent to which workers are permitted to participate in decision making. In more routine kinds of work employees had less opportunity to become involved in the decisions being made in the plant. Two other measures of structure, distance between supervisors and subordinates and employee autonomy, showed no relationship with the routineness of the work.

Hickson, Pugh, and Pheysey (1969) report an

interesting study of forty-six work organizations located in Birmingham, England. Here technology was thought to have its broadest influence on the organizational structure of plants that hired a small number of employees. In larger firms the effects of technology appeared to be focused on the aspects of the organizational structure that were directly related to producing and distributing the firm's output. Inkson, Pugh, and Hickson (1970) supply us with confirmation of these results in a study involving forty English work organizations. As with the Hickson et al. study, size of the firm seemed to have a stronger bearing on organizational structure than did the nature of the technology used in doing the work. Hence in small plants, technology's influence on organizational structures appears to be a general one, influencing every level of the firm. With larger plants, however, the effects of technology seem to be confined to those levels of the organization that are most closely associated with producing and distributing.

It would appear to be too early to draw the conclusion that there is a direct and substantial relationship between the level of work technology and the structure of work organizations. Mohr (1971) reports only a weak association between the two, and Khandwalla (1974) presents evidence suggesting that the relation holds best for companies having high profit margins. Probably it would be safe to conclude that technology does exert some kind of influence on the structure of an organization, but the nature of this relationship will have to await advances in our experimental procedures, especially in the measurement of technological level and the quantification of the dimensions of organizational structure.

The Sociotechnical Design of Work

Recently there has been growing interest in modifying the social conditions of work in order to achieve a better match between the technical and the social dimensions of the job environment. From the perspective of this sociotechnical approach to job design, every work setting contains two closely interrelated systems: the technical system and the social system. The former involves the machines, equipment, procedures, and schedules of work, while the latter consists of the attitudes, beliefs, and feelings of the workers (Trist, Sussman, & Brown, 1977). A sociotechnical design is one that attempts to establish a congenial match between these two systems, and there is indication in the literature that these efforts can pay off with a more satisfying job environment and a more effective work group.

Sociotechnical design and analysis do not refer to a specific set of techniques and procedures. Furthermore, many of the reports that have been made concerning this approach take the form of studies that are more like case histories than tightly run experiments. For example, Trist, Sussman, and Brown (1977) describe an instance in which autonomous work groups were formed among groups of coal-mine work crews. These crews were responsible for digging and removing coal from the mine face, and changes were instituted that would give the work group more control over the work. For instance, during the study, management relinquished its right to direct crew members at the work site, there was increased freedom for workers to learn new jobs within their sections, and a new grievance system that handled complaints closer to the work site was installed. Subsequent experience with this autonomous-group approach provided encouragement that the design created a more satisfactory set of working conditions. All was not positive, but in the complicated set of events surrounding the experiment, many of which were not under the control of the researchers, there was evidence of improved safety, reduced accidents, lower production costs, and more favorable attitudes toward the work.

Work on sociotechnical systems has also given considerable emphasis to the need to establish collaborative relationships in work settings as a means of improving the general quality of work life (Appley & Winder, 1977). Contending that in many work settings competition among work associates is characteristic of the social environment, it is suggested that a collaborative orientation be established in order to solve many of the pressing environmental problems. Collaboration refers to an

approach to social relations built on a set of values that leads individuals to

1. Share mutual aspirations and a common conceptual framework
2. Interact with one another in a manner that is characterized by fairness and a commitment to a sense of justice

3. Be consciously aware of their motives toward others
4. Express concern for others and share with them a commitment to work that is a matter of choice

Advocates of this approach contend that when there is a commitment to planned change within an organization, it is possible to move toward a climate of work that reflects this collaborative orientation. Visionary in its outlook and futuristic in its directions, this movement toward collaborative work is worth watching, if for no other reason than that it expresses many of the values and long-term objectives shared by many social scientists.

SUMMARY COMMENTS

In the light of the studies reviewed in this chapter, we should stop and ask how far the social sciences have come in answering some of the more fundamental questions that may be asked concerning technology and work. In doing so we find that some areas of the literature give us a clearer picture than do others. For instance, we probably are in a better position to comment on the effects of technology on the structure of occupational fields than on the psychological consequences of different technologies. In many instances there is evidence that technology has created whole new job classifications, while at the same time it has contributed to the elimination of others. Technological change has exerted a significant influence on the nature of the various job categories that make up the labor market. A substantial increase in the number of managerial, professional, scientific, and engineering jobs testifies to the expanding technical character of work; and the emergence of what may be called a service economy represents a major shift away from the traditional idea that work involves making something.

Reflecting the rapid changes occurring in the nature of jobs, work careers have tended to become more varied in occupational field. Educational requirements for many jobs have been upgraded and revised, and a growing proportion of the labor force has received formal training beyond the high school diploma. Hence, there have been profound changes taking place in the composition of the labor force, which have paralleled the changes taking place in the structure and content of occupational fields. In varying degrees, technological innovation has been a contributing factor to these changes in work.

In facing this changing structure of work, many have raised questions regarding the psychological consequences involved. There is a widely shared fear that technology has often deprived jobs of any potential for personal satisfaction and fulfillment. Empty work, work that lacks challenge and variety, that does not provide enjoyment and self-esteem, is often seen as the residue that remains after technology has taken the psychological substance out of a job. Alienation is a term often applied to the psychological consequences of technological change, and numerous case studies and anecdotal reports have described the feelings of powerlessness and detachment generated by jobs that have been altered by technology. Yet there is a substantial amount of evidence indicating that job satisfaction is quite high, even in those industries that are most often associated with such things as extreme job specialization and machine pacing. In addition, there is a good possibility that the impact of job content, instead of producing the same psychological consequences for every worker, is dependent upon a variety of factors that lie in the worker's background and that vary widely among workers.

In considering adjustments to technological change, a major factor is probably to be found in the expectations workers have concerning the nature of the work role and the norms governing individual responsibilities and commitments to work. More information is needed about the type of individual who best adjusts to a particular job, but there is also a need for well-constructed theoretical models that can broaden our understanding of the relationships among jobs, human attributes, and psychological adjustment.

In reviewing the literature on technological change, one can easily come away with the impression that there are certain kinds of structural deficiencies in jobs that can lead to psychological difficulties that persist as long as the individual holds the job. This is probably true in many instances, but comparatively little attention has been paid to the ability of workers to adjust to the requirements of work and eventually make a reasonably satisfactory accommodation to the situation. Walker's (1957) description of the events surrounding transfer to a new automated steel mill illustrates something about the worker's flexibility in adjusting to changing circumstances. In this study, after an initial period during which workers complained about the new dimensions of their jobs, there followed a time in which attitudes toward work moved from negative to positive. Furthermore, it was those aspects of the new job that were initially disliked that eventually became some of the more frequently mentioned reasons for liking the more highly automated situation. At present we are in a very poor position to comment in any depth about the long-term implications of technological change, but at the very least we should keep the idea of human adaptability in mind when we consider the problem of worker reaction to a changing technology.

The study of the psychological and social effects of technological innovation is perhaps one of the most important areas of inquiry to engage the attention of social scientists. Our lack of a satisfactory understanding of the consequences of these changes cannot be used to caution those in other technical fields to slow their achievements. We must, however, continue to seek new insights into these problems and must continue to encourage all to think of the social and psychological consequences, else we shall continue to find ourselves following our own technologies rather than leading them toward a more just and satisfying social world.

16
Women at Work

Of all the changes taking place in the labor force, none has been more visible or more significant than the increase in the number of women who hold jobs. This growth in women's rate of participation in paid work has been a steady one, reflecting trends that have been evident for over a century. For example, in 1870 women composed 14.7 percent of the labor force; by 1920 they accounted for 20.5 percent, and by 1972 their participation rate had increased to 43.5 percent. In 1977, 56 percent of all women over 16 worked at least some of the time during the year (Young, 1979).

No single factor can be identified as the sole cause of these changes. Economic trends, technological developments both at the workplace and at home, wars that have called women into jobs previously held by men, and a growing demand for more equitable treatment in society have all combined to produce this continuing expansion of the woman's role. But whatever the causes, the social-psychological implications of this trend are extensive and important. For instance, virtually every dimension of family life has had to adapt to women's new work roles. The wife's contribution to the family income has weakened a traditional source of male power (breadwinning). Child-rearing practices and sex-role differentiation have had to undergo substantial changes in order to adjust to the fact that many families now contribute eighty, not forty, hours to work activities.

In this chapter we will consider a number of issues that relate to women and work. One principal concern will be with the effects of sociali-zation on the work experience of women. At a very early age females are brought under the influence of a complicated set of social traditions and practices that lead them toward certain kinds of work roles. Customarily, their two major choices have been between the role of wife and mother, and a work career that takes the woman away from home. If she chose the work role, then there was "woman's work," a segment of the job market reserved for women. These jobs are often rather routine, carrying with them comparatively low wages and little chance for advancement. The woman who chooses to pursue a career that takes her outside these traditional work areas faces a new set of problems that are both social and psychological in their nature. Ranging from internal conflicts concerning a sense of feminine identity to organizational barriers that discourage career development, these workers face employment situations that may require considerable adaptability and resilience. The present chapter will attempt to consider some of the factors that have been found to be important in the career choices that an increasing number of women are making.

As a general aim, we will try to determine whether there is anything unique about women's response to work. How do they respond to various work incentives, what are their career expectations and aspirations, what are their principal sources of job satisfaction? Is there anything associated with the way children are raised in our culture that makes a woman's response to the work setting any different from that of a man? Both social and psychological factors will be considered. For example, one important social question concerns changing family roles. To what extent do men share the household chores that were previously assigned to women? Do men assume a more active role in the care of children when the mother enters the job market? Overall, what are the marital consequences of women's entry into the labor market?

Of the many psychological issues relating to women at work, one of the more interesting concerns the expectations and aspirations women tend to bring into the job market. Not only does there seem to be an increase in the level of confidence and optimism that women express concerning the nature of work and its availability; these positive feelings are also associated with personal conflict when they are brought up against some of the more traditional ideas that women may have developed. For instance, some social scientists contend that there are social forces at work that tend to make women less competitive and more fearful of success. There are others who maintain that a number of women experience a sense of guilt when they choose a work career over the more traditional marriage-related role. This chapter will consider these and other psychological issues, but before doing so, it would probably be prudent to look more closely at some of the information that is available concerning the changing character of women's role in the workplace.

SOCIAL INDICATORS

There are many who see women's changing work roles as an expression of a recent social movement to achieve equity for women in a broad range of social affairs. In some respects this is true, but by and large the movement of women into various sectors of the job market is a trend that has been visible for decades, and its consistency is most interesting. For the past century there has been a steady increase in women's participation in paid work, with no significant reversal in trend being evident throughout this long period (see Table 16.1). Perhaps one can better gauge the magnitude of these changes by noting that from 1950 to 1975 the entry of women into places of

TABLE 16.1   Labor-Force Participation Rates by Sex From 1890 to 1980

Year	Percent Participation[1]		
	Total	Women	Men
1890	52.2	18.2	84.3
1900	53.7	20.0	85.7
1920	54.3	22.7	84.6
1940	52.4	27.9	82.5
1950	59.9	33.9	86.8
1960	57.3	37.8	80.4
1970	61.3	43.4	80.6
1980	62.8	51.7	78.0

[1]Percent estimates before 1940 obtained from the Decennial Census; estimates 1940 to the present obtained from Labor Department average monthly employment data.

Sources: *Statistical history of the United States from colonial times to the present: 1976.* Data from 1980 obtained from U.S. Department of Labor, *Employment and earnings*, 1980, *28*(1), 26.

work has accounted for over three-fifths of all the net additions to the labor force (Sum, 1977).

Male Participation

Correlated with the rise in women's participation rates has been a steady decline in the rate of male participation in the labor market. In 1950, for example, 86.4 percent of all men 16 years of age or over were found in the labor force. By 1976 this figure had fallen to 77.5 percent (Bednarzik & Klein, 1977). Although the greatest decline in male participation rates has been among younger (16–25) and older (55–64) workers, there has also been a noticeable drop among males in the prime working years (25–54 years). Deutermann (1977) suggests that schooling and early retirement account for the decline among younger and older workers, but the reasons are more obscure when it comes to the 25- to 54-year group. To what extent the entrance of women into the job market is a factor in this decline is uncertain; however, almost half of these prime-working-age nonparticipants who lived with their wives reported that their wives were employed. The most frequently mentioned reason for not working, health, was reported by about 45 percent of this 25- to 54-year

FIGURE 16.1 Employed Persons by Sex and Occupation.

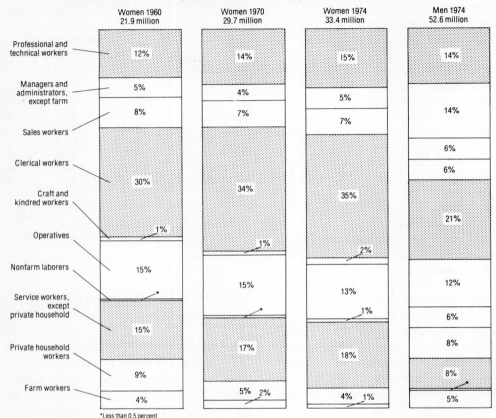

	Women 1960 21.9 million	Women 1970 29.7 million	Women 1974 33.4 million	Men 1974 52.6 million
Professional and technical workers	12%	14%	15%	14%
Managers and administrators, except farm	5%	4%	5%	14%
Sales workers	8%	7%	7%	
Clerical workers				6%
				6%
	30%	34%	35%	
Craft and kindred workers				21%
Operatives	1%	1%	2%	
Nonfarm laborers	15%	15%	13%	12%
Service workers, except private household	*	*	1%	6%
	15%			8%
Private household workers		17%	18%	
	9%			8%
Farm workers	4%	5% 2%	4% 1%	5%

*Less than 0.5 percent

Notice how gradually shifts in occupational groups have been occurring. This slow pace is representative of many changes that have been taking place in work phenomena.

Source: *U.S. working women.* **U.S. Department of Labor, Bulletin 1980, 1975.**

age group, but whatever the reasons, there is clear evidence that there has been a significant change in the rates of men's and women's participation in work. Rising rates for women and declining rates for men describe the changing composition of the national labor force.

Women's Participation and Age

The change in women's rate of participation in paid work has not been uniform for all ages. Female teenagers have been entering the labor market in increasing numbers. In 1974, 40 percent of women 16 and 17, and 58 percent of women 18 and 19 years old were active in the labor force (Grossman, 1975). The highest rate of female participation, however, is found among young women 20 to 24 (63 percent). For ten years, beginning in 1964, this group increased its rate of participation by almost 1.5 percent each year, in large measure as a consequence of the fact that an increasing proportion of these women were remaining unmarried or were marrying and not having children at an early age. Between the ages of 25 and 44, more than half (53 percent) of all women worked in paid jobs.

We find in these labor statistics clear evidence

**TABLE 16.2   Occupational Distribution of Employed Women
1962 and 1974**

Occupational Group	Employed Women		Women as a percent of all employed	
	1962	1974	1962	1974
All employed	23,029	33,417	33.9	38.9
Professional	2890	4992	35.9	40.5
Managerial	1138	1650	15.3	18.5
Sales	1715	2265	39.2	41.8
Clerical	6918	11,676	68.8	77.6
Craft workers	232	511	2.5	4.5
Operatives	3392	4331	25.9	31.1
Nonfarm laborers	94	354	2.6	8.1
Farmers and farm managers	132	98	5.1	6.0
Farm laborers	730	385	32.0	27.4
Service workers, except private household	3457	5955	53.5	58.7
Private household	2330	1201	97.3	97.8

Source: Garfinkle, S. H. Occupations of women and black workers, 1962–1974. *Monthly Labor Review,* 1975, *98*(4), p. 27.

that women are moving into the labor market in increasing numbers. Younger workers, responding to changing patterns of marriage and to growing economic pressures, are entering the labor market and staying there for longer periods of time (Fullerton & Byrne, 1976). Women in the prime work age, 25 to 54, have also shown growing rates of involvement with paid work, whereas there has been a slight decline in the rate of participation for women 55 and older. This latter finding parallels the trends that are evident among men, and it probably reflects improved economic conditions that make early retirement a more realistic alternative.

Where Women Work

In spite of the fact that women are found in the labor force in ever increasing numbers, the pattern of their employment has not undergone radical change. Statistical studies (Waldman & McEaddy, 1974) show that women are occupying the same kinds of jobs they have held in past decades. Clerical work, teaching, and retail sales account for a large number of jobs held by women. Garfinkle (1975) reports that in 1974 women accounted for

77.6 percent of all employees in clerical occupations and 58.7 percent of all service workers (see Table 16.2). Women also accounted for 98 percent of all registered nurses and over 84 percent of all elementary school teachers. Granted, there have been signs of change in many occupational categories, but the truth of the matter remains that those occupations that in the 1960s accounted for large concentrations of female employment remained in the middle 1970s the principal sources of work for women.

There have been important signs of the beginning of change in the occupational location of women workers. By and large, there is evidence of a shift in employment; jobs that traditionally have been dominated by one sex are beginning to employ more of the other sex. This trend is operating in both directions. For example, in 1962, 86.5 percent of all elementary teachers were women; by 1974 this figure dropped to 84.3 percent. In 1962, 97.2 percent of all judges and lawyers were men; by 1974 this figure had dropped to 93 percent. Hence for a variety of reasons, one important one being federal legislation discouraging discrimination in hiring, there have been noticeable, although in some instances small, changes in the distribution of the sexes among the various occupational fields. The labor market still contains, however, many jobs that are viewed primarily as men's or women's work.

SOCIALIZATION, SEX ROLES, AND WORK

The behavior we see in others is usually the result of a long and complicated learning period during which the individual is trained to adjust to the social world. This training and the persons who provide it are parts of a complex mechanism called *socialization*. Socialization refers to social learning, and it is a process that leads to the development of social habits, that is, ways of reacting to other people. In most instances these habits are supportive of the social system into which the person is being initiated; and as a result, socialization most often leads to behaviors that are positively sanctioned by the society. When we are "good," those around us reward this behavior. When we are "bad," we are punished. Socialization, therefore, is a global concept referring to every facet of social learning. It is a term that is used to express the fact that much of our behavior bears the stamp of the social environment in which we have been reared.

Socialization and Personality

As social habits develop, they become relatively permanent parts of the personality; hence, the influence of the social environment becomes an integral part of the psychology of the person. The social world becomes an indivisible part of one's psychological makeup and as a consequence, it is often difficult to recognize the social origins of many behaviors. What expresses itself as the individual personality is often an expression of a set of social influences that are common to many who live in the same culture.

Agents

The agents of socialization are other persons and groups who possess the psychological re-

sources—that is, rewards and punishments—that facilitate learning new social behaviors. The family is usually thought to be the principal socializing agent. It is here that the individual is introduced to a social world that broadens with age to include the school, peer groups, and other socializing influences. It is within the family that individuals become acquainted with the model of society that serves as the basis of their understanding of the social world and how it works. This social model includes a wide assortment of positions and status relationships, and surrounding each is a set of expectations concerning how people who occupy these positions *should behave*. The rabbi or priest *should* be devout and dignified; the mother, loving and generous; the executive, confident and dynamic. Thus, it is within these social models that we find prescriptions concerning how people in different social positions *should act*, and these prescriptions can play a significant part in determining how they *will* behave.

Roles

Social behaviors are often described in terms of the concept of role. A role is a set of expectations regarding what is appropriate behavior for individuals who occupy a given social position, a set of ideas concerning how a person *should* behave. Role consideration enters into the relationships between people. What one may see in the interaction between a teacher and a student, for example, is not only an expression of two unique personalities, but a behavioral exchange that is influenced by the role commitments made by each. Teachers behave in a fashion that is consistent with their concept of the teacher role; students react in accordance with the requirements of the student role. Violations of these role relationships (for example, a student's display of arrogance, a teacher's indifference to a student's efforts to learn) are considered to be inappropriate.

The roles adopted by an individual often serve several psychological functions. In some instances they function to give direction to the individual's behavior. In other instances they function to evaluate and interpret the behavior of others with whom the person comes into contact. Some roles are incorporated into the self-concept and play a part in defining the individual's sense of identity. "Who am I?" a person asks. "I am honest, intelligent, a police officer, a woman." The self is identified through a number of role commitments, some of which concern personal attributes; others refer to social position.

Each role plays a part in defining the behaviors that are available to the person. For instance, a commitment to the role of an honest person encourages the individual to draw on certain kinds of responses (truthfulness) and avoid certain others (lying, cheating). Hence a role often functions to set limits on the behaviors that may be used by the individual. We tend to draw on behaviors that are role consistent, but these kinds of actions do not exhaust all the responses that might be made. All persons have access to behaviors that they rarely if ever employ, because these acts would be incompatible with the role commitments they have made. A role, therefore, is associated with both a cluster of role-consistent behaviors and a cluster of role-inconsistent behaviors. Hence, to know something about a person's role commitments is to gain insight into the categories of behavior the person often uses and the kinds of behaviors that person normally avoids.

Sex Roles

Of all the role commitments made by the individual, none is more basic than the commitment made to the person's sex. A sex role refers to sets of beliefs and attitudes concerning the behaviors and dispositions thought to be appropriate for the members of a given sex. When these views are held by a large number of people, they are called sex-role *stereotypes*. Most of us are familiar with these stereotypes; men are aggressive, independent, competitive, and emotionally controlled; women are nonaggressive, dependent, noncompetitive, and emotionally volatile. Men hunt, play poker, watch professional football. Women watch soap operas, go to bridal showers, knit sweaters. Perhaps to some extent these behaviors originate in the biological differences separating the two

sexes, but by and large, the major contributor to these roles seems to be found in the different patterns of socialization to which men and women are exposed.

Sex-Role Differentiation. Beginning with the earliest phases of childhood, parental behavior often is found to be different for girls and boys. For example, Goldberg and Lewis (1969) observed a group of mothers interacting with their six-month-old babies and found different patterns of parenting behavior for girls and boys. Mothers of girls touched their babies more, vocalized to them more, and frequently breast-fed them. When these same infants reached the age of thirteen months, they showed similar role differences in their interaction with their mothers. For instance, girls touched their mothers and talked to them more than did boys.

As time progresses, boys are exposed to parenting techniques that place emphasis on achievement, competition, the control of feelings (big boys don't cry), and concern for rule conformity (Block, 1973). For girls, stress is placed on developing satisfying interpersonal relationships, being open about their feelings, and showing affection. By an early age, sex-role stereotypes seem to be well established (Schlossberg & Goodman, 1972; Broverman et al., 1972). Furthermore, the characteristics commonly associated with the male role are often more highly valued by both men and women (Brown, 1958; Sherriffs & McKee, 1957). Hence, part of the feminine role is a belief that women have negative attributes and undesirable traits (Sherriffs & McKee, 1957). These beliefs often have a profound psychological effect on the individual. Block, von der Lippe, and Block (1973) maintain that sex-role stereotypes commonly associated with men tend to expand the personal options that are available, while female sex roles tend to restrict alternatives. Adopting these traditional stereotypes results in self-perceptions that determine the kinds of activities that people believe to be appropriate for themselves. Career choice and work activities are a case in point.

Sex Roles and Work

Sex-role stereotypes operate to restrict the kind of work available for men and women. Opportunities for employment are often restricted by the sex-role perceptions held by those who are in a position to hire women. Hence women have been denied access to certain jobs not only by their own sex-role attitudes, but also by sets of firmly entrenched sex-role stereotypes that operate in the work organization to make a variety of positions unavailable to them (Bem and Bem, 1973).

Block et al. (1973) maintain that socialization often encourages nurturant, submissive, and conservative behaviors in women, and as a consequence, jobs that draw heavily on these behaviors (teaching, nursing, secretarial work) are often seen as women's work. Therefore, as a function of a socialization process from which a woman obtains a view of herself, a woman often approaches the job market in search of work that is compatible with the sex-role commitments she has made. In doing so she often finds a job market in which these stereotypes are reflected in the hiring practices that operate.

Social scientists have tried to identify several patterns that describe the typical female work careers that emerge from this situation. Osipow (1975), for example, suggests that one may think of women's work careers in terms of three broad patterns:

---

1. *The Homemaker*—A career in which the woman never engages in any significant paid work outside the role of housewife, mother, and wife.
2. *Traditional Work*—A career that involves the woman in work of the type traditionally associated with female sex stereotypes. In this pattern the woman may or may not be married and she may leave the labor force for periods of time to bear and raise children.
3. *Pioneer Work Pattern*—Those displaying this career pattern may or may not be married. For a significant portion of her adult life the woman engages in paid work that brings her into competition with men in areas of work usually associated with the male role. She shows a significant commitment to work and to moving up in her vocation.

These patterns are the outcome of a number of social-psychological factors. Circumstances and opportunities lend an unpredictable component to the choice of careers, but the way people see themselves cannot be overlooked as an important contributor to the choices that are made.

The Androgynous Personality. Some argue that it is a mistake to describe personality in terms of the extent to which the individual draws on behaviors that are either masculine or feminine. To be sure, there are individuals whose commitment to a particular sex-linked role denies them access to those behaviors that are characteristic of the other sex. Hence, highly masculine males may be unable to draw on feminine behaviors, since to do so would entail an unacceptable violation of a self-view that is tightly bound up with male stereotypes.

Behaviors that are masculine or feminine do not necessarily exist in mutually exclusive categories. It is possible for an individual to be able to draw on both types of behavior, and to do so as the requirements of the situation dictate. From this perspective it is often inaccurate to describe an individual's personality in terms of a position on a scale that has masculinity at one end and femininity at the other. For some individuals the personality is not bound to a given sex stereotype, but is free to select masculine and feminine behaviors that are appropriate to meet the needs of the situation. Bem (1974) and Spence and Helmreich (1978) refer to this as an androgynous personality, and this type of structure serves as an alternative to those personality configurations that may best be described in terms of either masculine or feminine types.

The broader range of behavioral options that are associated with the androgynous male or female implies a personality structure that is more adaptable, and hence more likely to reflect signs of positive mental health. From a vocational perspective, the androgynous personality is associated with a range of occupational choices that is not limited to those jobs that are compatible with the traditional male-female image. Having a broader set of alternatives, the androgynous person would be expected to have a better chance of securing work that is psychologically fulfilling, and once having taken a job, to be better able to adapt to the full range of experiences that work and the employing organization can provide.

WOMEN AND THE CHOICE OF OCCUPATIONS

Why people end up in one occupation or another has, for a long time, attracted the attention of social scientists. To consider this question in the light of one's own career often leads to the conclusion that coincidence as much as anything else is responsible for the line of work one is following. The job one has often seems to be the result of the most superficial, or even fortuitous happenings. "I took a course in economics and admired the instructor; this led to my adopting economics as a major." "A friend of mine told me they were hiring down at the plant, and I went and applied for a job; I've been working there ever since." These and other such tales suggest that job selection and career development is mainly a combination of chance and the availability of specific opportunities.

Yet there is a considerable body of literature that suggests that the sorting out of people into various occupational fields is not a haphazard affair. Rather, it is an expression of the psychology of the individual and the social environment within which the individual has been reared. Recall from Chapter 8 that Holland (1973) identified occupational choice with six personality types according to which both people and jobs may be classified. Holland maintains that people tend to gravitate toward jobs that provide a work environment that is congruent with their dominant personality characteristics.

Super's Theory

Donald E. Super and his associates (Super, 1951, 1957; Super et al., 1963) present a somewhat similar point of view. They see an occupation as a social-psychological environment wherein an individual may play a role that is appropriate to one's self-concept.

In expressing a vocational preference, a person puts into occupational terminology his idea of the kind of person he is; that in entering an occupation, he seeks to implement a concept of himself; that in getting established in an occupation he achieves self actualization. (Super et al., 1963, p. 1)

What Super is saying is that as individuals mature they tend to develop ideas concerning the kinds of people typically found in various occupations; they also translate concepts they hold about themselves into these occupational terms. The choice of work is influenced by individuals' perceptions of the kind of person they are, compared to the kind of people they believe are found in a given line of work.

Super et al. (1963) maintain that this extension of one's self-concept into different occupational categories may be the result of several types of experiences. For example, one may identify with an adult who is in a particular occupational role, and this may cause this occupation to be seen as compatible with the kind of person one believes oneself to be. Or one may have direct experience with an occupation and find that it fits one's self-concept quite well. Or a person may have been successful in school subjects that are associated with a particular occupation.

An important part of the self-concept is the sex role the individual has adopted, and it is quite reasonable to expect that this aspect of the self will be translated into occupational terms. As a consequence, a woman whose self-concept includes the traditional sex-role stereotypes that are widely held in our culture, will often choose an occupation that has traditionally been reserved for women. Conversely, a woman who thinks of herself in terms of nontraditional sex roles is often found pursuing a career that involves activities usually thought of as men's work. A culture that trains its young people to draw clear distinctions between the personal attributes and abilities of men and women will find these distinctions operating in the selection of careers. Hence, according to this point of view, one important reason why we find large numbers of women entering nursing, secretarial work, and the teaching profession is that many of these women have been taught to think of themselves and these jobs in terms of very traditional sex-role stereotypes.

Research Evidence.   There is some support in the research literature for this kind of argument. Kotcher (1975), for example, found that in early adolescence young women who identify with male sex-role attributes tend to see themselves going into occupations that are traditionally male. As these self-concepts change in later adolescence and become more feminine, the occupational choices they make tend to involve more feminine kinds of jobs. This study, along with several others (for example, Richardson, 1975; Hanley, 1974), indicates that women tend to choose occupations that are compatible with the way they view themselves. Furthermore, women whose psychological needs are more closely related to those usually identified with a male role tend to choose occupations that are nontraditional. Trigg and Perlman (1976) found that women applying for training in nontraditional fields showed lower need for affiliation compared with applicants for training in traditional fields. They also considered being married and having children less important.

Interests, personality characteristics, self-concept, all have been linked with the occupation one chooses (Rand, 1968); even the content of one's daydreams has been found to relate to the career plans and academic choices one makes (Touchton & Magoon, 1977). When these psychological events are sorted into behaviors identified with male or female roles, they are often found to predict whether a woman will seek a career in male- or female-dominated segments of the job market.

Social Influences

A woman's self-concept is an important contributor to her decision to embark on a work career and to enter a traditional or a nontraditional sphere of work. This is not the only factor, however. Work careers, whether traditional or nontraditional, are often influenced by other people with whom we associate; and in the case of women, the literature shows us that it is not only parental influence but the influence of the significant male friends in their lives that contributes to the career choices that are made. Trigg and Perlman (1976) report that college-age women seeking nontraditional career goals tend to receive support from boyfriends who have positive attitudes toward this kind of work. Hanley (1974) also found that a group of college senior women who perceived approval from the significant males in their lives tended to maintain a high level of commitment to a work career as opposed to a career in homemaking.

Of course, there are many instances in which a woman finds a significant role model in other women. In certain cases the mother, especially if she has had a successful work career, can serve as a potent influence that directs a woman into a particular career channel. Teachers, friends, and admired public figures may all contribute to a woman's career directions. The main point is that the choice of careers is a matter that is vulnerable to influences from a wide range of significant people who enter an individual's life.

Pioneers, Traditionals, and Homemakers

We have already seen that social scientists have often found it convenient to classify women in three categories of career orientation. Persons entering areas of work that in the past have hired very few women are called *pioneers* or *innovators.* Those whose work takes them into jobs typically associated with women—nurses, teachers, and so forth—are called *traditionals,* while those who remain at home and care for the house and children are called *homemakers.*

Not all of these categories are of equal breadth. The homemaker group, for example, includes a very narrow set of work alternatives compared to the traditionals who are found in a wider variety of jobs. Pioneers, on the other hand, are to be found in a range of jobs that vary even more than is the case with the traditionals (Tangri, 1969). Hence, we might expect that with regard to a number of psychological variables there would be variation in the spread of differences found among the women in each of these three categories.

There is an abundance of evidence indicating that the three groups tend to differ from each other in a number of social and psychological characteristics. Tangri (1969), in studying samples of college women, found that pioneers tended to aspire to higher levels of personal accomplishment than did traditionals. They also expressed a higher level of commitment to their work than did the traditionals and were motivated to achieve by factors that were more intrinsic to their work than was the case for the traditionals. Several studies (Moore & Veres, 1976; Watley & Kaplan, 1971) suggest that the woman who is strongly committed to a work career and is pursuing innovative career plans tends to be more able scholastically. Wolkon (1972) finds that pioneers differ significantly from traditionals in the reasons behind their working. Pioneers show a stronger desire to work, and place higher value on such things as engaging in interesting activities and opportunity to master a challenging task. Oliver (1974) finds that women with high career orientation tend to show evidence of high need for achievement, and Lawlis and Crawford (1975) report that women who take jobs in male-dominated occupations are better able to deal with social relationships that are more complicated. Traditionals tend to see social relationships in a simpler fashion. These authors suggest that women who are embarking on careers that take them into pioneering areas will be confronted with social relationships involving both men and women. To be attracted to these more complex social situations the pioneer must have greater ability to cope with these social complexities.

One could continue to cite studies that point out social and psychological differences between women who adopt different career orientations. The main point, however, is that these social and psychological differences are thought to lie behind the choice of career, and they serve to dispose individuals to seek out work oportunities that are in harmony with their psychological makeups.

Personality, Sex Differences, and Occupational Choice

One viewpoint contends that there are important differences between men and women in many traits and that these characteristics are significant in determining occupational compatibility. As a consequence, the division of jobs into male and female occupations is a reflection of the differences that separate the two sexes. Although some of these traits are physical, for example, strength, many are associated with socialization practices that lead to separate patterns of interests and personality in men and women.

There is some support for the contention that men and women do differ in vocationally related characteristics (Gottfredson, Holland, & Gottfredson, 1974; Prediger & Hanson, 1976); but as one might suspect, there is considerable overlap between the two groups. Theories of vocational choice suggest that the movement of women into nontraditional jobs operates according to the same principles that govern men's movement into these jobs. That is, both women and men seek out occupations that are compatible with their psychological makeups. As a result, men and women in the same occupation should be found to have similar personality characteristics.

The research evidence that has been assembled to test this idea has not been particularly supportive. Rosenthal (1974) observed a national sample of women and concluded that a woman's occupational choice depends more on her present social circumstances than on her early socialization experiences. Oftentimes, the career followed by a woman is the result of an effort to balance economic objectives with the needs of her current family situation. The choice, according to Rosenthal, does not limit itself to that band of jobs in which a woman will find compatible work associates. Rather, vocational choice is an expression of more immediate and pragmatic considerations that relate to economics, family, and opportunities.

Prediger and Hanson (1976) analyzed data obtained from 39,000 men and women in 104 different occupations. These data contained personality measures that were expressed in terms of Holland's six personality types (see Chapter 5). Men and women working in the same occupation were compared, and the findings indicated substantial differences between the two sexes. These data show that men and women pursuing the same occupation do not necessarily display the same personality patterns. Furthermore, the differences that did exist were larger in situations in which women were working in nontraditional occupations.

Why these differences appeared is open to speculation. Perhaps, for some reason traceable to early learning, women may perceive the field of occupations differently than men. In doing so, they may translate a given self-concept into a different set of occupational categories. Furthermore, the nontraditional occupation for women is the traditional occupation for men. Embarking on a pioneering career, therefore, probably requires personal characteristics that are not needed by men who are following traditional career plans. As a case in point, Gump (1972) finds that women who actively pursue traditional sex-role goals show evidence of lower ego strength than do those who have nontraditional goals. Hence, the contrasts Prediger and Hanson report between men and women in the same occupations may well result from a comparison of one group of people following traditional career plans with another group that is following nontraditional plans.

Parental Models

The relationships that women establish with their parents have been shown to play a significant role in the career decisions they make. The father, in particular, has often been thought of as playing a critical part in the daughter's decision to seek a work career. The masculine role usually involves a high commitment to status, competence, and achievement, and these attributes are more closely associated with a work career than with the mother's homemaking role. As a result, it is often thought that women who pursue work careers would be expected to report that their fathers are a more important object of identification than would women who become homemakers. Several studies (Roe & Siegelman, 1964; Oliver, 1975) have, in fact, found this to be true, but there is a growing amount of evidence that suggests that the relationship is far from simple.

In those instances in which the mother has a work career of her own, there is evidence that she can provide a model with which the daughter can identify. Tangri (1969), for example, found that more highly educated working mothers do serve as important role models for women who are following nontraditional careers. Perhaps the social status of a working mother is higher than that of the homemaker, and as a consequence the working mother can provide the daughter with a more attractive role model. Both Douvan (1963) and Baruch (1974) have found this to be true. Baruch (1972) has also reported that the daughters of working mothers tend to place higher values on feminine competence than do women whose mothers do not work. Hence, it seems that both father and mother do play roles in providing a model that is used by the daughter in selecting and pursuing a work career. The status held by the parents and the extent to they have succeeded in their respective careers are important considerations underlying their influence as role models.

Organizational Influences

A number of factors have been found to influence women's choice of work careers (Stein & Bailey, 1973). Some of these factors are external, being found in the customs and practices of the society; others are internal, being part of the individual's psychological makeup. Recently much attention has been directed to certain personnel practices that operate to create barriers to women who are seeking nontraditional kinds of employment. Over the years work organizations have evolved personnel procedures that incorporate many of the traditional sex stereotypes that have led to the division of jobs into "women's work" and "men's work." Personnel officers and school officials have often served as "vocational gatekeepers" who directed women and men into lines of work that were generally thought to be "appropriate" for their sex roles. Every facet of a personnel program—recruitment, selection, placement, training, and promotion—could function to exclude people from certain kinds of work because of their sex. For example, Bem and Bem (1973) report evidence indicating that the wording of a job advertisement can serve to direct women away from jobs that are perceived as being more appropriate for men. Industry practices such as this have in the past been successful in maintaining traditional sex-linked differences in the assignment of jobs. Title VII of the Civil Rights Act of 1964 was written to prevent employers from discriminating against job applicants and employees on the basis of race, color, national origin, *and sex*. Directed toward biased recruiting and hiring practices, this act attempts to broaden the range of vocational choices that are available to all. In the light of this legislation, company personnel practices have been subject to reconsideration, and as a consequence one should expect gradual changes in the organizational impediments that function to identify certain jobs in terms of sex-related attributes.

Motivation to Avoid Success

Ambition, competitiveness, and success are attributes that usually are not associated with a feminine role. As a consequence, women who display these characteristics may be seen as unfeminine and as socially less attractive. Horner (1968, 1970, 1972) contends that these circumstances motivate many able women to fear and avoid success, since to achieve is to threaten the sex-role commitments that lie at the very foundation of the individual's self-concept. High-status jobs and challenging and demanding educational programs are less attractive to a woman whose apprehension of success leads

her into more traditional and lesser status vocations. The prospects of high achievement, therefore, often place women in conflict situations. To achieve is to attain desired goals; but at the same time, achievement threatens self-concepts that are fundamental to women's psychological adjustment. As a result, Horner argues, most women are motivated to avoid success. Furthermore, this motivation is probably stronger in women with high ability and high achievement needs.

Horner's Study. Horner (1968) reports a study in which men and women were asked to complete a story that involved a woman (a man for the male subjects) who displayed a high level of achievement. Ninety females completed the following story, "After first term finals Anne (John for the male subjects) finds herself at the top of her medical school class." In response to this successful female character, 65 percent of the women subjects expressed negative ideas, many of which dealt with the loss of femininity, social rejection, and personal or social destruction. Fewer than 10 percent of the male subjects responded negatively to the successful male character.

Horner (1972) contends that the motivation to avoid success stems from a person's expectation that success will lead to negative consequences. For many women the anticipation of success, therefore, results in anxiety, which can be reduced by the individual withdrawing from the situation. A psychological barrier is therefore established, which discourages an individual from actively striving for certain kinds of achievement. Horner maintains that the traditional child-rearing practices that are found in most middle-class families make achievement and femininity two incompatible goals. Male children, on the other hand, are exposed to parenting behaviors that form a positive link between masculinity and achievement. To achieve in the case of the male is to fulfill one's sex-role identity; for many women, success leads to a loss of sexual identity. The absence of a proportionate number of women in high-status, achievement-related occupations is, according to this point of view, a reflection of these learned impediments to success, which are more characteristic of women than men.

Other Studies.   Horner's work has stimulated a large amount of research activity, the results of which have demonstrated the complexity of this point of view. For example, there are wide individual differences among women in this negative orientation toward achievement, and these differences seem to be associated with a number of factors. There is evidence, for instance, that suggests that the motive to avoid success is more clearly visible in situations in which there are negative sanctions against feminine achievement—for example, as when all other members of the group are males. Others (Tomlinson-Keasey, 1974) report that married women display higher achievement motivation and lower avoidance of success than do unmarried women. Several studies (Tangri, 1972; Williams & King, 1976) find that fear of success does not correlate significantly with achievement in school or with the choice of a college major. These latter findings probably reflect the fact that the social environment of school places less severe negative sanctions on female achievement.

One important conclusion drawn by Horner and her associates is that the fear of success is a type of behavior that is most characteristic of women. The difference between the sexes is attributed to the different patterns of socialization to which men and women are exposed. Yet recent tests of this proposition have failed to find this kind of behavior occurring with higher frequency among women. Furthermore, when men and women who display fear of success are identified, there seems to be very little difference between them in the manner in which this behavior operates (Canavan-Gumpert, Garner, & Gumpert, 1978).

The fear of success emerges whenever success-fearing people approach a success experience, and during these times they display what Canavan-Gumpert and her associates call ''self-sabotage'' behaviors. Success-fearing persons do, however, value success, but their desire for success appears most clearly when they are distant from a goal. Success-fearing individuals also fear failure, and

this becomes evident in their behavior whenever a failure situation either has occurred or is about to occur. It is interesting to note that studies report evidence indicating that although the fear of failure is an integral part of the fear-of-success syndrome, it still does not disrupt or interfere with the individual's performance. In fact, failure may improve performance; subjects who do not fear success tend not to respond to failure in this fashion.

There is much more that could be said about this interesting aspect of human behavior, but the main point for this chapter is that there is reason to doubt that the fear of success is a motivational problem that is most frequently found in women. As a consequence, in thinking about women's employment and career development, it would appear to be risky to apply this fear-of-success concept as a general explanation for differences between men and women employees.

THE CONSEQUENCES OF WORK

Up to this point we have been interested in the events that lead up to the entry of women into the job market. Career plans and vocational choice, especially as observed in college-educated women, have received a great deal of attention from researchers; the social and psychological consequences of working, however, are questions that are equally important. For instance, are there demonstrable differences in the manner in which women and men adopt roles and adjust to them? To the extent that differences exist, are they traceable to patterns of socialization to which women and men are exposed or are they a function of the structural characteristics of our work organizations?

We know that a man's social position is, in large measure, calculated on the basis of the job he holds. What do we know about social position and the jobs women hold? For example, to what extent do jobs, as contrasted to marriage, contribute to the social mobility women experience? Do employed women occupy socioeconomic positions that are comparable to those held by men?

Social Mobility and Status Attainment

Surprisingly, there are, on the average, substantial similarities between employed men and women in both their levels of education and the socioeconomic status of their occupations (Treiman & Terrell, 1975; McClendon, 1976). To be sure, there are differences in the distribution of working males and females across different levels of education and occupational attainment. Working women, for example, are found to be more heavily concentrated in the middle regions of educational attainment, having left school after completing high school. A higher proportion of males, on the other hand, have either left school before reaching high school or have completed a college degree. Averaging the two distributions, however, places men and women at comparable positions on the scale of educational attainment.

There is little question that the single most important determinant of the level of occupational attainment is education. There is also little doubt that there is a clear difference in the distribution of men and women across the various occupational fields. Men and women are found to be concentrated in different lines of work. Yet there is evidence (Treiman & Terrell, 1975; McClendon, 1976) that white male and female occupational status structures are very much alike, even though these status structures are based on different types of jobs. In spite of the fact that men and women are found working in different jobs, when the socioeconomic status of their jobs is considered, the *averages* for both groups are surprisingly similar.

On first impression this statement does not seem to fit in with many of the beliefs that are currently held regarding sex-related inequities in hiring and pay. We often think of women being assigned to the less desirable jobs in the labor market, but these results begin to make better sense when one takes into consideration the fact that the socioeconomic status of a job is a reflection of several variables. Educational level of the job occupants, pay, and ratings of the prestige of the job combine into a measure of the overall socioeconomic status of the position. For one component of this measurement, pay, women earn substantially less than men, even when they are in the same jobs (U.S. Department of Labor, 1975). Compensating for this wage inequity, however, women tend to be more heavily concentrated in white-collar work, which generally has higher prestige than blue-collar jobs. In the national samples used by McClendon (1976), two-thirds of the women were found working in white-collar jobs, while only one-half of the male sample were found in these jobs. As a result, when the higher prestige of white-collar work was factored in with the lower pay received by women, there resulted a distribution of socioeconomic status that was similar to the one associated with men's jobs. Although one can find industries that place large numbers of women in low-status, blue-collar jobs, across all job categories we find that higher proportions of men tend to be hired for blue-collar jobs that are generally viewed as involving low-prestige work.

All this may be of little comfort to a woman who is holding down a low-paying job or one who is facing an employment market that reserves many of the more attractive jobs for men. The fact remains, however, that just as high-prestige, white-collar jobs are disproportionately occupied by men, so too are low-prestige, blue-collar jobs. When job prestige and pay are combined into a measure of the socioeconomic status of jobs, the distributions are quite similar for men and women.

Intergenerational Mobility

Many Americans share a belief that each new generation should prosper more than the previous generation. One aspect of this theme involves the belief that as one generation follows another, there should be a steady improvement in a family's social position. The social scientist refers to this movement from one social level to another as *intergenerational mobility*. Social movement, up or down, is often gauged by considering the status of jobs held by family members of two different generations. For example, respondents may be asked what kinds of jobs their fathers held and what kinds of jobs the respondents now hold. Compar-

FIGURE 16.2   **Median Usual Weekly Earnings of Full-time Women Wage and Salary Workers by Occupation and as a Percent of Men's Earnings.**

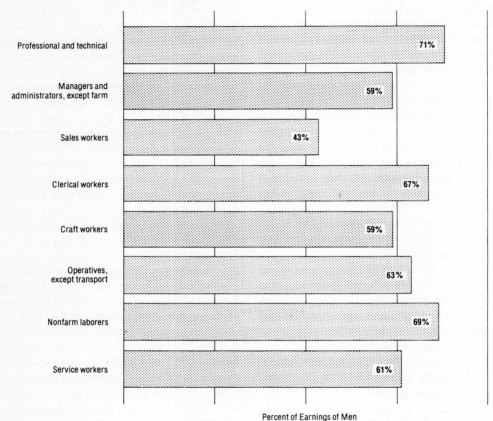

Professional and technical — 71%

Managers and administrators, except farm — 59%

Sales workers — 43%

Clerical workers — 67%

Craft workers — 59%

Operatives, except transport — 63%

Nonfarm laborers — 69%

Service workers — 61%

Percent of Earnings of Men

The usual weekly earnings of full-time women workers in eight broad occupational groups ranged from about 40 to 70 percent of the earnings of men.

Source: *U.S. working women.* U.S. Department of Labor, Bulletin 1980, 1975.

ison of the socioeconomic status of the two results in a measure of intergenerational mobility.

As a rule, the mechanisms for social mobility have been viewed as being different for men and women. Men are thought to improve their social standing primarily through the occupation they pursue, while women find social ascendency through marriage. Most of the information formerly available on this subject has referred to men. Recently, however, several studies (DeJong, Brawer, & Robin, 1971; Tyree & Treas, 1974;

Glenn, Ross, & Tully, 1974) have appeared that include women subjects, and we are beginning to get a clearer view of the movement of women up and down the social hierarchy.

The results of these studies show that women do experience social mobility as a function of the jobs they hold, but marriage seems to result in patterns of movement for women that are more similar to the patterns of social mobility that men experience through the jobs they hold (Tyree & Treas, 1974). In a recent study Glenn et al. (1974)

report that marriage choices of women result in much more fluid social movement than do the occupational choices made by men. In other words, women tend to move up *and down* the social scale more as a consequence of whom they marry than do men as the result of the jobs they select. There is also evidence of considerable downward mobility for women as the result of marriage, while similar amounts of downward movement were not seen in men as the result of the jobs they obtain. Women experience much more movement downward from their fathers' white-collar families to their husbands' blue-collar families. There seems to be a much more substantial barrier impeding the male's movement from white- to blue-collar social status.

Job Orientation

It is not difficult to find people who believe that there are substantial differences between men and women in their general orientation toward work. Considering the differences that have been observed in the socialization of males and females, it is easy to be led into assuming that there are many differences in the way men and women define what is and what is not important to them in their jobs, and the search for these differences has stimulated a goodly amount of research (Lyle & Ross, 1973). Differences between the sexes have been observed, but as a rule, these differences have been slight. When they do appear, sex differences in job orientation tend to involve women seeing greater importance in comfortable working conditions and congenial work associates, while men seem to see career success and pay as more important (Manhardt, 1972; Bartol, 1976). But there is reason to doubt whether even these differences can be attributed to the sex of the worker, since they often disappear when other variables are held constant. For example, Saleh and Lalljee (1969) found that job orientations of men and women were different when their sample included people who were in different jobs and at different job levels. When males and females on similar jobs were compared, however, these differences were no longer visible. Bartol (1976) reports sim-

ilar results. It would seem, therefore, that differences in job orientation, when they do occur, tend to be more closely tied in with the positions people hold and the training they receive than with their sex.

There is one interesting difference that has been observed in men's and women's orientation toward work, and that is that women are more accurately aware of men's orientation toward work. Burke (1966) reports two studies in which women were able to predict more accurately than men the opposite sex's preferences for the different rewards available at work. When asked about their own orientation toward their jobs, both men and women responded in a very similar fashion. When asked to predict what the opposite sex preferred, however, men showed very little understanding of the job conditions women subjects actually did prefer. Men tended to draw sharper distinctions between the sexes than did women.

Perhaps Burke's studies point out a general tendency on the part of people who occupy a privileged position in any social system to perceive clearly defined differences between themselves and those in less advantaged positions. Advantaged members tend to acknowledge the validity of the system that has vested them with rank and privilege. They see status differentials as an expression of real differences between the attributes people possess. Nonprivileged people, on the other hand, are probably more prone to minimize the differences that exist between themselves and those in favored circumstances. Traditionally, men have been given a number of social privileges. This is particularly true in the area of careers and occupations. Hence, when asked to describe certain psychological characteristics of men and women workers, men tend to draw clear distinctions; women tend to perceive few differences between themselves and men.

Women's Commitment to Work

It is often believed that commitment to a career is of secondary importance to women. Marriage and family roles are thought to be of much higher importance, and because of this, many employers claim that it is economically unrealistic to hire and train women for important jobs. Marriage plans, pregnancy, and child-care problems often make women's employment status appear to be unreliable. Traditionally, work for women occupied that period in life between the completion of schooling and marriage. According to this model, once married, a woman leaves the labor force and assumes household chores. Those who return to work at a later date do so to provide a supplementary income for the family. Under circumstances such as these, it is expected that a woman's commitment to long-term career plans will be rather low. But we are facing a changing vocational world, and this traditional career model may no longer apply to large numbers of women.

It is extremely difficult to measure long-range commitments of this sort, and as a consequence, there is no definitive answer to this question. There have been surveys, however, and many of them do show that a large number of women see their primary commitment involving their families and their husbands' careers. There is a growing list of surveys (Mishler, 1975), however, that indicate that there is an increasing number of women who want to participate in *both* family and work and who believe that a strong commitment to one does not preclude a strong commitment to the other. A study by Gannon and Hendrickson (1973) is a case in point. This study finds that working wives with a strong commitment to the family are just as likely to be committed to their jobs as wives with low family commitments. Hence, in spite of the traditional view, it is quite clear that women are psychologically capable of maintaining their family- and work-role involvements, and that family concerns do not necessarily reduce their commitment to their jobs.

Finances versus Fulfillment. What lies at the root of women's movement into the labor force is a topic that involves psychological, sociological, and economic variables. Economic motives have doubtless played a significant role in bringing large numbers of women into the labor force. The desire to improve a family's financial resources is a rea-

son that is found behind many women's decision to enter the labor force, and for a growing number of families, the woman's income represents the sole source of support. But are financial motives more important to women than ego needs?

A survey of working wives (Sobol, 1963) reports that financial reasons were the *most frequently* cited motives for working on their present jobs. In this sample, large numbers of women reported that they were working because "the family needs the money" or "to buy something." However, when a measure of long-range work commitment was considered (that is, to what extent does the wife plan to work in the future), actual family income, the income of either the husband or the wife, did not relate to these future work commitments. Sobol maintains that a woman's commitment to work is a function of the adequacy of a family's income *as it is viewed from the family's own standards*. It is not how much the family earns, but whether they see the family income as being adequate that is a major factor underlying a wife's commitment to work.

Financial needs, although frequently mentioned, were not the *most important* factors found underlying a woman's commitment to a career. Working to fill a need for accomplishment and working so as to be able to meet people or occupy one's time were found to be more highly related to a woman's future career plans. Hence, financial contribution to the family appears to be of secondary importance to a woman's commitment to work, when compared to the satisfactions that are obtained from the work itself and from the social setting of work. The point of all this is that when women are asked for their immediate reasons for working, financial motives are often cited, but when long-term career plans are considered, we find that financial incentives do not necessarily serve as the principal variable underlying their commitment.

Absences from Work. All this begs the question of whether women's commitment to work is comparable to that of men. The experimental problems associated with any direct comparison between the sexes would be substantial; there is, however, indirect evidence that is of some relevance to this question, even if it does not provide us with a final answer. Part of this evidence is found in a study of the pattern of women's job absences, which have been found to be correlated with the activities of her family. What these data show are that family needs often subordinate a woman's commitment to work, resulting in her absence from work.

Chadwick-Jones, Brown, and Nicholson (1973) carried out a study in which they plotted absences over a full year for a large group of women employed in the textile industry. Their data reflect noticeable increases in short-term absences that coincided with the husbands' work vacations and with the children's school holidays. Furthermore, childhood illness typically takes the mother away from the job, not the father. Hedges and Barnett (1972) cite the results of a survey that found that one-fourth of low-income, white mothers left their last jobs because of child-care problems. These authors also report that when the woman in the family works, there is often very little change in the hours invested in household activities by the man. The working woman often seems to face two jobs, household work and paid employment. Her dual role commitment, coupled with the general expectation that hers is the primary responsibility for house and child care, may influence job attendance and give the impression of low commitment to her job.

We find, therefore, a complicated picture of the level of involvement in work that characterizes women workers. On the positive side, there has been a steady increase in the rates of women's participation in work, not only in terms of job holding but in terms of the increasing length of their work career. There has also been a significant increase in the number of women who hold several jobs. Finally, there is evidence suggesting that for many women the primary factor behind their commitment to work is not family finances, but their own efforts to secure a more interesting set of life experiences. On the negative side, one might cite the attendance problems women sometimes have.

These attendance patterns, however, probably reflect women's burdensome commitment to both home and work roles, rather than a fundamental lack of interest and involvement with their work.

Satisfaction with Housework and Employment

In the light of much that is being said about the nature of homemaking, one might question whether women who are engaged in full-time housework are as satisfied with their work as are those who are employed outside the home. Over the recent past, housework has been undergoing a significant devaluation in status. The routine, the lack of mental challenge, and the short-term consequences of many household chores make homemaking appear to be a dull and unfulfilling occupation. Employment and the prospects of a career are often viewed as much more attractive alternatives. The freedom from the confinement of the home, the intellectual challenge, heightened status, and social opportunities are among the many positive characteristics associated with a job. From this perspective, therefore, a work career offers a woman much greater potential for happiness and a sense of esteem and fulfillment.

There are, however, difficulties connected with the work role that are more or less peculiar to women's employment. Instead of freeing women from the tedium of housework, outside employment is often taken on as an additional responsibility. Taking a job does not relieve a woman from the household tasks she carried out before finding employment; rather, she often winds up holding two sets of commitments. Hedges and Barnett (1972), for example, cite a survey that involved 1300 husband-and-wife families from a range of different social classes. This survey revealed that women who were employed more than 30 hours a week averaged 34 hours a week on household tasks, while women who did not hold jobs spent, on the average, 57 hours a week on their household duties. Hence, 30 or more hours of outside work reduced time spent in housework by only 23 hours. Apparently paid work does reduce a woman's investment in housework, but this reduction is often not proportionate to the time investment made in the job. Taking a job, therefore, appears to involve a lengthening of the workweek, and results in many women occupying the dual role of housewife and wage earner.

But these dual role commitments do not necessarily lead to conflict and dissatisfaction. The psychological rewards associated with the job may more than compensate for the added hours of work that housework and employment require, and there is evidence that indicates that women who hold outside jobs in addition to their homemaking responsibilities are more satisfied with their work than women who are engaged in full-time housework. Oakley (1974), in a study that interviewed a sample of forty London housewives, found that about 70 percent expressed dissatisfaction with their homemaking roles. Monotony was the principal complaint, followed by reports of loneliness, which was a consequence of the social isolation that often accompanies housework. Ferree (1976) interviewed a sample of urban housewives and found that these women did not prefer full-time housework to outside employment. Women with full-time jobs were found to be happier and felt that they were better off than women who were homemakers. Dissatisfaction with housework was traced to low status, social isolation, and a feeling of powerlessness. Perhaps more important, women who engaged in outside employment reported that they had better opportunity to achieve a feeling of self-esteem and competence. Homemakers found it difficult to see themselves as competent, and as a consequence they reported that they experienced little sense of esteem and fulfillment from the housework role. Interestingly, women who held part-time jobs appeared to be more satisfied than either the housewives or the full-time job holders. Part-time workers were also more interested in the nonfinancial aspects of their work.

All studies do not, however, indicate that women, as a group, tend to be dissatisfied with housework and prefer paid employment. Some surveys (Komarovsky, 1962; Weaver & Holmes, 1975; Arvey & Gross, 1977) indicate that many women appear to be quite contented with their homemaking roles. Komarovsky (1962), in a study of 58 blue-collar marriages, reports that although the homemaking role is not without significant frustration, the majority of the sample expressed a general acceptance of this kind of work and regarded it as a respected role for women. Observing the most satisfactory samples in this area of research, Weaver and Holmes (1975) analyzed data obtained from two surveys that utilized large probability samples of the total noninstitutionalized population of the United States, 18 years of age or older. Respondents were asked; "On the whole, how satisfied are you with the work you do— would you say that you are very satisfied, moderately satisfied, satisfied, a little dissatisfied, or very dissatisfied?" The results indicate that among white females, 52 percent who had full-time jobs and 53 percent who were full-time housewives reported that they were very satisfied with their line of work. Among those who perceived the family's income as below that of the average American family, housewives were significantly *more* satisfied with their work than were women who were employed full time.

Some might argue that women who hold full-time jobs should be less satisfied with their work than women who are full-time housewives. This point of view contends that much of women's social training is directed toward preparing them for marriage and family roles; hence the homemaker's job fits in better with this kind of early training. The work role, on the other hand, does not receive the same prominence in the social preparation of women for adulthood. Yet the research that has been reported thus far does not permit us to conclude that work results in feelings of general discontentment. There is some evidence, however, that social class is an important consideration in determining women's reaction to the dual homemaking and work role. It is assumed that women from working-class families tend to adjust more comfortably to the homemaking role than do women from middle- and upper-class families, yet even this assumption finds contradictions in the literature (Komarovsky, 1962; Ferree, 1976). Therefore it is probably true that a whole constellation of factors moderates the adjustment of a woman to the homemaking and job roles. Social class, educational level, parental role models, husband's income, and community resources for volunteer and avocational activities all combine to determine whether a woman is satisfied with a homemaking or a job role. Hence, at the present time the research literature does not permit us to conclude that either housewives or jobholders are more, or less, satisfied with the work they do.

Job and Life Satisfaction

It is often thought that job satisfaction is related to an individual's general satisfaction with life. The job is such a significant dimension of the individual's total experience that satisfaction with work encourages satisfaction with life in general. This conclusion may be drawn from studies that have attempted to correlate measures of job and life satisfaction, but a closer examination of this literature reveals that many of these studies have observed only male jobholders. A 1957 study by Brayfield and Wells is one exception, since it did compute the relationship between job and life satisfaction separately for 41 male and 52 female Civil Service employees. Here a positive relationship was found between the two measures only for the male sample. For the women surveyed, satisfaction with a job did not correlate significantly with the satisfaction expressed with life. Women who were dissatisfied with their jobs were not necessarily dissatisfied with their lives. This study was interpreted to be an indication of the relative importance of the work role for men and the comparative unimportance of the work role for women. Women were seen as being more interested in their families; and as a consequence, life satisfaction was seen to be more significantly influenced by this role than by the experience of work. But since the Brayfield and Wells study, many social changes have taken place that might lead one to question the current validity of this interpretation. It seems reasonable, in the light of contemporary trends, to doubt that job satisfaction continues to exist in a psychological compartment apart from the individual's general satisfaction with life.

There is a more recent study that seems to bear out these suspicions. This study reports a significant relationship between job and life satisfaction among a large group of women university employees. Kavanagh and Halpern (1977) conducted the study, using the same test instruments as Brayfield and Wells on a group of 411 women found in clerical, faculty, and supervisory positions in a university. For the total group combined, and for each separate job level included in the study, there appeared to be a significant positive correlation between job and life satisfaction. Since the sample used in this study was not comparable to that employed earlier by Brayfield and Wells, it is impossible to attribute these different results entirely to the changing social climate surrounding women's work; it clearly calls the earlier set of results into question, however, and puts Brayfield and Wells's interpretation under a shadow.

Work and Mental Health

There is a considerable amount of evidence indicating that women show a much higher incidence of psychological distress than do men (Gove and Tudor, 1973). Community surveys, admissions to in-patient treatment programs, or participation in out-patient care all reveal that women experience more emotional problems. Gove and Tudor see the role of the housewife, especially as it has changed over the recent past, as a particularly significant contributor to the emotional difficulties women experience. According to this point of view, men have a much broader range of role alternatives from which they may seek satisfaction. Jobs that are more challenging, family, community, and avocational activities all provide men with a wider set of role options that are available to meet the emotional stresses of life. Women have fewer resources of this sort from which to obtain personal gratification; and as a consequence, they experience higher rates of psychological distress. There is also some evidence (Singer, 1975) that suggests that women are exposed to a larger number of life stresses than men.

Given these results, one may wonder about the role played by paid employment in women's psychological adjustment. Certainly a job leads to improved financial circumstances, as well as providing a woman with a wider range of role alternatives. To the extent that this is true, one might argue that a job would broaden and enrich a woman's life and result in more positive mental health. Therefore, employed women, as a group, should display better mental health than comparable groups of women who pursue homemaking roles.

There is another point of view. Considering the fact that employment is often not a substitute commitment but rather a responsibility added to housework, employed women may have to cope with a more demanding and more complicated life. As a result, a job may confront a woman with a role conflict that pits home and family demands against the demands made by the job. Under these circumstances, mental health would be expected to suffer, and homemakers should show evidence of better psychological adjustment than women who are employed.

Research Evidence. Turning to the research that has been done on this question, one finds a number of studies that have compared homemakers and employed persons on a variety of measures that reflect mental health. These studies yield a mixed picture regarding the psychological significance of paid work. When compared to women who are engaged in full-time housework, women employed outside the home have, at times, been found to show evidence of better mental health (Dupuy et al., 1970; Briggs, Laperriere, & Greden, 1965; Mostow and Newberry, 1975). There have been other studies (Jordan-Viola, Fassberg, & Viola, 1976; Newman, Whittemore, & Newman, 1973) that suggest that psychological problems may be associated with women's full-time employment. There also have been studies (Powell, 1975; Powell and Reznikoff, 1976) that have been unable to find differences in the mental-health status of homemakers and employed women.

These studies show quite clearly that broad generalizations should not be made concerning the mental-health consequences of women's employment. Variables associated with the home, job, and the individual combine to determine whether homemaking or employment is psychologically more positive. Each work situation presents a woman with a unique pattern of problems and stresses, although there may be certain types of difficulties frequently faced by working women. For instance, Skvorc (1975) reports finding structural barriers that prevented women from moving up in an engineering department of a large corporation. These structural barriers consisted of organizational policies and practices that reflected the male-dominated power structure that operated the management divisions of the corporation. Associated with positions of higher status were increased opportunities for satisfaction and reduced alienation. As a consequence, women experienced significantly less satisfaction and more alienation than men, simply as the result of these structural impediments to promotion. Women who work in an organization that is free of these barriers to promotion should report more positive mental health. The HEW study (Dupuy et al., 1970) reports that women in higher-status jobs report significantly fewer signs of psychological distress than do women who occupy jobs of lower status. Powell and Reznikoff (1976) find that attitudinal variables influence the level of psychiatric impairment found in working women. Measuring sex-role attitudes, Powell and Reznikoff found that women who maintained more contemporary sex-role viewpoints exhibited a higher incidence of psychiatric symptoms.

The problem of employment and mental health is doubtless similar for both men and women. In both cases no general statement is possible concerning the psychological implications of employment, since too many other variables play a part in determining the quality of psychological adjustment. Many of the same variables that influence this relationship in men operate with women. Status, for example, seems to be one such factor, with high-status jobs, whether held by men or women, being associated with relatively better mental health. Hence, we tentatively conclude that the same factors that moderate the mental-health implications of women's employment also serve to moderate the mental-health implications of male employment. Personality, job structure and job-person fit determine whether a job will enhance or diminish an individual's general emotional adjustment.

THE FAMILY AND WORK

It is no longer appropriate to think of women, when considering their options for adult life, as facing a work choice that is limited to either employment or homemaking. Current evidence indicates that a large and increasing number of women see both employment and homemaking as adult roles that may be held simultaneously (for example, Bronzaft, 1974), and there is evidence that indicates that these life plans are being translated into action (Hayghe, 1973; Leon and Bednarzik, 1978; Smith, 1977). To take but one example, Smith (1977) reports that between 1971 and 1975, 75 percent of the increase in women's participation in work occurred among married women. Furthermore, of those who are entering the labor force, the greatest increase has been found among women who have children under six. The data are clear; for an increasing number of women, marriage and motherhood no longer serve as insurmountable obstacles to employment and a career.

Popular Concerns

Evidence of a substantial increase in the number of multiple-career families has been the cause of much concern among social analysts. Questions have been raised regarding the consequences of these trends, especially as they may produce strains on husband-and-wife relationships or on the personality and social development of children. In the search for a standard for defining a psychologically healthy environment in which to rear children, for example, many have brought forward traditional views of the family and its functions. From this perspective, a family pattern with a father who is employed, a mother who remains at home, and children who are under the mother's full-time supervision whenever they are not in school is considered to be a "natural" family pattern. Maternal employment is equated with the partial abandonment of the children, and great concern is expressed about the quality of care these children receive, and the effects multiple parenting has on their psychological development.

These misgivings are not without foundation. For instance, one may point to the fact that most preschool children who have working mothers are not cared for in organized day-care centers staffed by trained personnel. Rather, most of these children are taken to other homes (Bureau of the Census, 1976), where the quality of care varies widely. High delinquency rates and a variety of school problems are also pointed to as an argument that maternal employment has resulted in the widespread neglect of children.

Research. It is comforting to learn that as a general rule the effects of a mother working do not appear to be as costly to the children as had been feared by some. Those who would condemn all working mothers would be hard pressed to find solid support for their position in the research literature. But all is not positive by any means, and there is enough of a negative nature to suggest that some considerable thought should be given to the decision to enter the work force, when there are very young children in the home. Although research has rejected the idea that all maternal employment is bad for the children, there is good evidence to indicate that it often does have some kind of effect on them, and in what follows we will consider some of these influences.

Age of Child. Perhaps one of the more important aspects of this question concerns whether there are critical years in the life of the young child when it is important for the mother to be present full time in the home. Popular belief holds that the absence of the mother from the home during the preschool years is risky. Yet with very young children, that is, below two years, there are several studies that indicate that the basic psychological attachment of the child to the parent is not nec-

FIGURE 16.3   Social Indicators for Families Headed by Women.

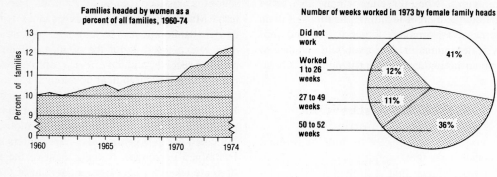

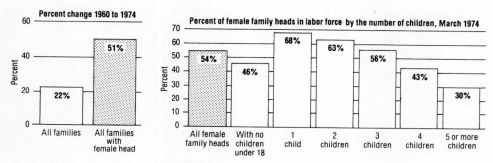

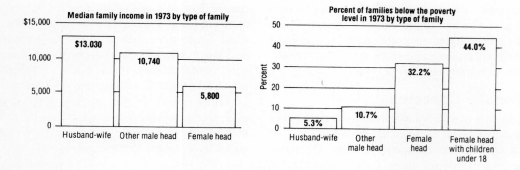

Families headed by women account for a significant and growing share of all American families. On the average, half of the women who head families are in the labor force, but proportionately more female than male family heads are below the poverty line.

Source: *U.S. working women.* U.S. Department of Labor, Bulletin 1980, 1975.

essarily disturbed by the parent being away from home during the day. What seems to be important, for children of both working and nonworking mothers, is the quality of parental care they receive when the parent is in the home (Kotelchuck, 1971; Caldwell et al., 1970; Maccoby & Feldman, 1972). The extent of contact while the parent is at home, the level of stimulation provided, and the quality of caring shown by the parent are all important factors. When these aspects of the parent-child relationship are good, then the fact that both parents are away from the home during working hours does not appear in the literature as a negative factor undermining the child's early attachment to the parent.

But apart from the strong psychological bond that is built between the mother and the child, there are personality facets that are being molded during these early years, and there is some reason to be concerned about the effects of maternal employment on these behaviors. Particularly when the child is assigned to substitute care before the age

FIGURE 16.4   Labor Force Participation Rates of Married or Formerly Married Women under Age 45.

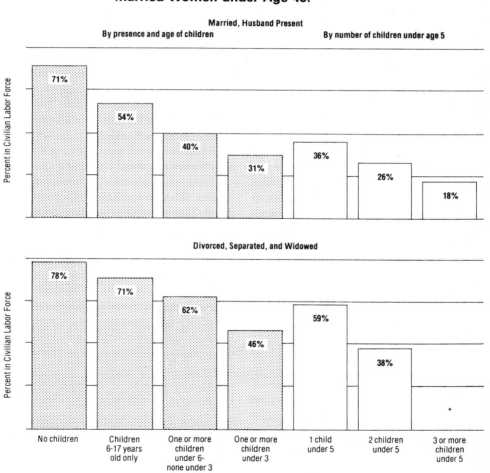

Married, Husband Present

By presence and age of children   By number of children under age 5

71%   54%   40%   31%   36%   26%   18%

Percent in Civilian Labor Force

Divorced, Separated, and Widowed

78%   71%   62%   46%   59%   38%   *

Percent in Civilian Labor Force

No children | Children 6-17 years old only | One or more children under 6- none under 3 | One or more children under 3 | 1 child under 5 | 2 children under 5 | 3 or more children under 5

* Not available; base population less than 75,000 women.

The presence of children, especially preschoolers, reduces the likelihood of labor force participation among married women in the typical child-bearing ages. This is true for divorced and separated women as well.

Source: *U.S. working women.* U.S. Department of Labor, Bulletin 1980, 1975.

of three is there an increased chance that such a program will have a significant effect on the developing personality. This is not to say that this influence will necessarily be an unhealthy one; just that the directions and consequences of personality development will be altered by these experiences. It is merely a question of the kind of behavior we want to develop in our children, and who is better able to achieve these behavioral objectives.

There is some evidence, particularly in the case of boys, that substitute parenting leads to a behavioral style that is somewhat less conforming, more aggressive and self-reliant. How these characteristics manifest themselves in adult life is a matter about which we know very little. Nevertheless, one may wonder whether the development of early self-sufficiency will yield a child who is capable of establishing the kind of affectional ties that serve in adulthood to sustain a marriage bond.

This is all very speculative thinking, but it does seem reasonable to contend that the entire slant of a child's approach to social relations could be influenced significantly by early nursery or day-care programs. One should emphasize, however, that the research thus far reported suggests that these influences generally do not lead to psychopathology (Burchinal and Rossman, 1961). Much needs to be done in this area; however, the importance of these questions and the uncertainties of the research findings counsel caution to those who would ignore the effects of maternal employment on the development of young children.

Attitude of Mother. Although when considered alone, maternal employment has not usually been linked to severe psychological problems in children, there are other variables that place the situation in another light, when considered together with maternal employment. One of these variables is the mother's attitude toward her job; another is the educational level of the mother (Yarrow et al., 1962; Hoffman, 1963; Woods, 1972). In general, mothers who work because they want a fuller life and who are satisfied with the work they do are often able to provide a reasonably good child-rearing environment. Women who dislike their jobs

and who are working for reasons that do not relate to their own psychological needs have been found to have difficulties in child rearing. Hoffman (1963), for example, reports a study in which working mothers who disliked their jobs were found to be less involved with their children. Mothers who liked their jobs were seen by their children as being a more significant source of positive emotions such as smiles and encouragement; they also tended to use milder discipline on their children.

Compensation. There is also evidence that working mothers, especially those who have higher levels of education, try to compensate for their absence and provide the child with a more stimulating home environment (Yarrow et al., 1962; Jones, Lundsteen, & Michael, 1967). These mothers were found to plan a wider variety of activities while they were at home with the children; they also were found reading more to their children, although it is not definite whether this is attributable to their working or to their general interest in educational attainment. Hoffman (1963) found that working mothers may not just compensate for their absence, but overcompensate. For example, she reports that mothers who worked tended to avoid inconveniencing their children with requests for help around the house. They tended to be nondisciplinarians and their children tended to be less assertive and ineffective in their relations with their peers. Teachers' ratings indicated that these children were not doing as well in their school work as their peers who were children of nonworking mothers, and their performance on school intelligence tests were lower. All these things combined led Hoffman to suspect that there are times when a working mother, possibly because of feelings of guilt, tries to compensate for her absence from the home, and in doing so she overcompensates.

Quality of Substitute Care. The quality of substitute care has also been shown to contribute significantly to determining whether a mother's employment does or does not have a detrimental effect on the young child. Moore (1963, 1964, 1969) carried out a series of studies in which children who had received substitute day care for at least one preschool year were compared with children who had not been involved in such a program. Day-care programs were classified as being stable (the same persons involved during the child's tenure in the program) or unstable (changes in the day-care personnel), and comparisons were made at ages 6 and 11.

At both 6 and 11, there were relatively few differences between children who had been raised exclusively by their mothers and those who had been exposed to stable substitute parenting. The few differences that did appear (for example, at 11, boys who had been in stable day-care programs were more aggressive and less conforming than were those raised exclusively by their mothers) did not seem to indicate worrisome levels of psychological disturbance. Day care that began before the age of two seemed to leave a more visible mark on the child; but although the age at which the child was introduced to substitute parenting was important, Moore (1969) concludes that the stability of the substitute-care program was of principal importance. He reports that the one group of children showing clear signs of damage were those who had been exposed to unstable day-care arrangements.

School-Age Children

Reviews of the literature dealing with school-age children (Hoffman, 1974; Etaugh, 1974; Poznanski, Maxey, & Marsden, 1970; Howell, 1973a, 1973b; Seiden, 1976) reveal that serious psychological impairment is not often associated with maternal employment. To be sure, there have been noted some effects attributed to the absence of the mother during working hours. For example, working mothers often provide the child with a different role model of both herself and, at times, the father. Children of employed mothers have often been found to have less traditional attitudes concerning male and female roles. Along similar lines, working mothers tend to give the child somewhat different kinds of child training. In general, children

of working mothers who have no college training are often given more responsibility around the home (Yarrow et al., 1962); mothers tend to place greater emphasis on training children to be less dependent and more self-sufficient. College-trained mothers, on the other hand, especially when they have young children, tend to play a more protective and nurturant role, giving their children fewer household responsibilities and not encouraging them to be independent of other family members.

It is difficult to explain why these differences exist in the families of college-and non-college-trained working mothers. Some (for example, Hoffman, 1963) suggest that a sense of guilt accompanies a mother's involvement in work that takes her away from the home; and these feelings, perhaps because of greater exposure to the child-rearing literature, are more keenly felt by college-trained mothers. There are also higher prospects that the college-trained women, since family income is probably higher, are more likely to employ part-time household help.

Academic Achievement.   Does the fact that a mother works away from the home have any significance for the school performance of her children? This is a question that has been raised in numerous studies, but unfortunately little consistency can be found in the results. Whenever effects have been observed, however, they have tended to be relatively slight, and they have been moderated by a number of other variables, such as the educational level of the mother, the family's social class, the age and sex of the children, and the status of the mother's job. There is one interesting trend that bears mentioning, and that is the fact that maternal employment seems to have a more visible effect on boys than on girls. Numerous studies have been unable to demonstrate a clear and substantial effect of maternal employment on the school achievement of girls. There have been instances, however, in which school achievement has been lower for boys of working mothers. We need more information concerning this distinction between girls and boys before launching into any elaborate explanations, but one is still tempted to speculate that there may be something associated with the sex role traditionally assigned to male children that makes home experiences more significant. The fact that boys are encouraged to be more aggressive, more competitive, and less demonstrative may require a base of emotional support in the home that is more critical for them than it is for girls. We need more research on this topic, but we should point out that this is an important trend, one that requires further investigation.

Women's Employment and Marriage

We now turn to a question that has received considerable research attention and that represents a matter that has great significance for a society that is experiencing such a rapid increase in the rate of participation of women in work. This question is, does the fact that both the man and the woman in a family hold jobs place additional strains on the marriage relationship and make a congenial marriage less likely? In answering this question, one thing appears to be fairly clear: when a married woman finds employment, the household roles of both husband and wife undergo change. In spite of the fact that employed wives often retain a primary responsibility for household maintenance, when they enter the labor force they do not do as much housework and their husbands do more (Blood, 1963). Part of this change involves the wife restricting her participation in masculine tasks, while the husband takes on tasks that are usually associated with women. Also, at upper-income levels there is often an increase in family expenditures for part-time housekeeping services and labor-saving devices.

Conflict.   Accompanying this shift in marriage roles is an increase in conflict that occurs between husbands and wives (Nye, 1963). Conflict seems to arise in those areas of family living that are most directly affected by the wife's new role, such as responsibility for household tasks and child-care obligations. This is particularly true with families

in which the husband's income is reasonably high. Blood (1963) finds that in families in which the husband's income is rather low, a wife's employment often is associated with an increase in conflict concerning finances. Why this occurs is open to speculation; perhaps a second job encourages a family to expand its standard of living beyond the limits of the combined income. Perhaps a second income is accompanied by a shift in the power of the wife in matters of family decision making. There is some evidence to support this latter possibility; Heer (1958) reports that in working-class families the employed wife exerts significantly more influence in family decision making than does the working wife in a middle-class family.

Scanzoni (1978) contends that work may also have an influence on the *nature* of the conflict relationship that exists between husband and wife. Marriage involves power, negotiation, and conflict, and it is often the case that women's employment will alter some aspects of this system. For example, each member of the marriage holds certain power that can be manipulated to attain desired goals. A traditional source of male power has, in one way or another, been linked to his role as breadwinner and provider. Scanzoni reports that traditional women try to bargain with their husbands by appealing to family objectives. She argues that the desired course of action is reasonable in the light of the well-being of the family. Nontraditional women more often argue on the basis of their own personal interests, and the more status women have, the greater is the likelihood that marriage negotiations will revolve around these personal objectives. Since the work role often enhances women's status and power, there is an increased likelihood that more egalitarian roles will develop. Scanzoni maintains that under these circumstances employed women often become more effective bargainers. They become tougher bargainers in the sense that they obtain more of what they want. They control more of the family's resources, and as a consequence they can play a more assertive role in family conflict.

We will have to leave the resolution of this question to further research, but on the basis of the

FIGURE 16.5   Wives with Earnings as a Percent of Family Income (1974)

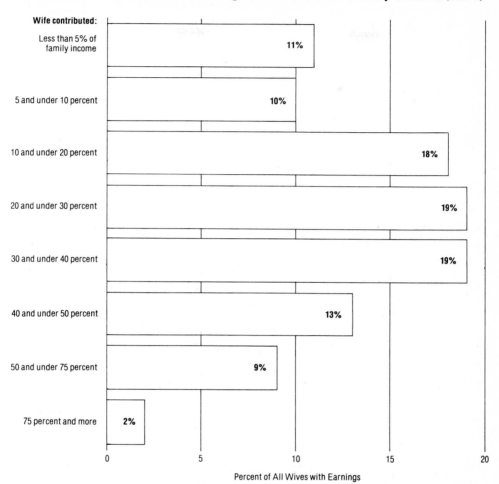

Percent of All Wives with Earnings

In families where the wife was an earner, she most commonly contributed between 20 and 40 percent of the family income. Notice that only 11 percent of working wives contributed 50 percent or more of the family income.

Source: *U.S. working women.* U.S. Department of Labor, Bulletin 1980, 1975.

evidence that is presently available, it seems reasonable to view the entrance of a wife into the labor force as being accompanied by a shift in the role responsibilities assumed by husband and wife and an increase in the level of conflict over matters that relate directly to the wife's employment.

Marital Happiness.   Even though the available research suggests that working wives are often found in families that display higher levels of conflict, there is little evidence that this conflict leads, as a general rule, to marital unhappiness. To be sure, there are situations where a wife's employment is linked to higher marital tensions and decreased husband-and-wife sociability (Orden & Bradburn, 1969), but it is uncertain whether the added tensions that accompany a wife's employment add significantly to the psychological bur-

TABLE 16.3   Median Usual Weekly Earnings of Full-Time Wage and Salary Workers by Sex, 1967 to 1980

| | Usual weekly earnings | | | | Women's earnings as percent of men's |
| | In current dollars | | In 1967 dollars | | |
Year	Women	Men	Women	Men	
May of:					
1967	78	125	78	125	62
1969	86	142	79	130	61
1970	94	151	81	131	62
1971	100	162	83	134	62
1972	106	168	85	135	63
1973	116	188	88	143	62
1974	124	204	85	140	61
1975	137	221	86	138	62
1976	145	234	86	138	62
1977	156	253	86	139	62
1978	166	272	85	140	61
1979[1]					
2nd quarter	183	295	85	137	62
1980:					
2nd quarter	200	317	81	129	63

Source: U.S. Department of Labor. *Perspectives on working women.* Bulletin 2080, 1980.

dens that are associated with marriage itself. For example, Gove and Tudor (1973) cite evidence indicating that signs of real psychological distress are significantly higher for married women than for unmarried ones.

One of the more influential factors associated with the effect of a wife's employment on marital relationships is the attitude the husband and the wife have toward the job the wife holds. Nye (1963), for instance, found that in instances in which either party expresses dissatisfaction with the wife's occupational role there is an increased chance for marital unhappiness. It should be pointed out that in Nye's sample there were relatively few husbands who did express disapproval of the wife's employment, and as a result, overall there was no difference in expressed happiness in marriages in families where the mother did and in families where the mother did not work.

Orden and Bradburn (1969) found that both the husband and the wife are less happy if the wife works because of economic necessity than if she works for more personal motives. These researchers also report that when there are preschool children in the family, marital relationships were better when the mother did not work. In families with grade school and high school children, maternal employment did not seem to disturb the marriage relationship. Hence, even though we are unable to draw a general conclusion regarding the marital implications of women's employment, it does seem relatively safe to conclude that in families in which the wife holds a job, marital relations are just as happy as other marriages, provided negative attitudes are not applied to the wife's employment by either spouse.

Comment

On first impression the research on marriage relationships and women's employment presents us with a picture of contradictions. On the one hand, there is evidence that a wife's employment often results in increased conflict concerning certain aspects of family living. On the other hand, the research that is available gives us no reason to conclude that employed wives are less happy in their marriages than wives who remain at home full time. Of course, under certain circumstances the marriages of working wives are less happy than those of wives who are not employed. The presence of preschool children in the home is one aggravating condition that relates to the marital problems of the wife who holds a job. Negative attitudes toward the wife's job, held by either husband or wife, is another factor associated with negative effects of women's employment.

There are instances, however, in which a wife's employment has a constructive influence on a marriage. In spite of the increased conflicts, which are probably superficial in many instances, there are compensating advantages that offset these negative aspects. For example, there is evidence that when husband and wife pursue the same professional careers they are both more productive at their work than are their unmarried counterparts (Martin, Berry, & Jacobsen, 1975; Heckman, Bryson, & Bryson, 1977). Increased professional productivity usually leads to increased recognition and higher levels of self-esteem; in these instances dual-career marriages may be reasonably satisfactory.

The income generated by a wife's job broadens a family's alternatives regarding leisure and life style, and this contributes positively to marital happiness. A job also frees wives from the social isolation that often surrounds housework, and improved opportunities for social contact can serve a positive role in removing frustrations that may strain a marriage. The whole question of the marital consequence of female employment seems to boil down to the question, under what circumstances does a wife's employment have a positive or negative influence on a marriage? Each marriage probably experiences profits and losses from a wife's membership in the labor force; our present problem is to determine the circumstances that lead to marital liabilities and gains.

WOMEN AND WORK LEADERSHIP

Recently Sturdivant and Adler (1975) reported on a survey of the characteristics of the executive officers who were found at the top of America's 300 largest industrial organizations. These executives formed a rather homogeneous group. They were predominantly Caucasian, Protestant, and Republican. They were raised in relatively affluent families living in the eastern United States, and were educated in a handful of prestigious universities. Along with all this, *not one of them was a woman*. Of course, one occasionally reads about a woman who occupies a position of substantial leadership in a business enterprise, but the fact remains that top-level executive positions are virtually the exclusive domain of the male. For a variety of reasons, women have not found their way into positions of work leadership, and this is true both in occupations that are viewed as being feminine and those viewed as being masculine. For example, Kadushin (1976) cites evidence indicating that in the field of social work, where women account for a large majority of the professional personnel, men tend to be advanced more rapidly to positions of administration. Gross and Trusk (1976) cite statistics indicating that although men comprise only 15 percent of elementary school teachers, they account for 79 percent of elementary school principals. It would be fruitless to cite additional evidence for what is an obvious fact: work leadership is the traditional preserve of the male.

It is sometimes argued that women are ill suited for positions of work leadership, and that part of this problem stems from the negative reactions of male employees who find it difficult to adjust to women supervisors. Other times it is said that because of the patterns of socialization that characterize the early learning of many girls, women do not have the psychological attributes that executive positions demand. Women are seen as not possessing the competitive drive, the ambition, and the aspiration for power and success that have been associated with positions high on the corporate lad-

FIGURE 16.6   Profile of a Woman Officer

Title

Chairman, Vice Chairman, President	1.4%
Group VP, Senior VP, and Vice President	24.1
Second Vice President	2.5
Assistant Vice President	7.0
Secretary	11.5
Assistant Secretary	39.5
Treasurer	1.2
Assistant Treasurer	6.8
Other	6.0
	100.0%

Type of Employer

Industrial	61%
Non-Industrial	39
	100%

Base

East	40%
Midwest	29
South and Southwest	15
West	16
	100%

Inside Director

Yes	6.4%
No	93.6
	100.0%

Outside Directorships

Yes	11.8%
No	88.2
	100.0%

Age

Under 30	6.4%
30-34	11.0
35-39	15.1
40-44	13.2
45-49	13.7
50-54	15.5
55 and over	25.1
	100.0%

Cash Compensation (Salary and Bonus)

Less than $20,000	10.1%
$20,000-29,999	28.7
$30,000-39,999	15.2
$40,000-49,999	16.6
$50,000-59,999	10.6
$60,000-69,999	5.5
$70,000-79,999	4.1
$80,000 or more	9.2
	100.0%

Perquisites

Medical Examination	59.3%
Stock Options	48.1
Extraordinary Insurance Coverage	47.7
Stock Purchase Plan	33.3
Club Membership	20.8
Automobile	19.9
Deferred Compensation	15.3
Financial Counseling	12.5
Performance Shares	10.2
Low-cost Loans	9.7
Vacation Retreat	3.7
Management Contract	3.2
None	12.5

(Results do not add to 100% due to multiple responses)

Career Continuity

Employed continuously, no family responsibilities	39.5%
Employed continuously, family responsibilities	50.5
Interrupted career for family responsibilities	10.0
	100.0%

Number of Employers

1	15.8%
2	23.4
3	17.8
4	22.0
5 or more	21.0
	100.0%

Years With Present Employer

0-5	21.5%
6-10	19.2
11-15	13.2
16-20	12.3
21-25	12.8
26 or more	21.0
	100.0%

Source of Present Position

Promoted from within	76.4%
Executive recruiter	4.5
Company made direct contact with me	12.7
Other	6.4
	100.0%

Hours Devoted to Work

40 or less	13.7%
41-50	43.8
51-60	35.2
More than 60	7.3
	100.0%

Education

High School	16.9%
Attended College	26.9
Undergraduate Degree	20.1
Graduate Study	10.5
Graduate Degree	25.6
	100.0%

Timing of Career Decision

Before high school	9.7%
During high school	24.5
During college	19.0
While on first job in business	33.9
Other	12.9
	100.0%

Thinking Regarding Future

Stay in present position	24.0%
Advance to higher level in same organization	42.4
Move to another organization if blocked	33.6
	100.0%

Satisfaction With Progress

Very high	34.8%
High	42.2
Average	21.1
Low	1.4
Very low	.5
	100.0%

Pleasure Derived From Work

Work and pleasure are one	16.8%
Work affords above average pleasure	55.3
Work affords average pleasure	23.3
Work affords below average pleasure	1.4
Work and pleasure are separate and distinct	3.2
	100.0%

In 1979 Heidrick and Struggles, Inc., a management consulting firm, surveyed 485 women who held officer rank at the corporate level in the nation's 1000 leading industrials and 50 leading banks. Forty-six percent responded (223), and the data in the figure summarize the survey's major findings.

Source: Heidrick and Struggles, Inc., *Profile of a woman officer*. Chicago: Heidrick & Struggles, Inc., 1979.

der. Along these lines, women are often viewed as lacking the commitment to work that is necessary for upward mobility in large organizations.

Arguments such as these are usually vacuous, their main flaw being found in the sweeping generalities they advance. Closer and more reasoned consideration of these issues usually reveals the existence of a much more complicated state of affairs, and these complications discourage generalizations that apply to all women and all work situations. In such circumstances one must be especially vigilant not to let personal wishes be substituted for the truth as it is available to us through the scientific literature. When this literature is incomplete, as it often is, then one must reserve an element of doubt in one's thinking. When doubt is coupled with curiosity, then one is in a position to deal effectively with a subject. This is the basis of all good scientific work.

Attitudinal Barriers

With regard to women's and men's qualifications for and success in positions of work leadership, there is little research that directly points to substantial differences between the two sexes. The major reason for the paucity of women in these high positions appears to lie not in unequal distributions of ability, but in the structure of a society that both trains women to avoid certain kinds of leadership roles and places external barriers before those who do enter the labor force in an attempt to achieve executive status. Of these external barriers, perhaps the most potent are the attitudes and beliefs of males who occupy positions of leadership (Schein, 1973). Of course, these attitudes are a product of the same kind of socializing influences that lead women to direct their vocational activities away from executive jobs.

An early study by Bowman, Wortney and Greyser (1965) asked male executives to express their attitudes on women being appointed to executive positions. In responding, 51 percent of the executives believed that women were temperamentally unsuited for management. Only 21 percent felt they would be comfortable with a female boss, and about a third of the group believed that women

managers have a bad effect on employee morale.

Often male attitudes do not discriminate between the sexes on the basis of abilities; rather, they involve social rules that govern relations between the sexes, requiring of men certain kinds of courtesy and politeness and requiring that women maintain a subordinate role (Bass, Krusell, & Alexander, 1971). It should be emphasized, however, that it is not only males who hold the attitudes that impede women's occupational success. Women have been found sharing with men the belief that women are poorly equipped for management responsibilities (Schein, 1975; O'Leary, 1974). We have already considered studies dealing with women's tendency to devalue feminine traits relative to traits usually associated with males. There is also evidence indicating that men and women tend to evaluate success and failure in different ways. For example, Feather and Simon (1975) found that women tend to upgrade successful men relative to unsuccessful men, but tend to downgrade successful women relative to women who are unsuccessful. Male occupational success was seen as being more important in determining one's status with others than was women's work success. In another study, Feather (1975) found women indicating that they felt a woman functioning in a nontraditional occupational role would not be as happy about success as a man and would be unhappier about failure.

These studies indicate that women tend to evaluate the consequences of success and failure as a function of whether it is a man or a woman involved in the job. The studies also reveal that in the eyes of women, occupational success is more positive when it is experienced by men, and this is especially true when the success occurs in an occupation that is deemed to be appropriate for the sex of the individual. These are attitudes that can serve to discourage women from seeking out the competitive and risky organizational channels that lead to positions of executive prominence. The paucity of women in executive roles, therefore, is in part the result of a complex of sex-stereotyped attitudes held by both women and men, which tend to define certain kinds of leadership positions as being off-limits for those who are committed to a feminine role.

Performance in Management Jobs

There is comparatively little information concerning the performance of women in management positions relative to the performance of men (Terborg, 1977). What little there is indicates that differences, when they do appear, tend to be rather slight. There have been indications of motivational differences between men and women managers, with men being more strongly motivated by pay and women being more highly motivated by the difficulty of the job and the responsibilities connected with the work (Shapiro, 1975). Helmich (1974) has also found a sample of women executives who tended to be more task oriented than their male counterparts.

One of the more frequently mentioned problems women managers face is the widespread belief that other workers, both men and women, do not like to work under a woman supervisor. In keeping with this point of view, Bass et al. (1971) found that male managers who had worked with women expressed more negative attitudes toward women in management than had male managers who had not worked with women. Bartol (1974), however, found no adverse reactions to female leaders in groups of males who were participating in management games. In fact, Bartol reports that males who were functioning under a female leader who displayed high need for dominance tended to express higher satisfaction with some aspects of group activity than were males who were led by a woman who had low dominance needs. This finding does not appear to be in keeping with Terborg's (1977) suggestion that reactions to a female leader are dependent on whether her behavior is congruent with the sex role thought to be appropriate for women. When her conduct is consistent with this female role, then the reaction to her supervision tends to be positive. Negative reactions would be expected when a woman manager behaves in a fashion thought to be more appropriate for a male.

This leads us to question whether women, when they do obtain positions in management, are exposed to evaluations that are more stringent than are those applied to their male counterparts. All the literature pointing to the effects of attitudes on women's careers suggest that these negative influences would continue to operate when actual job performance was evaluated. Yet research has not supported this expectation. In fact, there are some studies (Epstein, 1970; Hamner et al., 1974; Bigoness, 1976) that indicate that women are sometimes given more liberal evaluations than are men. Garland (1977) suggests that women may be held up to double standards. Before achieving a position of leadership women are subject to attitudes that tend to be stereotyped and that judge them more unfavorably than they do men. After they move into management positions, however, their ability and level of performance play the critical role in evaluations. Hence, when in a position where they can display evidence of achievement, women appear to be subjected to standards of evaluation that are similar to those applied to men. There may even be a tendency for these standards to be somewhat more lenient.

There is also fragmentary information indicating that women's adjustments to the requirements of a large organization do not differ from the patterns of adjustment observed in men (Miner, 1974; Bedeian, Armenakis, & Kemp, 1976; Wanous, 1976; Lirtzman & Wahba, 1972). For example, the job of an executive has many attributes that are political in nature. Interpersonal relations, power exchanges, and coalition formation account for an important part of the executive's efforts to maintain control over a large organization. Lirtzman and Wahba (1972) present evidence indicating that there is little difference in the strategies adopted by men and women in forming coalitions in situations containing risk and uncertainty. Both male and female subjects tended to seek out allies who would maximize the payoff that was expected from the competitive situation.

When the available studies are brought together it is easy to see that our information concerning women's performance in executive jobs is mostly incomplete. At present we must content ourselves with information concerning primarily the factors that serve to bar women from occupational ascendancy. Nevertheless, the research that is available does not provide anything like a solid base of support for the negative attitudes that tend to discourage the promotion of women into high executive positions. Of course one must bear in mind that the apprenticeship that most executive positions require is quite long. As a result, one might hope that as time progresses, opportunities will open up for women and bring an increasing number of them into positions that will be fulfilling and in which they can competently serve.

SUMMARY COMMENTS

In certain respects the literature on women at work is a surprising one, in that it has thus far been unable to point up a large number of important differences between men's and women's job potential for performance. On the other hand, the research on early socialization has been much more successful in demonstrating contrasts between the social environments in which girls and boys are raised. This suggests that the principal variables that explain women's role in the various occupational fields are found in sets of attitudes and beliefs that serve to give direction to their search for jobs and their commitment to work objectives. This is not to say that the socialization process rarely leaves its stamp on women's job performance. We have referred to some evidence that suggests that men and women approach interpersonal relations in different ways. But when it comes to the realm of abilities and talents, even

physical strength (Wardle, 1976), there is little in the research literature that would exclude women from all but a very few jobs.

The entrance of large numbers of women into the labor force has raised questions about the effects of work on the family. To be sure, the research that is now available has demonstrated that maternal employment has had an effect on child rearing and husband-and-wife relations in many families. These effects have been both positive and negative, and we are beginning to get a better picture of the conditions that lead to family strains when the wife takes on dual career commitments of homemaker and employee. But at the present time we are unable to find convincing evidence that maternal employment leads, as a general rule, to severe psychological distress among members of a family. There is reason to believe that under the proper circumstances women with families find employment a rewarding addition to their lives, both in terms of their direct work experiences and in terms of the new economic opportunities their income may provide.

A new concept of woman, mother, and wife has become more visible throughout the past decades. The change will continue to evolve. The life of the woman worker is becoming more fulfilling and more complicated at the same time. With complications, there are greater risks to be taken, and these may best be dealt with in the light of increasing scientific information concerning the social psychology of work. We all have an important interest in seeing that this research continues to focus on those aspects of our lives that involve so much of our psychological resources.

BIBLIOGRAPHY

Abdel-Halim, A., & Rowland, K. M. Some personality determinants of the effects of participation: A further investigation. *Personnel Psychology,* 1976, *29,* 41–55.

Abramson, E. W. Projected demand for and supply of Ph.D. manpower, 1972–1985. *Monthly Labor Review,* 1975, *98,* 52–53.

Ackoff, R. L. Management misinformation systems. *Management Science,* 1967, *14,* 147–156.

Adams, J. S. Wage inequities, productivity and work quality. *Industrial Relations,* 1963, *3,* 9–16.

Adams, J. S. Inequity in social exchanges. In L. Berkowitz (Ed.), *Advances in experimental social psychology.* New York: Academic Press, 1965.

Adams, J. S., & Jacobsen, P. R. Effects of wage inequities on work quality. *Journal of Abnormal and Social Psychology,* 1964, *69,* 19–25.

Adams, J. S., & Rosenbaum, W. B. The relationship of worker productivity to cognitive dissonance about wage inequities. *Journal of Applied Psychology,* 1962, *46,* 161–164.

Aldridge, J. F. Emotional illness and the working environment. *Ergonomics,* 1970, *13,* 613–621.

Allen, R. F., & Silverzweig, S. Group norms: Their influence on training effectiveness. In R. L. Craig, *Training and developmental handbook.* New York: McGraw-Hill, 1976.

Allen, T. J., & Cohen, S. I. Information flow in research and development laboratories. *Administrative Science Quarterly,* 1969, *14,* 12–20.

Almond, G. A., & Verba, S. *The civic culture.* Princeton, N.J.: Princeton University Press, 1960.

Alvarez, R. Informal reactions to deviance in simulated work organizations: A laboratory experiment. *American Sociological Review,* 1968, *33,* 893–912.

Ammerman, H. L., & Essex, D. W. Performance content for job training. Volume 4: Deriving performance requirements for training research and development. Columbus: Ohio State University, Center for Vocational Education, Series 124, 1977.

Anderson, C. W. The relation between speaking times and decision in the employment interview. *Journal of Applied Psychology,* 1960, *44,* 267–268.

Anderson, M. *Welfare.* Stanford, Cal.: Hoover Press, 1978.

Andrews, F. M., & Farris, G. F. Supervisory practices and innovation in scientific teams. *Personnel Psychology,* 1967, *20,* 497–515.

Andrews, I. R. Wage inequity and job performance. *Journal of Applied Psychology,* 1967, *51,* 39–45.

Andrews, I. R., & Henry, M. M. Management attitudes toward pay. *Industrial Relations,* 1963, *3,* 29–39.

Andrews, I. R., & Valenzi, E. Overpay inequity or self-image as a worker: A critical examination of an experimental induction procedure. *Organizational Behavior and Human Performance,* 1970, *53,* 22–27.

Appelbaum, L. Officer turnover and salary structures in local unions. *Industrial and Labor Relations Review,* 1966, *19,* 224–230.

Appley, D. G., & Winder, A. E. An evolving definition of collaboration and some implications for the world of work. *Journal of Applied Behavioral Science,* 1977, *13,* 279–291.

Argyris, C. *Personality and organization.* New York: Harper, 1957.

Argyris, C. *Integrating the individual and the organization.* New York: Wiley, 1964.

Argyris, C. *Intervention theory and method.* Reading, Mass.: Addison-Wesley, 1970.

Armknecht, P. A., & Early, J. L. Quits in manufacturing: A study of their causes. *Monthly Labor Review,* 1972, *95*(11), 31–37.

Arvey, R. D., & Gross, R. H. Satisfaction levels and correlates of satisfaction in the homemaker job. *Journal of Vocational Behavior,* 1977, *10*(1), 13–24.

Ash, P. The SRA employee inventory—a statistical analysis. *Personnel Psychology,* 1954, *7,* 337–364.

Ash, P. The parties to the grievance. *Personnel Psychology,* 1970, *23,* 13–37.

Ash, R. A., & Edgell, S. L. A note on the readability of the Position Analysis Questionnaire (PAQ). *Journal of Applied Psychology,* 1975, *60,* 765–766.

Asher, J. J. The biographical item: Can it be improved? *Personnel Psychology,* 1972, *25,* 251–269.

Asher, J. J., & Sciarrino, J. A. Realistic work sample tests; A review. *Personnel Psychology,* 1974, *27,* 519–533.

Athanassiades, J. C. *Distortion of upward communication as a function of a subordinates security level, his achievement motives, and organizational authority structure.* Unpublished doctoral dissertation, New York University, 1971.

Avery, D. D., & Cross, H. A. *Experimental methodology in psychology.* Belmont, Cal.: Wadsworth, 1978.

Bahn, C. Counter training problems. *Personnel Journal*, 1973, *28*, 1068–1072.

Baird, J. C., & Noma, E. *Fundamentals of scaling and psychophysics*. New York: Wiley, 1978.

Bandura, A. *Psychosocial modeling: Conflicting theories*. Chicago: Aldine-Atherton, 1971.

Barnard, C. I. *The functions of the executive*. Cambridge, Mass.: Harvard University Press, 1938.

Barnlund, D. C., & Harland, C. Propinquity and prestige as determinants of communication networks. *Sociometry*, 1963, *26*, 467–479.

Bartol, K. M. Male versus female leaders: The effect of leader need for dominance on follower satisfaction. *Academy of Management Journal*, 1974, *17*, 225–233.

Bartol, K. M. Relationship of sex and professional training area to job orientation. *Journal of Applied Psychology*, 1976, *61*, 368–370.

Baruch, G. K. Maternal influences upon college women's attitudes toward women and work. *Developmental Psychology*, 1972, *6*, 32–37.

Baruch, G. K. Maternal career-orientation as related to parental identification in college women. *Journal of Vocational Behavior*, 1974, *4*, 173–180.

Bass, B. M. Effects on the subsequent performance of negotiations of studying issues or planning strategies alone or in groups. *Psychological Monographs*, 1966, *80*(Whole No. 6).

Bass, B. M. Ability, values and concepts of equitable salary increases in exercise compensation. *Journal of Applied Psychology*, 1968, *52*, 299–303.

Bass, B. M., & Barrett, G. V. *Man work and organizations: An introduction to industrial and organizational psychology* (2nd ed.). Boston: Allyn and Bacon, 1981.

Bass, B. M., Cascio, W. F., McPherson, J., & Tragash, H. J. PROSPER, training and research for increasing management awareness of affirmative action in race relations. *Academy of Management Journal*, 1976, *19*, 353–369.

Bass, B. M., Krusell, J., & Alexander, R. A. Male managers' attitudes toward working women. *American Behavioral Scientist*, 1971, *15*, 221–236.

Bass, B. M., & Mitchell, C. W. Influences on the felt need for collective bargaining by business and science professionals. *Journal of Applied Psychology*, 1976, *61*, 770–773.

Baumgartel, H. Using employee questionnaire results for improving organizations. *Kansas Business Review*, 1959, *12*, 2–6.

Baumgartel, H., & Goldstein, G. Some human consequences of technical change. *Personnel Administration*, 1961, *24*, 485–489.

Baumgartel, H., & Jeanpierre, F. Applying new knowledge in the back-home setting: A study of Indian manager's adaptive efforts. *Journal of Applied Behavioral Science*, 1972, *8*, 674–694.

Baumhart, R. *Ethics in business*. New York: Holt, Rinehart and Winston, 1968.

Bavelas, A. A mathematical model for group structures. *Applied Anthropology*, 1948, *7*(3), 16–30.

Bavelas, A. Communication patterns in task oriented groups. In H. Lasswell & D. Lerner, *The policy sciences*. Stanford, Cal: Stanford University Press, 1950.

Beatty, R. W. Blacks as supervisors: A study of training, job performance and employer's expectations. *Academy of Management Journal*, 1973, *16*, 196–206.

Bedeian, A. G., Armenakis, A. A., & Kemp, B. W. Relation of sex to perceived legitimacy of organizational influence. *Journal of Psychology*, 1976, *94*, 93–99.

Bednarzik, R. W., & Klein, D. P. Labor force trend: A synthesis and analysis. *Monthly Labor Review*, 1977, *100*(10), 3–11.

Beehr, T. A., & Newman, J. E. Job stress, employee health, and organizational effectiveness: A facet analysis, model and literature review. *Personnel Psychology*, 1978, 31, 665–699.

Beehr, T. A., Walsh, J. T., & Taber, T. D. Relationship of stress to individually and organizationally valued states. *Journal of Applied Psychology*, 1976, *61*, 41–47.

Behling, O., Labovitz, G., & Gainer, M. College recruiting: A theoretical base. *Personnel Journal*, 1968, *47*, 13–19.

Behrend, H. The effort bargain. *Industrial and Labor Relations Review*, 1957, *10*, 503–515.

Bell, D. *The coming of post-industrial society*. New York: Basic Books, 1973.

Bem, S. L. The measurement of psychological androgyny. *Journal of Consulting and Clinical Psychology*, 1974, *42*, 155–162.

Bem, S. L., & Bem, D. J. Does sex-biased job advertising aid and abet sex discrimination. *Journal of Applied Social Psychology*, 1973, *3*, 6–18.

Bendig, A. W. The reliability of self-ratings as a function of the amount of verbal anchoring and of the number of categories on the scale. *Journal of Applied Psychology*, 1953, *37*, 38–41.

Bendig, A. W. Reliability and the number of rating scale categories. *Journal of Applied Psychology*, 1954, *38*, 38–40.

Bentz, V. J. The Sears experience in the investigation, description and prediction of executive behavior. In J. A. Myers, Jr. (Ed.), *Predicting managerial success*. Ann Arbor, Mich.: Braun and Brumfield, Inc., 1968.

Berkowitz, L. The contagion of violence. In W. J. Arnold & M. M. Page (Eds.), *Nebraska Symposium on Motivation*, 1970, *18*, 95–136.

Berkowitz, L., & Lundy, R. M. Personality characteristics related to susceptibility to influence by peers or authority figures. *Journal of Personality*, 1957, *25*, 306–316.

Berkun, N. M., Bialek, H. M., Kern, R. P., & Yagi, K. Experimental studies of psychological stress in man. *Psychological Monographs*, 1962, *76*(15, Whole No. 534).

Berlew, D. E., & Hall, D. T. The socialization of managers: Effects of expectations on performance. *Administrative Science Quarterly*, 1966, *11*, 207–223.

Bernardin, H. J. Behavioral expectation scales versus summated scales: A fairer comparison. *Journal of Applied Psychology*, 1977, *62*, 422–427.

Bernardin, H. J. Effects of rater training on licensing and halo errors in student ratings of instructors. *Journal of Applied Psychology*, 1978, *63*, 301–308.

Bernardin, H. J., Alvares, K. M., & Cranny, C. J. A recomparison of behavioral expectation scales to summated scales. *Journal of Applied Psychology*, 1976, *61*, 564–570.

Bernardin, H. J., & Pence, E. C. Effects of rater training: Creating new response sets and decreasing accuracy. *Journal of Applied Psychology*, 1980, *65*, 60–66.

Bernardin, H. J., & Walter, C. S. Effects of rater training and diary-keeping on psychometric error in rating. *Journal of Applied Psychology*, 1977, *62*, 64–69.

Bettelheim, B. Individual and mass behavior in extreme situations. *Journal of Abnormal and Social Psychology*, 1943, *38*, 417–452.

Biderman, A. D. Sequels to a military career: The retired military. In M. Janowitz, *The new military*. New York: Russell Sage Foundation, 1964.

Bigoness, W. J. Effects of applicant's sex, race and performance on employer's performance ratings: Some additional findings. *Journal of Applied Psychology*, 1976, *61*, 80–84.

Bigoness, W. J. Correlates of faculty attitudes toward collective bargaining. *Journal of Applied Psychology*, 1978, *63*, 228–233.

Biles, G. E. Allegiances of unionized public employees toward employer and union. *Public Personnel Management*, 1974, *3*, 1965–169.

Blake, R. R., & Mouton, J. S. *The new managerial grid*. Houston: Gulf, 1978.

Blanz, F., & Ghiselli, E. E. The mixed standard scale: A new rating system. *Personnel Psychology*, 1972, *25*, 185–199.

Blau, P. M. *Exchange and power in social life*. New York: Wiley, 1964.

Blau, P. M., & Duncan, O. D. *The American occupational structure*. New York: Wiley, 1967.

Blauner, R. *Alienation and freedom*. Chicago: University of Chicago Press, 1964.

Bledsoe, J. C., & Brown, S. E. Factor structure of the Minnesota Satisfaction Questionnaire. *Perceptual and Motor Skills*, 1977, *45*, 301–302.

Block, J. H. Conceptions of sex role: Some cross-cultural and longitudinal perspectives. *American Psychologist*, 1973, *28*, 513–526.

Block, J., Von der Lippe, A., & Block, J. H. Sex-role and socialization patterns: Some personality concomitants and environmental antecedents. *Journal of Consulting Psychology*, 1973, *41*, 321–341.

Blood, M. R., & Hulin, C. L. Alienation, environmental characteristics and worker responses. *Journal of Applied Psychology*, 1967, *51*, 284–290.

Blood, R. O., Jr. The husband-wife relationship. In F. I. Nye & L. W. Hoffman (Eds.), *The employed mother in America*. Chicago: Rand McNally, 1963.

Blum, F. H. *Toward a democratic work process*. New York: Harper, 1953.

Blum, M. L., & Naylor, J. C. *Industrial psychology: Its theoretical and social foundations*. New York: Harper & Row, 1968.

Blumberg, H. H. Communication of interpersonal evaluations. *Journal of Personality and Social Psychology*, 1972, *23*, 157–162.

Blume, N. Union worker attitudes toward open housing: The case of the UAW in the Toledo metropolitan area. *Phylon*, 1973, *34*, 63–72.

Boehm, V. R. Negro-white differences in validity of employment and training selection procedures. *Journal of Applied Psychology*, 1972, *56*, 33–39.

Boehm, V. R. Differential prediction: A methodological artifact. *Journal of Applied Psychology*, 1977, *62*, 146–154.

Bogard, H. M. Union and management trainees—a comparative study of personality and occupational choice. *Journal of Applied Psychology*, 1960, *44*, 56–63.

Bok, D. C., & Dunlop, J. T. *Labor and the American community*. New York: Simon and Schuster, 1970.

Bolster, F. I., & Springbett, B. M. The reaction of interviewers to favorable and unfavorable information. *Journal of Applied Psychology*, 1961, *45*, 97–103.

Borman, W. C. The rating of individuals in organizations: An alternate approach. *Organizational Behavior and Human Performance*, 1974, *12*, 105–124.

Borman, W. C. Effect of instructions to avoid halo error on reliability and validity of performance evaluation ratings. *Journal of Applied Psychology*, 1975, *60*, 556–560.

Borman, W. C. Exploring the upper limits of reliability and validity in job performance ratings. *Journal of Applied Psychology*, 1978, *63*, 135–144.

Borman, W. C. Format and training effects on rating accuracy and rater errors. *Journal of Applied Psychology*, 1979, *64*, 410–421.

Borman, W. C., & Dunnette, M. D. Behavior-based versus trait-oriented performance ratings: An empirical study. *Journal of Applied Psychology*, 1975, *60*, 561–565.

Borman, W. C., & Vallon, W. R. A view of what can happen when behavioral expectation scales are developed in one setting and used in another. *Journal of Applied Psychology*, 1974, *59*, 197–201.

Borresen, H. A. The effects of instructions and item content on three types of ratings. *Educational and Psychological Measurements*, 1967, *27*, 855–962.

Boulding, K. E., & Spivey, W. A. *Linear programming and the theory of the firm*. New York: Macmillan, 1960.

Bowers, D. G. OD techniques and their results in 23 organizations: The Michigan ICL study. *Journal of Applied Behavioral Science*, 1973, *9*, 21–43.

Bowers, D. G., & Franklin, J. L. Survey-guided development: Using human resources measurement in organizational change. *Journal of Contemporary Business*, 1972, *1*, 43–56.

Bowman, G. W. What helps or harms promotability? *Harvard Business Review*, 1964, *42*(1), 6–26, 184–196.

Bowman, G., Wortney, B. N., & Greyser, S. H. Are women executives people? *Harvard Business Review*, 1965, *43*, 14–28, 164–178.

Bradburn, N. *The structure of psychological well being*. Chicago: Aldine Press, 1969.

Bray, D. W., & Campbell, R. J. Selections of salesmen by means of an assessment center. *Journal of Applied Psychology*, 1968, *52*, 36–41.

Bray, D. W., & Grant, D. L. The assessment center in the measurement of potential for business management. *Psychological Monographs*, 1966, *80*(17, Whole No. 625).

Brayfield, A. H., & Crockett, W. H. Employee attitudes and employee performance. *Psychological Bulletin*, 1955, *52*, 396–424.

Brayfield, A. H., & Wells, R. V. Interrelationships among measures of job satisfaction and general satisfaction. *Journal of Applied Psychology*, 1957, *41*, 201–205.

Brehm, J., & Festinger, L. Pressures toward uniformity of performance in groups. *Human Relations*, 1957, *10*, 85–91.

Briggs, P. F., Laperriere, R., & Greden, J. Working outside the home and the occurrence of depression in middle-aged women. *Mental Hygiene*, 1965, *49*, 438–442.

Bright, J. R. *Automation and management*. Boston: Graduate School of Business Administration, Harvard University, 1958.

Britt, D., & Galle, O. R. Industrial conflict and unionization. *American Sociological Review*, 1972, *37*, 46–57.

Brodsky, C. M. *The harassed worker*. Lexington, Mass.: D. C. Heath, 1976.

Brogden, H. E., & Taylor, E. K. The dollar criterion—applying the cost accounting concept to criterion construction. *Personnel Psychology*, 1950, *3*, 133–154.

Bronzaft, A. L. College women want a career, marriage and children. *Psychological Reports*, 1974, *35*, 1031–1034.

Broverman, I. K., Vogel, S., Broverman, D., Clarkson, I., & Rosenkrantz, P. Sex-role stereotypes: A current appraisal. *Journal of Social Issues*, 1972, *28*, 59–79.

Brown, B. S. *Participative management practices and attitudes*. Unpublished doctoral dissertation, The American University, 1977.

Brown, D. G. Sex role development in a changing culture. *Psychological Bulletin*, 1958, *55*, 232–242.

Brown, J. S. *The motivation of behavior*. New York: McGraw-Hill, 1961.

Brown, R., & Ford, M. Address in American English. *Journal of Abnormal and Social Psychology*, 1961, *62*, 375–385.

Brua, L. A. Who are the top managers? II. Directors compared. In B. Taylor (Ed.), *Business strategy and planning*. London: Longman, 1973.

Brumback, G. B., Employee attitude surveys. *Personnel Administration*, 1972, *35*, 27–34.

Bruner, J. S., Matter, J. S., & Papanek, M. L. Breadth of learning as a function of drive level and mechanization. *Psychological Review*, 1955, *62*, 1–10.

Buchholz, R. A. The belief structure of managers relative to work concepts measured by a factor analytic model. *Personnel Psychology*, 1977, *30*, 567–587.

Buck, V. E. *Working under pressure*. London: Granada Publishing, 1972.

Buel, W. D. The validity of behavioral rating scale items for the assessment of individual creativity. *Journal of Applied Psychology*, 1960, *44*, 407–412.

Bull, S. G., & Dizney, H. F. Epistemic curiosity-arousing prequestions: Their effects on long term retention. *Journal of Educational Psychology*, 1973, *65*, 45–49.

Bunney, W. E., & Hamburg, D. A. Methods for reliable longitudinal observation of behavior. *Archives of General Psychiatry*, 1963, *9*, 280–294.

Burchinal, L. G., & Rossman, J. Relationships among maternal employment indices and developmental characteristics of children. *Marriage and Family Living*, 1961, *23*, 334–340.

Bureau of the Census. Daytime care of children: October 1974 and February 1975. *Current Population Reports—Series P-20*, 1976, 298.

Bureau of the Census. *Statistical abstract of the United States, bicentennial issue*. Washington, D. C.: Bureau of the Census, Department of Commerce, 1976.

Bureau of National Affairs, Inc. *Management performance appraisal programs*. Washington, D.C.: Bureau of National Affairs, Inc., 1974.

Burgoyne, J. G., & Cooper, C. L. Evaluation methodology. *Journal of Occupational Psychology*, 1975, *48*, 53–62.

Burke, R. Differences in perception of desired job characteristics of the same sex and the opposite sex. *Journal of Genetic Psychology*, 1966, *109*, 37–46.

Burke, R. J. Managerial satisfaction with various work and non-work life roles. *Studies in Personnel Psychology*, 1973, *5*(1), 53–62.

Burke, R. J., Weitzel, W., & Weir, T. Characteristics of effective employee performance review and development interviews: Replications and extension. *Personnel Psychology*, 1978, *31*, 903–919.

Burnaska, R. F. The effects of behavior modeling training upon manager's behaviors and employee's perceptions. *Personnel Psychology*, 1976, *29*, 329–335.

Burnaska, R. F., & Hollmann, T. D. An empirical comparison of the relative effects of rater response biases on three rating scale formats. *Journal of Applied Psychology*, 1974, *59*, 307–312.

Burns, T. The directions of activity and communication in a department executive group. *Human Relations*, 1954, *7*, 73–97.

Buros, O. K. *The eighth mental measurements yearbook* (Vol. 1 and 2). Highland Park, N.J.: The Gryphon Press, 1978.

Butler, R. P., & Jaffee, C. L. Effects of incentive, feedback and manner of presenting the feedback on leader behavior. *Journal of Applied Psychology*, 1974, *59*, 332–336.

Byham, W. C. Assessment center for spotting future managers. *Harvard Business Review*, July 1970, *48*, 150–160.

Byham, W. C. The assessment center as an aid in management development. *Training and Development Journal*, 1971, *25*, 10–22.

Byham, W. C., & Spitzer, M. E. *The law and personnel testing*. New York: American Management Association, 1971.

Caldwell, B. M., Wright, C. M., Honig, A. S., & Tannenbaum, J. Infant day-care and attachment. *American Journal of Orthopsychiatry*, 1970, *40*, 397–412.

Cammann, C., Quinn, R. P., Beehr, T. A., & Gupta, N. *Effectiveness in work roles report 1: Validating quality of employment indicators*. Ann Arbor, Mich.: Survey Research Center, 1975.

Campbell, D. T., & Stanley, J. C. *Experimental and quasi-experimental designs for research*. Chicago: Rand McNally, 1963.

Campbell, J. P. Psychometric theory. In M. D. Dunnette, *Handbook of industrial and organizational psychology*. Chicago: Rand McNally, 1976.

Campbell, J. P., Dunnette, M. D., Avery, R. D., & Hellevik, L. V. The development and evaluation of behaviorally based rating scales. *Journal of Applied Psychology*, 1973, *57*, 15–22.

Canavan-Gumpert, D., Garner, K., & Gumpert, P. *The success-fearing personality*. Lexington, Mass.: Lexington Books, 1978.

Cantril, H. *The pattern of human concerns*. New Brunswick, N.J.: Rutgers University Press, 1966.

Carlson, R. E. Effect of applicant sample on ratings of valid information in an employment setting. *Journal of Applied Psychology*, 1970, *54*, 217–222.

Carlson, S. *Executive behavior*. Stockholm: Strömbergs, 1951.

Caro, P. W., Jr. Adaptive training—an application to flight simulation. *Human Factors,* 1969, *11,* 569–576.

Carrell, M. R., & Elbert, N. F. Some personal and organizational determinants of job satisfaction of postal clerks. *Academy of Management Journal,* 1974, *17,* 368–372.

Carroll, S., Paine, F. T., & Ivancevich, J. J. The relative effectiveness of training methods—expert opinion and research. *Personnel Psychology,* 1972, *25,* 495–509.

Cartwright, D., & Zander, A. *Group dynamics—research and theory.* Evanston, Ill.: Row, Peterson, 1960.

Cascio, W. F. Accuracy of verifiable biographical information blank responses. *Journal of Applied Psychology,* 1975, *60,* 767–769.

Cascio, W. F. Turnover, biographical data and fair employment practice. *Journal of Applied Psychology,* 1976, *61,* 576–580.

Cascio, W. F., & Silbey, V. Utility of the assessment center as a selection device. *Journal of Applied Psychology,* 1979, *64,* 107–118.

Cascio, W. F., & Valenzi, E. R. Behaviorally anchored rating scales: Effects of education and job experience of raters and ratees. *Journal of Applied Psychology,* 1977, *62,* 278–282.

Cass, J. *The significance of children's play.* London: B. T. Batsford, Ltd., 1971.

Centers, R., & Bugental, D. E. Intrinsic and extrinsic job motivation among different segments of the working population. *Journal of Applied Psychology,* 1966, *50,* 193–197.

Cervin, V. Experimental investigation of behavior in social situations: I Behavior under opposition. *Canadian Journal of Psychology,* 1955, *9,* 107–116.

Cervin, V. Individual behavior in social situations: Its relation to anxiety, neuroticism and group solidarity. *Journal of Experimental Psychology,* 1956, *51,* 161–168.

Chadwick-Jones, J. K. *Automation and behavior.* New York: Wiley, 1969.

Chadwick-Jones, J. K., Brown, C. A., & Nicholson, N. A-type and B-type absence: Empirical trends for women employees. *Occupational Psychology,* 1973, *47,* 75–80.

Chamberlain, N. W., & Cullen, D. E. *The labor sector* (2nd ed.). New York: McGraw-Hill, 1971.

Charner, I. Investing in your employee's future. *Training and Development Journal,* 1980, *34,* 100–104.

Cherrington, D. J., Reitz, H. J., & Scott, W. E. Effects of contingent and non-contingent reward on the relationship between satisfaction and task performance. *Journal of Applied Psychology,* 1971, *55,* 531–536.

Chinoy, E. *Automobile workers and the American dream.* New York: Doubleday, 1955.

Christal, R. E. *The United States Air Force occupational research project.* (AFHRL Technical Report No. 77–34). San Antonio, Texas: Brooks Air Force Base, 1974.

Christie, L. S., Luce, R. D., & Macy, J. *Communication and learning in task-oriented groups.* (Technical Report No. 231). Boston, Mass.: Research Laboratory of Electronics, Massachusetts Institute of Technology, 1952.

Cleary, T. A. Test bias: Prediction of grades of Negro and white students in integrated colleges. *Journal of Educational Measurement,* 1968, *5,* 115–124.

Cline, V. W., Tucker, M. F., & Anderson, D. R. The prediction of creativity and other performance measures among pharmaceutical students. *Psychological Reports,* 1966, *19,* 951–954.

Coates, C. H., & Pellegrin, R. J. Executives and supervisors: A situational theory of differential occupational mobility. *Social Forces,* 1956, *35,* 121–126.

Cobb, S. Role responsibility: The differentiation of a concept. In A. McLean (Ed.), *Occupational stress.* Springfield, Ill.: Charles C Thomas, 1974.

Cobb, S., & Kasl, S. V. Some medical aspects of unemployment. In G. M. Shatto (Ed.), *Employment of the middle-aged: Papers from industrial gerontology seminars.* Springfield, Ill.: Charles C Thomas, 1972.

Coch, L., & French, J. R. P. Overcoming resistance to change. *Human Relations,* 1948, *1,* 512–532.

Cogan, J. F. *Negative income taxation and labor supply: New evidence from the New Jersey-Pennsylvania experiment.* Santa Monica, Cal.: Rand Corporation, 1978.

Cohen, A. M., Robinson, E. L., & Edwards, J. L. Experiments in organizational embeddedness. *Administrative Science Quarterly,* 1969, *14,* 208–221.

Cohen, A. R. Upward communication in experimentally created hierarchies. *Human Relations,* 1958, *11,* 41–53.

Cohen, S. L., & Bunker, K. A. Subtle effects of sex role stereotype on recruiters' hiring decision. *Journal of Applied Psychology,* 1975, *60,* 566–572.

Cohn, E., & Lewis, N. Employer's experience in retaining hard-core hires. *Industrial Relations,* 1975, *14,* 55–62.

Cole, N. S. Bias in selection. *Journal of Educational Measurement*, 1973, *10*, 237–255.

Coleman, J. F., Blake, R. R., & Mouton, J. S. Task difficulty and conformity pressures. *Journal of Abnormal and Social Psychology*, 1958, *57*, 120–122.

Coleman, R. J. The chief executive: His personality characteristics and the firm's growth rate. *Personnel Journal*, 1970, *49*, 994–1001.

Comrey, A. L., High, W. S., & Wilson, R. C. Factors influencing organizational effectiveness VII: A survey of aircraft supervisors. *Personnel Psychology*, 1955, *8*, 245–257.

Comrey, A. L., Pfiffner, J. M., & Beem, H. P. Factors influencing organizational effectiveness I: The U.S. forest survey. *Personnel Psychology*, 1952, *5*, 307–328.

Connolly, T., & Miklausich, V. M. Some effects of feedback error in diagnostic decision tasks. *Academy of Management Journal*, 1978, *21*, 301–307.

Constantin, S. U. An investigation of information favorability in the employment interview. *Journal of Applied Psychology*, 1976, *61*, 743–749.

Cook, F. G., Clark, S. C., Roberts, K., & Semeonoff, E. Are white-collar trade unionists different? *Sociology of Work and Occupations*, 1978, *5*, 235–245.

Cook, T. D., & Campbell, D. T. The design and conduct of quasi-experiments and true experiments in field settings. In M. D. Dunnette, *Handbook of industrial and organizational psychology*. Chicago; Rand McNally, 1976.

Cook, T. D., & Campbell, D. T. *Quasi experimentation: Design and analysis issues for field settings*. Chicago: Rand McNally, 1979.

Cooper, C. L., & Mangham, I. L. *T-groups: A survey of research*. London: Wiley, 1971.

Cooper, C. L., & Marshall, J. Occupational sources of stress: A review of the literature relating to coronary heart disease and mental health. *Journal of Occupational Psychology*, 1976, *49*, 11–28.

Cox, J. A., & Krumboltz, J. D. Racial bias in peer ratings of basic airmen. *Sociometry*, 1958, *21*, 292–299.

Cozan, L. W. Forced-choice: Better than other rating methods? *Personnel Psychology*, 1959, *36*, 80–83.

Cronbach, L. J. Test validation. In R. L. Thorndike, *Educational measurement* (2nd ed.). Washington, D. C.: American Council on Education, 1971.

Crossman, E. R. F. W., & Laner, S. *The impact of technological change on manpower and skill demand: Case study data and policy implications*. Berkeley: Department of Industrial Engineering and Operations Research, University of California, 1969.

Crow, W. J. The effects of training upon accuracy and variability in interpersonal perception. *Journal of Abnormal and Social Psychology*, 1957, *55*, 355–359.

Culbertson, K., & Thompson, M. An analysis of supervisory training needs. *Training and Development Journal*, 1980, *34*, 58–62.

Cummin, P. C. TAT correlates of executive performance. *Journal of Applied Psychology*, 1967, *51*, 78–81.

Cummings, T. G., & Manring, S. L. The relationship between worker alienation and work related behavior. *Journal of Vocational Behavior*, 1977, *10*, 167–179.

Cummings, T. G., Molloy, E. S., & Glen, R. A methodological critique of fifty-eight selected work experiments. *Human Relations*, 1977, *30*, 675–708.

Dalton, M. The industrial "rate-buster": A characterization. *Applied Anthropology*, 1948, *7*, 5–18.

Dalton, M. *Men who manage*. New York: Wiley, 1959.

Daniel, W. W. Automation and the quality of work. *New Society*, May 29, 1969.

Dansereau, F., Cashman, J., & Graen, G. Instrumentality theory and equity theory as complementary approaches in predicting relationship of leadership and turnover among managers. *Organizational Behavior and Human Performance*, 1973, *10*, 184–200.

Dansereau, F., Graen, G., & Haga, W. J. A vertical dyad linkage approach to leadership in formal organizations. *Organizational Behavior and Human Performance*, 1975, *13*, 46–78.

Darlington, R. B. Another look at "culture fairness." *Journal of Educational Measurement*, 1971, *8*, 71–82.

Davis, K. Management communication and the grapevine. *Harvard Business Review*, 1953, *31*(5), 44–49.

Dawis, R. V., Lofquist, L. H., & Weiss, D. J. A theory of work adjustment (Rev. ed.). *Minnesota Studies in Vocational Rehabilitation*, 1968, *23*.

Dawis, R. V., Pinto, P. P., Weitzel, W., & Nezzer, M. Describing organizations as reinforcer systems: A new use for job satisfaction and employee attitude surveys. *Journal of Vocational Behavior*, 1974, *4*, 55–66.

Dean, L. R. Union activity and dual loyalty. *Industrial Labor Relations Review*, 1954, *7*, 526–536. (a)

Dean, L. R. Social integration, attitudes and union activity. *Industrial Labor Relations Review*, 1954, *8*, 48–56. (b) deCharms, R. *Personal causation: The internal affective determinants of behavior.* New York; Academic Press, 1968.

Deci, E. L. Effects of externally mediated rewards on intrinsic motivation. *Journal of Personality and Social Psychology,* 1971, *18,* 105–115.

Deci, E. L. Intrinsic motivation, extrinsic reinforcement and inequity. *Journal of Personality and Social Psychology,* 1972, *22,* 113–120.

Deci, E. L. *Intrinsic motivation.* New York: Plenum Press, 1975.

The decision to retire: A canvas of possibilities. *Monthly Labor Review,* 1966, *89*(1), III-IV.

DeGrazia, S. *On time, work, and leisure.* Garden City, N.Y.: Doubleday, 1964.

DeJong, P. Y., Brawer, M. J., & Robin, S. S. Patterns of female intergenerational occupational mobility: A comparison with male patterns of intergenerational occupational mobility. *American Sociological Review,* 1971, *36,* 1033–1042.

Dentler, R. A., & Erikson, K. T. The functions of deviance in groups. *Social Problems,* 1959, *7,* 98–107.

Derber, M., Chalmers, W. E., & Edelman, M. T. Types and variants in local union management relationships. *Human Organizations,* 1962–63, *21,* 264–271.

DeSola-Pool, I. The head of the company: Conceptions of role and identity. *Behavioral Science,* 1964, *9,* 147–155.

Deutermann, W. V., Jr. Another look at working-age men who are not in the labor force. *Monthly Labor Review,* 1977, *100*(6), 9–14.

Dicesare, C. B. Changes in the occupational structure of U. S. jobs. *Monthly Labor Review,* 1975, *98*(3), 24–34.

Dictionary of 500 largest U. S. industrial corporations. *Fortune,* 1977, *95*(5), 364–386.

Dittes, J. E., & Kelley, H. H. Effects of different conditions of acceptance upon conformity to group norms. *Journal of Abnormal and Social Psychology,* 1956, *53,* 100–107.

Dossett, D. L., Latham, G. P., & Mitchell, T. R. Effects of assigned versus participatively set goals, knowledge of results and individual differences on employee behavior when goal difficulty is held constant. *Journal of Applied Psychology,* 1979, *64,* 291–298.

Douvan, D. Employment and the adolescent. In F. Nye & L. Hoffman (Eds.), *The employed mother in America.* Chicago: Rand McNally, 1963.

Downey, H. K., Sheridan, J. E., & Slocum, J. W. The path-goal theory of leadership: A longitudinal analysis. *Organizational Behavior and Human Performance,* 1976, *16,* 156–176.

Downey, R. G., Medland, F. F., & Yates, L. G. Evaluation of a peer rating system for predicting subsequent promotion of senior military officers. *Journal of Applied Psychology,* 1976, *61,* 206–209.

Drabek, T. E., & Hass, J. E. Laboratory simulation of organizational stress. *American Sociological Review,* 1969, *34,* 223–238.

Dubin, R. S. Industrial workers' worlds: A study of the central life interests of industrial workers. *Social Problems,* 1956, *3,* 131–142.

Dubin, R. S., & Goldman, D. R. Central life interests of American middle managers and specialists. *Journal of Vocational Behavior,* 1972, *2,* 133–141.

Dubin, R. S., & Spray, S. Executive behavior and interaction. *Industrial Relations,* 1964, *3,* 99–108.

Duell, O. K. Effect of type of objective level of test questions, and the judged importance of tested materials upon posttest performance. *Journal of Educational Psychology,* 1974, *66,* 225–232.

Duffy, N. F. The skilled worker and his union. *Journal of Industrial Relations,* 1960, *2,* 99–109.

Dunnette, M. D., & Borman, W. C. Personnel selection and classification systems. *Annual Review of Psychology,* 1979, *30,* 477–525.

Dunnette, M. D., & Campbell, J. P. Laboratory education: Impact on people and organizations. *Industrial Relations,* 1968, *8,* 1–27.

Dunnette, M. D., & Motowidlo, S. J. *Development of a personnel selection and career assessment system for police officers for patrol, investigative, supervisory and command positions.* Minneapolis, Minn.: Personnel Decisions, Inc., 1975.

Dupuy, H. J., Engle, A., Devine, B. K., Scanlon, J., & Querec, L. Selected symptoms of psychological distress. *Vital and Health Statistics (DHEW),* 1970, Series 11.

Easterbrook, J. A. The effect of emotion on utilization and the organization of behavior. *Psychological Review,* 1959, 66, 183–201.

Edwards, A. L. *Techniques of attitude scale construction.* New York: Appleton-Century-Crofts, 1957.

Eisele, C. F. Organization size, technology and frequency of strikes. *Industrial and Labor Relations Review,* 1974, *27,* 560–571.

Elzey, F. F. *A programmed introduction to statistics.* Belmont, Cal: Wadsworth, 1966.

England, G. W., Agarwal, N. C., & Trerise, R. E. Union leaders and managers: A comparison of value systems. *Industrial Relations,* 1971, *10,* 211–226.

Epstein, C. F. *Women's place*. Berkeley, Cal.: University of California Press, 1970.

Erickson, J. M., Pugh, W. M., & Gunderson, E. K. Status congruency as a predictor of job satisfaction and life stress. *Journal of Applied Psychology,* 1972, *56,* 523–525.

Etaugh, C. Effects of maternal employment on children: A review of the research. *Merrill Palmer Quarterly,* 1974, *20,* 70–98.

Etzioni, A. *A comparative analysis of complex organizations.* New York: Free Press, 1961.

Etzioni-Halevy, E. Patterns of conflict generation and conflict "absorption." The cases of Israeli labor and ethnic conflicts. *Journal of Conflict Resolution,* 1975, *19,* 286–309.

Evans, M. G. The moderating effects of internal versus external control on the relationship between various aspects of job satisfaction. *Studies in Personnel Psychology,* 1973, *5,* 37–46.

Evans, M. G., & Molinari, L. Equity, piece-rate overpayment, and job security: Some effects on performance. *Journal of Applied Psychology,* 1970, *54,* 105–114.

Exline, R. V., & Ziller, R. C. Status congruency and interpersonal conflict in decision making groups. *Human Relations,* 1959, *12,* 147–162.

Farr, J. L. Response requirements and primacy-recency effects in a simulated selection interview. *Journal of Applied Psychology,* 1973, *57,* 228–232.

Farr, J. L., O'Leary, B. S., & Bartlett, C. J. Ethnic group membership as a moderator of the prediction of job performance. *Personnel Psychology,* 1971, *24,* 609–636.

Farr, J. L., O'Leary, B. S., & Bartlett, C. J. Effect of a work sample test upon self-selection and turnover of job applicants, *Journal of Applied Psychology,* 1973, *58,* 283–285.

Farr, J. L. Vance, R. J., & McIntyre, R. M. Further examination of the relationship between reward contingency and intrinsic motivation. *Organizational Behavior and Human Performance,* 1977, *20,* 31–53.

Farr, R. M. On the nature of attributional artifacts in qualitative research; Herzberg's two-factor theory of work motivation. *Journal of Occupational Psychology,* 1977, *50,* 3–14.

Farris, G. F. Organizational factors and individual performance; A longitudinal study. *Journal of Applied Psychology,* 1969, *53,* 87–92.

Farris, G. F. A predictive study of turnover. *Personnel Psychology,* 1971, *24,* 311–328.

Farris, G. F., & Lim, F. G. Effects of performance on leadership cohesiveness, influence, satisfaction and subsequent performance. *Journal of Applied Psychology,* 1969, *53,* 490–497.

Faunce, W. A. The automobile industry. In H. B. Jacobson & J. S. Roucek (Eds.), *Automation and society.* New York: Philosophical Library, 1959.

Faunce, W. A. Automation and the division of labor. *Social Problems,* 1965, *13,* 149–160.

Feather, N. T. Positive and negative reactions to male and female success and failure in relation to the perceived status and sex-typed appropriateness of occupations. *Journal of Personality and Social Psychology,* 1975, *31,* 536–548.

Feather, N. T., & Simon, J. G. Reactions to male and female success and failure in sex-linked occupations: Impressions of personality, causal attributions, and perceived likelihood of different consequences. *Journal of Personality and Social Psychology,* 1975, *31,* 20–31.

Federal Register. Uniform guidelines on employee selection. *Federal Register,* August 25, 1978, *43,* 38290–38315.

Felton, J. S., & Cole, R. The high cost of heart disease. *Circulation,* 1963, *27,* 957–962.

Fenchel, G. H., Monderer, J. H., & Hartley, E. L. Subjective status and the equilibration hypothesis. *Journal of Abnormal and Social Psychology,* 1951, *46,* 476–479.

Fenz, W. D. Conflict and stress as related to physiological activation and sensory, perceptual, and cognitive functioning. *Psychological Monographs,* 1964, *78*(8, Whole No. 585).

Ferree, M. M. Working-class jobs: Housework and paid work as sources of satisfaction. *Social Problems,* 1976, *23,* 431–441.

Fiedler, F. E. The leader's psychological distance and group effectiveness. In D. Cartwright & A. Zander, *Group dynamics* (2nd ed.). New York: Harper and Row, 1960, 586–606.

Fiedler, F. E. A contingency model of leadership effectiveness. In L. Berkowitz, *Advances in experimental social psychology.* New York: Academic Press, 1964.

Fiedler, F. E. *A theory of leadership effectiveness.* New York: McGraw-Hill, 1967.

Fiedler, F. E. Personality, motivational systems and behavior of high and low LPC persons. *Human Relations,* 1972, *25,* 391–412.

Fiedler, F. E., & Chemers, M. M. *Leadership and effective management.* Glenview, Ill.: Scott, Foresman, 1974.

Fiedler, F. E., & Mahar, L. A field experiment validating contingency model leadership training. *Journal of Applied Psychology,* 1979, *64,* 247–254.

Finkel, R. B. Management assessment centers. In M. D. Dunnette, *Handbook of industrial and organizational psychology.* Chicago: Rand McNally, 1976.

Finn, R. H. Effects of some variations in rating scale characteristics on the means and reliabilities of ratings. *Educational and Psychological Measurement,* 1972, *32,* 255–265.

Finn, R. H., & Lee, S. M. Salary equity; Its determination, analysis and correlates. *Journal of Applied Psychology,* 1972, *56,* 283–292.

Fisher, C. D. Transmission of positive and negative feedback to subordinates: A laboratory investigation. *Journal of Applied Psychology,* 1979, *64,* 533–540.

Fisher, D. J. *A case study of the success syndrome in high-achieving executives within a corporate structure.* Unpublished doctoral dissertation, University of Michigan, 1976.

Flanagan, J. C. Critical requirements: A new approach to employee evaluation. *Personnel Psychology,* 1949, *2,* 419–425.

Flanagan, J. C. The critical incident technique. *Psychological Bulletin,* 1954, *51,* 327–358.

Flaugher, R. L. The many definitions of test bias. *American Psychologist,* 1978, *33,* 671–679.

Fleishman, E. A. Toward a taxonomy of human performance. *American Psychologist,* 1975, *30,* 1127–1149.

Fleishman, E. A., & Berniger, J. One way to reduce office turnover, *Personnel,* 1960, *37,* 63–69.

Fleishman, E. A., & Harris, E. F. Patterns of leadership behavior related to employee grievances and turnover. *Personnel Psychology,* 1962, *15,* 43–56.

Fleishman, E. A., Harris, E. F., & Burtt, H. E. *Leadership and supervision in industry.* Columbus: Ohio State University, Bureau of Educational Research, 1955.

Fleishman, E. A. & Peters, D. R. Interpersonal values, leadership attitudes and managerial "success." *Personnel Psychology,* 1962, *15,* 127–143.

Flemming, A. J. Executive stress: Excessive or not? *Advanced Management,* 1962, *27,* 11–12.

Form, W. H. Occupational and social integration of automobile workers in four countries: A comparative study. *International Journal of Comparative Sociology,* 1969, *10*(March-June), 1–2, 95–116.

Form, W. H. Technology and social behavior in four countries: A sociotechnical perspective. *American Sociological Review,* 1972, *37,* 727–738.

Form, W. H. Job vs. political unionism: A cross-national comparison. *Industrial Relations,* 1973, *12,* 224–238.(a)

Form, W. H. Auto workers and their machines: A study of work, factory, and job satisfaction in four countries. *Social Forces,* 1973, *52,* 1–15.(b)

Fortune. The Fortune directory of the 500 largest U.S. industrial corporations. *Fortune,* 1979, *99*(5), 268–295.

Fossum, J. A. Urban-rural differences in job satisfaction. *Industrial and Labor Relations Review,* 1974, *27,* 405–409.

Frank, L. L., & Hackman, J. R. A failure of job enrichment: The case of the change that wasn't. *Journal of Applied Behavioral Science,* 1975, *11,* 413–436.

Frankenhaeuser, M. Quality of life: Criteria for behavioral adjustment. *International Journal of Psychology,* 1977, *12*(2), 99–110.

Frase, L. T. Integration of written text. *Journal of Educational Psychology,* 1973, *65,* 252–261.

Frase, L. T. Prose processing. In G. Bower, *Psychology of learning and motivation* (Vol. 9). New York: Academic Press, 1975.

Frase, L. T., & Kreitzberg, V. S. Effect of topical and indirect learning directions on prose recall. *Journal of Educational Psychology,* 1975, *67,* 320–324.

French, J. R. P. Person-role fit. In A. McLean, *Occupational stress.* Springfield, Ill.: Charles C Thomas, 1974.

French, J. R. P., & Caplan, R. D. Organizational stress and individual strain. In A. J. Marrow (Ed.), *The failure of success.* New York: AMACOM, 1973.

French, J. R. P., & Kahn, R. A programmatic approach to studying the industrial environment and mental health. *Journal of Social Issues,* 1962, *18*(3), 1–47.

Friedlander, F. Motivation to work and organizational performance. *Journal of Applied Psychology,* 1966, *50,* 143–152.(a)

Friedlander, F. Importance of work versus manwork among socially and occupationally stratified groups. *Journal of Applied Psychology,* 1966, *50,* 437–441.(b)

Friedlander, F., & Greenberg, S. Effect of climate job attitudes, training and organizational climate on performance of the hard-core unemployed. *Journal of Applied Psychology,* 1971, *55,* 289–295.

Friedman, M. D., & Rosenman, R. H. *Type A behavior and your heart.* New York: Knopf, 1974.

Fullan, M. Industrial technology and worker integration in the organization. *American Sociological Review,* 1970, *35,* 1028–1039.

Fullerton, H. N., Jr., & Byrne, J. J. Length of working life for men and women, 1970. *Monthly Labor Review,* 1976, *99*(2), 31–35.

Gage, N. L., Leavitt, G. S., & Stone, G. C. The psychological meaning of acquiescence set for authoritarianism. *Journal of Abnormal and Social Psychology,* 1957, *55,* 98–103.

Gagne, R. Simulators. In R. Glaser (Ed.), *Training research and education.* Washington, D.C.: Office of Naval Research, Psychological Services Division, 1961.

Gagne, R. M. Military training and principles of learning. *American Psychologist,* 1962, *18,* 83–91.

Gagne, R. M. *Essentials of learning for instruction.* Hinsdale, Ill.: Dryden Press, 1974.

Gagne, R. M., & Briggs, L. J. *Principles of instructional design.* New York: Holt, Rinehart and Winston, 1974.

Galanter, E. The direct measurement of utility and subjective probability. *American Journal of Psychology,* 1962, *75,* 208–220.

Galinsky, M. D. Personality development and vocational choice of clinical psychologists and physicists. *Journal of Counseling Psychology,* 1962, *9,* 299–305.

Gallup, P. Gallup poll. *New York Times,* March 27, 1973, p. 22.

Gandz, J., & Murray, V. V. The experience of workplace politics. *Academy of Management Journal,* 1980, *23,* 237–251.

Gannon, M. J., & Hendrickson, D. H. Career orientation and job satisfaction among working wives. *Journal of Applied Psychology,* 1973, *57,* 339–340.

Gardell, B. Psychological and social problems of industrial work in affluent societies. *International Journal of Psychology,* 1977, *12*(2), 125–134.

Garfinkle, S. H. Occupations of women and black workers, 1962–1974. *Monthly Labor Review,* 1975, *98*(4), 25–29.

Garland, H. The effects of piece-rate underpayment and overpayment on job performance: A test of equity theory with a new induction procedure. *Journal of Applied Social Psychology,* 1973, *3,* 325–334.

Garland, H. Sometimes nothing succeeds like success: Reactions to success and failure in sex-linked occupations. *Psychology of Women Quarterly,* 1977, *2,* 50–61.

Gavin, J. F. Occupational mental health—forces and trends. *Personnel Journal,* 1977, *56,* 198–201.

Gavin, J. F., & Howe, J. G. Psychological climate: Some theoretical and empirical considerations. *Behavioral Science,* 1975, *20,* 228–240.

Gechman, A. S., & Wiener, Y. Job involvement and satisfaction as related to mental health and personal time devoted to work. *Journal of Applied Psychology,* 1975, *60,* 521–523.

Gemmill, G. R., & Heisler, W. J. Machiavellianism as a factor in managerial job strain, job satisfaction, and upward mobility. *Academy of Management Journal,* 1972, *15,* 51–62.

Georgopoulos, B. S., Mahoney, G. M., and Jones, N. W. A path-goal approach to productivity. *Journal of Applied Psychology,* 1957, *41,* 345–353.

Getman, J. G., Goldberg, S. B., & Herman, J. B. *Union representation elections: Law and reality.* New York: Russell Sage Foundation, 1976.

Ghiselli, E. E. *The validity of occupational aptitude tests.* New York: Wiley, 1966.

Ghiselli, E. E., & Haire, M. The validation of selection tests in the light of the dynamic character of criteria. *Personnel Psychology,* 1960, *13,* 225–231.

Gibbons, R. W. Showdown at Lordstown. *Commonweal,* 1972, *95,* 523–524.

Gibson, J. L., & Klein, S. M. Employee attitudes as a function of age and length of service; A reconceptualization. *Academy of Management Journal,* 1970, *13,* 411–425.

Giles, B. A., & Barrett, G. V. Utility of merit increases. *Journal of Applied Psychology,* 1971, *55,* 103–109.

Gilmer, B. V. H. Psychological aspects of women in industry. *Personnel Psychology,* 1957, *10,* 439–452.

Gilmore, D. C., Beehr, T. A., & Richter, D. J. Effects of leader behaviors on subordinate performance and satisfaction: A laboratory experiment with student employees. *Journal of Applied Psychology,* 1979, *64,* 166–172.

Glenn, N. D., Ross, A. A., & Tully, J. C. Patterns of intergenerational mobility of females through marriage. *American Sociological Review,* 1974, *39,* 683–699.

Gluskinos, U. M., & Kestleman, B. Management and union leaders' perception of work needs as compared with self-reported needs. *Proceedings of the Annual Convention of the American Psychological Association,* 1970, *5,* 603–604. (Part 2)

Goldberg, S., & Lewis, M. Play behavior in the year-old infant; Early sex differences. *Child Development,* 1969, *40,* 21–31.

Goldman, D. R. Managerial mobility motivation and central life interest. *American Sociological Review,* 1973, *38,* 119–126.

Goldstein, A. P., & Sorcher, M. *Changing supervisor behavior.* New York: Pergamon, 1974.

Goldstein, B. Some aspects of the nature of unionism

among salaried professionals in industry. *American Sociological Review*, 1955, *20*, 199–205.

Goldstein, I. L. The application blank: How honest are the responses? *Journal of Applied Psychology*, 1971, *55*, 491–492.

Goldstein, I. L. *Training: Program development and evaluation*. Monterey, Cal.: Brooks-Cole, 1974.

Goldstein, I. L. Training in work organizations. *Annual Review of Psychology*, 1980, *31*, 229–272.

Goldthorpe, J. H. Attitudes and behavior of car assembly workers: A deviant case and a theoretical critique. *British Journal of Sociology*, 1966, *17*, 227–244.

Goodman, P. S. Effect of perceived inequity on salary allocation decision. *Journal of Applied Psychology*, 1975, *60*, 372–375.

Goodman, P., & Friedmen, A. An examination of the effect of wage inequity in the hourly condition. *Organizational Behavior and Human Performance*, 1968, *3*, 340–352.

Goodman, P., Furcon, J., & Rose, J. Examination of some measures of creative ability by the multitrait-multimethod martrix. *Journal of Applied Psychology*, 1969, *53*, 240–243.

Goodman, P., & Salipante, P., Jr. Organizational rewards and retention of the hard-core unemployed. *Journal of Applied Psychology*, 1976, *61*, 12–21.

Goodwin, L. *Do the poor want to work?* Washington, D.C.: Brookings Institution, 1972.

Gordon, M. E., Philpot, J. W., Burt, R. E., Thompson, C. A., & Spiller, W. E. Commitment to the union: Development of a measure and an examination of its correlates. *Journal of Applied Psychology*, 1980, *65*, 479–499.

Gore, S. *The influence of social support and related variables in ameliorating the consequences of job loss*. Unpublished doctoral dissertation, University of Pennsylvania, 1973.

Gottfredson, G. D., Holland, J. L., & Gottfredson, L. S. *The relation of vocational aspirations and assessments to employment reality—Research report 181*. Baltimore, Md.: Center for Social Organization of Schools, The John Hopkins University, 1974.

Gottfredson, L. S. *A multiple-labor market model of occupational achievement—Research report 225*. Baltimore, Md.: Center for Social Organization of Schools, The John Hopkins University, 1977.

Gouldner, A. W. *Patterns of industrial bureaucracy*. New York: Free Press, 1954.

Gouldner, A. W. Cosmopolitans and locals: Toward an analysis of latent social roles—I. *Administrative Science Quarterly*, 1958, *3*, 281–306.(a)

Gouldner, A. W. Cosmopolitans and locals. Toward an analysis of latent social roles—II. *Administrative Science Quarterly*, 1958, *3*, 444–480.(b)

Gove, W. R., & Tudor, E. Adult sex roles and mental illness. In J. Huber (Ed.), *Changing women in a changing society*. Chicago: University of Chicago Press, 1973.

Gowler, D., & Legge, K. (Eds.) *Managerial stress*. New York: Wiley, 1975.

Graen, G. Role making processes within complex organizations. In M. D. Dunnette (Ed.), *Handbook of industrial and organizational psychology*. Chicago: Rand McNally, 1976.

Graen, G., & Shiemann, W. Leader-member agreement: A vertical dyad linkage approach. *Journal of Applied Psychology*, 1978, *63*, 206–212.

Grant, D. L. Analysis of management potential. *Proceedings of the Meeting of the Eastern Psychological Association*, 1965.

Greenberg, J. The Protestant work ethic and reactions to negative performance evaluations on a laboratory task. *Journal of Applied Psychology*, 1977, *62*, 682–690.

Greene, C. N. Relationships between role accuracy, compliance, performance evaluation, and satisfaction within managerial dyads. *Academy of Management Journal*, 1972, *15*, 205–215.

Greene, C. N. Causal connections among managers' merit pay, job satisfaction, and performance. *Journal of Applied Psychology*, 1973, *58*, 85–100.

Greene, C. N., & Organ, D. W. An evaluation of causal models linking the received role with job satisfaction. *Administrative Science Quarterly*, 1973, *18*, 95–103.

Greenwood, J. W. Management stressors. In A. McLean, *Reducing occupational stress*. Washington, D.C.: U.S. Department of Health, Education and Welfare, National Institute for Occupational Safety and Health, 1978.

Greller, M. M., & Herold, D. M. Sources of feedback: A preliminary investigation. *Organizational Behavior and Human Performance*, 1975, *13*, 244–256.

Grimsley, G., & Jarrett, H. F. The relation of past managerial achievement to test measure obtained in the employment situation: Methodology and results. *Personnel Psychology*, 1973, *26*, 31–48.

Gross, A. L., & Su, W. Defining a "fair" or "unbiased" selection model; A question of utilities. *Journal of Applied Psychology*, 1975, *60*, 345–351.

Gross, N., & Trusk, A. E. *The sex factor and the management of schools*. New York: Wiley, 1976.

Grossman, A. S. Women in the labor force: The early years. *Monthly Labor Review,* 1975, *98*(4), 3–9.

Gruenfeld, L. W. A study of the motivation of industrial supervisors. *Personnel Psychology,* 1962, *15,* 303–314.

Gruenfeld, L. W., & Weissenberg, P. Field independence and articulation of sources of job satisfaction. *Journal of Applied Psychology,* 1970, *54,* 424–426.

Guest, R. H. Of time and the foreman. *Personnel,* 1956, *32,* 478–486.

Guetzkow, H., & Dill, W. R. Factors in the organizational development of task-oriented groups. *Sociometry,* 1957, *20,* 175–203.

Guetzkow, H., & Simon, H. The impact of certain communication nets upon organization and performance in task oriented groups. *Management Science,* 1955, *1,* 233–250.

Guilford, J. P. *Psychometric methods* (2nd ed.). New York: McGraw-Hill, 1954.

Guion, R. M. Industrial morale: The problem of terminology. *Personnel Psychology,* 1958, *11,* 59–64.

Guion, R. M. Criterion measurement and personnel judgment. *Personnel Psychology,* 1961, *14,* 141–149.

Guion, R. M. *Personnel testing.* New York: McGraw-Hill, 1965.

Guion, R. M. Employment tests and discriminatory hiring. *Industrial Relations,* 1966, *5,* 20–37.

Guion, R. M. Recruiting, selection and job placement. In M. D. Dunnette (Ed.), *Handbook of industrial and organizational psychology.* Chicago: Rand McNally, 1976.

Guion, R. M., & Landy, F. J. The meaning of work and the motivation to work. *Organizational Behavior and Human Performance,* 1972, *7,* 308–339.

Gump, J. P. Sex-role attitudes and psychological well-being. *Journal of Social Issues,* 1972, *28,* 79–92.

Gurin, G., Veroff, J., & Feld, S. *Americans view their mental health.* New York: Basic Books, 1960.

Hackman, J. R. Work redesign. In J. R. Hackman & J. L. Suttles (Eds.), *Improving life at work: Behavioral science approaches to organizational change.* Pacific Palisades, Cal.: Goodyear, 1977.

Hackman, J. R., & Oldham, G. R. Motivation through the design of work: Test of a theory. *Organizational Behavior and Human Performance,* 1976, *16,* 250–279.

Haefner, J. E. Race, age, sex, and competence as factors in employer selection of the disadvantaged. *Journal of Applied Psychology,* 1977, *62,* 199–202.

Hagburg, E. C. Correlates of organizational partic-

ipation: An examination of factors affecting union membership activity. *Pacific Sociological Review,* 1966, *9,* 15–21.

Hage, J., & Aiken, M. Routine technology, social structure and organizational goals. *Administrative Science Quarterly,* 1969, *14,* 366–377.

Haire, M. Role-perception in labor-management relations: An experimental approach. *Industrial and Labor Relations Review,* 1955, *8,* 204–216.

Hakel, M. D., Hollmann, T. D., & Dunnette, M. D. Accuracy of interviewers, certified public accountants, and students in identifying the interests of accountants. *Journal of Applied Psychology,* 1970, *54,* 115–119.

Hakel, M. D., Ohnesorge, J. P., & Dunnette, M. D. Interviewer evaluations of job applicants' resumés as a function of the qualifications of the immediately preceding applicants: An examination of contrast effects. *Journal of Applied Psychology,* 1970, *54,* 27–30.

Halaby, C. N. Bureaucratic promotion criteria. *Administrative Science Quarterly,* 1978, *23,* 466–484.

Hall, D. T., & Mansfield, R. Organizational and individual response to external stress. *Administrative Science Quarterly,* 1971, *16,* 533–547.

Hall, D. T., & Mansfield, R. Relationships of age and seniority with career variables of engineers and scientists. *Journal of Applied Psychology,* 1975, *60,* 201–210.

Hall, D. T., Schneider, B., & Nygren, H. T. Personal factors in organizational identification. *Administrative Science Quarterly,* 1970, *15,* 176–190.

Hammer, P. G., & Chapin, F. S. *Human time allocation: A case study of Washington, D.C.* University of North Carolina, Center for Urban and Regional Studies, 1972.

Hamner, W. C., Kim, J. S., Baird, L., & Bigoness, W. J. Race and sex as determinants of ratings by potential employers in a simulated work-sampling task. *Journal of Applied Psychology,* 1974, *59,* 705–711.

Hamner, W. C., & Smith, F. J. Work attitudes as predictors of unionization activity. *Journal of Applied Psychology,* 1978, *63,* 415–421.

Hamner, W. C., & Tosi, H. Relationship or role conflict and role ambiguity to job involvement measures. *Journal of Applied Psychology,* 1974, *4,* 497–499.

Hanley, M. A. *Factors of achievement and femininity as predictors of career commitment in college senior women.* Unpublished doctoral dissertation, Boston University, 1974.

Harris, T. C., & Locke, E. A. Replication of white-collar-blue-collar differences in sources of satisfaction and dissatisfaction. *Journal of Applied Psychology,* 1974, *59,* 369–370.

Hart, H. H. The identification with the machine. *American Imago,* 1953, *10,* 95–111.

Harvey, O. J., & Consalvi, C. Status and conformity to pressures in informal groups. *Journal of Abnormal and Social Psychology,* 1960, *60,* 182–187.

Hayghe, H. Labor force activity of married women. *Monthly Labor Review,* 1973, *96*(4), 31–40.

Hays, W. L. *Statistics for the social sciences.* 2nd ed. New York: Holt, Rinehart and Winston, 1973.

Haythorn, W., Couch, A., Haefner, D., Langham, P., & Carter, L. The behavior of authoritarian and equalitarian personalities in small groups. *Human Relations,* 1956, *9,* 57–74.(a)

Haythorn, W., Couch, A., Haefner, D., Langham, P., & Carter, L. The effects of varying combinations of authoritarian and equalitarian leaders and followers. *Journal of Abnormal and Social Psychology,* 1956, *53,* 210–219.(b)

Heckman, N. A., Bryson, R., & Bryson, J. B. Problems of professional couples: A content analysis. *Journal of Marriage and the Family,* 1977, *39,* 323–330.

Heckscher, A., & DeGrazia, S. Executive leisure. *Harvard Business Review,* 1959, *37,* 6–7.

Hedges, J. N. Unscheduled absences from work— an update. *Monthly Labor Review,* 1975, *98,* 36–38.

Hedges, J. N., & Barnett, J. K. Working women and the division of household tasks. *Monthly Labor Review,* 1972, *95*(4), 9–14.

Hedges, J. N., & Taylor, D. E. Recent trends in worktime: Hours edge downward. *Monthly Labor Review,* 1980, *103,* 3–11.

Heer, D. M. Dominance and the working wife. *Social Forces,* 1958, *26,* 341–347.

Heidrich & Struggles, Inc. *Profile of a president.* Chicago: Heidrick & Struggles, 1972, 1977, 1980.

Hellervik, L. W., Hunt, A., & Silzer, R. F. *An assessment center for selecting account executives.* Minneapolis, Minn.: Personnel Decisions, Inc., 1976.

Helmich, D. L. Male and female presidents: Some implications of leadership style. *Human Resources Management,* 1974, *13,* 25–26.

Helson, H., Blake, R. R., Mouton, J. S., & Olmstead, J. A. Attitudes as adjustments to stimulus background and residual factors. *Journal of Abnormal and Social Psychology,* 1956, 314–322.

Hemphill, J. K. *Leader behavior description.* Columbus: Ohio State University, Personnel Research Board, 1950.

Hendrick, C., & Constantini, A. F. Effects of varying trait inconsistency and response requirements on the primacy effect in impression formation. *Journal of Personality and Social Psychology,* 1970, *15,* 158–164.

Heneman, H. G., Schwab, D. P., Huett, D. L., & Ford, J. J. Interviewer validity as a function of interview structure, biographical data and interviewee order. *Journal of Applied Psychology,* 1975, *60,* 748–753.

Henry, W. E. The business executive: Psychodynamics of a social role. *American Journal of Sociology,* 1949, *54,* 286–291.

Herman, J. B., Dunham, R. B., & Hulin, C. L. Organizational structure, demographic characteristics, and employee responses. *Organizational Behavior and Human Performance,* 1975, *13,* 206–232.

Herman, J. B., & Hulin, C. L. Studying organizational attitudes from individual and organizational frames of reference. *Organizational Behavior and Human Performance,* 1972, *8,* 84–108.

Herrick, J. S. Work motives of female executives. *Public Personnel Management,* 1973, *2*(5), 380–387.

Herzberg, F. *Work and the nature of man.* Cleveland, Ohio: World, 1966.

Herzberg, F. *The managerial choice.* Homewood, Ill.: Dow Jones-Irwin, 1976.

Herzberg, F., Mausner, B., Peterson, R. O., & Capwell, D. F. *Job attitudes: Review of research and opinions.* Pittsburgh: Psychological Service of Pittsburgh, 1957.

Herzberg, F., Mausner, B., & Snyderman, B. *The motivation to work.* New York: Wiley, 1959.

Heslin, R., & Blake, B. Performance as a function of payment, commitment, and task interest. *Psychonomic Science,* 1969, *15,* 323–324.

Hickson, D. J. Motives of people who restrict their output. *Occupational Psychology,* 1961, *35,* 110–121.

Hickson, D. J., Pugh, D. S., & Pheysey, D. C. Operations technology and organization structure: A reappraisal. *Administrative Science Quarterly,* 1969, *14,* 378–397.

Hinrichs, J. R. A replicated study of job satisfaction dimensions. *Personnel Psychology,* 1968, *4,* 479–500.

Hinrichs, J. R. Correlates of employee evaluations of pay increases. *Journal of Applied Psychology,* 1969, *53,* 481–489.(a)

Hinrichs, J. R. Comparison of "real-life" assessments of management potential with situational exercises, paper-and-pencil ability tests, and personality inventories. *Journal of Applied Psychology,* 1969, *53,* 425–432.(b)

Hinrichs, J. R. Personnel training. In M. D. Dunnette, *Handbook of industrial and organizational psychology.* Chicago: Rand McNally, 1976.

Hise, R. T. Effect of close supervision on productivity of simulated managerial decision-making groups. *Business Studies,* North Texas State University, 1968 (Fall), 96–104.

Hodge, R. W., Siegel, P. M., & Rossi, P. H. Occupational prestige in the United States, 1925–1963. *American Journal of Sociology,* 1964, *70,* 290–292.

Hoffman, L. W. Mother's enjoyment of work and effects on the child. In F. I. Nye and L. W. Hoffman (Eds.), *The employed mother in America.* Chicago: Rand McNally, 1963.

Hoffman, L. W. Effects of maternal employment on the child—A review of the research. *Developmental Psychology,* 1974, *10,* 204–228.

Holland, J. L. *The psychology of vocational choice.* Waltham, Mass.: Blaisdell, 1966.

Holland, J. L. *Making vocational choices: A theory of careers.* Englewood Cliffs, N.J.: Prentice-Hall, 1973.

Holland, J. L., Whitney, D. R., Cole, N. S., & Richards, J. M., Jr. *An empirical occupational classification derived from a theory of personality and intended for practice and research—ACT research report no. 29.* Iowa City: The American College Testing Program, 1969.

Hollander, E. P. Conformity, status, and idiosyncratic credit. *Psychological Review,* 1958, *65,* 117–127.

Hollander, E. P. Competence and conformity in the acceptance of influence. *Journal of Abnormal and Social Psychology,* 1960, *61,* 361–365.

Hollander, E. P. Some effects of perceived status on response to innovative behavior. *Journal of Abnormal and Social Psychology,* 1961, *63,* 247–250.

Hollander, E. P. *Leaders, groups and influence.* New York: Oxford University Press, 1964.

Hollingshead, A. B., & Redlich, F. C. *Social class and mental illness.* New York: Wiley, 1958.

Hollman, T. D. Employment interviewers' errors in processing positive and negative information. *Journal of Applied Psychology,* 1972, *56,* 130–134.

Holmes, T. H., & Masuda, M. Life change and illness susceptibility. In J. P. Scott & E. C. Senay (Eds.), *Separation and depression.* Washington, D.C.: American Association for the Advancement of Science, Publication no. 94, 1973.

Hom, P. W., Katerberg, R., & Hulin, C. L. Comparative examination of three approaches to the prediction of turnover. *Journal of Applied Psychology,* 1979, *64,* 280–290.

Homans, G. C. *The human group.* New York: Harcourt, Brace, & World, 1950.

Homans, G. C. Human behavior as exchange. *American Journal of Sociology,* 1958, *63,* 597–606.

Homans, G. C. *Social behavior: Its elementary forms.* New York: Harcourt, Brace & World, 1961.

Hoos, I. R. When the computer takes over the office. *Harvard Business Review,* 1960, *38,* 102–112.

Hoos, I. R. *Automation in the office.* Washington, D.C.: Public Affairs Press, 1961.

Hoppock, R. *Job satisfaction.* New York: Harper, 1935.

Horn, P. W., Katerberg, R., & Hulin, C. Comparative examination of three approaches to the prediction of turnover. *Journal of Applied Psychology,* 1979, *64,* 280–290.

Horner, M. S. *Sex differences in achievement motivation and performance in competitive and non-competitive situations.* Unpublished doctoral disseration, University of Michigan, 1968.

Horner, M. S. Femininity and successful achievement: A basic inconsistency. In J. Bardwick, E. M. Douvan, M. S. Horner, & D. Gutman (Eds.), *Feminine personality and conflict.* Belmont, Cal.: Brooks-Cole, 1970.

Horner, M. S. Toward an understanding of achievement-related conflicts in women. *Journal of Social Issues,* 1972, *28*(2), 157–175.

House, R. J. A path-goal theory of leader effectiveness. *Administrative Science Quarterly,* 1971, *16,* 321–328.

House, R. J., & Rizzo, J. R. Role conflict and ambiguity as critical variables in a model of organizational behavior. *Organizational Behavior and Human Performance,* 1972, *7,* 467–505.

House, R. J., & Wigdor, L. A. Herzberg's dual-factor theory of job satisfaction and motivation: A review of the evidence and a criterion. *Personnel Psychology,* 1967, *20,* 369–390.

Howard, J. H., Cunningham, D. A., & Rechnitzer, P. A. Work patterns associated with type A behavior: A managerial population. *Human Relations,* 1977, *30,* 825–836.

Howell, M. C. Employed mothers and their families I. *Pediatrics,* 1973, *52,* 252–263.(a)

Howell, M. C. Employed mothers and their families II. *Pediatrics,* 1973, *52,* 327–343.(b)

Howells, J. M., & Brosnan, P. The ability to predict workers' preferences: A research exercise. *Human Relations,* 1972, *25,* 265–281.

Huck, J. R. Assessment centers: A review of the

external and internal validities. *Personnel Psychology,* 1973, *26,* 191–212.

Hulin, C. L., & Blood, M. J. Job enlargement, individual differences, and worker responses. *Psychological Bulletin,* 1968, *69,* 41–55.

Hunt, J. G. Fiedler's leadership contingency model: An empirical test in three organizations. *Organizational Behavior and Human Performance,* 1967, *2,* 290–308.

Hunter, J. E., & Schmidt, F. L. Critical analyses of the statistical and ethnical implications of various implications of test bias. *Psychological Bulletin,* 1976, *83,* 1053–1071.

Hurwitz, J., Zander, A., & Hymovitch, B. Some effects of power on the relations among group members. In D. Cartwright & A. Zander, *Group dynamics: Research and theory.* Evanston, Ill.: Row, Peterson, 1960.

Husaini, B. A., & Geschwender, J. A. Some correlates of attitudes toward membership in white-collar unions. *Southwestern Social Science Quarterly,* 1968, *48,* 595–602.

Huszczo, G. E. *The relative importance of variables related to participation in union activities.* Unpublished doctoral dissertation, Michigan State University, 1975.

Ilgen, D. R. Attendance behavior: A reevaluation of Latham and Purcell's conclusions. *Journal of Applied Psychology,* 1977, *62,* 230–233.

Ilgen, D. R., Fisher, C. D., & Taylor, M. S. Consequences of individual feedback on behavior in organizations. *Journal of Applied Psychology,* 1979, *64,* 349–371.

Indik, B. P. Some effects of organizational size on members' attitudes and behavior. *Human Relations,* 1963, *16,* 369–384.

Indik, B. P. Organization size and member participation: Some empirical tests of alternative explanations. *Human Relations,* 1965, *18,* 339–350.

Indik, B. P., Georgopolous, B. S., & Seashore, S. E. Superior-subordinate relationships and performance. *Personnel Psychology,* 1961, *14,* 357–374.

Inkeles, A. Industrial man: The relation of status to experience, perception and value. *American Journal of Sociology,* 1960, *66,* 1–31.

Inkeles, A., & Rossi, P. H. National comparisons of occupational prestige. *American Journal of Sociology,* 1956, *61,* 329–339.

Inkson, J. H. K., Pugh, D. S., & Hickson, D. J. Organization context and structure: An abbreviated replication. *Administrative Science Quarterly,* 1970, *15,* 318–329.

Inkson, Kerr, & Simpson, D. The assembly-line and alienation: A participant observer study in the meat-freezing industry. *New Zealand Psychologist,* 1975 (November), *42,* 44–45.

Institute of Industrial Relations Attitudes toward unionism of active and passive members. *Monthly Labor Review,* 1966, *89,* 175–177.

Iris, B., & Barrett, G. W. Some relations between job and life situation and job importance. *Journal of Applied Psychology,* 1972, *56,* 301–304.

Isard, E. S. The relationship between item ambiguity and discriminating power in a forced-choice scale. *Journal of Applied Psychology,* 1956, *40,* 266–268.

Ivancevich, J. M. Different goal setting treatments and their effects on performance and job satisfaction. *Academy of Management Journal,* 1977, *20,* 406–419.

Ivancevich, J. M. Longitudinal study of the effects of rater training on psychometric error in ratings. *Journal of Applied Psychology,* 1979, *64,* 502–508.

Jackall, R. *Workers in a labyrinth.* Montclair, N.J.: Allanheld, Osmun & Co., 1978.

Jackson, E. F. Status consistency and symptoms of stress. *Sociological Review,* 1962, *27,* 469–480.

Jackson, J. Structural characteristics of norms. In N. B. Henry (Ed.), *Dynamics of instructional groups.* Chicago: University of Chicago Press, 1960.

Jackson, J. Structural characteristics of norms. In I. D. Steiner & M. Fishbein (Eds.), *Current studies in social psychology.* New York: Holt, Rinehart and Winston, 1965.

Jackson, J. A conceptual and measurement model for norms and roles..*Pacific Sociological Review,* 1966, *9,* 35–47.

Jago, A. *Hierarchical level determinants of participative leader behavior.* Unpublished doctoral dissertation, Yale University, 1977.

James, L. R. Criterion models and construct validity for criteria. *Psychological Bulletin,* 1973, *80,* 75–83.

Janis, I. L. *Air war and emotional stress.* New York: McGraw-Hill, 1951.

Janis, I. L. *Air war and emotional stress.* New York: McGraw-Hill, 1958.

Janis, I. L. *Victims of group think: A psychological study of foreign-policy decisions and fiascos.* Boston: Houghton Mifflin, 1972.

Jaques, E. *Measurement of responsibility.* Cambridge, Mass.: Harvard University Press, 1956.

Jaques, E. *Equitable payment.* New York: Wiley, 1961.

Jaques, E. *Work, creativity, and social justice.* New York: International Universities Press, 1970.

Jenkins, C. D. Psychologic and social precursors of coronary disease. *New England Journal of Medicine,* 1971, *284,* 244–255.

Jenkins, C. D., Zyzanski, S. J., & Rosenman, R. H. Progress toward validation of a computer scored test for the type A coronary prone behavior pattern. *Psychosomatic Medicine,* 1971, *33,* 193–202.

Jenkins, G. D., & Taber, T. A. Monte Carlo study of factors affecting three indices of composite scale reliability. *Journal of Applied Psychology,* 1977, *62,* 392–398.

Jennings, E. E. *The mobile executive.* New York: McGraw-Hill, 1971.

Jennings, E. E. *The executive in crisis.* New York: McGraw-Hill, 1972.

Johnson, D. P. Social organization of an industrial work group: Emergence and adaptation to environmental change. *The Sociological Quarterly,* 1974, *15,* 109–126.

Johnson, G. H. An instrument for the measurement of job satisfaction. *Personnel Psychology,* 1955, *8,* 27–37.

Jones, A. P., James, L. R., & Bruni, J. R. Perceived leadership behavior and employee confidence in the leader as moderated by job involvement. *Journal of Applied Psychology,* 1975, *60,* 146–149.

Jones, E. E., Gergen, K. J., & Jones, R. C. Tactics of ingratiation among leaders and subordinates in a status hierarchy. *Psychological Monographs,* 1963, *77,* 566.

Jones, J. B., Lundsteen, S. W., & Michael, W. B. The relationship of the professional employment status of mothers to reading achievement of sixth-grade children. *California Journal of Educational Research,* 1967, *43,* 102–108.

Jones, S. C. Some determinants of interpersonal evaluating behavior. *Journal of Personality and Social Psychology,* 1966, *3,* 397–403.

Jones, W. H., Rambo, W. W., & Finney, P. D. The relationship between political ideology and information as a function of participation. *The Journal of Social Psychology,* 1975, *95,* 221–225.

Jordan-Viola, E., Fassberg, S., & Viola, M. T. Feminism, androgyny, and anxiety. *Journal of Consulting and Clinical Psychology,* 1976, *44,* 870–871.

Julian, J. Compliance patterns and communication blocks in complex organizations. *American Sociological Review,* 1966, *31,* 382–389.

Jurgensen, C. E. Selected factors which influence job preferences. *Journal of Applied Psychology,* 1947, *31,* 553–564.

Jurgensen, C. E. Job preference (What makes a job good or bad?) *Journal of Applied Psychology,* 1978, *63,* 267–276.

Jury, P. A., Weitzel, W., Davis, R. V., & Pinto, P. R. The relation of sample demographic characteristics to job satisfaction—Technical report. *Industrial Relations Center—University of Minnesota,* 1971.

Kadushin, A. Men in a woman's profession. *Social Work,* 1976, *21,* 440–447.

Kagan, J., & Mussen, P. H. Dependency themes on the TAT and group conformity. *Journal of Consulting Psychology,* 1956, *20,* 29–32.

Kahn, R. L. Human relations on the shop floor. In E. M. Hugh-Jones (Ed.), *Human relations and modern management.* Chicago: Quadrangle Books, 1959.

Kahn, R. L. The meaning of work: Interpretation and proposals for measurement. In A. Campbell & P. E. Converse, *The human meaning of social change.* New York: Russell Sage Foundation, 1972.

Kahn, R. L. Conflict, ambiguity and overload: Three elements in job stress. In A. McLean, *Occupational stress.* Springfield, Ill.: Charles C Thomas, 1974.

Kahn, R. L., & Katz, D. Leadership practices in relation to productivity and morale. In D. Cartwright & A. Zander, *Group dynamics* (2nd ed.). New York: Harper & Row, 1960.

Kahn, R., Wolfe, D. M., Quinn, R. P. Snoek, J. D., & Rosenthal, R. A. *Organizational stress: Studies in role conflict and ambiguity.* New York: Wiley, 1964.

Kane, J. S., & Lawler, E. E., III. Methods of peer assessment. *Psychological Bulletin,* 1978, *85,* 555–586.

Kanouse, D. E., & Hanson, L. R., Jr. Negativity in evaluations. In E. E. Jones (Ed.), *Attribution: Perceiving the causes of behavior.* Morristown, N.J.: General Learning Corporation, 1972.

Kanter, R. M. *Men and women of the corporation.* New York: Basic Books, 1977.

Kanungo, R. N. The concepts of alienation and involvement revisited. *Psychological Bulletin,* 1979, *86,* 119–138.

Kaplan, H. J. *Effects of degree of cooperation and affiliation on conforming behavior in adolescents.* Unpublished doctoral dissertation. Syracuse University, 1961.

Kaplan, H. R., & Tausky, C. Work and the welfare Cadillac: The function of and commitment to work among the hard core unemployed. *Social Problems,* 1972, *19,* 469–483.

Karabenick, S. A., & Meisels, M. Effects of performance evaluation on interpersonal distance. *Journal of Personality,* 1972, *40,* 275–286.

Kasl, S. V. Mental health and work environment: An examination of the evidence. *Journal of Occupational Medicine*, 1973, *15*, 509–518.

Kasl, S. V. Epidemiological contributions to the study of work stress. In C. L. Cooper & R. Payne (Eds.), *Stress at work*. New York: Wiley, 1978.

Kasl, S. V., & Cobb, S. Effects of parental status incongruence and discrepancy on physical and mental health of adult offspring. *Journal of Personality and Social Psychology Monograph*, 1967, *7*(Whole Number 642).

Kasl, S. V., & French, J. R. P. The effects of occupational status on physical and mental health. *Journal of Social Issues*, 1962, *18*, 67–89.

Katz, D. The attitude survey approach. In A. Kornhauser (Ed.), *Psychology of labor-management relations*. Champaign, Ill.: Industrial Relations Research Association, 1949.

Katz, D., & Kahn, R. L. *The social psychology of organizations*. New York: Wiley, 1966.

Katz, D., & Kahn, R. L. *The social psychology of organizations*. New York: Wiley, 1978.

Katz, D., Maccoby, N., Gurin, G., & Floor, L. *Productivity, supervision and morale among railroad workers*. Ann Arbor: University of Michigan, Institute for Social Research, 1951.

Katz, D., Maccoby, N., & Morse, N. C. *Productivity, supervision and morale in an office situation*. Ann Arbor: University of Michigan, Institute for Social Research, 1950.

Kavanagh, M. J., & Halpern, M. The impact of job level and sex differences on the relationship between life and job satisfaction. *Academy of Management Journal*, 1977, *20*, 66–73.

Kay, E., Meyer, H. H., & French, J. R. P. Effects of threat in a performance appraisal interview. *Journal of Applied Psychology*, 1965, *49*, 311–317.

Kay, R., & Meyer, H. H. The development of a job activity questionnaire for production foremen. *Personnel Psychology*, 1962, *15*, 411–418.

Keeley, M. Subjective performance evaluation and person-role conflict under conditions of uncertainty. *Academy of Management Journal*, 1977, *20*, 301–314.

Keller, R. T. Role conflict and ambiguity: Correlates with job satisfaction and values. *Personnel Psychology*, 1975, *28*, 57–64.

Kelley, H. H. Communication in experimentally created hierarchies. *Human Relations*, 1951, *4*, 39–56.

Kelley, H. H., & Shapiro, M. M. An experiment on conformity to group norms where conformity is detri-mental to group achievement. *American Sociological Review*, 1954, *19*, 667–677.

Kelly, J. The study of executive behavior by activity sampling. *Human Relations*, 1964, *17*, 277–287.

Kennedy, J. E., & O'Neill, H. E. Job content and worker's opinions. *Journal of Applied Psychology*, 1958, *42*, 372–375.

Kerr, C., & Siegel, A. The interindustry propensity to strike—An international comparison. In A. Kornhauser, R. Dubin, & A. M. Ross, *Industrial conflict*. New York: McGraw-Hill, 1954.

Kesselman, G. A., Wood, M. T., & Hagen, E. L. Relationships between performance and satisfaction under contingent and noncontingent reward systems. *Journal of Applied Psychology*, 1974, *59*, 374–376.

Khandwalla, P. N. Mass output orientation of operations technology and organizational structure. *Administrative Science Quarterly*, 1974, *19*, 74–97.

Kidd, J. B., & Morgan, J. R. A predictive information system for management. *Operational Research Quarterly*, 1969, *20*, 149–170.

Kilbridge, M. D. Turnover, absence, and transfer rates as indicators of employee dissatisfaction with repetitive work. *Industrial and Labor Relations Review*, 1961, *15*, 21–32.

Kirsch, B. A., & Lengermann, J. J. An empirical test of Robert Blauner's ideas on alienation in work as applied to different type jobs in a white-collar setting. *Sociology and Social Research*, 1971, *56*, 180–194.

Kirchner, W. K., & Reisberg, D. J. Relationship between supervisory and subordinate ratings for technical personnel. *Journal of Industrial Psychology*, 1965, *3*, 57–60.

Klein, D. P. Women in the labor force: The middle years. *Monthly Labor Review*, 1975, *98*(11), 1975.

Klein, S. M. *Workers under stress*. Lexington: University of Kentucky Press, 1971.

Klein, S. M. Pay factors as predictors to satisfaction: A comparison of reinforcement, equity, and expectancy. *Academy of Management Journal*, 1973, *16*, 598–610.

Klein, S. M., & Maher, J. R. Education level and satisfaction with pay. *Personnel Psychology*, 1966, *19*, 195–208.

Kleiner, R. J., & Parker, S. Goal-striving, social status and mental disorder: A research review. *American Sociological Review*, 1963, *28*, 189–203.

Klimoski, R. J., & London, M. Role of the rater in performance appraisal. *Journal of Applied Psychology*, 1974, *59*, 445–451.

Koch, J. L., & Steers, R. M. Job attachment, satisfaction and turnover among public sector employees. *Journal of Vocational Behavior*, 1978, *12*, 119–128.

Komarovsky, M. *Blue-collar marriage*. New York: Random House, 1962.

Korman, A. K. The prediction of managerial performance: A review. *Personnel Psychology*, 1968, *21*, 295–322.

Korman, A. K. Expectancies as determinants of performance. *Journal of Applied Psychology*, 1971, *55*, 218–222.

Kornhauser, A. *Mental health of the industrial worker*. New York: Wiley, 1965.

Kotcher, E. V. *Sex-role identity and career goals in adolescent women*. Unpublished doctoral dissertation, Hofstra University, 1975.

Kotelchuck, M. *The nature of the child's tie to the father*. Unpublished doctoral dissertation, Harvard University, 1971.

Kraut, A. I. New frontiers for assessment centers. *Personnel*, 1976, *53*, 30–38.

Krebs, A. M. Two determinants of conformity: Age of independence training and n-achievement. *Journal of Abnormal and Social Psychology*, 1958, *56*, 130–131.

Kritsikis, S. P., Heineman, A. L., & Eitner, S. The correlation of angina pectoris with biological disposition, psychological and sociological antecedents. *German Health*, 1965, *23*, 1878–1885.

Krivonos, P. D., Byrne, D., & Friedrich, G. W. The effect of attitude similarity on task performance. *Journal of Applied Social Psychology*, 1976, *6*, 307–313.

Kruglanski, A. W., Riter, A., Arazi, D., Agassi, R., Monteqio, J., Peri, I., & Peretz, M. Effects of task-intrinsic rewards upon extrinsic and intrinsic motivation. *Journal of Personality and Social Psychology*, 1975, *31*, 699–705.

Kuhn, J. W. Success and failure in organizing professional engineers. *Proceedings of the Industrial Relations Research Association*, 1963, *16*, 194–208.

Kutscher, R. E., Mark, J. A., & Norsworthy, J. R. The productivity slowdown and the outlook to 1985. *Monthly Labor Review*, 1977, *100*(5), 3–8.

Lacey, D. W. Holland's vocational models: A study of work groups and need satisfaction. *Journal of Vocational Behavior*, 1971, *1*, 105–122.

La Follette, W. R., & Sims, H. P. Is satisfaction redundant with organizational climate? *Organizational Behavior and Human Performance*, 1975, *13*, 257–278.

Lammers, C. J. Strikes and mutinies: A comparative study of organizational conflicts between rulers and ruled. *Administrative Science Quarterly*, 1969, *14*, 558–572.

Landy, F. J. An opponent process theory of job satisfaction. *Journal of Applied Psychology*, 1978, *63*, 533–547.

Landy, F. J., Barnes, J. L., & Murphy, K. R. Correlates of perceived fairness and accuracy of performance evaluation. *Journal of Applied Psychology*, 1978, *63*, 751–754.

Landy, F. J., & Farr, J. L. Performance rating. *Psychological Bulletin*, 1980, *87*, 72–107.

Landy, F. J., Farr, J. L., Saal, F. G., & Freytag, W. R. Behaviorally anchored scales for rating the performance of police officers. *Journal of Applied Psychology*, 1976, *61*, 752–758.

Landy, F. J., & Guion, R. M. Development of scales for the measurement of work motivation. *Organizational Behavior and Human Performance*, 1970, *5*, 93–103.

Lane, I. M., & Messé, L. A. Equity and the distribution of rewards. *Journal of Personality and Social Psychology*, 1971, *20*, 1–17.

Lane, I. M., & Messé, L. A. Distribution of insufficient and oversufficient rewards. *Journal of Personality and Social Psychology*, 1972, *21*, 228–233.

Langner, T. S., & Michael, S. T. *Life stress and mental health*. New York: Free Press of Glencoe, 1963.

Larwood, L., & Whittaker, W. Managerial myopia: Self-serving biases in organizational planning. *Journal of Applied Psychology*, 1977, *62*, 194–198.

Latham, G. P., Fay, C. H., & Saari, L. M. The development of behavioral observation scales for appraising the performance of foremen. *Personnel Psychology*, 1979, *32*, 299–311.

Latham, G. P., Mitchell, T. R., & Dossett, D. L. Importance of participative goal setting and anticipated rewards on goal difficulty and job performance. *Journal of Applied Psychology*, 1978, *63*, 163–171.

Latham, G. P., & Pursell, E. D. Measuring absenteeism from the opposite side of the coin. *Journal of Applied Psychology*, 1975, *60*, 369–371.

Latham, G. P., & Wexley, K. N. *Increasing productivity through performance appraisal*. Reading, Mass.: Addison-Wesley, 1981.

Latham, G. P., & Yukl, G. A. Assigned versus participative goal setting with educated and uneducated wood workers. *Journal of Applied Psychology*, 1975, *60*, 299–302.

Laurent, H. *The validation of aids for identification*

of management potential. Paper presented at the meeting of the American Psychological Association, St. Louis, 1962.

Lawler, E. E. Managers' perceptions of their subordinates' pay and of their superiors' pay. *Personnel Psychology,* 1965, *18,* 413–423.

Lawler, E. E. The mythology of management compensation. *California Management Review,* 1966, *9,* 11–22. (a)

Lawler, E. E. Managers' attitudes toward how their pay is and should be determined. *Journal of Applied Psychology,* 1966, *50,* 273–279. (b)

Lawler, E. E. Secrecy about management compensation: Are there hidden costs? *Organizational Behavior and Human Performance,* 1967, *2,* 182–188.

Lawler, E. E. Effects of hourly overpayment on productivity and work quality. *Journal of Personality and Social Psychology,* 1968, *10,* 306–313.

Lawler, E. E. Effects of task factors on job attitudes and behavior: A symposium: III Job design and employee motivation. *Personnel Psychology,* 1969, *22,* 426–435.

Lawler, E. E. *Pay and organizational effectiveness.* New York: McGraw-Hill, 1971.

Lawler, E. E., & Hall, D. T. Relationships of job characteristics to job involvement, satisfaction and intrinsic motivation. *Journal of Applied Psychology,* 1970, *54,* 305–312.

Lawler, E. E., Hall, D. T., & Oldham, G. R. Organizational climate: Relationship to organizational structure, process and performance. *Organizational Behavior and Human Performance,* 1974, *11,* 139–155.

Lawler, E. E., Koplin, C. A., Young, T. F., & Fadem, J. A. Inequity reduction over time in an induced overpayment situation. *Organizational Behavior and Human Performance,* 1968, *3,* 253–268.

Lawler, E. E., and Levin, E. Union officer's perceptions of members' pay preferences. *Industrial and Labor Relations Review,* 1968, *21,* 509–517.

Lawler, E. E., & Porter, L. W. Perceptions regarding management compensation. *Industrial Relations,* 1963, *3,* 41–49.

Lawler, E. E., & Porter, L. W. Predicting managers' pay and their satisfaction with their pay. *Personnel Psychology,* 1966, *19,* 363–373.

Lawlis, G. E., & Crawford, J. D. Cognitive differentiation in women and pioneer-traditional vocational choices. *Journal of Vocational Behavior,* 1975, *6,* 263–267.

Lawrence, P. R., & Lorsch, J. W. Differentiation and integration in complex organizations. *Administrative Science Quarterly,* 1967, *12,* 1–47.

Lawrence, P. R., & Lorsch, J. W. *Developing organizations: Diagnosis action.* Reading, Mass.: Addison-Wesley, 1969.

Lawshe, C. H., Bolda, R. A., & Brune, R. L. Studies in management training evaluation: I Scaling responses to human relations training cases. *Journal of Applied Psychology,* 1958, *42,* 396–398.

Lawshe, C. H., Bolda, R. A., & Brune, R. L. Studies in management training evaluation: II The effects of exposure to role playing. *Journal of Applied Psychology,* 1959, *43,* 287–292.

Lawson, T. E. Gagne's learning theory applied to technical instruction. *Training and Development Journal,* 1974, *28*(4), 32–40.

Lazarus, R. *Psychological stress and the coping process.* New York: McGraw-Hill, 1966.

Leavitt, H. J. Some effects of certain communication patterns on group performance. *Journal of Abnormal and Social Psychology,* 1951, *46,* 38–50.

Leavitt, H. J., & Mueller, R. A. H. Some effects of feedback on communciation. *Human Relations,* 1951, *4,* 401–410.

Lee, R., & Booth, J. M. A utility analysis of a weighted application blank designed to predict turnover for clerical employees. *Journal of Applied Psychology,* 1974, *59,* 516–518.

Lefkowitz, J. Effect of training on the productivity and tenure of sewing machine operators. *Journal of Applied Psychology,* 1970, *54,* 81–86.

Leon, C., & Bednarzik, R. W. A profile of women on part-time schedules. *Monthly Labor Review,* 1978, *101*(10), 3–12.

Lepkowski, J. R. Development of a forced-choice rating scale for engineer evaluation. *Journal of Applied Psychology,* 1963, *47,* 87–88.

Lissitz, R. W., & Green, S. B. Effect of the number of scale points on reliability. *Journal of Applied Psychology,* 1975, *60,* 10–13.

Levine, J., Laffal, J., Berkowitz, M., Lindeman, J., & Drevdahl, J. Conforming behavior of psychiatric and medical patients. *Journal of Abnormal and Social Psychology,* 1954, *49,* 251–255.

Levitan, U. M. *Status in human organizations as a determinant of mental health and performance.* Unpublished doctoral dissertation, Michigan State University, 1971.

Lewin, A. Y., & Zwany, A. Peer nominations: A model literature critique and a paradigm for research. *Personnel Psychology,* 1976, *29,* 423–447.

Lewin, K. Group decision and social change. In T. M. Newcomb & E. L. Hartley, *Readings in social psychology.* New York: Holt, 1947.

Lieberman, S. The relationship between attitudes and roles: A natural field experiment. *American Psychologist,* 1954, *9,* 418–419.

Likert, R. *New patterns in management.* New York: McGraw-Hill, 1961. (a)

Likert, R. An emerging theory of organizations, leadership and management. In L. Petrullo & B. M. Bass, *Leadership and interpersonal behavior.* New York: Holt, 1961. (b)

Linn, R. L. Single group validity, differential validity and differential prediction. *Journal of Applied Psychology,* 1978, *63,* 507–512.

Lippitt, R., & White, R. K. An experimental study of leadership and group life. In T. M. Newcomb & E. L. Hartley, *Readings in social psychology.* New York: Holt, 1947.

Lipset, S. M. *Political man.* New York: Doubleday, 1960.

Lipset, S. M. Trade unions and social structure: II. *Industrial Relations,* 1962, *1*(Pt. 2), 89–110.

Lipset, S. M., Trow, M., & Coleman, J. *Union democracy.* Garden City, N.Y.: Doubleday, 1956.

Lirtzman, S. I., & Wahba, M. A. Determinants of coalitional behavior of men and women. *Journal of Applied Psychology,* 1972, *56,* 406–411.

Litwin, G., & Stringer, R. *Motivation and organizational climate.* Cambridge, Mass.: Harvard University Press, 1968.

Locke, E. A. What is job satisfaction? *Organizational Behavior and Human Performance,* 1969, *4,* 309–336.

Locke, E. A. Satisfiers and dissatisfiers among white-collar and blue-collar employees. *Journal of Applied Psychology,* 1973, *58,* 67–76.

Locke, E. A. Nature and causes of job satisfaction. In M. D. Dunnette (Ed.), *Handbook of industrial and organizational psychology.* Chicago: Rand McNally, 1976.

Locke, E. A. The myths of behavior mod in organizations. *Academy of Management Review,* 1977, *2,* 543–553.

Locke, E. A., Sirota, D., & Wolfson, A. D. An experimental case study of the success and failures of job enrichment in a government agency. *Journal of Applied Psychology,* 1976, *61,* 701–711.

Lodahl, T. M. Patterns of job attitudes in two assembly technologies. *Administrative Science Quarterly,* 1964, *8,* 482–519.

Lodahl, T. M., & Kejner, M. The definition and measurement of job involvement. *Journal of Applied Psychology,* 1965, *49,* 24–33.

Lofquist, L. H., & Dawis, R. V. *Adjustment to work.* New York: Appleton-Century-Crofts, 1969.

Lofquist, L. H., & Dawis, R. V. Vocational needs, work reinforcers, and job satisfaction. *Vocational Guidance Quarterly,* 1975, *24,* 132–139.

Lowin, A., & Craig, J. R. The influence of level of performance on managerial style: An experimental object-lesson in the ambiguity of correlational data. *Organizational Behavior and Human Performance,* 1968, *3,* 440–458.

Lyle, J., & Ross, J. L. *Women in industry: Employment patterns of women in corporate America.* Lexington, Mass.: Lexington Books: 1973.

Lyon, H. L., & Ivancevich, J. M. An exploratory investigation of organizational climate and job satisfaction in a hospital. *Academy of Management Journal,* 1974, *17,* 635–648.

Lyons, T. F. Role clarity, need for clarity, satisfaction, tension and withdrawal. *Organizational Behavior and Human Performance,* 1971, *6,* 99–110.

Lyons, T. F. Turnover and absenteeism: A review of relationships and shared correlates. *Personnel Psychology,* 1972, *25,* 271–281.

McClelland, D. C. *The achieving society.* Princeton, N.J.: Van Nostrand, 1961.

McClelland, D. C. *Power: The inner experience.* New York: Irvington Publishers, 1975.

McClelland, D. C., & Burnham, D. H. Power is the great motivator. *Harvard Business Review,* 1976, *54,* 100–110.

McClendon, McK. J. The occupational status attainment process of males and females. *American Sociological Review,* 1976, *41,* 52–64.

McCormick, E. J. Job and task analysis. In M. D. Dunnette, *Handbook of industrial and organizational psychology.* Chicago: Rand McNally, 1976.

McCormick, E. J., & Bachus, J. A. Paired comparison ratings. I. The effect on ratings of reduction in the number of pairs. *Journal of Applied Psychology,* 1952, *36,* 123–127.

McCormick, E. J., DeNisi, A. S., & Shaw, J. B. Use of the Position Analysis Questionnaire (PAQ) for establishing the job content validity of tests. *Journal of Applied Psychology,* 1979, *64,* 51–56.

McCormick, E. J., & Ilgen, D. R. *Industrial psychology.* Englewood Cliffs, N.J.: Prentice-Hall, 1980.

McCormick, E. J., Jeanneret, P. R., & Meacham,

R. C. A study of job characteristics and job dimensions based on the Position Analyses Questionnaire (PAQ). *Journal of Applied Psychology,* 1972, *56;* 347–368.

McGehee, P. E., & Teevan, R. C. Conformity behavior and need for affiliation. *Journal of Social Psychology,* 1967, *72,* 117–121.

McGehee, W., & Thayer, P. W. *Training in business and industry.* New York: Wiley, 1961.

McGrath, G. E. Stress and behavior in organizations. In M. D. Dunnette (Ed.), *Handbook of industrial and organizational psychology,* Chicago: Rand McNally, 1976.

McGregor, D. *The human side of enterprise.* New York: McGraw-Hill, 1960.

McKeachie, W. J. Instructional psychology. *Annual Review of Psychology,* 1974, *25,* 161–194.

McLean, A. A. Emotional problems of businessmen. *Advanced Management,* 1960, *25,* 9–10.

Maccoby, E. E., & Feldman, S. S. Mother attachment and stranger-reactions in the third year of life. *Monographs of the Society for Research in Development,* 1972, *37*(1, Serial No. 146).

Mager, R. F., & Pipe, P. *Analyzing performance problems.* Belmont, Cal.: Fearon, 1970.

Maher, J. R., & Piersol, D. T. Perceived clarity of individual job objectives and of group mission as correlates of organizational morale. *Journal of Communication,* 1970, *20,* 125–133.

Mahone, C. Fear of failure and unrealistic vocational aspiration. *Journal of Abnormal and Social Psychology,* 1960, *60,* 253–261.

Mahoney, T. A., Jerdee, T. H., & Carroll, S. J. The job(s) of management. *Industrial Relations,* 1965, *4,* 97–110.

Maier, N. R. F. The quality of group decisions as influenced by the discussion leader. *Human Relations,* 1950, *3,* 155–174.

Maier, N. R. F. *Principles of human relations.* New York: Wiley, 1952.

Maier, N. R. F. *Problem-solving discussion and conferences: Leadership methods and skills.* New York: McGraw-Hill, 1963.

Maier, N. R. F. The subordinate's role in the delegation process. *Personnel Psychology,* 1968, *21,* 179–191.

Maier, N. R. F. Problems in delegation. *Personnel Psychology,* 1969, *22,* 131–139.

Maier, N. R. F. *Problem solving and creativity.* Belmont, Cal.: Brooks-Cole, 1970.

Maier, N. R. F., Hoffman, L., Hoover, J., & Read, W. Superior-subordinate communications in management. *American Management Review Research Studies,* 1961, No. *52.*

Maier, N. R. F., & Solem, A. R. The contribution of a discussion leader to the quality of group thinking: The effective use of minority opinion. *Human Relations,* 1952, *5,* 277–288.

Maier, N. R. F., & Thurber, J. A. Problems in delegation. *Personnel Psychology,* 1969, *22,* 131–139.

Mandell, M. M. Supervisory characteristics and ratings: A summary of recent research. *Personnel Psychology,* 1956, *32,* 435–440.

Mandell, M. M., & Duckworth, P. The supervisor's job: A survey. *Personnel,* 1955, *31,* 456–462.

Manhardt, P. J. Job orientation of male and female college graduates in business. *Personnel Psychology,* 1972, *25,* 361–368.

Mann, F. C., & Hoffman, L. R. *Automation and the worker.* New York: Henry Holt, 1960.

Mannheim, B. A comparative study of work centrality, job rewards and satisfaction. *Sociology of Work and Occupations,* 1975, *2,* 79–102.

Mansfield, R. The initiates of graduates in industry: The resolution of identity-stress as a determinant of job satisfaction in the early months at work. *Human Relations,* 1972, *25,* 77–86.

March, J. G., & Simon, H. A. *Organizations.* New York: Wiley, 1958.

Markey, V. K. Psychological need relationships in dyadic attraction and rejection. *Psychological Reports,* 1973, *32,* 111–123.

Marlatt, G. A., & Perry, M. A. Modeling methods. In F. H., Kanfer & A. P. Goldstein, *Helping people change.* New York: Pergamon Press, 1975.

Marlowe, D. Relationship among direct and indirect measures of the achievement motive and overt behavior. *Journal of Consulting Psychology,* 1959, *23,* 329–332.

Marrett, C. B., Hage, J., & Aiken, M. Communication and satisfaction in organization. *Human Relations,* 1975, *28,* 611–626.

Martin, B. The assessment of anxiety by physiological behavior measures. *Psychological Bulletin,* 1961, *58,* 234–255.

Martin, T. W., Berry, K. J., & Jacobsen, R. B. The impact of dual-career marriages on female professional careers: An empirical test of a parsonian hypothesis. *Journal of Marriage and the Family,* 1975, *37,* 734–742.

Maslow, A. H. A theory of human motivation. *Psychological Review,* 1943, *50,* 370–396.

Maslow, A. H. *Motivation and personality.* New York: Harper, 1954.

Maslow, A. H. *Motivation and personality* (2nd ed.). New York: Harper & Row, 1970.

Matthews, K. A., & Saal, F. E. Relationship of the Type A coronary-prone behavior pattern to achievement, power and affiliation motives. *Psychosomatic Medicine,* 1978, *40,* 631–636.

Maurer, J. G. *Work role involvement of industrial supervisors.* East Lansing: Michigan State University, 1969.

Mausner, B., & Bloch, B. L. A study of the additivity of variables affecting social interaction. *Journal of Abnormal and Social Psychology,* 1957, *54,* 250–256.

May, M. A., & Lumsdaine, A. A. *Learning from films.* New Haven, Conn.: Yale University Press, 1958.

Mayfield, E. C. The selection interview: A reevaluation of published research. *Personnel Psychology,* 1964, *17,* 239–260.

Mayfield, E. C., & Carlson, R. E. Selection interview decisions: First results from a long-term research project. *Personnel Psychology,* 1966, *19,* 41–53.

Meier, R. L. Human time allocation: A basis for social accounts. *Journal of the American Institute of Planners,* 1959, *25,* 27–33.

Merton, R. K. *Social theory and social structure* (rev. ed.). New York: Free Press, 1957.

Messer, E. F. Thirty-eight years is a plenty. *Civil Service Journal,* 1964, *5*(2), 6–8.

Messick, D. M. To join or not to join: An approach to the unionization decision. *Organizational Behavior and Human Performance,* 1973, *10,* 145–156.

Messick, D. M. When a little group interest goes a long way: A note on social motives and union joining. *Organizational Behavior and Human Performance,* 1974, *12,* 331–334.

Metropolitan Life Insurance Company. Longevity of corporate executives. *Statistical Bulletin,* 1974, *55,* 2–4.

Mettlin, C., & Woelfel, J. Interpersonal influence and symptoms of stress. *Journal of Health and Social Behavior,* 1974, *15,* 311–319.

Meyer, H., Walker, W., & Sitivin, G. Motive patterns and risk preferences associated with entrepreneurship. *Journal of Abnormal and Social Psychology,* 1961, *63,* 570–574.

Meyer, H. H., Kay, E., & French, J. R. P. Jr. Split roles in performance appraisal. *Harvard Business Review,* 1965, *43,* 123–129.

Milbrath, L. W. *Political participation.* Chicago: Rand McNally, 1965.

Miles, M. B., Hornstein, H. A., Callahan, D. M., Calder, P. H., & Schiavo, R. S. The consequences of survey feedback. In W. G. Bennis, K. D. Beene, & R. Chin (Eds.), *The planning of change* (2nd ed.). New York: Holt, Rinehart and Winston, 1969.

Miles, R. E., & Ritchie, J. B. Leadership attitudes among union officials. *Industrial Relations,* 1968, *8*(1), 108–117.

Miles, R. H. An empirical test of causal inference between role perceptions of conflict and ambiguity and various personal outcomes. *Journal of Applied Psychology,* 1975, *60,* 334–339.

Milkovich, G. T., & Anderson, P. H. Management compensation and secrecy policy. *Personnel Psychology,* 1972, *25,* 293–302.

Miller, E. L. Job attitudes of national union officials: Perceptions of the importance of certain personality traits as a function of job level and union organization structure. *Personnel Psychology,* 1966, *19,* 394–410.

Miller, G. G. Some considerations in the design and utilization of simulations for technical training. *AFHRL Technical Report (Texas),* 1974, *74–65.*

Miner, J. B. Motivation to manage among women: Studies of business managers and educational administrators. *Journal of Vocational Behavior,* 1974, *5,* 197–208.

Miner, J. B., & Anderson, J. K. The postwar occupational adjustment of emotionally disturbed soldiers. *Journal of Applied Psychology,* 1958, *42,* 317–322.

Miner, J. B., & Culver, J. E. Some aspects of the executive personality. *Journal of Applied Psychology,* 1955, *39,* 348–353.

Mintzberg, H. Managerial work: Analysis from observation. In B. Taylor (Ed.), *Business strategy and planning.* London: Longman, 1973.

Mishler, S. A. Barriers to the career development of women. In S. H. Osipow (Ed.), *Emerging woman: Career analysis and outlooks.* Columbus, Ohio: Charles Merrill, 1975.

Mobley, W. H., Horner, S. O., & Hollingsworth, A. T. An evaluation of precursors of hospital employee turnover. *Journal of Applied Psychology,* 1978, *63,* 408–414.

Moeller, G., & Aplezweig, M. H. A motivational factor in conformity. *Journal of Abnormal and Social Psychology,* 1957, *55,* 114–120.

Mohr, L. Organizational technology and organizational structure. *Administrative Science Quarterly,* 1971, *16,* 444–459.

Monthly Labor Review. Attitudes toward unionism

of active and passive members. *Monthly Labor Review,* 1966, 89(2), 175–177.

Moore, K. M., & Veres, H. C. Traditional and innovative career plans of two-year college women. *Journal of College Student Personnel,* 1976, *17,* 34–38.

Moore, L. M., & Baron, R. M. Effects of wage inequities on work attitudes and performance. *Journal of Experimental Social Psychology,* 1973, *9*(1), 1–16.

Moore, M. L., & Dutton, P. Training needs analysis: Review and critique. *Academy of Management Review,* 1978, *3,* 532–545.

Moore, T. W. Effects on the children. In S. Yudkin & A. Holme, *Working mothers and their children.* London: Michael Joseph, 1963.

Moore, T. W. Children of full-time and part-time mothers. *International Journal of Social Psychiatry,* 1964, No. 2. (Special Congress Issue)

Moore, T. W. Stress in normal childhood. *Human Relations,* 1969, *22,* 235–250.

Morrison, R. E., & Sebold, M. Personal characteristics differentiating female executive from female non-executive personnel. *Journal of Applied Psychology,* 1974, *59,* 656–659.

Morse, J. J., & Lorsch, J. W. Beyond theory Y. *Harvard Business Review,* 1970, *48*(3), 61–68.

Morse, N. C., & Weiss, R. S. The function and meaning of work and the job. *American Sociological Review,* 1955, *20,* 191–198.

Moses, J. L., & Ritchie, R. J. Supervisory relationships training: A behavioral evaluation of a behavior modeling program. *Personnel Psychology,* 1976, *29,* 337–343.

Mostow, E., & Newberry, P. Work role and depression in women: A comparison of workers and housewives in treatment. *American Journal of Orthopsychiatry,* 1975, *45,* 538–548.

Mueller, E. *Technological advance in an expanding economy.* Ann Arbor: Institute for Social Research, University of Michigan, 1969.

Mulder, M., & Stemerding, A. Threat, attraction to group, and need for strong leadership. *Human Relations,* 1963, *16,* 317–334.

Munson, F. The trade union as an organization. *Monthly Labor Review,* 1965, *88,* 497–501.

Münsterberg, H. *Psychology and industrial efficiency.* Boston: Houghton Mifflin, 1913.

Nash, A. N., Muczyk, J. P., & Vettori, F. L. The relative practical effectiveness of programmed instruction. *Personnel Psychology,* 1971, *24,* 397–418.

National Opinion Research Center. Jobs and occupations: A popular evaluation. *Opinion News,* 1947, *9,* 3–13.

Nealey, S. M. Determining worker preferences among employee benefit programs. *Journal of Applied Psychology,* 1964, *48,* 7–12.

Nealey, S. M., & Goodale, J. G. Worker preferences among time-off benefits and pay. *Journal of Applied Psychology,* 1967, *51,* 357–361.

Neeley, J. D. A test of the need gratification theory of job satisfaction. *Journal of Applied Psychology,* 1973, *57,* 86–88.

Neff, F. W. Survey research: A tool for problem diagnosis and improvement in organizations. In S. M. Miller & A. W. Gouldner (Eds.), *Applied sociology.* New York: Free Press, 1965.

Nevo, B. Using biographical information to predict success of men and women in the Army. *Journal of Applied Psychology,* 1976, *61,* 106–108.

Newman, J. E. Understanding the organization structure—job attitude relationship through perceptions of the work environment. *Organizational Behavior and Human Performance,* 1975, *14,* 371–397.

Newman, J. E., & Beehr, T. A. Personal and organizational strategies for handling job stress: A review of research and opinion. *Personnel Psychology,* 1979, *32,* 1–43.

Newman, J. F., Whittemore, K. R., & Newman, H. G. Women in the labor force and suicide. *Social Problems,* 1973, *21,* 220–230.

Newman, J. M. Discrimination in recruitment: An empirical analysis. *Industrial and Labor Relations Review,* 1978, *32,* 15–23.

Newman, J. M., & Krzystofiak, F. Self-reports versus unobtrusive measures: Balancing method variance and ethical concerns in employment discrimination research. *Journal of Applied Psychology,* 1979, *64,* 82–85.

Nieva, V. F. *Supervisor-subordinate similarity: A determinant of subordinate ratings and rewards.* Unpublished doctoral dissertation, University of Michigan, 1976.

Noll, E. C. Adjustment in major roles II: Work. In N. Bradburn, *The structure of psychological well being.* Chicago: Aldine Press, 1968.

Notz, W. W. Work motivation and the negative effects of extrinsic rewards. *American Psychologist,* 1975, *30,* 884–891.

Nye, F. I. Marital interaction. In F. I. Nye & L. W. Hoffman, *The employed mother in America.* Chicago: Rand McNally, 1963.

Oakley, A. *The sociology of housework*. New York: Random House, 1974.

Obradovic, J. Modification of the forced-choice method as a criterion of job proficiency. *Journal of Applied Psychology*, 1970, *54*, 228–233.

Office of the Federal Register. *U.S. Government Manual, 1979–1980*. Washington, D.C.: National Archives and Records Service, 1979.

O'Keefe, R. D., Kernaghan, J. A., & Rubenstein, A. H. Group cohesiveness: A factor in the adoption of innovations among scientific work groups. *Small Group Behavior*, 1975, *6*(3), 282–292.

O'Leary, V. E. Some attitudinal barriers to occupational aspirations in women. *Psychological Bulletin*, 1974, *81*, 809–826.

Oliver, L. W. Achievement and affiliation motivation in career-oriented and homemaking-oriented college women. *Journal of Vocational Behavior*, 1974, *4*, 275–281.

Oliver, L. W. The relationship of parental attitudes and parent identification to career and homemaking orientation in college women. *Journal of Vocational Behavior*, 1975, *7*, 1–12.

Opsahl, R. L., & Dunnette, M. D. The role of financial compensation in industrial motivation. *Psychological Bulletin*, 1966, *66*, 94–118.

Orden, S. R., & Bradburn, N. M. Working wives and marriage happiness. *American Journal of Sociology*, 1969, *74*, 392–407.

O'Reilly, C. A. Supervisors and peers as information-sources, group supportiveness and individual decision-making performance. *Journal of Applied Psychology*, 1977, *62*, 632–635.

O'Reilly, C. A., & Roberts, K. H. Information filtration in organizations: Three experiments. *Organizational Behavior and Human Performance*, 1974, *11*, 253–265.

O'Reilly, C. A., & Roberts, K. H. Task group structure, communication, and effectiveness in three organizations. *Journal of Applied Psychology*, 1977, *62*, 674–681.

O'Reilly, C. A., & Weitz, B. A. Managing marginal employees: The use of warnings and dismissals. *Administrative Science Quarterly*, 1980, *25*, 467–484.

Organ, D. W. Inferences about trends in labor force satisfaction: A causal-correlation analysis. *Academy of Management Journal*, 1977, *20*, 510–519.

Organ, D. W., & Greene, C. N. Role ambiguity, locus of control, and work satisfaction. *Journal of Applied Psychology*, 1974, *59*, 101–102.

Orne, M. T. On the social psychology of the psychology experiment: With particular reference to demand characteristics and their implications. *American Psychologist*, 1962, *17*, 776–783.

Orpen, C., & Pinshaw, J. An empirical examination of the need-gratification theory of job satisfaction. *Journal of Social Psychology*, 1975, *96*, 139–140.

Orzack, L. H. Work as a central life interest of professionals. *Social Problems*, 1959, *7*, 125–132.

Osipow, S. H., *Emerging woman: Career analysis and outlooks*. Columbus, Ohio: Charles E. Merrill, 1975.

Otto, C. P., & Glaser, R. O. *The management of training: A handbook for training and development personnel*. Reading, Mass.: Addison-Wesley, 1970.

Pace, L. A., & Schoenfeldt, L. F. Legal concerns in the use of weighted applications. *Personnel Psychology*, 1977, *30*, 159–166.

Parker, S. R. Type of work, friendship patterns and leisure. *Human Relations*, 1964, *17*, 215–219.

Parnes, H. S. *Union strike votes*. Princeton, N.J.: Princeton University Press, 1956.

Patchen, M. *The choice of wage comparisons*. Englewood Cliffs, N.J.: Prentice-Hall, 1961.

Patchen, M. *Participation, achievement and involvement on the job*. Englewood Cliffs, N.J.: Prentice-Hall, 1970.

Patrick, J., & Stammers, R. Computer assisted learning and occupational training. *British Journal of Educational Technology*, 1977, *8*, 253–267.

Paykel, E. S. Life events and depression: A controlled study. *Archives of General Psychiatry*, 1969, *21*, 753–760.

Paykel, E. S. Life events and acute depression. In J. P. Scott & E. C. Senay (Eds.), *Separation and depression*. Washington, D.C.: American Association for the Advancement of Science, No. 94, 1973.

Penzer, W. N. Education level and satisfaction with pay: An attempted replication. *Personnel Psychology*, 1969, *22*, 185–199.

Pepitone, A. Attributions of causality, social attitudes, and cognitive matching processes. In R. Tagiuri & L. Petrullo (Eds.), *Person perception and interpersonal behavior*. Stanford, Cal.: Stanford University Press, 1958, 258–276.

Perline, M. M., & Lorenz, V. R. Factors influencing member participation in trade union activities. *American Journal of Economics and Sociology*, 1970, *29*, 425–437.

Perrow, C. A framework for the comparative analysis of organizations. *American Sociological Review,* 1967, *32,* 194–208.

Peters, L. H., & Terborg, J. R. The effects of temporal placement of unfavorable information and of attitude similarity on personnel selection decisions. *Organizational Behavior and Human Performance,* 1975, *13,* 279–292.

Pieters, G. R., Hundert, A. T., & Beer, M. Predicting organizational choice: A post-hoc analysis. *Proceedings of the 76th Annual Convention of the American Psychological Association,* 1968.

Pinto, P. R., & Davis, T. C. The moderating effect of need type on the prediction of overall job satisfaction. *Journal of Vocational Behavior,* 1974, *4,* 339–348.

Piotrowski, Z. A. Consistently successful and failing top business executives: An inkblot study. In G. Fisher, *The frontiers of management psychology.* New York: Harper & Row, 1964.

Planty, E. G., McCord, W. S., & Efferson, C. A. *Training employees and managers.* New York: Ronald Press, 1948.

Plotkin, L. Coal handling, steamfitting, psychology and the law. *American Psychologist,* 1972, *27,* 202–204.

Porter, L. W. A study of perceived need satisfaction in bottom and middle management jobs. *Journal of Applied Psychology,* 1961, *45,* 1–10.

Porter, L. W. Job attitudes in management: I Perceived deficiencies in need fulfillment as a function of job level. *Journal of Applied Psychology,* 1962, *46,* 375–384.

Porter, L. W. Job attitudes in management: II Perceived importance of needs as a function of job level. *Journal of Applied Psychology,* 1963, *47,* 141–148. (a)

Porter, L. W. Job attitudes in management: III Perceived deficiencies in need fulfillment as a function of line versus staff type of job. *Journal of Applied Psychology,* 1963, *47,* 267–275. (b)

Porter, L. W. Job attitudes in management: IV Perceived deficiencies in need fulfillment as a function of size of company. *Journal of Applied Psychology,* 1963, *47,* 386–397. (c)

Porter, L. W., & Lawler, E. E. The effects of tall and flat organization structures on managerial job satisfaction. *Personnel Psychology,* 1964, *17,* 135–148.

Porter, L. W., & Lawler, E. E. Properties of organization structure in relation to job attitudes and job behavior. *Psychological Bulletin,* 1965, *64,* 23–51.

Porter, L. W., & Lawler, E. E. *Managerial attitudes and performance.* Homewood, Ill.: Richard D. Irwin, 1968.

Porter, L. W., & Siegel, J. Relationships of tall and flat organization structures to the satisfaction of foreign managers. *Personnel Psychology,* 1965, *18,* 379–392.

Porter, L. W., & Steers, R. M. Organizational, work and personal factors in employee turnover and absenteeism. *Psychological Bulletin,* 1973, *80,* 151–176.

Postman, L., & Bruner, J. S. Perception under stress. *Psychological Review,* 1948, *55,* 314–324.

Poulton, E. C. Blue collar stressors. In C. L. Cooper & R. Payne (Eds.), *Stress at work,* 1978.

Powell, B. *Role conflict and symptoms of psychological distress in college educated women.* Unpublished doctoral dissertation, Fordham University, 1975.

Powell, B., & Reznikoff, M. Role conflict and symptoms of psychological distress in college-educated women. *Journal of Consulting and Clinical Psychology,* 1976, *44,* 473–479.

Powell, R. Elements of executive promotion. *California Management Review,* 1963, *6,* 83–90.

Poznanski, E., Maxey, A., & Marsden, G. Clinical implications of maternal employment: A review of research. *Journal of the American Academy of Child Psychiatry,* 1970, *9,* 741–761.

Prediger, D. J., & Hanson, G. R. Holland's theory of careers applied to women and men: Analysis of implicit assumptions. *Journal of Vocational Behavior,* 1976, *8,* 167–184.

Presthus, R. *The organizational society.* New York: Vintage Books, 1962.

Pritchard, R. D., Campbell, K. M., & Campbell, D. J. Effects of extrinsic financial rewards on intrinsic motivation. *Journal of Applied Psychology,* 1977, *62,* 9–15.

Pritchard, R. D., Dunnette, M. D., & Jorgenson, D. O. Effects of perceptions of equity and inequity on worker performance and satisfaction. *Journal of Applied Psychology,* 1972, *56,* 75–94.

Pitchard, R. D., & Karasick, B. W. The effects of organizational climate on managerial job performance and job satisfaction. *Organizational Behavior and Human Performance,* 1973, *9,* 126–146.

Pruden, H. O. The upward mobile, indifferent, and ambivalent typology of managers. *Academy of Management Journal,* 1973, *16,* 454–464.

Pryer, M. W., & Bass, B. M. Some effects of feedback behavior in groups. *Sociometry,* 1959, *22,* 56–63.

Purcell, T. V. *Blue collar man.* Cambridge, Mass.: Harvard University Press, 1960.

Quinn, R. P., & Shepard, L. J. *The 1972–73 quality of employment survey: Descriptive statistics with comparison data from the 1969–70 survey of working conditions.* Ann Arbor: Institute for Social Research, University of Michigan, 1974.

Quinn, R. P., Staines, G. L., & McCollogh, M. R. *Job satisfaction: Is there a trend?* Washington, D.C.: U. S. Government Printing Office, 1974.

Rabbie, J. M. Differential preference for companionship under threat. *Journal of Abnormal and Social Psychology,* 1963, *67,* 643–648.

Rabinowitz, S., & Hall, D. T. Organizational research on job involvement. *Psychological Bulletin,* 1977, *84,* 265–288.

Radloff, R., & Helmreich, R. *Groups under stress: Psychological research in SEALAB II.* New York: Appleton-Crofts, 1968.

Rambo, W. W. The construction and analysis of a leadership behavior checklist. *Journal of Applied Psychology,* 1958, *42,* 409–415.

Rambo, W. W. The effects of partial pairing on scale values derived from the method of paired comparisons. *Journal of Applied Psychology,* 1959, *43,* 379–381 (a).

Rambo, W. W. Paired comparison scale value variability as a function of partial pairing. *Psychological Reports,* 1959, *5,* 341–344 (b).

Rambo, W. W., Chomiak, A. M., & Price, J. M. *A longitudinal study of output rates: Production in cut and sew trades.* (Tech. Rep.). Stillwater, Okla.: Oklahoma State University, 1981.

Rambo, W. W., & Finney, P. D. Liberal and conservative: Differential response to social pressures generated in a laboratory setting. *Experimental Study of Politics,* 1974, *3,* 38–53.

Rambo, W. W., Jones, W. H., & Finney, P. D. Some correlates of the level of constraint in a system of social attitudes. *The Journal of Psychology,* 1973, *83,* 89–94.

Rand, L. Masculinity or femininity? Differentiating career-oriented and homemaking-oriented college freshmen women. *Journal of Counseling Psychology,* 1968, *15,* 444–450.

Randle, C. W. How to identify promotable executives. *Harvard Business Review,* 1956, *34*(3), 122–134.

Rawls, D. J., & Rawls, J. R. Personality characteristics and personal history data of successful and less successful executives. *Psychological Reports,* 1968, *23,* 1032–1034.

Read, W. Upward communication in industrial hierarchies. *Human Relations,* 1962, *15,* 3–16.

Reilly, R. R., Tenopyr, M. L., & Sperling, S. M. Effects of job previews on job acceptance and survival of telephone operator candidates. *Journal of Applied Psychology,* 1979, *64,* 218–220.

Rennie, T. A. C., & Srole, L. Social class prevalence and distribution of psychosomatic conditions in an urban population. *Psychosomatic Medicine,* 1956, *18,* 449–456.

Rezler, J. *Automation and industrial labor.* New York: Random House, 1969.

Richardson, M. S. Self-concepts in the career orientation of college women. *Journal of Counseling Psychology,* 1975, 22(2), 122–126.

Roach, D. E. Dimensions of employee morale. *Personnel Psychology,* 1958, *11,* 419–431.

Robertson, I., & Downs, S. Learning and the prediction of performance: Development of trainability testing in the United Kingdom. *Journal of Applied Psychology,* 1979, *64,* 42–50.

Robinson, J. P., Athanasiou, R., & Head, K. B. *Measures of occupational attitudes and occupational characteristics.* Ann Arbor: Institute for Social Research, University of Michigan, 1969.

Robinson, J. P., & Converse, P. E. *Summary of United States time use survey.* Ann Arbor: University of Michigan, Survey Research Center, 1966.

Roe, A. *The psychology of occupations.* New York: Wiley, 1956.

Roe, A., & Siegelman, M. *Origin of interests. American inquiry studies—no. 1.* Washington, D.C.: American Personnel and Guidance Association, 1964.

Roethlisberger, F. J., & Dickson, W. J. *Management and the worker.* Cambridge, Mass.: Harvard University Press, 1939.

Rogoff, N. *Recent trends in occupational mobility.* Glencoe, Ill.: Free Press, 1953.

Rogow, R. Membership participation and centralized control. *Industrial Relations,* 1968, *7,* 132–145.

Ronan, W. W. A study of and some concepts concerning labor turnover. *Occupational Psychology,* 1967, *41,* 193–202.

Ronan, W. W., & Organt, G. J. Determinants of pay and pay satisfaction. *Personnel Psychology,* 1973, *26,* 503–520.

Rose, A. M. *Union solidarity.* Minneapolis: University of Minnesota Press, 1952.

Rosen, E. The executive personality. *Personnel,* 1959, *36,* 10–20.

Rosen, H. Desirable attributes of work: Four levels

of management describe their job environments. *Journal of Applied Psychology*, 1961, *45*, 156–160.

Rosen, H., & Weaver, C. Motivation in management: A study of four managerial levels. *Journal of Applied Psychology*, 1960, *44*, 386–392.

Rosen, S., & Tesser, A. On reluctance to communicate undesirable information: The mum effect. *Sociometry*, 1970, *33*, 253–263.

Rosenberg, M. *Occupations and values*. Glencoe, Ill.: Free Press, 1957.

Rosenfeld, C. Multiple job holding holds steady in 1978. *Monthly Labor Review*, 1979, *102*(2), 59–61.

Rosenman, R. H. The role of behavior patterns and neurogenic factors in the pathogenesis of coronary heart disease. In R. S. Elliot (Ed.), *Stress and the heart*. New York: Futura, 1974.

Rosenman, R. H., & Friedman, M. M. Observations on the pathogenesis of coronary heart disease. *Nutrition News*, 1971, *34*, 9–14.

Rosenthal, E. R. *Structural patterns of women's occupational choice*. Unpublished doctoral dissertation, Cornell University, 1974.

Rosenthal, R. *Experimenter effects in behavioral research*. New York: Appleton-Century-Crofts, 1966.

Ross, A. M. The prospects for industrial conflict. *Industrial Relations*, 1961, *1*, 57–74.

Ross, A. M., & Hartman, P. T. *Changing patterns of industrial conflict*. New York: Wiley, 1960.

Rothaus, P., Morton, R. B., & Hanson, P. G. Performance appraisal and psychological distance. *Journal of Applied Psychology*, 1965, *49*, 48–54.

Rothe, H. F. Output rates among industrial employees. *Journal of Applied Psychology*, 1978, *63*, 40–46.

Rotter, J. B. Generalized expectancies for internal versus external control of reinforcement. *Psychological Monographs*, 1966, *80*(1, Whole No. 609).

Roy, D. F. Quota restriction and goldbricking in a machine shop. *American Journal of Sociology*, 1952, *57*, 427–442.

Roy, D. F. Work satisfaction and social reward in quota achievement: An analysis of piecework incentive. *American Sociological Review*, 1953, *18*, 507–514.

Roy, D. F. Banana time: Job satisfaction and informal interaction. *Human Organizations*, 1960, *18*, 158–168.

Ruda, E., & Albright, L. E. Racial differences on selection instruments related to subsequent job performance. *Personnel Psychology*, 1968, *21*, 31–41.

Saal, F. E. Job involvement: A multivariate approach. *Journal of Applied Psychology*, 1978, *63*, 53–61.

Saal, F. E., Downey, R. G., and Lahey, M. A. Rating the ratings: Assessing the psychometric quality of rating data. *Psychological Bulletin*, 1980, *88*, 413–428.

Saal, F. E., & Landy, F. J., The mixed standard rating scale: An evaluation. *Organizational Behavior and Human Performance*, 1977, *18*, 19–35.

Sainsbury, P. Psychosomatic disorders and neurosis in outpatients attending a general hospital. *Journal of Psychosomatic Research*, 1960, *4*, 261–273.

Salancik, G. R., & Pfeffer, J. An examination of need satisfaction models of job attitudes. *Administrative Science Quarterly*, 1977, *22*, 427–456.

Saleh, S. D., & Lalljee, M. Sex and job orientation. *Personnel Psychology*, 1969, *22*, 465–471.

Saleh, S. D., & Singh, T. N. Work values of white-collar employees as a function of sociological background. *Journal of Applied Psychology*, 1973, *58*, 131–133.

Sales, S. M. Some effects of role overload and role underload. *Organizational Behavior and Human Performance*, 1970, *5*, 592–608.

Salipante, P., Jr., & Goodman, P. Training, counseling, and retention of the hard-core unemployed. *Journal of Applied Psychology*, 1976, *61*, 1–11.

Samelson, F. Conforming behavior under two conditions of conflict in the cognitive field. *Journal of Abnormal and Social Psychology*, 1957, *55*, 181–187.

Sanford, F. H. Leadership identification and acceptance. In H. Guetzkow, *Groups, leadership, and men*. Pittsburgh, Pa.: Carnegie Press, 1951, p. 155–176.

Sarnoff, I., & Zimbardo, P. G. Anxiety, fear and social affiliation. *Journal of Abnormal and Social Psychology*, 1961, *62*, 356–363.

Sayles, L. R. *Behavior of industrial work groups: Prediction and control*. New York: Wiley, 1958.

Sayles, L. R., & Strauss, G. *The local union*. New York: Harper, 1953.

Scandura, J. M. Structural approach to instructional problems. *American Psychologist*, 1977, *32*, 33–53.

Scanzoni, J. *Sex roles, women's work, and marital conflict*. Lexington, Mass.: D. C. Heath, 1978.

Schachter, S. *The psychology of affiliation*. Stanford, Cal.: Stanford University Press, 1959.

Schachter, S., Ellertson, N., McBride, D., & Gregory, D. An experimental study of cohesiveness and productivity. *Human Relations*, 1951, *4*, 229–238.

Schachter, S., Willerman, B., Festinger, L., & Hyman, R. Emotional disruption and industrial productivity. *Journal of Applied Psychology*, 1961, *45*, 201–213.

Schein, V. E. The relationship between sex-role stereotypes and requisite management characteristics. *Journal of Applied Psychology*, 1973, *57*, 95–100.

Schenkel, K. F., Dewire, J. E., & Ronan, W. W. One in every crowd? The chronic grievant. *Proceedings of the 81st Annual Convention of the American Psychological Association*, 1973, 583–584.

Schlossberg, N. K., & Goodman, J. A woman's place: Children's sex stereotyping of occupations. *Vocational Guidance Quarterly*, 1972, *20*, 266–270.

Schmideberg, M. Some observations on individual reactions to air raids. *International Journal of Psychoanalysis*, 1942, *23*, 146–176.

Schmidt, F. L., & Hunter, J. E. The future of criterion-related validity. *Personnel Psychology*, 1980, *33*, 41–60.

Schmidt, F. L., Hunter, J. E., McKenzie, R. C., & Muldrow, T. W. Impact of valid selection procedures on work-force productivity. *Journal of Applied Psychology*, 1979, *64*, 609–626.

Schmidt, F. L., Hunter, J. E., & Urry, V. W. Statistical power in criterion-related validity studies. *Journal of Applied Psychology*, 1976, *61*, 473–485.

Schmidt, F. L., & Johnson, R. H. Effect of race on peer ratings in an industrial situation. *Journal of Applied Psychology*, 1973, *57*, 237–241.

Schmitt, N. Social and situational determinants of interview decisions: Implications for the employment interview. *Personnel Psychology*, 1976, *29*, 79–101.

Schmitt, N., & Coyle, B. W. Applicant decisions in the employment interview. *Journal of Applied Psychology*, 1976, *61*, 184–192.

Schneider, B., & Snyder, R. A. Some relationships between job satisfaction and organizational climate. *Journal of Applied Psychology*, 1975, *60*, 318–328.

Schnieder, J. *The effects of success and failure goal-related performance feedback on cognitive determinants of motivation*. Unpublished doctoral dissertation, University of Maryland, 1972.

Schneider, J., & Locke, E. A. A critique of Herzberg's incident classification system and a suggested revision. *Organizational Behavior and Human Performance*, 1971, *6*, 441–457.

Schneier, C. E. Operational utility and psychometric characteristics of behavioral expectation scales: A cognitive reinterpretation. *Journal of Applied Psychology*, 1977, *62*, 541–548.

Schneier, C. E., & Beatty, R. W. The influence of role prescriptions on the performance appraisal process. *Academy of Management Journal*, 1978, *21*, 129–135.

Schneier, C. E., Beatty, R. W., and Beatty, J. R. *An empirical investigation of perceptions of rater behavior frequency and rater behavior change using behavioral expectation scales (BES)*. Unpublished doctoral dissertation, University of Maryland, 1976.

Schoonmaker, A. N. *Anxiety and the executive*. New York: The American Management Association, 1969.

Schriesheim, C. A. Job satisfaction, attitudes toward unions and rating in a union representation election. *Journal of Applied Psychology*, 1978, *63*, 548–552.

Schriesheim, C. A., & Von Glinow, M. A. The path-goal theory of leadership: A theoretical and empirical analysis. *Academy of Management Journal*, 1977, *20*, 398–404.

Schuler, R. S., Worker background and job satisfaction. *Industrial and Labor Relations Review*, 1973, *26*, 851–953.

Schuler, R. S. Role perceptions, satisfaction and performance: A partial reconciliation. *Journal of Applied Psychology*, 1975, *60*, 683–687.

Schuster, J. R., & Clark, B. Individual differences related to feelings toward pay. *Personnel Psychology*, 1970, *23*, 591–604.

Schwab, D. P., & Heneman, H. G. Age and satisfaction with dimensions of work. *Journal of Vocational Behavior*, 1977, *10*, 212–220.

Schwartz, M. M., Stark, H. F., & Schiffman, H. R. Responses of union and management leaders to emotionally-toned industrial relations terms. *Personnel Psychology*, 1970, *23*, 361–376.

Schwyhart, W. R., & Smith, P. C. Factors in the job involvement of middle managers. *Journal of Applied Psychology*, 1972, *56*, 227–233.

Scofield, R. W. *The role of college education in occupational mobility*. Unpublished doctoral dissertation, University of Chicago, 1956.

Scott, W. E., & Hamner, W. C. The influence of variations in performance profiles on the performance evaluation process: An examination of the validity of the criterion. *Organizational Behavior and Human Performance*, 1975, *14*, 360–370.

Scoville, J. G. *The job content of the U.S. economy*. New York: McGraw-Hill, 1969.

Searls, D. J., Brauch, G. N., & Miskimins, R. W. Work values of the chronically unemployed. *Journal of Applied Psychology*, 1974, *59*, 93–95.

Seashore, S. *Group cohesiveness in the industrial*

work group. Ann Arbor: Institute for Social Research, University of Michigan, 1954.

Seashore, S. E. A survey of working conditions in the United States. *Studies in Personnel Psychology*, 1972, *4*, 7–20.

Seashore, S. E. Job satisfaction: A dynamic predictor of adaptive and defensive behavior. *Studies in Personnel Psychology*, 1973, *5*, 7–20.

Segal, S. J. A psychoanalytic analysis of personality factors in vocational choice. *Journal of Counseling Psychology*, 1961, *8*, 202–210.

Seiden, A. M. Overview: Research on the psychology of women: II. Women in families, work, and psychotherapy. *American Journal of Psychiatry*, 1976, *133*, 1111–1123.

Seidman, J., London, J., Karsh, B., & Tagliacozzo, D. L. *The worker views his union*. Chicago: University of Chicago Press, 1951.

Sekscenski, E. S. Job tenure declines as work force changes. *Monthly Labor Review*, 1979, *102*(12), 48–55.

Seltzer, R. A. Computer-assisted instruction—what it can and cannot do. *American Psychologist*, 1971, *26*, 373–377.

Shapiro, H. J. Job motivations of males and females: An empirical study. *Psychological Reports*, 1975, *36*, 647–654.

Sharon, A. T., & Bartlett, C. J. Effect of instructional conditions in producing leniency on two types of rating scales. *Personnel Psychology*, 1969, *22*, 251–263.

Shaw, M. E. *Scaling group tasks: A method for dimensional analysis*. (Tech. Rep. No. 1). Gainesville: University of Florida, 1963.

Shaw, M. E. Communication networks. In L. Berkowitz (Ed.), *Advances in experimental social psychology*. New York: Academic Press, 1964.

Sheard, J. L. Intrasubject prediction of preferences for organizational types. *Journal of Applied Psychology*, 1970, *54*, 248–252.

Sheikh, M. J. *Executive behavior: A temporal analysis*. Unpublished doctoral dissertation, University of Southern California School of Public Administration, 1966.

Shepard, J. M. Functional specialization and work attitudes. *Industrial Relations*, 1969, *8*, 185–194.

Shepard, J. M. Functional specialization, alienation and job satisfaction. *Industrial and Labor Relations Review*, 1970, *23*, 207–219.

Shepard, J. M. *Automation and alienation: A study of office and factory workers*. Cambridge, Mass.: M.I.T. Press, 1971.

Shepard, J. M. Technology, alienation and job satisfaction. *Annual Review of Sociology*, 1977, *3*, 1–21.

Sheppard, H. L., & Herrick, N. Q. *Where have all the robots gone?* New York: Free Press, 1972.

Sheppard, H. L., & Stern, J. L. Impact of automation on workers in supplier plants. *Labor Law Journal*, 1957, *8*, 714–718.

Sheridan, J. E., & Slocum, J. W. The direction of the causal relationship between job satisfaction and work performance. *Organizational Behavior and Human Performance*, 1975, *14*, 159–172.

Sherif, M. A study of some social factors in perception. *Archives of Psychology*, 1935, *27*, No. 187.

Sherif, M. *The psychology of social norms*. New York: Harper, 1936.

Sherriffs, A. C., & McKee, J. P. Qualitative aspects of beliefs about men and women. *Journal of Personality*, 1957, *25*, 451–464.

Shirom, A., Eden, D., Silberwasser, S., & Kellerman, J. J. Job stresses and risk factors in coronary heart disease among occupational categories in kibbutzim. *Social Science and Medicine*, 1973, *7*, 875–892.

Shlensky, B. C. Determinants of turnover in training programs for the disadvantaged. *Personnel Administration*, 1972, *35*, 53–61.

Siassi, I., Crocetti, G., & Spiro, H. R. Emotional health, life and job satisfaction in aging workers. *Industrial Gerontology*, 1975, *2*, 289–296.

Siegal, A. I., & Bergman, B. A. A job learning approach to performance prediction. *Personnel Psychology*, 1975, *28*, 325–339.

Siegal, J. P., & Bowen, D. Satisfaction and performance: Causal relationships and moderating effects. *Journal of Vocational Behavior*, 1971, *1*, 263–269.

Siegal, J. P., & Ghiselli, E. E. Managerial talent, pay and age. *Journal of Vocational Behavior*, 1971, *1*, 129–135.

Siegel, A. L., & Ruh, R. A. Job involvement, participation in decision making, personal background, and job behavior. *Organizational Behavior and Human Performance*, 1973, *9*, 318–327.

Silverman, R. E. Anxiety and the mode of response. *Journal of Abnormal and Social Psychology*, 1954, *49*, 538–542.

Simmons, L. M. H. Computer assisted learning in British Airways. In R. Hooper & I. Toye (Eds.), *Computer assisted learning in the United Kingdom*. London: Council for Educational Technology, 1975.

Simon, H. A. *Administrative behavior*. New York: Macmillan, 1947.

Simon, H. A. *Administrative behavior* (2nd ed.). New York: Macmillan, 1957. (a)

Simon, H. A. *Models of man*. New York: Wiley, 1957. (b)

Simpson, R. L., & Simpson, I. H. Correlates and estimation of occupational prestige. *American Journal of Sociology*, 1960, *66*, 135–140.

Simpson, R. L., & Simpson, I. H. Social origins, occupational advice, occupational values and work careers. *Social Forces*, 1962, *40*, 264–271.

Singer, J. N. *Job strain as a function of job and life stresses*. Unpublished doctoral dissertation, Colorado State University, 1975.

Singh, T. N., & Baumgartel, H. Background factors in airline mechanics work motivations: A research note. *Journal of Applied Psychology*, 1966, *50*, 357–359.

Sistrunk, F., & McDavid, J. W. Achievement motivation, affiliation motivation, and task difficulty as determinants of social conformity. *Journal of Social Psychology*, 1965, *66*, 41–50.

Sjoberg, G. Politics, ethics and evaluation research. In M. Guttentag & E. L. Struening (Eds.), *Handbook of evaluation research* (Vol. 2). Beverly Hills: Sage, 1975.

Skvorc, L. R. *Women in industry: Alienation, satisfaction, and change*. Unpublished doctoral dissertation, Case Western Reserve University, 1975.

Slobin, D., Miller, S., & Porter, L. W. Forms of address and social relations in a business organization. *Journal of Personality and Social Psychology*, 1968, *8*, 289–293.

Slocum, W. L., & Musgrave, P. W. Towards a sociological theory of occupational choice. *The Sociological Review*, 1967, *15*, 33–46.

Smart, J. C. Environments as reinforcer-systems in the study of job satisfaction. *Journal of Vocational Behavior*, 1975, *6*, 337–347.

Smith, F. J., & Kerr, W. A. Turnover factors as assessed by the exit interview. *Journal of Applied Psychology*, 1953, *37*, 352–355.

Smith, F., Roberts, K. H., & Hulin, C. L. Ten year job satisfaction trends in a stable organization. *Academy of Management Journal*, 1976, *19*, 462–469.

Smith, F. J., Scott, K. D., & Hulin, C. L. Trends in job-related attitudes of managerial and professional employees. *Academy of Management Journal*, 1977, *20*, 454–460.

Smith, P. B. Controlled studies of the outcome of sensitivity training. *Psychological Bulletin*, 1975, *82*, 597–622.

Smith, P. C. Behaviors, results and organizational effectiveness. In M. D. Dunnette (Ed.), *Handbook of industrial and organizational psychology*. Chicago: Rand McNally, 1976.

Smith, P. C., & Kendall, L. M. Retranslation of expectations: An approach to the construction of unambiguous anchors for rating scales. *Journal of Applied Psychology*, 1963, *47*, 149–155.

Smith, P. C., Kendall, L. M., & Hulin, C. L. *The measurement of satisfaction in work and retirement*. Chicago: Rand McNally, 1969.

Smith, P. E. Management modeling training to improve morale and customer satisfaction. *Personnel Psychology*, 1976, *29*, 251–259.

Smith, R. E. Sources of growth of the female labor force, 1971–1975. *Monthly Labor Review*, 1977, *100*(8), 27–29.

Snowman, J., & Cunningham, D. J. A comparison of pictoral and written adjunct aids in learning from text. *Journal of Educational Psychology*, 1975, *67*, 307–311.

Snyder, R. A., & Hammer, T. H. A note on the generality of managers' job perceptions of union members. *Journal of Social Psychology*, 1977, *103*, 323–324.

Sobol, M. G. Commitment to work. In F. I. Nye & L. W. Hoffman, *The employed mother in America*. Chicago: Rand McNally, 1963.

Soliman, H. M. Motivation-hygiene theory of job attitudes: An empirical investigation and an attempt to reconcile both the one and the two factor theories of job attitudes. *Journal of Applied Psychology*, 1970, *54*, 452–461.

Solomon, R. L. An extension of control group design. *Psychological Bulletin*, 1949, *46*, 137–150.

Solomon, R. L., & Corbit, J. D. An opponent process theory of motivation: I Temporal dynamics of affect. *Psychological Review*, 1974, *81*, 119–145.

Sommers, D., & Eck, A. Occupational mobility in the American labor force. *Monthly Labor Review*, 1977, *100*(1), 3–13.

Sorcher, M. A behavior modification approach to supervisory training. *Professional Psychology*, 1971, *2*, 401–402.

Spence, J. T., & Helmreich, R. L. *Masculinity and femininity: Their psychological dimensions, correlates and antecedents*. Austin: University of Texas Press, 1978.

Spinrad, W. Correlates of trade union participation. *American Sociological Review,* 1960, *25,* 237–244.

Spool, M. D. Training programs for observers of behavior: A review. *Personnel Psychology,* 1978, *31,* 853–888.

Springbett, B. M. Factors affecting the final decision in the employment interview. *Canadian Journal of Psychology,* 1958, *12,* 13–22.

Stagner, R. Dual allegiance as a problem in modern society. *Personnel Psychology,* 1954, *7,* 41–47.

Stagner, R. *The psychology of industrial conflict.* New York: Wiley, 1956.

Stagner, R. Boredom on the assembly line: Age and personality variables. *Industrial Gerontology,* 1974, *2,* 23–44.

Starcevich, M. M. Job factor importance for job satisfaction and dissatisfaction across different occupational levels. *Journal of Applied Psychology,* 1972, *56,* 467–471.

Stedry, A. C., & Kay, E. The effects of goal difficulty on performance. *Behavioral Science,* 1966, *11,* 459–470.

Stein, E. The dilemma of union democracy. *American Academy of Political and Social Science,* 1963, *350,* 46–54.

Stein, H. S., & Bailey, M. M. The socialization of achievement orientation in females. *Psychological Bulletin,* 1973, *80,* 345–366.

Stewart, R. H. Effect of continuous responding on the order effect in personality impression formation. *Journal of Personality and Social Psychology,* 1965, *1,* 161–165.

Stogdill, R. M. Validity of leader behavior descriptions. *Personnel Psychology,* 1969, *22,* 153–158.

Stogdill, R. M. *Handbook of leadership.* New York: Free Press, 1974.

Stogdill, R. M., Goode, O. S., & Day, D. R. New leader behavior description subscales. *Journal of Psychology,* 1962, *54,* 259–269.

Stogdill, R. M., Goode, O. S., & Day, D. R. The leader behavior of corporation presidents. *Personnel Psychology,* 1963, *16,* 127–132. (a)

Stogdill, R. M., Goode, O. S., & Day, D. R. The leader behavior of United States senators. *Journal of Psychology,* 1963, *56,* 3–8. (b)

Stogdill, R. M., Goode, O. S., & Day, D. R. The leader behavior of presidents of labor unions. *Personnel Psychology,* 1964, *17,* 49–57.

Stogdill, R. M., Scott, E. L., & Jaynes, W. E. *Leadership and role expectation.* Columbus: Ohio State University Bureau of Business Research, 1956.

Strauss, G. Professional or employee oriented: Dilemma for engineering unions. *Industrial and Labor Relations Review,* 1964, *17,* 519–533.

Strauss, G. Related instruction: Basic problems and issues. In *Research in apprenticeship training.* Milwaukee: The University of Wisconsin, Center for Vocational and Technical Education, 1967.

Sturdivant, F. D., & Adler, R. D. Executive origins: Still a gray flannel world? *Harvard Business Review,* 1976, *54,* 125–132.

Sum, A. M. Female labor force participation: why projections have been low. *Monthly Labor Review,* 1977, *100*(7), 18–24.

Sundby, E. A. *A study of personality and social variables related to conformity.* Unpublished doctoral dissertation, Vanderbilt University, 1962.

Super, D. E. Vocational adjustment: Implementing a self-concept. *Occupations,* 1951, *30,* 88–92.

Super, D. E. *The psychology of careers.* New York: Harper, 1957.

Super, D. E., & Crites, S. D. *Appraising vocational fitness* (Rev. ed.). New York: Harper & Row, 1962.

Super, D. E., Starishevsky, R., Matlin, N., & Jordaan, J. P. *Career development: Self-concept theory.* New York: College Entrance Examination Board, 1963.

Surber, J. R., & Anderson, R. C. Delay-retention effect in natural classroom settings. *Journal of Educational Psychology,* 1975, *67,* 170–173.

Sussman, G. I. Process design, automation and worker alienation. *Industrial Relations,* 1972, *11,* 34–45.

Sussman, L. Perceived message distortion: Or you can fool some of the supervisors some of the time. *Personnel Journal,* 1974, *53,* 679–682.

Sutton, H., & Porter, L. W. A study of the grapevine in a governmental organization. *Personnel Psychology,* 1968, *21,* 223–230.

Sypher, H. E. Task productivity of continuing and zero-history groups in two communication networks. *Perceptual and Motor Skills,* 1977, *44*(3, Pt. 2), 1333–1334.

Szalai, A. Differential evaluation of time-budget for comparative purposes. In R. L. Merritt & S. Rokkan (Eds.), *Comparing nations: The use of qualitative data in cross-national research.* New Haven, Conn.: Yale University Press, 1966. (a)

Szalai, A. Trends in comparative time-budget research. *American Behavioral Scientist*, 1966, *9*, 3–8. (b)

Tangri, S. S. *Role-innovation in occupational choice among college women*. Unpublished doctoral dissertation, University of Michigan, 1969.

Tangri, S. S. Determinants of occupational role innovations among college women. *Journal of Social Issues*, 1972, *28*, 177–179.

Tannenbaum, A. S., & Kahn, R. L. *Participation in union locals*. Evanston, Ill.: Row, Peterson, 1958.

Tausky, C. Meanings of work among blue-collar men. *Pacific Sociological Review*, 1969, *12*, 49–55.

Tausky, C., & Dubin, R. Career anchorage: Managerial mobility motivations. *American Sociological Review*, 1965, *30*, 725–735.

Taussig, F. W., & Joslyn, C. S. *American business leaders*. New York: Macmillan, 1932.

Taylor, C. W., Price, P. B., Richards, J. M., & Jacobsen, T. L. An investigation of the criterion problem for a medical school faculty. *Journal of Applied Psychology*, 1965, *49*, 399–406.

Taylor, D. E. Absent workers and lost work hours, May 1978. *Monthly Labor Review*, 1979, *102*(8), 51–52.

Taylor, D. W. Decision making and problem solving. In J. G. March, *Handbook of organizations*. Chicago: Rand McNally, 1965.

Taylor, E. K., Schneider, D. E., & Clay, H. C. Short forced-choice ratings work. *Personnel Psychology*, 1954, *7*, 245–252.

Taylor, H. C. Job satisfaction and quality of working life: A reassessment. *Journal of Occupational Psychology*, 1977, *50*, 243–252.

Taylor, H. C., & Bowers, D. G. *Survey of organizations: A machine scored standardized questionnaire instrument*. Ann Arbor: Institute for Social Research, The University of Michigan, 1972.

Taylor, L. *Occupational sociology*. New York: Oxford University Press, 1968.

Taylor, R. C., & Russell, J. T. The relationship of validity coefficients to the practical effectivenss of tests in selection. *Journal of Applied Psychology*, 1939, *23*, 565–578.

Terborg, J. R. Women in management: A research review. *Journal of Applied Psychology*, 1977, *62*, 647–664.

Terborg, J. R., Castore, C., & DeNinno, J. A. A longitudinal field investigation of the impact of group composition on group performance and cohesion. *Jour-*

nal of Personality and Social Psychology*, 1976, *34*, 782–790.

Tesser, A., & Rosen, S. The reluctance to transmit bad news. In L. Berkowitz (Ed.), *Advances in experimental social psychology* (Vol. 8). New York: Academic Press, 1975.

Thayer, P. W., & McGehee, W. On the effectiveness of not holding a formal training course. *Personnel Psychology*, 1977, *30*, 455–456.

Thorndike, R. L. *Personnel selection*. New York: Wiley, 1949.

Thorndike, R.￨L. Concepts of culture fairness. *Journal of Educational Measurement*, 1971, *8*, 63–70.

Tom, V. R. The role of personality and organizational images in the recruiting process. *Organizational Behavior and Human Performance*, 1971, *6*, 573–592.

Tomlinson-Keasey, C. Role variables: Their influence on female motivational constructs. *Journal of Counseling Psychology*, 1974, *21*, 232–237.

Torgerson, W. S. *Theory and method of scaling*. New York: Wiley, 1958.

Tornow, W. W., & Dunnette, M. D. *Development and use of an input-outcome checklist to identify persons differentially susceptible to conditioning of over and under reward in work setting* (Tech. Rep. 4004). Minneapolis: University of Minnesota, 1970.

Tosi, H. A reexamination of personality as a determinant of the effects of participation. *Personnel Psychology*, 1970, *23*, 91–99.

Tosi, H. Organizational stress as a moderator of the relationship between influence and role response. *Academy of Management Journal*, 1971, *14*, 7–20.

Tosi, H., & Tosi, D. I. Some correlates of role conflict and ambiguity among public school teachers. *Journal of Human Relations*, 1970, *18*, 1068–1075.

Tosti, D. T. Behavior modeling: A process. *Training and Development Journal*, 1980, *34*, 70–74.

Touchton, J. G., & Magoon, T. M. Occupational daydreams as predictors of vocational plans of college women. *Journal of Vocational Behavior*, 1977, *10*, 156–166.

Treiman, D. J., & Terrell, K. Sex and the process of status attainment: A comparison of working women and men. *American Sociological Review*, 1975, *40*, 174–200.

Triandis, H. D., Feldman, J. M., & Weldon, D. E. Designing preemployment training for the hard to employ: A cross-cultural psychological approach. *Journal of Applied Psychology*, 1974, *59*, 687–693.

Triandis, H. C., Feldman, J. M., & Weldon, D. E.

Ecosystem distrust and the hard-to-employ. *Journal of Applied Psychology,* 1975, *60,* 44–56.

Trigg, L. J., & Perlman, D. Social influences on women's pursuit of a nontraditional career. *Psychology of Women Quarterly,* 1976, *1*(2) 138–150.

Trist, E. R., Sussman, G. I., & Brown, G. R. An experiment in autonomous working in an American underground coal mine. *Human Relations,* 1977, *30,* 201–236.

Troxell, J. P. Elements in job satisfaction. *Personnel,* 1954, *31,* 199–205.

Tucker, D. H., & Rowe, P. M. Relationship between expectancy, causal attributions and final hiring in the employment interview. *Journal of Applied Psychology,* 1979, *64,* 27–34.

Turner, A. N., & Lawrence, P. R. *Industrial jobs and the worker.* Boston: Harvard Graduate School of Business Administration, 1965.

Turner, A. N., & Miclette, A. L. Sources of satisfaction in repetitive work. *Occupational Psychology,* 1962, *36,* 215–231.

Turner, W. W. Dimensions of foremen performance: A factor analysis of criterion measures. *Journal of Applied Psychology,* 1960, *44,* 216–223.

Tuttle, T. C., Gould, R. B., & Hazel, J. T. Dimensions of job satisfaction: Initial development of the air force occupational attitude inventory. *U. S. Air Force Human Resources Laboratory,* 1975, No. 75.

Tyree, A., & Treas, J. The occupational and marital mobility of women. *American Sociological Review,* 1974, *39,* 294–302.

Umstat, D. D., Bell, C. H., & Mitchell, T. R. Effects of job enrichment and task goals on satisfaction and productivity: Implications for job design. *Journal of Applied Psychology,* 1976, *61,* 379–394.

U.S. Department of Health, Education, and Welfare. *Work in America.* Cambridge, Mass.: HEW, 1973.

U.S. Department of Labor. *Selected earnings and demographic characteristics of union members.* Bureau of Labor Statistics, Bulletin 417, 1970.

U.S. Department of Labor. *Directory of national unions and employee associations,* 1973. Bureau of Labor Statistics, 1974.

U.S. Department of Labor. *Characteristics of major collective bargaining agreements,* July 1974. Bureau of Labor Statistics, Bulletin 1888, 1975.

U.S. Department of Labor. *U. S. working women.* Washington, D.C.: U. S. Department of Labor, Bulletin, 1980, 1975.

U.S. Department of Labor. *Statistical history of the United States from colonial times to the present: 1976.* Washington, D.C.: Government Printing Office, 1976.

U.S. Department of Labor. *Employment and earnings.* Washington, D.C.: U. S. Department of Labor, 1976, *22*(2), 105.

U.S. Department of Labor. *Employment and earnings.* Washington, D.C.: U. S. Department of Labor, 1977, *23*(1), 10.

U.S. Department of Labor. *Employment and Earnings.* Washington, D.C.: U. S. Department of Labor, 1980, *28*(1), 26.

Uphoff, W. H., & Dunnette, M. D. *Understanding the union member.* Minneapolis: University of Minnesota Press, 1956.

Valenzi, E. R., & Andrews, I. R. Effect of hourly overpay and underpay inequity when tested with new induction procedure. *Journal of Applied Psychology,* 1971, *55,* 22–27.

Veroff, J., Atkinson, J. W., Feld, S. E., & Gurin, G. The use of thematic apperception to assess motivation in a nationwide interview study. *Psychological Monographs,* 1960, *12*.

Viteles, M. *Industrial psychology.* New York: Norton, 1932.

Von Wiegan, R. A. The crucial role of management and labor in employee alcoholism programs. In *Occupational health and safety symposia.* Symposium presented by the U. S. Dept. of Health, Education and Welfare, 1976.

Vroom, V. H. *Some personality determinants of the effects of participation.* Englewood Cliffs, N.J.: Prentice-Hall, 1960.

Vroom, V. H. Ego-involvement, job satisfaction and job performance. *Personnel Psychology,* 1962, *15,* 159–177.

Vroom, V. H. *Work and motivation.* New York: Wiley, 1964.

Vroom, V. H. Leadership. In M. D. Dunnette (Ed.), *Handbook of industrial and organizational psychology.* Chicago: Rand McNally, 1976. (a)

Vroom, V. H. Can leaders learn to lead? *Organizational Dynamics,* 1976, *4,* 17–28. (b)

Vroom, V. H., & Jago, A. G. On the validity of the Vroom-Yetton model. *Journal of Applied Psychology,* 1978, *63,* 151–162.

Vroom, V. H., & Yetton, P. W. *Leadership and decision making.* Pittsburgh: University of Pittsburgh Press, 1973.

Wagner, R. V. Complementary needs, role expectation, interpersonal attraction and the stability of working relationships. *Journal of Personality and Social Psychology,* 1975, *32,* 116–121.

Waldman, E., Grossman, A. S., Hayghe, H., & Johnson, B. L. Working mothers in the 1970's: A look at the statistics. *Monthly Labor Review,* 1979, *102*(10), 39–56.

Waldman, E., & McEaddy, B. J. Where women work—an analysis by industry and occupation. *Monthly Labor Review,* 1974, *98*(5), 3–13.

Walker, C. R. *Toward the automatic factory: A case study of men and machines.* New Haven, Conn.: Yale University Press, 1957.

Walker, C. R., & Guest, R. H. *The man on the assembly line.* Cambridge, Mass.: Harvard University Press, 1952.

Wall, T. D. Overall job satisfaction in relation to "social desirability," age, length of employment and social class. *British Journal of Social and Clinical Psychology,* 1972, *11,* 79–81.

Wanous, J. P. Occupational preference: Perceptions of valence and instrumentalities and objective data. *Journal of Applied Psychology,* 1972, *56,* 152–155.

Wanous, J. P. Effects of a realistic job preview on job acceptance, job attitude and job survival. *Journal of Applied Psychology,* 1973, *58,* 327–332.

Wanous, J. P. Organizational entry: From native expectations to realistic beliefs. *Journal of Applied Psychology,* 1976, *61,* 22–29.

Wanous, J. P., & Lawler, E. E. Measurement and meaning of job satisfaction. *Journal of Applied Psychology,* 1972, *56,* 95–105.

Wardle, M. G. Women's psychological reactions to physically demanding work. *Psychology of Women Quarterly,* 1976, *1*(2), 151–159.

Wardwell, W. I., Hyman, M. M., & Bahnson, C. B. Stress and coronary disease in three field studies. *Journal of Chronic Diseases,* 1964, *17,* 73–94.

Warmke, D. L., & Billings, R. S. Comparison of training methods for improving the psychometric quality of experimental and administrative performance ratings. *Journal of Applied Psychology,* 1979, *64,* 124–131.

Warner, W. L., & Abegglen, J. C. *Big business leaders in America.* New York: Harper, 1955. (a)

Warner, W. L., & Abegglen, J. C. *Occupational mobility.* Minneapolis: University of Minnesota Press, 1955. (b)

Warner, W. L., & Low, J. D. *The social system of the modern factory* (Vol. 1, Yankee City Series). New Haven, Conn.: Yale University Press, 1947.

Warner, W. L., Van Riper, P. P., Martin, N. H., & Collins, O. F. *The American federal executive.* New Haven, Conn.: Yale University Press, 1963.

Warr, P., & Wall, T. *Work and well-being.* Harmondsworth, Middlesex, England: Penguin Books, 1975.

Waters, L. K. A note on the "fakability" of forced-choice scales. *Personnel Psychology,* 1965, *2,* 187–192.

Waters, L. K., & Roach, D. E. Relationship between job attitudes and two forms of withdrawal from the work situation. *Journal of Applied Psychology,* 1971, *55,* 92–94.

Waters, L. K., & Roach, D. Job attitudes as predictors of termination and absenteeism: Consistency over time and across organizational units. *Journal of Applied Psychology,* 1973, *57,* 341–342.

Waters, L. K., & Roach, D. Job satisfaction, behavioral intention, and absenteeism as predictors of turnover. *Personnel Psychology,* 1979, *32,* 393–397.

Watley, D. J., & Kaplan, R. Career or marriage? Aspirations and achievements of able young women. *Journal of Vocational Behavior,* 1971, *1*(1), 29–43.

Watts, H. W., & Rees, A. *The New Jersey income-maintenance experiment, Vol. II, labor-supply responses.* New York: Academic Press, 1977.

Weaver, C. H. The quantification of the frame of reference in labor-management communication. *Journal of Applied Psychology,* 1958, *42,* 1–9.

Weaver, C. N., & Holmes, S. L. A comparative study of the work satisfaction of females with full-time employment and full-time housekeeping. *Journal of Applied Psychology,* 1975, *60,* 117–118.

Webb, W. B. The problem of obtaining negative nominations in peer ratings. *Personnel Psychology,* 1955, *8,* 61–64.

Weber, M. [*Essays in sociology*](H. H. Gerth & C. W. Mills, Eds. and trans.). London: Oxford University Press, 1946.

Weiner, B. New conceptions in the study of achievement motivation. In B. A. Maher (Ed.), *Progress in experimental personality research* (Vol. 5). New York: Academic Press, 1970.

Weiss, D. J., Dawis, R. V., England, G. W., & Lofquist, L. H. Manual for the Minnesota satisfaction questionnaire. *Minnesota Studies in Vocational Rehabilitation,* 1967, *22,* entire publication.

Weissenberg, P., & Gruenfeld, L. W. Relationship between job satisfaction and job involvement. *Journal of Applied Psychology,* 1968, *52,* 469–473.

Wellman, D. The wrong way to find jobs for Negroes. *Trans-action*, 1968, *5*, 9–18.

Wernimont, P. F. Intrinsic and extrinsic factors in job satisfaction. *Journal of Applied Psychology*, 1966, *50*, 41–50.

Wherry, R. J. An orthogonal re-rotation of the Baehr and Ash studies of the SRA employee inventory. *Personnel Psychology*, 1954, *7*, 365–380.

Wherry, R. J. Industrial morale (a symposium): IV Factor analysis of morale data. *Personnel Psychology*, 1958, *11*, 78–89.

White, J. K., & Ruh, R. A. Effects of personal values on the relationship between participation and job attitudes. *Administrative Science Quarterly*, 1973, *18*, 506–514.

Whyte, W. F. *Human relations in the restaurant industry*. New York: McGraw-Hill, 1948.

Wickert, F. R. Turnover and employees' feelings of ego-involvement in the day-to-day operations of a company. *Personnel Psychology*, 1951, *4*, 185–197.

Wickesberg, A. K. Communication networks in the business organization structure. *Academy of Management Journal*, 1968, *11*, 253–262.

Widick, B. J. Sweethearts or adversaries? *The Nation*, 1973, *216*, 792–794.

Wilensky, H. L. The uneven distribution of leisure: The impact of economic growth on "free time." *Social Problems*, 1961, *9*, 32–56.

Williams, D., & King, M. Sex role attitudes and fear of success as correlates of sex role behavior. *Journal of College Student Personnel*, 1976, *17*, 480–484.

Wilson, C. Identify needs with costs in mind. *Training and Development Journal*, 1980, *34*, 58–62.

Wirich, R. *Mate-selection: A study of complementary needs*. New York: Harper, 1958.

Wittrock, M. C., & Lumsdaine, A. A. Instructional psychology. *Annual Review of Psychology*, 1977, *28*, 417–459.

Wolf, M. Need gratification theory: A theoretical reformulation of job satisfaction-dissatisfaction and job motivation. *Journal of Applied Psychology*, 1970, *54*, 87–94.

Wolfenstein, M. *Disaster*. Glencoe, Ill.: Free Press, 1957.

Wolkon, K. A. Pioneer vs. traditional: Two distinct vocational patterns of college alumnae. *Journal of Vocational Behavior*, 1972, *2*, 275–282.

Won, G., & Yamamura, D. Career orientation of local union leadership: A case study. *Sociology and Social Research*, 1968, *52*, 243–252.

Wood, D. A. Effect of worker orientation differences on job attitude correlates. *Journal of Applied Psychology*, 1974, *59*, 54–60.

Wood, I., & Lawler, E. E. Effects of piece-rate overpayment on productivity. *Journal of Applied Psychology*, 1970, *54*, 234–238.

Woods, M. B. The unsupervised child of the working mother. *Developmental Psychology*, 1972, *6*, 14–25.

Woodward, J. *Industrial organization: Theory and practice*. London: Oxford University Press, 1965.

Wool, H. What's wrong with work in America? *Monthly Labor Review*, 1973, *96*(3), 38–44.

Wool, H. Future labor supply for lower level occupations. *Monthly Labor Review*, 1976, *99*(3), 22–31.

Worthy, J. C. Factors influencing employee morale. *Harvard Business Review*, 1950, *28*(1), 61–73.

Yarrow, M. R., Scott, P., DeLeeuw, L., & Heinig, C. Child-rearing in families of working and nonworking mothers. *Sociometry*, 1962, *25*, 122–140.

Young, A. McD. Work experience of the population in 1977. *Monthly Labor Review*, 1979, *102*(3), 53–57.

Young, A. McD. Work experience of the population in 1978. *Monthly Labor Review*, 1980, *103*, 43–47.

Zaleznik, A., Ondrack, J., & Silver, A. Social class, occupation and mental illness. In A. McLean, *Mental health and work organizations*. Chicago: Rand McNally, 1970.

Zander, A., & Quinn, R. The social environment and mental health: A review of past research at the Institute for Social Research. *Journal of Social Issues*, 1967, *18*, 48–66.

Zedeck, S., Imparato, N., Krausz, M., & Oleno, T. Development of behaviorally anchored rating scales as a function of organizational level. *Journal of Applied Psychology*, 1974, *59*, 249–252.

Zedeck, S., & Smith, P. C. A psychological determination of equitable pay. *Journal of Applied Psychology*, 1968, *52*, 343–347.

Zeitlin, L. R. A little larceny can do a lot for employee morale. *Psychology Today*, 1971, *5*(1), 22–26.

Zimbardo, P., & Fromica, R. Emotional comparison and self-esteem as determinants of affiliation. *Journal of Personality*, 1963, *31*, 141–162.

Name Index

Subject index

Problem:

Compare different departments (& admin) at BSU on job satisfaction.

– note problems involved